MW01629906

EXPERIENCING LAW SERIES™

EXPERIENCING ARBITRATION

Michael Nolan
Partner
Milbank LLP

Frédéric G. Sourgens
Professor of Law
Washburn University School of Law

WEST ACADEMIC PUBLISHING

© 2019 LEG, Inc. d/b/a West Academic
    444 Cedar Street, Suite 700
    St. Paul, MN 55101
    1-877-888-1330
West, West Academic Publishing, and West Academic are trademarks of West Publishing Corporation, used under license.

Printed in the United States of America

ISBN: 978-1-64020-846-9

User Instructions

It is the fastest way to obscurity to title any writing "Preface." To title a writing "user instructions" is a close second. We have nevertheless chanced our luck in the hope that our readers might happen upon the user instructions some time *after* having gotten frustrated with one aspect of the book or another on their own and then done the unthinkable—open the instruction manual. (In any event, that is how the authors feel when they open the instruction to any gizmo or thingamajic only *after* having assembled the rather complicated contraption and finding that they cannot find where the "blasted last piece goes.")

The point of the book is to give you an insight into how you would handle arbitration work for your clients in an arbitration practice. It is intended as an intensely practical, experience-based toolkit for you to learn the ins and outs of the world of arbitration. When one of the authors arrived as a junior lawyer to practice with the other, he frequently found that law school education would have been significantly more helpful if it had provided such a toolkit. As it turns out, it had not. But the co-author did. This is just such a toolkit. And it was actually "user tested"—by the authors themselves.

In order to use the book in the manner in which it was intended, it would be most helpful for the reader to begin—and again this is hardly intuitive—in the beginning of each chapter. The first step is to read the fact scenario. This fact scenario is like the client question that starts the associate on their path. The fact scenario is in fact based on actual cases and problems. These problems sometimes are ripped from the (legal) headlines. More often, however, they are taken from past experiences of the authors—altered and adapted for this book to serve an educational purpose and further significantly anonymized to protect the private information of the parties (see the chapter on "confidentiality," below). As you puzzle over the questions presented by the fact scenario, consider that the scenarios in fact are the kind of things you will be expected to do as a midlevel associate in legal practice—and that this book therefore tries to get you—to use a tired trope—not only practice ready, but also "lateral ready."

Any scenario inevitably requires the associate to do legal research. The materials excerpted in each chapter is the initial legal research that you would do to complete the tasks set out in the fact scenarios. The point of the materials is not so much that you read them to prepare for a Socratic engagement with your instructors. It is to help you figure out how to solve the problems your client has asked you. It is to help you strategize and see the warts of any approach you might choose. And it is to help you write the work product you would deliver to your client. The notes and questions are intended to help you on your way.

If you go through the task lists, you will then also author the kinds of work product that will form the start of a professional portfolio. Law firms frequently ask you for writing samples. They do so in part to see how you right and reason. But they mostly do so to see if you can help them provide legal advice to clients. A strong portfolio of writing samples that tracks the tasks an associate will do will help you show to law firms that you are in fact able to do so. It will also give you a starting point when you face these tasks for the first time in practice.

Should you wonder—"but what will this strange approach do for me now?" consider this. One of the tasks you will face on most bar exams is a "performance test." This performance test will ask you to write a piece of work product on the basis of a closed packet of materials. The chapters each are organized to give you practice at precisely that kind of exercise. So—getting ready to practice will also help you with your bar studies. (Or—more precisely— to get the kind of transferable lawyering skills that the bar thinks are sufficiently essential to your future success to test you on them on the bar exam.)

Before letting you go to test your mettle with the tasks, we have to say a very public thank you to the people without whom this project would not have been possible. First of all, we would like to say thank you to Erin Culbertson and Julia Duke, as well as Annette Chase at Milbank. Their help has been invaluable. We also would like to thank Anna Murphy, who as a summer associate helped to test and iron out the kinks of the manuscript.

We also need to thank the Washburn law school community. The book was tried out on scores of students over the years. The most recent crew in fact read the text with an eye to its publication. We therefore owe a thank you Michael Abbott, Othman Aloraini, Abduh Asiri, Andy Bailey, Spencer Bailly, Noah Hahs, Dennis Kirk, Sullivan Manion, Madison McKay, Clara Melero, Elena Nedelea, Ahmed Rajhi, Laura Riggs-Johnson, Jordan Shaw, John Singer, Jason Steele, Tiffany Thomas, Peter Tuttle, and Lauren Young. It also benefited from many conversations with Washburn's civil procedure faculty, so thanks are also due to Professor Rory D. Bahadur and Professor Alex Glashausser.

Finally, a thank you to close friends with whom we used to practice through the years and without whom the actual work upon which this book is based would not have been possible—or not nearly as much as fun. So thank you, Teddy Baldwin, Lesley Benn, Elitza Popova-Talty, and thank you to a constant friend who never dodged a phone call to talk about the next idea for a chapter—John V. Work.

Freddy Sourgens, Topeka, KS, Feb. 19, 2019

Summary of Contents

PART IV. PROCEDURAL ISSUES IN ARBITRATION

PART V. PROVING FACTS IN ARBITRATION

PART VI. ARBITRAL ADVOCACY

PART VII. THE AWARD

Table of Contents

PART II. PROFESSIONAL RESPONSIBILITY IN ARBITRATION PROCEEDINGS

PART III. THE ARBITRAL TRIBUNAL

Chapter 9. Methods of Appointing an Arbitral Tribunal 243

PART IV. PROCEDURAL ISSUES IN ARBITRATION

PART V. PROVING FACTS IN ARBITRATION

Table of Cases

The principal cases are in bold type.

EXPERIENCING ARBITRATION

CHAPTER 1

Introduction to Arbitration

Why does arbitration matter? It is certainly a controversial form of dispute resolution and not the hoped for "panacea" to streamline the crowded dockets of state and federal courts. Although arbitration has received its fair share of praise (usually from the Supreme Court and arbitral institutions), it also is the subject of rather extensive criticism. Consumer protection groups frequently complain about the arbitration clauses embedded in everyday consumer contracts, which these groups say frustrate any right for the consumer to bring a claim related to the product or service in question. This external criticism could move, and *has* moved, law makers to limit some forms of arbitration—although these efforts usually have been thwarted by the United States Supreme Court, as you will see throughout the book. These critiques—although certainly valid in some instances—can safely be relegated to policy clashes and need not worry the aspiring arbitration practitioner.

A far more credible threat for arbitration is that the business community is joining the chorus of arbitration naysayers. Business leaders allege the cost of arbitration is growing out of proportion with its supposed benefit. Further, the promised efficiencies of faster dispute resolution that many people associate with arbitration tend to be overstated in complex arbitrations. These large arbitrations may drag on as long as any federal litigation, and even spawn extensive litigation. Such complaints should be taken very seriously by practitioners of arbitration because they affect whether or not arbitration will maintain staying power as form of dispute resolution.

Despite these credible threats to arbitration's longevity, they do not seem to have an immediate impact on its popularity. As proof, the American Arbitration Association continues to register approximately 400 commercial cases a month, it oversaw approximately 1857 employment arbitrations in 2012, and even supervised some 143,000 insurance arbitrations in New York state in that timeframe alone. Regardless of arbitration's criticism, there is still an intact and rather healthy practice for those wishing to specialize in arbitration, or even sub-specialize in, say, employment or insurance arbitration.

Given the vocal criticism of arbitration coming even from the business community, why does arbitration remain such a popular form of dispute resolution? The answer is the significant *control* parties may assume over the arbitration process.

Parties control a host of the arbitration's aspects, as will be discussed throughout this textbook. As an overview, the parties exercise dominion over the following:

1. Selecting the arbitrators who will form the tribunal overseeing the arbitration (*i.e.*, "constitution of the tribunal").[1] The arbitrators serve as both finder of fact and legal decisionmakers for the dispute. This power to select the arbitrators in effect means that the parties have the power to pick judge *and* jury for their dispute.

2. Determining the rules of procedure the arbitral tribunal must apply to the dispute. In litigation, the state or federal government provide the rules of procedure a court must apply to the dispute. There is reasonably little leeway for the parties to change these rules of procedure and substitute with them their own. In arbitration, however, the parties can freely fashion their own rules of procedure. This means that the parties have the power to set out how much if any discovery they will be entitled to, whether the tribunal has the power to issue temporary restraining orders, or whether the tribunal must issue an award in a certain manner.

3. Deciding whether or not class action will be available. Many consumer litigations in particular are only feasible if a large group of similarly situated plaintiffs can sue as a class. The group then shares in litigation costs. This is important as many harms individual consumers suffer are less than the cost of litigating a dispute—assume that a leading online retailer breaches the same terms and conditions with each of its customers for each transaction, doing harm to the customers at an average rate of $1 per transaction. An active online shopper may well incur damages in the amount of $500 per year. But even over a period of multiple years, it may simply not be worthwhile for the online to sue. A group as small as 1,000 online shoppers, however,

---

[1] See Part III.

would likely suffer a loss that is sufficiently great to justify incurring the cost of litigation. Class actions in court proceedings make it possible for such groups to pursue class claims. Arbitration agreements importantly can limit the availability of such class claims simply by requiring customers to agree to arbitration. This is thus a significant tool to limit exposure for businesses transacting on reasonable similar terms with large groups of customers—and a hidden cost for the customers, which they should bear in mind when determining whether a particular deal is "worth it."

4.   Exercising even broader control with regard to the privacy of the arbitration. Most court proceedings are public. It is possible for interested persons—including reporters—to sit in the courtroom and observe proceedings. The filings made by the litigants as part of the proceedings can also be accessed by third parties with relative ease. This means that litigation is in many instances an exercise of airing one's dirty laundry in public—with all of the reputational risk this entails. Arbitration allows the parties to create a greater environment of privacy for their disputes. As discussed below, arbitration is not a means to keep disputes confidential. But prying eyes will have to look much harder to find the information they seek—and frequently cannot do so until after a dispute has been resolved.

5.   Wielding substantial control over the manner of enforcement of their award following the conclusion of the proceeding. "Let's prepare the appeal." That is something that most losing commercial litigants will hear from their counsel at the end of a trial. Litigation, in other words, allows the parties to drag out the enforcement of a verdict. Arbitration on its face is not subject to such an appeal—one cannot appeal the result of an arbitration to a court as a matter of right. This means that the parties can get to a faster resolution of their claims. On the other hand, parties can agree ahead of time to submit the result of an arbitration to a second, "appeals" arbitration. If the parties seek to have greater comfort with the legal correctness of a decision, they can contract to achieve this comfort in arbitration. But neither party can impose the burdens of appeal on the other after the fact.

The significant discretion of the parties persuades stakeholders to return to arbitration—even in light of its perceived imperfections. These imperfections in fact appear not to be the in the nature of arbitration itself, but rather arise out of how it is practiced. Happy clients are repeat clients, thus behooves lawyers and law students to learn more about how the control in question can be expertly exercised to achieve competing goals (i.e., finality and speed of the process vs. "correctness" of its ultimate result), master the arbitration process.

Fact Scenario

You represent a baseball player in a grievance arbitration. The baseball league, which employed the player suspended the player without pay for a period of 100 games for use of a banned substance. The league relied for its suspension on an investigative report concluding that the player used performance enhancing drugs rather than a positive drug test. Your client has retained you to challenge the suspension in arbitration. Your client insists that he has never tested positive for a banned substance in a league sanctioned test and that he therefore should not be suspended. After you discuss the case with your client, your client discloses that he inquired about the side-effects of human growth hormone by email to one of his offseason physical trainers. He says he still has the email. Do you volunteer this evidence in an arbitration governed by the following clause?

8.   Evidence.

The Parties may offer any evidence they wish. The arbitral tribunal shall have the power to order the Parties to produce such additional evidence as it deems necessary to an understanding and determination of the dispute. The arbitral tribunal is not bound by any rules of evidence and shall be the judge of the relevancy and materiality of the evidence offered or ordered to be produced.

PART I

The Arbitration Clause

The core distinction of arbitration from litigation is the consensual nature of arbitration. The Federal Arbitration Act provides that

> A written provision in any maritime transaction or a contract evidencing a transaction involving commerce to settle by arbitration a controversy thereafter arising out of such contract or transaction, or the refusal to perform the whole or any part thereof, or an agreement in writing to submit to arbitration an existing controversy arising out of such a contract, transaction, or refusal, shall be valid, irrevocable, and enforceable, save upon such grounds as exist at law or in equity for the revocation of any contract.[1]

The first important limitation is that arbitration is available only if parties to a transaction or controversy agree to its use. Consent to arbitration must either flow from a "written provision in . . . a transaction" or "an agreement in writing to submit to arbitration an existing controversy."[2]

> This limitation of party consent applies not only to the availability of arbitration *as such*, but also to the scope of the agreement to arbitrate. Once the parties have included an arbitration clause in an agreement, they are not automatically bound to submit any and all disputes to arbitration. Rather, the requirement of a written consent applies to a specific "controversy" to be settled in arbitration.[3] Consequently, it must be proved that the written consent to arbitration in fact applies to any given dispute. A further important limitation apparent on the face of the Federal Arbitration Act is its application to written agreements "in any maritime transaction" or "contract[s] evidencing a transaction involving commerce."[4] As one commentator noted: The section defining 'commerce' states that it means interstate commerce or international commerce. To a modern reader, this definition may

---

[1]   Federal Arbitration Act ("FAA"), 9 U.S.C. § 2 (1947).

[2]   *Id.*

[3]   *Id.*

[4]   *Id.*

evoke the vast sweep of current Commerce Clause power, which reaches almost all economic activity. But at the time of the FAA's enactment, in 1925, the scope of federal regulatory power was, of course, much narrower. And although federal authority substantially expanded through the course of the New Deal and then World War II, the Supreme Court did not expand the scope of the FAA to match the full reach of that expanded constitutional power [until 1984].[5]

Traditionally, the scope of arbitration under the FAA tended to cover business-to-business transactions, negotiated by relatively sophisticated parties wishing to resolve their disputes quietly outside of the bustle of the courts.

The arrival of the form contract, together with a change in U.S. Supreme Court jurisprudence, have significantly changed this nature of arbitration. Currently, arbitration clauses are frequently included in any kind of boiler plate agreement, and such agreements are often (if not always) enforced. This simple shift has transformed arbitration from an exceptional means of dispute resolution to the normal form of dispute resolution in many, if not most, commercial settings. Part I of the textbook will introduce you to the arbitration clause as the cornerstone of the arbitral process.

---

[5] Aaron-Andrew P. Bruhl, *The Unconscionability Game: Strategic Judging and the Evolution of Federal Arbitration Law*, 33 N.Y.U. L. REV. 1420, 1427–31 (2008).

CHAPTER 2

Development of the Law Governing Arbitration Clauses

This chapter sets out the historical development of U.S. Supreme Court jurisprudence on the permissible scope of arbitration clauses. First, this chapter begins with Supreme Court decisions that have expanded the scope of federal jurisdiction under the FAA over arbitrations. Second, this chapter traces the development of the scope of "controversies" that can be submitted to arbitration and the displacement of the federal judiciary—to the benefit of arbitral jurisdiction—in controversies involving federal statutory claims. The result of this historical development is that an arbitration clause, if artfully drafted, can cover almost any potential dispute. These two aspects form the background against which Chapter 2 must be understood.

Fact Scenario

Donny Standon is a college student who works as a waiter at a Kansas City "Pear Grove" restaurant. He began working for the company when he was 16 years old. The restaurant is part of a national chain. The terms of Mr. Standon's employment are included in an Employee Manual that is updated from time to time by the company. Three years ago, the Employee Manual was updated to include the following arbitration clause:

> In consideration of the Company offering you employment and employing you, you and the company each agree that, provided, when appropriate, the employee, complies with the company's open door policy and/or compliance resolution procedure, the employee and the company agree to resolve any claims pursuant to the company's rules and procedures for alternative resolution of employment-related disputes, as promulgated by company from time to time (the "Rules"). The Company will make available or provide a copy of the rules upon written request of the employee.

At the same time the arbitration clause was introduced, the Employee Manual also updated policies for tardiness, conversion of kitchen supplies by staff, and unpaid sick leave.

Two years ago, the company changed the Rules so as to permit itself to have a choice whether to litigate claims against employees or submit these claims to arbitration. It continued to require that the employee had to submit these claims to arbitration. The clause also expressly prohibited class arbitration by employees against the company for any claim arising out of, or relating to, their employment at Pear Grove.

Donny Standon is part of a putative class action commenced by Pear Grove employees. The class action asserts that Pear Grove systematically defrauded its employees with regard to payment of their wages. They allege that Pear Grove incorrectly identified tax withholdings and, in fact, kept part of the allegedly withheld money for its own account. Among other causes of action, the class asserts that Pear Grove violated the United States Racketeer Influenced and Corrupt Organizations Act (RICO). Prepare arguments for either Standon or the Pear Grove regarding the separability issue[1] raised by this fact pattern.

Readings

A) The Reach of the Federal Arbitration Act

Arbitration displaces ordinary judicial remedies. The current development of Supreme Court jurisprudence has brought about an expansion of federal power—and a displacement of state regulatory authority—over which disputes may be submitted to arbitration.

The Federal Arbitration Act's scope is facially limited to "any maritime transaction" or "commerce."[2] The FAA defines "maritime transactions" as any matter that "would be embraced within admiralty jurisdiction."[3] The statute further defines "commerce" as follows:

> [C]ommerce among the several States or with foreign nations, or in any Territory of the United States or in the District of Columbia, or between any such Territory and another, or between any such Territory and any State or foreign nation, or between the District of Columbia and any State or Territory or foreign nation, but nothing herein contained shall apply to contracts of employment of seamen,

---

[1]   According to the separability principle, the invalidity of the underlying agreement will not have an impact on the arbitration clause; likewise, the invalidity of the arbitration clause will not render the underlying agreement invalid.

[2]   Federal Arbitration Act ("FAA"), 9 U.S.C. § 2. For a discussion of admiralty jurisdiction, *see* David J. Sharpe, *Admiralty Jurisdiction: The Power over Cases,* 79 TUL. L. REV. 1149 (2005).

[3]   FAA, 9 U.S.C. at § 1.

railroad employees, or any other class of workers engaged in foreign or interstate commerce.[4]

This definition of "commerce" derives from the power of Congress to "regulate Commerce with foreign Nations, and among the several States, and with the Indian Tribes."[5] The drafters of the FAA did not incorporate the scope of the Commerce Power merely by reference to "commerce," thus a statutory definition was required to define the scope of "commerce" in the FAA.

Depending upon the transaction involved, the determination of whether something constitutes "commerce" can be facially difficult to establish. Consider for instance the following scenarios:

1. A Kansas grocer buys wheat that is grown and harvested in Kansas from a Missouri wholesaler. The grain at issue in the transaction has never left the state of Kansas.

2. The same facts as scenario 1, except that the wholesaler is located in Kansas. The sale transaction, however, was completed online. Payment was made through intermediaries located in Utah and Delaware, respectively.

3. A Washington, D.C. shop sells a stroller to a family living in the District. The stroller was manufactured in the Netherlands and imported by a company in New York.

4. A multinational accounting firm enters into a services agreement with a hospitality company based in Washington, D.C. The services are actually rendered in Washington, D.C. by employees physically located in the multinational's Washington, D.C. office, which was set-up principally to handle this one sizeable account.

5. The same facts as in scenario 4, except assume that the Washington D.C. office of the multinational broke-off from its parent company. Assume further that the Washington, D.C. hospitality company receives money from franchises worldwide.

---

[4] *Id.*

[5] U.S. CONST. art. I, § 8 cl. 3.

1)   The Historical Starting Point

Bernhardt v. Polygraphic Co. of America

350 U.S. 198 (1956)

MR. JUSTICE DOUGLAS delivered the opinion of the Court.

This suit, removed from a Vermont court to the District Court on grounds of diversity of citizenship, was brought for damages for the discharge of petitioner under an employment contract. At the time the contract was made petitioner was a resident of New York. Respondent is a New York corporation. The contract was made in New York. Petitioner later became a resident of Vermont, where he was to perform his duties under the contract, and asserts his rights there.

The contract contains a provision that in case of any dispute the parties will submit the matter to arbitration under New York law by the American Arbitration Association, whose determination 'shall be final and absolute.' After the case had been removed to the District Court, respondent moved for a stay of the proceedings so that the controversy could go to arbitration in New York. The motion alleged that the law of New York governs the question whether the arbitration provision of the contract is binding.

The District Court ruled that under *Erie R. Co. v. Tompkins*, 304 U.S. 64, the arbitration provision of the contract was governed by Vermont law and that the law of Vermont makes revocable an agreement to arbitrate [*200] at any time before an award is actually made. The District Court therefore denied the stay. The Court of Appeals reversed. The case is here on a petition for certiorari which we granted, because of the doubtful application by the Court of Appeals of *Erie R. Co. v. Tompkins*.

A question under the United States Arbitration Act lies at the threshold of the case. Section 2 of that Act makes 'valid, irrevocable, and enforceable' provisions for arbitration in certain classes of contracts; and § 3 provides for a stay of actions in the federal courts of issues referable to arbitration under those contracts. Section 2 makes 'valid, irrevocable, and enforceable' only two types of contracts: those relating to a maritime transaction and those involving commerce. No maritime transaction is involved here. Nor does this contract evidence 'a transaction involving commerce' within the meaning of § 2 of the Act. There is no showing that petitioner [*201] while performing his duties under the employment contract was working 'in' commerce, was producing goods for commerce, or was engaging in activity that affected commerce, within the meaning of our decisions.

The Court of Appeals went on to hold that in any event § 3 of the Act stands on its own footing. It concluded that while § 2 makes enforceable arbitration agreements in maritime transactions and in transactions involving commerce, § 3 covers all arbitration agreements even though they do not involve maritime transactions or transactions in commerce. We disagree with that reading of the Act. Sections 1, 2, and 3 are integral parts of a whole. To be sure, § 3 does not repeat the words 'maritime transaction' or 'transaction involving commerce,' used in §§ 1 and 2. But §§ 1 and 2 define the field in which Congress was legislating. Since § 3 is a part of the regulatory scheme, we can only assume that the 'agreement in writing' for arbitration referred to in § 3 is the kind of agreement which §§ 1 and 2 have brought under federal regulation. There is no intimation or suggestion in the Committee Reports that §§ 1 and 2 cover a narrower field than § 3. On the contrary, S. Rep. No. 536, 68th Cong., 1st Sess., p. 2, states that § 1 defines the contracts to which 'the bill will be applicable.' And H.R. Rep. No. 96, 68th Cong., 1st Sess., p. 1, [*202] states that one foundation of the new regulating measure is 'the Federal control over interstate commerce and over admiralty.' If respondent's contention is correct, a constitutional question might be presented. *Erie R. Co. v. Tompkins* indicated that Congress does not have the constitutional authority to make the law that is applicable to controversies in diversity of citizenship cases.

. . . .

The question remains whether, apart from the Federal Act, a provision of a contract providing for arbitration is enforceable in a diversity case.

The Court of Appeals, in disagreeing with the District Court as to the effect of an arbitration agreement under *Erie R. Co. v. Tompkins,* followed its earlier decision of *Murray Oil Products Co. v. Mitsui & Co.,* 146 F.2d 381, 383, which held that, 'Arbitration is merely a form of trial, to be adopted in the action itself, in place of the trial at common law: it is like a reference to a master, or an 'advisory trial' under Federal Rules of Civil Procedure . . . .'

We disagree with that conclusion. We deal here with a right to recover that owes its existence to one of the States, not to the United States. The federal court enforces [*203] the state-created right by rules of procedure which it has acquired from the Federal Government and which therefore are not identical with those of the state courts. Yet, in spite of that difference in procedure, the federal court enforcing a state-created right in a diversity case is, as we said in

Guaranty Trust Co. v. York, 326 U.S. 99, 108, in substance 'only another court of the State.' The federal court therefore may not 'substantially affect the enforcement of the right as given by the State.' *Id.*, 109. If the federal court allows arbitration where the state court would disallow it, the outcome of litigation might depend on the courthouse where suit is brought. For the remedy by arbitration, whatever its merits or shortcomings, substantially affects the cause of action created by the State. The nature of the tribunal where suits are tried is an important part of the parcel of rights behind a cause of action. The change from a court of law to an arbitration panel may make a radical difference in ultimate result. Arbitration carries no right to trial by jury that is guaranteed both by the Seventh Amendment and by Ch. 1, Art. 12th, of the Vermont Constitution. Arbitrators do not have the benefit of judicial instruction on the law; they need not give their reasons for their results; the record of their proceedings is not as complete as it is in a court trial; and judicial review of an award is more limited than judicial review of a trial—all as discussed in *Wilko v. Swan*, 346 U.S. 427, 435–438. We said in the *York* case that 'The nub of the policy that underlies *Erie R. Co. v. Tompkins* is that for the same transaction the accident of a suit by a non-resident litigant in a federal court instead of in a State court a block away should not lead to a substantially different result.' 326 U.S., at 109. There would in our judgment be a resultant discrimination if the parties suing on a Vermont cause of action in the federal court were remitted to arbitration, while those suing in the Vermont court could not be.

The District Court found that if the parties were in a Vermont court, the agreement to submit to arbitration would not be binding and could be revoked at any time before an award was made. He gave as his authority *Mead's Admx v. Owen* and *Sartwell v. Sowles*, decided by the Supreme Court of Vermont. In the *Owen* case the court, in speaking of an agreement to arbitrate, held that '. . . either party may revoke the submission at any time before the publication of an award.' . . . We agree with [the District Judge] that if arbitration could not be compelled in the Vermont courts, it should not be compelled in the Federal District Court. . . .

       . . . .

The judgment of the Court of Appeals is reversed and the cause is remanded to the District Court for proceedings in conformity with this opinion.

Reversed and remanded

NOTES

Facts

1. Was there any argument at the beginning of the transaction that the agreement involved "commerce" as defined by the FAA? If so, what would that argument have been?

2. The Court stated in a footnote that it did not have to address the question whether the employment relationship fell within the exclusionary definition of "commerce" of the FAA. In your opinion, what kind of employment relationship should have been considered "commerce"? If you made an argument premised upon that opinion, what canon of statutory construction would you use to make that fact relevant?

3. How do you determine the scope of the "business" of the employer? How does the business of the employer matter to the "commerce" analysis?

Law

1. The Court refers in its decision to *Erie R. Co. v. Tompkins* 304 U.S. 64 (1938). What does *Erie* stand for? Why is *Erie* relevant to a question whether or not to apply the FAA?

2. In *N.L.R.B. v. Jones & Laughlin Steel Corp.*, 301 U.S. 1 (1937), the United States Supreme Court held that the National Labor Relations Act, 29 U.S.C. § 151 fell within Congress' commerce power to enact. The case concerned the asserted coercive and discriminatory treatment by an employer of its unionized employees. Review the case. Is the case consistent with the *Bernhardt* decision?

3. Is it legally relevant that the petitioner moved from New York to Vermont? Assume that the transaction had not concerned an employment relationship, but rather the construction and shipment of cabinets. Would the fact that the cabinets now would be constructed in Vermont and then shipped to New York have altered the outcome of the case? What is the best argument for a change in outcome? What is the best argument against?

4. The Court states without reference that "[t]here is no showing that petitioner while performing his duties under the employment contract was working 'in' commerce, was producing goods for commerce, or was engaging in activity that affected commerce, within the meaning of our decisions." *Bernhardt*, 350 U.S. at 200–01. Does this means that the Court assumed that the definition of "commerce" in the FAA was co-equal with the Commerce Power of the Constitution? Are there any other grounds

that you could cite to limit the definition on point in the FAA further? How?

2) *The Turning Point*

Prima Paint Corp. v. Flood & Conklin Mfg. Co.

388 U.S. 395 (1967)

MR. JUSTICE FORTAS delivered the opinion of the Court.

This case presents the question whether the federal court or an arbitrator is to resolve a claim of 'fraud in [*397] the inducement,' under a contract governed by the United States Arbitration Act of 1925, where there is no evidence that the contracting parties intended to withhold that issue from arbitration.

The question arises from the following set of facts. On October 7, 1964, respondent, Flood & Conklin Manufacturing Company, a New Jersey corporation, entered into what was styled a 'Consulting Agreement,' with petitioner, Prima Paint Corporation, a Maryland corporation. This agreement followed by less than three weeks the execution of a contract pursuant to which Prima Paint purchased F & C's paint business. The consulting agreement provided that for a six-year period F & C was to furnish advice and consultation 'in connection with the formulae, manufacturing operations, sales and servicing of Prima Trade Sales accounts.' These services were to be performed personally by F & C's chairman, Jerome K. Jelin, 'except in the event of his death or disability.' F & C bound itself for the duration of the contractual period to make no 'Trade Sales' of paint or paint products in its existing sales territory or to current customers. To the consulting agreement were appended lists of F & C customers, whose patronage was to be taken over by Prima Paint. In return for these lists, the covenant not to compete, and the services of Mr. Jelin, Prima Paint agreed to pay F & C certain percentages of its receipts from the listed customers and from all others, such payments not to exceed $225,000 over the life of the agreement. The agreement took into account the possibility that Prima Paint might encounter financial difficulties, including bankruptcy, but no corresponding reference was made to possible financial problems which might be encountered by F & C. The agreement stated that it 'embodies the entire understanding of the parties [*398] on the subject matter.' Finally, the parties agreed to a broad arbitration clause, which read in part:

'Any controversy or claim arising out of or relating to this Agreement, or the breach thereof, shall be settled by arbitration in the City of New York, in accordance with the rules then obtaining of the American Arbitration Association. . . .'

The first payment by Prima Paint to F & C under the consulting agreement was due on September 1, 1965. None was made on that date. Seventeen days later, Prima Paint did pay the appropriate amount, but into escrow. It notified attorneys for F & C that in various enumerated respects their client had broken both the consulting agreement and the earlier purchase agreement. Prima Paint's principal contention, so far as presently relevant, was that F & C had fraudulently represented that it was solvent and able to perform its contractual obligations, whereas it was in fact insolvent and intended to file a petition under Chapter XI of the Bankruptcy Act, 52 Stat. 905, 11 U.S.C. § 701 *et seq.*, shortly after execution of the consulting agreement. Prima Paint noted that such a petition was filed by F & C on October 14, 1964, one week after the contract had been signed. F & C's response, on October 25, was to serve a 'notice of intention to arbitrate.' On November 12, three days before expiration of its time to answer this 'notice,' Prima Paint filed suit in the United States District Court for the Southern District of New York, seeking rescission of the consulting agreement on the basis of the alleged fraudulent inducement. The complaint asserted that the federal court had diversity jurisdiction.

[*399] Contemporaneously with the filing of its complaint, Prima Paint petitioned the District Court for an order enjoining F & C from proceeding with the arbitration. F & C cross-moved to stay the court action pending arbitration. F & C contended that the issue presented—whether there was fraud in the inducement of the consulting agreement—was a question for the arbitrators and not for the District Court. . . .

The District Court granted F & C's motion to stay the action pending arbitration, holding that a charge of fraud in the inducement of a contract containing an arbitration clause as broad as this one was a question for the arbitrators and not for the court. . . . The Court of Appeals for the Second Circuit dismissed Prima Paint's appeal. It held that the contract in question evidenced a transaction involving interstate commerce; that under the controlling *Robert [*400] Lawrence Co.* decision a claim of fraud in the inducement of the contract generally—as opposed to the arbitration clause itself—is for the arbitrators and not for the courts; and that this rule—one of 'national substantive law'—governs even in the face of a contrary state rule. We agree, albeit for somewhat different reasons, and we affirm the decision below.

The key statutory provisions are §§ 2, 3, and 4 of the United States Arbitration Act of 1925. Section 2 provides that a written provision for arbitration 'in any maritime transaction or a contract evidencing a transaction involving commerce . . . shall be valid, irrevocable, and enforceable, save upon such grounds as exist at law or in equity for the revocation of any contract.' Section 3 requires a federal court in which suit has been brought 'upon any issue referable to arbitration under an agreement in writing for such arbitration' to stay the court action pending arbitration once it is satisfied that the issue is arbitrable under the agreement. Section 4 provides a federal remedy for a party 'aggrieved by the alleged failure, neglect, or refusal of another to arbitrate under a written agreement for arbitration,' and directs the federal court to order arbitration once it is satisfied that an agreement for arbitration has been made and has not been honored.

[*401] In *Bernhardt v. Polygraphic Co.*, 350 U.S. 198 (1956), this Court held that the stay provisions of § 3, invoked here by respondent F & C, apply only to the two kinds of contracts specified in §§ 1 and 2 of the Act, namely those in admiralty or evidencing transactions in 'commerce.' Our first question, then, is whether the consulting agreement between F & C and Prima Paint is such a contract. We agree with the Court of Appeals that it is. Prima Paint acquired a New Jersey paint business serving at least 175 wholesale clients in a number of States, and secured F & C's assistance in arranging the transfer of manufacturing and selling operations from New Jersey to Maryland. The consulting agreement was inextricably tied to this interstate transfer and to the continuing operations of an interstate manufacturing and wholesaling business. There could not be a clearer case of a contract evidencing a transaction in interstate commerce.[7]

[*402] Having determined that the contract in question is within the coverage of the Arbitration Act, we turn to the central issue in this case: whether a claim of fraud in the inducement of the entire contract is to be resolved by the

---

[7] It is suggested in dissent that, despite the absence of any language in the statute so indicating, we should construe it to apply only to 'contracts between merchants for the interstate shipment of goods.' Not only have we neither the desire nor the warrant so to amend the statute, but we find persuasive and authoritative evidence of a contrary legislative intent. See, *e.g.*, the House Report on this legislation which proclaims that 'the control over interstate commerce [one of the bases for the legislation] reaches not only the actual physical interstate shipment of goods but also contracts relating to interstate commerce.' H. R. Rep. No. 96, 68th Cong., 1st Sess., 1 (1924). We note, too, that were the dissent's curious narrowing of the statute correct, there would have been no necessity for Congress to have amended the statute to exclude certain kinds of employment contracts. See § 1. In any event, the anomaly urged upon us in dissent is manifested by the present case. It would be remarkable to say that a contract for the purchase of a single can of paint may evidence a transaction in interstate commerce, but that an agreement relating to the facilitation of the purchase of an entire interstate paint business and its re-establishment and operation in another State is not.

federal court, or whether the matter is to be referred to the arbitrators. The courts of appeals have differed in their approach to this question. The view of the Court of Appeals for the Second Circuit, as expressed in this case and in others, is that—*except where the parties otherwise intend*—arbitration clauses as a matter of federal law are 'separable' from the contracts in which they are embedded, and that where no claim is made that fraud was directed to the arbitration clause itself, a broad arbitration clause will be held to encompass arbitration of the claim that the contract itself was induced by fraud. . . .With respect to cases brought in federal court involving maritime contracts or those evidencing transactions in 'commerce,' we think that Congress has provided an explicit answer. That answer is to be found in § 4 of the Act, which provides a remedy to a party seeking to compel compliance with an arbitration agreement. Under § 4, with respect to a matter within the jurisdiction of the federal courts save for the existence of an arbitration clause, the federal court is instructed to order arbitration to proceed once it is satisfied that 'the making of the agreement for arbitration or the failure to comply [with the arbitration agreement] is not in issue.' Accordingly, if the claim is fraud in the inducement of the arbitration clause itself—an issue which [*404] goes to the 'making' of the agreement to arbitrate—the federal court may proceed to adjudicate it. But the statutory language does not permit the federal court to consider claims of fraud in the inducement of the contract generally. Section 4 does not expressly relate to situations like the present in which a stay is sought of a federal action in order that arbitration may proceed. But it is inconceivable that Congress intended the rule to differ depending upon which party to the arbitration agreement first invokes the assistance of a federal court. . . .

There remains the question whether such a rule is constitutionally permissible. The point is made that, whatever the nature of the contract involved here, this case is in federal court solely by reason of diversity of citizenship, and that since the decision in *Erie R. Co. v. Tompkins*, 304 U.S. 64 (1938), federal courts are bound in diversity cases to follow state rules of decision in matters which are 'substantive' rather than 'procedural,' [*405] or where the matter is 'outcome determinative.' *Guaranty Trust Co. v. York*, 326 U.S. 99 (1945). The question in this case, however, is not whether Congress may fashion federal substantive rules to govern questions arising in simple diversity cases. *See Bernhardt v. Polygraphic Co.*, 350 U.S. at 202. Rather, the question is whether Congress may prescribe how federal courts are to conduct themselves with respect to subject matter over which Congress plainly has power to legislate. The answer to that can only be in the affirmative. And it is clear beyond dispute that the federal arbitration statute is based upon and confined to the incontestable federal foundations of 'control over interstate commerce and over admiralty.' H. R. Rep. No. 96, 68th Cong., 1st Sess., 1 (1924); S. Rep. No. 536, 68th Cong., 1st Sess., 3 (1924).[13]

Non-congressional sponsors of the legislation agreed. As Mr. Charles L. Bernheimer, chairman of the Arbitration Committee of the New York Chamber of Commerce, told the Senate subcommittee, the proposed legislation 'follows the lines of the New York arbitration law, applying it to the fields wherein there is Federal jurisdiction. These fields are in admiralty and in foreign and interstate commerce.' Hearing on S. 4213 and S. 4214, before the Subcommittee of the Senate Committee on the Judiciary, 67th Cong., 4th Sess., 2 (1923). In the joint House and Senate hearings, Mr. Bernheimer answered 'Yes; entirely,' to the statement of the chairman, Senator Sterling, that 'What you have in mind is that this proposed legislation relates to contracts arising in interstate commerce.' Joint Hearings on S. 1005 and H. R. 646 before the Subcommittees of the Committees on the Judiciary, 68th Cong., 1st Sess., 7 (1924). Mr. Julius Henry Cohen, draftsman for the American Bar Association of the proposed bill, said the sponsor's goals were: 'First . . . to get a State statute, *and then to get a Federal law to cover interstate and Foreign commerce and admiralty*, and, third, to get a treaty with foreign countries.' Joint Hearings, supra, at 16 (emphasis added). See also Joint Hearings, supra, at 27–28 (statement of Mr. Alexander Rose). Mr. Cohen did submit a brief to the Subcommittee urging a jurisdictional base broader than the commerce and admiralty powers, Joint Hearings, supra, at 37–38, but there is no indication in the statute or in the legislative history that this invitation to go beyond those powers was accepted, and his own testimony took a much narrower tack.

. . . *Affirmed.*

MR. JUSTICE BLACK, with whom MR. JUSTICE DOUGLAS and MR. JUSTICE STEWART join, dissenting.

---

[13]   It is true that the Arbitration Act was passed 13 years before this Court's decision in *Erie R. Co. v. Tompkins, supra*, brought to an end the regime of *Swift v. Tyson*, 16 Pet. 1 (1842), and that at the time of enactment Congress had reason to believe that it still had power to create federal rules to govern questions of 'general law' arising in simple diversity cases—at least, absent any state statute to the contrary. If Congress relied at all on this 'oft-challenged' power, *see Erie R. Co.*, 304 U.S., at 69, it was only supplementary to the admiralty and commerce powers, which formed the principal bases of the legislation. Indeed, Congressman Graham, the bill's sponsor in the House, told his colleagues that it 'only affects contracts relating to interstate subjects and contracts in admiralty.' 65 Cong. Rec. 1931 (1924). The Senate Report on this legislation similarly indicated that the bill '[relates] to maritime transactions and to contracts in interstate and foreign commerce.' S. Rep. No. 536, 68th Cong., 1st Sess., 3 (1924).

The Court here holds that the United States Arbitration Act, 9 U.S.C. §§ 1–14, as a matter of federal substantive law, compels a party to a contract containing a written arbitration provision to carry out his 'arbitration agreement' even though a court might, after a fair trial, hold the entire contract—including the arbitration agreement—void because of fraud in the inducement. The Court holds, what is to me fantastic, that the legal issue of a contract's voidness because of fraud is to be decided by persons designated to arbitrate factual controversies arising out of a valid contract between the parties. And the arbitrators who the Court holds are to adjudicate the legal validity of the contract need not even be lawyers, and in all probability will be nonlawyers, wholly unqualified to decide legal issues, and even if qualified to apply the law, not bound to do so. I am by no means sure that thus forcing a person to forgo his opportunity to try his legal issues in the courts where, unlike the situation in arbitration, he may have a jury trial and right to appeal, is not a denial of due process of law. I am satisfied, however, that Congress did not impose any such procedures in the Arbitration Act. And I am fully satisfied that a [*408] reasonable and fair reading of that Act's language and history shows that both Congress and the framers of the Act were at great pains to emphasize that nonlawyers designated to adjust and arbitrate factual controversies arising out of valid contracts would not trespass upon the courts' prerogative to decide the legal question of whether any legal contract exists upon which to base an arbitration.

I.

The agreement involved here is a consulting agreement in which Flood & Conklin agreed to perform certain services for and not to compete with Prima Paint. The agreement contained an arbitration clause providing that 'any controversy or claim arising out of or relating to this Agreement . . . shall be settled by arbitration in the City of New York.' F & C, contending that Prima had failed to make a payment under the contract, sent Prima a 'Notice of Intention to Arbitrate' pursuant to the New York Arbitration Act. Invoking diversity jurisdiction, Prima brought this action in federal district court to rescind the entire consulting agreement on the ground of fraud. The fraud allegedly consisted of F & C's misrepresentation at the time the contract was made, that it was solvent and able to perform the agreement, while in fact it was completely insolvent. Prima alleged that it would not have made any contract at all with F & C but for this misrepresentation. Prima simply contended that there was never a meeting of minds between the parties. F & C moved to stay Prima's lawsuit for rescission pending arbitration of the fraud issue raised by Prima. The lower courts, relying on the [*409] Second Circuit's decision in *Robert Lawrence*

Co. v. Devonshire Fabrics, Inc., 271 F.2d 402, cert. granted, 362 U.S. 909, dismissed, 364 U.S. 801, held that, as a matter of 'national substantive law,' the arbitration clause in the contract is 'separable' from the rest of the contract and that allegations that go to the validity of the contract in general, as opposed to the arbitration clause in particular, are to be decided by the arbitrator, not the court.

The Court today affirms this holding for three reasons, none of which is supported by the language or history of the Arbitration Act. First, the Court holds that because the consulting agreement was intended to supplement a separate contract for the interstate transfer of assets, it is itself a 'contract evidencing a transaction involving commerce,' the language used by Congress to describe contracts the Act was designed to cover. But in light of the legislative history which indicates that the Act was to have a limited application to contracts between merchants for the interstate shipment of goods,[2] and in light of the express failure of Congress to use language [*410] making the Act applicable to all contracts which 'affect commerce,' the statutory language Congress normally uses when it wishes to exercise its full powers over commerce,[3] I am not at all certain that the Act was intended to apply to this consulting agreement. Second, the Court holds that the language of § 4 of the Act provides an 'explicit answer' to the question of whether the arbitration clause is 'separable' from the rest of the contract in which it is contained. Section 4 merely provides that the court must order arbitration if it is 'satisfied that the making of the agreement for

---

[2]   The principal support for the Act came from trade associations dealing in groceries and other perishables and from commercial and mercantile groups in the major trading centers. 50 A. B. A. Rep. 357 (1925). Practically all who testified in support of the bill before the Senate subcommittee in 1923 explained that the bill was designed to cover contracts between people in different States who produced, shipped, bought, or sold commodities. Hearing on S. 4213 and S. 4214 before the Subcommittee of the Senate Committee on the Judiciary, 67th Cong., 4th Sess., 3, 7, 9, 10 (1923). The same views were expressed in the 1924 hearings. When Senator Sterling suggested, 'What you have in mind is that this proposed legislation relates to contracts arising in interstate commerce,' Mr. Bernheimer, a chief exponent of the bill, replied: 'Yes; entirely. The farmer who will sell his carload of potatoes, from Wyoming, to a dealer in the State of New Jersey, for instance.' Joint Hearings on S. 1005 and H.R. 646 before the Subcommittees of the Committees on the Judiciary, 68th Cong., 1st Sess., 7. See also *id.*, at 27.

[3]   In some Acts Congress uses broad language and defines commerce to include even that which 'affects' commerce. Federal Employers' Liability Act, 35 Stat. 65, § 1, as amended, 45 U.S.C. § 51; National Labor Relations Act, 49 Stat. 450, § 2, as amended, 29 U.S.C. § 152(7). In other instances Congress has chosen more restrictive language. Fair Labor Standards Act of 1938, 52 Stat. 1062, § 6, as amended, 29 U.S.C. § 206. Prior to this case, this Court has always made careful inquiry to assure itself that it is applying a statute with the coverage that Congress intended, so that the meaning *in that statute* of 'commerce' will be neither expanded nor contracted. The Arbitration Act is an example of carefully limited language. It covers only those contracts 'involving commerce,' and nowhere is there a suggestion that it is meant to extend to contracts 'affecting commerce.' The Act not only uses narrow language, but also is completely without any declaration of some national interest to be served or some nationwide comprehensive scheme of regulation to be created, and this absence suggests that Congress did not intend to exert its full power over commerce.

arbitration . . . is not in issue.' That language, considered alone, far from providing an 'explicit answer,' merely poses the further question of what kind of allegations put the making of the arbitration agreement in issue. Since both the lower courts assumed that but for the federal Act, New York law might apply and that under New York law a general allegation of fraud in the inducement puts into issue the making of the agreement to arbitrate (considered inseparable [*411] under New York law from the rest of the contract), the Court necessarily holds that federal law determines whether certain allegations put the making of the arbitration agreement in issue. And the Court approves the Second Circuit's fashioning of a federal separability rule which overrides state law to the contrary. The Court thus holds that the Arbitration Act, designed to provide merely a procedural remedy which would not interfere with state substantive law, authorizes federal courts to fashion a federal rule to make arbitration clauses 'separable' and valid. And the Court approves a rule which is not only contrary to state law, but contrary to the intention of the parties and to accepted principles of contract law—a rule which indeed elevates arbitration provisions above all other contractual provisions. As the Court recognizes, that result was clearly not intended by Congress. Finally, the Court summarily disposes of the problem raised by *Erie R. Co. v. Tompkins*, 304 U.S. 64, recognized as a serious constitutional problem in *Bernhardt v. Polygraphic Co.*, 350 U.S. 198 by insufficiently supported assertions that it is 'clear beyond dispute' that Congress based the Arbitration Act on its power to regulate commerce and that 'if Congress relied at all on' its power to create federal law for diversity cases, such reliance 'was only supplementary.'

II.

[*412] Let us look briefly at the language of the Arbitration Act itself as Congress passed it. Section 2, the key provision of the Act, provides that '[a] written provision in . . . a contract . . . involving commerce to settle by arbitration a controversy thereafter arising out of such contract . . . shall be valid, irrevocable, and enforceable, *save upon such grounds as exist at law or in equity for the revocation of any contract.*' (Emphasis added.) Section 3 provides that 'if any suit . . . be brought . . . *upon any issue referable to arbitration* under an agreement in writing for such arbitration, the court . . . *upon being satisfied that the issue involved in such suit . . . is referable to arbitration under such an agreement,* shall . . . stay the trial of the action until such arbitration has been had . . .' (Emphasis added.) The language of these sections could not, I think, raise doubts about their meaning except to someone anxious to find doubts. They simply mean this: an arbitration agreement is to be enforced by a federal court unless the court, not the arbitrator,

finds grounds 'at law or in equity for the revocation of any contract.' Fraud, of course, is one of the most common grounds for revoking a contract. If the contract was procured by fraud, then, unless the defrauded party elects to affirm it, there is absolutely no contract, nothing to be arbitrated. Sections 2 and 3 of the Act assume the existence of a valid contract. They merely provide for enforcement where such a valid contract [*413] exists. These provisions were plainly designed to protect a person against whom arbitration is sought to be enforced from having to submit his legal issues as to validity of the contract to the arbitrator. The legislative history of the Act makes this clear. Senator Walsh of Montana, in hearings on the bill in 1923, observed, 'The court has got to hear and determine whether there is an agreement of arbitration, undoubtedly, and it is open to all defenses, equitable and legal, that would have existed at law . . . .' Mr. Piatt, who represented the American Bar Association which drafted and supported the Act, was even more explicit: 'I think this will operate something like an injunction process, except where he would attack it on the ground of fraud.' And then Senator Walsh replied: 'If he should attack it on the ground of fraud, *to rescind the whole thing*. . . . I presume that it merely [is] a question of whether he did make the arbitration agreement or not, . . . and then he would possibly set up that he was misled about the contract and entered into it by mistake . . . .' It is evident that Senator Walsh was referring to situations in which the validity of the entire contract is called into question. And Mr. Bernheimer, who represented one of the chambers of commerce in favor of the bill, assured the Senate subcommittee that 'the constitutional right to jury trial is adequately safeguarded' by the Act. Mr. Cohen, the American Bar Association's draftsman of the bill, assured the members of Congress that the Act would not impair the right to a jury trial, because it deprives a person of that right only when he has voluntarily and validly waived it by agreeing to submit certain [*414] disputes to arbitration. The court and a jury are to determine both the legal existence and scope of such an agreement. The members of Congress revealed an acute awareness of this problem. On several occasions they expressed opposition to a law which would enforce even a valid arbitration provision contained in a contract between parties of unequal bargaining power. Senator Walsh cited insurance, employment, construction, and shipping contracts as routinely containing arbitration clauses and being offered on a take-it-or-leave-it basis to captive customers or employees. He noted that such contracts 'are really not voluntarily [*sic*] things at all' because 'there is nothing for the man to do except to sign it; and then he surrenders his right to have his case tried by the court . . . .' He was emphatically assured by the supporters of the bill that it was not their intention to cover such cases. The significant thing is that Senator Walsh was not thinking in terms of the arbitration provisions being 'separable' parts of such contracts, parts which should be enforced without regard to why the entire contracts in which they were contained were agreed to. The issue for him was not whether an arbitration provision in a contract was made, but why, in the context of the entire contract and the circumstances [*415] of the parties, the entire contract was made. That is precisely the issue that a general allegation of fraud in the inducement raises: Prima contended that it would not have executed any contract, including the arbitration clause, if it were not for the fraudulent representations of F & C. Prima's agreement to an arbitration clause in a contract obtained by fraud was no more 'voluntary' than an insured's or employee's agreement to an arbitration clause in a contract obtained by superior bargaining power. . . .

III.

With such statutory language and legislative history, one can well wonder what is the basis for the Court's surprising departure from the Act's clear statement which expressly excepts from arbitration 'such grounds as exist at law or in equity for the revocation of any contract.' Credit for the creation of a rationalization to justify this statutory mutilation apparently must go to the Second Circuit' opinion in *Robert Lawrence Co. v. Devonshire Fabrics, Inc., supra.* In that decision Judge Medina undertook to resolve the serious constitutional problem which this Court had avoided in *Bernhardt* by holding the Act inapplicable to a diversity case involving an intrastate contract. That problem was whether the Arbitration [*417] Act, passed 13 years prior to *Erie R. Co. v. Tompkins,* 304 U.S. 64, could be constitutionally applied in a diversity case even though its application would require the federal court to enforce an agreement to arbitrate which the state court across the street would not enforce. *Bernhardt's* holding that arbitration is 'outcome determinative,' 350 U.S., at 203 and its recognition that there would be unconstitutional discrimination if an arbitration agreement were enforceable in federal court but not in the state court, *id.,* at 204, posed a choice of two alternatives for Judge Medina. If he held that the Arbitration Act rested solely on Congress' power, widely recognized in 1925 but negated in *Erie,* to prescribe general federal law applicable in diversity cases, he would be compelled to hold the Act unconstitutional as applied to diversity cases under *Erie* and *Bernhardt.* If he held that the Act rested on Congress' power to enact substantive law governing interstate commerce, then the *Erie-Bernhardt* problem would be avoided and the application of the Act to diversity cases involving commerce could be saved.

. . . .

Finally, there are clear indications in the legislative history that the Act was not intended to make arbitration agreements enforceable in state courts[23] or to provide an independent federal-question basis for jurisdiction in federal courts apart from diversity jurisdiction.[24] The absence of both of these effects—which normally follow from legislation of federal substantive law—seems to militate against the view that Congress was creating a body of federal substantive law.

Suffice it to say that Judge Medina chose the alternative of construing the Act to create federal substantive law in order to avoid its emasculation under *Erie* and *Bernhardt*. But Judge Medina was not content to stop there with a holding that the Act makes arbitration agreements in a contract involving commerce enforceable in federal court even though the basis of jurisdiction is diversity and state law does not enforce such [*421] agreements. The problem in *Robert Lawrence*, as here, was not whether an arbitration agreement is enforceable, for the New York Arbitration Act, upon which the federal Act was based, enforces an arbitration clause in the same terms as the federal Act. The problem in *Robert Lawrence*, and here, was rather whether the arbitration clause in a contract induced by fraud is 'separable.' Under New York law, it was not: general allegations of fraud in the inducement would, as a matter of state law, put in issue the making of the arbitration clause. So to avoid this application of state law, Judge Medina went further than holding that the federal Act makes agreements to arbitrate enforceable: he held that the Act creates a 'body of law' that 'encompasses questions of interpretation and construction as well as questions of validity, revocability and enforceability of arbitration agreements affecting interstate commerce or maritime affairs.' 271 F.2d at 409.

Thus, 35 years after the passage of the Arbitration Act, the Second Circuit completely rewrote it. Under its new formulation, § 2 now makes arbitration agreements enforceable 'save upon such grounds as exist at *federal* law for the revocation of any contract.' And under § 4, before enforcing an arbitration

---

[23]   *See, e.g.*, Cohen & Dayton, *supra*, at 277; Committee on Commerce, Trade & Commercial Law, *supra*, at 155, 156. Mr. Rose, representing the Arbitration Society of America, suggested that the Act might have the beneficial effect of encouraging States to enact similar laws, Joint Hearings, *supra*, at 28, but Mr. Cohen assured Congress: "Nor can it be said that the Congress of the United States, directing its own courts . . ., would infringe upon the provinces or prerogatives of the States. . . . The question of the enforcement relates to the law of remedies and not to substantive law. The rule must be changed for the jurisdiction in which the agreement is sought to be enforced . . . . There is no disposition therefore by means of the Federal bludgeon to force an individual State into an unwilling submission to arbitration enforcement." *Id.*, at 39–40.

[24]   This seems implicit in § 3's provision for a stay by a "court in which such suit is pending" and § 4's provision that enforcement may be ordered by "any United States district court which, save for such agreement, would have jurisdiction under Title 28, in a civil action or in admiralty of the subject matter of a suit arising out of the controversy between the parties."

agreement, the district court must be satisfied that 'the making of the agreement for arbitration, *as a matter of federal law*, is not in issue.' And then when Judge Medina turned to the task of 'the formulation of the principles of federal substantive law necessary for this purpose,' 271 F.2d, at 409, he formulated the separability rule which the Court today adopts—not because § 4 provided this rule as an 'explicit answer,' not because he looked to the intention of the parties, but because of his notion that the separability rule would further a 'liberal policy of promoting arbitration.' 271 F.2d, at 410.

[*422] Today, without expressly saying so, the Court does precisely what Judge Medina did in *Robert Lawrence*. It is not content to hold that the Act does all it was intended to do: make arbitration agreements enforceable in federal courts if they are valid and legally existent under state law. The Court holds that the Act gives federal courts the right to fashion federal law, inconsistent with state law, to determine whether an arbitration agreement was made and what it means. Even if Congress intended to create substantive rights by passage of the Act, I am wholly convinced that it did not intend to create such a sweeping body of federal substantive law completely to take away from the States their power to interpret contracts made by their own citizens in their own territory.

First. The legislative history is clear that Congress intended no such thing. Congress assumed that arbitration agreements were recognized as valid by state and federal law. Courts would give damages for their breach, but would simply refuse to specifically enforce them. Congress thus had one limited purpose in mind: to provide a party to such an agreement 'a remedy formerly denied him.' 'Arbitration under the Federal . . . [statute] is simply a new procedural remedy.' The Act 'creates no new legislation, grants no new rights, except a remedy to enforce. . . .' The drafters of the Act were very explicit:

> 'A Federal statute providing for the enforcement of arbitration agreements does relate solely to procedure [*423] of the Federal courts. *It is no infringement upon the right of each State to decide for itself what contracts shall or shall not exist under its laws.* To be sure *whether or not a contract exists is a question of the substantive law of the jurisdiction wherein the contract was made.*' Committee on Commerce, Trade & Commercial Law, The United States Arbitration Law and Its Application, 11 A. B. A. J. 153, 154. (Emphasis added.)

> 'Neither is it true that such a statute, declaring arbitration agreements to be valid, is the source of their existence as a matter of substantive law. . . .

'So far as the present law declares simply the policy of recognizing and enforcing arbitration agreements in the Federal courts it does not encroach upon the province of the individual States.' Cohen & Dayton, The New Federal Arbitration Law, 12 VA. L. REV. 265, 276–277.

All this indicates that the § 4 inquiry of whether the making of the arbitration agreement is in issue is to be determined by reference to state law, not federal law formulated by judges for the purpose of promoting arbitration.

Second. The avowed purpose of the Act was to place arbitration agreements 'upon the same footing as other contracts.' The separability rule which the Court applies to an arbitration clause does not result in equality between it and other clauses in the contract. I had always thought that a person who attacks a contract on the ground of fraud and seeks to rescind it has to seek rescission of the whole, not tidbits, and is not given the option of denying the existence of some clauses and affirming the existence of others. Here F & C agreed both to perform consulting services for Prima and not to [*424] compete with Prima. Would any court hold that those two agreements were separable, even though Prima in agreeing to pay F & C not to compete did not directly rely on F & C's representations of being solvent? The simple fact is that Prima would not have agreed to the covenant not to compete or to the arbitration clause but for F & C's fraudulent promise that it would be financially able to perform consulting services. . . .

. . . .

Under this test, all of Prima's promises were part of one, inseparable contract.

Third. It is clear that had this identical contract dispute been litigated in New York courts under its arbitration act, Prima would not be required to present its claims of fraud to the arbitrator if the state rule of nonseparability applies. The Court here does not hold today, as did Judge Medina, that the body of federal substantive law created by federal judges under the Arbitration Act is required to be applied by state courts. A holding to that effect—which the Court seems to leave up in the air—would flout the intention of the framers of the Act. Yet under this Court's opinion today—that the Act supplies not only the remedy of enforcement but a body of federal doctrines to determine the validity of an arbitration agreement—failure to make the Act [*425] applicable in state courts would give rise to 'forum shopping' and an unconstitutional discrimination that both *Erie* and *Bernhardt* were designed to eliminate. These problems are greatly reduced if the Act is limited, as it should be, to its proper scope: the mere enforcement in federal courts of valid arbitration agreements.

IV.

The Court's summary treatment of these issues has made it necessary for me to express my views at length. The plain purpose of the Act as written by Congress was this and no more: Congress wanted federal courts to enforce contracts to arbitrate and plainly said so in the Act. But Congress also plainly said that whether a contract containing an arbitration clause can be rescinded on the ground of fraud is to be decided by the courts and not by the arbitrators. Prima here challenged in the courts the validity of its alleged contract with F & C as a whole, not in fragments. If there has never been any valid contract, then there is not now and never has been anything to arbitrate. If Prima's allegations are true, the sum total of what the Court does here is to force Prima to arbitrate a contract which is void and unenforceable before arbitrators who are given the power to make final legal determinations of their own jurisdiction, not even subject to effective review by the highest court in the land. That is not what Congress said Prima must do. It seems to be what the Court thinks would promote the policy of arbitration. I am completely unable to agree to this new version of the Arbitration Act, a version which its own creator in *Robert Lawrence* practically admitted was judicial legislation. Congress might possibly have enacted such a version into law had it been able to foresee subsequent legal events, but I do not think this Court should do so.

I would reverse this case.

NOTES

Facts

1. What was the transaction at-issue in the case? How does the transaction differ from the one at-issue in *Bernhardt*? How were they similar? Did the court address these factual similarities/differences? What do you think motivated the court's treatment of the facts?

2. What was the jurisdictional basis upon which the U.S. Supreme Court heard the case? How does, or should, this procedural posture matter to the resolution of the case?

Law

1. What does the "separability doctrine" mean? How could one attack an arbitration agreement contained within a larger contract without also asserting that the contract as a whole is subject to the same defense?

2. What is the statutory basis for the separability doctrine? Was it applicable?

CHAPTER 3

The Contemporary Standard

In a series of decisions starting in 1984, the United States Supreme Court has fashioned the current standard applicable to arbitration in the United States. This standard provides a broad scope within which arbitration agreements will be enforced under the Federal Arbitration Act—even in the face of opposition by state legislation deeming the agreement unenforceable and state supreme courts holding that the underlying agreement in which the arbitration clause was contained was criminal in nature. As this section will introduce, this expansive scope of the Federal Arbitration Act at times can raise significant federalism questions.

As this section further explains, the contemporary standard provides significant latitude when it comes to the FAA's "writing requirement"—that is, the FAA does not apply to an arbitration agreement unless it is in "writing.". The FAA states

> A written provision in any maritime transaction or a contract evidencing a transaction involving commerce to settle by arbitration a controversy thereafter arising out of such contract or transaction, or the refusal to perform the whole or any part thereof, or an agreement in writing to submit to arbitration an existing controversy arising out of such a contract, transaction, or refusal, shall be valid, irrevocable, and enforceable, save upon such grounds as exist at law or in equity for the revocation of any contract.[1]

As this chapter will show, the original hostility and caution toward arbitration has worn-off in the modern age. Arbitration agreements are now enforced robustly. The law provides the drafters of arbitration agreements with unprecedented latitude in concluding their arbitration agreements. How to use this latitude will be discussed in the next section.

---

[1] Federal Arbitration Act ("FAA"), 9 U.S.C. § 2 (1947).

Fact Scenario

Dover, Inc. ("*Dover*") concluded a contract with Calais Fine Foods, LLC ("*Calais*") for the provision of catering services for the annual dinner at a large Pacific Rim software development conference it was hosting. Dover specified that Calais was to prepare gourmet foods, including "Fugu," a poisonous blowfish. Dover's president left the following voicemail on the digital answering machine of his Calais contact:

> "Doug, this is David from Dover. Listen, we would like you to cater the Tanaka wedding as discussed. We will pay you $50,000 for your "A-List" services per your website. Our guys really want to make sure that we get a great sushi chef who can prepare Fugu. Now listen, if there are any disputes relating to this agreement, we must arbitrate them according to the AAA commercial rules, okay. That is a deal-breaker on our side. Talk to you soon. Bye."

Doug Meirelsa returned the call, and also left a voicemail:

> "David, this Doug from Calais. We agree to cater the event per your voicemail. Just send the $17,500 down payment over and we will get started."

Dover made the down payment, and Calais catered the event. All of the guests who tried the Fugu within 30 minutes experienced numbness and tingling around the mouth, nausea, and vomiting. Dover subsequently did not pay the balance due on the contract, and Calais began court proceedings against Dover for payment of the outstanding amount on the contract. Dover moved to compel arbitration, providing the two voicemails (transcribed) as evidence of an arbitration agreement. What arguments should the respective parties advance that there was or was not a written agreement sufficient to meet the FAA requirements?

Readings

A) The Reach of the Federal Arbitration Act

Southland Corp. v. Keating

465 U.S. 1 (1984)

CHIEF JUSTICE BURGER delivered the opinion of the Court.

I

Appellant The Southland Corp. is the owner and franchisor of 7-Eleven convenience stores. Southland's standard franchise agreement provides each franchisee with a license to use certain registered trademarks, a lease or sublease of a convenience store owned or leased by Southland, inventory [*4] financing, and assistance in advertising and merchandising. The franchisees operate the stores, supply bookkeeping data, and pay Southland a fixed percentage of gross profits. The franchise agreement also contains the following provision requiring arbitration:

> *"Any controversy or claim arising out of or relating to this Agreement or the breach thereof shall be settled by arbitration in accordance with the Rules of the American Arbitration Association . . . and judgment upon any award rendered by the arbitrator may be entered in any court having jurisdiction thereof."*

Appellees are 7-Eleven franchisees. Between September 1975 and January 1977, several appellees filed individual actions against Southland in California Superior Court alleging, among other things, fraud, oral misrepresentation, breach of contract, breach of fiduciary duty, and violation of the disclosure requirements of the California Franchise Investment Law. Cal. Corp. Code Ann. § 31000 *et seq.* (West 1977). Southland's answer, in all but one of the individual actions, included the affirmative defense of failure to arbitrate.

In May 1977, appellee Keating filed a class action against Southland on behalf of a class that assertedly includes approximately 800 California franchisees. Keating's principal claims were substantially the same as those asserted by the other franchisees. After the various actions were consolidated, Southland petitioned to compel arbitration of the claims in all cases, and appellees moved for class certification.

The Superior Court granted Southland's motion to compel arbitration of all claims except those claims based on the Franchise Investment Law. The court did not pass on appellees' request for class certification. Southland appealed from the order insofar as it excluded from arbitration the claims based on the California statute. Appellees filed a petition for a writ of mandamus or prohibition in the California [*5] Court of Appeal arguing that the arbitration should proceed as a class action.

The California Court of Appeal reversed the trial court's refusal to compel arbitration of appellees' claims under the Franchise Investment Law. *Keating v. Superior Court, Alameda County*, 167 Cal. Rptr. 481 (1980). That court interpreted the arbitration clause to require arbitration of all claims asserted under the Franchise Investment Law, and construed the Franchise Investment Law not to invalidate such agreements to arbitrate. Alternatively, the court concluded that if the Franchise Investment Law rendered arbitration agreements involving commerce unenforceable, it would conflict with § 2 of the Federal Arbitration Act, 9 U.S.C. § 2, and therefore be invalid under the Supremacy Clause. 67 Cal. Rptr., at 493–494. The Court of Appeal also determined that there was no "insurmountable obstacle" to conducting an arbitration on a classwide basis, and issued a writ of mandate directing the trial court to conduct class-certification proceedings. *Id.*, at 492.

The California Supreme Court, by a vote of 4–2, reversed the ruling that claims asserted under the Franchise Investment Law are arbitrable. *Keating v. Superior Court of Alameda County*, 31 Cal. 3d 584, 645 P.2d 1192 (1982). The California Supreme Court interpreted the Franchise Investment Law to require judicial consideration of claims brought under that statute and concluded that the California statute did not contravene the federal Act. *Id.*, at 604, 645 P.2d 1203–1204. The court also remanded the case to the trial court for consideration of appellees' request for classwide arbitration.

[*6] We postponed consideration of the question of jurisdiction pending argument on the merits. We reverse in part and dismiss in part.

. . . .

III

As previously noted, the California Franchise Investment Law provides:

"Any condition, stipulation or provision purporting to bind any person acquiring any franchise to waive compliance with any provision of this law or any rule or order hereunder is void." Cal. Corp. Code Ann. § 31512 (West 1977).

The California Supreme Court interpreted this statute to require judicial consideration of claims brought under the state statute and accordingly refused to enforce the parties' contract to arbitrate such claims. So interpreted the

California Franchise Investment Law directly conflicts with § 2 of the Federal Arbitration Act and violates the Supremacy Clause.

In enacting § 2 of the federal Act, Congress declared a national policy favoring arbitration and withdrew the power of the states to require a judicial forum for the resolution of claims which the contracting parties agreed to resolve by arbitration. . . .

. . . .

We discern only two limitations on the enforceability of arbitration provisions governed by the Federal Arbitration [*11] Act: they must be part of a written maritime contract or a contract "evidencing a transaction involving commerce" and such clauses may be revoked upon "grounds as exist at law or in equity for the revocation of any contract." We see nothing in the Act indicating that the broad principle of enforceability is subject to any additional limitations under state law.

The Federal Arbitration Act rests on the authority of Congress to enact substantive rules under the Commerce Clause. In *Prima Paint Corp. v. Flood & Conklin Mfg. Co.*, 388 U.S. 395 (1967), the Court examined the legislative history of the Act and concluded that the statute "is based upon . . . the incontestable federal foundations of 'control over interstate commerce and over admiralty.' " *Id.*, at 405(quoting H. R. Rep. No. 96, 68th Cong., 1st Sess. 1 (1924)). The contract in *Prima Paint*, as here, contained an arbitration clause. One party in that case alleged that the other had committed fraud in the inducement of the contract, although not of arbitration clause in particular, and sought to have the claim of fraud adjudicated in federal court. The Court held that, notwithstanding a contrary state rule, consideration of a claim of fraud in the inducement of a contract "is for the arbitrators and not for the courts," 388 U.S., at 400. The Court relied for this holding on Congress' broad power to fashion substantive rules under the Commerce Clause.

At least since 1824 Congress' authority under the Commerce Clause has been held plenary. *Gibbons v. Ogden*, 9 Wheat. 1, 196 (1824). In the words of Chief Justice Marshall, [*12] the authority of Congress is "the power to regulate; that is, to prescribe the rule by which commerce is to be governed." *Ibid.* The statements of the Court in *Prima Paint* that the Arbitration Act was an exercise of the Commerce Clause power clearly implied that the substantive rules of the Act were to apply in state as well as federal courts. . . .

. . . .

Although the legislative history is not without ambiguities, there are strong indications that Congress had in mind something more than making arbitration agreements enforceable only in the federal courts. The House Report plainly suggests the more comprehensive objectives:

> "The purpose of this bill is to make valid and enforcible [sic] agreements for arbitration contained in *contracts involving [*13] interstate commerce* or within the jurisdiction or [sic] admiralty, *or* which may be the subject of litigation in the Federal courts." H. R. Rep. No. 96, 68th Cong., 1st Sess. 1 (1924) (emphasis added).

This broader purpose can also be inferred from the reality that Congress would be less likely to address a problem whose impact was confined to federal courts than a problem of large significance in the field of commerce. The Arbitration Act sought to "overcome the rule of equity, that equity will not specifically enforce [any] arbitration agreement." Hearing on S. 4213 and S. 4214 before a Subcommittee of the Senate Committee on the Judiciary, 67th Cong., 4th Sess. 6 (1923) (Senate Hearing) (remarks of Sen. Walsh). The House Report accompanying the bill stated:

> *"The need for the law arises from . . . the jealousy of the English courts for their own jurisdiction. . . . This jealousy survived for so [long] a period that the principle became firmly embedded in the English common law and was adopted with it by the American courts. The courts have felt that the precedent was too strongly fixed to be overturned without legislative enactment. . . ." H. R. Rep. No. 96, supra, at 1–2.*

Surely this makes clear that the House Report contemplated a broad reach of the Act, unencumbered by state-law constraints. As was stated in *Metro Industrial Painting Corp. v. Terminal Construction Co.*, 287 F.2d 382, 387 (CA2 1961) (Lumbard, C. J., concurring), "the purpose of the act was to assure those who desired arbitration and whose contracts related to interstate commerce that their expectations would not be undermined by federal judges, or . . . by state courts or legislatures." . . . .

. . . .

The problems Congress faced were therefore twofold: the old common-law hostility toward arbitration, and the failure of state arbitration statutes to mandate enforcement of arbitration agreements. To confine the scope of the Act to arbitrations sought to be enforced in federal courts would frustrate what we believe Congress intended to be a broad enactment appropriate in scope to meet the large problems Congress was addressing.

Justice O'CONNOR argues that Congress viewed the Arbitration Act "as a procedural statute, applicable only in federal courts." *Post*, at 25. If it is correct that Congress sought only to create a procedural remedy in the federal courts, there can be no explanation for the express limitation in the Arbitration Act to contracts "involving commerce." 9 U.S.C. § 2. For example, when Congress has authorized this Court to prescribe the rules of procedure in the federal courts of appeals, district courts, and bankruptcy courts, it has not limited the power of the Court to prescribe rules applicable only to causes of action involving commerce. . . .We would expect that if Congress, in enacting the Arbitration Act, was creating what it thought to be a procedural rule applicable only in federal courts, it would not so limit the Act to transactions involving commerce. On the other hand, Congress would need to call on the Commerce Clause if it intended the Act to apply in state courts. Yet at the same time, its reach would be limited to transactions involving interstate commerce. We therefore view the "involving commerce" requirement in § 2, not as an inexplicable limitation on the power of the federal courts, but as a necessary [*15] qualification on a statute intended to apply in state and federal courts.

. . . .

[*17] The judgment of the California Supreme Court denying enforcement of the arbitration agreement is reversed; as to the question whether the Federal Arbitration Act precludes a class-action arbitration and any other issues not raised in the California courts, no decision by this Court would be appropriate at this time. As to the latter issues, the case is remanded for further proceedings not inconsistent with this opinion.

It is so ordered.

JUSTICE O'CONNOR with whom JUSTICE REHNQUIST joins, dissenting.

Section 2 of the Federal Arbitration Act (FAA) (originally known as the "United States Arbitration Act") provides that a written arbitration agreement "shall be valid, irrevocable, [*22] and enforceable, save upon such grounds as exist at law or in equity for the revocation of any contract." Section 2 does not, on its face, identify which judicial forums are bound by its requirements or what procedures govern its enforcement. The FAA deals with these matters in §§ 3 and 4. Section 3 provides:

> "If any suit or proceeding be brought *in any of the courts of the United States* upon any issue referable to arbitration . . . the court . . . shall on application of one of the parties stay the trial of the action until such

arbitration has been had in accordance with the terms of the agreement . . . ."

Section 4 specifies that a party aggrieved by another's refusal to arbitrate

"may petition *any United States district court* which, save for such agreement, would have jurisdiction under title 28, in a civil action or in admiralty of the subject matter . . . for an order directing that such arbitration proceed in the manner provided for in such agreement. . . ."

Today, the Court takes the facial silence of § 2 as a license to declare that state as well as federal courts must apply § 2. In addition, though this is not spelled out in the opinion, the Court holds that in enforcing this newly discovered federal right state courts must follow procedures specified in § 3. The Court's decision is impelled by an understandable desire to encourage the use of arbitration, but it utterly fails to recognize [*23] the clear congressional intent underlying the FAA. Congress intended to require federal, not state, courts to respect arbitration agreements.

I

The FAA was enacted in 1925. As demonstrated *infra*, at 24–29, Congress thought it was exercising its power to dictate either procedure or "general federal law" in federal courts. The issue presented here is the result of three subsequent decisions of this Court.

In 1938 this Court decided *Erie R. Co. v. Tompkins*, 304 U.S. 64. *Erie* denied the federal government the power to create substantive law solely by virtue of the Article III power to control federal-court jurisdiction. Eighteen years later the Court decided *Bernhardt v. Polygraphic Co.*, 350 U.S. 198 (1956). *Bernhardt* held that the duty to arbitrate a contract dispute is outcome-determinative—*i. e.* "substantive"—and therefore a matter normally governed by state law in federal diversity cases.

Bernhardt gave rise to concern that the FAA could thereafter constitutionally be applied only in federal-court cases arising under federal law, not in diversity cases. In *Prima Paint Corp. v. Flood & Conklin Mfg. Co.*, 388 U.S. 395, 404–405 (1967), we addressed that concern, and held that the FAA may constitutionally be applied to proceedings in a federal diversity court. The FAA covers only contracts involving interstate commerce or maritime affairs, and Congress "plainly has the power to legislate" in that area. *Id.* at 405.

[*24] Nevertheless, the *Prima Paint* decision "carefully avoided any explicit endorsement of the view that the Arbitration Act embodied substantive policies that were to be applied to all contracts within its scope, whether sued on in state or federal courts." P. Bator, P. Mishkin, D. Shapiro, & H. Wechsler, Hart and Wechsler's The Federal Courts and the Federal System 731–732 (2d ed. 1973).FN6 Today's case is the first in which this Court has had occasion to determine whether the FAA applies to state-court proceedings. One statement on the subject did appear in *Moses H. Cone Memorial Hospital v. Mercury Construction Corp.*, 460 U.S. 1 (1983), but that case involved a federal, not a state, court proceeding; its dictum concerning the law applicable in state courts was wholly unnecessary to its holding.

II . . .

A

[*25] One rarely finds a legislative history as unambiguous as the FAA's. That history establishes conclusively that the 1925 Congress viewed the FAA as a procedural statute, applicable only in federal courts, derived, Congress believed, largely from the federal power to control the jurisdiction of the federal courts.

In 1925 Congress emphatically believed arbitration to be a matter of "procedure." At hearings on the Act congressional Subcommittees were told: "The theory on which you do this is that you have the right to tell the Federal courts how to proceed." The House Report on the FAA stated: "Whether an agreement for arbitration shall be enforced or not is a question of procedure. . . ." . . . .

Since *Bernhardt*, a right to arbitration has been characterized as "substantive," and that holding is not challenged here. But Congress in 1925 did not characterize the FAA as this Court did in 1956. Congress *believed* that the FAA established nothing more than a rule of procedure, a rule therefore applicable only in the federal courts.

If characterizing the FAA as procedural was not enough, the draftsmen of the Act, the House Report, and the early commentators all flatly stated that the Act was intended to affect only federal-court proceedings. Mr. Cohen, the American Bar Association member who drafted the bill, assured two congressional Subcommittees in joint hearings:

"Nor can it be said that the Congress of the United States, *directing its own courts* . . ., would infringe upon [*27] the provinces or prerogatives of the States. . . . [The] question of the enforcement relates to the law of remedies and not to substantive law. The rule must be changed for the jurisdiction in which the agreement is sought to be enforced. . . . There is no disposition therefore by means of the Federal bludgeon to force an individual State into an unwilling submission to arbitration enforcement."

. . . .

B

The structure of the FAA itself runs directly contrary to the reading the Court today gives to § 2. Sections 3 and 4 are the implementing provisions of the Act, and they expressly apply only to federal courts. Section 4 refers to the "United States district [courts]," and provides that it can be invoked only in a court that has jurisdiction under Title 28 of the United States Code. As originally enacted, § 3 referred, in the same terms as § 4, to "courts [or court] of the United States."[17] There has since been a minor amendment in § 4's phrasing, but no substantive change in either section's limitation to federal courts.[18] . . .

The *Prima Paint* majority gave full but precise effect to the original congressional intent—it recognized that notwithstanding the intervention of *Erie* the FAA's restrictive focus on maritime and interstate contracts permits its application in federal diversity courts. Today's decision, in contrast, glosses over both the careful crafting of *Prima Paint* and the historical reasons that made *Prima Paint* necessary, and gives the FAA a reach far broader than Congress intended. . . . .

IV

The Court, ante, at [pages] 15–16, rejects the idea of requiring the FAA to be applied only in federal courts partly out of concern with the problem of forum shopping. The concern is unfounded. Because the FAA makes the federal courts equally accessible to both parties to a dispute, no forum shopping would be possible even if we gave the FAA a construction [*34] faithful to the congressional intent. In controversies involving incomplete diversity of citizenship there is simply no access to federal court and therefore no possibility of forum shopping. In controversies *with* complete diversity of citizenship the

---

[17] The use of identical language in both sections was natural: § 3 applies when the party resisting arbitration initiates the federal-court action; § 4 applies to actions initiated by the party seeking to enforce an arbitration provision. Phrasing the two sections differently would have made no sense.

[18] . . . . Even without this history, § 3's "courts of the United States" is a term of art whose meaning is unmistakable. State courts are "in" but not "of" the United States. . . .

FAA grants federal-court access equally to both parties; no party can gain any advantage by forum shopping. Even when the party resisting arbitration initiates an action in state court, the opposing party can invoke FAA § 4 and promptly secure a federal-court order to compel arbitration. See, *e.g., Moses H. Cone Memorial Hospital v. Mercury Construction Corp.*, 460 U.S. 1 (1983).

Ironically, the FAA was passed specifically to rectify forum-shopping problems created by this Court's decision in *Swift v. Tyson*, 16 Pet. 1 (1842). By 1925 several major commercial States had passed state arbitration laws, but the federal courts refused to enforce those laws in diversity cases. The drafters of the FAA might have anticipated *Bernhardt* by legislation and required federal diversity courts to adopt the arbitration law of the State in which they sat. But they deliberately chose a different approach. As was pointed out at congressional hearings, an additional goal of the Act was to make arbitration agreements enforceable even in federal courts located in States that had no arbitration law. The drafters' plan for maintaining reasonable harmony between state and federal practices was not to bludgeon States into compliance, but rather to adopt a uniform federal law, patterned after New York's path-breaking state statute, and simultaneously to press for passage of coordinated [*35] state legislation. The key language of the Uniform Act for Commercial Arbitration was, accordingly, identical to that in § 2 of the FAA.

In summary, forum-shopping concerns in connection with the FAA are a distraction that do not withstand scrutiny. The Court ignores the drafters' carefully devised plan for dealing with those problems.

V

Today's decision adds yet another chapter to the FAA's already colorful history. In 1842 this Court's ruling in *Swift v. Tyson, supra*, set up a major obstacle to the enforcement of state arbitration laws in federal diversity courts. In 1925 Congress sought to rectify the problem by enacting the FAA; the intent was to create uniform law binding only in the federal courts. In *Erie R. Co. v. Tompkins*, 304 U.S. 64 (1938), and then in *Bernhardt Polygraphic Co.*, 350 U.S. 198 (1956), this Court significantly curtailed federal power. In 1967 our decision in *Prima Paint* upheld the application of the FAA in a *federal-court* proceeding as a valid exercise of Congress's Commerce Clause and admiralty powers. Today the Court discovers a federal right in FAA § 2 that the state courts must enforce. Apparently confident that state courts are not competent to devise their own procedures for protecting the newly discovered federal right, the Court summarily prescribes a specific procedure, found nowhere in § 2 or its common-law origins, that the state courts are to follow.

[*36] Today's decision is unfaithful to congressional intent, unnecessary, and, in light of the FAA's antecedents and the intervening contraction of federal power, inexplicable. Although arbitration is a worthy alternative to litigation, today's exercise in judicial revisionism goes too far. I respectfully dissent.

NOTES

Facts

1. What is the cause of action on the basis of which the plaintiffs have commenced court proceedings? Do the plaintiffs bring a cause of action that sounds in contract or does it have some other basis? If it is not an action for breach of contract, how does the cause of action relate to the contract?

2. How have the plaintiffs organized their claim? Do you think that they will be able to maintain the same procedural posture in arbitration?

3. To what disputes does the arbitration clause apply? Is there a way to re-plead the dispute to bring it clearly outside of the scope of the arbitration agreement?

Law

1. On what basis did the California courts consider the arbitration agreement? An arbitration statute? Some other statute?

2. Was there any allegation on the parts of Southland that the transactions at-issue in the suit had any direct nexus to interstate commerce? What link is there?

Buckeye Check Cashing, Inc. v. Cardegna

546 U.S. 440 (2006)

The following case arose from a dispute involving a check cashing business and its clients. Buckeye Check Cashing would provide its clients with cash in exchange for a personal check. Buckeye charged a fee for these transactions. Each transaction was covered by a contract providing that, at the election of either party, any dispute would be submitted to arbitration. Buckeye's clients initiated a class action lawsuit in Florida state court alleging that Buckeye charged usurious rates, and thus, the contracts were illegal. Buckeye filed a motion to compel arbitration. The trial court dismissed the motion because the contract containing the arbitration clause was illegal and void ab initio. The state district court of appeals reversed on the ground that an arbitration clause is separate from the rest of the contract and, as the plaintiffs did not allege the arbitration agreement was illegal, the dispute should proceed to arbitration. The Florida Supreme Court reversed holding that the concept of separability could not save an arbitration clause in an illegal contract because this would essentially revive the legal contract. Buckeye appealed.

JUSTICE SCALIA delivered the opinion of the Court.

We decide whether a court or an arbitrator should consider the claim that a contract containing an arbitration provision is void for illegality.

. . . .

In *Prima Paint Corp. v. Flood & Conklin Mfg. Co.*, 388 U.S. 395, 87 S. Ct. 1801, 18 L. Ed. 2d 1270 (1967), we addressed the question of who—court or arbitrator—decides these two types of challenges. The issue in the case was "whether a claim of fraud in the inducement of the entire contract is to be resolved by the federal [*445] court, or whether the matter is to be referred to the arbitrators." *Id.*, at 402, 87 S. Ct. 1801, 18 L. Ed. 2d 1270. Guided by § 4 of the FAA, we held that "if the claim is fraud in the inducement of the arbitration clause itself—an issue which goes to the making of the agreement to arbitrate— the federal court may proceed to adjudicate it. But the statutory language does not permit the federal court to consider claims of fraud in the inducement of the contract generally." *Id.*, at 403–404, 87 S. Ct. 1801, 18 L. Ed. 2d 1270 (internal quotation marks and footnote omitted). We rejected the view that the question of "severability" was one of state law, so that if state law held the arbitration provision not to be severable a challenge to the contract as a whole would be decided by the court. See *id.*, at 400, 402–403, 87 S. Ct. 1801, 18 L. Ed. 2d 1270.

Subsequently, in *Southland Corp.*, we held that the FAA "created a body of federal substantive law," which was "applicable in state and federal courts." 465 U.S., at 12, 104 S. Ct. 852, 79 L. Ed. 2d 1 (internal quotation marks omitted). We rejected the view that state law could bar enforcement of § 2, even in the context of state-law claims brought in state court. . . .

B

Prima Paint and *Southland* answer the question presented here by establishing three propositions. First, as a matter of substantive federal arbitration law, an arbitration provision is severable from the remainder of the contract. Second, unless the challenge is to the arbitration clause itself, [*466] the issue of the contract's validity is considered by the arbitrator in the first instance. Third, this arbitration law applies in state as well as federal courts. The parties have not requested, and we do not undertake, reconsideration of those holdings. Applying them to this case, we conclude that because respondents challenge the Agreement, but not specifically its arbitration provisions, those provisions are enforceable apart from the remainder of the contract. The challenge should therefore be considered by an arbitrator, not a court.

In declining to apply *Prima Paint*'s rule of severability, the Florida Supreme Court relied on the distinction between void and voidable contracts. "Florida public policy and contract law," it concluded, permit "no severable, or salvageable, parts of a contract found illegal and void under Florida law." 894 So. 2d, at 864. *Prima Paint* makes this conclusion irrelevant. That case rejected application of state severability rules to the arbitration agreement *without discussing* whether the challenge at issue would have rendered the contract void or voidable. . . . Indeed, the opinion expressly disclaimed any need to decide what state-law remedy was available. . . . Likewise in *Southland*, which arose in state court, we did not ask whether the several challenges made there—fraud, misrepresentation, breach of contract, breach of fiduciary duty, and violation of the California Franchise Investment Law—would render the contract void or voidable. We simply rejected the proposition that the enforceability of the arbitration agreement turned on the state legislature's judgment concerning the forum for enforcement of the state-law cause of action. . . . So also here, we cannot accept the Florida Supreme Court's conclusion that enforceability of the arbitration agreement should turn on "Florida public policy and contract law," 894 So. 2d, at 864.

[*447] C

Respondents assert that *Prima Paint*'s rule of severability does not apply in state court. They argue that *Prima Paint* interpreted only §§ 3 and 4—two of the FAA's procedural provisions, which appear to apply by their terms only in federal court—but not § 2, the only provision that we have applied in state court. This does not accurately describe *Prima Paint*. Although § 4, in particular, had much to do with *Prima Paint*'s understanding of the rule of severability, this rule ultimately arises out of § 2, the FAA's substantive command that arbitration agreements be treated like all other contracts. The rule of severability establishes how this equal-footing guarantee for "a written [arbitration] provision" is to be implemented. Respondents' reading of *Prima Paint* as establishing nothing more than a federal-court rule of procedure also runs contrary to *Southland*'s understanding of that case. One of the bases for *Southland*'s application of § 2 in state court was precisely *Prima Paint*'s "reliance for [its] holding on Congress' broad power to fashion substantive rules under the Commerce Clause." 465 U.S., at 11, 104 S. Ct. 852, 79 L. Ed. 2d 1 . . . . *Southland* itself refused to "believe Congress intended to limit the Arbitration Act to disputes subject only to *federal-court* jurisdiction." 465 U.S., at 15, 104 S. Ct. 852, 79 L. Ed. 2d 1.

Respondents point to the language of § 2, which renders "valid, irrevocable, and enforceable" "a written provision in" or "an agreement in writing to submit to arbitration an existing controversy arising out of" a "contract." Since, respondents argue, the only arbitration agreements to which § 2 applies are those involving a "contract," and since an agreement void *ab initio* under state law is not a "contract," there is no "written provision" in or "controversy arising out of" a "contract," to which § 2 can apply. This argument echoes [*448] Justice Black's dissent in *Prima Paint*: "Sections 2 and 3 of the Act assume the existence of a valid contract. They merely provide for enforcement where such a valid contract exists." 388 U.S., at 412–413, 87 S. Ct. 1801, 18 L. Ed. 2d 1270. We do not read "contract" so narrowly. The word appears four times in § 2. Its last appearance is in the final clause, which allows a challenge to an arbitration provision "upon such grounds as exist at law or in equity for the revocation of any *contract*." (Emphasis added.) There can be no doubt that "contract" as used this last time must include contracts that later prove to be void. Otherwise, the grounds for revocation would be limited to those that rendered a contract voidable—which would mean (implausibly) that an arbitration agreement could be challenged as voidable but not as void. Because the sentence's final use of "contract" so obviously includes putative contracts, we will not read the same word earlier in the same sentence to have a more narrow meaning. We note that neither *Prima Paint* nor *Southland* lends support to respondents' reading; as we have discussed, neither case turned on whether the challenge at issue would render the contract voidable or void.

* * *

It is true, as respondents assert, that the *Prima Paint* rule permits a court to enforce an arbitration agreement in a contract that the arbitrator later finds to be void. But it is equally true that respondents' approach permits a court to deny effect to an arbitration provision in a contract that [*449] the court later finds to be perfectly enforceable. *Prima Paint* resolved this conundrum—and resolved it in favor of the separate enforceability of arbitration provisions. We reaffirm today that, regardless of whether the challenge is brought in federal or state court, a challenge to the validity of the contract as a whole, and not specifically to the arbitration clause, must go to the arbitrator.

The judgment of the Florida Supreme Court is reversed, and the case is remanded for further proceedings not inconsistent with this opinion.

It is so ordered.

NOTES

1.   What was the factual basis for the Florida court to strike down the contract? Do you think that Buckeye committed a crime? Does it matter?

2.   Is there ever a situation in which it is possible to attack an arbitration clause because the contract is to commit a crime? How about a contract killing agreement that contains an arbitration clause between Assassins, Inc. and Corporate Sabotage, LLC? Would a court compel arbitration if Assassins sought payment from Corporate Sabotage? Why? Why not?

B)   The Writing Requirement

As already stated in the introduction, the Federal Arbitration Act requires that the undertaking to arbitrate be "written." As a reminder, it provides that:

> A written provision in any maritime transaction or a contract evidencing a transaction involving commerce to settle by arbitration a controversy thereafter arising out of such contract or transaction, or the refusal to perform the whole or any part thereof, or an agreement in writing to submit to arbitration an existing controversy arising out of such a contract, transaction, or refusal, shall be valid, irrevocable, and enforceable, save upon such grounds as exist at law or in equity for the revocation of any contract.[2]

Requirements that undertakings be in writing in order to be enforceable are common. Thus, the statute of frauds in the common law of contracts typically provides that:

> Unless additional requirements are prescribed by the particular statute, a contract within the Statute of Frauds is enforceable if it is evidenced by any writing, signed by or on behalf of the party to be charged, which
>
> (a)   reasonably identifies the subject matter of the contract,

---

[2]   Federal Arbitration Act ("FAA"), 9 U.S.C. § 2 (1947).

(b)   is sufficient to indicate that a contract with respect thereto has been made between the parties or offered by the signer to the other party, and

(c)   states with reasonable certainty the essential terms of the unperformed promises in the contract.[3]

As the cases in this section outline, the writing requirement in the FAA differs in important respects from the requirements of a writing for purposes of the statute of frauds. As you read the cases, consider how these differences manifest themselves, how they impact the drafting of arbitration clauses, and how they could be used potentially to defeat a consent to arbitration that would not meet the requirements of the statute of frauds.

Caley v. Gulfstream Aerospace Corp.

428 F.3d 1359 (11th Cir. 2005)

The following excerpt is from a case that is reflective of the interpretation of the FAA's writing requirement by the majority of U.S. Circuit Courts of Appeals

HULL, J.

I.   BACKGROUND

A.   *Dispute Resolution Policy*

Each of the plaintiffs is a current or former employee of Gulfstream and was employed at Gulfstream's Savannah, Georgia, facility during the relevant period from the summer of 2002 until the spring of 2003. During the summer of 2002, Gulfstream adopted the DRP[4] to serve as its exclusive method for resolving covered employment-related disputes between itself and its employees.

On or about July 15, 2002, Gulfstream mailed to all of the workers employed at its Savannah facility a copy of the DRP, an explanatory cover letter, and a question-and-answer form. An outside company mailed the documents by first-class mail to the employee addresses on file with Gulfstream's human resources department. In addition, Gulfstream placed the DRP and accompanying documents on the company intranet accessible by the plaintiffs. Gulfstream also distributed the DRP electronically through the Management Newsletter emailed to approximately 1,000 employees. Gulfstream also posted

---

3   RESTATEMENT (SECOND) OF CONTRACTS § 131 (AM. LAW INST. 1981).

4   Editors' Note: DRP refers to Gulfstream's dispute resolution policy.

notices relating to the DRP's implementation, but not the DRP itself, on thirteen bulletin boards throughout the Savannah facility.

The explanatory cover letter, mailed with the DRP on July 15, 2002, read in part as follows: "The DRP will become the exclusive procedure to resolve covered workplace disputes—so you should carefully read the enclosed brochure. This policy, which will become effective on August 1, 2002, will be a *condition of continued employment*. All covered claims will be subject to this DRP at that time." (Emphasis added.)

In addition, the DRP itself included the following clause explaining that the DRP was a contract and that an employee's continuation of employment constituted acceptance:

Acceptance/No Change in Terms of Employment

*[*1365] The submission of an application, acceptance of employment or the continuation of employment by an individual shall be deemed to be acceptance of the DRP. No signature shall be required for the policy to be applicable. The mutual obligations set forth in this DRP shall constitute a contract between the Employee and the Company but shall not change an Employee's at-will relationship or any term of any other contract or agreement between the Company and Employee. This Policy shall constitute the entire agreement between the Employee and Company for the resolution of Covered Claims.*

The DRP established a four-level dispute-resolution process, as follows: Level One: Human Resources Review; Level Two: Management Panel Review; Level Three: Mediation; Level Four: Arbitration. The DRP explained how each level would work and set forth specific discovery rules.

The DRP also contained a time-based waiver applicable to employees. Specifically, the DRP provided that an employee's failure to submit a covered claim to the next level within thirty days of the final determination at a given level would waive the employee's rights to pursue the covered claim. While an employee was required to proceed through each level sequentially, the DRP specified that Gulfstream "may elect to bypass one or more steps prior to arbitration for disputes with applicants for employment, with former employees, or if the Company is the initiating party." In addition, no time-based waiver applied to Gulfstream under the DRP.

The DRP defined "covered claims" as employment-related claims . . . of a legal right, obligation or entitlement regarding or arising from the employment relationship." The DRP further provided that Covered Claims include, but are not limited to the following: [a enumerated list of claims and included a list of claims that were excluded from the DRP's coverage].

. . . .

The DRP further provided that for certain limited claims, either the employee or Gulfstream "may . . . apply to any court of competent jurisdiction and seek interim provisional, injunctive, or other equitable relief until the arbitration award is rendered or the Covered Claim is otherwise resolved." None of the claims in this case falls within this provision.

The DRP explicitly provided that it was "the sole and exclusive forum and remedy for all Covered Claims." It further provided that the employee and Gulfstream waived any right to jury trial, as follows: "The Employee and Company agree and hereby waive any right to jury trial for any Covered Claim."

Finally, the DRP provided that Gulfstream retained the right to modify or terminate the DRP on thirty days' written notice and that the policy in effect at the time a claim was received would govern the process by which the claim was determined.

In March 2003, Gulfstream modified certain terms of the DRP and noticed and distributed it by the same methods as the original version. The terms of the modified DRP were substantially similar. However, the revised DRP provided that the employee agreed that no "Covered Claim" may be brought as a class or collective action under the DRP. The revised DRP also stated that the employee's continued employment would constitute acceptance. The effective date of the modification was April 10, 2003, and each of the plaintiffs was employed when notice of the modification to the DRP was given and on the effective date.

B.   *Plaintiffs' Lawsuits*

On November 17, 2003, the plaintiffs filed two related complaints seeking damages and equitable relief from defendants Gulfstream and its parent company, General Dynamics Corporation ("General Dynamics"). In *Caley, et al. v. Gulfstream Aerospace Corp. and General Dynamics Corp.*, the plaintiffs' complaint asserted claims on behalf of an estimated class of two hundred workers under the FLSA, charging that the defendants deliberately mischaracterized the plaintiffs as exempt from overtime pay requirements and therefore failed to pay the plaintiffs for hours worked in excess of forty per week. The same counsel filed the complaint in *Jackson, et al. v. Gulfstream Aerospace Corp. and General Dynamics Corp.* on behalf of an estimated class of one hundred workers, charging the same defendants with ADEA and ERISA violations, asserting other Georgia-law contract claims, and alleging individual claims of race discrimination, a retaliation claim, and a gender discrimination claim under Title VII and an FLSA retaliation claim on behalf of certain plaintiffs.

In response to the complaints, the defendants filed motions to compel arbitration [*1367] and to dismiss both actions. On March 10, 2004, General Dynamics (later joined by Gulfstream) moved to treat the *Caley* and *Jackson* actions as related. The motion was granted on March 26, 2004 . [sic]

On August 24, 2004, the district court entered an order granting the defendants' motions to compel arbitration and to dismiss.

The plaintiffs now appeal. This appeal concerns the validity of Gulfstream's DRP, which includes a requirement to arbitrate certain types of employment-related claims, including those asserted by the plaintiffs in these cases.

II. DISCUSSION

. . . .

B. *"Written Agreement" Requirement in the FAA*

The plaintiffs first argue that the DRP is not an "agreement in writing" for purposes of FAA enforcement because it is not signed by both parties. We reject this argument because while the FAA requires that the arbitration agreement be in writing, it does not require that it be signed by the parties.

We begin with § 2 of the FAA, which provides that "[a] written provision" to arbitrate shall be enforceable, as follows:

> A *written provision* in any maritime transaction or *a contract* evidencing a transaction involving commerce *to settle by arbitration a controversy* thereafter arising out of such contract or transaction, or the refusal to perform the whole or any part thereof, or an agreement in writing to submit to arbitration an existing controversy arising out of such a contract, transaction, or refusal, *shall be valid, irrevocable, and enforceable,* save upon such grounds as exist at law or in equity for the revocation of any contract.

9 U.S.C. § 2 (emphasis added). Similarly, the FAA's enforcement sections require a court to stay a proceeding where the issue in the proceeding "is referable to arbitration under an *agreement in writing* for such arbitration," 9 U.S.C. § 3 (emphasis added), and provide for a "party aggrieved by the alleged failure,

neglect, or refusal of another to arbitrate under a *written agreement* for arbitration" to petition a district court for an order directing that arbitration proceed, 9 U.S.C. § 4 (emphasis added). The FAA thus uses the [*1369] statutory language of "[a] written provision" in a contract, "agreement in writing," and "written agreement," which we collectively refer to as the "written agreement" requirement.

We readily conclude that no signature is needed to satisfy the FAA's written agreement requirement. First, the plain language of § 2 requires that the arbitration provision be "written." It does not, however, require that the agreement to arbitrate be signed by either party; nor does any other provision of the FAA. As the Tenth Circuit has explained, "Decisions under the Federal Arbitration Act . . . have held it not necessary that there be a simple integrated writing or that a party sign the writing containing the arbitration clause. All that is required is that the arbitration provision be in writing." *Medical Dev. Corp. v. Indus. Molding Corp.*, 479 F.2d 345, 348 (10th Cir. 1973) (citations omitted) . . . .

Second, the overwhelming weight of authority supports the view that no signature is required to meet the FAA's "written" requirement. . . . Indeed, this Court has found no decision to the contrary.

Here, the DRP is indisputably in writing. Although the employees' acceptance was by continuing their employment and was not in writing, all material terms—including the manner of acceptance—were set forth in the written DRP. The DRP stated that it was a contract and constituted the entire agreement between the employee and Gulfstream as to covered claims. Nothing in the FAA suggests [*1370] that a "written provision" must be signed to be enforceable. Accordingly, we conclude that the DRP is a written agreement to arbitrate for purposes of the FAA.

. . . .

NOTES

1. Would the contract have satisfied the requirements of the statute of frauds discussed above?

2. Whose writing contained the arbitration provision? How do you establish if a contract was ever formed?

3. Consider again the doctrine of separability. Assume that a transaction falling within the statute of frauds contains an arbitration clause. Assume further that the transaction is memorialized in writing by one party and submitted for agreement to the other, but the other party does not sign it,

instead calls over the phone to voice its agreement. Does the arbitration agreement fall with the contract in which it is contained?

Campbell v. Gen. Dynamics Gov't Sys. Corp.

407 F.3d 546 (1st Cir. 2005)

SEYLA, CIRCUIT JUDGE. This appeal calls upon us to consider the enforceability of a mandatory arbitration agreement, contained in a dispute resolution policy linked to an e-mailed company-wide announcement, insofar as it applies to employment discrimination claims brought under the Americans with Disabilities Act (ADA). Our analysis turns on whether the employer provided minimally sufficient notice of the contractual nature of the e-mailed policy and of the concomitant waiver of an employee's right to access a judicial forum. Weighing all the attendant circumstances, we conclude that the notice was wanting and that, therefore, enforcement of the waiver would be inappropriate. Consequently, we uphold the district court's denial of the employer's motion to stay proceedings and compel the employee to submit his claim to arbitration.

I.   BACKGROUND

For a period of nearly three years, plaintiff-appellee Roderick Campbell toiled as an at-will employee of General Dynamics Government Systems Corporation. Starting on June 6, 2000, the plaintiff held a full-time, salaried position.

On April 30, 2001, at 1:54 p.m., General Dynamics sent an e-mail announcement to its entire work force regarding the implementation of a new dispute resolution policy (the Policy). The tag line of the e-mail indicated that the sender was "Broadcaster, NDHM [*NDHM.Broadcaster(at)GD-NS.Com*]" and its subject heading read "G. DeMuro—New Dispute Resolution Policy." The message consisted of a page-long letter from Gerard DeMuro, the president of General Dynamics. In the introductory [*548] paragraphs, DeMuro pointed out that General Dynamics was "a leader in a very competitive marketplace," that its success depended on its employees, and that it was committed to "open, forthright and honest communication," especially in the context of "addressing and resolving employee issues concerning legally protected rights and matters." Subsequent paragraphs explained that the company had developed the Policy as a means to handle legal issues arising out of workplace disputes. The e-mail then limned the Policy's four-step approach to dispute resolution, describing the last step as "arbitration by a qualified and independent arbitrator."

The e-mail made no mention of whether (or how) the Policy would affect an employee's right to access a judicial forum with respect to workplace disputes. Moreover, it neither specified that the Policy contained an agreement to arbitrate that would become binding upon continued employment nor indicated whether the term "workplace disputes" included those giving rise to federal statutory claims. The text of the Policy was not part of the e-mail proper, although the company posted the Policy on its intranet (its internal corporate network).

The e-mail did state that the Policy would become effective on May 1, 2001 (the day following its transmission). It also urged recipients to "review the enclosed materials carefully, as the [Policy] is an essential element of your employment relationship." Those with questions were invited to contact the company's vice-president of human resources.

The phrase "enclosed materials" was an apparent reference to two embedded links located at the bottom of the e-mail. Each link provided access to a document that the recipient could view by moving a cursor over the link and clicking on it. The first link was labeled "Brochure: *http://csconnect.gd-cs.com/hr/dispute_resolution.htm*"; clicking on it would have provided access to a two-page brochure that detailed how the Policy worked. Upon reading the second page of that brochure, the recipient would have learned that company employees who "continue [their] current employment after the effective date of the [Policy's] adoption" would be "covered" by its terms and that the Policy would encompass, among other things, "[e]mployment discrimination and harassment claims, based on, for example, age, race, sex, religion, national origin, veteran status, citizenship, disability or other characteristics protected by law." In a shaded box in the lower right-hand corner of that page, the recipient would have found the following statement:

> *The Company has adopted this four-step policy as the exclusive means of resolving workplace disputes for legally protected rights. If an employee files a lawsuit against the Company, the Company will ask the court to dismiss the lawsuit and refer it to the [Policy].*

Clicking on the second link, entitled "Handbook: *http://csconnect.gd-cs.com/hr/DRP_Handbook_2.doc*," would have provided access to a dispute resolution handbook, which contained the full text of the Policy (designated as "Human Resources Policy 402"), a flow chart illustrating how the Policy worked, forms for filing claims at each of the four levels, and a compendium of questions that the company thought might arise.

No part of the e-mail communication required a response acknowledging receipt of the Policy or signifying that a recipient had read and understood its terms. Although General Dynamics set up a tracking log to monitor whether each of its employees opened the e-mail—the record indicates that the plaintiff opened the e-mail [*549] two minutes after it was sent—it did not take any steps to record whether its employees clicked on the embedded links to peruse either the brochure or the handbook. Moreover, General Dynamics has not supplied any evidence to contradict the plaintiff's claim that he never read or saw the brochure, the handbook, or the Policy prior to his termination.

II.   TRAVEL OF THE CASE

On December 30, 2002, General Dynamics terminated the plaintiff's employment on account of persistent absenteeism and tardiness. Alleging that these infractions (and, hence, his dismissal) stemmed from a medical condition known as sleep apnea that General Dynamics should have accommodated, the plaintiff filed an administrative complaint with the proper agency charging discrimination on the basis of disability. He later withdrew that complaint and sued General Dynamics in a Massachusetts state court under the ADA, 42 U.S.C. §§ 12101–12213, and Mass. Gen. Laws ch. 151B, § 4.

General Dynamics removed the action to the federal district court. *See* 28 U.S.C. §§ 1331, 1367, 1441. It thereupon filed an answer in which it asserted, among other things, that the court could not try the plaintiff's claims because they were subject to resolution under the Policy. To give teeth to this defense, the company invoked the Federal Arbitration Act (FAA), 9 U.S.C. §§ 1–16, and moved to stay the court proceedings and compel the plaintiff to submit his claims to arbitration. *See id.* §§ 3, 4. In an accompanying memorandum, it contended that the Policy forged an enforceable agreement to arbitrate all employment-related claims and maintained that the Policy's four-step framework was the exclusive means for resolution of the plaintiff's claims.

The plaintiff opposed that motion, moved to strike the company's affirmative defense, and asked the court to impose sanctions. His opposition posited (i) that an e-mail communication is not a writing and, therefore, the Policy did not satisfy the "written provision" requirement of 9 U.S.C. § 2 and (ii) that, in all events, the Policy was unenforceable because the company's e-mail communication had failed to give the plaintiff adequate notice that the Policy was intended to form a binding agreement to arbitrate. . . .

The district court determined that the company's efforts to notify the plaintiff about the Policy were insufficient to extinguish his right to a judicial forum vis-à-vis his disability discrimination claims. . . . Accordingly, it denied the motion to stay proceedings and compel arbitration. *Id.* at 150.

In reaching those conclusions, the court focused on the characteristics of e-mail as a form of notification and declared that "a mass email message, without more, fails to constitute the minimal level of notice required" to enforce an agreement to arbitrate ADA claims. *Id.* at 149. The court added that the Policy could not be enforced under Massachusetts contract law because the plaintiff lacked knowledge of the offer and, therefore, any apparent acceptance of the terms of the Policy that might otherwise be inferable from his continued employment was nugatory. . . . Because it viewed the inadequacy of notice as dispositive, the court declined to reach the question of whether an electronic communication can constitute a written agreement within the purview of the FAA. *See id.* at 150. In a separate order, the court struck the related affirmative defense, *see supra* note 3, and denied the plaintiff's request for sanctions.

General Dynamics now appeals both the denial of its motion to stay proceedings and compel arbitration and the order striking its affirmative defense. The district court has stayed the proceedings below pending the resolution of this interlocutory appeal.

. . . .

Congress passed the FAA to overcome a history of judicial hostility to arbitration agreements. . . . Its aim was to "place such agreements upon the same footing as other contracts." *Allied-Bruce Terminix Cos. v. Dobson*, 513 U.S. 265, 271, 130 L. Ed. 2d 753, 115 S. Ct. 834 (1995). As enacted, the FAA promotes a liberal federal policy favoring arbitration and guarantees that "[a] written provision in . . . a contract evidencing a transaction involving commerce to settle by arbitration a controversy thereafter arising out of such contract or transaction . . . shall be valid, irrevocable, and enforceable, save upon such grounds as exist at law or in [*552] equity for the revocation of any contract." 9 U.S.C. § 2. . . .

[W]e must inquire whether General Dynamics's e-mail announcement of the Policy provided sufficient notice to the plaintiff that his continued employment would constitute a waiver of his right to litigate any employment-related ADA claim, thereby rendering judicial enforcement of that waiver appropriate. . . .

As an initial matter, this case requires us to consider the proper weight that the choice of a mass e-mail as a means of communication bears on this multi-factor inquiry. The district court sharply discounted General Dynamics's case based on its use of this particular medium. . . . We question the extent of that discount; in our view, an e-mail, properly couched, can be an appropriate medium for forming an arbitration agreement. Withal, we do not read the district court's opinion as holding to the contrary—that would be incorrect—but as enumerating several ways in which General Dynamics readily and inexpensively could have made this particular e-mail notice more informative. . . . We nonetheless acknowledge that the district court's opinion does exhibit a high degree of skepticism about the use of e-mail in this context. We do not share that skepticism: we easily can envision circumstances in which a straightforward e-mail, [*556] explicitly delineating an arbitration agreement, would be appropriate.

In all events, the Electronic Signatures in Global and National Commerce Act (E-Sign Act), Pub. L. No. 106–229, 114 Stat. 464 (2000) (codified at 15 U.S.C. §§ 7001–7031), likely precludes any flat rule that a contract to arbitrate is unenforceable under the ADA solely because its promulgator chose to use e-mail as the medium to effectuate the agreement. The E-Sign Act provides in pertinent part:

> *Notwithstanding any statute, regulation, or other rule of law (other than this subchapter and subchapter II of this chapter), with respect to any transaction in or affecting interstate or foreign commerce—(1) a signature, contract, or other record relating to such transaction may not be denied legal effect, validity, or enforceability solely because it is in electronic form.*

15 U.S.C. § 7001(a). This statute definitively resolves the issue, left open by the district court, . . . as to whether an e-mail agreement to arbitrate is unenforceable under the FAA because it does not satisfy the FAA's "written provision" requirement, 9 U.S.C. § 2. By its plain terms, the E-Sign Act prohibits any interpretation of the FAA's "written provision" requirement that would preclude giving legal effect to an agreement solely on the basis that it was in electronic form. *See Specht v. Netscape Communications Corp.*, 306 F.3d 17, 26 n.11 (2d Cir. 2002).

[The court nevertheless confirmed the District Court's holding on other grounds.]

NOTES

1. As you read the case, consider the definition of "writing" and "record" for purposes of the UCC. If this definition were applied to determine the meaning of a "written arbitration provision" for purposes of the FAA, how would *Campbell* have come out? In the context of commercial arbitration

of contracts for the sale of goods, should the FAA be interpreted in light of this distinction?

<u>U.C.C. § 1–201 (AM. LAW INST. 2018)</u>

. . . .

(31) "Record" means information that is inscribed in a tangible medium or that is stored in an electronic or other medium and is retrievable in perceivable form.

. . . .

(43) "Writing" includes printing, typewriting, or any other intentional reduction to tangible form. "Written" has a corresponding meaning.

2. The Uniform Arbitration Act departs from the FAA. It requires that an arbitration provision be contained in a "record" and defines "record" consistently with the UCC. Do you think that the FAA should be interpreted consistently with the Uniform Arbitration Act? What counsels against such a reading?

<u>U.S. Uniform Arbitration Act[5]</u>

Section 1. Definitions. In this [Act]:

. . . .

(6) "Record" means information that is inscribed on a tangible medium or that is stored in an electronic or other medium and is retrievable in perceivable form.

. . . .

Section 6.   Validity of Agreement to Arbitrate.

(a)   An agreement contained in a record to submit to arbitration any existing or subsequent controversy arising between the parties to the agreement is valid, enforceable, and irrevocable except upon a ground that exists at law or in equity for the revocation of a contract.

---

[5]   UNIF. ARB. ACT § 1 (NAT'L CONFERENCE OF COMM'R ON UNIF. STATE LAWS 2000).

CHAPTER 4

Arbitrability

Arbitration covers a large swath of disputes from commercial disputes, to consumer disputes, labor disputes, insurance disputes, construction disputes, and so forth. Nonetheless, it is a matter of some controversy what disputes in fact can be submitted to arbitration and which disputes are reserved for resolution in the courts.

The issue whether certain types of disputes are capable of resolution by means of arbitration already played a role in some of the cases discussed in Chapter 2. Thus, one of the questions raised in *Southland* was whether statutory claims under the California Franchise Investment Act could be submitted to arbitration or whether the statute foreclosed submission to arbitration. We focused on the case in that context to show how the Federal Arbitration Act has come to encompass a far broader array of clauses than was the case in *Bernhardt* (excerpted in Chapter 1). *Southland* similarly foreshadows the interesting question: are there certain disputes that simply cannot be submitted to arbitration? Courts addressing this question frequently speak of the "arbitrability" of the dispute.

The outer limits of arbitrability appear obvious at first glance. First, constitutional guarantees curtail the availability of arbitration in criminal cases. Second, regulatory disputes appear ill-suited for arbitration. But what about civil cases that allege anti-trust or securities laws claims? How about arbitrations addressing RICO claims? And if antitrust, securities, and RICO claims are arbitrable, are there any other claims that private parties cannot agree ahead of time to submit to arbitration? This chapter will explore the problem in the context of traditional cases addressing securities and antitrust claims, and then in the scenario of RICO claims.

Fact Scenario

The Board of Regents of a state university system is voting to adopt the following change to its policy regarding suspensions:

> The chief executive officer of a state university has the authority to suspend, dismiss, or terminate from employment any faculty or staff

member who makes improper use of social media. "Social media" means any facility for online publication and commentary, including but not limited to blogs, wikis, and social networking sites such as Facebook, LinkedIn, Twitter, Flickr, and YouTube. "Improper use of social media" means making a communication through social media that:

i.   directly incites violence or other immediate breach of the peace;

ii.   when made pursuant to (i.e. in furtherance of) the employee's official duties, is contrary to the best interest of the university.

The state university handbook further provides that all disputes regarding termination of the employment relationship shall be submitted to arbitration by a panel to be designated for such disputes by the state governor.

The state board revisits the change after the suspension of a political science professor. The professor tweeted "#NRA are murderers" after a recent mass shooting at a mall. A key question in the proceedings will be whether the Fourteenth Amendment is implicated by the decision to suspend the professor. Develop arguments for and against arbitrability of this dispute.

Readings

A) Arbitrating Claims Under Securities Laws

This section looks at two early Supreme Court cases, *Wilko v. Swan* and *Scherk v. Alberto-Culver Co,* that set the stage for the discussion of arbitrability of statutory claims. As you read these cases, consider whether *Scherk* remains consistent with *Wilko* or whether it departs from earlier jurisprudence, much in the same way that *Southland* departed from *Bernhardt.*

We will circle back to arbitrating claims under U.S. securities laws at the end of the Chapter. When we reprise the question of arbitrability of claims raised under securities laws, focus on how the law on arbitrability developed over time—and how you can anticipate it moving in the future. These considerations are of significance in drafting arbitral agreements meant to govern long-term agreements and commercial relationships.

Wilko v. Swan

346 U.S. 427 (1953)

MR. JUSTICE REED delivered the opinion of the Court.

This action by petitioner, a customer, against respondents, partners in a securities brokerage firm, was brought in the United States District Court for the Southern District of New York, to recover damages under s 12(2) of the Securities Act of 1933.[1] The complaint alleged that on or about January 17, 1951, through the instrumentalities of interstate commerce, petitioner was induced by Hayden, Stone and Company to purchase 1,600 shares of the common stock of Air Associates, Incorporated, by false representations that pursuant to a merger contract with the Borg Warner Corporation, Air Associates' stock would be valued at $6.00 per share over the then current market price, and that financial interests were buying up the stock for the speculative profit. It was alleged that he was not told that Haven B. Page (also named as a defendant but not involved in this review), a director of, and counsel for, Air Associates was then selling his own Air Associates' stock, including some or all that petitioner purchased. Two weeks after the purchase, petitioner disposed of the stock at a loss. Claiming that the loss was due to the firm's misrepresentations and omission of information concerning Mr. Page, he sought damages.

Without answering the complaint, the respondent moved to stay the trial of the action pursuant to s 3 of the United States Arbitration Act until an arbitration in accordance with the terms of identical margin agreements was had. An affidavit accompanied the motion stating that the parties' relationship was controlled by the terms of the agreements and that while the firm was willing to arbitrate petitioner had failed to seek or proceed with any arbitration of the controversy.

Finding that the margin agreements provide that arbitration should be the method of settling all future controversies, the District Court held that the

---

[1]   15 U.S.C.A. s 77l(2), provides: 'Any person who-* * *'(2) sells a security (whether or not exempted by the provisions of section 77c of this title, other than paragraph (2) of subsection (a) of section 77c of this title), by the use of any means or instruments of transportation or communication in interstate commerce or of the mails, by means of a prospectus or oral communication, which includes an untrue statement of a material fact or omits to state a material fact necessary in order to make the statements, in the light of the circumstances under which they were made, not misleading (the purchaser not knowing of such untruth or omission), and who shall not sustain the burden of proof that he did not know, and in the exercise of reasonable care could not have known, of such untruth or omission, shall be liable to the person purchasing such security from him, who may sue either at law or in equity in any court of competent jurisdiction, to recover the consideration paid for such security with interest thereon, less the amount of any income received thereon, upon the tender of such security, or for damages if he no longer owns the security.'

agreement to arbitrate deprived petitioner of the advantageous court remedy afforded by the Securities Act, and denied the stay. A divided Court of Appeals concluded that the Act did not prohibit the agreement to refer future controversies to arbitration, and reversed.

The question is whether an agreement to arbitrate a future controversy is a 'condition, stipulation, or provision binding any person acquiring any security to waive compliance with any provision' of the Securities Act which s 14[6] declares 'void.'

In response to a Presidential message urging that there be added to the ancient rule of caveat emptor the further doctrine of 'let the seller also beware,' Congress passed the Securities Act of 1933. Designed to protect investors, the Act requires issuers, underwriters, and dealers to make full and fair disclosure of the character of securities sold in interstate and foreign commerce and to prevent fraud in their sale. To effectuate this policy, s 12(2) created a special right to recover for misrepresentation which differs substantially from the common-law action in that the seller is made to assume the burden of proving lack of scienter. The Act's special right is enforceable in any court of competent jurisdiction-federal or state-and removal from a state court is prohibited. If suit be brought in a federal court, the purchaser has a wide choice of venue, the privilege of nation-wide service of process and the jurisdictional $3,000 requirement of diversity cases is inapplicable.

The United States Arbitration Act establishes by statute the desirability of arbitration as an alternative to the complications of litigation. The reports of both Houses on that Act stress the need for avoiding the delay and expense of litigation, and practice under its terms raises hope for its usefulness both in controversies based on statutes or on standards otherwise created. This hospitable attitude of legislatures and courts toward arbitration, however, does not solve our question as to the validity of petitioner's stipulation by the margin agreements, set out below, to submit to arbitration controversies that might arise from the transactions.

Respondent asserts that arbitration is merely a form of trial to be used in lieu of a trial at law, and therefore no conflict exists between the Securities Act and the United States Arbitration Act either in their language or in the congressional purposes in their enactment. Each may function within its own

---

[6]   Section 14 provides: 'Any condition, stipulation, or provision binding any person acquiring any security to waive compliance with any provision of this subchapter or of the rules and regulations of the Commission shall be void.'

scope, the former to protect investors and the latter to simplify recovery for actionable violations of law by issuers or dealers in securities.

The words of s 14, note 6, supra, void any 'stipulation' waiving compliance with any 'provision' of the Securities Act. This arrangement to arbitrate is a 'stipulation,' and we think the right to select the judicial forum is the kind of 'provision' that cannot be waived under s 14 of the Securities Act. While a buyer and seller of securities, under some circumstances, may deal at arm's length on equal terms, it is clear that the Securities Act was drafted with an eye to the disadvantages under which buyers labor. Issuers of and dealers in securities have better opportunities to investigate and appraise the prospective earnings and business plans affecting securities than buyers. It is therefore reasonable for Congress to put buyers of securities covered by that Act on a different basis from other purchasers.

When the security buyer, prior to any violation of the Securities Act, waives his right to sue in courts, he gives up more than would a participant in other business transactions. The security buyer has a wider choice of courts and venue. He thus surrenders one of the advantages the Act gives him and surrenders it at a time when he is less able to judge the weight of the handicap the Securities Act places upon his adversary.

Even though the provisions of the Securities Act, advantageous to the buyer, apply, their effectiveness in application is lessened in arbitration as compared to judicial proceedings. Determination of the quality of a commodity or the amount of money due under a contract is not the type of issue here involved. This case requires subjective findings on the purpose and knowledge of an alleged violator of the Act. They must be not only determined but applied by the arbitrators without judicial instruction on the law. As their award may be made without explanation of their reasons and without a complete record of their proceedings, the arbitrators' conception of the legal meaning of such statutory requirements as 'burden of proof,' 'reasonable care' or 'material fact,' cannot be examined. Power to vacate an award is limited. While it may be true, as the Court of Appeals thought, that a failure of the arbitrators to decide in accordance with the provisions of the Securities Act would 'constitute grounds for vacating the award pursuant to section 10 of the Federal Arbitration Act,' that failure would need to be made clearly to appear. In unrestricted submission, such as the present margin agreements envisage, the interpretations of the law by the arbitrators in contrast to manifest disregard are not subject, in the federal courts, to judicial review for error in interpretation. As the protective provisions of the Securities Act require the exercise of judicial direction to fairly assure their effectiveness, it seems to us that Congress must have intended s 14, to apply to waiver of judicial trial and review.

This accords with *Boyd v. Grand Trunk Western R. Co.* We there held invalid a stipulation restricting an employee's choice of venue in an action under the Federal Employers' Liability Act Section 6 of that Act permitted suit in any one of several localities and s 5 forbade a common carrier's exempting itself from any liability under the Act.[28] Section 5 had been adopted to avoid contracts waiving employers' liability. It is to be noted that in words it forbade exemption only from 'liability.' We said the right to select the 'forum' even after the creation of a liability is a 'substantial right' and that the agreement, restricting that choice, would thwart the express purpose of the statute. We need not and do not go so far in this present case. By the terms of the agreement to arbitrate, petitioner is restricted in his choice of forum prior to the existence of a controversy. While the Securities Act does not require petitioner to sue, a waiver in advance of a controversy stands upon a different footing.

Two policies, not easily reconcilable, are involved in this case. Congress has afforded participants in transactions subject to its legislative power an opportunity generally to secure prompt, economical and adequate solution of controversies through arbitration if the parties are willing to accept less certainty of legally correct adjustment. On the other hand, it has enacted the Securities Act to protect the rights of investors and has forbidden a waiver of any of those rights. Recognizing the advantages that prior agreements for arbitration may provide for the solution of commercial controversies, we decide that the intention of Congress concerning the sale of securities is better carried out by holding invalid such an agreement for arbitration of issues arising under the Act.

Reversed.

NOTES

Facts

1. The Court styles the action as one between "a customer against . . . partners in a securities brokerage firm". What is the transaction at issue? How much money do you suppose must have been at issue? Consider that the

---

[28] s 5 of the Federal Employers' Liability Act, 35 Stat. 66, 45 U.S.C. s 55, 45 U.S.C.A. s 55, provides: 'Any contract, rule, regulation, or device whatsoever, the purpose or intent of which shall be to enable any common carrier to exempt itself from any liability created by this chapter, shall to that extent be void * * *.'

promised profit margin appears to have been $9,600 in 1951 dollars. Inflation adjusted, this comes to approximately $90,000 in today's money.

2.   Does the pitch ring any alarm bells? What problems do you see?

Law

1.   In your view, was the Court's decision narrow or broad? If broad, what standard do you understand the Court to have set?

Scherk v. Alberto-Culver Co.

417 U.S. 506 (1974)

MR. JUSTICE STEWART delivered the opinion of the Court.

Alberto-Culver Co., the respondent, is an American company incorporated in Delaware with its principal office in Illinois. It manufactures and distributes toiletries and hair products in this country and abroad. During the 1960's Alberto-Culver decided to expand its overseas operations, and as part of this program it approached the petitioner Fritz Scherk, a German citizen residing at the time of trial in Switzerland. Scherk was the owner of three interrelated business entities, organized under the laws of Germany and Liechtenstein, that were engaged in the manufacture of toiletries and the licensing of trademarks for such toiletries. In February 1969 a contract was signed in Vienna, Austria, which provided for the transfer of the ownership of Scherk's enterprises to Alberto-Culver, along with all rights held by these enterprises to trademarks in cosmetic goods. The contract contained a number of express warranties whereby Scherk guaranteed the sole and unencumbered ownership of these trademarks. In addition, the contract contained an arbitration clause providing that 'any controversy or claim (that) shall arise out of this agreement or the breach thereof' would be referred to arbitration before the International Chamber of Commerce in Paris, France, and that '(t)he laws of the State of Illinois, U.S.A. shall apply to and govern this agreement, its interpretation and performance.'

The closing of the transaction took place in Geneva, Switzerland, in June 1969. Nearly one year later Alberto-Culver allegedly discovered that the trademark rights purchased under the contract were subject to substantial encumbrances that threatened to give others superior rights to the trademarks and to restrict or preclude Alberto-Culver's use of them. Alberto-Culver thereupon tendered back to Scherk the property that had been transferred to it and offered to rescind the contract. Upon Scherk's refusal, Alberto-Culver commenced this action for damages and other relief in a Federal District Court in Illinois, contending that Scherk's fraudulent representations concerning the status of the trademark rights constituted violations of s 10(b) of the Securities Exchange Act of 1934, 48 Stat. 891, 15 U.S.C. s 78j(b), and Rule 10b–5 promulgated thereunder, 17 CFR s 240.10b–5.

In response, Scherk filed a motion to dismiss the action for want of personal and subject-matter jurisdiction as well as on the basis of *forum non conveniens*, or, alternatively, to stay the action pending arbitration in Paris pursuant to the agreement of the parties. Alberto-Culver, in turn, opposed this motion and sought a preliminary injunction restraining the prosecution of arbitration proceedings. On December 2, 1971, the District Court denied Scherk's motion to dismiss, and, on January 14, 1972, it granted a preliminary order enjoining Scherk from proceeding with arbitration. In taking these actions the court relied entirely on this Court's decision in *Wilko v. Swan*, 346 U.S. 427, which held that an agreement to arbitrate could not preclude a buyer of a security from seeking a judicial remedy under the Securities Act of 1933, in view of the language of s 14 of that Act, barring '(a)ny condition, stipulation, or provision binding any person acquiring any security to waive compliance with any provision of this subchapter . . . .' The Court of Appeals for the Seventh Circuit, with one judge dissenting, affirmed, upon what it considered the controlling authority of the *Wilko* decision. Because of the importance of the question presented we granted Scherk's petition for a writ of certiorari.

I

The United States Arbitration Act, now 9 U.S.C. s 1 et seq., reversing centuries of judicial hostility to arbitration agreements, was designed to allow parties to avoid 'the costliness and delays of litigation,' and to place arbitration agreements 'upon the same footing as other contracts . . . .' H.R.Rep.No.96, 68th Cong., 1st Sess., 1, 2 (1924); see also S.Rep.No.536, 68th Cong., 1st Sess. (1924). Accordingly the Act provides that an arbitration agreement such as is here involved 'shall be valid, irrevocable, and enforceable, save upon such grounds as exist at law or in equity for the revocation of any contract.' 9 U.S.C. s 2.

In *Wilko v. Swan*, supra, this Court acknowledged that the Act reflects a legislative recognition of the 'desirability of arbitration as an alternative to the complications of litigation,' but nonetheless declined to apply the Act's provisions. That case involved an agreement between Anthony Wilko and Hayden, Stone & Co., a large brokerage firm, under which Wilko agreed to purchase on margin a number of shares of a corporation's common stock. Wilko alleged that his purchase of the stock was induced by false representations on the part of the defendant concerning the value of the shares, and he brought suit for damages under s 12(2) of the Securities Act of 1933. The defendant responded that Wilko had agreed to submit all controversies arising out of the purchase to arbitration, and that this agreement, contained in a written margin contract between the parties, should be given full effect under the Arbitration Act.

The Court found that '(t)wo policies, not easily reconcilable, are involved in this case.' On the one hand, the Arbitration Act stressed 'the need for avoiding the delay and expense of litigation,' id., at 431, 74 S.Ct., at 185, and directed that such agreements be 'valid, irrevocable, and enforceable' in federal courts. On the other hand, the Securities Act of 1933 was '(d)esigned to protect investors' and to require 'issuers, underwriters, and dealers to make full and fair disclosure of the character of securities sold in interstate and foreign commerce and to prevent fraud in their sale,' by creating 'a special right to recover for misrepresentation . . . .'. In particular, the Court noted that s 14 of the Securities Act, provides:

> *'Any condition, stipulation, or provision binding any person acquiring any security to waive compliance with any provision of this subchapter or of the rules and regulations of the Commission shall be void.'*

The Court ruled that an agreement to arbitrate 'is a 'stipulation,' and (that) the right to select the judicial forum is the kind of 'provision' that cannot be waived under s 14 of the Securities Act.' Thus, Wilko's advance agreement to arbitrate any disputes subsequently arising out of his contract to purchase the securities was unenforceable under the terms of s 14 of the Securities Act of 1933.

Alberto-Culver, relying on this precedent, contends that the District Court and Court of Appeals were correct in holding that its agreement to arbitrate disputes arising under the contract with Scherk is similarly unenforceable in view of its contentions that Scherk's conduct constituted violations of the Securities Exchange Act of 1934 and rules promulgated thereunder. For the reasons that follow, we reject this contention and hold that the provisions of the Arbitration Act cannot be ignored in this case.

Accepting the premise that the operative portions of the language of the 1933 Act relied upon in *Wilko* are contained in the Securities Exchange Act of 1934, the respondent's reliance on *Wilko* in this case ignores the significant and, we find, crucial differences between the agreement involved in *Wilko* and the one signed by the parties here. Alberto-Culver's contract to purchase the business entities belonging to Scherk was a truly international agreement. Alberto-Culver is an American corporation with its principal place of business and the vast bulk of its activity in this country, while Scherk is a citizen of Germany whose companies were organized under the laws of Germany and Liechtenstein. The negotiations leading to the signing of the contract in Austria and to the closing in Switzerland took place in the United States, England, and Germany, and involved consultations with legal and trademark experts from each of those countries and from Liechtenstein. Finally, and most significantly, the subject matter of the contract concerned the sale of business enterprises organized under the laws of and primarily situated in European countries, whose activities were largely, if not entirely, directed to European markets.

Such a contract involves considerations and policies significantly different from those found controlling in *Wilko*. In *Wilko*, quite apart from the arbitration provision, there was no question but that the laws of the United States generally, and the federal securities laws in particular, would govern disputes arising out of the stock-purchase agreement. The parties, the negotiations, and the subject matter of the contract were all situated in this country, and no credible claim could have been entertained that any international conflict-of-laws problems would arise. In this case, by contrast, in the absence of the arbitration provision considerable uncertainty existed at the time of the agreement, and still exists, concerning the law applicable to the resolution of disputes arising out of the contract.

Such uncertainty will almost inevitably exist with respect to any contract touching two or more countries, each with its own substantive laws and conflict-of-laws rules. A contractual provision specifying in advance the forum in which disputes shall be litigated and the law to be applied is, therefore, an almost indispensable precondition to achievement of the orderliness and predictability essential to any international business transaction. Furthermore, such a provision obviates the danger that a dispute under the agreement might be submitted to a forum hostile to the interests of one of the parties or unfamiliar with the problem area involved.

A parochial refusal by the courts of one country to enforce an international arbitration agreement would not only frustrate these purposes, but would invite unseemly and mutually destructive jockeying by the parties to secure tactical litigation advantages.

The exception to the clear provisions of the Arbitration Act carved out by *Wilko* is simply inapposite to a case such as the one before us. In *Wilko* the Court reasoned that '(w)hen the security buyer, prior to any violation of the Securities Act, waives his right to sue in courts, he gives up more than would a participant in other business transactions. The security buyer has a wider choice of courts and venue. He thus surrenders one of the advantages the Act gives him . . . .' In the context of an international contract, however, these advantages become chimerical since, as indicated above, an opposing party may by speedy resort to a foreign court block or hinder access to the American court of the purchaser's choice.

For all these reasons we hold that the agreement of the parties in this case to arbitrate any dispute arising out of their international commercial transaction is to be respected and enforced by the federal courts in accord with the explicit provisions of the Arbitration Act.

Accordingly, the judgment of the Court of Appeals is reversed and the case is remanded to that court with directions to remand to the District Court for further proceedings consistent with this opinion.

It is so ordered. Reversed and remanded.

NOTES

Facts

1. Who is the plaintiff in the original action? What does the plaintiff seek to achieve? Could it have achieved the same objective with a claim for breach of contract in arbitration?

2. Does it matter that one of the parties, Alberto-Culver Co., is a U.S. company traded on the NY Stock Exchange? Should it matter? Why?

3. Assume that Scherk is a German citizen residing in Europe. How would you ordinarily have to enforce a U.S. judgment against Scherk? Should that affect your litigation strategy in similar circumstances? Why?

Law

1. Is the Court's holding limited to international cases? If so, what is the criteria for defining a case as "international"? Could one set the foundation for an international case simply by incorporating a special purpose vehicle outside of the U.S.? Would that not undercut the regulatory purposes of U.S. Securities Laws?

2. Does the Federal Arbitration Act on its face permit a distinction between domestic and international arbitrations? Assume that the Federal Arbitration Act in later sections also includes two international conventions governing the enforcement of arbitration clauses. Does that change your analysis? Should the Court have premised its analysis exclusively on these international conventions?

3. Read the following story published by the National Law Journal. Hal Scott & Leslie Silverman, SEC's Silent Opposition to Arbitration Bylaws is Speaking Volumes (Aug. 12, 2013), http://capmktsreg.org/2013/08/secs-silent-opposition-to-arbitration-bylaws-is-speaking-volumes/. Does this story shed some light upon whether the Scherk holding might hold beyond the international context? How?

B) Arbitrating Antitrust Claims

Mitsubishi Motors is a leading case in U.S. jurisprudence regarding arbitration, and the excerpt below addresses the issue of the "arbitrability" of antitrust claims.

Mitsubishi Motors Corp. v.
Soler Chrysler-Plymouth, Inc.

473 U.S. 614 (1985)

Mitsubishi entered into an agreement with Soler for the sale of cars. The agreement contained the following arbitration clause:

> *All disputes controversies or differences which may arise between [Mitsubishi] and [Soler] out of or in relation to Articles I-B through V of this Agreement or for the breach thereof, shall be finally settled by arbitration in Japan in accordance with the rules and regulations of the Japanese Commercial Arbitration Association.*

Following a market downturn, a dispute arose between Mitsubishi and Soler concerning the sales volume agreed upon in the contract. Mitsubishi sought to compel arbitration. Soler filed a counterclaim in the district court asserting, *inter alia*, claims under the Sherman Act alleging Mitsubishi was engaged in a conspiracy to restrain trade. Premised upon the counterclaim, the district court refused to compel arbitration because antitrust claims are typically inappropriate for arbitration. The United States Court of Appeals for the First Circuit reversed and the Supreme Court granted certiorari.

Justice Blackmun delivered the opinion of the Court.

We now turn to consider whether Soler's antitrust claims are nonarbitrable even though it has agreed to arbitrate them. In holding that they are not, the Court of Appeals followed the decision of the Second Circuit in *American Safety Equipment Corp. v. J. P. Maguire & Co.*, 391 F.2d 821 (1968). Notwithstanding the absence of any explicit support for such an exception in either the Sherman Act or the Federal Arbitration Act, the Second Circuit there reasoned that "the pervasive public interest in enforcement of the antitrust laws, and the nature of the claims that arise in such cases, combine to make . . . antitrust claims . . . inappropriate for arbitration." *Id., at 827–828*. We find it unnecessary to assess the legitimacy of the *American Safety* doctrine as applied to agreements to arbitrate arising from domestic transactions. As in *Scherk v. Alberto-Culver Co.*, 417 U.S. 506 (1974), we conclude that concerns of international comity, respect for the capacities of foreign and transnational tribunals, and sensitivity to the need of the international commercial system for predictability in the resolution of disputes require that we enforce the parties' agreement, even assuming that a contrary result would be forthcoming in a domestic context.

Even before *Scherk*, this Court had recognized the utility of forum-selection clauses in international transactions. In *The Bremen, supra*, an American oil company, seeking to evade a contractual choice of an English forum and, by implication, English law, filed a suit in admiralty in a United States District Court against the German corporation which had contracted to tow its rig to a location in the Adriatic Sea. Notwithstanding the possibility that the English court would enforce provisions in the towage contract exculpating the German party which an American court would refuse to enforce, this Court gave effect to the choice-of-forum clause. It observed:

> *"The expansion of American business and industry will hardly be encouraged if, notwithstanding solemn contracts, we insist on a parochial concept that all disputes must be resolved under our laws and in our courts. . . . We cannot have trade and commerce in world markets and international waters exclusively on our terms, governed by our laws, and resolved in our courts." 407 U.S., at 9.*

Recognizing that "agreeing in advance on a forum acceptable to both parties is an indispensable element in international trade, commerce, and contracting," *id., at 13–14*, the decision in *The Bremen* clearly eschewed a provincial solicitude for the jurisdiction of domestic forums.

Identical considerations governed the Court's decision in *Scherk*, which categorized "[an] agreement to arbitrate before a specified tribunal [as], in effect, a specialized kind of forum-selection clause that posits not only the situs of suit but also the procedure to be used in resolving the dispute." 417 U.S., at 519. In *Scherk*, the American company Alberto-Culver purchased several interrelated business enterprises, organized under the laws of Germany and Liechtenstein, as well as the rights held by those enterprises in certain trademarks, from a German citizen who at the time of trial resided in Switzerland. Although the contract of sale contained a clause providing for arbitration before the International Chamber of Commerce in Paris of "any controversy or claim [arising] out of this agreement or the breach thereof," Alberto-Culver subsequently brought suit against Scherk in a Federal District Court in Illinois, alleging that Scherk had violated *§ 10(b)* of the Securities Exchange Act of 1934 by fraudulently misrepresenting the status of the trademarks as unencumbered. The District Court denied a motion to stay the proceedings before it and enjoined the parties from going forward before the arbitral tribunal in Paris. The Court of Appeals for the Seventh Circuit affirmed, relying on this Court's holding in *Wilko v. Swan*, 346 U.S. 427 (1953), that agreements to arbitrate disputes arising under the Securities Act of 1933 are nonarbitrable. This Court reversed, enforcing the arbitration agreement even while assuming for purposes of the decision that the controversy would be nonarbitrable under the holding of *Wilko* had it arisen out of a domestic transaction. Again, the Court emphasized:

> *"A contractual provision specifying in advance the forum in which disputes shall be litigated and the law to be applied is . . . an almost indispensable precondition to achievement of the orderliness and predictability essential to any international business transaction. . . .*
>
> *"A parochial refusal by the courts of one country to enforce an international arbitration agreement would not only frustrate these purposes, but would invite unseemly and mutually destructive jockeying by the parties to secure tactical litigation advantages. . . . [It would] damage the fabric of international commerce and trade, and imperil the willingness and ability of businessmen to enter into international commercial agreements." 417 U.S., at 516–517.*

Accordingly, the Court held Alberto-Culver to its bargain, sending it to the international arbitral tribunal before which it had agreed to seek its remedies.

The Bremen and *Scherk* establish a strong presumption in favor of enforcement of freely negotiated contractual choice-of-forum provisions. Here, as in *Scherk*, that presumption is reinforced by the emphatic federal policy in favor of arbitral dispute resolution. And at least since this Nation's accession in 1970 to the Convention, see [1970] 21 U.S.T. 2517, T.I.A.S. 6997, and the implementation of the Convention in the same year by amendment of the Federal Arbitration Act, that federal policy applies with special force in the field of international commerce. Thus, we must weigh the concerns of *American Safety* against a strong belief in the efficacy of arbitral procedures for the resolution of international commercial disputes and an equal commitment to the enforcement of freely negotiated choice-of-forum clauses.

At the outset, we confess to some skepticism of certain aspects of the *American Safety* doctrine. As distilled by the First Circuit, 723 F.2d, at 162, the doctrine comprises four ingredients. First, private parties play a pivotal role in aiding governmental enforcement of the antitrust laws by means of the private action for treble damages. Second, "the strong possibility that contracts which generate antitrust disputes may be contracts of adhesion militates against automatic forum determination by contract." Third, antitrust issues, prone to complication, require sophisticated legal and economic analysis, and thus are "ill-adapted to strengths of the arbitral process, *i. e.,* expedition, minimal requirements of written rationale, simplicity, resort to basic concepts of common sense and simple equity." Finally, just as "issues of war and peace are too important to be vested in the generals, . . . decisions as to antitrust regulation of business are too important to be lodged in arbitrators chosen from the business community—particularly those from a foreign community that has had no experience with or exposure to our law and values." See *American Safety*, 391 F.2d, at 826–827.

Initially, we find the second concern unjustified. The mere appearance of an antitrust dispute does not alone warrant invalidation of the selected forum on the undemonstrated assumption that the arbitration clause is tainted. A party resisting arbitration of course may attack directly the validity of the agreement to arbitrate. See *Prima Paint Corp. v. Flood & Conklin Mfg. Co.*, 388 U.S. 395 (1967). [. . .]

Next, potential complexity should not suffice to ward off arbitration. We might well have some doubt that even the courts following *American Safety* subscribe fully to the view that antitrust matters are inherently insusceptible to resolution by arbitration, as these same courts have agreed that an undertaking to arbitrate antitrust claims entered into *after* the dispute arises is acceptable. [. . .] And the vertical restraints which most frequently give birth to antitrust claims covered by an arbitration agreement will not often occasion the monstrous proceedings that have given antitrust litigation an image of intractability. [. . .] In sum, the factor of potential complexity alone does not persuade us that an arbitral tribunal could not properly handle an antitrust matter.

For similar reasons, we also reject the proposition that an arbitration panel will pose too great a danger of innate hostility to the constraints on business conduct that antitrust law imposes. International arbitrators frequently are drawn from the legal as well as the business community; where the dispute has an important legal component, the parties and the arbitral body with whose assistance they have agreed to settle their dispute can be expected to select arbitrators accordingly. We decline to indulge the presumption that the parties and arbitral body conducting a proceeding will be unable or unwilling to retain competent, conscientious, and impartial arbitrators.

We are left, then, with the core of the *American Safety* doctrine—the fundamental importance to American democratic capitalism of the regime of the antitrust laws. [. . .] As the Court of Appeals pointed out:

> " 'A claim under the antitrust laws is not merely a private matter. The Sherman Act is designed to promote the national interest in a competitive economy; thus, the plaintiff asserting his rights under the Act has been likened to a private attorney-general who protects the public's interest.' " *723 F.2d, at 168*, quoting *American Safety, 391 F.2d, at 826.*

The importance of the private damages remedy, however, does not compel the conclusion that it may not be sought outside an American court. Notwithstanding its important incidental policing function, the treble-damages cause of action conferred on private parties by *§ 4* of the Clayton Act, *15 U. S. C. § 15*, and pursued by Soler here by way of its third counterclaim, seeks primarily to enable an injured competitor to gain compensation for that injury.

"Section 4 . . . is in essence a remedial provision. It provides treble damages to '[any] person who shall be injured in his business or property by reason of anything forbidden in the antitrust laws . . . .' *Brunswick Corp. v. Pueblo Bowl-O-Mat, Inc.,* 429 U.S. 477, 485–486 (1977).

There is no reason to assume at the outset of the dispute that international arbitration will not provide an adequate mechanism. To be sure, the international arbitral tribunal owes no prior allegiance to the legal norms of particular states; hence, it has no direct obligation to vindicate their statutory dictates. The tribunal, however, is bound to effectuate the intentions of the parties. Where the parties have agreed that the arbitral body is to decide a defined set of claims which includes, as in these cases, those arising from the application of American antitrust law, the tribunal therefore should be bound to decide that dispute in accord with the national law giving rise to the claim. Cf. *Wilko v. Swan,*

346 U.S., at 433–434. And so long as the prospective litigant effectively may vindicate its statutory cause of action in the arbitral forum, the statute will continue to serve both its remedial and deterrent function.

Having permitted the arbitration to go forward, the national courts of the United States will have the opportunity at the award-enforcement stage to ensure that the legitimate interest in the enforcement of the antitrust laws has been addressed.

The judgment of the Court of Appeals is affirmed in part and reversed in part, and the cases are remanded for further proceedings consistent with this opinion.

It is so ordered.

NOTES

Facts

1. What is the nature of the underlying agreement? Is it domestic? Is it international? Are the parties sophisticated? Do any of these facts appear to make a difference in the Court's reasoning?

2. As a matter of litigating strategy, who seeks to compel arbitration and who seeks to defeat arbitration? Does the underlying claim brought to defeat arbitration appear to you to be what the dispute between the parties is actually about? Does it matter

Law

1. In his dissent, Justice Stevens noted that until the Court's decision in *Mitsubishi Motors* all the Supreme Court cases enforcing arbitration agreements were regarding contract claims rather than statutory claims— especially those statutory claims with only an "indirect relationship to the contract." Do you think there is a principled distinction between contract claims and statutory claims such that arbitration would be inappropriate for statutory claims? What do you make of Justice Stevens' argument that arbitration is inappropriate for statutory claims due to the need for consistent interpretation of statutory rights? Is this argument weakened by the fact that even courts do not always necessarily agree on statutory interpretation, and unless and until Congress or the Supreme Court propounds an "official" interpretation, courts can interpret the statute differently?

2. In his dissent in *Mitsubishi Motors*, Justice Stevens argues: "The Court has repeatedly held that a decision by Congress to create a special statutory remedy renders a private agreement to arbitrate a federal statutory claims unenforceable." 473 U.S. at 650. Moreover, he notes that treble damages in antitrust claims can be brought only in U.S. district courts, which according to Justice Stevens, further evinces Congress' intent to limit the fora capable of entertaining antitrust claims. Do you find this reasoning persuasive?

3. The Court in *Mitsubishi Motors* emphasized that the agreement was international and that the principle of comity counseled in favor of enforcing the arbitration agreement. Justice Stevens did not accept this rationale, arguing that if, as the Court suggested, antitrust claims are not capable of being arbitrated pursuant to an arbitration clause in a domestic contract, antitrust claims should not be capable of being arbitrated pursuant to an arbitration clause in an international contract. Stevens distinguished *Scherk* on the grounds that the claims in that case were premised on foreign law while the merits of the claims in *Mitsubishi Motors* were entirely controlled by U.S. law. Moreover, the federal claim in *Scherk* was not expressly authorized by Congress and was almost identical to the breach of warranty contract claim also brought in the case. Do you think these are valid distinctions?

4. In support of his argument that the United States' international law commitments did not compel the holding in *Mitsubishi Motors*, Justice Stevens cited Article V(2)(a) of the New York Convention, which contemplates non-recognition and non-enforcement if, *inter alia*, the matter is not capable of settlement by arbitration under the laws of the State where such recognition and enforcement is sought. Given this provision, do you think the Court made too much of international comity? Is Justice Stevens' reliance misplaced because the New York Convention governs enforcement of an arbitral award rather than enforcement of an arbitration agreement?

C) RICO Claims and Securities Claims Revisited

Shearson/American Exp., Inc. v. McMahon

482 U.S. 220 (1987)

JUSTICE O'CONNOR delivered the opinion of the Court.

This case presents two questions regarding the enforceability of predispute arbitration agreements between brokerage firms and their customers. The first is whether a claim brought under § 10(b) of the Securities Exchange Act of 1934 (Exchange Act), must be sent to arbitration in accordance with the terms of an arbitration agreement. The second is whether a claim brought under the Racketeer Influenced and Corrupt Organizations Act (RICO), 18 U.S.C. § 1961 et seq., must be arbitrated in accordance with the terms of such an agreement.

I

Between 1980 and 1982, respondents Eugene and Julia McMahon, individually and as trustees for various pension and profit-sharing plans, were customers of petitioner Shearson/American Express Inc. (Shearson), a brokerage firm registered with the Securities and Exchange Commission (SEC or Commission). Two customer agreements signed by Julia McMahon provided for arbitration of any controversy relating to the accounts the McMahons maintained with Shearson. The arbitration provision provided in relevant part as follows:

> "Unless unenforceable due to federal or state law, any controversy arising out of or relating to my accounts, to transactions with you for me or to this agreement or the breach thereof, shall be settled by arbitration in accordance with the rules, then in effect, of the National Association of Securities Dealers, Inc. or the Boards of Directors of the New York Stock Exchange, Inc. and/or the American Stock Exchange, Inc. as I may elect."

In October 1984, the McMahons filed an amended complaint against Shearson and petitioner Mary Ann McNulty, the registered representative who handled their accounts, in the United States District Court for the Southern District of New York. The complaint alleged that McNulty, with Shearson's knowledge, had violated § 10(b) of the Exchange Act and Rule 10b–5, 17 CFR § 240.10b–5 (1986), by engaging in fraudulent, excessive trading on respondents' accounts and by making false statements and omitting material facts from the advice given to respondents. The complaint also alleged a RICO claim, 18 U.S.C. § 1962(c), and state law claims for fraud and breach of fiduciary duties.

Relying on the customer agreements, petitioners moved to compel arbitration of the McMahons' claims pursuant to § 3 of the Federal Arbitration Act, 9 U.S.C. § 3. The District Court granted the motion in part. The court first rejected the McMahons' contention that the arbitration agreements were unenforceable as contracts of adhesion. It then found that the McMahons' § 10(b) claims were arbitrable under the terms of the agreement, concluding that such a result followed from this Court's decision in *Dean Witter Reynolds Inc. v. Byrd*, 470 U.S. 213 (1985), and the "strong national policy favoring the enforcement of arbitration agreements." The District Court also held that the McMahons' state law claims were arbitrable under *Dean Witter Reynolds Inc. v. Byrd*, supra. It concluded, however, that the McMahons' RICO claim was not arbitrable "because of the important federal policies inherent in the enforcement of RICO by the federal courts."

The Court of Appeals affirmed the District Court on the state law and RICO claims, but it reversed on the Exchange Act claims. With respect to the RICO claim, the Court of Appeals concluded that "public policy" considerations made it "inappropriat[e]" to apply the provisions of the Arbitration Act to RICO suits. The court reasoned that RICO claims are "not merely a private matter." Because a RICO plaintiff may be likened to a "private attorney general" protecting the public interest, the Court of Appeals concluded that such claims should be adjudicated only in a judicial forum. It distinguished this Court's reasoning in *Mitsubishi Motors Corp. v. Soler Chrysler-Plymouth, Inc.*, 473 U.S. 614 (1985), concerning the arbitrability of antitrust claims, on the ground that it involved international business transactions and did not affect the law "as applied to agreements to arbitrate arising from domestic transactions."

II

The Federal Arbitration Act, 9 U.S.C. § 1 et seq., provides the starting point for answering the questions raised in this case. The Act was intended to "revers[e] centuries of judicial hostility to arbitration agreements," *Scherk v. Alberto-Culver Co.*, supra, 417 U.S., at 510, 94 S.Ct., at 2453, by "plac[ing] arbitration agreements 'upon the same footing as other contracts.'" The Arbitration Act accomplishes this purpose by providing that arbitration agreements "shall be valid, irrevocable, and enforceable, save upon such grounds as exist at law or in equity for the revocation of any contract."

The Arbitration Act thus establishes a "federal policy favoring arbitration," requiring that "we rigorously enforce agreements to arbitrate." This duty to enforce arbitration agreements is not diminished when a party bound by an agreement raises a claim founded on statutory rights. As we observed in *Mitsubishi Motors Corp. v. Soler Chrysler-Plymouth, Inc.*, "we are well past the time when judicial suspicion of the desirability of arbitration and of the competence of arbitral tribunals" should inhibit enforcement of the Act " 'in controversies based on statutes.' " Absent a well-founded claim that an arbitration agreement resulted from the sort of fraud or excessive economic power that "would provide grounds 'for the revocation of any contract,' " the Arbitration Act "provides no basis for disfavoring agreements to arbitrate statutory claims by skewing the otherwise hospitable inquiry into arbitrability."

The Arbitration Act, standing alone, therefore mandates enforcement of agreements to arbitrate statutory claims. Like any statutory directive, the Arbitration Act's mandate may be overridden by a contrary congressional command. The burden is on the party opposing arbitration, however, to show that Congress intended to preclude a waiver of judicial remedies for the statutory rights at issue. If Congress did intend to limit or prohibit waiver of a judicial forum for a particular claim, such an intent "will be deducible from [the statute's] text or legislative history," ibid., or from an inherent conflict between arbitration and the statute's underlying purposes.

To defeat application of the Arbitration Act in this case, therefore, the McMahons must demonstrate that Congress intended to make an exception to the Arbitration Act for claims arising under RICO and the Exchange Act, an intention discernible from the text, history, or purposes of the statute. We examine the McMahons' arguments regarding the Exchange Act and RICO in turn.

III

When Congress enacted the Exchange Act in 1934, it did not specifically address the question of the arbitrability of § 10(b) claims. The McMahons contend, however, that congressional intent to require a judicial forum for the resolution of § 10(b) claims can be deduced from § 29(a) of the Exchange Act, 15 U.S.C. § 78cc(a), which declares void "[a]ny condition, stipulation, or provision binding any person to waive compliance with any provision of [the Act]."

First, we reject the McMahons' argument that § 29(a) forbids waiver of § 27 of the Exchange Act, 15 U.S.C. § 78aa. Section 27 provides in relevant part:

"The district courts of the United States . . . shall have exclusive jurisdiction of violations of this title or the rules and regulations thereunder, and of all suits in equity and actions at law brought to enforce any liability or duty created by this title or the rules and regulations thereunder."

The McMahons contend that an agreement to waive this jurisdictional provision is unenforceable because § 29(a) voids the waiver of "any provision" of the Exchange Act. The language of § 29(a), however, does not reach so far. What the antiwaiver provision of § 29(a) forbids is enforcement of agreements to waive "compliance" with the provisions of the statute. But § 27 itself does not impose any duty with which persons trading in securities must "comply." By its terms, § 29(a) only prohibits waiver of the substantive obligations imposed by the Exchange Act. Because § 27 does not impose any statutory duties, its waiver does not constitute a waiver of "compliance with any provision" of the Exchange Act under § 29(a).

We do not read *Wilko v. Swan*, 346 U.S. 427, 74 S.Ct., 182, 98 L.Ed. 168 (1953), as compelling a different result. In *Wilko*, the Court held that a predispute agreement could not be enforced to compel arbitration of a claim arising under § 12(2) of the Securities Act, 15 U.S.C. § 77 l(2). The basis for the ruling was § 14 of the Securities Act, which, like § 29(a) of the Exchange Act, declares void any stipulation "to waive compliance with any provision" of the statute. At the beginning of its analysis, the *Wilko* Court stated that the Securities Act's jurisdictional provision was "the kind of 'provision' that cannot be waived under § 14 of the Securities Act." 346 U.S., at 435, 74 S.Ct., at 186. This statement, however, can only be understood in the context of the Court's ensuing discussion explaining why arbitration was inadequate as a means of enforcing "the provisions of the Securities Act, advantageous to the buyer." Ibid. The conclusion in *Wilko* was expressly based on the Court's belief that a judicial forum was needed to protect the substantive rights created by the Securities Act: "As the protective provisions of the Securities Act require the exercise of judicial direction to fairly assure their effectiveness, it seems to us that Congress must have intended § 14 . . . to apply to waiver of judicial trial and review." *Id.*, at 437, 74 S.Ct., at 188. Wilko must be understood, therefore, as holding that the plaintiff's waiver of the "right to select the judicial forum," *id.*, at 435, 74 S.Ct., at 186, was unenforceable only because arbitration was judged inadequate to enforce the statutory rights created by § 12(2).

Indeed, any different reading of *Wilko* would be inconsistent with this Court's decision in *Scherk v. Alberto-Culver Co.*, 417 U.S. 506, 94 S.Ct. 2449, 41

L.Ed.2d 270 (1974). In *Scherk*, the Court upheld enforcement of a predispute agreement to arbitrate Exchange Act claims by parties to an international contract. The *Scherk* Court assumed for purposes of its opinion that *Wilko* applied to the Exchange Act, but it determined that an international contract "involve[d] considerations and policies significantly different from those found controlling in *Wilko*." 417 U.S., at 515, 94 S.Ct., at 2455. The Court reasoned that arbitration reduced the uncertainty of international contracts and obviated the danger that a dispute might be submitted to a hostile or unfamiliar forum. At the same time, the Court noted that the advantages of judicial resolution were diminished by the possibility that the opposing party would make "speedy resort to a foreign court." *Id.*, at 518, 94 S.Ct., at 2456. The decision in Scherk thus turned on the Court's judgment that under the circumstances of that case, arbitration was an adequate substitute for adjudication as a means of enforcing the parties' statutory rights. *Scherk* supports our understanding that *Wilko* must be read as barring waiver of a judicial forum only where arbitration is inadequate to protect the substantive rights at issue. At the same time, it confirms that where arbitration does provide an adequate means of enforcing the provisions of the Exchange Act, § 29(a) does not void a predispute waiver of § 27—*Scherk* upheld enforcement of just such a waiver.

The other reason advanced by the McMahons for finding a waiver of their § 10(b) rights is that arbitration does "weaken their ability to recover under the [Exchange] Act." Ibid. That is the heart of the Court's decision in *Wilko*, and respondents urge that we should follow its reasoning. *Wilko* listed several grounds why, in the Court's view, the "effectiveness [of the Act's provisions] in application is lessened in arbitration." 346 U.S., at 435, 74 S.Ct., at 185. First, the *Wilko* Court believed that arbitration proceedings were not suited to cases requiring "subjective findings on the purpose and knowledge of an alleged violator." *Wilko* also was concerned that arbitrators must make legal determinations "without judicial instruction on the law," and that an arbitration award "may be made without explanation of [the arbitrator's] reasons and without a complete record of their proceedings." *Id.*, at 436, 74 S.Ct., at 187. Finally, *Wilko* noted that the "[p]ower to vacate an award is limited," and that "interpretations of the law by the arbitrators in contrast to manifest disregard are not subject, in the federal courts, to judicial review for error in interpretation." *Wilko* concluded that in view of these drawbacks to arbitration, § 12(2) claims "require[d] the exercise of judicial direction to fairly assure their effectiveness." *Id.*, at 437, 74 S.Ct., at 187.

As Justice Frankfurter noted in his dissent in *Wilko*, the Court's opinion did not rest on any evidence, either "in the record . . . [or] in the facts of which [it could] take judicial notice," that "the arbitral system . . . would not afford the plaintiff the rights to which he is entitled." *Id.*, at 439, 74 S.Ct., at 189. Instead, the reasons given in Wilko reflect a general suspicion of the desirability of arbitration and the competence of arbitral tribunals-most apply with no greater force to the arbitration of securities disputes than to the arbitration of legal disputes generally. It is difficult to reconcile Wilko's mistrust of the arbitral process with this Court's subsequent *232 decisions involving the Arbitration Act. See, e.g., *Mitsubishi Motors Corp. v. Soler Chrysler-Plymouth, Inc.*, supra; *Dean Witter Reynolds Inc. v. Byrd*, 470 U.S. 213, 105 S.Ct. 1238, 84 L.Ed.2d 158 (1985); *Southland Corp. v. Keating*, 465 U.S. 1, 104 S.Ct. 852, 79 L.Ed.2d 1 (1984); *Moses H. Cone Memorial Hospital v. Mercury Construction Corp.*, 460 U.S. 1, 103 S.Ct. 927, 74 L.Ed.2d 765 (1983); *Scherk v. Alberto-Culver Co.*, 417 U.S. 506, 94 S.Ct. 2449, 41 L.Ed.2d 270 (1974).

Indeed, most of the reasons given in *Wilko* have been rejected subsequently by the Court as a basis for holding claims to be nonarbitrable. In Mitsubishi, for example, we recognized that arbitral tribunals are readily capable of handling the factual and legal complexities of antitrust claims, notwithstanding the absence of judicial instruction and supervision. *See* 473 U.S., at 633–634, 105 S.Ct., at 3357–3358. Likewise, we have concluded that the streamlined procedures of arbitration do not entail any consequential restriction on substantive rights. *Id.*, at 628, 105 S.Ct., at 3354. Finally, we have indicated that there is no reason to assume at the outset that arbitrators will not follow the law; although judicial scrutiny of arbitration awards necessarily is limited, such review is sufficient to ensure that arbitrators comply with the requirements of the statute. See *id.*, at 636–637, and n. 19, 105 S.Ct., at 3359, and n. 19 (declining to assume that arbitration will not be resolved in accordance with statutory law, but reserving consideration of "effect of an arbitral tribunal's failure to take cognizance of the statutory cause of action on the claimant's capacity to reinstate suit in federal court").

The suitability of arbitration as a means of enforcing Exchange Act rights is evident from our decision in *Scherk*. Although the holding in that case was limited to international agreements, the competence of arbitral tribunals to resolve § 10(b) claims is the same in both settings. Courts likewise have routinely enforced agreements to arbitrate § 10(b) claims where both parties are members of a securities exchange or the National Association of Securities Dealers (NASD), suggesting that arbitral tribunals are fully capable of handling such matters. *See, e.g., Axelrod & Co. v. Kordich, Victor & Neufeld*, 320 F.Supp. 193 (SDNY 1970), aff'd, 451 F.2d 838 (CA2 1971); *Brown v. Gilligan, Will & Co.*, 287 F.Supp. 766 (SDNY 1968). And courts uniformly have concluded that Wilko does not apply to the submission to arbitration of existing disputes, *see, e.g., Gardner v. Shearson, Hammill & Co.*, 433 F.2d 367 (CA5 1970); *Moran v. Paine, Webber, Jackson & Curtis*, 389 F.2d 242 (CA3 1968), even though the inherent suitability of arbitration as a means of resolving § 10(b) claims remains unchanged. Cf. *Mitsubishi*, 473 U.S., at 633, 105 S.Ct., at 3357.

Thus, the mistrust of arbitration that formed the basis for the *Wilko* opinion in 1953 is difficult to square with the assessment of arbitration that has prevailed since that time. This is especially so in light of the intervening changes in the regulatory structure of the securities laws. Even if *Wilko*'s assumptions regarding arbitration were valid at the time *Wilko* was decided, most certainly they do not hold true today for arbitration procedures subject to the SEC's oversight authority.

In 1953, when *Wilko* was decided, the Commission had only limited authority over the rules governing self-regulatory organizations (SROs)-the national securities exchanges and registered securities associations-and this authority appears not to have included any authority at all over their arbitration rules. *See Brief for Securities and Exchange Commission as Amicus Curiae* 14–15. Since the 1975 amendments to § 19 of the Exchange Act, however, the Commission has had expansive power to ensure the adequacy of the arbitration procedures employed by the SROs. No proposed rule change may take effect unless the SEC finds that the proposed rule is consistent with the requirements of the Exchange Act, 15 U.S.C. § 78s(b)(2); and the Commission has the power, on its own initiative, to "abrogate, add to, and delete from" any SRO rule if it finds such changes necessary or appropriate to further the objectives of the Act, 15 U.S.C. § 78s(c). In short, the Commission has broad authority to oversee and to *234 regulate the rules adopted by the SROs relating to customer disputes, including the power to mandate the adoption of any rules it deems necessary to ensure that arbitration procedures adequately protect statutory rights.

In the exercise of its regulatory authority, the SEC has specifically approved the arbitration procedures of the New York Stock Exchange, the American Stock Exchange, and the NASD, the organizations mentioned in the arbitration agreement at issue in this case. We conclude that where, as in this case, the prescribed procedures are subject to the Commission's § 19 authority, an arbitration agreement does not effect a waiver of the protections of the Act. While *stare decisis* concerns may counsel against upsetting *Wilko*'s contrary conclusion under the Securities Act, we refuse to extend *Wilko*'s reasoning to the Exchange Act in light of these intervening regulatory developments. The McMahons' agreement to submit to arbitration therefore is not tantamount to an impermissible waiver of the McMahons' rights under § 10(b), and the agreement is not void on that basis under § 29(a).

IV

Unlike the Exchange Act, there is nothing in the text of the RICO statute that even arguably evinces congressional intent to exclude civil RICO claims from the dictates of the Arbitration Act. This silence in the text is matched by silence in the statute's legislative history. The private treble-damages provision codified as 18 U.S.C. § 1964(c) was added to the House version of the bill after the bill had been passed by the Senate, and it received only abbreviated discussion in either House. There is no hint in these legislative debates that Congress intended for RICO treble-damages claims to be excluded from the ambit of the Arbitration Act.

Because RICO's text and legislative history fail to reveal any intent to override the provisions of the Arbitration Act, the McMahons must argue that there is an irreconcilable conflict between arbitration and RICO's underlying purposes. Our decision in *Mitsubishi Motors Corp. v. Soler Chrysler-Plymouth, Inc.,* 473 U.S. 614, 105 S.Ct. 3346, 87 L.Ed.2d 444 (1985), however, already has addressed many of the grounds given by the McMahons to support this claim. In *Mitsubishi*, we held that nothing in the nature of the federal antitrust laws prohibits parties from agreeing to arbitrate antitrust claims arising out of international commercial transactions. Although the holding in *Mitsubishi* was limited to the international context, much of its reasoning is equally applicable here. Thus, for example, the McMahons have argued that RICO claims are too complex to be subject to arbitration. We determined in *Mitsubishi*, however, that "potential complexity should not suffice to ward off arbitration." Antitrust matters are every bit as complex as RICO claims, but we found that the "adaptability and access to expertise" characteristic of arbitration rebutted the view "that an arbitral tribunal could not properly handle an antitrust matter."

Likewise, the McMahons contend that the "overlap" between RICO's civil and criminal provisions renders § 1964(c) claims nonarbitrable. Yet § 1964(c) is no different in this respect from the federal antitrust laws. In *Sedima, S.P.R.L. v. Imrex Co.* we rejected the view that § 1964(c) "provide[s] civil remedies for offenses criminal in nature." In doing so, this Court observed: "[T]he fact that conduct can result in both criminal liability and treble damages does not mean that there is not a bona fide civil action. The familiar provisions for both criminal liability and treble damages under the antitrust laws indicate as much." *Mitsubishi* recognized that treble-damages suits for claims arising under § 1 of the Sherman Act may be subject to arbitration, even though such conduct may also give rise to claims of criminal liability. We similarly find that the criminal provisions of RICO do not preclude arbitration of bona fide civil actions brought under § 1964(c).

The McMahons' final argument is that the public interest in the enforcement of RICO precludes its submission to arbitration. *Mitsubishi* again is relevant to the question. In that case we thoroughly examined the legislative intent behind § 4 of the Clayton Act in assaying whether the importance of the private treble-damages remedy in enforcing the antitrust laws precluded arbitration of § 4 claims. We found that "[n]otwithstanding its important incidental policing function, the treble-damages cause of action ... seeks primarily to enable an injured competitor to gain compensation for that injury." Emphasizing the priority of the compensatory function of § 4 over its deterrent function, *Mitsubishi* concluded that "so long as the prospective litigant effectively may vindicate its statutory cause of action in the arbitral forum, the statute will continue to serve both its remedial and deterrent function."

The legislative history of § 1964(c) reveals the same emphasis on the remedial role of the treble-damages provision. In introducing the treble-damages provision to the House Judiciary Committee, Representative Steiger stressed that "those who have been wronged by organized crime should at least be given access to a legal remedy." Hearings on S. 30 and Related Proposals before Subcommittee No. 5 of the House Committee on the Judiciary, 91st Cong., 2d Sess., 520 (1970). The policing function of § 1964(c), although important, was a secondary concern. During the congressional debates on § 1964(c), Representative Steiger again emphasized the remedial purpose of the provision: "It is the intent of this body, I am certain, to see that innocent parties who are the victims of organized crime have a right to obtain proper redress. . . . It represents the one opportunity for those of us who have been seriously affected by organized crime activity to recover." 116 Cong.Rec. 35346–35347 (1970). This focus on the remedial function of § 1964(c) is reinforced by the recurrent references in the legislative debates to § 4 of the Clayton Act as the model for the RICO treble-damages provision. See, e.g., 116 Cong.Rec. 35346 (statement of Rep. Poff) (RICO provision "has its counterpart almost in haec verba in the antitrust statutes"); id., at 25190 (statement of Sen. McClellan) (proposed amendment would "authorize private civil damage suits based upon the concept of section 4 of the Clayton Antitrust Act"). *See generally Sedima, S.P.R.L. v. Imrex Co.*, 473 U.S., at 489, 105 S.Ct., at 3281 ("The clearest current in [RICO's] history is the reliance on the Clayton Act model").

Not only does *Mitsubishi* support the arbitrability of RICO claims, but there is even more reason to suppose that arbitration will adequately serve the purposes of RICO than that it will adequately protect private enforcement of the antitrust laws. Antitrust violations generally have a widespread impact on national markets as a whole, and the antitrust treble-damages provision gives private parties an incentive to bring civil suits that serve to advance the national interest in a competitive economy. RICO's drafters likewise sought to provide vigorous incentives for plaintiffs to pursue RICO claims that would advance society's fight against organized crime. But in fact RICO actions are seldom asserted "against the archetypal, intimidating mobster." The special incentives necessary to encourage civil enforcement actions against organized crime do not support nonarbitrability of run-of-the-mill civil RICO claims brought against legitimate enterprises. The private attorney general role for the typical RICO plaintiff is simply less plausible than it is for the typical antitrust plaintiff, and does not support a finding that there is an irreconcilable conflict between arbitration and enforcement of the RICO statute.

In sum, we find no basis for concluding that Congress intended to prevent enforcement of agreements to arbitrate RICO claims. The McMahons may effectively vindicate their RICO claim in an arbitral forum, and therefore there is no inherent conflict between arbitration and the purposes underlying § 1964(c). Moreover, nothing in RICO's text or legislative history otherwise demonstrates congressional intent to make an exception to the Arbitration Act for RICO claims. Accordingly, the McMahons, "having made the bargain to arbitrate," will be held to their bargain. Their RICO claim is arbitrable under the terms of the Arbitration Act.

NOTES

Facts

1. What was the alleged wrongdoing here? Why would the defendant have engaged in that wrongdoing?

2. Who are the plaintiffs? On whose behalf do they bring the claims? How much money was at stake here?

3.   Do you think the plaintiffs would have been at a significant disadvantage, economically, in prosecuting their claims in arbitration? Are they consumers without means or industry knowledge?

Law

1.   What test does the Court establish in order to determine whether a statute renders claims inarbitrable? Does the Court establish a single test or two different tests, and if two, what are they?

2.   What still remains good law from the *Wilko* decision?

D) Federalism and Arbitrability—Renewed Rumblings

The discussion in the last chapter has shown that under current Supreme Court jurisprudence, the role for state law and state courts in limiting arbitration is very limited. This does not mean, however, that state courts do not nevertheless attempt to protect the weaker party against perceived exploitative arbitration agreements. The case excerpted below is one example of such a case. It addresses the hot button issue (already alluded to in many of the cases above) of mandatory arbitration imposed through an employment agreement.

Northern Kentucky Area Development District v. Snyder

No. 2017–SC–000277–DG, 2018 WL 4628143 (Ky. Sept. 27, 2018)
(footnotes omitted)

[*1] Kentucky Revised Statute ("KRS") 336.700(2) prohibits employers from conditioning employment on an existing employee's or prospective employee's agreement to "waive, arbitrate, or otherwise diminish any existing or future claim, right, or benefit to which the employee or person seeking employment would otherwise be entitled. . . ." When Northern Kentucky Area Development District ("NKADD") conditioned Danielle Snyder's continued employment on her agreement to arbitrate any dispute that may arise between them, that agreement violated KRS 336.700(2). As a result, the arbitration agreement between NKADD and Snyder—the enforcement of which is the basis of the case before us today—is unenforceable as a matter of state statutory law.

NKADD correctly asserts that the Federal Arbitration Act ("FAA") broadly prohibits discrimination against arbitration agreements. It then argues that the FAA preempts the operation of KRS 336.700(2) under the facts of this case. But, rejecting NKADD's argument, we hold that no such discrimination occurred here because KRS 336.700(2) does not prohibit arbitration agreements, limit the power of persons to enter voluntarily into arbitration agreements, or single out arbitration agreements in any way. Correctly viewed, KRS 336.700(2) is an anti-discrimination statute that prohibits employers from conditioning employment on an agreement to, not only arbitration, but also any waiver or diminution of the employee's existing or future rights or claims for benefits arising out of employment. So, on discretionary review, we affirm for different reasons the Court of Appeals' decision that affirmed the trial court's order denying NKADD's motion to compel enforcement of the arbitration agreement. And we remand this case to the trial court for further proceedings consistent with this opinion.

I.   BACKGROUND.

NKADD is a government entity created under KRS 147A.050 et. seq. It is funded by taxpayers to administer social programs in an eight-county area of Northern Kentucky. It receives federal funds for various social programs, including an elder-abuse program, a long-term-care ombudsman program, and a family caregiver program. Additionally, using federal funds, NKADD partners with local food banks to distribute food to lower-income households and administers a small-business loan fund. It also provides employment services through its Northern Kentucky Workforce Investment Board to supply workers to businesses and participates in a regional public-private partnership working to supply employees to businesses in the Northern Kentucky-Greater Cincinnati area.

Danielle Snyder worked for NKADD as an administrative purchasing agent. While employed there, Snyder had to sign an arbitration agreement mandating arbitration of any dispute she had with NKADD. The agreement makes clear, "As a condition of employment with the District, you will be required to sign the attached arbitration agreement." Additionally, "You may revoke your acceptance of the agreement by communicating your rejection in writing to the District within five days after you sign it. However, because the agreement is a condition of employment, your employment and/or consideration for employment will end via resignation or withdrawal from the process."

[*2] Snyder filed an action in the trial court asserting claims under the Kentucky Whistleblower Act ("KWA") and the Kentucky Wages and Hours Act ("KWHA") after NKADD terminated her employment. NKADD filed a

motion to stay the proceedings and compel arbitration based on the arbitration agreement. The circuit court denied NKADD's motion, and NKADD appealed.

The Court of Appeals affirmed the trial court's denial, explaining that NKADD is a creature of statute, and the wording of two Kentucky statutes, which purportedly prohibit an employer's conditioning employment on the employee's agreement to arbitrate any disputes, makes ultra vires any arbitration contract by NKADD forcing arbitration in this way. Therefore, the Court of Appeals reasoned, the FAA cannot compel arbitration between the parties because NKADD never had the authority to enter into an arbitration agreement in the first place, and "federal law does not pre-empt the authority of the Commonwealth to deny the authority of its [agencies] to enter into arbitration agreements."

II.   ANALYSIS.

We granted NKADD's motion for discretionary review to consider whether the FAA preempts Kentucky's legislative enactment to preserve employee rights, KRS 336.700(2), because it seeks, among other broadly stated areas, to prohibit employers from conditioning employment on the employee's agreement to a contract provision mandating arbitration in the event of a dispute between them. We ultimately conclude that the statute does not run afoul of the FAA under the facts of this case. But first, we must determine whether NKADD truly does not have the power to condition employment on agreement to arbitration.

A.   NKADD and its power.

"[A]dministrative agencies have no inherent authority and may exercise only such authority as may be legislatively conferred." It is axiomatic that NKADD, as a state agency, only has the power that the General Assembly gives it.

NKADD exists by virtue of KRS 147A.050(7). The precise legal term to describe the creature NKADD may be elusive, but the parties and the lower courts have not quibbled over the fact that NKADD is a Kentucky state agency.

Like all area development districts, NKADD is operated by state employees under KRS 147A.060 and 147A.070 and receives taxpayer funding. The governing body of NKADD, its board of directors, entirely derives its power from KRS 147A.080 and 147A.090, the statutes that detail all of the power that the General Assembly has granted to NKADD. Among other powers, the board of directors may "[m]ake and enter into all contracts or agreements necessary or incidental to the performance of its duties" and "[p]erform such other and further acts as may be necessary to carry out the duties and responsibilities created by KRS 147A.050 to 147A.120."

The text of these statutes alone does not explicitly allow NKADD to mandate agreement to arbitration as a condition of employment. At best, the power to condition employment on agreement to arbitration may be implied by the broad language used in the statutory provisions outlining NKADD's powers and responsibilities.

Regardless, we find explicit statutory limitation on the ability of NKADD to condition employment on agreement to arbitration. KRS 336.700(2) states:

> [*3] Notwithstanding any provision of the Kentucky Revised Statutes to the contrary, no employer shall require as a condition or precondition of employment that any employee or person seeking employment waive, arbitrate, or otherwise diminish any existing or future claim, right, or benefit to which the employee or person seeking employment would otherwise be entitled under any provision of the Kentucky Revised Statutes or any federal law.

KRS 336.700(1) defines employer to mean "any person, either individual, corporation, partnership, agency, or firm, that employs an employee."

The parties do not challenge the applicability of KRS 336.700(2) to NKADD in this case. Indeed, KRS 147.080(10) deems an "area development district organization" a "public agency," which appears to fall within the ambit of the definition of employer in KRS 336.700(1), which includes "agenc[ies]."

Although one could argue that the definition of employer in KRS 336.700(1) appears to contemplate private, not public, entities, we dealt with a similar situation in Madison County Fiscal Court v. Kentucky Labor Cabinet. There, we considered the exact same definition of employer for the purpose of the applicability of KRS 337.285, the wage and hour requirements for overtime pay, to public entities, including the Madison County Fiscal Court, Central Campbell County Fire District, and ten municipal corporations.8 We concluded "municipal corporations" fell within the ambit of "corporation[s]" as included within the definition of employer. In conformance with the spirit of Madison County, we find NKADD, an agency of the Commonwealth, constitutes an "agency" contemplated by the definition of employer in KRS 336.700(1) such that KRS 336.700(2) applies.

We conclude that Kentucky state-created entities do not have the power to compel, as a condition of employment, any employee agree to arbitrate any claim, right, or benefit he or she may have against NKADD. Although NKADD appears to have broad power to enter into agreements and define the terms of those agreements, KRS 336.700(2) acts expressly prohibits NKADD from conditioning employment on an agreement to arbitrate.

We therefore conclude that the General Assembly intended to forbid NKADD from having the power to condition employment on agreement to arbitration by the express language of KRS 336.700(2).

When a government entity acts beyond its power by violating an express statutory prohibition, its actions are said to be "ultra vires . . . and therefore . . . void." KRS 336.700(2) is a direct limitation on the power of state agencies to condition employment of their state employees on agreement to an arbitration clause; in fact, this statute outright prohibits such act. Because NKADD, a state agency affected by the prohibitions of KRS 336.700(2), never had the power to force Snyder to agree to arbitrate disputes arising between them as a condition of her employment, the resulting arbitration agreement is void.

B.   The FAA does not preempt KRS 336.700(2) in this case.

[*4] Although we have determined that NKADD acted beyond its power when forcing Snyder to agree to arbitrate disputes arising between them as a condition of her employment, we nonetheless must determine if the FAA nullifies this conclusion because of its preemptive effect on laws discriminating against arbitration.

The U.S. Supreme Court defined the parameters of the FAA, the law at issue in this case, most recently in *Kindred Nursing Centers Ltd. Partnership v. Clark.* "The Federal Arbitration Act makes arbitration agreements 'valid, irrevocable, and enforceable, save upon such grounds as exist at law or in equity for the revocation of any contract.' " "[9 U.S.C. § 2] establishes an equal-treatment principle: A court may invalidate an arbitration agreement based on 'generally applicable contract defenses' like fraud or unconscionability, but not on legal rules that 'apply only to arbitration or that derive their meaning from the fact that an agreement to arbitrate is at issue.' " "The FAA thus preempts any state rule discriminating on its face against arbitration—for example, a 'law prohibit[ing] outright the arbitration of a particular type of claim.' " "And not only that: The Act also displaces any rule that covertly accomplishes the same objective by disfavoring contracts that (oh so coincidentally) have the defining features of arbitration agreements."

The broad preemptive effect of the FAA is undeniable. But we fail to see how a law, in this case KRS 336.700(2), that does not actually attack, single out, or specifically discriminate against arbitration agreements must yield to the FAA.

We cannot read KRS 336.700(2) as evidencing hostility to arbitration agreements. KRS 336.700(2) does not prevent NKADD, any state entity, or any private entity, from agreeing to arbitration. KRS 336.700(2) simply prevents NKADD from conditioning employment on the employee's agreement to arbitration. This is the key distinction supporting the reason the FAA does not apply to preempt KRS 336.700(2). That statute only proscribes conditioning employment on agreement to arbitration, not the act of agreeing to arbitration.

Moreover, KRS 336.700(2) does not single out arbitration clauses. KRS 336.700(2) prevents the conditioning of employment on an employee's agreement to waive or otherwise diminish "any existing or future claim, right, or benefit to which the employee or person seeking employment would otherwise be entitled . . . ." This not only means that an employer cannot force the employee to agree to arbitration on penalty of termination but also means that an employer cannot force an employee to, for example, waive all rights to file KWA claims against the employer. In this way, KRS 336.700(2) is a law of general applicability that prevents employers from conditioning employment on the employee's agreement to forego the exercise of all rights against the employer.

KRS 336.700(2) is not a law that discriminates or singles out arbitration clauses. It is a law that prohibits employers from firing or failing to hire on the condition that the employee or prospective employee waive all existing rights that employee would otherwise have against the employer. More importantly, KRS 336.700(2) does nothing to discriminate against arbitration clauses—it only prevents an employer from terminating or refusing to hire an individual who refuses to agree to such a clause.

[*5] Even the broadest construction of the reach of the FAA would not allow employers to fire or hire an employee or prospective employee based on that employee's willingness or unwillingness to sign an arbitration agreement. It is true that the U.S. Supreme Court recently expanded the reach of the FAA: "[T]he Act cares not only about the 'enforce[ment]' of arbitration agreements, but also about their initial 'valid[ity]'—that is, about what it takes to enter into them. . . . A rule selectively finding arbitration contracts invalid because improperly formed fares no better under the Act than a rule selectively refusing to enforce those agreements once properly made."

As stated, however, KRS 336.700(2) does not "selectively find[ ] arbitration contracts invalid"; rather, KRS 336.700(2) prevents an employer from entering into any agreement whatsoever that conditions employment on the employee's agreement to waive any and all rights against the employer. Moreover, KRS 336.700(2) does not invalidate arbitration contracts because they are arbitration contracts; KRS 336.700(2) only invalidates arbitration contracts when the employer evidences an intent to fire or refuse to hire an employee because of that employee's unwillingness to sign such a contract. This is not an attack on the arbitration agreement—it is an attack on the employer for basing employment decisions on whether the employee is willing to sign an arbitration agreement.

A comparison to the rule at issue in Kindred Nursing may be of benefit: "[A]n agent c[an] deprive her principal of an 'adjudication by judge or jury' only if the power of attorney 'expressly so provides.' " The U.S. Supreme Court identified that this rule "fails to put arbitration agreements on an equal plane with other contracts" and "singl[ed] out [arbitration agreements] for disfavored treatment" because "the [Kentucky Supreme Court] nowhere cautioned that an attorney-in-fact would not need a specific authorization to, say, sell her principal's furniture or commit her principal to a non-disclosure agreement." Finally, the U.S. Supreme Court noted, "A rule selectively finding arbitration contracts invalid because improperly formed fares no better under the Act . . . ."

The preempted rule at issue in Kindred Nursing stated that a person acting under a power-of-attorney may never enter into an arbitration agreement on the principal's behalf unless the principal provides express written assent to such. The rule singled out arbitration agreements because the rule only required specific written authorization for an agent acting under a power-of-attorney to enter into an arbitration agreement and not any other type of agreement.

This is different from KRS 336.700(2). The statute does not single out arbitration agreements—it makes clear that any contract that waives or limits an employee's rights against the employer is void if employment was predicated on signing the agreement. Apart from arbitration agreements, this would include, to name a couple of examples, an agreement whereby the employee waives the ability to file a KWA claim against the employer, or an agreement that limits the amount of damages the employee can recover against the employer.

KRS 336.700(2) is not an anti-arbitration clause provision—it is an anti-employment discrimination provision. KRS 336.700(2) uniformly voids any agreement diminishing an employee's rights against an employer when that agreement had to be signed by the employee on penalty of termination or as a predicate to working for that employer. As such, we hold that the FAA does not preempt KRS 336.700(2) because it does not discriminate against arbitration agreements but rather the conditioning of employment on an employee's agreement to arbitrate.

III. CONCLUSION.

[*6] NKADD acted beyond the scope of its power when it conditioned Snyder's employment on her willingness to sign an arbitration agreement. So NKADD's act of doing so is beyond the limits of its legislative grant of authority, rendering the arbitration agreement itself void. The FAA does not mandate a contrary holding because it does not preempt KRS 336.700(2) in this case. We affirm the result reached by the Court of Appeals for the reasons stated in this opinion and remand this case to the trial court for further proceedings consistent with this opinion.

NOTES

Facts

1. Who is NKADD? What is the statutory regime that applies to it and why? Is that relationship any different from one that would apply to an ordinary business?

2. What relationship does the arbitration clause affect? What relationship is covered by the statute?

Law

1. What is the argument that the FAA preempts Kentucky law? Does that argument follow from the earlier jurisprudence discussed in prior chapters?

2. What distinctions can you draw between the earlier jurisprudence and this case? If the case would be argued before the U.S. Supreme Court, how would you approach the argument for each side as to whether these distinctions are sufficient to bring this case outside the scope of existing Supreme Court jurisprudence?

3. NKADD retains you after the Kentucky Supreme Court decision to determine how it should restructure its operations for new employees. NKADD would much prefer to be able to arbitrate disputes with future employees than be forced to go to court. Is there any avenue available by which NKADD could still insist on arbitration?

CHAPTER 5

Drafting an Effective Arbitration Clause (Scope and Procedure)

As discussed in the previous chapters, the Federal Arbitration Act, as interpreted by United States federal courts, gives broad latitude to the kind of disputes that *can* be submitted to arbitration. As this chapter will highlight, this does not mean that the phrasing of every arbitration clause will reach all arbitrable disputes. Rather, the clause itself can impose further voluntary restrictions on the arbitrability of disputes. In drafting and interpreting arbitration clauses, it is therefore important to use canons of construction to give effect to the contracting parties' business agreements.

Drafting an effective arbitration clause requires more than simply considering what types of disputes should be encompassed by the parties' commitment to arbitrate. Additional key questions are when and how disputes should be arbitrated. A current trend in arbitral practice is to rely upon multi-tiered dispute resolution provisions, which can combine mandatory settlement negotiation attempts, mediations and arbitration among other ADR tools. Arbitration is only one aspect of these provisions. It is thus necessary to draft effective conditions that frame and/or limit the parties' agreement to arbitrate.

This chapter will explore techniques to draft (and defend) arbitration clauses that achieve the intended substantive and procedural goals of the parties negotiating them. Although the chapter discusses various techniques of drafting arbitration clauses, it will use as its default position the AAA's model arbitration clause for commercial disputes:

> Any controversy or claim arising out of or relating to this contract, or the breach thereof, shall be settled by arbitration administered by the American Arbitration Association under its Commercial Arbitration Rules, and judgment on the award rendered by the arbitrator(s) may be entered in any court having jurisdiction thereof.

Fact Scenario

Mendoza Vineyards LLC ("*Mendoza*"), a California vintner, enters into a contract with Barrelling Oaks Inc. ("*Barrelling*"), a Minnesota company specializing in the fabrication of oak barrels for use in wine making. Barrelling produces its barrels from American white oak. Mendoza is looking to purchase 100 Bordeaux-type barrels each year for its wine production (each barrel holds 225 liters). Barrelling anticipates that it will age *Faber Unum* wine in these barrels for 5 years, and then reuse the barrels for maturing its *Rusticum* line for a period of 2 years.

Mendoza and Barrelling are discussing the terms of the arbitration clause. The following is the last email exchange between their respective counsel:

From: Langley Martin
To: Robby Parker
Re: Arbitration Clause

Robby,

My client agrees to your suggestion. Why don't we exchange draft clauses by email next week.

Regards,

Langley

From: Robby Parker
To: Langley Martin
Re: Arbitration Clause

Langley,

My client told me that they are okay with the exclusion you suggest. To the extent that we make any kind of exclusions, my client also would want to make sure that we do not arbitrate any express warranties claims. Other than that, I think we should be good to go.

Regards,

Robby

From: Langley Martin
To: Robby Parker
Re: Arbitration Clause

Robby,

My client is okay with the idea of an arbitration clause. There is one thing that we would very much like to avoid submitting to arbitration—to the extent that there is anything to do with food safety, we must submit those disputes to litigation so that we can bring in our suppliers to any lawsuit, as well. You understand that we could not do that in arbitration. That would be a deal breaker for us—but you understand we never anticipate any of those issues coming up.

Regards,

Langley

Using the AAA Commercial Arbitration Clause as a model, draft the arbitration clause for Robby or Langley. Consider that each side might have a slightly different interest in wording the exclusion.

Readings

A) Disputes "Arising out of" and Disputes "Relating to" a Contract

This section addresses the key distinction in arbitration jurisprudence between clauses that require arbitration of disputes "arising out of" and disputes "relating to" the transaction. This distinction typically governs whether the arbitration clause can reach claims relating to the commercial relationship between the parties created by the transaction documents.

Thus, the first step in drafting an arbitration clause should be to address this distinction. As you read the materials below, consider the choice underlying the drafting of the AAA's model clause, which encompasses both claims "arising out of or relating to this contract."

1) *The U.S. Approach*

Personal Security & Safety Systems Inc. v. Motorola Inc.

297 F.3d 388 (5th Cir. 2002)

JOLLY, J.

Motorola, Inc. appeals the district court's denial of its motion to compel arbitration of claims raised by Personal Security and Safety Systems, Inc. ("PSSI"). In 2000, PSSI filed suit against Motorola alleging that Motorola breached a stock purchase agreement with PSSI and made fraudulent misrepresentations during the negotiations leading up to the agreement. Although the stock purchase agreement did not include an arbitration clause, Motorola moved to compel arbitration based on a provision in a licensing agreement that was executed alongside the stock purchase agreement as part of a broader contractual arrangement. The district court initially granted Motorola's motion, but it later reconsidered its decision and denied the motion.

The central issue in this appeal is whether PSSI's claims under the stock purchase agreement fall within the scope of the broad arbitration provision in the licensing agreement. We hold that the licensing agreement's arbitration provision governs claims arising out of the stock purchase agreement because the agreements were executed together as part of the same overall transaction and therefore are properly construed together. We further hold that a forum selection clause in the stock purchase agreement does not operate to preclude arbitration of claims arising out of that agreement. Accordingly, we reverse the district court's denial of Motorola's motion to compel arbitration and remand to the district court for entry of an order staying the litigation and requiring the parties to submit their dispute to binding arbitration.

I

The underlying dispute in this case stems from Motorola's abortive strategic investment in PSSI. Before its demise in 1999, PSSI was a small start-up company engaged in the development and sale of specialized security systems—primarily a "Personal 911 System" that allowed individuals to summon help from within a limited geographic area by means of a wireless communications device. Although it had made substantial progress in developing the technology for the Personal 911 System by 1997, PSSI did not have sufficient capital to complete development of the system or to install the system at customer sites. At about the same time, Motorola was in the process of developing a similar localized security system for use in the hospitality industry, but its technology was significantly less developed than PSSI's technology.

Seeing an opportunity for collaboration, Motorola initiated discussions with PSSI in June 1997 concerning a possible investment in PSSI that would give Motorola access to PSSI's technology. On December 17, 1997, PSSI and Motorola executed three agreements in connection with this investment: a Stock Purchase Agreement, a Product Development and License Agreement, and a

Shareholders Agreement. Each of these agreements played a particular role in the overall transaction.

Under the Stock Purchase Agreement, Motorola agreed to provide twelve million dollars in financing in return for a convertible debenture and a nine percent equity stake in PSSI. The financing was to come in three parts. First, Motorola paid PSSI one million dollars in cash and forgave a one million dollar interim loan that it had provided to PSSI during the negotiations. Second, Motorola loaned PSSI five million dollars to finance the development of the existing Personal 911 System. Third, Motorola agreed to provide up to five million dollars to finance the installation of the existing Personal 911 System at customer sites once PSSI secured purchase contracts for the system.

Under the Product Development Agreement, the parties agreed to collaborate on the development of new communications technologies based on the existing PSSI system. The Product Development Agreement also defines in detail the parties' respective rights to existing intellectual property and to any new, jointly-developed intellectual property. The Shareholders Agreement, which is not directly at issue in this litigation, defines shareholder rights.

In May 1999, PSSI completed development of its Personal 911 System, and several customers committed to purchase the system. Relying on the terms of the Stock Purchase Agreement, PSSI asked Motorola to provide it with financing to install the system at the customer sites. When Motorola refused to disburse the requested funds, PSSI filed a complaint in federal district court alleging that (1) Motorola's refusal to provide financing constituted a breach of the Stock Purchase Agreement and (2) Motorola made fraudulent representations during negotiations to induce PSSI to enter into the agreement. Invoking the arbitration provision in the Product Development Agreement, Motorola filed a motion to stay the proceedings and to compel arbitration. The district court ultimately denied Motorola's motion, and Motorola now appeals pursuant to 9 U.S.C. § 16. The proceedings in the district court have been stayed pending the appeal.

II

The primary issue in this appeal is whether the arbitration provision in the Product Development Agreement applies to PSSI's claims arising under the Stock Purchase Agreement. Motorola argues that PSSI's claims fall within the broad scope of the arbitration provision because the Stock Purchase Agreement and the Product Development Agreement were executed together as part of the same transaction and therefore must be construed together. PSSI responds that the two agreements are independent, freestanding contracts. Because PSSI's claims rely solely on the Stock Purchase Agreement and because the arbitration provision in the Product Development Agreement does not expressly apply to claims arising under other agreements, PSSI maintains that the arbitration provision does not reach claims under the Stock Purchase Agreement. Instead, PSSI argues that the forum selection clause in the Stock Purchase Agreement controls, and the claims stated in its complaint must be litigated in a court located in Texas.

The district court agreed with PSSI and denied Motorola's motion to compel arbitration. We review de novo the district court's denial of a motion to compel arbitration. *See OPE Int'l LP v. Chet Morrison Contractors, Inc.*, 258 F.3d 443, 445 (5th Cir. 2001).

A

We begin our inquiry by outlining the basic principles that inform federal law in this area. The Supreme Court has made it clear that the Federal Arbitration Act, 9 U.S.C. § 3, establishes a "liberal policy favoring arbitration" and a "strong federal policy in favor of enforcing arbitration agreements." *Texaco Exploration & Prod. Co. v. AmClyde Engineered Prods. Co.*, 243 F.3d 906, 909 (5th Cir. 2001) (citations and internal quotation marks omitted). Of course, this general policy is not without limits. Because arbitration is necessarily a matter of contract, courts may require a party to submit a dispute to arbitration only if the party has expressly agreed to do so. *See AT&T Tech., Inc. v. Communications Workers of Am.*, 475 U.S. 643, 648, 89 L. Ed. 2d 648, 106 S. Ct. 1415 (1986); *see also Volt Info. Sciences, Inc. v. Bd. of Trustees*, 489 U.S. 468, 478, 103 L. Ed. 2d 488, 109 S. Ct. 1248 (1989) ("[The FAA] simply requires courts to enforce privately negotiated agreements to arbitrate, like other contracts, in accordance with their terms.").

To ascertain whether the parties have agreed to arbitrate a particular claim, we must determine: "(1) whether there is a valid agreement to arbitrate between the parties; and (2) whether the dispute in question falls within the scope of that arbitration agreement." *OPE Int'l*, 258 F.3d at 445 (citations and internal quotation marks omitted). In view of the policy favoring arbitration, we ordinarily "resolve doubts concerning the scope of coverage of an arbitration clause in favor of arbitration." *Neal v. Hardee's Food Systems, Inc.*, 918 F.2d 34, 37 (5th Cir. 1990); *see also Moses H. Cone Mem. Hosp. v. Mercury Constr. Corp.*, 460 U.S. 1, 24–25, 74 L. Ed. 2d 765, 103 S. Ct. 927 (1983) (same). As a consequence, a valid agreement to arbitrate applies "unless it can be said with positive assurance that [the] arbitration clause is not susceptible of an interpretation which would cover the dispute at issue." *Neal*, 918 F.2d at 37 (internal citations and quotation marks omitted). With these principles in mind, we now turn to the arbitration provision in this case.

B

Motorola and PSSI agree that the Product Development Agreement contains a valid arbitration provision and that there are no external constraints that preclude arbitration of PSSI's claims. Thus, the central question is whether the arbitration provision covers the claims—arising solely out of the Stock Purchase Agreement—alleged in PSSI's amended complaint. Stated in terms of the applicable caselaw, the question is whether we can say "with positive assurance" that the arbitration provision in the Product Development Agreement is not susceptible of an interpretation that would cover those claims.

We start, as always, with the language of the arbitration provision itself. Paragraph 14.2 of the Product Development Agreement provides, in relevant part:

> [T]he parties hereby agree to resolve by binding arbitration any and all claims, demands, actions, disputes, controversies, damages, losses, liabilities, judgments, payments of interest, penalties, enforcement of settlement agreements, deficiencies, any and all demands not yet matured into the foregoing, and other matters in question arising out of or relating to this Agreement (all of which are referred to as "Claims"), even though some or all of such Claims allegedly are extra-contractual in nature and even though some or all of such Claims sound in contract, tort or otherwise, at law or in equity, in accordance with Commercial Arbitration Rules . . . of the American Arbitration Association . . . .

Where, as here, an arbitration provision purports to cover all disputes "related to" or "connected with" the agreement, we have held that the provision is "not limited to claims that literally 'arise under the contract,' but rather embraces all disputes between the parties having a significant relationship to the contract regardless of the label attached to the dispute." *Pennzoil Exploration and Production Co. v. Ramco Energy Ltd.*, 139 F.3d 1061, 1067 (5th Cir. 1998). Thus, PSSI must arbitrate its dispute with Motorola if the allegations of fraud and breach of the Stock Purchase Agreement have a "significant relationship to" the subject matter of the transaction.

PSSI argues that the arbitration provision does not apply in this case because it governs only those claims related to the Product Development Agreement, while the claims stated in PSSI's complaint arise under an entirely separate agreement. It is well established, however, that "under general principles of contract law, separate agreements executed contemporaneously by the same parties, for the same purposes, and as part of the same transaction, are to be construed together." *Neal v. Hardee's Food Systems, Inc.*, 918 F.2d 34, 37 (5th Cir. 1990) (citations omitted); *see also* Restatement (Second) of Contracts § 202(2) (1979) (same); *Richland Plantation Co. v. Justiss-Mears Oil Co.*, Inc., 671 F.2d 154, 156 (5th Cir. 1982) ("When several documents represent one agreement, all must be construed together in an attempt to discern the intent of the parties, reconciling apparently conflicting provisions and attempting to give effect to all of them, if possible." (citations omitted)).

In the present case, the Stock Purchase Agreement and the Product Development Agreement were both key elements of a transaction in which Motorola agreed to provide financing in return for a stake in PSSI and access to PSSI's technology. Although the Stock Purchase Agreement and the Product Development Agreement govern different facets of the parties' relationship, the agreements must be construed together because they were executed at the same time as part of the same overall transaction. Indeed, each agreement expressly anticipates the execution of the other, and the parties attached a form of the Product Development Agreement as an exhibit to the Stock Purchase Agreement. As we observed in *Neal,* 918 F.2d at 37, "although the parties used multiple agreements to delineate their relationship, each agreement was dependent upon the entire transaction. . . . The individual agreements were integral and interrelated parts of the one deal."

PSSI argues that this view runs contrary to the intent of the parties in this case because the arbitration provision was in an ancillary agreement and was therefore not intended to govern the parties' entire relationship. Even assuming that the Stock Purchase Agreement is the heart of the transaction at issue here, however, this fact is not dispositive because the arbitration provision is contained in an agreement that was essential to the overall transaction.

As we explained earlier, the thrust of the transaction was relatively straightforward. In return for providing funds to complete the development and installation of PSSI's Personal 911 System, Motorola received a minority stake in PSSI (with an option to purchase a larger stake) *and* it received access to PSSI's technology to facilitate the joint development of future products. It seems clear that the Product Development Agreement, which governed access to each party's intellectual property as well as the parties' joint development efforts, was a central part of this transaction. Although the arbitration provision in the Product Development Agreement is somewhat narrower than the provision at issue in *Neal*, we conclude that it is sufficiently broad to cover all disputes related to the entire transaction. It is of no moment that each element of the transaction focuses on a different aspect of the transaction and could be a valid free-standing contract.

In sum, we hold that, where the parties include a broad arbitration provision in an agreement that is "essential" to the overall transaction, we will presume that they intended the clause to reach all aspects of the transaction—including those aspects governed by other contemporaneously executed agreements that are part of the same transaction. Thus, in the absence of a contrary expression of intent in the Stock Purchase Agreement, the arbitration provision in the Product Development Agreement covers all disputes related to the subject matter of the entire transaction between PSSI and Motorola. Because we cannot say "with positive assurance that [the] arbitration clause is not susceptible of an interpretation which would cover the dispute at issue," we find that it applies to PSSI's claims under the Stock Purchase Agreement.

C

PSSI argues that, even assuming the arbitration provision in the Product Development Agreement can be construed to cover claims arising out of the Stock Purchase Agreement, the forum selection clause in the Stock Purchase Agreement forecloses this interpretation. Paragraph 6.7 of the Stock Purchase Agreement provides:

> *Governing Law.* THIS AGREEMENT SHALL BE GOVERNED BY AND CONSTRUED IN ACCORDANCE WITH THE LAWS OF THE STATE OF TEXAS. ANY SUIT OR PROCEEDING BROUGHT HEREUNDER SHALL BE SUBJECT TO THE EXCLUSIVE JURISDICTION OF THE COURTS LOCATED IN TEXAS.

Focusing on the term "exclusive jurisdiction," PSSI reads this provision to mean that any dispute arising out of the Stock Purchase Agreement must be litigated in Texas courts. PSSI argues that, because the parties "intended to confer solely upon Texas courts the power to decide" any dispute brought under the Stock Purchase Agreement, the parties expressly excluded the use of arbitration to resolve such a dispute.

We do not find PSSI's interpretation of the forum selection clause persuasive. Standing alone, one could plausibly read the forum selection clause to mean that Texas courts have the exclusive power to resolve all disputes arising under the Stock Purchase Agreement. But the forum selection clause does not stand alone. To the contrary, we must interpret the forum selection clause in the context of the entire contractual arrangement and we must give effect to all of the terms of that arrangement. *See Richland Plantation Co. v. Justiss-Mears Oil Co., Inc.*, 671 F.2d 154, 156 (5th Cir. 1982) ("When several documents represent one agreement, all must be construed together in an attempt to discern the intent of the parties, reconciling apparently conflicting provisions and attempting to give effect to all of them, if possible."). Given our conclusion that the arbitration provision in the Product Development Agreement applies to all claims related to the overall transaction, we must therefore interpret the forum selection provision in the Stock Purchase Agreement in a manner that is consistent with the arbitration provision.

Reading the two provisions together, it becomes clear that the forum selection clause does not require the parties to litigate all claims in Texas courts, nor does it expressly forbid arbitration of claims arising under the Stock Purchase Agreement. Instead, we interpret the forum selection clause to mean that the parties must litigate in Texas courts only those disputes that are not subject to arbitration—for example, a suit to challenge the validity or application of the arbitration clause or an action to enforce an arbitration award. Rather than covering all "disputes" or all "claims" like the arbitration provision in the Product Development Agreement, the forum selection clause confers "exclusive jurisdiction" on Texas courts only with respect to "any suit or proceeding." This limitation suggests that the parties intended the clause to apply only in the event of a non-arbitrable dispute that must be litigated in court.

Thus, read together with the arbitration provision, the forum selection clause in the Stock Purchase Agreement does not operate to bar arbitration of disputes where otherwise required by contract. Consequently, we conclude that the claims in PSSI's complaint must be arbitrated in accordance with the terms of the Product Development Agreement.

III

For the reasons set out above, we REVERSE the judgment of the district court denying Motorola's motion to compel arbitration of PSSI's claims and REMAND for entry of an order staying the litigation and requiring the parties to submit their dispute to binding arbitration.

REVERSED and REMANDED

NOTES

Facts

1. How many contracts were at issue in the dispute? Did each of them have dispute resolution provisions? How different was the wording of the dispute resolution provisions?

2. What was the overall transaction the parties were trying to structure? How did each of the component agreements contribute to this transaction structure? What part of the transaction generated the bulk of the economic value here?

3. What do you think the parties originally intended by including the dispute resolution clauses in the various contracts? Did the Court's holding to your mind comport with the parties' original intent?

Law

1. What operative language did the court focus upon in making its determination regarding the scope of the arbitration clause?

2. As you can see, the parties modified the AAA Model Commercial Arbitration Clause. Did those modifications have any consequence for Court's holding? Do you think the Court would have ruled the same way had the parties simply included the AAA Model Commercial Arbitration Clause?

3. Assume you were tasked with redrafting the provisions of similarly worded transaction documents after the Motorola decision was issued. How would you approach re-drafting the transaction documents to give effect to the choice of forum clause in the Stock Purchase Agreement without otherwise reducing the scope of the arbitration clause in the Product Development Agreement?

B) Narrowly Tailoring the Arbitration Clause

As the *Motorola* case show, the parties to a transaction may wish to limit their agreement to arbitrate to only certain kinds of disputes—such as disputes that courts define as "arising out of" or "relating to" an agreement—as apparently was the case in *Motorola*. It is thus necessary to tailor narrowly an arbitration clause to satisfy the business objectives of the parties.

There is a significant danger that construction of an arbitration agreement when faced with an actual dispute will lead to unintended circumstances. The potential for unanticipated circumstances presents a significant disincentive to tailoring dispute resolution clauses too narrowly. For example, a clause that is narrowly tailored to the resolution of disputes "arising out of the breach of an agreement" may not be sufficiently capacious to cover disputes regarding the occurrence or non-occurrence of a condition set out in the agreement. As a condition cannot be breached, the narrow clause on its face would not apply to the dispute. The party seeking to invoke the clause would certainly submit that there was a breach because it deemed the event covered by the condition to have occurred. But the occurrence of the event is a condition *sine qua non* of breach. As that issue was not submitted to arbitration, the parties might have to litigate the occurrence of the event to then arbitrate the question of breach of contract.

As you read the case below, consider what the parties likely sought to submit to arbitration and how the actual dispute created a controversy as to the applicability of the arbitration clause.

Cummings v. FedEx Ground Package System, Inc.

404 F.3d 1258 (10th Cir. 2005)

LUCERO, CIRCUIT JUDGE.

This appeal involves a dispute regarding the scope of a narrowly drawn arbitration clause. The district court denied a motion by defendant FedEx Ground Package System, Inc. ("FedEx"), to compel arbitration of two claims contained in a complaint filed against it by plaintiffs Gary Cummings, James Bittle, and Sean Steiner. In June 2003, the plaintiffs brought suit against FedEx in Colorado state court asserting claims for rescission, fraud, negligent misrepresentation, breach of contract, breach of the covenant of good faith, and deceptive trade practices. FedEx removed the case to federal court on the basis of diversity jurisdiction, and then filed a motion to dismiss the action under Fed.R.Civ.P. 12(b)(1) and to compel arbitration, citing an arbitration clause in agreements signed by each plaintiff. Plaintiffs amended their complaint to clarify that their claims are based solely on oral representations allegedly made by FedEx, not on the written agreements. FedEx reasserted its motion to dismiss and to compel arbitration of the amended complaint. The district court denied FedEx's motion, ruling that the nature of plaintiffs' claims fell outside the scope of the arbitration clause. We exercise jurisdiction pursuant to 9 U.S.C. § 16(a)(1)(C) and affirm.

BACKGROUND

Plaintiffs entered into separate, but for all relevant purposes identical, contracts with FedEx to serve as package delivery contractors. Plaintiffs allege in their complaint that, prior to the execution of any agreement, FedEx made oral representations to them concerning the amount of income plaintiffs would earn based on their workload and assigned delivery route, as well as the assistance that FedEx would provide them. Each plaintiff alleges that, in response to FedEx advertisements, he met with a FedEx regional recruiter to inquire about acquiring a FedEx delivery route. The complaint alleges a FedEx recruiter told each plaintiff he would be assigned a route and that, if he worked between ten and twelve hours a day, he would earn approximately $1,500 a week, plus bonuses, on that route. Plaintiffs also allege the FedEx recruiter told them they were required to purchase a truck, but that FedEx would assist them in reselling their route and the truck if they left FedEx.

Each plaintiff later signed FedEx's form Pick-Up and Delivery Contractor Operating Agreement (the "Operating Agreement"), and, as required, purchased a FedEx truck. Each was assigned a delivery route, originating from a Colorado FedEx facility. The plaintiffs allege that, despite working in excess of the recommended hours per day, they were never able to earn close to the amount of money represented by FedEx on their assigned route; Cummings and Bittle allege they were unable to earn more than $400 a week, despite working more than twelve hours a day. All of the plaintiffs resigned from FedEx in 2001. They allege that FedEx refused to assist them in selling their trucks.

In its motion to compel arbitration, FedEx cites the following arbitration clause contained in each Operating Agreement:

> 12.3   Arbitration of Asserted Wrongful Termination. In the event FedEx Ground acts to terminate this Agreement (which acts shall include any claim by [plaintiff] of constructive termination) and [plaintiff] disagrees with such termination or asserts that the *actions* of [defendant] are not authorized under the terms of this Agreement, then each such disagreement (but no others) shall be settled by arbitration in accordance with the Commercial Arbitration Rules of the American Arbitration Association (AAA). . . .

The arbitration clause also includes a requirement that claims be submitted to arbitration within ninety days of any wrongful termination. Plaintiffs did not submit any claims to arbitration, and FedEx contends they would now be time-barred from doing so.

Although plaintiffs' amended complaint asserts eight claims, FedEx only contends two claims are subject to arbitration: the fourth claim, for breach of implied contract, and the fifth claim, for breach of the implied duty of good faith and fair dealing arising out of an implied contract. The fourth claim alleges that:

> FedEx contracted with Plaintiffs, either directly or through promissory estoppel, to aid the Plaintiffs in selling their routes and or trucks if things did not work out. Such agreement does not arise from the *terms* of the written Contract supplied by FedEx. FedEx breached this agreement with Plaintiffs and Plaintiffs have been damaged thereby.

The fifth claim alleges that:

> Plaintiffs had an implied contractual relationship with FedEx concerning income, time to complete routes and aid in selling trucks and routes upon termination, and implied thereby is the *covenant* of good faith and fair dealing. By failing to inform Plaintiffs of the efforts necessary to make the type of money being represented, by failing to aid Plaintiffs in selling their routes or trucks, and by other similar or related acts, FedEx has breached the covenant of good faith and fair dealing with the Plaintiffs. Plaintiffs have been damaged by such breach.

In rejecting FedEx's argument that these two claims were subject to arbitration, the district court first noted that the clause is a narrow one, which limits arbitration to very specific types of disputes. By its terms, the arbitration clause in the Operating Agreement only covers acts by FedEx to terminate the Operating Agreement or acts claimed by plaintiffs to constitute a constructive termination of the Operating Agreement.

ANALYSIS

"To determine whether a particular dispute falls within the scope of an agreement's arbitration clause, a court should undertake a three-part inquiry." Louis Dreyfus Negoce S.A. v. Blystad Shipping & Trading Inc., 252 F.3d 218, 224 (2d Cir.2001).

First, recognizing there is some range in the breadth of arbitration clauses, a court should classify the particular clause as either broad or narrow. Next, if reviewing a narrow clause, the court must determine whether the dispute is over an issue that is on its face within the purview of the clause, or over a collateral issue that is somehow connected to the main agreement that contains the arbitration clause. Where the arbitration clause is narrow, a collateral matter will generally be ruled beyond its purview. Where the arbitration clause is broad, there arises a presumption of arbitrability and arbitration of even a collateral matter will be ordered if the claim alleged implicates issues of contract construction or the parties' rights and obligations under it.

On appeal, FedEx argues that the factual underpinning of plaintiffs' fourth and fifth claims is the allegation that FedEx either directly or indirectly terminated the Operating Agreement. FedEx states that all doubts as to the scope of the arbitration clause should be construed in favor of arbitration, and argues that because the claims bear a significant relationship to the Operating Agreement, they necessarily arise out of this contract. This argument overlooks, however, the narrow scope of the arbitration clause.

It is true that "[t]he Supreme Court has long recognized and enforced a liberal federal policy favoring arbitration agreements," and that "[u]nder this policy, the doubts concerning the scope of arbitrable issues should be resolved in favor of arbitration." However, "arbitration is a matter of contract and a party cannot be required to submit to arbitration any dispute which he has not agreed so to submit." When an arbitration clause is narrowly drawn, the policy in favor of arbitration does not have the "strong effect here that it would have if we were construing a broad arbitration clause."

Here, as the district court ruled, we are presented with a narrowly drawn arbitration clause. It is not the type of broad provision that "refer[s] all disputes arising out of a contract to arbitration." Rather, the parties clearly manifested an intent to narrowly limit arbitration to specific disputes regarding the termination of the Operating Agreement. In construing the scope of a narrow arbitration clause, we must take care to carry out the specific and limited intent of parties.

Under a narrow arbitration clause, a dispute is subject to arbitration only if it relates to an issue that is on its face within the purview of the clause, and collateral matters will generally be beyond its purview. The arbitration clause in this case manifests an obvious intent to be narrowly construed. Thus, a dispute that is merely collateral to the Operating Agreement is beyond the purview of this narrow arbitration clause.

We agree with the district court that plaintiffs do not allege that FedEx actually or constructively terminated the Operating Agreement, which, according to its unambiguous terms, are the only disputes subject to arbitration.

The subject matter of the claims-oral representations and implied agreements concerning income and truck resale assistance made prior to the execution of the Operating Agreement-is not reasonably factually related to a dispute over the termination, direct or otherwise, of the Operating Agreement. Notably, the Third Circuit has construed the same arbitration clause very narrowly. The arbitration clause in the Operating Agreement states that, should a dispute be submitted to arbitration, the arbitrator shall only have authority to determine whether the termination was within the terms of the Operating Agreement. FedEx has successfully argued that the identical arbitration clause is so narrow as to preclude an arbitrator from ruling that FedEx denied a contractor due process in terminating his agreement. If the clause does not give an arbitrator authority over a dispute as related to termination as the procedures used in the termination, it does not encompass an even broader dispute such as whether enforceable oral representations were made prior to and apart from the written terms of the Operating Agreement.

In summary, given the narrow scope of the arbitration clause, we conclude that the district court correctly ruled that the fourth and fifth claims of plaintiffs' complaint are not disputes within the scope of the arbitration agreement. The judgment of the district court is AFFIRMED.

NOTES

Facts

1. What are the fourth and fifth claims at issue here and how do they relate to the contract? Could you reformulate these claims as wrongful termination claims?

2. What is the argument advanced by FedEx that the claims are actually wrongful termination claims? Does the argument pass the "smell test"? What facts would you need to develop to improve upon the argument?

3. The Court references FedEx's conduct in the interpretation of its own arbitration clause. Do you think that the Court would have interpreted the clause differently without this conduct? How would you counsel your clients to avoid the "sauce-for-the-goose, sauce-for-the-gander" problem?

Law

1. What is a "collateral matter"? How does the court go about determining whether a dispute is "collateral" or not?

2.   Is there a technique you could use in order to limit an arbitration clause in certain regards (for instance, exclude mail fraud and wire fraud claims from arbitration) while at the time keeping claims collateral to the reminder of the contract within the scope of the arbitration clause? How would you do so?

C) Who Determines Jurisdiction?

A different issue arises regarding the question of who determines the arbitral tribunal's jurisdiction over the dispute—the courts or the arbitral tribunal? The AAA's model arbitration clause addresses this issue by reference. It states that the dispute "shall be settled by arbitration administered by the American Arbitration Association under its Commercial Arbitration Rules." Commercial Arbitration Rule 7 then goes on to state that

> The arbitrator shall have the power to rule on his or her own jurisdiction, including any objections with respect to the existence, scope, or validity of the arbitration agreement or to the arbitrability of any claim or counterclaim.

> The arbitrator shall have the power to determine the existence or validity of a contract of which an arbitration clause forms a part. Such an arbitration clause shall be treated as an agreement independent of the other terms of the contract. A decision by the arbitrator that the contract is null and void shall not for that reason alone render invalid the arbitration clause.

> A party must object to the jurisdiction of the arbitrator or to the arbitrability of a claim or counterclaim no later than the filing of the answering statement to the claim or counterclaim that gives rise to the objection. The arbitrator may rule on such objections as a preliminary matter or as part of the final award.

The use of the AAA model clause refers the parties and the arbitrators to the relevant AAA rules for a more precise definition of arbitral powers. Commercial Arbitration Rule 7 expressly bestows the power to determine jurisdiction upon the arbitral tribunal. It further provides the mandatory means by which a party can object to jurisdiction and the consequence of a failure to object in this way. The materials below outline why the clause was model drafted in this manner and who has competence to decide upon questions that touch on a tribunal's jurisdiction if the arbitration agreement is silent.

First Options of Chicago, Inc. v. Kaplan

514 U.S. 938 (1995)

First Options, a stock clearing company, entered into a debt "workout" agreement with MK Investments and Manuel Kaplan and his wife. Mr. Kaplan owned MK Investments. The workout agreement consisted of four documents only one of which contained an arbitration clause. When a dispute arose regarding payments, First Options filed notice of arbitration. MK Investments agreed to submit to arbitration because it had signed all four documents, including the one with the arbitration clause. However, the Kaplans challenged the jurisdiction of the arbitral tribunal on the grounds that they had not signed the document with the arbitration clause and that their dispute with First Options was not arbitrable. The arbitral tribunal found that it had jurisdiction over the entirety of the dispute and after a hearing on the merits rendered an award in favor of First Options. The Kaplans filed in U.S. district court to vacate the award while First Options sought to have the court confirm the award. The district court confirmed the award. However, the 3rd Circuit Court of Appeals reversed, finding that the dispute with the Kaplans was not arbitrable. First Options appealed.

JUSTICE BREYER delivered the opinion of the Court.

[. . .]

The first question—the standard of review applied to an arbitrator's decision about arbitrability—is a narrow one. To understand just how narrow, consider three types of disagreement present in this case. First, the Kaplans and First Options disagree about whether the Kaplans are personally liable for MKI's debt to First Options. That disagreement makes up the *merits* of the dispute. Second, they disagree about whether they agreed to arbitrate the merits. That disagreement is about the *arbitrability* of the dispute. Third, they disagree about *who should have the primary power to decide the second matter.* Does that power belong primarily to the arbitrators (because the court reviews their arbitrability decision deferentially) or to the court (because the court makes up its mind about arbitrability independently)? We consider here only this third question.

Although the question is a narrow one, it has a certain practical importance. That is because a party who has not agreed to arbitrate will normally have a right to a court's decision about the merits of its dispute (say, as here, its obligation under a contract). But, where the party has agreed to arbitrate, he or she, in effect, has relinquished much of that right's practical value. The party still can ask a court to review the arbitrator's decision, but the court will set that decision aside only in very unusual circumstances. [. . .] Hence, who—court or arbitrator—has the primary authority to decide whether a party has agreed to arbitrate can make a critical difference to a party resisting arbitration.

We believe the answer to the "who" question (*i. e.*, the standard-of-review question) is fairly simple. Just as the arbitrability of the merits of a dispute depends upon whether the parties agreed to arbitrate that dispute, see, *e. g., Mastrobuono* v. *Shearson Lehman Hutton, Inc., ante,* at 57; *Mitsubishi Motors Corp. v. Soler Chrysler-Plymouth, Inc.,* 473 U.S. 614, 626, 87 L. Ed. 2d 444, 105 S. Ct. 3346 (1985), so the question "who has the primary power to decide arbitrability" turns upon what the parties agreed about *that* matter. Did the parties agree to submit the arbitrability question itself to arbitration? If so, then the court's standard for reviewing the arbitrator's decision about *that* matter should not differ from the standard courts apply when they review any other matter that parties have agreed to arbitrate. See *AT&T Technologies, Inc. v. Communications Workers,* 475 U.S. 643, 649, 89 L. Ed. 2d 648, 106 S. Ct. 1415 (1986) (parties may agree to arbitrate arbitrability); *Steelworkers v. Warrior & Gulf Nav. Co.,* 363 U.S. 574, 583, n. 7, 4 L. Ed. 2d 1409, 80 S. Ct. 1347 (1960) (same). That is to say, the court should give considerable leeway to the arbitrator, setting aside his or her decision only in certain narrow circumstances. See, *e. g., 9 U.S.C. § 10.* If, on the other hand, the parties did *not* agree to submit the arbitrability question itself to arbitration, then the court should decide that question just as it would decide any other question that the parties did not submit to arbitration, namely, independently. These two answers flow inexorably from the fact that arbitration is simply a matter of contract between the parties; it is a way to resolve those disputes—but only those disputes—that the parties have agreed to submit to arbitration. See, *e. g., AT&T Technologies, supra, at 649; Mastrobuono, ante,* at 57–58, and n. 9; *Allied-Bruce Terminix Cos. v. Dobson,* 513 U.S. 265, 271, 130 L. Ed. 2d 753, 115 S. Ct. 834 (1995); *Mitsubishi Motors Corp., supra, at 625–626.*

We agree with First Options, therefore, that a court must defer to an arbitrator's arbitrability decision when the parties submitted that matter to arbitration. Nevertheless, that conclusion does not help First Options win this case. That is because a fair and complete answer to the standard-of-review question requires a word about how a court should decide whether the parties have agreed to submit the arbitrability issue to arbitration. And, that word makes clear that the Kaplans did not agree to arbitrate arbitrability here.

When deciding whether the parties agreed to arbitrate a certain matter (including arbitrability), courts generally (though with a qualification we discuss below) should apply ordinary state-law principles that govern the formation of contracts.

This Court, however, has (as we just said) added an important qualification, applicable when courts decide whether a party has agreed that arbitrators should decide arbitrability: Courts should not assume that the parties agreed to arbitrate arbitrability unless there is "clea[r] and unmistakabl[e]" evidence that they did so. In this manner the law treats silence or ambiguity about the question *"who* (primarily) should decide arbitrability" differently from the way it treats silence or ambiguity about the question *"whether* a particular merits-related dispute is arbitrable because it is within the scope of a valid arbitration agreement"—for in respect to this latter question the law reverses the presumption. See *Mitsubishi Motors, supra, at 626* (" 'Any doubts concerning the scope of arbitrable issues should be resolved in favor of arbitration' ")

On the record before us, First Options cannot show that the Kaplans clearly agreed to have the arbitrators decide (*i. e.,* to arbitrate) the question of arbitrability. First Options relies on the Kaplans' filing with the arbitrators a written memorandum objecting to the arbitrators' jurisdiction. But merely arguing the arbitrability issue to an arbitrator does not indicate a clear willingness to arbitrate that issue, *i. e.,* a willingness to be effectively bound by the arbitrator's decision on that point. To the contrary, insofar as the Kaplans were forcefully objecting to the arbitrators deciding their dispute with First Options, one naturally would think that they did *not* want the arbitrators to have binding authority over them. This conclusion draws added support from (1) an obvious explanation for the Kaplans' presence before the arbitrators (*i. e.,* that MKI, Mr. Kaplan's wholly owned firm, was arbitrating workout agreement matters); and (2) Third Circuit law that suggested that the Kaplans might argue arbitrability to the arbitrators without losing their right to independent court review.

First Options makes several counterarguments: (1) that the Kaplans had other ways to get an independent court decision on the question of arbitrability without arguing the issue to the arbitrators (*e. g.,* by trying to enjoin the arbitration, or by refusing to participate in the arbitration and then defending against a court petition First Options would have brought to compel arbitration, see *9 U.S.C. § 4*); (2) that permitting parties to argue arbitrability to an arbitrator without being bound by the result would cause delay and waste in the resolution of disputes; and (3) that the Arbitration Act therefore requires a presumption that the Kaplans agreed to be bound by the arbitrators' decision, not the contrary. The first of these points, however, while true, simply does not say anything about whether the Kaplans intended to be bound by the arbitrators' decision. The second point, too, is inconclusive, for factual circumstances vary too greatly to permit a confident conclusion about whether allowing the arbitrator to make an initial (but independently reviewable) arbitrability determination would, in general, slow down the dispute resolution process. And, the third point is legally erroneous, for there is no strong arbitration-related policy favoring First Options in respect to its particular argument here. After all, the basic objective in this area is not to resolve disputes in the quickest manner possible, no matter what the parties' wishes, *Dean Witter Reynolds, supra, at 219–220*, but to ensure that commercial arbitration agreements, like other contracts, " 'are enforced according to their terms,' " *Mastrobuono, ante*, at 54 (quoting *Volt Information Sciences*, 489 U.S. at 479), and according to the intentions of the parties, *Mitsubishi Motors*, 473 U.S. at 626. See *Allied-Bruce*, 513 U.S. at 271. That policy favors the Kaplans, not First Options.

We conclude that, because the Kaplans did not clearly agree to submit the question of arbitrability to arbitration, the Court of Appeals was correct in finding that the arbitrability of the Kaplan/First Options dispute was subject to independent review by the courts.

[. . .]

The judgment of the Court of Appeals is affirmed.

It is so ordered.

NOTES

Facts

1. What evidence did First Options rely upon to prove that the question of whether the dispute could be resolved in arbitration should be submitted to the arbitrator? What other evidence would be relevant?

2. How would First Options have to change the arbitration clause in order to provide such clear evidence?

Law

1. The Court uses the term "arbitrability" throughout this decision. As is obvious on the face of the decision, the Court does not use the term "arbitrability" in the sense discussed in the previous chapter—*i.e.*, in the sense of a subject matter that *per se* can or cannot be submitted to arbitration. How does the Court here use the term arbitrability? How does that relate to the usage of the term arbitrability in the last chapter?

2.   How do the facts here differ from *Motorola*? Are the facts here stronger or weaker than the facts in *Motorola* to suggest that the parties really did intend to arbitrate their disputes?

Howsam v. Dean Witter Reynolds, Inc.

537 U.S. 79 (2002)

The *Howsam* case arose from a dispute regarding investment advice Dean Witter had provided to one of its clients. The arbitration agreement contained in the contract allowed the client to choose the arbitral forum from the self-regulating agency of which Dean Witter was a member. The client chose to arbitrate before the National Association of Securities Dealers (NASD). Dean Witter brought suit in U.S. district court for an order declaring the dispute not arbitrable on the grounds that the NASD's rules provided that a dispute would not be eligible for arbitration if six years had elapsed since the event giving rise to the dispute. Dean Witter also sought an injunction against further attempts to arbitrate the dispute. The district court dismissed the case holding that the decision as to arbitrability should be decided by the arbitral tribunal. The Tenth Circuit Court of Appeals reversed, holding that the court should decide issues of arbitrability. The client appealed.

JUSTICE BREYER delivered the opinion of the Court.

This case focuses upon an arbitration rule of the National Association of Securities Dealers (NASD). The rule states that no dispute "shall be eligible for submission to arbitration . . . where six (6) years have elapsed from the occurrence or event giving rise to the . . . dispute." NASD Code of Arbitration Procedure § 10304 (1984) (NASD Code or Code). We must decide whether a court or an NASD arbitrator should apply the rule to the underlying controversy. We conclude that the matter is for the arbitrator.

After the Uniform Submission Agreement was executed, Dean Witter filed this lawsuit in Federal District Court. It asked the court to declare that the dispute was "ineligible for arbitration" because it was more than six years old. App. 45. And it sought an injunction that would prohibit Howsam from proceeding in arbitration. The District Court dismissed the action on the ground that the NASD arbitrator, not the court, should interpret and apply the NASD rule. The Court of Appeals for the Tenth Circuit, however, reversed. 261 F.3d 956 (2001). In its view, application of the NASD rule presented a question of the underlying dispute's "arbitrability"; and the presumption is that a court, not an arbitrator, will ordinarily decide an "arbitrability" question. See, *e.g., First*

Options of Chicago, Inc. v. Kaplan, 514 U.S. 938, 131 L. Ed. 2d 985, 115 S. Ct. 1920 (1995).

II

This Court has determined that "arbitration is a matter of contract and a party cannot be required to submit to arbitration any dispute which he has not agreed so to submit." Although the Court has also long recognized and enforced a "liberal federal policy favoring arbitration agreements," it has made clear that there is an exception to this policy: The question whether the parties have submitted a particular dispute to arbitration, *i.e.*, the *"question of arbitrability,"* is "an issue for judicial determination [u]nless the parties clearly and unmistakably provide otherwise." We must decide here whether application of the NASD time limit provision falls into the scope of this last-mentioned interpretive rule.

Linguistically speaking, one might call any potentially dispositive gateway question a "question of arbitrability," for its answer will determine whether the underlying controversy will proceed to arbitration on the merits. The Court's case law, however, makes clear that, for purposes of applying the interpretive rule, the phrase "question of arbitrability" has a far more limited scope. See 514 U.S. at 942. The Court has found the phrase applicable in the kind of narrow circumstance where contracting parties would likely have expected a court to have decided the gateway matter, where they are not likely to have thought that they had agreed that an arbitrator would do so, and, consequently, where reference of the gateway dispute to the court avoids the risk of forcing parties to arbitrate a matter that they may well not have agreed to arbitrate.

Thus, a gateway dispute about whether the parties are bound by a given arbitration clause raises a "question of arbitrability" for a court to decide. Similarly, a disagreement about whether an arbitration clause in a concededly binding contract applies to a particular type of controversy is for the court.

At the same time the Court has found the phrase "question of arbitrability" *not* applicable in other kinds of general circumstance where parties would likely expect that an arbitrator would decide the gateway matter. Thus " 'procedural' questions which grow out of the dispute and bear on its final disposition" are presumptively *not* for the judge, but for an arbitrator, to decide. So, too, the presumption is that the arbitrator should decide "allegations of waiver, delay, or a like defense to arbitrability." Indeed, the Revised Uniform Arbitration Act of 2000 (RUAA), seeking to "incorporate the holdings of the vast majority of state courts and the law that has developed under the [Federal Arbitration Act]," states that an "arbitrator shall decide whether a condition precedent to arbitrability has been fulfilled." RUAA § 6(c) and comment 2, 7 U. L. A. 12–13 (Supp. 2002). And the comments add that "in the absence of an agreement to the contrary, issues of substantive arbitrability . . . are for a court to decide and issues of procedural arbitrability, *i.e.,* whether prerequisites such as *time limits,* notice, laches, estoppel, and other conditions precedent to an obligation to arbitrate have been met, are for the arbitrators to decide." *Id.,* § 6, comment 2, 7 U. L. A., at 13 (emphasis added).

Following this precedent, we find that the applicability of the NASD time limit rule is a matter presumptively for the arbitrator, not for the judge. The time limit rule closely resembles the gateway questions that this Court has found not to be "questions of arbitrability." Such a dispute seems an "aspect of the [controversy] which called the grievance procedures into play."

Moreover, the NASD arbitrators, comparatively more expert about the meaning of their own rule, are comparatively better able to interpret and to apply it. In the absence of any statement to the contrary in the arbitration agreement, it is reasonable to infer that the parties intended the agreement to reflect that understanding. And for the law to assume an expectation that aligns (1) decisionmaker with (2) comparative expertise will help better to secure a fair and expeditious resolution of the underlying controversy—a goal of arbitration systems and judicial systems alike.

We consequently conclude that the NASD's time limit rule falls within the class of gateway procedural disputes that do not present what our cases have called "questions of arbitrability." And the strong pro-court presumption as to the parties' likely intent does not apply.

[. . .]

IV

For these reasons, the judgment of the Tenth Circuit is

Reversed.

NOTES

Facts

1. What was the issue on the basis of which Dean Witter sought an injunction providing that the dispute could not be submitted to arbitration?

2. How did the arbitration clause address this issue? How did the arbitration rules address this issue? How did the arbitration clause refer to the arbitration rules?

Law

1. How can one distinguish between procedural issues and issues of consent? How about fulfilment of a condition precedent? Is that not a question of arbitrability?

Rent-a-Center, West, Inc. v. Jackson

561 U.S. 63 (2010) (footnotes omitted)

In the following case, Antonio Jackson filed an employment discrimination suit in U.S. district court against his employer, Rent-a-Center. Rent-a-Center filed a motion to compel arbitration pursuant to the employment contract which contained an arbitration clause which specifically provided that "[t]he Arbitrator, and not any federal, state, or local court or agency, shall have exclusive authority to resolve any dispute relating to the interpretation, applicability, enforceability or formation of this Agreement including, but not limited to any claim that all or any part of this Agreement is void or voidable." Jackson argued the arbitration agreement was unconscionable. The district court granted Rent-a-Center's motion to compel arbitration. However, the Ninth Circuit Court of Appeals reversed. Rent-a-Center appealed.

JUSTICE SCALIA delivered the opinion of the Court.

We consider whether, under the Federal Arbitration Act (FAA or Act), *9 U.S.C. §§ 1–16*, a district court may decide a claim that an arbitration agreement is unconscionable, where the agreement explicitly assigns that decision to the arbitrator.

The Agreement here contains multiple "written provision[s]" to "settle by arbitration a controversy," *§ 2*. Two are relevant to our discussion. First, the section titled "Claims Covered By The Agreement" provides for arbitration of all "past, present or future" disputes arising out of Jackson's employment with Rent-A-Center. App. 29. Second, the section titled "Arbitration Procedures" provides that "[t]he Arbitrator . . . shall have exclusive authority to resolve any dispute relating to the . . . enforceability . . . of this Agreement including, but not limited to any claim that all or any part of this Agreement is void or voidable." *Id.*, at 32, 34. The current "controversy" between the parties is whether the Agreement is unconscionable. It is the second provision, which delegates resolution of that controversy to the arbitrator, that Rent-A-Center seeks to enforce. Adopting the terminology used by the parties, we will refer to it as the delegation provision.

The delegation provision is an agreement to arbitrate threshold issues concerning the arbitration agreement. We have recognized that parties can agree to arbitrate "gateway" questions of "arbitrability," such as whether the parties have agreed to arbitrate or whether their agreement covers a particular controversy. See, *e.g.*, *Howsam*, 537 U.S., at 83–85, 123 S. Ct. 588, 154 L. Ed. 2d 491; *Green Tree Financial Corp. v. Bazzle*, 539 U.S. 444, 452, 123 S. Ct. 2402, 156 L. Ed. 2d 414 (2003) (plurality opinion). This line of cases merely reflects the principle that arbitration is a matter of contract. See *First Options of Chicago, Inc. v. Kaplan*, 514 U.S. 938, 943, 115 S. Ct. 1920, 131 L. Ed. 2d 985 (1995). An agreement to arbitrate a gateway issue is simply an additional, antecedent agreement the party seeking arbitration asks the federal court to enforce, and the FAA operates on this additional arbitration agreement just as it does on any other. The additional agreement is valid under *§ 2* "save upon such grounds as exist at law or in equity for the revocation of any contract," and federal courts can enforce the agreement by staying federal litigation under *§ 3* and compelling arbitration under *§ 4*. The question before us, then, is whether the delegation provision is valid under *§ 2*.

B

There are two types of validity challenges under *§ 2*: "One type challenges specifically the validity of the agreement to arbitrate," and "[t]he other challenges the contract as a whole, either on a ground that directly affects the entire agreement (*e.g.*, the agreement was fraudulently induced), or on the ground that the illegality of one of the contract's provisions renders the whole contract invalid." *Buckeye*, 546 U.S., at 444, 126 S. Ct. 1204, 163 L. Ed. 2d 1038. In a line of cases neither party has asked us to overrule, we held that only the first type of challenge is relevant to a court's determination whether the arbitration agreement at issue is enforceable. See *Prima Paint Corp. v. Flood & Conklin Mfg. Co.*, 388 U.S. 395, 403–404, 87 S. Ct. 1801, 18 L. Ed. 2d 1270 (1967); *Buckeye, supra*, at 444–446, 126 S. Ct. 1204, 163 L. Ed. 2d 1038; *Preston v. Ferrer*, 552 U.S. 346, 353–354, 128 S. Ct. 978, 169 L. Ed. 2d 917 (2008). That is because *§ 2* states that a "written provision" "to settle by arbitration a controversy" is "valid, irrevocable, and enforceable" *without mention* of the validity of the contract in which it is contained. Thus, a party's challenge to another provision of the contract, or to the contract as a whole, does not prevent a court from enforcing a specific agreement to arbitrate. "[A]s a matter of substantive federal arbitration law, an arbitration provision is severable from the remainder of the contract." *Buckeye*, 546 U.S., at 445, 126 S. Ct. 1204, 163 L. Ed. 2d 1038; see also *id.*, at 447, 126 S. Ct. 1204, 163 L. Ed. 2d 1038 (the severability rule is based on *§ 2*).

But that agreements to arbitrate are severable does not mean that they are unassailable. If a party challenges the validity under § 2 of the precise agreement to arbitrate at issue, the federal court must consider the challenge before ordering compliance with that agreement under § 4. In *Prima Paint*, for example, if the claim had been "fraud in the inducement of the arbitration clause itself," then the court would have considered it. 388 U.S., at 403–404, 87 S. Ct. 1801, 18 L. Ed. 2d 1270. "To immunize an arbitration agreement from judicial challenge on the ground of fraud in the inducement would be to elevate it over other forms of contract," *id.*, at 404, n. 12, 87 S. Ct. 1801, 18 L. Ed. 2d 1270. In some cases the claimed basis of invalidity for the contract as a whole will be much easier to establish than the same basis as applied only to the severable agreement to arbitrate. Thus, in an employment contract many elements of alleged unconscionability applicable to the entire contract (outrageously low wages, for example) would not affect the agreement to arbitrate alone. But even where that is not the case—as in *Prima Paint* itself, where the alleged fraud that induced the whole contract equally induced the agreement to arbitrate which was part of that contract—we nonetheless require the basis of challenge to be directed specifically to the agreement to arbitrate before the court will intervene.

Here, the "written provision . . . to settle by arbitration a controversy," *9 U.S.C. § 2*, that Rent-A-Center asks us to enforce is the delegation provision— the provision that gave the arbitrator "exclusive authority to resolve any dispute relating to the . . . enforceability . . . of this Agreement," App. 34. The "remainder of the contract," *Buckeye, supra,* at 445, 126 S. Ct. 1204, 163 L. Ed. 2d 1038, is the rest of the agreement to arbitrate claims arising out of Jackson's employment with Rent-A-Center. To be sure this case differs from *Prima Paint, Buckeye,* and *Preston,* in that the arbitration provisions sought to be enforced in those cases were contained in contracts unrelated to arbitration—contracts for consulting services, see *Prima Paint,* supra, at 397, 87 S. Ct. 1801, 18 L. Ed. 2d 1270, check-cashing services, see *Buckeye,* supra, at 442, 126 S. Ct. 1204, 163 L. Ed. 2d 1038, and "personal management" or "talent agent" services, see *Preston, supra,* at 352, 128 S. Ct. 978, 169 L. Ed. 2d 917. In this case, the underlying contract is itself an arbitration agreement. But that makes no difference. Application of the severability rule does not depend on the substance of the remainder of the contract. *Section 2* operates on the specific "written provision" to "settle by arbitration a controversy" that the party seeks to enforce. Accordingly, unless Jackson challenged the delegation provision specifically, we must treat it as valid under § 2, and must enforce it under §§ 3 and 4, leaving any challenge to the validity of the Agreement as a whole for the arbitrator.

C

The District Court correctly concluded that Jackson challenged only the validity of the contract as a whole. Nowhere in his opposition to Rent-A-Center's motion to compel arbitration did he even mention the delegation provision. [. . .]

The arguments Jackson made in his response to Rent-A-Center's motion to compel arbitration support this conclusion. Jackson stated that "the *entire agreement* seems drawn to provide [Rent-A-Center] with undue advantages should an employment-related dispute arise." *Id.*, at 44 (emphasis added). At one point, he argued that the limitations on discovery "further suppor[t] [his] contention that the *arbitration agreement as a whole* is substantively unconscionable." *Ibid.* (emphasis added). And before this Court, Jackson describes his challenge in the District Court as follows: He "opposed the motion to compel on the ground that the *entire arbitration agreement*, including the delegation clause, was unconscionable." Brief for Respondent 55 (emphasis added). That is an accurate description of his filings.

As required to make out a claim of unconscionability under Nevada law, see 581 F.3d at 919, he contended that the Agreement was both procedurally and substantively unconscionable. It was procedurally unconscionable, he argued, because it "was imposed as a condition of employment and was non-negotiable." App. 41. But we need not consider that claim because none of Jackson's substantive unconscionability challenges was specific to the delegation provision. [. . .]

Jackson's other two substantive unconscionability arguments assailed arbitration procedures called for by the contract—the fee-splitting arrangement and the limitations on discovery—procedures that were to be used during arbitration under *both* the agreement to arbitrate employment-related disputes *and* the delegation provision. [. . .] Jackson, however, did not make any arguments specific to the delegation provision; he argued that the fee-sharing and discovery procedures rendered the *entire* Agreement invalid.

Jackson's appeal to the Ninth Circuit confirms that he did not contest the validity of the delegation provision in particular. [. . .] Finally, he repeated the argument made in his District Court filings, that under state law the unconscionable clauses could not be severed from the arbitration agreement, see *id.*, at 8–9. The point of this argument, of course, is that the Agreement *as a whole* is unconscionable under state law.

Jackson repeated that argument before this Court. At oral argument, counsel stated: "There are certain elements of the arbitration agreement that are unconscionable and, under Nevada law, which would render the *entire arbitration agreement* unconscionable." Tr. of Oral Arg. 43 (emphasis added). And again, he stated, "we've got both certain provisions that are unconscionable, that under Nevada law render the *entire agreement* unconscionable . . ., and that's what the Court is to rely on." *Id.*, at 43–44 (emphasis added).

[. . .]

We reverse the judgment of the Court of Appeals for the Ninth Circuit.

It is so ordered.

D) Multitiered Dispute Resolution

The use of multitiered dispute resolution is becoming increasingly common, but it presents a challenge for the effective drafting of arbitration clauses. Any contentious dispute resolution mechanism has significant downsides. It tends to escalate the dispute and stand in the way of the continued performance of the contract. The dispute further can create reputation damage to the parties. Finally, arbitrations do not resolve disputes immediately. Rather, evidence must be gathered, presented, and then mulled by a tribunal before the issuance of an ultimate award. For this reason, businesses frequently prefer to avoid even arbitration as a means to resolve their disputes. To do this, parties include dispute resolution mechanisms that should be exhausted before they proceed to arbitration. These mechanisms can include facilitative alternative dispute resolution tools such as mandatory negotiation or mediation to evaluative tools such as early neutral evaluation. Sophisticated parties may combine these different tools in provisions such as MED-ARB or ARB-MED provisions.

The most significant challenge arises in the context of an alleged non-fulfillment of a condition to arbitration. These cases present the question who determines whether or not the condition to the arbitration undertaking is itself submitted to arbitration. What happens if a party "jumps the gun" and submits a dispute to arbitration before using the other dispute resolution tools included in the clause? A clause may state "the parties shall submit any dispute to mediation. After the conclusion of the mediation, either party may commence an arbitration proceeding with regard to such a dispute." Is the question of whether the mediation provision was satisfied—and thus whether the parties have consented to arbitration of the dispute—one that should be submitted to the arbitrators or to the courts?

As you can see from the case below, the controversy over who determines whether a condition to arbitration has been fulfilled can lead to unanticipated results. As you read the case, consider how the problem could have been avoided by clearer drafting of the arbitration agreement.

Republic of Argentina v. BG Group PLC

665 F.3d 1363 (2012)

ROGERS, CIRCUIT JUDGE:

The Republic of Argentina appeals the denial of its motion to vacate an arbitral award on the principal ground that the arbitral panel exceeded its authority by ignoring the terms of the parties' agreement. That agreement, in the form of a Bilateral Investment Treaty between the United Kingdom of Great Britain and Northern Ireland, and Argentina ("the Treaty"), provides that disputes between an investor and the host State will be resolved in the host State's courts. If, however, no final court ruling is forthcoming within eighteen months or the dispute is unresolved after a court ruling, the Treaty provides that resort may then be had to arbitration. BG Group, PLC, a British corporation and investor in Argentina gas companies pursuant to the Treaty, invoked the arbitration clause without first filing a claim in the Argentine courts. The arbitral panel nonetheless ruled it had jurisdiction, found Argentina had violated the Treaty, and awarded BG Group damages.

Although the scope of judicial review of the substance of arbitral awards is exceedingly narrow, it is well settled that an arbitrator cannot ignore the intent of the contracting parties. Where, as here, the result of the arbitral award was to ignore the terms of the Treaty and shift the risk that the Argentine courts might not resolve BG Group's claim within eighteen months pursuant to Article 8(2) of the Treaty, the arbitral panel rendered a decision wholly based on outside legal sources and without regard to the contracting parties' agreement establishing a precondition to arbitration. Accordingly, we reverse the orders denying the motion to vacate and granting the cross-motion to confirm, and we vacate the Final Award.

I.

The Bilateral Investment Treaty between the United Kingdom and Argentina was signed December 11, 1990, and became effective on February 19, 1993. It aimed to promote a favorable investment environment between the contracting parties following Argentina's economic reformation to reduce inflation and the public debt. As relevant, Article 8(1) of the Treaty provides that disputes between an investor under the Treaty and the host State that "have not been amicably settled shall be submitted, at the request of one of the Parties to the dispute, to the decision of the competent tribunal of the Contracting Party in whose territory the investment was made." Article 8(2) sets the conditions by which such a dispute may be submitted to international arbitration:

> (a)   if one of the Parties so requests, in any of the following circumstances:
>
> (i)   where, after a period of eighteen months has elapsed from the moment when the dispute was submitted to the competent tribunal of the Contracting Party in whose territory the investment was made, the said tribunal has not given its final decision;
>
> (ii)   where the final decision of the aforementioned tribunal has been made but the Parties are still in dispute; [or]
>
> (b)   where the Contracting Party and the investor of the other Contracting Party have so agreed.

Art. 8(2) (emphasis added). Article 8(3) provides that if, after three months from written notification of the claim, the parties to the dispute are unable to agree on one of the described arbitration procedures, then "the Parties to the dispute shall be bound to submit it to arbitration under the Arbitration Rules of the United Nations Commission on International Trade Law ["UNCITRAL Rules"]," although they can modify these rules. Article 8(4) instructs that "[t]he arbitral tribunal shall decide the dispute in accordance with the provisions of this Agreement [i.e., the Treaty], the laws of the Contracting Party involved in the dispute, including its rules on conflict of laws, the terms of any specific agreement concluded in relation to such an investment and the applicable principles of international law."

Around the time the Treaty took effect, as part of its economic reformation, Argentina privatized the state-owned gas transportation and distribution company, Gas del Estado, and established a 1:1 fixed parity between the Argentine peso and the U.S. dollar. Gas del Estado was split into two transportation companies and eight distribution companies, one of which was MetroGAS. MetroGAS was granted a thirty-five year exclusive license to distribute gas in the city of Buenos Aires and portions of the surrounding metropolitan area, and the license provided that tariffs would be calculated in U.S. dollars and expressed in pesos. One provision of MetroGAS's license provided that adjustments to tariffs would be made every six months for inflation, in accordance with the United States Product Price Index ("PPI"). MetroGAS was entitled to review of its tariffs every five years to ensure reasonable returns. BG Group eventually acquired a 54.67 percent interest in Gas Argentino, S.A. ("GASA"), which in turn owned seventy percent of MetroGAS. In addition, BG Group invested directly in MetroGAS, and by 1998 held a 45.11 percent interest in MetroGAS.

The Argentine economy collapsed in late 2001 and early 2002 following, Argentina explained, the collapse of the Brazilian currency, a run on Argentine banks, and the withholding of a billion dollar loan installment by the International Monetary Fund. In response, Argentina enacted Emergency Law 25,561 on January 6, 2002, to terminate the currency board that had pegged the peso to the U.S. dollar, to convert U.S. dollar based adjustment clauses in agreements to peso-based adjustment clauses, to prohibit inflation adjustments based on foreign price indices (e.g., the PPI), and to convert dollar-based tariffs into peso-based tariffs at a rate of one peso to one U.S. dollar. Argentina also established, by Resolution 308/02 and Decree 1090/02, a renegotiation process for public service contracts (excluding any licensee who sought redress in court or arbitration). And on March 2, 2002, Argentina adopted Decree 214/02, Article 12 of which stayed for 180 days the compliance with injunctions and execution of final judgments in lawsuits brought on account of the Emergency Law's effect on the financial system.

Eight months after the stay under Article 12 of Decree 214/02 had expired, BG Group filed a Notice of Arbitration, on April 25, 2003, pursuant to Article 8(3) of the Treaty. When it was unable to reach agreement with Argentina on an alternate forum, BG Group submitted to arbitration under the UNCITRAL Rules. As characterized by the Arbitral Panel, a ministerial opinion (appearing in an article by the former Argentina Attorney General and Minister of Justice) submitted by BG Group estimated that it would take six years to resolve BG Group's claim in the Argentine courts, and BG Group therefore viewed the requirement in Article 8(2) of the Treaty as "senseless," Final Award ¶ 142, and saw no reason to wait eighteen months before requesting arbitration. Alternatively, BG Group argued that customary international law did not require exhaustion of local remedies, and that Article 3 of the Treaty, the Most Favored Nation Clause, obviated the requirement that it seek recourse in Argentine courts given that Argentina's investment treaty with the United States lacked such a requirement.

The Arbitral Panel issued a Final Award on December 24, 2007, in Washington, D.C. The Panel determined it had jurisdiction. It rejected BG

Group's arguments that the dispute was arbitrable because an Argentine court would not resolve the dispute within eighteen months and that international law did not require exhaustion of local remedies. Instead, the Panel concluded that although BG Group did not seek recourse in Argentine courts for the eighteen month period required by Article 8(2) of the Treaty, that provision could not, "[a]s a matter of Treaty interpretation ... be construed as an absolute impediment to arbitration." Final Award ¶ 147. Citing Article 32 of the Vienna Convention, the Panel concluded that because Argentina by emergency decrees had restricted access to its courts and had excluded from the renegotiation process any licensee that sought redress, a literal reading of the Treaty would produce an "absurd and unreasonable result." Id. The Panel thus found it unnecessary to decide whether Article 3 of the Treaty made Article 8(1) and (2) inoperative.

Argentina petitioned to vacate or modify the Final Award pursuant to the FAA, 9 U.S.C. §§ 10(a) & 11.FN4 BG Group filed an opposition and a cross-motion for recognition and enforcement of the Final Award, and for a prejudgment bond. Following further filings in opposition or reply, the district court denied vacatur and granted enforcement. Argentina appeals; our review of the district court's findings of fact is for clear error and our review of questions of law is de novo.

II.

The "gateway" question in this appeal is arbitrability: when the United Kingdom and Argentina executed the Treaty, did they, as contracting parties, intend that an investor under the Treaty could seek arbitration without first fulfilling Article 8(1)'s requirement that recourse initially be sought in a court of the contracting party where the investment was made? That question raises the antecedent question of whether the contracting parties intended the answer to be provided by a court or an arbitrator.

The Supreme Court has held that the intent of the contracting parties controls whether the answer to the question of arbitrability is to be provided by a court or an arbitrator. "Courts should not assume that the parties agreed to arbitrate arbitrability unless there is 'clea[r] and unmistakabl[e]' evidence that they did so." Thus, in "construing an arbitration clause, courts and arbitrators must 'give effect to the contractual rights and expectations of the parties.' "

In *Howsam v. Dean Witter*, the Court provided guidance on the circumstances in which a court, rather than the arbitrator, is to decide a "question of arbitrability," A court will decide the question in the kind of narrow circumstances where the contracting parties would likely have expected a court to have decided the gateway matter, where they are not likely to have thought that they had agreed that an arbitrator would do so, and, consequently, where reference of the gateway dispute to the court avoids the risk of forcing parties to arbitrate a matter that they may well not have agreed to arbitrate.

In such circumstances, where "the parties did not agree to submit the arbitrability question itself to arbitration, then the district court should decide that question ... independently." If, on the other hand, there is clear and unmistakable evidence that the parties intended for the arbitrator to decide the question of arbitrability, a district court's review of the arbitrator's decision on that matter "should not differ from the standard courts apply when they review any other matter that parties have agreed to arbitrate. . . . That is to say, the court should give considerable leeway to the arbitrator, setting aside his or her decision only in certain narrow circumstances." Id. (internal citations omitted).

Any concession by Argentina was ... limited to stating that the parties agreed the issue of arbitrability would be decided by an arbitrator if the aggrieved party had first sought relief in an Argentine court, pursuant to Article 8(1) and (2) of the Treaty. Indeed, its counsel made the point explicit in responding to the district court's next inquiry about whether the Treaty provided that the UNCITRAL Rules would apply if there were no agreement on an arbitral forum. See id. at 4–5. Argentina's counsel stated: "The fundamental issue[ ] here and that's our first objection is that [under the terms of the Treaty] Argentina's consent to arbitration had a very important condition. And that condition was that the dispute had to be submitted for 18 months to local courts to an Argentine judge." Id. at 5. The transcript thus demonstrates, when the statement by Argentina's counsel on which the district court relied is viewed in context, that the district court clearly erred in finding that Argentina had conceded that the arbitrator had the power to determine arbitrability under the circumstances.

A temporal analysis of the Treaty confirms this conclusion. Article 8(3) of the Treaty provides for the procedure to be followed once the possibility of arbitration is triggered, but only after an Argentine court first has an opportunity to resolve the dispute. Under Article 8(3), if the parties do not agree on an arbitration forum or procedure, the UNCITRAL Rules will govern resolution of the dispute; the UNCITRAL Rules grant the arbitrator the power to determine issues of arbitrability.[5] Thus, once Article 8(3) of the Treaty is

---

[5]   Article 21(1) of the UNCITRAL Arbitration Rules, G.A. Res. 31/98, art. 21, para. 1, U.N. Doc. A/RES/31/98 (Dec. 15, 1976), provides that "[t]he arbitral tribunal shall have the power to rule on objections that it has no jurisdiction" to hear the arbitration.

triggered, the Treaty's incorporation of the UNCITRAL Rules provides "clear[ ] and unmistakabl[e] evidence," that the parties intended for the arbitrator to decide questions of arbitrability. But the Treaty's incorporation of the UNCITRAL Rules has a temporal limitation: the Rules are not triggered until after an investor has first, pursuant to Article 8(1) and (2), sought recourse, for eighteen months, in a court of the contracting party where the investment was made.

The Treaty does not directly answer whether the contracting parties intended a court or the arbitrator to determine questions of arbitrability where the precondition of resort to a contracting party's court pursuant to Article 8(1) and (2) is disregarded by an investor. By comparison, the Treaty states in Article 9(2) that should a dispute arise between the contracting parties themselves, the United Kingdom and Argentina, and it is not resolved through diplomatic channels, the dispute will go directly to arbitration. Article 9(5) provides that "[t]he [arbitral] tribunal shall determine its own procedure." This provision indicates that the contracting parties were aware of how to provide an arbitrator with the authority to determine a "question of arbitrability," and suggests that the absence of such language in Article 8(1) and (2) was intentional. It also underscores the importance the contracting parties ascribed to Article 8(1) and (2), counseling against a reading that would render its requirements inoperative.

Furthermore, the contracting parties likely never conceived of the need to specify that a court should decide whether Article 8(1) and (2)'s requirement that disputes first be brought to a court should be respected. The Treaty provides a prime example of a situation where the "parties would likely have expected a court" to decide arbitrability. *Howsam*, 537 U.S. at 83, 123 S.Ct. 588. It would be odd to assume that where the gateway provision itself is resort to a court, the parties would have been surprised to have a court, and not an arbitrator, decide whether the gateway provision should be followed. At the very least, there is no clear and unmistakable evidence, that the contracting parties intended an arbitrator to decide the gateway question.

Because the Treaty provides that a precondition to arbitration of an investor's claim is an initial resort to a contracting party's court, and the Treaty is silent on who decides arbitrability when that precondition is disregarded, we hold that the question of arbitrability is an independent question of law for the court to decide. See id. The district court therefore erred as a matter of law by failing to determine whether there was clear and unmistakable evidence that the contracting parties intended the arbitrator to decide arbitrability where BG

Group disregarded the requirements of Article 8(1) and (2) of the Treaty to initially seek resolution of its dispute with Argentina in an Argentine court.

Accordingly, "[b]ecause we conclude that there can be only one possible outcome on the [arbitrability question] before us," namely, that BG Group was required to commence a lawsuit in Argentina's courts and wait eighteen months before filing for arbitration pursuant to Article 8(3) if the dispute remained, we reverse the orders denying the motion to vacate and granting the cross-motion to confirm the Final Award, and we vacate the Final Award.

CHAPTER 6

Drafting an Effective Arbitration Clause (Class Actions)

Two of the key issues in arbitration concern whether one can arbitrate disputes as a class action, and whether waivers of class arbitration are effective. The issue is currently hotly contested in appellate litigation—and has generated a growing number of U.S. Supreme Court jurisprudence.

In order to understand fully the subject's importance, consider why there are class action mechanisms in the U.S. These mechanisms provide a means through which a large number of similar claims can be effectively—and consistently—adjudicated or settled. Further, class actions provide a way for a large group of plaintiffs to aggregate their resources to shoulder the expense of litigation. Thus, at its best, class action permits the holders of comparatively small claims to have a "day in court" that they otherwise might never be able to afford. It is because of this second advantage of class action that almost every consumer is regularly told by mail that he or she has been the beneficiary of a class settlement. (Although the delivery of course means that many contemporary papyrophobic consumers simply never actually receive this notice but alas, the courts have yet to allow you to choose to go "paperless.")

The virtues and vices of class actions are a hotly debated topic in their own right. Much of this spirited debate applies with equal force to class arbitrations. What is special about arbitration, however, is that it provides a means of both gatekeeping and enforcing specific mechanisms for the resolution of class claims. In this sense, arbitration is ahead of litigation in providing a marketplace of varying forms of dispute resolution.

This chapter will not go into the details of arbitrating class disputes. Rather, it will introduce the questions of whether and how arbitration clauses must be drafted in order to address the potential of class claims.

Fact Scenario

Topeka Home Cinemas LLC is an independent retail store selling and installing home theater systems. In November 2017, it entered into an agreement with Totalila Distribution LLC, a wholly-owned subsidiary of Totalila, a Japanese electronics company. Totalila sells home theater systems, including large screen LCD television sets. Its LCD line is broken into three classes: Premium, Super-Premium and Excelsoir. Premium and Super-Premium televisions are available in 45", 52", 62" and 76". Excelsoir televisions are available in 55", 65", 75", 85", and 157".

Topeka Home Cinemas LLC noticed an arbitration clause in its agreement with Totalila Distribution and inquired whether the clause was in fact the most recent version of the model arbitration clause. Totalila Distribution confirmed as much. The AAA amended its Commercial Arbitration Rules most recently in October 2013. The standard arbitration clause appearing in the AAA Commercial Arbitration Rules states as follows:

> *Any controversy or claim arising out of or relating to this contract, or the breach thereof, shall be settled by arbitration administered by the American Arbitration Association under its Commercial Arbitration Rules, and judgment on the award rendered by the arbitrator(s) may be entered in any court having jurisdiction thereof.*

In 2018, the Department of Justice determined that Totalila and several of its competitors fixed prices on LCD televisions in violation of U.S. antitrust laws. Topeka Home Cinemas purchased the following LCD televisions in December 2017 from Totalila:

1. Premium—52", 62"

2. Super-Premium—62", 76"

3. Excelsoir—55"

Topeka Home Cinemas files an arbitration against Totalila, asserting violation of U.S. antitrust laws and further states that it files its arbitration as a class action. Topeka Home Cinemas attaches letters from 14 mid-Western retailers who entered into agreements with Totalila around the same time period and purchased every kind of Totalila LCD television for the 2017 Christmas season. Totalila's documents show that it sold televisions to 1,768 independent retailers in the U.S. in the relevant time period.

Readings

A) What Is a Class Action?

Federal Rules of Civil Procedure, Rule 23

(a) Prerequisites. One or more members of a class may sue or be sued as representative parties on behalf of all members only if:

(1) the class is so numerous that joinder of all members is impracticable;

(2) there are questions of law or fact common to the class;

(3) the claims or defenses of the representative parties are typical of the claims or defenses of the class; and

(4) the representative parties will fairly and adequately protect the interests of the class.

(b) Types of Class Actions. A class action may be maintained if Rule 23(a) is satisfied and if:

(1) prosecuting separate actions by or against individual class members would create a risk of:

(A) inconsistent or varying adjudications with respect to individual class members that would establish incompatible standards of conduct for the party opposing the class; or

(B) adjudications with respect to individual class members that, as a practical matter, would be dispositive of the interests of the other members not parties to the individual adjudications or would substantially impair or impede their ability to protect their interests;

(2) the party opposing the class has acted or refused to act on grounds that apply generally to the class, so that final injunctive relief or corresponding declaratory relief is appropriate respecting the class as a whole; or

(3) the court finds that the questions of law or fact common to class members predominate over any questions affecting only individual members, and that a class action is superior to other available methods for fairly and efficiently adjudicating the controversy. The matters pertinent to these findings include:

(A) the class members' interests in individually controlling the prosecution or defense of separate actions;

(B)   the extent and nature of any litigation concerning the controversy already begun by or against class members;

(C)   the desirability or undesirability of concentrating the litigation of the claims in the particular forum; and

(D)   the likely difficulties in managing a class action.

. . .

In re American Medical Systems, Inc.

75 F.3d 1069 (6th Cir. 1996)

SUHRHEINRICH, CIRCUIT JUDGE.

Petitioners American Medical Systems ("AMS") and Pfizer, Inc., defendants below, both seek a writ of mandamus directing the district court to vacate orders conditionally certifying a class in a products liability suit involving penile prostheses.

I.

Since 1973, AMS, a wholly-owned subsidiary of Pfizer, has manufactured and marketed penile prostheses, which are used to treat impotence. The plaintiffs, respondents in this proceeding, all use or have used AMS' products.

Plaintiff Paul Vorhis was implanted with an AMS penile prosthesis on April 25, 1989. It failed to function in January of 1993, and Vorhis had the prosthesis replaced with an AMS 700 Ultrex prosthesis in May 1993. This second prosthesis caused him pain and discomfort, and plaintiff had it removed in August of 1993 and replaced with a third AMS prosthesis, with which he is presently satisfied. Vorhis filed this action against defendant AMS in the Southern District of Ohio on December 5, 1994, individually and on behalf of others similarly situated who suffered damages as a result of the implantation of penile prostheses manufactured by AMS. The complaint alleges strict product liability, negligence, breach of implied and express warranties, fraud and punitive damages, and seeks a declaratory judgment for medical monitoring.

On December 29, 1994, Vorhis filed a motion for class certification. On January 5, 1995, the district judge entered an order setting a hearing for January 27, 1995, later extended to February 24, 1995.

On January 20, 1995, AMS moved to stay or defer a ruling on the class certification question, based on virtually identical actions that had been previously filed. On February 14, 1995, AMS also filed a motion to dismiss based on lack of personal jurisdiction or to transfer based on improper venue. The district judge never ruled on either motion.

After expedited discovery, AMS submitted a brief in opposition to the class certification motion on February 17, 1995. Plaintiff filed his reply brief on February 23, 1995.

On February 28, 1995, the district judge issued a two-page order stating, "based upon the information currently available to it, that class certification appears to be the most efficient and appropriate manner in which to handle this matter," and promised a "further order outlining the reasoning supporting that conclusion" to follow. The order was conditional, subject to decertification at any time, and conditioned further "upon class counsel acting to amend the complaint within thirty (30) days . . . in order to add additional plaintiffs who qualify as appropriate class representatives and who are free of the alleged infirmities on which Defendant's objections to the suitability of the current Plaintiff/class representative are premised."

III.

A.

We begin our analysis by considering whether the lower court committed patent error. We address in tandem petitioners' contentions that the lower court disregarded the standards for class certification and certified a class despite the absence of an adequate factual record establishing the elements of Rule 23.

The Supreme Court has required district courts to conduct a "rigorous analysis" into whether the prerequisites of Rule 23 are met before certifying a class. The trial court has broad discretion in deciding whether to certify a class, but that discretion must be exercised within the framework of Rule 23.

A class is not maintainable as a class action by virtue of its designation as such in the pleadings. Although a hearing prior to the class determination is not always required, "it may be necessary for the court to probe behind the pleadings before coming to rest on the certification question."

The party seeking the class certification bears the burden of proof. Subsection (a) of Rule 23 contains four prerequisites which must all be met before a class can be certified. Once those conditions are satisfied, the party seeking certification must also demonstrate that it falls within at least one of the subcategories of Rule 23(b). We shall examine each of these factors individually.

1.

The first subdivision of Rule 23(a)(1) requires that the class be "so numerous that joinder of all members is impracticable." "The reason for [the impracticability] requirement is obvious. Only when joinder is impracticable is there a need for a class action device." There is no strict numerical test for determining impracticability of joinder. Rather, "[t]he numerosity requirement requires examination of the specific facts of each case and imposes no absolute limitations." When class size reaches substantial proportions, however, the impracticability requirement is usually satisfied by the numbers alone.

In the original complaint, Vorhis alleged that although he was unable to state the exact size of the class, "members of the class number at least in the thousands." The first amended complaint modified that estimate to "over 150,000." The district judge's finding of a class of 15,000 to 120,000 persons may not be unreasonable, especially since AMS has been producing penile prostheses for over twenty years, and has the largest share of the penile implant market. Defendant, moreover, does not contest this factor.

2.

Rule 23(a)(2) requires that for certification there must be "questions of law or fact common to the class." The commonality requirement is interdependent with the impracticability of joinder requirement, and the "tests together form the underlying conceptual basis supporting class actions." As the Supreme Court described in *Falcon*:

> The class-action was designed as "an exception to the usual rule that litigation is conducted by and on behalf of the individual named parties only." Class relief "is 'peculiarly appropriate' when the 'issues involved are common to the class as a whole' and when they 'turn on questions of law applicable in the same manner to each member of the class." For in such cases, "the class-action device saves the resources of both the courts and the parties by permitting an issue potentially affecting every [class member] to be litigated in an economical fashion under Rule 23."

> 457 U.S. at 155.

The commonality test "is qualitative rather than quantitative, that is, there need be only a single issue common to all members of the class." But, as we shall see, there is an important check on this requirement under Rule 23(b)(3).

Plaintiffs' complaint and class certification motion simply allege in general terms that there are common issues without identifying any particular defect common to all plaintiffs. Yet AMS introduced uncontradicted evidence that since 1973 AMS has produced at least ten different models, and that these models have been modified over the years. Plaintiffs' claims of strict liability, fraudulent misrepresentation to both the FDA and the medical community, negligent testing, design and manufacture, and failure to warn will differ depending upon the model and the year it was issued.

Proofs as to strict liability, negligence, failure to warn, breach of express and implied warranties will also vary from plaintiff to plaintiff because complications with an AMS device may be due to a variety of factors, including surgical error, improper use of the device, anatomical incompatibility, infection, device malfunction, or psychological problems. Furthermore, each plaintiff's urologist would also be required to testify to determine what oral and written statements were made to the physician, and what he in turn told the patient, as well as to issues of reliance, causation and damages.

The amended complaint reflects that the plaintiffs received different models and have different complaints regarding each of those models. In the absence of more specific allegations and/or proof of commonality of any factual or legal claims, plaintiffs have failed to meet their burden of proof on Rule 23(a)(2).

This failure of proof highlights the error of the district judge. Despite evidence in the record presented by the nonmoving party that at least ten different models existed, testimony from a urologist that there is no "common cause" of prostheses malfunction, and conclusory allegations by the party with the burden of proof on certification, we find not even the hint of any serious consideration by the judge of commonality.

3.

Rule 23(a)(3) requires that "claims or defenses of the representative parties [be] typical of the claims or defenses of the class."

Typicality determines whether a sufficient relationship exists between the injury to the named plaintiff and the conduct affecting the class, so that the court may properly attribute a collective nature to the challenged conduct. In other words, when such a relationship is shown, a plaintiff's injury arises from or is directly related to a wrong to a class, and that wrong includes the wrong to the plaintiff. Thus, a plaintiff's claim is typical if it arises from the same event or practice or course of conduct that gives rise to the claims of other class members, and if his or her claims are based on the same legal theory.

Vorhis' claim relates to a previous AMS penile prosthesis which, several years after insertion, allegedly could not be inflated due to a possible leak in the input tube of a CX device. This in turn may have been caused by rear-tip extender surgery Vorhis had in 1990, in an attempt to increase penile length that was lost through surgery to correct a curvature of his penis. Based on what little we have to go on, it is hard to imagine that Vorhis' claim is typical of the class certified in this case.

Because the district judge issued its amended order of certification before discovery of the plaintiffs other than Vorhis, we have less information about them. However, we know from the amended complaint that each plaintiff used a different model, and each experienced a distinct difficulty. York claims that his 700 inflatable penile prosthesis fails to fully inflate. Kennedy alleges that his Ultrex inflatable penile prosthesis malfunctioned because the cylinders and pump leaked. Finally, Gordy maintains that his Hyrdoflex failed, and that his current implant, the Dynaflex prosthesis, inflates on one side only. These allegations fail to establish a claim typical to each other, let alone a class.

Once again, it should have been obvious to the district judge that it needed to "probe behind the pleadings" before concluding that the typicality requirement was met. Instead, the district judge gave no serious consideration to this factor, but simply mimicked the language of the rule. This was error.

4.

Rule 23(a)(4) allows certification only if "the representative parties will fairly and adequately protect the interests of the class." This prerequisite is essential to due process, because a final judgment in a class action is binding on all class members.

In *Senter*, we articulated two criteria for determining adequacy of representation: "1) the representative must have common interests with unnamed members of the class, and 2) it must appear that the representatives will vigorously prosecute the interests of the class through qualified counsel." *Senter*, 532 F.2d at 525. The adequate representation requirement overlaps with the typicality requirement because in the absence of typical claims, the class representative has no incentives to pursue the claims of the other class members.

Although the district judge considered the qualifications of plaintiff's counsel, he made no finding on the first *Senter* criterion, and did not consider whether Vorhis or the other plaintiffs would "vigorously prosecute the interests of the class." AMS raised a serious question as to Vorhis' suitability to serve as a class representative given his history of psychological problems.

As amply illustrated, plaintiffs' complaint and class certification motion simply allege the elements of Rule 23(a) in conclusory terms without submitting any persuasive evidence to show that these factors are met. Because the plaintiffs did not create a factual record, and petitioners have demonstrated that the products at issue are very different and that each plaintiff's claim is unique, class certification was inappropriate.

NOTES

Facts

1. What was the cause of action asserted by Mr. Vorhis?

2. From the excerpted material, do you see any allegation of a factual common denominator for the claims?

3. What different fact pattern could overcome the shortcomings identified by the judge?

Law

1. What is the significance of placing the burden of proof on a party seeking class certification?

2. What procedural mechanisms are necessary in order to carry the burden of proof? What difficulties would a party face seeking to satisfy this burden in arbitration?

B)   Drafting Arbitration Clauses in Light of Class Issues

The U.S. Supreme Court in a line of recent cases faced the question of how to deal with class actions in the context of arbitrations. The Court determined that there were three critical questions it would have to answer. *First*, who would determine whether an arbitration clause permits class arbitration—and certify the class. *Second*, what to do with clauses that are facially silent on the issue of class arbitration. *Third*, how to respond to challenges to clearly worded class action waivers in arbitration clauses.

With regard to the first question, the Court follows its jurisprudence on arbitrability. The question of whether an arbitration clause permits class arbitration falls to the arbitrator—to the extent the question of arbitrability is submitted to arbitration in the first instance. As we have discussed in prior chapters, arbitration clauses typically deal with this issue by reference. The clauses refer the parties to arbitration under certain kinds of arbitration rules. These arbitration rules in turn bestow upon the tribunal the authority to deal with questions of arbitral jurisdiction. As a drafting matter, it is therefore important to bear this jurisprudence in mind when addressing class action questions.

Determining *who* is authorized to make a determination of the underlying question of class arbitration does not fully resolve the issue how the arbitrator is supposed to do so. Many arbitration clauses remain facially silent on the issue of class arbitration. They simply refer questions to arbitration. What is an arbitrator to do under those circumstances? The Court has answered this question with some initial clarity—the arbitrator may interpret the clause. The arbitrator therefore may deem a clause as sufficiently capacious to allow for class arbitration upon a reasonable interpretation. But the arbitrator may not impose class arbitration as a matter of policy if the parties stipulate that neither party intended to reach the question of class arbitration by their clause.

The question which remains to be answered under this second question is what to do with the "clever" arbitrator who imposes a policy judgment upon the parties clothed as textual interpretation of the clause. The direction so far appears to direct arbitrators to justify their results by means of a certain method. It also appears to direct parties wishing to submit disputes to class arbitration not to stipulate that the clause was truly silent on the question of class arbitration, i.e., they should always submit that class arbitrations fall within the intended scope of the clause. But should one police this argumentative regress? The Court so far was not called upon to resolve the issue. In the end, the current guidance that *does* exist points to deference to the arbitrator.

The final question is whether clearly worded class action waivers can be attacked collaterally. So far, the Court has resoundingly answered that any judicial collateral attack on the enforceability of class action waivers will fail. The Court has addressed such challenges on policy grounds, asserted inconsistencies between the waiver and state law, and asserted inconsistencies between the waiver and federal regulatory interpretation of federal law. In each of these instances, the Court has rejected attempts to overcome the waiver. It is unlikely that the Court will change course. A well worded waiver, in other words, will survive judicial scrutiny.

This leaves another question unanswered. What happens if the arbitrator refuses to honor a waiver? This question reintroduces the concerns discussed above that an arbitrator is not allowed to make policy decisions. But what if the arbitrator finds a way to sidestep the waiver by interpreting it and finding it inapplicable? Again, this scenario has not yet arisen. Drafters should be mindful of this development and draft their clauses as clearly as possible to avoid any unexpected surprises.

The Court has also not yet determined—and it is difficult to see how it could determine—whether class certification itself was appropriate. This issue would have to be resolved exclusively within the arbitration context and thus places significant strain on arbitral institutions to design arbitration rules to deal with these challenges. Following the discussion of the Supreme Court cases, you will find a short overview of how the AAA has dealt with this issue.

1)   *Supreme Court Jurisprudence on Class Arbitration*

Who Determines Class Arbitrability?

Green Tree Financial Corp. v. Bazzle

539 U.S. 444 (2003)

This case concerns contracts between a commercial lender and its customers, each of which contains a clause providing for arbitration of all contract-related disputes. The Supreme Court of South Carolina held (1) that the arbitration clauses are silent as to whether arbitration might take the form of class arbitration, and (2) that, in that circumstance, South Carolina law interprets the contracts as permitting class arbitration.

We are faced at the outset with a problem concerning the contracts' silence. Are the contracts in fact silent, or do they forbid class arbitration as petitioner Green Tree Financial Corp. contends? Given the South Carolina Supreme Court's holding, it is important to resolve that question. But we cannot do so, not simply because it is a matter of state law, but also because it is a matter for the arbitrator to decide. Because the record suggests that the parties have not yet received an arbitrator's decision on that question of contract interpretation, we vacate the judgment of the South Carolina Supreme Court and remand the case so that this question may be resolved in arbitration.

I

In 1995, respondents Lynn and Burt Bazzle secured a home improvement loan from petitioner Green Tree. The Bazzles and Green Tree entered into a contract, governed by South Carolina law, which included the following arbitration clause:

"ARBITRATION-All disputes, claims, or controversies arising from or relating to this contract or the relationships which result from this contract . . . shall be resolved by binding arbitration by one arbitrator selected by us with consent of you. This arbitration contract is made pursuant to a transaction in interstate commerce, and shall be governed by the Federal Arbitration Act at 9 U.S.C. section 1. . . . THE PARTIES VOLUNTARILY AND KNOWINGLY WAIVE ANY RIGHT THEY HAVE TO A JURY TRIAL, EITHER PURSUANT TO ARBITRATION UNDER THIS CLAUSE OR PURSUANT TO A COURT ACTION BY U.S. (AS PROVIDED HEREIN) . . . . The parties agree and understand that the arbitrator shall have all powers provided by the law and the contract. These powers shall include all legal and equitable remedies, including, but not limited to, money damages, declaratory relief, and injunctive relief." App. 34 (emphasis added, capitalization in original).

Respondents Daniel Lackey and George and Florine Buggs entered into loan contracts and security agreements for the purchase of mobile homes with Green Tree. These agreements contained arbitration clauses that were, in all relevant respects, identical to the Bazzles' arbitration clause. (Their contracts substitute the word "you" with the word "Buyer[s]" in the italicized phrase.)

At the time of the loan transactions, Green Tree apparently failed to provide these customers with a legally required form that would have told them that they had a right to name their own lawyers and insurance agents and would have provided space for them to write in those names. The two sets of customers before us now as respondents each filed separate actions in South Carolina state courts, complaining that this failure violated South Carolina law and seeking damages.

In April 1997, the Bazzles asked the court to certify their claims as a class action. Green Tree sought to stay the court proceedings and compel arbitration. On January 5, 1998, the court both (1) certified a class action and (2) entered an order compelling arbitration. App. 7. Green Tree then selected an arbitrator with the Bazzles' consent. And the arbitrator, administering the proceeding as a class arbitration, eventually awarded the class $10,935,000 in statutory damages, along with attorney's fees. The trial court confirmed the award, App. to Pet. for Cert. 27a–35a, and Green Tree appealed to the South Carolina Court of Appeals claiming, among other things, that class arbitration was legally impermissible.

Lackey and the Buggses had earlier begun a similar court proceeding in which they, too, sought class certification. Green Tree moved to compel arbitration. The trial court initially denied the motion, finding the arbitration agreement unenforceable, but Green Tree pursued an interlocutory appeal and the State Court of Appeals reversed. The parties then chose an arbitrator, indeed the same arbitrator who was subsequently selected to arbitrate the Bazzles' dispute.

In December 1998, the arbitrator certified a class in arbitration. The arbitrator proceeded to hear the matter, ultimately ruled in favor of the class, and awarded the class $9,200,000 in statutory damages in addition to attorney's fees. The trial court confirmed the award. Green Tree appealed to the South Carolina Court of Appeals claiming, among other things, that class arbitration was legally impermissible.

The South Carolina Supreme Court withdrew both cases from the Court of Appeals, assumed jurisdiction, and consolidated the proceedings. That court then held that the contracts were silent in respect to class arbitration, that they consequently authorized class arbitration, and that arbitration had properly taken that form. We granted certiorari to consider whether that holding is consistent with the Federal Arbitration Act.

II

The South Carolina Supreme Court's determination that the contracts are silent in respect to class arbitration raises a preliminary question. Green Tree argued there, as it argues here, that the contracts are not silent-that they forbid class arbitration. And we must deal with that argument at the outset, for if it is right, then the South Carolina court's holding is flawed on its own terms; that court neither said nor implied that it would have authorized class arbitration had the parties' arbitration agreement forbidden it.

Whether Green Tree is right about the contracts themselves presents a disputed issue of contract interpretation. THE CHIEF JUSTICE believes that Green Tree is right; indeed, that Green Tree is so clearly right that we should ignore the fact that state law, not federal law, normally governs such matters, and reverse the South Carolina Supreme Court outright. THE CHIEF JUSTICE points out that the contracts say that disputes "shall be resolved . . . by one arbitrator selected by us [Green Tree] with consent of you [Green Tree's customer]." And it finds that class arbitration is clearly inconsistent with this requirement. After all, class arbitration involves an arbitration, not simply between Green Tree and a named customer, but also between Green Tree and other (represented) customers, all taking place before the arbitrator chosen to arbitrate the initial, named customer's dispute.

We do not believe, however, that the contracts' language is as clear as THE CHIEF JUSTICE believes. The class arbitrator was "selected by" Green Tree "with consent of" Green Tree's customers, the named plaintiffs. And insofar as the other class members agreed to proceed in class arbitration, they consented as well.

Of course, Green Tree did not independently select this arbitrator to arbitrate its disputes with the other class members. But whether the contracts contain this additional requirement is a question that the literal terms of the contracts do not decide. The contracts simply say (I) "selected by us [Green Tree]." And that is literally what occurred. The contracts do not say (II) "selected by us [Green Tree] to arbitrate this dispute and no other (even identical) dispute with another customer." The question whether (I) in fact implicitly means (II) is the question at issue: Do the contracts forbid class arbitration? Given the broad authority the contracts elsewhere bestow upon the arbitrator, see, e.g., App. to Pet. for Cert. 110a (the contracts grant to the arbitrator "all powers," including certain equitable powers "provided by the law and the contract"), the answer to this question is not completely obvious.

At the same time, we cannot automatically accept the South Carolina Supreme Court's resolution of this contract-interpretation question. Under the terms of the parties' contracts, the question-whether the agreement forbids class arbitration-is for the arbitrator to decide. The parties agreed to submit to the arbitrator "[a]ll disputes, claims, or controversies arising from or relating to this contract or the relationships which result from this contract." Ibid. (emphasis added). And the dispute about what the arbitration contract in each case means (i.e., whether it forbids the use of class arbitration procedures) is a dispute "relating to this contract" and the resulting "relationships." Hence the parties seem to have agreed that an arbitrator, not a judge, would answer the relevant question. And if there is doubt about that matter-about the " 'scope of arbitrable issues' "—we should resolve that doubt " 'in favor of arbitration.' "

In certain limited circumstances, courts assume that the parties intended courts, not arbitrators, to decide a particular arbitration-related matter (in the absence of "clea[r] and unmistakabl[e]" evidence to the contrary). These limited instances typically involve matters of a kind that "contracting parties would likely have expected a court" to decide. They include certain gateway matters, such as whether the parties have a valid arbitration agreement at all or whether a concededly binding arbitration clause applies to a certain type of controversy.

The question here-whether the contracts forbid class arbitration-does not fall into this narrow exception. It concerns neither the validity of the arbitration clause nor its applicability to the underlying dispute between the parties. Unlike *First Options*, the question is not whether the parties wanted a judge or an arbitrator to decide whether they agreed to arbitrate a matter. Rather the relevant question here is what kind of arbitration proceeding the parties agreed to. That question does not concern a state statute or judicial procedures. It concerns contract interpretation and arbitration procedures. Arbitrators are well situated to answer that question. Given these considerations, along with the arbitration contracts' sweeping language concerning the scope of the questions committed to arbitration, this matter of contract interpretation should be for the arbitrator, not the courts, to decide.

III

With respect to this underlying question-whether the arbitration contracts forbid class arbitration-the parties have not yet obtained the arbitration decision that their contracts foresee. As far as concerns the *Bazzle* plaintiffs, the South Carolina Supreme Court wrote that the "trial court" issued "an order granting class certification" and the arbitrator subsequently "administered" class arbitration proceedings "without further involvement of the trial court." Green Tree adds that "the class arbitration was imposed on the parties and the arbitrator by the South Carolina trial court." Respondents now deny that this was so, but we can find no convincing record support for that denial.

A far as concerns the Lackey plaintiffs, what happened in arbitration is less clear. On the one hand, the Lackey arbitrator (the same individual who later arbitrated the *Bazzle* dispute) wrote: "I determined that a class action should proceed in arbitration based upon my careful review of the broadly drafted arbitration clause prepared by Green Tree." App. to Pet. for Cert. 84a (emphasis added). And respondents suggested at oral argument that the arbitrator's decision was independently made.

On the other hand, the Lackey arbitrator decided this question after the South Carolina trial court had determined that the identical contract in the *Bazzle* case authorized class arbitration procedures. And there is no question that the arbitrator was aware of the *Bazzle* decision, since the Lackey plaintiffs had argued to the arbitrator that it should impose class arbitration procedures in part because the state trial court in *Bazzle* had done so. In the court proceedings below (where Green Tree took the opposite position), the Lackey plaintiffs maintained that "to the extent" the arbitrator decided that the contracts permitted class procedures (in the Lackey case or the Bazzle case), "it was a reaffirmation and/or adoption of [the Bazzle c]ourt's prior determination."

On balance, there is at least a strong likelihood in *Lackey* as well as in *Bazzle* that the arbitrator's decision reflected a court's interpretation of the contracts rather than an arbitrator's interpretation. That being so, we remand the case so that the arbitrator may decide the question of contract interpretation-thereby enforcing the parties' arbitration agreements according to their terms. 9 U.S.C. § 2.

The judgment of the South Carolina Supreme Court is vacated, and the case is remanded for further proceedings.

So ordered.

NOTES

Facts

1. What was the cause of action asserted by the Bazzles? Do the facts suggest that the lender acted intentionally? Why would it do so?

2. How large do you suppose the class certified was? If you had to establish a putative class, how would you draw it?

3. The arbitration clause does not appear to have been specifically negotiated. Do you think that the lenders anticipated that their clause could be used for purposes of class arbitration? Do you think their counsel should have warned them of that possibility?

Law

1. If the case had been handled in court, what would the Bazzles have needed to establish to certify a class under the circumstances under the pillars of class certification discussed in the previous section? How would they have discharged their burden of proof?

2. If you represented the lenders, what would have been your strongest arguments to fight class certification? What evidence would you try to find to support your argument? Would such a defense be easier in arbitration than it is in litigation? Why or why not?

3. How could you interpret the arbitration clause excerpted in the case to permit class arbitration? What would be your strongest argument?

4. What do you think the lenders argued on this point? What would be their strongest argument?

Reviewing Arbitral Decisions on Class Arbitrability

Stolt-Nielsen S.A. v. AnimalFeeds International Corp.

559 U.S. 662 (2010)

JUSTICE ALITO delivered the opinion of the Court.

We granted certiorari in this case to decide whether imposing class arbitration on parties whose arbitration clauses are "silent" on that issue is consistent with the Federal Arbitration Act (FAA), 9 U.S.C. § 1 et seq.

I

A

Petitioners are shipping companies that serve a large share of the world market for parcel tankers—seagoing vessels with compartments that are separately chartered to customers wishing to ship liquids in small quantities. One of those customers is AnimalFeeds International Corp. (hereinafter AnimalFeeds), which supplies raw ingredients, such as fish oil, to animal-feed producers around the world. AnimalFeeds ships its goods pursuant to a standard contract known in the maritime trade as a charter party.[1] Numerous charter parties are in regular use, and the charter party that AnimalFeeds uses is known as the "Vegoilvoy" charter party. Petitioners assert, without contradiction, that charterers like AnimalFeeds, or their agents—not the shipowners—typically select the particular charter party that governs their shipments.

Adopted in 1950, the Vegoilvoy charter party contains the following arbitration clause:

> "Arbitration. Any dispute arising from the making, performance or termination of this Charter Party shall be settled in New York, Owner and Charterer each appointing an arbitrator, who shall be a merchant, broker or individual experienced in the shipping business; the two thus chosen, if they cannot agree, shall nominate a third arbitrator who shall be an Admiralty lawyer. Such arbitration shall be conducted in conformity with the provisions and procedure of the United States

---

[1] "[C]harter parties are commonly drafted using highly standardized forms specific to the particular trades and business needs of the parties." Comment, A Comparative Analysis of Charter Party Agreements "Subject to" Respective American and British Laws and Decisions . . . It's All in the Details, 26 Tulane Mar. L.J. 291, 294 (2001–2002).

Arbitration Act [i.e., the FAA], and a judgment of the Court shall be entered upon any award made by said arbitrator."

In 2003, a Department of Justice criminal investigation revealed that petitioners were engaging in an illegal price-fixing conspiracy. When AnimalFeeds learned of this, it brought a putative class action against petitioners in the District Court for the Eastern District of Pennsylvania, asserting antitrust claims for supracompetitive prices that petitioners allegedly charged their customers over a period of several years.

Other charterers brought similar suits. In one of these, the District Court for the District of Connecticut held that the charterers' claims were not subject to arbitration under the applicable arbitration clause, but the Second Circuit reversed. While that appeal was pending, the Judicial Panel on Multidistrict Litigation ordered the consolidation of then-pending actions against petitioners, including AnimalFeeds' action, in the District of Connecticut. The parties agree that as a consequence of these judgments and orders, AnimalFeeds and petitioners must arbitrate their antitrust dispute.

B

In 2005, AnimalFeeds served petitioners with a demand for class arbitration, designating New York City as the place of arbitration and seeking to represent a class of "[a]ll direct purchasers of parcel tanker transportation services globally for bulk liquid chemicals, edible oils, acids, and other specialty liquids from [petitioners] at any time during the period from August 1, 1998, to November 30, 2002." The parties entered into a supplemental agreement providing for the question of class arbitration to be submitted to a panel of three arbitrators who were to "follow and be bound by Rules 3 through 7 of the American Arbitration Association's Supplementary Rules for Class Arbitrations (as effective Oct. 8, 2003)." These rules (hereinafter Class Rules) were developed by the American Arbitration Association (AAA) after our decision in *Green Tree Financial Corp. v. Bazzle*, 539 U.S. 444 (2003), and Class Rule 3, in accordance with the plurality opinion in that case, requires an arbitrator, as a threshold matter, to determine "whether the applicable arbitration clause permits the arbitration to proceed on behalf of or against a class."

The parties selected a panel of arbitrators and stipulated that the arbitration clause was "silent" with respect to class arbitration. Counsel for AnimalFeeds explained to the arbitration panel that the term "silent" did not simply mean that the clause made no express reference to class arbitration. Rather, he said, "[a]ll the parties agree that when a contract is silent on an issue there's been no agreement that has been reached on that issue."

After hearing argument and evidence, including testimony from petitioners' experts regarding arbitration customs and usage in the maritime trade, the arbitrators concluded that the arbitration clause allowed for class arbitration. They found persuasive the fact that other arbitrators ruling after *Bazzle* had construed "a wide variety of clauses in a wide variety of settings as allowing for class arbitration," but the panel acknowledged that none of these decisions was "exactly comparable" to the present dispute. Petitioners' expert evidence did not show an "inten[t] to preclude class arbitration," the arbitrators reasoned, and petitioners' argument would leave "no basis for a class action absent express agreement among all parties and the putative class members."

The arbitrators stayed the proceeding to allow the parties to seek judicial review, and petitioners filed an application to vacate the arbitrators' award in the District Court for the Southern District of New York. The District Court vacated the award, concluding that the arbitrators' decision was made in "manifest disregard" of the law insofar as the arbitrators failed to conduct a choice-of-law analysis. Had such an analysis been conducted, the District Court held, the arbitrators would have applied the rule of federal maritime law requiring that contracts be interpreted in light of custom and usage.

AnimalFeeds appealed to the Court of Appeals, which reversed. [T]he Court of Appeals concluded that, because petitioners had cited no authority applying a federal maritime rule of custom and usage against class arbitration, the arbitrators' decision was not in manifest disregard of federal maritime law. Nor had the arbitrators manifestly disregarded New York law, the Court of Appeals continued, since nothing in New York case law established a rule against class arbitration.

II

A

Petitioners contend that the decision of the arbitration panel must be vacated, but in order to obtain that relief, they must clear a high hurdle. It is not enough for petitioners to show that the panel committed an error—or even a serious error. "It is only when [an] arbitrator strays from interpretation and application of the agreement and effectively 'dispense[s] his own brand of industrial justice' that his decision may be unenforceable." In that situation, an arbitration decision may be vacated under § 10(a)(4) of the FAA on the ground that the arbitrator "exceeded [his] powers," for the task of an arbitrator is to interpret and enforce a contract, not to make public policy. In this case, we must conclude that what the arbitration panel did was simply to impose its own view of sound policy regarding class arbitration.

B

1

[T]he panel appears to have rested its decision on AnimalFeeds' public policy argument. Because the parties agreed their agreement was "silent" in the sense that they had not reached any agreement on the issue of class arbitration, the arbitrators' proper task was to identify the rule of law that governs in that situation. Had they engaged in that undertaking, they presumably would have looked either to the FAA itself or to one of the two bodies of law that the parties claimed were governing, *i.e.*, either federal maritime law or New York law. But the panel did not consider whether the FAA provides the rule of decision in such a situation; nor did the panel attempt to determine what rule would govern under either maritime or New York law in the case of a "silent" contract. Instead, the panel based its decision on post-*Bazzle* arbitral decisions that "construed a wide variety of clauses in a wide variety of settings as allowing for class arbitration." The panel did not mention whether any of these decisions were based on a rule derived from the FAA or on maritime or New York law.[4]

Rather than inquiring whether the FAA, maritime law, or New York law contains a "default rule" under which an arbitration clause is construed as allowing class arbitration in the absence of express consent, the panel proceeded as if it had the authority of a common-law court to develop what it viewed as the best rule to be applied in such a situation. Perceiving a post-*Bazzle* consensus among arbitrators that class arbitration is beneficial in "a wide variety of settings," the panel considered only whether there was any good reason not to follow that consensus in this case. The panel was not persuaded by "court cases denying consolidation of arbitrations," by undisputed evidence that the

---

[4]   The panel's reliance on these arbitral awards confirms that the panel's decision was not based on a determination regarding the parties' intent. All of the arbitral awards were made under the AAA's Class Rules, which were adopted in 2003, and thus none was available when the parties here entered into the Vegoilvoy charter party during the class period ranging from 1998 to 2002. Indeed, at the hearing before the panel, counsel for AnimalFeeds conceded that "[w]hen you talk about expectations, virtually every one of the arbitration clauses that were the subject of the 25 AAA decisions were drafted before [*Bazzle*]. So therefore, if you are going to talk about the parties' intentions, pre-[*Bazzle*] class arbitrations were not common, post [*Bazzle*] they are common." Moreover, in its award, the panel appeared to acknowledge that none of the cited arbitration awards involved a contract between sophisticated business entities.

Vegoilvoy charter party had "never been the basis of a class action," or by expert opinion that "sophisticated, multinational commercial parties of the type that are sought to be included in the class would never intend that the arbitration clauses would permit a class arbitration.". Accordingly, finding no convincing ground for departing from the post-*Bazzle* arbitral consensus, the panel held that class arbitration was permitted in this case. The conclusion is inescapable that the panel simply imposed its own conception of sound policy.

III

A

The arbitration panel thought that *Bazzle* "controlled" the "resolution" of the question whether the Vegoilvoy charter party "permit[s] this arbitration to proceed on behalf of a class," but that understanding was incorrect.

Bazzle concerned contracts between a commercial lender (Green Tree) and its customers. These contracts contained an arbitration clause but did not expressly mention class arbitration. Nevertheless, an arbitrator conducted class arbitration proceedings and entered awards for the customers.

The South Carolina Supreme Court affirmed the awards. After discussing both Seventh Circuit precedent holding that a court lacks authority to order classwide arbitration under § 4 of the FAA, and conflicting California precedent, the State Supreme Court elected to follow the California approach, which it characterized as permitting a trial court to "order class-wide arbitration under adhesive but enforceable franchise contracts," Under this approach, the South Carolina court observed, a trial judge must "[b]alanc[e] the potential inequities and inefficiencies" of requiring each aggrieved party to proceed on an individual basis against "resulting prejudice to the drafting party" and should take into account factors such as "efficiency" and "equity."

Applying these standards to the case before it, the South Carolina Supreme Court found that the arbitration clause in the Green Tree contracts was "silent regarding class-wide arbitration." Id., at 263, 569 S.E.2d, at 359 (emphasis deleted). The Court described its holding as follows:

> "[W]e . . . hold that class-wide arbitration may be ordered when the arbitration agreement is silent if it would serve efficiency and equity, and would not result in prejudice. If we enforced a mandatory, adhesive arbitration clause, but prohibited class actions in arbitration where the agreement is silent, the drafting party could effectively

prevent class actions against it without having to say it was doing so in the agreement." Id., at 266, 569 S.E.2d, at 360 (footnote omitted).

When *Bazzle* reached this Court, no single rationale commanded a majority. The opinions of the Justices who joined the judgment—that is, the plurality opinion and Justice STEVENS' opinion—collectively addressed three separate questions. The first was which decision maker (court or arbitrator) should decide whether the contracts in question were "silent" on the issue of class arbitration. The second was what standard the appropriate decision maker should apply in determining whether a contract allows class arbitration. (For example, does the FAA entirely preclude class arbitration? Does the FAA permit class arbitration only under limited circumstances, such as when the contract expressly so provides? Or is this question left entirely to state law?) The final question was whether, under whatever standard is appropriate, class arbitration had been properly ordered in the case at hand.

The plurality opinion decided only the first question, concluding that the arbitrator and not a court should decide whether the contracts were indeed "silent" on the issue of class arbitration. The plurality noted that, "[i]n certain limited circumstances," involving "gateway matters, such as whether the parties have a valid arbitration agreement at all or whether a concededly binding arbitration clause applies to a certain type of controversy," it is assumed "that the parties intended courts, not arbitrators," to make the decision. But the plurality opined that the question whether a contract with an arbitration clause forbids class arbitration "does not fall into this narrow exception." The plurality therefore concluded that the decision of the State Supreme Court should be vacated and that the case should be remanded for a decision by the arbitrator on the question whether the contracts were indeed "silent." The plurality did not decide either the second or the third question noted above.

B

Unfortunately, the opinions in *Bazzle* appear to have baffled the parties in this case at the time of the arbitration proceeding. For one thing, the parties appear to have believed that the judgment in *Bazzle* requires an arbitrator, not a court, to decide whether a contract permits class arbitration. In fact, however, only the plurality decided that question. But we need not revisit that question here because the parties' supplemental agreement expressly assigned this issue to the arbitration panel, and no party argues that this assignment was impermissible.

Unfortunately, however, both the parties and the arbitration panel seem to have misunderstood *Bazzle* in another respect, namely, that it established the standard to be applied by a decisionmaker in determining whether a contract may permissibly be interpreted to allow class arbitration. The arbitration panel began its discussion by stating that the parties "differ regarding the rule of interpretation to be gleaned from [the *Bazzle*] decision." The panel continued:

> "Claimants argue that *Bazzle* requires clear language that forbids class arbitration in order to bar a class action. The Panel, however, agrees with Respondents that the test is a more general one—arbitrators must look to the language of the parties' agreement to ascertain the parties' intention whether they intended to permit or to preclude class action."

As we have explained, however, *Bazzle* did not establish the rule to be applied in deciding whether class arbitration is permitted. The decision in *Bazzle* left that question open, and we turn to it now.

IV

While the interpretation of an arbitration agreement is generally a matter of state law, the FAA imposes certain rules of fundamental importance, including the basic precept that arbitration "is a matter of consent, not coercion."

A

Whether enforcing an agreement to arbitrate or construing an arbitration clause, courts and arbitrators must "give effect to the contractual rights and expectations of the parties." In this endeavor, "as with any other contract, the parties' intentions control." This is because an arbitrator derives his or her powers from the parties' agreement to forgo the legal process and submit their disputes to private dispute resolution.

Underscoring the consensual nature of private dispute resolution, we have held that parties are " 'generally free to structure their arbitration agreements as they see fit.' "

We think it is also clear from our precedents and the contractual nature of arbitration that parties may specify with whom they choose to arbitrate their disputes. It falls to courts and arbitrators to give effect to these contractual limitations, and when doing so, courts and arbitrators must not lose sight of the purpose of the exercise: to give effect to the intent of the parties.

B

From these principles, it follows that a party may not be compelled under the FAA to submit to class arbitration unless there is a contractual basis for concluding that the party agreed to do so. In this case, however, the arbitration panel imposed class arbitration even though the parties concurred that they had reached "no agreement" on that issue. The critical point, in the view of the arbitration panel, was that petitioners did not "establish that the parties to the charter agreements intended to preclude class arbitration." Even though the parties are sophisticated business entities, even though there is no tradition of class arbitration under maritime law, and even though AnimalFeeds does not dispute that it is customary for the shipper to choose the charter party that is used for a particular shipment, the panel regarded the agreement's silence on the question of class arbitration as dispositive. The panel's conclusion is fundamentally at war with the foundational FAA principle that arbitration is a matter of consent.

In certain contexts, it is appropriate to presume that parties that enter into an arbitration agreement implicitly authorize the arbitrator to adopt such procedures as are necessary to give effect to the parties' agreement. Thus, we have said that " ' "procedural" questions which grow out of the dispute and bear on its final disposition' are presumptively not for the judge, but for an arbitrator, to decide." This recognition is grounded in the background principle that "[w]hen the parties to a bargain sufficiently defined to be a contract have not agreed with respect to a term which is essential to a determination of their rights and duties, a term which is reasonable in the circumstances is supplied by the court."

An implicit agreement to authorize class-action arbitration, however, is not a term that the arbitrator may infer solely from the fact of the parties' agreement to arbitrate. This is so because class-action arbitration changes the nature of arbitration to such a degree that it cannot be presumed the parties consented to it by simply agreeing to submit their disputes to an arbitrator. In bilateral arbitration, parties forgo the procedural rigor and appellate review of the courts in order to realize the benefits of private dispute resolution: lower costs, greater efficiency and speed, and the ability to choose expert adjudicators to resolve specialized disputes. But the relative benefits of class-action arbitration are much less assured, giving reason to doubt the parties' mutual consent to resolve *686 disputes through class-wide arbitration.

Consider just some of the fundamental changes brought about by the shift from bilateral arbitration to class-action arbitration. An arbitrator chosen according to an agreed-upon procedure, see, e.g., supra, at ___, no longer resolves a single dispute between the parties to a single agreement, but instead resolves many disputes between hundreds or perhaps even thousands of parties. Under the Class Rules, "the presumption of privacy and confidentiality" that applies in many bilateral arbitrations "shall not apply in class arbitrations," thus potentially frustrating the parties' assumptions when they agreed to arbitrate. The arbitrator's award no longer purports to bind just the parties to a single arbitration agreement, but adjudicates the rights of absent parties as well. And the commercial stakes of class-action arbitration are comparable to those of class-action litigation, even though the scope of judicial review is much more limited. We think that the differences between bilateral and class-action arbitration are too great for arbitrators to presume, consistent with their limited powers under the FAA, that the parties' mere silence on the issue of class-action arbitration constitutes consent to resolve their disputes in class proceedings.

V

For these reasons, the judgment of the Court of Appeals is reversed, and the case is remanded for further proceedings consistent with this opinion.

It is so ordered.

NOTES

Facts

1. What was the cause of action asserted by the class plaintiffs? How did the plaintiffs learn about their cause of action? How would this help to meet the requirements for class certification?

2. In your estimation, would the number of members of the certified class be larger than 100 individuals? 1,000? 1,000,000? If you had to establish a putative class, how would you draw it?

3. What did you make of the parties' understanding as to the significance of the silence of the arbitration clause on class arbitration?

Law

1. Did the Court conclude that the clause did not reach class arbitration, or did the Court conclude that the arbitrators had not appropriately established that the clause reached class arbitration? What is the difference?

2. Assume you were faced with a similar arbitration clause class certification issue. How would you argue your case for class arbitration? What evidence would you need in order to meet the *Stolt-Nielsen* standard?

Oxford Health Plans LLC v. Sutter

569 U.S. 564 (2013) (citations omitted)

Class arbitration is a matter of consent: An arbitrator may employ class procedures only if the parties have authorized them. In this case, an arbitrator found that the parties' contract provided for class arbitration. The question presented is whether in doing so he "exceeded [his] powers" under § 10(a)(4) of the Federal Arbitration Act (FAA or Act), 9 U.S.C. § 1 et seq. We conclude that the arbitrator's decision survives the limited judicial review § 10(a)(4) allows.

I

Respondent John Sutter, a pediatrician, entered into a contract with petitioner Oxford Health Plans, a health insurance company. Sutter agreed to provide medical care to members of Oxford's network, and Oxford agreed to pay for those services at prescribed rates. Several years later, Sutter filed suit against Oxford in New Jersey Superior Court on behalf of himself and a proposed class of other New Jersey physicians under contract with Oxford. The complaint alleged that Oxford had failed to make full and prompt payment to the doctors, in violation of their agreements and various state laws.

Oxford moved to compel arbitration of Sutter's claims, relying on the following clause in their contract:

> "No civil action concerning any dispute arising under this Agreement shall be instituted before any court, and all such disputes shall be submitted to final and binding arbitration in New Jersey, pursuant to the rules of the American Arbitration Association with one arbitrator."

The state court granted Oxford's motion, thus referring the suit to arbitration.

The parties agreed that the arbitrator should decide whether their contract authorized class arbitration, and he determined that it did. Noting that the question turned on "construction of the parties' agreement," the arbitrator focused on the text of the arbitration clause quoted above. He reasoned that the clause sent to arbitration *567 "the same universal class of disputes" that it barred the parties from bringing "as civil actions" in court: The "intent of the clause" was "to vest in the arbitration process everything that is prohibited from the court process." And a class action, the arbitrator continued, "is plainly one of the possible forms of civil action that could be brought in a court" absent the agreement. Accordingly, he concluded that "on its face, the arbitration clause . . . expresses the parties' intent that class arbitration can be maintained."

Oxford filed a motion in federal court to vacate the arbitrator's decision on the ground that he had "exceeded [his] powers" under § 10(a)(4) of the FAA. The District Court denied the motion, and the Court of Appeals for the Third Circuit affirmed.

While the arbitration proceeded, this Court held in *Stolt-Nielsen* that "a party may not be compelled under the FAA to submit to class arbitration unless there is a contractual basis for concluding that the party agreed to do so." The parties in *Stolt-Nielsen* had stipulated that they had never reached an agreement on class arbitration. Relying on § 10(a)(4), we vacated the arbitrators' decision approving class proceedings because, in the absence of such an agreement, the arbitrators had "simply . . . imposed [their] own view of sound policy."

Oxford immediately asked the arbitrator to reconsider his decision on class arbitration in light of *Stolt-Nielsen*. The arbitrator issued a new opinion holding that *Stolt-Nielsen* had no effect on the case because this agreement authorized class arbitration. Unlike in *Stolt-Nielsen*, the arbitrator explained, the parties here disputed the meaning of their contract; he had therefore been required "to construe the arbitration clause in the ordinary way to glean the parties' intent." And in performing that task, the arbitrator continued, he had "found that the arbitration clause *568 unambiguously evinced an intention to allow class arbitration." The arbitrator concluded by reconfirming his reasons for so construing the clause.

Oxford then returned to federal court, renewing its effort to vacate the arbitrator's decision under § 10(a)(4). Once again, the District Court denied the motion, and the Third Circuit affirmed. [. . .]

II

Under the FAA, courts may vacate an arbitrator's decision "only in very unusual circumstances." That limited judicial review, we have explained, "maintain[s] arbitration's essential virtue of resolving disputes straightaway." If parties could take "full-bore legal and evidentiary appeals," arbitration would become "merely a prelude *569 to a more cumbersome and time-consuming judicial review process."

Here, Oxford invokes § 10(a)(4) of the Act, which authorizes a federal court to set aside an arbitral award "where the arbitrator[ ] exceeded [his] powers." A party seeking relief under that provision bears a heavy burden. "It is not enough . . . to show that the [arbitrator] committed an error—or even a serious error." Because the parties "bargained for the arbitrator's construction of their agreement," an arbitral decision "even arguably construing or applying the contract" must stand, regardless of a court's view of its (de)merits. Only if "the arbitrator act[s] outside the scope of his contractually delegated authority"—issuing an award that "simply reflect[s] [his] own notions of [economic] justice" rather than "draw[ing] its essence from the contract"—may a court overturn his determination. So the sole question for us is whether the arbitrator (even arguably) interpreted the parties' contract, not whether he got its meaning right or wrong.

*570 And we have already all but answered that question just by summarizing the arbitrator's decisions; they are, through and through, interpretations of the parties' agreement. The arbitrator's first ruling recited the "question of construction" the parties had submitted to him: "whether [their] Agreement allows for class action arbitration." To resolve that matter, the arbitrator focused on the arbitration clause's text, analyzing (whether correctly or not makes no difference) the scope of both what it barred from court and what it sent to arbitration. The arbitrator concluded, based on that textual exegesis, that the clause "on its face . . . expresses the parties' intent that class action arbitration can be maintained." When Oxford requested reconsideration in light of *Stolt-Nielsen*, the arbitrator explained that his prior decision was "concerned solely with the parties' intent as evidenced by the words of the arbitration clause itself." He then ran through his textual analysis again, and reiterated his conclusion: "[T]he text of the clause itself authorizes" class arbitration. Twice, then, the arbitrator did what the parties had asked: He considered their contract and decided whether it reflected an agreement to permit class proceedings. That suffices to show that the arbitrator did not "exceed[ ] [his] powers." § 10(a)(4).

Oxford's contrary view relies principally on *Stolt-Nielsen*. As noted earlier, we found there that an arbitration panel exceeded its powers under § 10(a)(4) when it ordered a party to submit to class arbitration. Oxford takes that decision to mean that "even the 'high hurdle' of Section 10(a)(4) review is overcome when an arbitrator imposes *571 class arbitration without a sufficient contractual basis.". Under *Stolt-Nielsen*, Oxford asserts, a court may thus vacate "as ultra vires" an arbitral decision like this one for misconstruing a contract to approve class proceedings.

But Oxford misreads *Stolt-Nielsen*: We overturned the arbitral decision there because it lacked any contractual basis for ordering class procedures, not because it lacked, in Oxford's terminology, a "sufficient" one. The parties in *Stolt-Nielsen* had entered into an unusual stipulation that they had never reached an agreement on class arbitration. In that circumstance, we noted, the panel's decision was not—indeed, could not have been—"based on a determination regarding the parties' intent." Nor, we continued, did the panel attempt to ascertain whether federal or state law established a "default rule" to take effect absent an agreement. Instead, "the panel simply imposed its own conception of sound policy" when it ordered class proceedings. But "the task of an arbitrator," we stated, "is to interpret and enforce a contract, not to make public policy." In "impos[ing] its own policy choice," the panel "thus exceeded its powers."

The contrast with this case is stark. In *Stolt-Nielsen*, the arbitrators did not construe the parties' contract, and did not identify any agreement authorizing class proceedings. So in setting aside the arbitrators' decision, we found not that they had misinterpreted the contract, but that they had abandoned their interpretive role. Here, the arbitrator did construe the contract (focusing, per usual, on its language), and did find an agreement to permit class arbitration. So to overturn his decision, we would have to rely on a finding that he misapprehended the parties' intent. But § 10(a)(4) *572 bars that course: It permits courts to vacate an arbitral decision only when the arbitrator strayed from his delegated task of interpreting a contract, not when he performed that task poorly. Stolt-Nielsen and this case thus fall on opposite sides of the line that § 10(a)(4) draws to delimit judicial review of arbitral decisions.

The remainder of Oxford's argument addresses merely the merits: . . . . At bottom, Oxford maintains, this is a garden-variety arbitration clause, lacking any of the terms or features that would indicate an agreement to use class procedures.

We reject this argument because, and only because, it is not properly addressed to a court. Nothing we say in this opinion should be taken to reflect any agreement with the arbitrator's contract interpretation, or any quarrel with Oxford's contrary reading. All we say is that convincing a court of an arbitrator's error—even his grave error—is not enough. So long as the arbitrator was "arguably construing" the contract—which this one was—a court may not correct his mistakes under § 10(a)(4). The potential for those mistakes is the price of agreeing to *573 arbitration. As we have held before, we hold again: "It is the arbitrator's construction [of the contract] which was bargained for; and so far as the arbitrator's decision concerns construction of the contract, the courts have no business overruling him because their interpretation of the contract is different from his." The arbitrator's construction holds, however good, bad, or ugly.

In sum, Oxford chose arbitration, and it must now live with that choice. Oxford agreed with Sutter that an arbitrator should determine what their contract meant, including whether its terms approved class arbitration. The arbitrator did what the parties requested: He provided an interpretation of the contract resolving that disputed issue. His interpretation went against Oxford, maybe mistakenly so. But still, Oxford does not get to rerun the matter in a court. Under § 10(a)(4), the question for a judge is not whether the arbitrator construed the parties' contract correctly, but whether he construed it at all. Because he did, and therefore did not "exceed his powers," we cannot give Oxford the relief it wants. We accordingly affirm the judgment of the Court of Appeals.

It is so ordered.

NOTES

Facts

1. Did the parties negotiate the arbitration clause? Where did the arbitration clause come from?

2. What was the difference in language between the Stolt-Nielsen clause and the Oxford Health Plans LLC clause? Did either clause expressly address the underlying issue of class certification?

3. What would be the consequence for the interested parties if the arbitrator had found that the clause does not permit class arbitration?

Law

1. What is the key difference between the arbitrator's approach in *Oxford Health Plan LLC* and *Stolt-Nielsen*? Is it a blue print for argument to or decisions by arbitrators about class certification issues?

2. What is the rationale for the Court's approach in *Oxford Health Plan LLC*? Is it consistent with *Stolt-Nielsen*? How would it respond to an argument that the arbitrator decided in bad faith to impose a policy preference on the parties?

3. How should the parties using model clauses respond to this development? Is there a way for the parties using the model clauses to add information to their negotiations to "salt the record?"

Class Action Waivers

AT&T Mobility LLC v. Concepcion

563 U.S. 333 (2011)

JUSTICE SCALIA delivered the opinion of the Court.

Section 2 of the Federal Arbitration Act (FAA) makes agreements to arbitrate "valid, irrevocable, and enforceable, save upon such grounds as exist at law or in equity for the revocation of any contract." 9 U.S.C. § 2. We consider whether the FAA prohibits States from conditioning the enforceability of certain arbitration agreements on the availability of classwide arbitration procedures.

I

In February 2002, Vincent and Liza Concepcion entered into an agreement for the sale and servicing of cellular telephones with AT & T Mobility LCC (AT & T). The contract provided for arbitration of all disputes between the parties, but required that claims be brought in the parties' "individual capacity, and not as a plaintiff or class member in any purported class or representative proceeding." The agreement authorized AT & T to make unilateral amendments, which it did to the arbitration provision on several occasions. The version at issue in this case reflects revisions made in December 2006, which the parties agree are controlling.

The revised agreement provides that customers may initiate dispute proceedings by completing a one-page Notice of Dispute form available on AT & T's Web site. AT & T may then offer to settle the claim; if it does not, or if the dispute is not resolved within 30 days, the customer may invoke arbitration by filing a separate Demand for Arbitration, also available on AT & T's Web site. In the event the parties proceed to arbitration, the agreement specifies that AT & T must pay all costs for nonfrivolous claims; that arbitration must take place in the county in which the customer is billed; that, for claims of $10,000 or less, the customer may choose whether the arbitration proceeds in person, by telephone, or based only on submissions; that either party may bring a claim in small claims court in lieu of arbitration; and that the arbitrator may award any form of individual relief, including injunctions and presumably punitive damages. The agreement, moreover, denies AT & T any ability to seek reimbursement of its attorney's fees, and, in the event that a customer receives an arbitration award greater than AT & T's last written settlement offer, requires AT & T to pay a $7,500 minimum recovery and twice the amount of the claimant's attorney's fees.

The Concepcions purchased AT & T service, which was advertised as including the provision of free phones; they were not charged for the phones, but they were charged $30.22 in sales tax based on the phones' retail value. In March 2006, the Concepcions filed a complaint against AT & T in the United States District Court for the Southern District of California. The complaint was later consolidated with a putative class action alleging, among other things, that AT & T had engaged in false advertising and fraud by charging sales tax on phones it advertised as free.

In March 2008, AT & T moved to compel arbitration under the terms of its contract with the Concepcions. The Concepcions opposed the motion, contending that the arbitration agreement was unconscionable and unlawfully exculpatory under California law because it disallowed classwide procedures. The District Court denied AT & T's motion. It described AT & T's arbitration agreement favorably, noting, for example, that the informal dispute-resolution process was "quick, easy to use" and likely to "promp[t] full or . . . even excess payment to the customer without the need to arbitrate or litigate"; that the $7,500 premium functioned as "a substantial inducement for the consumer to pursue the claim in arbitration" if a dispute was not resolved informally; and that consumers who were members of a class would likely be worse off. Nevertheless, relying on the California Supreme Court's decision in *Discover Bank v. Superior Court*, 36 Cal.4th 148 (2005), the court found that the arbitration provision was unconscionable because AT & T had not shown that bilateral arbitration adequately substituted for the deterrent effects of class actions.

The Ninth Circuit affirmed, also finding the provision unconscionable under California law as announced in Discover Bank. It also held that the Discover Bank rule was not preempted by the FAA because that rule was simply "a refinement of the unconscionability analysis applicable to contracts generally in California." In response to AT & T's argument that the Concepcions' interpretation of California law discriminated against arbitration, the Ninth Circuit rejected the contention that " 'class proceedings will reduce the efficiency and expeditiousness of arbitration' " and noted that " 'Discover Bank placed arbitration agreements with class action waivers on the exact same footing as contracts that bar class action litigation outside the context of arbitration.' "

II

The FAA was enacted in 1925 in response to widespread judicial hostility to arbitration agreements. Section 2 provides, in relevant part, as follows:

> "A written provision in any maritime transaction or a contract evidencing a transaction involving commerce to settle by arbitration a controversy thereafter arising out of such contract or transaction . . . shall be valid, irrevocable, and enforceable, save upon such grounds as exist at law or in equity for the revocation of any contract." 9 U.S.C. § 2.

The final phrase of § 2 . . . permits arbitration agreements to be declared unenforceable "upon such grounds as exist at law or in equity for the revocation of any contract." This saving clause permits agreements to arbitrate to be invalidated by "generally applicable contract defenses, such as fraud, duress, or unconscionability," but not by defenses that apply only to arbitration or that derive their meaning from the fact that an agreement to arbitrate is at issue. The question in this case is whether § 2 preempts California's rule classifying most collective-arbitration waivers in consumer contracts as unconscionable. We refer to this rule as the *Discover Bank* rule.

Under California law, courts may refuse to enforce any contract found "to have been unconscionable at the time it was made," or may "limit the application of any unconscionable clause." A finding of unconscionability requires "a 'procedural' and a 'substantive' element, the former focusing on 'oppression' or 'surprise' due to unequal bargaining power, the latter on 'overly harsh' or 'one-sided' results."

In *Discover Bank*, the California Supreme Court applied this framework to class-action waivers in arbitration agreements and held as follows:

> "[W]hen the waiver is found in a consumer contract of adhesion in a setting in which disputes between the contracting parties predictably involve small amounts of damages, and when it is alleged that the party with the superior bargaining power has carried out a scheme to deliberately cheat large numbers of consumers out of individually small sums of money, then . . . the waiver becomes in practice the exemption of the party 'from responsibility for [its] own fraud, or willful injury to the person or property of another.' Under these circumstances, such waivers are unconscionable under California law and should not be enforced."

California courts have frequently applied this rule to find arbitration agreements unconscionable.

III

A

The Concepcions argue that the Discover Bank rule, given its origins in California's unconscionability doctrine and California's policy against exculpation, is a ground that "exist[s] at law or in equity for the revocation of any contract" under FAA § 2. Moreover, they argue that even if we construe the Discover Bank rule as a prohibition on collective-action waivers rather than simply an application of unconscionability, the rule would still be applicable to all dispute-resolution contracts, since California prohibits waivers of class litigation as well.

When state law prohibits outright the arbitration of a particular type of claim, the analysis is straightforward: The conflicting rule is displaced by the FAA. But the inquiry becomes more complex when a doctrine normally thought to be generally applicable, such as duress or, as relevant here, unconscionability, is alleged to have been applied in a fashion that disfavors arbitration. In *Perry v. Thomas*, 482 U.S. 483 (1987), for example, we noted that the FAA's preemptive effect might extend even to grounds traditionally thought to exist 'at law or in equity for the revocation of any contract.'

An obvious illustration of this point would be a case finding unconscionable or unenforceable as against public policy consumer arbitration agreements that fail to provide for judicially monitored discovery. The rationalizations for such a holding are neither difficult to imagine nor different in kind from those articulated in *Discover Bank*. A court might reason that no consumer would knowingly waive his right to full discovery, as this would enable companies to hide their wrongdoing. Or the court might simply say that such agreements are exculpatory—restricting discovery would be of greater benefit to the company than the consumer, since the former is more likely to be sued than to sue. And, the reasoning would continue, because such a rule applies the general principle of unconscionability or public-policy disapproval of exculpatory agreements, it is applicable to "any" contract and thus preserved by § 2 of the FAA. In practice, of course, the rule would have a disproportionate impact on arbitration agreements; but it would presumably apply to contracts purporting to restrict discovery in litigation as well.

The Concepcions suggest that all this is just a parade of horribles, and no genuine worry. "Rules aimed at destroying arbitration" or "demanding procedures incompatible with arbitration," they concede, "would be preempted by the FAA because they cannot sensibly be reconciled with Section 2." The "grounds" available under § 2's saving clause, they admit, "should not be construed to include a State's mere preference for procedures that are incompatible with arbitration and 'would wholly eviscerate arbitration agreements.' " Id., at 33 (quoting *Carter v. SSC Odin Operating Co., LLC*, 237 Ill.2d 30, 50, 340 Ill.Dec. 196, 927 N.E.2d 1207, 1220 (2010)).

We largely agree. Although § 2's saving clause preserves generally applicable contract defenses, nothing in it suggests an intent to preserve state-law rules that stand as an obstacle to the accomplishment of the FAA's objectives. As we have said, a federal statute's saving clause " 'cannot in reason be construed as [allowing] a common law right, the continued existence of which would be absolutely inconsistent with the provisions of the act. In other words, the act cannot be held to destroy itself.' "

We differ with the Concepcions only in the application of this analysis to the matter before us. We do not agree that rules requiring judicially monitored discovery or adherence to the Federal Rules of Evidence are "a far cry from this case." The overarching purpose of the FAA is to ensure the enforcement of arbitration agreements according to their terms so as to facilitate streamlined proceedings. Requiring the availability of classwide arbitration interferes with fundamental attributes of arbitration and thus creates a scheme inconsistent with the FAA.

B

The "principal purpose" of the FAA is to "ensur[e] that private arbitration agreements are enforced according to their terms." This purpose is readily apparent from the FAA's text.

The point of affording parties discretion in designing arbitration processes is to allow for efficient, streamlined procedures tailored to the type of dispute. It can be specified, for example, that the decisionmaker be a specialist in the relevant field, or that proceedings be kept confidential to protect trade secrets. And the informality of arbitral proceedings is itself desirable, reducing the cost and increasing the speed of dispute resolution.

California's *Discover Bank* rule . . . interferes with arbitration. Although the rule does not require classwide arbitration, it allows any party to a consumer contract to demand it ex post. The rule is limited to adhesion contracts, but the times in which consumer contracts were anything other than adhesive are long past. The rule also requires that damages be predictably small, and that the consumer allege a scheme to cheat consumers. The former requirement, however, is toothless and malleable (the Ninth Circuit has held that damages of $4,000 are sufficiently small, *see Oestreicher v. Alienware Corp.*, 322 Fed.Appx. 489, 492 (2009) (unpublished)), and the latter has no limiting effect, as all that is required is an allegation. Consumers remain free to bring and resolve their disputes on a bilateral basis under *Discover Bank*, and some may well do so; but there is little incentive for lawyers to arbitrate on behalf of individuals when they may do so for a class and reap far higher fees in the process. And faced with inevitable class arbitration, companies would have less incentive to continue resolving potentially duplicative claims on an individual basis.

Although we have had little occasion to examine classwide arbitration, our decision in *Stolt-Nielsen* is instructive. In that case we held that an arbitration panel exceeded its power under § 10(a)(4) of the FAA by imposing class procedures based on policy judgments rather than the arbitration agreement itself or some background principle of contract law that would affect its interpretation. We then held that the agreement at issue, which was silent on the question of class procedures, could not be interpreted to allow them because the "changes brought about by the shift from bilateral arbitration to class-action arbitration" are "fundamental." This is obvious as a structural matter: Classwide arbitration includes absent parties, necessitating additional and different procedures and involving higher stakes. Confidentiality becomes more difficult. And while it is theoretically possible to select an arbitrator with some expertise relevant to the class-certification question, arbitrators are not generally knowledgeable in the often-dominant procedural aspects of certification, such as the protection of absent parties. The conclusion follows that class arbitration, to the extent it is manufactured by Discover Bank rather than consensual, is inconsistent with the FAA.

First, the switch from bilateral to class arbitration sacrifices the principal advantage of arbitration—its informality—and makes the process slower, more costly, and more likely to generate procedural morass than final judgment.

Second, class arbitration requires procedural formality. The AAA's rules governing class arbitrations mimic the Federal Rules of Civil Procedure for class litigation. Compare AAA, Supplementary Rules for Class Arbitrations (effective Oct. 8, 2003), online at http://www.adr.org/sp.asp?id=21936, with Fed. Rule Civ. Proc. 23. And while parties can alter those procedures by contract, an alternative is not obvious.

Third, class arbitration greatly increases risks to defendants. Informal procedures do of course have a cost: The absence of multilayered review makes it more likely that errors will go uncorrected. Defendants are willing to accept the costs of these errors in arbitration, since their impact is limited to the size of individual disputes, and presumably outweighed by savings from avoiding the courts. But when damages allegedly owed to tens of thousands of potential claimants are aggregated and decided at once, the risk of an error will often become unacceptable. Faced with even a small chance of a devastating loss, defendants will be pressured into settling questionable claims. Other courts have noted the risk of *"in terrorem"* settlements that class actions entail, and class arbitration would be no different.

Arbitration is poorly suited to the higher stakes of class litigation. In litigation, a defendant may appeal a certification decision on an interlocutory basis and, if unsuccessful, may appeal from a final judgment as well. Questions of law are reviewed de novo and questions of fact for clear error. In contrast, 9 U.S.C. § 10 allows a court to vacate an arbitral award only where the award "was procured by corruption, fraud, or undue means"; "there was evident partiality or corruption in the arbitrators"; "the arbitrators were guilty of misconduct in refusing to postpone the hearing . . . or in refusing to hear evidence pertinent and material to the controversy[,] or of any other misbehavior by which the rights of any party have been prejudiced"; or if the "arbitrators exceeded their powers, or so imperfectly executed them that a mutual, final, and definite award . . . was not made." The AAA rules do authorize judicial review of certification decisions, but this review is unlikely to have much effect given these limitations; review under § 10 focuses on misconduct rather than mistake. And parties may not contractually expand the grounds or nature of judicial review. We find it hard to believe that defendants would bet the company with no effective means of review, and even harder to believe that Congress would have intended to allow state courts to force such a decision.

The Concepcions contend that because parties may and sometimes do agree to aggregation, class procedures are not necessarily incompatible with arbitration. But the same could be said about procedures that the Concepcions admit States may not superimpose on arbitration: Parties could agree to arbitrate pursuant to the Federal Rules of Civil Procedure, or pursuant to a discovery process rivaling that in litigation. Arbitration is a matter of contract, and the FAA requires courts to honor parties' expectations. But what the parties in the aforementioned examples would have agreed to is not arbitration as envisioned by the FAA, lacks its benefits, and therefore may not be required by state law.

The dissent claims that class proceedings are necessary to prosecute small-dollar claims that might otherwise slip through the legal system. But States cannot require a procedure that is inconsistent with the FAA, even if it is desirable for unrelated reasons. Moreover, the claim here was most unlikely to go unresolved. As noted earlier, the arbitration agreement provides that AT & T will pay claimants a minimum of $7,500 and twice their attorney's fees if they obtain an arbitration award greater than AT & T's last settlement offer. The District Court found this scheme sufficient to provide incentive for the individual prosecution of meritorious claims that are not immediately settled, and the Ninth Circuit admitted that aggrieved customers who filed claims would be "essentially guarantee[d]" to be made whole. Indeed, the District Court concluded that the Concepcions were better off under their arbitration agreement with AT & T than they would have been as participants in a class action, which "could take months, if not years, and which may merely yield an opportunity to submit a claim for recovery of a small percentage of a few dollars."

Because it "stands as an obstacle to the accomplishment and execution of the full purposes and objectives of Congress," California's Discover Bank rule is preempted by the FAA. The judgment of the Ninth Circuit is reversed, and the case is remanded for further proceedings consistent with this opinion.

It is so ordered.

NOTES

Facts

1. What precisely was the challenge to the arbitration clause in this instance? Did it concern the contract as a whole, or did it concern the arbitration provision specifically?

2. How was dispute resolution under the clause structured? Could you make an argument that the clause was unconscionable?

3. In light of the provisions in the clause, in what circumstances would plaintiffs be financially better off filing a successful class action litigation rather than an arbitration? Does the court's reasoning deal adequately with this type of case?

Law

1. Compare the decision in *AT&T* to the decision in *Buckeye Cashing* discussed in Chapter 3. How do the challenges to the arbitration provisions in both

cases develop? Did the factual precedent of the *AT&T* challenge satisfy the standard set out in *Buckeye Cashing?*

2.   Consider the reverse question: Would the *Buckeye Cashing* facts have satisfied the standard set out in *AT&T?*

3.   You have been hired as counsel to the Texas legislature. The Texas legislature is considering legislation to protect consumers against abusive commercial terms, including arbitration clauses, in contracts of adhesion,. How would you draft the legislation to prohibit class action waivers in arbitration without running afoul of the *AT&T* and *Buckeye Cashing* standards?

American Express Co. v. Italian Colors Restaurant

570 U.S. 228 (2013) (citations omitted)

JUSTICE SCALIA delivered the opinion of the Court.

*231 We consider whether a contractual waiver of class arbitration is enforceable under the Federal Arbitration Act when the plaintiff's cost of individually arbitrating a federal statutory claim exceeds the potential recovery.

I

Respondents are merchants who accept American Express cards. Their agreement with petitioners—American Express and a wholly owned subsidiary—contains a clause that requires all disputes between the parties to be resolved by arbitration. The agreement also provides that "[t]here shall be no right or authority for any Claims to be arbitrated on a class action basis."

Respondents brought a class action against petitioners for violations of the federal antitrust laws. According to respondents, American Express used its monopoly power in the market for charge cards to force merchants to accept credit cards at rates approximately 30% higher than the fees for competing credit cards. This tying arrangement, respondents said, violated § 1 of the Sherman Act. They sought treble damages for the class under § 4 of the Clayton Act.

Petitioners moved to compel individual arbitration under the Federal Arbitration Act (FAA), 9 U.S.C. § 1 et seq. In resisting the motion, respondents submitted a declaration from an economist who estimated that the cost of an expert analysis necessary to prove the antitrust claims would be "at least several hundred thousand dollars, and might exceed $1 million," while the maximum recovery for an individual plaintiff would be $12,850, or $38,549 when trebled. App. 93. The District Court granted the motion and dismissed *232 the lawsuits. The Court of Appeals reversed and remanded for further proceedings. It held that because respondents had established that "they would incur prohibitive costs if compelled to arbitrate under the class action waiver," the waiver was unenforceable and the arbitration could not proceed. In re American Express Merchants' Litigation, 554 F.3d 300, 315–316 (C.A.2 2009).

[. . .]

II

Congress enacted the FAA in response to widespread judicial hostility to arbitration. [. . .] [Its] text reflects the overarching principle that arbitration is a matter of contract. And consistent with that text, courts must "rigorously enforce" arbitration agreements according to their terms, including terms that "specify with whom [the parties] choose to arbitrate their disputes," and "the rules under which that arbitration will be conducted," That holds true for claims that allege a violation of a federal statute, unless the FAA's mandate has been " 'overridden by a contrary congressional command.' ".

III

No contrary congressional command requires us to reject the waiver of class arbitration here. Respondents argue that requiring them to litigate their claims individually—as they contracted to do—would contravene the policies of the antitrust laws. But the antitrust laws do not guarantee an affordable procedural path to the vindication of every claim. Congress has taken some measures to facilitate the litigation of antitrust claims—for example, it enacted a multiplied-damages remedy. See 15 U.S.C. § 15 (treble damages). In enacting such measures, Congress has told us that it is willing to go, in certain respects, beyond the normal limits of law in advancing its goals of deterring and remedying unlawful trade practice. But to say that Congress must have intended *234 whatever departures from those normal limits advance antitrust goals is simply irrational. "[N]o legislation pursues its purposes at all costs."

The antitrust laws do not "evinc[e] an intention to preclude a waiver" of class-action procedure. The Sherman and Clayton Acts make no mention of class actions. In fact, they were enacted decades before the advent of Federal Rule of Civil Procedure 23, which was "designed to allow an exception to the usual rule that litigation is conducted by and on behalf of the individual named parties only." [. . .]

IV

Our finding of no "contrary congressional command" does not end the case. Respondents invoke a judge-made exception to the FAA which, they say, serves to harmonize competing federal policies by allowing courts to invalidate agreements that prevent the "effective vindication" of a federal statutory right. Enforcing the waiver of class arbitration bars effective vindication, respondents contend, because they have no economic incentive to pursue their antitrust claims individually in arbitration.

The "effective vindication" exception to which respondents allude originated as dictum in *Mitsubishi Motors*, where we expressed a willingness to invalidate, on "public policy" grounds, arbitration agreements that "operat[e] . . . as a prospective waiver of a party's right to pursue statutory remedies." Dismissing concerns that the arbitral forum was inadequate, we said that "so long as the prospective litigant effectively may vindicate its statutory cause of action in the arbitral forum, the statute will continue to serve both its remedial and deterrent function." Subsequent cases have similarly asserted the existence of an "effective vindication" exception, but have similarly declined to apply it to invalidate the arbitration agreement at issue.

*236 And we do so again here. As we have described, the exception finds its origin in the desire to prevent "prospective waiver of a party's right to pursue statutory remedies,". That would certainly cover a provision in an arbitration agreement forbidding the assertion of certain statutory rights. And it would perhaps cover filing and administrative fees attached to arbitration that are so high as to make access. But the fact that it is not worth the expense involved in proving a statutory remedy does not constitute the elimination of the right to pursue that remedy. The class-action waiver merely limits arbitration to the two contracting parties. It no more eliminates those parties' right to pursue their statutory remedy than did federal law before its adoption of the class action for legal relief in 1938.

[. . .]

The regime established by the Court of Appeals' decision would require— before a plaintiff can be held to contractually agreed bilateral arbitration—that a federal court determine (and the parties litigate) the legal requirements for success on the merits claim-by-claim and theory-by-theory, the evidence necessary to meet those requirements, the cost of developing *239 that evidence, and the damages that would be recovered in the event of success. Such a preliminary litigating hurdle would undoubtedly destroy the prospect of speedy resolution that arbitration in general and bilateral arbitration in particular was meant to secure. The FAA does not sanction such a judicially created superstructure.

The judgment of the Court of Appeals is reversed.

It is so ordered.

NOTES

Facts

1.   Did the arbitration clause directly address the question of class arbitration?

2.   Do you think the arbitration clause determined who would decide questions of arbitrability, the judge or the arbitrator? Is this a fact the Court discusses? Is this surprising?

3.   Do you see how the Supreme Court's jurisprudence affected the drafting of arbitration clauses? Look at how sophisticated parties responded to the Court's cases and what avenues this has left for litigants seeking to attack arbitration clauses/waiver of class arbitration.

Law

1.   What is the Court's basis for decision, a concern for arbitrability or a question of construction of the arbitration agreement?

2.   The Court in *AT&T Mobility, LLC v. Concepcion*, 563 U.S. 333 (2011) and *DIRECTV, Inc. v. Imburgia*, 136 S. Ct. 463 (2015) further addressed that state statutes, which sought to render class action waivers in certain kinds of contracts unenforceable to be preempted by the Federal Arbitration Act. In essence, this development suggests that only federal law can create causes of actions which would invalidate arbitration class action waivers. As a matter of constitutional analysis, does this surprise you?

3.   What is the result under *Stolt-Nielsen* and *Oxford Health Plan LLC* if an arbitrator certifies a class arbitration under the Italian Colors arbitration clause? Does it matter if the arbitrator bases her decision on policy grounds?

4.   How about if the arbitrator construes the arbitration clause as follows: "The intention of the parties in agreeing to a waiver of class actions was intended to cover only cases in which it would be economical to pursue individual claims. The remainder of the contract in which the arbitration clause is included details specific individual obligations of the parties

towards each other. The waiver therefore is most clearly intended to cover the matters included in the contract, together with the naturally occurring statutory claims arising out of a breach of contract. My construction of the waiver extends it no further. As the cause of action as pled in this case falls outside of this scope of the true construction of the waiver, I certify the class."

Epic Systems Corp v. Lewis

138 S.Ct. 1612 (2018) (citations omitted)

JUSTICE GORSUCH delivered the opinion of the Court.

Should employees and employers be allowed to agree that any disputes between them will be resolved through one-on-one arbitration? Or should employees always be permitted to bring their claims in class or collective actions, no matter what they agreed with their employers?

As a matter of policy these questions are surely debatable. But as a matter of law the answer is clear. In the Federal Arbitration Act, Congress has instructed federal courts to enforce arbitration agreements according to their terms—including terms providing for individualized proceedings. Nor can we agree with the employees' suggestion that the National Labor Relations Act (NLRA) offers a conflicting command. It is this Court's duty to interpret Congress's statutes as a harmonious whole rather than at war with one another. And abiding that duty here leads to an unmistakable conclusion. The NLRA secures to employees rights to organize unions and bargain collectively, but it says nothing about how judges and arbitrators must try legal disputes that leave the workplace and enter the courtroom or arbitral forum. This Court has never read a right to class actions into the NLRA—and for three quarters of a century neither did the National Labor Relations Board. Far from conflicting, the Arbitration Act and the NLRA have long enjoyed separate spheres of influence and neither permits this Court to declare the parties' agreements unlawful.

I

The three cases before us differ in detail but not in substance. Take *Ernst & Young LLP v. Morris*. There Ernst & Young and one of its junior accountants, Stephen Morris, entered into an agreement providing that they would arbitrate any disputes that might arise between them. The agreement stated that the employee could choose the arbitration provider and that the arbitrator could "grant any relief that could be granted by . . . a court" in the relevant jurisdiction.

*1620 The agreement also specified individualized arbitration, with claims "pertaining to different [e]mployees [to] be heard in separate proceedings."

After his employment ended, and despite having agreed to arbitrate claims against the firm, Mr. Morris sued Ernst & Young in federal court. He alleged that the firm had misclassified its junior accountants as professional employees and violated the federal Fair Labor Standards Act (FLSA) and California law by paying them salaries without overtime pay. Although the arbitration agreement provided for individualized proceedings, Mr. Morris sought to litigate the federal claim on behalf of a nationwide class under the FLSA's collective action provision, 29 U.S.C. § 216(b). He sought to pursue the state law claim as a class action under Federal Rule of Civil Procedure 23.

Ernst & Young replied with a motion to compel arbitration. The district court granted the request, but the Ninth Circuit reversed this judgment. 834 F.3d 975 (2016). The Ninth Circuit recognized that the Arbitration Act generally requires courts to enforce arbitration agreements as written. But the court reasoned that the statute's "saving clause," *see* 9 U.S.C. § 2, removes this obligation if an arbitration agreement violates some other federal law. And the court concluded that an agreement requiring individualized arbitration proceedings violates the NLRA by barring employees from engaging in the "concerted activit[y]," 29 U.S.C. § 157, of pursuing claims as a class or collective action.

[. . .]

Although the Arbitration Act and the NLRA have long coexisted—they date from 1925 and 1935, respectively—the suggestion they might conflict is something quite new. Until a couple of years ago, courts more or less agreed that arbitration agreements like those before us must be enforced according to their terms.

The National Labor Relations Board's general counsel expressed much the same view in 2010. [. . .] But recently things have shifted. In 2012, the Board—for the first time in the 77 years since the NLRA's adoption—asserted that the NLRA effectively nullifies the Arbitration Act in cases like ours. Initially, this agency decision received a cool reception in court. In the last two years, though, some circuits have either agreed with the Board's conclusion or *1621 thought themselves obliged to defer to it under *Chevron U.S.A. Inc. v. Natural Resources Defense Council, Inc.*, 467 U.S. 837 (1984). [. . .]

II

We begin with the Arbitration Act and the question of its saving clause.

Congress adopted the Arbitration Act in 1925 in response to a perception that courts were unduly hostile to arbitration. [. . .] The Act, this Court has said, establishes "a liberal federal policy favoring arbitration agreements.". Not only did Congress require courts to respect and enforce agreements to arbitrate; it also specifically directed them to respect and enforce the parties' chosen arbitration procedures. [. . .]

On first blush, these emphatic directions would seem to resolve any argument under the Arbitration Act. The parties before us contracted for arbitration. They proceeded to specify the rules that would govern their arbitrations, indicating their intention to use individualized rather than class or collective action procedures. And this much the Arbitration Act seems to protect pretty absolutely. You might wonder if the balance Congress struck in 1925 between arbitration *1622 and litigation should be revisited in light of more contemporary developments. You might even ask if the Act was good policy when enacted. But all the same you might find it difficult to see how to avoid the statute's application.

Still, the employees suggest the Arbitration Act's saving clause creates an exception for cases like theirs. By its terms, the saving clause allows courts to refuse to enforce arbitration agreements "upon such grounds as exist at law or in equity for the revocation of any contract." § 2. That provision applies here, the employees tell us, because the NLRA renders their particular class and collective action waivers illegal. In their view, illegality under the NLRA is a "ground" that "exists at law . . . for the revocation" of their arbitration agreements, at least to the extent those agreements prohibit class or collective action proceedings.

The problem with this line of argument is fundamental. Put to the side the question whether the saving clause was designed to save not only state law defenses but also defenses allegedly arising from federal statutes. Put to the side the question of what it takes to qualify as a ground for "revocation" of a contract. Put to the side for the moment, too, even the question whether the NLRA actually renders class and collective action waivers illegal. Assuming (but not granting) the employees could satisfactorily answer all those questions, the saving clause still can't save their cause.

It can't because the saving clause recognizes only defenses that apply to "any" contract. In this way the clause establishes a sort of "equal-treatment" rule for arbitration contracts. The clause "permits agreements to arbitrate to be invalidated by 'generally applicable contract defenses, such as fraud, duress, or unconscionability.' " At the same time, the clause offers no refuge for "defenses that apply only to arbitration or that derive their meaning from the fact that an agreement to arbitrate is at issue." Under our precedent, this means the saving clause does not save defenses that target arbitration either by name or by more subtle methods, such as by "interfer[ing] with fundamental attributes of arbitration."

This is where the employees' argument stumbles. They don't suggest that their arbitration agreements were extracted, say, by an act of fraud or duress or in some other unconscionable way that would render any contract unenforceable. Instead, they object to their agreements precisely because they require individualized arbitration proceedings instead of class or collective ones. And by attacking (only) the individualized nature of the arbitration proceedings, the employees' argument seeks to interfere with one of arbitration's fundamental attributes.

[. . .]

The employees' efforts to distinguish Concepcion fall short. They note that their putative NLRA defense would render an agreement "illegal" as a matter of federal statutory law rather than "unconscionable" as a matter of state common law. But we don't see how that distinction makes any difference in light of *Concepcion*'s rationale and rule. Illegality, like unconscionability, may be a traditional, generally applicable contract defense in many cases, including arbitration cases. But an argument that a contract is unenforceable just because it requires bilateral arbitration is a different creature. A defense of that kind, *Concepcion* tells us, is one that impermissibly disfavors arbitration whether it sounds in illegality or unconscionability. The law of precedent teaches that like cases should generally be treated alike, and appropriate respect for that principle means the Arbitration Act's saving clause can no more save the defense at issue in these cases than it did the defense at issue in Concepcion. At the end of our encounter with the Arbitration Act, then, it appears just as it did at the beginning: a congressional command requiring us to enforce, not override, the terms of the arbitration agreements before us.

III

But that's not the end of it. Even if the Arbitration Act normally requires us to *1624 enforce arbitration agreements like theirs, the employees reply that the NLRA overrides that guidance in these cases and commands us to hold their agreements unlawful yet.

This argument faces a stout uphill climb. When confronted with two Acts of Congress allegedly touching on the same topic, this Court is not at "liberty to pick and choose among congressional enactments" and must instead strive " 'to give effect to both.' " A party seeking to suggest that two statutes cannot be harmonized, and that one displaces the other, bears the heavy burden of showing " 'a clearly expressed congressional intention' " that such a result should follow. The intention must be " 'clear and manifest.' " And in approaching a claimed conflict, we come armed with the "stron[g] presum[ption]" that repeals by implication are "disfavored" and that "Congress will specifically address" preexisting law when it wishes to suspend its normal operations in a later statute.

These rules exist for good reasons. Respect for Congress as drafter counsels against too easily finding irreconcilable conflicts in its work. More than that, respect for the separation of powers counsels restraint. Allowing judges to pick and choose between statutes risks transforming them from expounders of what the law is into policymakers choosing what the law should be. Our rules aiming for harmony over conflict in statutory interpretation grow from an appreciation that it's the job of Congress by legislation, not this Court by supposition, both to write the laws and to repeal them.

Seeking to demonstrate an irreconcilable statutory conflict even in light of these demanding standards, the employees point to Section 7 of the NLRA. That provision guarantees workers

> "the right to self-organization, to form, join, or assist labor organizations, to bargain collectively through representatives of their own choosing, and to engage in other concerted activities for the purpose of collective bargaining or other mutual aid or protection."
> 29 U.S.C. § 157.

From this language, the employees ask us to infer a clear and manifest congressional command to displace the Arbitration Act and outlaw agreements like theirs.

But that much inference is more than this Court may make. Section 7 focuses on the right to organize unions and bargain collectively. It may permit unions to bargain to prohibit arbitration. But it does not express approval or disapproval of arbitration. It does not mention class or collective action procedures. It does not even hint at a wish to displace the Arbitration Act—let alone accomplish that much clearly and manifestly, as our precedents demand.

Neither should any of this come as a surprise. The notion that Section 7 confers a right to class or collective actions seems pretty unlikely when you recall that procedures like that were hardly known when the NLRA was adopted in 1935. Federal Rule of Civil Procedure 23 didn't create the modern class action until 1966; class arbitration didn't emerge until later still; and even the Fair Labor Standards Act's collective action provision postdated Section 7 by years. And while some forms of group litigation existed even in 1935, Section 7's failure to mention them only reinforces that the statute doesn't speak to such procedures.

A close look at the employees' best evidence of a potential conflict turns out to reveal no conflict at all. The employees direct our attention to the term "other concerted activities for the purpose of . . . other mutual aid or protection." This catchall term, they say, can be read to include class and collective legal actions. But the term appears at the end of a detailed list of activities speaking of "self-organization," "form[ing], join[ing], or assist[ing] labor organizations," and "bargain[ing] collectively." 29 U.S.C. § 157. And where, as here, a more general term follows more specific terms in a list, the general term is usually understood to " 'embrace only objects similar in nature to those objects enumerated by the preceding specific words.' ". All of which suggests that the term "other concerted activities" should, like the terms that precede it, serve to protect things employees "just do" for themselves in the course of exercising their right to free association in the workplace, rather than "the highly regulated, courtroom-bound 'activities' of class and joint litigation." *Alternative Entertainment*, 858 F.3d, at 414–415 (Sutton, J., concurring in part and dissenting in part) (emphasis deleted). None of the preceding and more specific terms speaks to the procedures judges or arbitrators must apply in disputes that leave the workplace and enter the courtroom or arbitral forum, and there is no textually sound reason to suppose the final catchall term should bear such a radically different object than all its predecessors.

[. . .]

Telling, too, is the fact that when Congress wants to mandate particular dispute resolution procedures it knows exactly how to do so. Congress has spoken often and clearly to the procedures for resolving "actions," "claims," "charges," and "cases" in statute after statute. E.g., 29 U.S.C. §§ 216(b), 626; 42 U.S.C. §§ 2000e–5(b), (f)(3)–(5). Congress has likewise shown that it knows how to override the Arbitration Act when it wishes—by explaining, for example, that, "[n]otwithstanding any other provision of law, . . . arbitration may be used . . .

only if" certain conditions are met, 15 U.S.C. § 1226(a)(2); or that "[n]o predispute arbitration agreement shall be valid or enforceable" in other circumstances, 7 U.S.C. § 26(n)(2); 12 U.S.C. § 5567(d)(2); or that requiring a party to arbitrate is "unlawful" in other circumstances yet, 10 U.S.C. § 987(e)(3). The fact that we have nothing like that here is further evidence that Section 7 does nothing to address the question of class and collective actions.

[. . .]

What all these textual and contextual clues indicate, our precedents confirm. In many cases over many years, this Court has heard and rejected efforts to conjure conflicts between the Arbitration Act and other federal statutes. In fact, this Court has rejected every such effort to date (save one temporary exception since overruled), with statutes ranging from the Sherman and Clayton Acts to the Age Discrimination in Employment Act, the Credit Repair Organizations Act, the Securities Act of 1933, the Securities Exchange Act of 1934, and the Racketeer Influenced and Corrupt Organizations Act. Throughout, we have made clear that even a statute's express provision for collective legal actions does not necessarily mean that it precludes " 'individual attempts at conciliation' " through arbitration. And we've stressed that the absence of any specific statutory discussion of arbitration or class actions is an important and telling clue that Congress has not displaced the Arbitration Act. Given so much precedent pointing so strongly in one direction, we do not see how we might faithfully turn the other way here.

[. . .]

With so much against them in the statute and our precedent, the employees end by seeking shelter in *Chevron*. Even if this Court doesn't see what they see in Section 7, the employees say we must rule for them anyway because of the deference this Court owes to an administrative agency's interpretation of the law. To be sure, the employees do not wish us to defer to the general counsel's judgment in 2010 that the NLRA and the Arbitration Act coexist peaceably; they wish us to defer instead to the Board's 2012 opinion suggesting the NLRA displaces the Arbitration Act. No party to these cases has asked us to reconsider *Chevron* deference. *Cf. SAS Institute Inc. v. Iancu*, ___ U.S. ___, ___, 138 S.Ct. 1348, 1358, ___ L.Ed.2d ___ (2018). But even under Chevron's terms, no deference is due. To show why, it suffices to outline just a few of the most obvious reasons.

The *Chevron* Court justified deference on the premise that a statutory ambiguity represents an "implicit" delegation to an agency to interpret a "statute which it administers." Here, though, the Board hasn't just sought to interpret its statute, the NLRA, in isolation; it has sought to interpret this statute in a way that limits the work of a second statute, the Arbitration Act. And on no account might we agree that Congress implicitly delegated to an agency authority to address the meaning of a second statute it does not administer. One of *Chevron*'s essential premises is simply missing here.

It's easy, too, to see why the "reconciliation" of distinct statutory regimes "is a matter for the courts," not agencies. An agency eager to advance its statutory mission, but without any particular interest in or expertise with a second statute, might (as here) seek to diminish the second statute's scope in favor of a more expansive interpretation of its own—effectively " 'bootstrap[ping] itself into an area in which it has no jurisdiction.' " All of which threatens to undo rather than honor legislative intentions. To preserve the balance Congress struck in its statutes, courts must exercise independent interpretive judgment.

[. . .]

The policy may be debatable but the law is clear: Congress has instructed that arbitration agreements like those before us must be enforced as written. While Congress is of course always free to amend this judgment, we see nothing suggesting it did so in the NLRA—much less that it manifested a clear intention to displace the Arbitration Act. Because we can easily read Congress's statutes to work in harmony, that is where our duty lies. The judgments in Epic, No. 16–285, and Ernst & Young, No. 16–300, are reversed, and the cases are remanded for further proceedings consistent with this opinion. The judgment in Murphy Oil, No. 16–307, is affirmed.

So ordered.

NOTES

1.   What are the conflicts at issue in this case? A potential conflict between federal laws? A conflict between regulations and federal laws? A conflict between the interpretation by the executive of a federal law and the interpretation by the judiciary of another federal law?

2.   The *Epic Systems* decision provides fascinating insight into the direction of the post-Scalia Court on many subjects including arbitration. Note the discussion of *Chevron* deference. Justice Gorsuch appears to sending reasonably clear signals of his views.

3.   Is there any way left to attack class action waivers in arbitration clauses?

2)   *Class Certification in AAA Arbitration*

AAA Supplementary Rules for Class Arbitrations (effective October 8, 2003)

1.   Applicability

(a)   These Supplementary Rules for Class Arbitrations ("Supplementary Rules") shall apply to any dispute arising out of an agreement that provides for arbitration pursuant to any of the rules of the American Arbitration Association ("AAA") where a party submits a dispute to arbitration on behalf of or against a class or purported class, and shall supplement any other applicable AAA rules. These Supplementary Rules shall also apply whenever a court refers a matter pleaded as a class action to the AAA for administration, or when a party to a pending AAA arbitration asserts new claims on behalf of or against a class or purported class.

(b)   Where inconsistencies exist between these Supplementary Rules and other AAA rules that apply to the dispute, these Supplementary Rules will govern. The arbitrator shall have the authority to resolve any inconsistency between any agreement of the parties and these Supplementary Rules, and in doing so shall endeavor to avoid any prejudice to the interests of absent members of a class or purported class.

(c)   Whenever a court has, by order, addressed and resolved any matter that would otherwise be decided by an arbitrator under these Supplementary Rules, the arbitrator shall follow the order of the court.

. . .

4.   Class Certification

(a)   Prerequisites to a Class Arbitration

If the arbitrator is satisfied that the arbitration clause permits the arbitration to proceed as a class arbitration, as provided in Rule 3, or where a court has ordered that an arbitrator determine whether a class arbitration may be maintained, the arbitrator shall determine whether the arbitration should proceed as a class arbitration. For that purpose, the arbitrator shall consider the criteria enumerated in this Rule 4 and any law or agreement of the parties the arbitrator determines applies to the arbitration. In doing so, the arbitrator shall determine whether one or more members of a class may act in the arbitration as representative parties on behalf of all members of the class described. The arbitrator shall permit a representative to do so only if each of the following conditions is met:

(1) the class is so numerous that joinder of separate arbitrations on behalf of all members is impracticable;

(2) there are questions of law or fact common to the class;

(3) the claims or defenses of the representative parties are typical of the claims or defenses of the class;

(4) the representative parties will fairly and adequately protect the interests of the class;

(5) counsel selected to represent the class will fairly and adequately protect the interests of the class; and

(6) each class member has entered into an agreement containing an arbitration clause which is substantially similar to that signed by the class representative(s) and each of the other class members.

(b) Class Arbitrations Maintainable

An arbitration may be maintained as a class arbitration if the prerequisites of subdivision (a) are satisfied, and in addition, the arbitrator finds that the questions of law or fact common to the members of the class predominate over any questions affecting only individual members, and that a class arbitration is superior to other available methods for the fair and efficient adjudication of the controversy. The matters pertinent to the findings include:

(1) the interest of members of the class in individually controlling the prosecution or defense of separate arbitrations;

(2) the extent and nature of any other proceedings concerning the controversy already commenced by or against members of the class;

(3) the desirability or undesirability of concentrating the determination of the claims in a single arbitral forum; and

(4) the difficulties likely to be encountered in the management of a class arbitration.

5. Class Determination Award

(a) The arbitrator's determination concerning whether an arbitration should proceed as a class arbitration shall be set forth in a reasoned, partial final award (the "Class Determination Award"), which shall address each of the matters set forth in Rule 4.

(b)   A Class Determination Award certifying a class arbitration shall define the class, identify the class representative(s) and counsel, and shall set forth the class claims, issues, or defenses. A copy of the proposed Notice of Class Determination (see Rule 6), specifying the intended mode of delivery of the Notice to the class members, shall be attached to the award.

(c)   The Class Determination Award shall state when and how members of the class may be excluded from the class arbitration. If an arbitrator concludes that some exceptional circumstance, such as the need to resolve claims seeking injunctive relief or claims to a limited fund, makes it inappropriate to allow class members to request exclusion, the Class Determination Award shall explain the reasons for that conclusion.

(d)   The arbitrator shall stay all proceedings following the issuance of the Class Determination Award for a period of at least 30 days to permit any party to move a court of competent jurisdiction to confirm or to vacate the Class Determination Award. Once all parties inform the arbitrator in writing during the period of the stay that they do not intend to seek judicial review of the Class Determination Award, or once the requisite time period expires without any party having informed the arbitrator that it has done so, the arbitrator may proceed with the arbitration on the basis stated in the Class Determination Award. If any party informs the arbitrator within the period provided that it has sought judicial review, the arbitrator may stay further proceedings, or some part of them, until the arbitrator is informed of the ruling of the court.

(e)   A Class Determination Award may be altered or amended by the arbitrator before a final award is rendered.

6.   Notice of Class Determination

(a)   In any arbitration administered under these Supplementary Rules, the arbitrator shall, after expiration of the stay following the Class Determination Award, direct that class members be provided the best notice practicable under the circumstances (the "Notice of Class Determination"). The Notice of Class Determination shall be given to all members who can be identified through reasonable effort.

(b)   The Notice of Class Determination must concisely and clearly state in plain, easily understood language:

(1)   the nature of the action;

(2)   the definition of the class certified;

(3)   the class claims, issues, or defenses;

(4)   that a class member may enter an appearance through counsel if the member so desires, and that any class member may attend the hearings;

(5)   that the arbitrator will exclude from the class any member who requests exclusion, stating when and how members may elect to be excluded;

(6)   the binding effect of a class judgment on class members;

(7)   the identity and biographical information about the arbitrator, the class representative(s) and class counsel that have been approved by the arbitrator to represent the class; and

(8)   how and to whom a class member may communicate about the class arbitration, including information about the AAA Class Arbitration Docket (see Rule 9).

NOTES

1.   How do the requirements of Supplementary Rule 4 compare to Federal Rule of Civil Procedure 23? Consider not just the language of each set of rules, but also the application of Federal Rule of Civil Procedure 23 in *In re American Medical Supplies.*

2.   Why do the Supplementary Rules require a separate Class Determination Award? What significance do you assign to the requirement that it be "reasoned"?

3.   Would it not be easier to defend decisions if there were no reasons stated? Does *Stolt-Nielsen* change your opinion on this point?

PART II

Professional Responsibility in Arbitration Proceedings

Arbitration poses particular professional challenges for attorneys appearing as counsel. The two chapters below outline two particular sets of problems facing counsel in arbitrations that may not otherwise arise in the context of litigation.

The first challenge for transactional attorneys in particular concerns the confidentiality of arbitration proceedings. The private nature of arbitration is one of the benefits of arbitration. Some transactional counsel may assume that this privacy entails a certain amount of confidentiality and advise their clients to enter into arbitration provisions on this basis. As the first chapter below outlines, such advice may be inaccurate. Counsel advising clients competently on the consequences of entering into an arbitration clause should therefore be aware of these problems.

Similarly, arbitration counsel should be careful, as well. A client may well be willing to be more forthcoming in an arbitration if it believes that the proceedings are confidential. They may be willing to submit sensitive materials as part of its affirmative case in the belief that no third parties would be able to gain access to these materials. As outlined below, this, too, is inaccurate. For instance, if the parties insist upon a reasoned award in their arbitration clause, an arbitrator might well summarize or quote the sensitive information at issue. The award then might surface during the attempts by the winning party to enforce it. The sensitive materials might then, too, turn up in public and be viewable by third parties. Chapter 7 will outline how to advise clients appropriately with regard to their confidentiality concerns.

Chapter 8 then addresses the problem of counsel conduct in arbitration. Most counsel are naturally respectful of judges. After all, if counsel fail to act professionally and ethically in a litigation, judges have significant contempt powers at their disposal to hold them accountable. Arbitrators do not have such contempt powers at their disposal. This means that there is a significant temptation to act with greater professional "freedom" in the arbitration setting.

Chapter 8 outlines the differences between litigation and arbitration in this respect. It also starts to outline the tools available to parties and arbitrators to rectify this apparent gap in the tribunal's powers. Effective advocacy in the arbitration setting require a careful understanding of these background conditions against which arbitrations take place to address the occasional professional shortcoming of participants in the arbitral process—and explain the consequences of potential (in)actions to one's own client.

CHAPTER 7

Confidentiality

Confidentiality is a uniquely important concern in arbitration. One or all parties to an arbitration agreement frequently do not wish to air their dispute in public and hope that arbitration will help them achieve this goal.

Although most parties to a proceeding would agree in the abstract that confidentiality is a virtue of the arbitral process, there is no consensus on what comprises confidentiality in arbitration. Thus, most users of arbitration would prefer that sensitive information submitted as part of the arbitration process not be used for any other purpose. But many commercial users of arbitration may have a statutory requirement to disclose the fact of the arbitration as part of their financial disclosures (after all, there is a risk they might lose or fail to recover a significant sum due to the arbitration). Further, most winners in arbitration would like to notify the world of the vindication of their rights—especially when the result is not consistent with the expectations set by reporting about the dispute before arbitration commenced. As discussed below, all of these issues can pose problems if not appropriately considered at the front-end.

Worse still, there are many issues as to which confidentiality simply cannot be guaranteed in arbitration. Information that a party gathers in an arbitration can frequently be used in other contexts. That information is not confidential in the sense that it cannot be used by the parties short of a confidentiality or non-disclosure agreement. Further, third parties can gain access to arbitration materials by means of discovery in litigation. And the general public might gain access to arbitral awards when the winning party seeks to enforce the award. It is therefore paramount to inform clients about the level of protection they can expect in the arbitral process. This may inform how the case is ultimately pled— and what evidence is volunteered by the parties. To be a competent, professional attorney advising clients about arbitration, a lawyer must have an in-depth understanding as to how these confidentiality issues are resolved in practice.

Fact Scenario

You represent Tesla Kitchens Corp. (*"Tesla"*), a company that manufactures induction cooktops for General Dynamics, Inc. (*"GDI"*) appliances. GDI used technology similar to the technology developed by your client in its new line of Gordon Remsay Pro Chef appliances. Tesla and GDI agree to arbitrate their disputes. The arbitration clause contained the following confidentiality provision:

> *"Except as may be required by law, neither a party nor its representatives may disclose materials relating to patent and other intellectual property rights generated in the context of, or submitted in, any arbitration hereunder without the prior written consent of (all/ both) parties."*

Your client instituted an AAA arbitration against GDI pursuant to the AAA Commercial Rules alleging patent infringement, breach of the cooktop supply agreement, and various violations of statutes. Your client succeeded on the breach of contract counts. All other counts were dismissed. The parties received a reasoned award that goes into great length about Tesla's business and operational model as part of the discussion of the breach of contract claim. The award dismisses all claims other than the breach of contract claim summarily, without any in-depth discussion of those claims.

Tesla's demands for payment of the award have gone unanswered. Tesla has tasked you with seeking to enforce the award and collect against GDI assets in San Francisco. Your client does not wish for the award to become part of the public record due to the sensitive discussion of its business and operation model. How do you maximize your chances of successfully filing an action for enforcement of the award under seal in the United States District Court for the Northern District of California?

Readings

A) Arbitration Confidentiality in US Court Decisions

In considering the extent to which confidentiality should be applied to an arbitral proceeding, the first question is whether U.S. court decisions recognize blanket confidentiality of arbitration proceedings. This issue can arise, for example, when courts (1) imply a confidentiality agreement between the parties if the arbitration clause is silent on the issue of confidentiality, (2) find an arbitration privilege if arbitration materials are requested by third parties in discovery; or (3) consider whether documents submitted in court proceedings relating to an arbitration can be filed under seal.

1) *Implied Confidentiality?*

A.T. v. State Farm Mutual Auto Insurance Co.

989 P.2d 219 (Colo. Ct. App. 1999)

Opinion by JUDGE NEY.

Plaintiff, A.T., appeals the summary judgment entered in favor of defendant, State Farm Automobile Insurance Company, and the court's denial of her motion to amend her complaint. We affirm.

Plaintiff, a self-employed chiropractor, sustained injuries in an auto accident. She filed three separate actions against State Farm, her insurer. Plaintiff's claim for uninsured motorist benefits was submitted to arbitration and an award was entered in her favor. The other two suits involved claims for personal injury protection and they were dismissed.

In the course of pursuing her claims, plaintiff provided medical records regarding her mental and psychological history and treatment. These records disclosed that plaintiff had been diagnosed with a psychological disorder.

Thereafter, plaintiff testified as an expert medical witness in litigation between one of her chiropractic patients and State Farm. State Farm's attorney cross-examined plaintiff, during her voir dire examination, about her psychological history and treatment, including the psychological disorder diagnosis.

Plaintiff asserted that the use of her medical history by State Farm was not authorized and brought this action against State Farm based on disclosure of confidential information. Her amended complaint includes five causes of action: extreme and outrageous conduct, intentional interference with a contractual relationship, bad faith breach of contract, breach of fiduciary duty, negligence, and breach of a confidential relationship.

Plaintiff then moved to amend her complaint to include the claim of invasion of privacy. State Farm moved for summary judgment and plaintiff filed a cross-motion for summary judgment. After a hearing on these motions, the trial court granted summary judgment in favor of State Farm, and denied plaintiff's motion to amend her complaint.

I.

The threshold issue is whether the trial court erred, as a matter of law, by determining that plaintiff's medical information disclosed during the uninsured motorist benefits arbitration was not confidential. Plaintiff argues that the arbitration proceeding was private and that the disclosed information is confidential. We disagree.

Because the facts of the case are undisputed and the court disposed of defendant's other arguments, the determinative legal issue for the trial court was whether the information disclosed in the arbitration proceeding was confidential.

The court found that the parties had not entered into a confidentiality agreement or disclosure-restriction provision regarding the arbitration. No protective order was sought by plaintiff or obtained from the arbitrators or the court. The court found that this arbitration was not conducted under the rules of the American Arbitration Association, which would have provided confidentiality, but rather, under the Uniform Arbitration Act of 1975, § 13–22–201, et seq., C.R.S.1998, which is silent on confidentiality.

The court concluded that because the arbitration statute provides that an arbitration award can be filed, enforced, and challenged in court, an arbitration record may become an open public record. Therefore, because the plaintiff did not obtain a confidentiality or protective order or agreement, the record was available for use by State Farm in later, separate litigation.

Because the trial court's factual findings are undisputed and we agree with its conclusions of law, we conclude that the summary judgment was proper. *See Walcott v. Total Petroleum, Inc.*, 964 P.2d 609 (Colo.App.1998).

There is a presumption that the public has access to court records. *Anderson v. Home Insurance Co.*, 924 P.2d 1123 (Colo.App.1996).

Because an arbitration record is potentially public in nature and plaintiff failed proactively to preserve it as confidential, we agree with the trial court's conclusion that the plaintiff's medical information disclosed in the arbitration proceeding was not confidential.

We also agree with the trial court's qualification that its conclusion does not render the entire arbitration akin to a public record available to anyone for any purpose. We hold only that the arbitration record, under the facts here, was available to defendant to use in another unrelated case in which plaintiff was involved.

Accordingly, because all of the plaintiff's claims in her first amended complaint essentially depend on the disclosed information being confidential, the trial court was correct in concluding that all such claims fail.

II.

Plaintiff also contends that the trial court committed reversible error by denying her motion to amend her complaint to include the claim of invasion of privacy. Again, we disagree.

The plaintiff's claim of invasion of privacy relies on *Robert C. Ozer, P.C. v. Borquez*, 940 P.2d 371 (Colo.1997), which concluded that invasion of privacy based on the unreasonable publication of one's private life is a cognizable tort. However, an element of that tort is that the published information is private. See *Ozer v. Borquez*, supra.

The trial court concluded, on undisputed evidence, that the information was disclosed in an arbitration that was not made private or confidential. Therefore, the plaintiff waived, at least as to State Farm's use, the confidentiality that might otherwise attach to that information. The trial court therefore concluded that the claim of invasion of privacy would necessarily fail.

We agree with the trial court's conclusion that because the disclosed information was no longer private, plaintiff's claim of invasion of privacy would fail. Thus, the court's refusal to permit amendment of the complaint to include such claim was not erroneous.

The judgment and order are affirmed.

NOTES

Facts

1. Who sought to introduce information discovered in the arbitration in later proceedings? How did that party learn of the existence of the arbitration (and thus knew of the potential to use that information)? How did that party come into possession of the materials at issue?

2. What was the information at issue in this case? How was it relevant to the arbitration? How was it relevant to the litigation?

3. Was there any confidentiality agreement between the parties?

Law

1. Would there have been an argument to exclude the material at issue from the arbitration? Is the psychological disorder included in the medical history relevant to the claim? Is its disclosure prejudicial? Is there a privilege which might have been invoked with regard to the disorder in question?

What do you think would have been the result in the arbitration had A.T. redacted the disorder and refused to produce it?

2. If you represent a client in a similar situation, what would you ask the arbitrator for as an alternative to excluding the evidence in question? In framing your request, consider whether the arbitrator has the authority to issue you relief you request. Consult the Commercial Arbitration Rules of the AAA for guidance.

3. To avoid the potential of information discovered or learned during an arbitration to be used outside of an arbitration, many parties will include express confidentiality agreements in their arbitration clauses. There are many problems with this approach. For one, consider that your client may have an obligation to make certain disclosures about the arbitration itself. Perhaps even more importantly, what remedy is there to prevent the disclosure of information learned in the arbitration? How effective do you think that remedy is? You will encounter this issue again in section C below.

2) *Third-Party Discovery of Arbitration Materials*

The case in this section addresses the ability of non-parties to an arbitration to discover material submitted in the arbitration or the result of the arbitration. In response, parties will argue that arbitration is by its very nature a confidential process and as such should be covered by the privileges that ordinarily attach to other forms of alternative dispute resolution, such as mediation.

This argument has so far not fared successfully in U.S. court proceedings (although some foreign jurisdictions have taken a different approach). The lack of such confidentiality protections means that your client can rely only upon evidentiary privileges that might otherwise protect the underlying information.

Of course, the reverse is also true: it is not necessarily the case that submission of materials in an arbitration means that they thereby become public or lose all confidentiality protections. A party to a litigation could well have framed discovery requests for the information at issue in other ways. As you read the case, ask yourself what the difficulty would have been in formulating such discovery requests.

Kimberly-Clark Worldwide, Inc. v. First Quality Baby Products LLC

447 Fed.Appx. 217 (Fed. Cir. 2011)

Lourie, Circuit Judge.

Kimberly-Clark Worldwide, Inc. ("K-C") appeals from the district court's orders compelling discovery relating to three alternative dispute resolution agreements and the proceedings that occurred pursuant to those agreements. In this appeal, K-C challenges the district court's holding that the sought information is not privileged. Because the district court did not abuse its discretion in finding that K-C had failed to show that a privilege shielded the requested information from discovery, we affirm.

Background

I.

This patent case relates to disposable absorbent products, such as diapers. K-C competes in that market with First Quality Baby Products, LLC; First Quality Products, Inc.; First Quality Retail Services LLC; and First Quality Hygienic, Inc. (collectively, "First Quality"). The issue in this appeal, however, does not relate to the underlying technology, but the discoverability of information relating to three alternative dispute resolution proceedings between K-C and Proctor & Gamble ("P&G") that involved patents at issue in this case.

Prior to filing suit against First Quality, K-C was involved in patent infringement disputes with a number of companies, including P&G. Initially, the parties filed patent infringement claims in federal court. Subsequently, between 1994 and 2003, K-C and P&G entered into a series of agreements that constructed a dispute resolution process to help resolve the parties' disputes.

Three of these agreements, each entitled Dispute Resolution Agreement, are at issue here, and each agreement contains similar terms relevant to this appeal.[1] First, the Dispute Resolution Agreements provided a dispute resolution framework. Under the Agreements, a panel of arbitrators would issue a "clear and concise decision." However, the decision would be non-binding and each party retained the right to seek *de novo* judicial resolution. The decision would

---

[1]   The parties had marked the Dispute Resolution Agreements as Confidential. At oral argument, however, the parties agreed to waive the confidentiality restriction to allow the court to discuss the Agreements' terms in an opinion. Oral Arg. at 0:11–1:20, available at http://oralarguments.cafc. uscourts.gov/default.aspx?fl=2011–1157.mp3. We discuss the terms of the Agreements only to the extent necessary to resolve the parties' disputes.

issue after the parties presented their cases at a hearing. Generally, the proceedings would be governed by federal law on procedure, burdens of proof, and substantive patent issues. At all times, the parties were prohibited from communicating *ex parte* with the arbitrators.

Second, the Dispute Resolution Agreements detailed pre-hearing, hearing, and post-hearing procedures. The Agreements provided for limited discovery, including document requests, depositions, and exchanges of claim charts and other disclosures. The Agreements appointed an arbitrator to resolve discovery disputes, and the parties were prohibited from communicating *ex parte* with the arbitrator. The Agreements also allowed the parties to file briefs. At the hearing, the parties would present argument and testimony, and submit other forms of evidence. The panel would then issue a decision. The Agreements required the initial panel decision to contain specific findings of fact and conclusions of law in compliance with the Federal Rules of Civil Procedure. After the issuance of the decision, the losing party could appeal to a second panel of arbitrators who would review the decision.

Third, the Agreements contained fee-shifting provisions. The party that did not prevail at the hearing was responsible for paying the arbitrators' fees for the proceeding. In addition, if a party's appeal from the initial decision was not justified, the losing party was responsible for the opposing party's attorney fees.

Finally, two of the Agreements contained a stipulation that allowed P&G to limit its liability if it did not prevail before the first panel of arbitrators or on appeal. The provision provided that if P&G ceased making, using, or selling infringing products in the United States within six months of the original decision, K-C would not file suit against P&G and would not seek past damages.

It appears that K-C and P&G conducted proceedings under the Agreements. Eventually, K-C and P&G settled their disputes.

II.

In 2009, K-C sued First Quality, alleging that First Quality infringed a number of patents, including patents that had been at issue in the proceedings conducted under the Dispute Resolution Agreements. After becoming aware of the Agreements, First Quality moved to compel production of discovery relating to the Agreements and the underlying proceedings. K-C opposed production on the basis that the materials were privileged and not discoverable.

The district court granted First Quality's motion. The district court concluded that "mediation is not an adversarial process," but instead is "a procedure by which parties reach a mutual agreement with the aid of a third-party who assists in fostering communication between the parties, and does not act as a decision-maker." Order at 3. Applying that definition, the court concluded that the Agreements created an arbitration proceeding, not a mediation. Id. at 3–4. While the court concluded that a federal mediation privilege was warranted, it concluded that the proceedings structured by the Dispute Resolution Agreements fell outside that privilege. Id. at 4.

K-C moved for reconsideration, and the district court denied K-C's motion. Rather than conclude that the Dispute Resolution Agreements created a mediative process, the court concluded that the Agreements created a "quasi-judicial procedure" by which the parties "obtained a decision from a panel of neutral arbitrators." Order on Reconsideration at 2. The district court specifically focused on the adversarial nature of the proceedings structured in the Agreements—prohibiting ex parte communications with the arbitrators; providing for formal pretrial disclosures, discovery, and hearings; requiring the decision to comply with the Federal Rules of Civil Procedure; providing for an appeals process; and including fee-shifting provisions. Id.

Discussion

Under Federal Rule of Civil Procedure 26(b)(1), a party may obtain discovery regarding "any nonprivileged matter that is relevant to any party's claim or defense." K-C does not question that First Quality has requested relevant information. Rather, K-C argues that information created under the Dispute Resolution Agreements is privileged. K-C presents a two-step argument. First, K-C argues that federal courts should recognize a mediation privilege under the authority provided by Federal Rule of Evidence 501. Second, K-C argues that the proceedings under the Agreements were mediations. Thus, concludes K-C, the district court erred in compelling production of information that is covered by a federal mediation privilege.

We disagree. The Dispute Resolution Agreements set up an arbitration proceeding, not mediation. The Agreements set up an adversarial proceeding in which a panel specifically denoted as "arbitrators" issued formal findings of fact and conclusions of law. As part of the proceeding, the parties would serve briefs and claim charts and undertake discovery, including depositions. The parties then, at a formal hearing, would present argument, documentary evidence, and testimony, including testimony on cross-examination. At all times, ex parte communication with the arbitrators was prohibited. The arbitrators were to render a "clear and concise decision." Thus, the process under the Agreements generally resembled an adversarial proceeding in court, not mediation.

Despite the adversarial nature of the arbitration proceedings delineated in the Agreements, K-C argues that the proceedings were mediative because the decisions issued by the arbitrators were "non-binding" and had the purpose of facilitating settlement. That argument is unpersuasive. As an initial matter, under the Agreements, the decisions would affect the parties' legal rights. The parties stipulated that P&G would avoid liability for past damages if it ceased infringing activities within six months of the issuance of an adverse decision. In addition, an arbitration panel's decision would trigger fee-shifting provisions.

In any event, arbitration does not necessarily become a mediative process simply because an arbitration panel's decision is "non-binding." In addition, under the Dispute Resolution Agreements, there was no framework to allow a party and a neutral to openly and freely discuss a party's case. In fact, the Agreements discouraged a party from freely discussing the weak points in its case—the Agreements barred ex parte communications with the arbitrators and contain "loser pays" fee-shifting provisions. Thus, even if K-C has correctly characterized the decisions as "non-binding," that distinction is not sufficient in this case to rebrand the adversarial arbitration proceedings as mediations.

Finally, while the designation of the panel as "arbitrators" is not conclusive on the issue before us, the parties in the prior cases had the opportunity to choose the language of their agreement, and that language certainly carries some weight as it applies to K-C here.

Because we conclude that K-C failed to show that the district court abused its discretion in concluding that the Dispute Resolution Agreements did not provide for mediation, we decline to determine if, in light of reason and experience, we should recognize a mediation privilege.

Conclusion

We have considered K-C's remaining arguments and conclude that they are without merit. For the foregoing reasons, the order of the district court is

AFFIRMED.

NOTES

Facts

1.   What is the case about? Why does First Quality Baby Products want access to information from the arbitration proceedings?

2.   Assume that there had not been a dispute resolution process. How would First Quality Baby Products likely have sought the information in question?

3.   How sensitive do you think the information at issue is? What type of material do you expect will be produced?

Law

1.   The court treats the proceeding as an arbitration. Why? Do you agree?

2.   The court notes that the proceeding was not non-binding. Does it follow that the proceedings were binding in the typical sense of the word? Does it matter?

3.   Assume that one of the parties failed to perform as required by the dispute resolution clause after the arbitration was concluded, i.e., failed to abide by the "arbitral award" or equivalent decision. What would have been that party's remedy: Direct enforcement of an arbitral award or a breach of contract action? How would either outcome change your answer to question 2?

4.   If the process discussed in the case does not qualify for an evidentiary privilege, how do you think a typical AAA arbitration will fare? What arguments would you be left with in that context? How successful do you think they will be?

3)   *Filing for Enforcement of Arbitral Awards Under Seal*

If parties fail to settle their case as part of the arbitration process, the tribunal will eventually issue an award. In many instances, parties will either comply with the award or will reach settlement at this point to avoid a lengthy enforcement fight. In some instances, however, parties simply will not perform and not negotiate even in the face of an adverse award. In those circumstances, the party that prevailed in arbitration will need to seek recognition and enforcement of the award in domestic court.

The court proceedings themselves pose a confidentiality issue because documents filed with the court are typically publicly available (at least in the United States). In the federal courts, it is even possible to view filings remotely using web-based services such as Pacer. Thus, at the very least, the initial filing attaching the arbitral award may become public. Worse still, the arbitral award, which is likely attached to the initial pleading as an exhibit, may also become part of the public record. Searching for such public records is one of the best ways to undercut the confidentiality of arbitration.

Court filings are not always open to the public, however, as it is possible to file sensitive materials "under seal." The right to do so is set out, for instance, in the Federal Rules of Civil Procedure.

Federal Rules of Civil Procedure, Rule 5.2

(a) REDACTED FILINGS. Unless the court orders otherwise, in an electronic or paper filing with the court that contains an individual's social-security number, taxpayer-identification number, or birth date, the name of an individual known to be a minor, or a financial-account number, a party or nonparty making the filing may include only:

(1) the last four digits of the social-security number and taxpayer-identification number;

(2) the year of the individual's birth;

(3) the minor's initials; and

(4) the last four digits of the financial-account number.

(b) EXEMPTIONS FROM THE REDACTION REQUIREMENT. The redaction requirement does not apply to the following:

(1) a financial-account number that identifies the property allegedly subject to forfeiture in a forfeiture proceeding;

(2) the record of an administrative or agency proceeding;

(3) the official record of a state-court proceeding;

(4) the record of a court or tribunal, if that record was not subject to the redaction requirement when originally filed;

(5) a filing covered by Rule 5.2(c) or (d); and

(6) a pro se filing in an action brought under 28 U.S.C. §§ 2241, 2254, or 2255.

(d) FILINGS MADE UNDER SEAL. The court may order that a filing be made under seal without redaction. The court may later unseal the filing or order the person who made the filing to file a redacted version for the public record.

(e) PROTECTIVE ORDERS. For good cause, the court may by order in a case:

(1) require redaction of additional information; or

(2) limit or prohibit a nonparty's remote electronic access to a document filed with the court.

(f)   OPTION FOR ADDITIONAL UNREDACTED FILING UNDER SEAL. A person making a redacted filing may also file an unredacted copy under seal. The court must retain the unredacted copy as part of the record.

(g)   OPTION FOR FILING A REFERENCE LIST. A filing that contains redacted information may be filed together with a reference list that identifies each item of redacted information and specifies an appropriate identifier that uniquely corresponds to each item listed. The list must be filed under seal and may be amended as of right. Any reference in the case to a listed identifier will be construed to refer to the corresponding item of information.

(h)   WAIVER OF PROTECTION OF IDENTIFIERS. A person waives the protection of Rule 5.2(a) as to the person's own information by filing it without redaction and not under seal.

Notes

1.   Filing under seal is only one of the potential options available under Federal Rules of Civil Procedure Rule 5.2. What other options may be available? What is the showing they require?

2.   Does Rule 5.2 tell you how to file under seal? Do you have to initiate the action first and then move to seal, or can you initiate the action to confirm an arbitral award under seal from the beginning?

United States District Court for the Northern District of California, Local Civil Rule 79–5

79–5. Filing Documents Under Seal in Civil Cases

(a)   This Rule Applies to Electronic and Manually-Filed Sealed Documents. The procedures and requirements set forth in Civil L.R. 79–5 apply to both the e-filing of sealed documents submitted by registered e-filers in e-filing cases; and the manual filing of sealed documents submitted by non-e-filers and/or in non-e-filing cases. For the purposes of Civil L.R. 79–5, "file" means: (1) to electronically file ("e-file") a document that is submitted by a registered e-filer in a case that is subject to e-filing; or (2) to manually file a document when it is submitted by a party that is not permitted to e-file and/or in a case that is not subject to e-filing. See Civil L.R. 5–1(b) for an explanation of cases and parties subject to e-filing.

(b)   Specific Court Order Required. Except as provided in Civil L.R. 79–5(c), no document may be filed under seal (i.e., closed to inspection by the public) except pursuant to a court order that authorizes the sealing of the particular document, or portions thereof. A sealing order may issue only upon a request that establishes that the document, or portions thereof, are privileged, protectable as a trade secret or otherwise entitled to protection under the law (hereinafter referred to as "sealable"). The request must be narrowly tailored to seek sealing only of sealable material, and must conform with Civil L.R. 79–5(d).

(c) Documents that May Be Filed Under Seal Before Obtaining a Specific Court Order. Only the unredacted version of a document sought to be sealed, may be filed under seal before a sealing order is obtained, as permitted by Civil L.R. 79–5(c)(1)(D).

(d) Request to File Document, or Portions Thereof, Under Seal. A party seeking to file a document, or portions thereof, under seal ("the Submitting Party") must: (1) File an Administrative Motion to File Under Seal, in conformance with Civil L.R. 7–11. The administrative motion must be accompanied by the following attachments:

(A) A declaration establishing that the document sought to be filed under seal, or portions thereof, are sealable. Reference to a stipulation or protective order that allows a party to designate certain documents as confidential is not sufficient to establish that a document, or portions thereof, are sealable. The procedures detailed in Civil L.R. 79–5(e) apply to requests to seal in which the sole basis for sealing is that the document(s) at issue were previously designated as confidential or subject to a protective order.

(B) A proposed order that is narrowly tailored to seal only the sealable material, and which lists in table format each document or portion thereof that is sought to be sealed.

(C) A redacted version of the document that is sought to be filed under seal. The redacted version shall prominently display the notation "REDACTED VERSION OF DOCUMENT(S) SOUGHT TO BE SEALED." A redacted version need not be filed if the submitting party is seeking to file the entire document under seal.

(D) An unredacted version of the document sought to be filed under seal. The unredacted version must indicate, by highlighting or other clear method, the portions of the document that have been omitted from the redacted version, and prominently display the notation "UNREDACTED VERSION OF DOCUMENT(S) SOUGHT TO BE SEALED." The unredacted version may be filed under seal pursuant to Civil L.R. 79–5(c) before the sealing order is obtained. Instructions for e-filing documents under seal can be found on the ECF website.

(2) Provide a courtesy copy of the administrative motion, declaration, proposed order, and both the redacted and unredacted versions of all documents sought to be sealed, in accordance with Civil L.R. 5–1(e)(7).

The courtesy copy of unredacted declarations and exhibits should be presented in the same form as if no sealing order was being sought. In other words, if a party is seeking to file under seal one or more exhibits to a declaration, or portions thereof, the courtesy copy should include the declaration with all of the exhibits attached, including the exhibits, or portions thereof, sought to be filed under seal, with the portions to be sealed highlighted or clearly noted as subject to a sealing motion.

The courtesy copy should be an exact copy of what was filed, and for e-filed documents the ECF header should appear at the top of each page. The courtesy copy must be contained in a sealed envelope or other suitable container with a cover sheet affixed to the envelope or container, setting forth the information required by Civil L.R. 3–4(a) and prominently displaying the notation "COURTESY [or CHAMBERS] COPY—DOCUMENTS SUBMITTED UNDER SEAL."

The courtesy copies of sealed documents will be disposed of in accordance with the assigned judge's discretion. Ordinarily these copies will be recycled, not shredded, unless special arrangements are made.

(e) Documents Designated as Confidential or Subject to a Protective Order. If the Submitting Party is seeking to file under seal a document designated as confidential by the opposing party or a non-party pursuant to a protective order, or a document containing information so designated by an opposing party or a non-party, the Submitting Party's declaration in support of the Administrative Motion to File Under Seal must identify the document or portions thereof which contain the designated confidential material and identify the party that has designated the material as confidential ("the Designating Party"). The declaration must be served on the Designating Party on the same day it is filed and a proof of such service must also be filed. (1) Within 4 days of the filing of the Administrative Motion to File Under Seal, the Designating Party must file a declaration as required by subsection 79–5(d)(1)(A) establishing that all of the designated material is sealable.

(2) If the Designating Party does not file a responsive declaration as required by subsection 79–5(e)(1) and the Administrative Motion to File Under Seal is

denied, the Submitting Party may file the document in the public record no earlier than 4 days, and no later than 10 days, after the motion is denied. A Judge may delay the public docketing of the document upon a showing of good cause.

(g)   Effect of Seal. Unless otherwise ordered by the Court, any document filed under seal shall be kept from public inspection, including inspection by attorneys and parties to the action, during the pendency of the case. Any document filed under seal in a civil case shall, upon request, be open to public inspection without further action by the Court 10 years from the date the case is closed. However, a Submitting Party or a Designating Party may, upon showing good cause at the conclusion of a case, seek an order to extend the sealing to a specific date beyond the 10 years provided by this rule. Nothing in this rule is intended to affect the normal records disposition policy of the United States Courts.

NOTE

1.   How would you proceed if you sought to enforce an arbitral award under seal in the Northern District of California?

Reinsurance Corp.-U.S. Branch v. Argonaut Ins. Co.

Nos. 07 Civ. 8196(PKC), 07 Civ. 8350(PKC), 2008 WL 1805459
(S.D.N.Y. Apr. 21, 2008)

P. KEVIN CASTEL, DISTRICT JUDGE.

This is a further Order on the sealing of submissions on petitions to confirm arbitration awards in the above actions. This Court's initial Memorandum and Order required the parties to demonstrate why any filings on these petitions ought to remain under seal. *ABC v. DEF*, 07 Civ. 8196(PKC) and *ABC v. XYZ*, 07 Civ. 8350(PKC) (S.D.N.Y. Nov. 28, 2007) (citing *United States v. Amodeo*, 44 F.3d 141, 145 (2d Cir.1995) ("Amodeo I") and *Lugosch v. Pyramid Co. of Onondaga*, 435 F.3d 110, 119–120 (2d Cir.2006)).

In my Further Memorandum and Order on Sealed Submissions, dated January 4, 2008, I concluded that the arbitration awards were judicial documents to which the presumption of access attaches. "Arbitration remains a species of contract and, in the absence of some governing principle of law (e.g. in the regulatory requirements), parties are permitted to keep their private undertakings from the prying eyes of others. The circumstance changes when a party seeks to enforce in federal court the fruits of their private agreement to arbitrate, i.e. the arbitration award." (at p. 3.)

Acknowledging that it was a "close question" and that the Court reserved the right to revisit the issue, this Court concluded that balancing the competing considerations against the presumption of access favored the continued sealing of the arbitration awards. "[D]isclosure of the decretal portions of the awards does present the risk that it will impair GlobalRe's negotiating position with other reinsurers and that such interest outweigh the public's right of access." (at p. 4.)

Respondent Argonaut Insurance Company has moved this Court to reconsider its ruling and unseal the final arbitration awards. Today, I held a hearing at which I gave Global Reinsurance Corporation-US Branch ("GlobalRe") an opportunity to explain the manner in which the language of the arbitration awards might impair its relationships with retrocessionaires and others participants in the reinsurance industry. GlobalRe did not endeavor to argue that disclosure of any language in the awards would cause it direct or immediate harm. It relied upon its assessment of the danger of a slippery slope that might impair the exchange of information between parties to a reinsurance agreement because of the fear of eventual disclosure. Because such a fear is not justified as applied to the bare bones relief granted or denied in arbitration preceding, it does not provide an adequate basis to overcome the presumption of access.

The federal policy in favor of arbitration is promoted by permitting one of the principle advantages of arbitration-confidentiality-to be achieved. In the ordinary course, a petition to confirm or vacate an arbitration award ought not require a court to review all testimony and documentary evidence before the arbitration panel. "Normally, confirmation of an arbitration award is 'a summary proceeding that merely makes what is already a final arbitration award a judgment of the court," and the court "must grant" the award "unless the award is vacated, modified, or corrected." 9 U.S.C. § 9. The arbitrator's rationale for an award need not be explained, and the award should be confirmed 'if a ground for the arbitrator's decision can be inferred from the facts of the case,' " *D.H. Blair & Co., Inc. v. Gottdiener*, 462 F.3d 95, 110 (2d Cir.2006) (quoting *Florasynth, Inc. v. Pickholz*, 750 F.2d 171, 176 (2d Cir.1984) and *Barbier v. Shearson Lehman Hutton, Inc.*, 948 F.2d 117, 121 (2d Cir.1991)). The arbitration award is often a statement of the relief granted or denied without explanation of the arbitrators' reasoning process. Because it is at the heart of what the Court is asked to act upon, the parties must demonstrate why the presumption of access should be overcome. *Lugosch v. Pyramid Co. of Onondaga*, 435 F.3d at 119–120. Here, the party seeking to maintain confidentiality has failed to adequately do so.

A final judgment compelling actions under pain of the Court's contempt power is a form of injunction. It ought to place the parties and all readers on notice of that which is required or prohibited A final judgment which incorporates another document by reference, such as a sealed arbitration award, would run afoul of Rule 65(d)(1)(B) & (C), Fed.R.Civ.P., which requires that every injunction "state its terms specifically" and "describe in reasonable detail-and not by referring to the complaint or other document-the act or acts restrained or required." In circumstances where an arbitration award is confirmed, the public in the usual case has a right to know what the Court has done.

On this record, the motion to reconsider (Docket # 28) is granted and the arbitration awards (Miletic Decl., 07 Civ. 8196(PKC) at Ex. H; Miletic Decl., 07 Civ. 8350(PKC) at Ex. J & K) are ordered unsealed.

SO ORDERED.

NOTES

Facts

1.	Why do you think Argonaut sought to unseal the arbitral award?

Law

1.	Discussing the case, one commentator noted that the greater the amount of detail in a decision, and thus the greater the need for filing an award under seal, the higher the likelihood that an application to file under seal a motion for enforcement of an arbitral award will be rejected. *See* Laura A. Kaster, *Confidentiality in U.S. Arbitration,* 5(1) N.Y. Disp. Resol. L. 22 (2012). Do you agree with that reading? If not, what standard should courts apply?

## B)	Confidentiality Under AAA Arbitration Rules

In the absence of a confidentiality agreement, parties may rely upon the arbitration rules, incorporated by reference into their contractual agreements, to provide some additional confidentiality protections. We will discuss in the context of confidentiality provisions more generally whether such confidentiality provisions are effective against third parties seeking discovery of arbitration materials. For current purposes, consider whether such an incorporation by reference would make a difference in the *State Farm* and *Argonaut* cases.

AAA Employment Arbitration Rules (effective Nov. 1, 2009)

23.   Confidentiality

The arbitrator shall maintain the confidentiality of the arbitration and shall have the authority to make appropriate rulings to safeguard that confidentiality, unless the parties agree otherwise or the law provides to the contrary.

AAA International Arbitration Rules (effective June 1, 2009)

Article 34

Confidential information disclosed during the proceedings by the parties or by witnesses shall not be divulged by an arbitrator or by the administrator. Except as provided in Article 27, unless otherwise agreed by the parties, or required by applicable law, the members of the tribunal and the administrator shall keep confidential all matters relating to the arbitration or the award.

AAA Commercial Arbitration Rules (effective Oct. 17, 2013)

R–23.   Enforcement Powers of the Arbitrator

The arbitrator shall have the authority to issue any orders necessary to enforce the provisions of rules R–21 and R–22 and to otherwise achieve a fair, efficient and economical resolution of the case, including, without limitation:

(a)   conditioning any exchange or production of confidential documents and information, and the admission of confidential evidence at the hearing, on appropriate orders to preserve such confidentiality;

(b)   imposing reasonable search parameters for electronic and other documents if the parties are unable to agree;

(c)   allocating costs of producing documentation, including electronically stored documentation;

(d)   in the case of willful non-compliance with any order issued by the arbitrator, drawing adverse inferences, excluding evidence and other submissions, and/or making special allocations of costs or an interim award of costs arising from such non-compliance; and

(e)   issuing any other enforcement orders which the arbitrator is empowered to issue under applicable law.

R–51.   Release of Documents for Judicial Proceedings

The AAA shall, upon the written request of a party to the arbitration, furnish to the party, at its expense, copies or certified copies of any papers in the AAA's possession that are not determined by the AAA to be privileged or confidential.

London Court of International Arbitration Rules

Article 30 Confidentiality

30.1   Unless the parties expressly agree in writing to the contrary, the parties undertake as a general principle to keep confidential all awards in their arbitration, together with all materials in the proceedings created for the purpose of the arbitration and all other documents produced by another party in the proceedings not otherwise in the public domain—save and to the extent that disclosure may be required of a party by legal duty, to protect or pursue a legal right or to enforce or challenge an award in bona fide legal proceedings before a state court or other judicial authority.

30.2   The deliberations of the Arbitral Tribunal are likewise confidential to its members, save and to the extent that disclosure of an arbitrator's refusal to participate in the arbitration is required of the other members of the Arbitral Tribunal under Articles 10, 12 and 26.

30.3   The LCIA Court does not publish any award or any part

C) The Limited Reach of Confidentiality Agreements

In light of the case law and arbitration rules surveyed so far, it is advisable to discuss with your client whether to insist on a confidentiality agreement as part of the arbitration clause. There is no one-size-fits-all approach, as the confidentiality agreement will have to take into account relevant reporting obligations, as well as the commercial interests of the parties.

The AAA's International Centre for Dispute Resolution provides the following relevant guidance for the drafting of confidentiality clauses. The guidance is greatly relevant even outside of the context of international disputes:

CONFIDENTIALITY CLAUSE

The type of contract may also call for additional language. So, for example, parties to an exclusive information contract or sensitive technology contract may wish to consider a confidentiality provision in their agreement. Parties to international contracts frequently mistake privacy, which is a standard feature of international commercial arbitration, for the obligation to maintain confidentiality, which absent party agreement under the ICDR International Arbitration Rules will extend only to the arbitrator and the ICDR. Parties should also be aware of the limits of party agreement to confidentiality as regards non-signatories to the agreement such as witnesses and the requirements of law otherwise.

The ICDR Model Confidentiality Clause is as follows:

"Except as may be required by law, neither a party nor its representatives may disclose the existence, content, or results of any arbitration hereunder without the prior written consent of (all/ both) parties."

International Centre for Dispute Resolution, Guide to Drafting International Dispute Resolution Clauses.

This model clause provides a good starting point for confidentiality clauses. Notice, however, that disclosure of the existence of an arbitration proceeding itself is prohibited except as required by law. For some clients, this may be too high of a confidentiality bar from a public relations point of view.

Even with the strong model language, the reach of the language will be limited with regard to non-parties. Consider the following case in which a non-party to an arbitration seeks discovery of arbitration materials.

Gotham Holdings, LP v. Health Grades, Inc.

580 F.3d 664 (7th Cir. 2009)

EASTERBROOK, CHIEF JUDGE.

Gotham Holdings is a plaintiff, and Health Grades a plaintiff, and Health Grades a defendant, in litigation pending in the Southern District of New York. (Although there are multiple plaintiffs, we use one name to denote all.) Health Grades contends in the New York case that an arbitration award supports its view of the merits. It tendered the award and some of the documents exchanged in the arbitration. When Gotham Holdings asked to see related documents, Health Grades balked, observing that the parties to the arbitration (Health Grades and Hewitt Associates, LLC) had pledged confidentiality. Gotham Holdings rejoined that, by relying on the award, Health Grades had waived confidentiality. When Health Grades refused to budge from its position,

Gotham Holdings served a subpoena on Hewitt Associates and moved to enforce it in the Northern District of Illinois, where Hewitt Associates' principal offices are located. See Fed.R.Civ.P. 34(c), 45.

No one contends that the subpoena exceeds the bounds set by Fed.R.Civ.P. 26(b)(1), and the district court directed Hewitt Associates to produce the documents. Hewitt Associates is willing to hand them over. But the district court issued a stay pending Health Grades' appeal. Because the discovery deadline in the New York suit is approaching, and the documents covered by the subpoena may lead to additional discovery requests in New York, we granted Gotham Holdings' request to expedite the appeal. It has been submitted on the briefs to the motions panel that granted the request for expedited consideration.

We affirm the district court's decision, for two reasons. First, ¶ 6 of the agreement between Health Grades and Hewitt Associates provides that materials from the arbitration may be disclosed in response to a subpoena. Second, even if the agreement had purported to block disclosure, such a provision would be ineffectual. Contracts bind only the parties. No one can "agree" with someone else that a stranger's resort to discovery under the Federal Rules of Civil Procedure will be cut off. We applied this principle in *Jepson, Inc. v. Makita Electric Works, Ltd.*, 30 F.3d 854 (7th Cir.1994), to confidentiality agreements reached during litigation. That conclusion is equally applicable to confidentiality agreements that accompany arbitration. Indeed, we have stated more broadly that a person's desire for confidentiality is not honored in litigation. Trade secrets, privileges, and statutes or rules requiring confidentiality must be respected, see Fed.R.Civ.P. 45(c)(3)(A)(iii), but litigants' preference for secrecy does not create a legal bar to disclosure.

Health Grades and Hewitt Associates were entitled to agree that they would not voluntarily disclose any information related to the arbitration. See *ITT Educational Services, Inc. v. Arce*, 533 F.3d 342, 347–48 (5th Cir.2008). Disclosure would be authorized only when a third party had a legal right of access. That's what ¶ 6 of this agreement does: The parties promised to keep their mouths (and files) shut unless a subpoena required a turnover. Gotham Holdings is entitled to compulsory process to acquire documents from third parties. Health Grades does not argue that any privilege protects this material. The Supreme Court has expressed reluctance to create new privileges, see *University of Pennsylvania v. EEOC*, 493 U.S. 182, 110 S.Ct. 577, 107 L.Ed.2d 571 (1990) (declining to create an "academic deliberations privilege"), and Health Grades does not attempt to show that an "arbitration privilege" would be appropriate under the Court's standards.

According to Health Grades, access to the information would undermine the national policy favoring arbitration. There is no such policy. Arbitration agreements are optional and enforced just like other contracts. 9 U.S.C. § 2. The Federal Arbitration Act eliminates hostility to private dispute resolution; it does not create a preference for that process. "There is no federal policy favoring arbitration under a certain set of procedural rules; the federal policy is simply to ensure the enforceability, according to their terms, of private agreements to arbitrate." *Volt Information Sciences, Inc. v. Stanford University*, 489 U.S. 468, 476, 109 S.Ct. 1248, 103 L.Ed.2d 488 (1989). People do not "violate" or "undermine" any federal policy if they litigate rather than arbitrate. Federal policy favors arbitration only in the sense that it favors contracts in general.

The Federal Arbitration Act does not promote arbitration at the expense of strangers. Suppose Health Grades and Hewitt Associates had agreed between themselves that Gotham Holdings would pay the arbitrators' fees. That would make arbitration more attractive, but no one would think the agreement enforceable; third parties' rights may be affected only with their consent. Just so here. Gotham Holdings has an entitlement to material information in the hands of Hewitt Associates. Nothing that Health Grades and Hewitt Associates can do or say, separately or collectively, can affect that legal right. We concluded in *Teamsters Negotiating Committee v. Troha*, 328 F.3d 325 (7th Cir.2003), that parties to a labor arbitration may use subpoenas to obtain information from third parties. It would be weird to treat this as a one-way street, so that parties to arbitration may obtain, but need not divulge, information relevant to the resolution of other disputes.

Hewitt Associates does not contend that the subpoena is unduly burdensome. No one contends that a recognized privilege applies to these documents. So the subpoena was properly enforced. The stay is lifted, and the judgment is affirmed. The mandate will issue today.

CHAPTER 8

Sanctions

Kristin Blankley's 2012 article surveying the field of arbitration ethics characterized arbitration as the "Wild West" in terms of the ethics on display by parties and counsel.[1] The article noted, correctly, that this "Wild West" increasingly is policed by tribunals that are willing to use their powers to sanction parties in the arbitration and by outside regulators that are willing to take a closer look at the conduct of counsel.[2] The same comment has also been made—and studied in detail—in the international arbitration context.[3]

This chapter discusses the various ways in which both clients and their counsel misbehave in arbitral proceedings, and how this behavior has been addressed in practice, with very real consequences. The material is broken out into two sections: sanctions of the parties and sanctions of counsel. Consider that in actual practice, however, the same underlying conduct is likely to give rise to sanctions for both the parties and their counsel.

Fact Scenario

Perigord Corp. (*"Perigord"*) and Catalan Inc. (*"Catalan"*) entered into a merger agreement. The agreement would have created the largest computing company in the world. Perigord structured the merger through a share purchase, purchasing 75% of shares in Catalan from its dominant shareholder L. Metti. A month prior to the shareholder holder meeting of Catalan at which the merger was to be ratified by the shareholders, Perigord was investigated by the French authorities for large scale tax fraud. At the shareholder meeting, the proxies voted by Perigord were not counted. A new board of directors was elected— each director handpicked by Metti. The new board declared the share transfer to be in violation of the company bylaws and cancelled the shares at issue, reissuing them to Metti-owned companies.

The merger agreement contained an arbitration clause. The clause called for AAA arbitration pursuant to the commercial arbitration rules. After a

---

[1]   Kristen Blankley, *Taming the Wild West of Arbitration Ethics*, 60 KAN. L. REV. 925 (2012).

[2]   *Id.*

[3]   CATHERINE A. ROGERS, ETHICS IN INTERNATIONAL ARBITRATION (2014).

|209|

tribunal was constituted, Perigord requested in discovery that Catalan produce the agreements pursuant to which Catalan reissued the shares at issue in the dispute. Its stated reason for seeking the documents was to prove that there was collusion between the company and the would-be shareholders in ousting Perigord. Counsel for Catalan admitted to the existence of these documents, but submitted a sworn affidavit from the company's CEO that the documents were sensitive and would not be produced as part of the arbitration process under any circumstances. After much back and forth with the tribunal, counsel for Catalan provided an excerpted version of the key document, which contained the price provision of the agreement. This price provision showed that the new shareholders agreed to pay in excess of the price paid by Perigord for the same shares. This evidence, Catalan's counsel submitted, should put to rest the argument that there was any collusion.

Perigord suspects that the purchase price was to be financed by Catalan itself in a different part of the contract that had not been produced—or that there was some other evidence of collusion (why else hide the document in its entirety?). Perigord instructs you to be as aggressive as possible in light of what it viewed to be unethical and sanctionable conduct by Catalan and its counsel. How do you proceed and why?

Readings

A) Sanctions of Parties in Litigation

To understand how sanctions of parties to an arbitration proceeding work, it is important to recall the power of courts to order sanctions against the parties. A key provision available in federal court is Rule 11 of the Federal Rules of Civil Procedure.

Federal Rules of Civil Procedure, Rule 11

(a)   Signature. Every pleading, written motion, and other paper must be signed by at least one attorney of record in the attorney's name—or by a party personally if the party is unrepresented. The paper must state the signer's address, e-mail address, and telephone number. Unless a rule or statute specifically states otherwise, a pleading need not be verified or accompanied by an affidavit. The court must strike an unsigned paper unless the omission is promptly corrected after being called to the attorney's or party's attention.

(b)   Representations to the Court. By presenting to the court a pleading, written motion, or other paper—whether by signing, filing, submitting, or later advocating it—an attorney or unrepresented party certifies that to the best of the person's knowledge, information, and belief, formed after an inquiry reasonable under the circumstances:

(1)   it is not being presented for any improper purpose, such as to harass, cause unnecessary delay, or needlessly increase the cost of litigation;

(2)   the claims, defenses, and other legal contentions are warranted by existing law or by a nonfrivolous argument for extending, modifying, or reversing existing law or for establishing new law;

(3)   the factual contentions have evidentiary support or, if specifically so identified, will likely have evidentiary support after a reasonable opportunity for further investigation or discovery; and

(4)   the denials of factual contentions are warranted on the evidence or, if specifically so identified, are reasonably based on belief or a lack of information.

(c)   Sanctions.

(1)   In General. If, after notice and a reasonable opportunity to respond, the court determines that Rule 11(b) has been violated, the court may impose an appropriate sanction on any attorney, law firm, or party that violated the rule or is responsible for the violation. Absent exceptional circumstances, a law firm must be held jointly responsible for a violation committed by its partner, associate, or employee.

(2)   Motion for Sanctions. A motion for sanctions must be made separately from any other motion and must describe the specific conduct that allegedly violates Rule 11(b). The motion must be served under Rule 5, but it must not be filed or be presented to the court if the challenged paper, claim, defense, contention, or denial is withdrawn or appropriately corrected within 21 days after service or within another time the court sets. If warranted, the court may award to the prevailing party the reasonable expenses, including attorney's fees, incurred for the motion.

(3)   On the Court's Initiative. On its own, the court may order an attorney, law firm, or party to show cause why conduct specifically described in the order has not violated Rule 11(b).

(4)   Nature of a Sanction. A sanction imposed under this rule must be limited to what suffices to deter repetition of the conduct or comparable conduct by others similarly situated. The sanction may include nonmonetary directives; an order to pay a penalty into court; or, if imposed on motion and warranted for effective deterrence, an order directing payment to the movant of part or all of

the reasonable attorney's fees and other expenses directly resulting from the violation.

(5)   Limitations on Monetary Sanctions. The court must not impose a monetary sanction:

(A)   against a represented party for violating Rule 11(b)(2); or

(B)   on its own, unless it issued the show-cause order under Rule 11(c)(3) before voluntary dismissal or settlement of the claims made by or against the party that is, or whose attorneys are, to be sanctioned.

(6)   Requirements for an Order. An order imposing a sanction must describe the sanctioned conduct and explain the basis for the sanction.

(d)   Inapplicability to Discovery. This rule does not apply to disclosures and discovery requests, responses, objections, and motions under Rules 26 through 37.

B)   Sanction of Parties to Arbitration

In the arbitration context, however, there are no uniform rules governing arbitral proceedings. Further, even when there are rules permitting an arbitrator to impose sanctions, it is unclear whether arbitrators would be willing to issue such sanctions, except in extreme circumstances. The readings in this section set out typical arbitration rules, and then discuss how and when arbitrators may sanction parties in arbitral proceedings, either directory or indirectly (in the form of evidentiary findings or adverse inferences).

1)   *Arbitral Rules on Sanctions*

AAA Commercial Arbitration Rules

R–23.   Enforcement Powers of the Arbitrator

The arbitrator shall have the authority to issue any orders necessary to enforce the provisions of rules R–21 and R–22 and to otherwise achieve a fair, efficient and economical resolution of the case, including, without limitation:

(a)   conditioning any exchange or production of confidential documents and information, and the admission of confidential evidence at the hearing, on appropriate orders to preserve such confidentiality;

(b)   imposing reasonable search parameters for electronic and other documents if the parties are unable to agree;

(c)   allocating costs of producing documentation, including electronically stored documentation;

(d)   in the case of willful non-compliance with any order issued by the arbitrator, drawing adverse inferences, excluding evidence and other submissions, and/or making special allocations of costs or an interim award of costs arising from such non-compliance; and

(e)   issuing any other enforcement orders which the arbitrator is empowered to issue under applicable law.

* * *

R–47.   Scope of Award

(a)   The arbitrator may grant any remedy or relief that the arbitrator deems just and equitable and within the scope of the agreement of the parties, including, but not limited to, specific performance of a contract.

(b)   In addition to a final award, the arbitrator may make other decisions, including interim, interlocutory, or partial rulings, orders, and awards. In any interim, interlocutory, or partial award, the arbitrator may assess and apportion the fees, expenses, and compensation related to such award as the arbitrator determines is appropriate.

(c)   In the final award, the arbitrator shall assess the fees, expenses, and compensation provided in Sections R–53, R–54, and R–55. The arbitrator may apportion such fees, expenses, and compensation among the parties in such amounts as the arbitrator determines is appropriate.

(d)   The award of the arbitrator(s) may include:

i.   interest at such rate and from such date as the arbitrator(s) may deem appropriate; and

ii.   an award of attorneys' fees if all parties have requested such an award or it is authorized by law or their arbitration agreement.

* * *

R–53.   Administrative Fees

As a not-for-profit organization, the AAA shall prescribe administrative fees to compensate it for the cost of providing administrative services. The fees in effect when the fee or charge is incurred shall be applicable. The filing fee shall be advanced by the party or parties making a claim or counterclaim, subject to final apportionment by the arbitrator in the award. The AAA may, in the event of extreme hardship on the part of any party, defer or reduce the administrative fees.

R–54.   Expenses

The expenses of witnesses for either side shall be paid by the party producing such witnesses. All other expenses of the arbitration, including required travel and other expenses of the arbitrator, AAA representatives, and any witness and the cost of any proof produced at the direct request of the arbitrator, shall be borne equally by the parties, unless they agree otherwise or unless the arbitrator in the award assesses such expenses or any part thereof against any specified party or parties.

R–55.   Neutral Arbitrator's Compensation

(a)   Arbitrators shall be compensated at a rate consistent with the arbitrator's stated rate of compensation.

(b)   If there is disagreement concerning the terms of compensation, an appropriate rate shall be established with the arbitrator by the AAA and confirmed to the parties.

(c)   Any arrangement for the compensation of a neutral arbitrator shall be made through the AAA and not directly between the parties and the arbitrator.

NOTES

1.   What kind of "sanctions" is an arbitrator empowered to order under the rules? Against whom may an arbitrator do so—the parties or their counsel?

2.   What are the different bases upon which an arbitrator may impose such sanctions under the rules?

3.   What is the most effective tool at an arbitrator's disposal?

2) *Sanctions in Reported Arbitral Decisions*

This section outlines reported decisions describing two different ways in which arbitral tribunals have imposed sanctions against a party. The first, at issue in *Verve*, concerns the arbitrator's ability to draw adverse inferences. The second, at issue in *Morgan Stanley* and *ReliaStar*, concerns the outright imposition of sanctions.

As you read these decisions, consider what the procedural misconduct was and who was ultimately to blame for it. Would the party have a claim against the attorney in this context? What would an attorney have to do in order to avoid a malpractice suit or complaint to a professional ethics board?

Verve Communications Pvt. Ltd. v. Software International Inc.

No. 11–1280 (FLW), 2011 WL 5508636 (D.N.J. Nov. 9, 2011)

WOLFSON, DISTRICT JUDGE.

Plaintiff Verve Communications Pvt. Ltd. ("Verve") brought an action in the Chancery Division, Superior Court of New Jersey, Somerset County, to confirm an arbitration award against Defendant Software International, Inc.'s ("SII's"). SII removed the case to this Court and, by way of cross-motion, seeks to have that award vacated. Having reviewed the parties' submissions, the Court now denies SII's cross-motion to vacate and grants Verve's motion to confirm the arbitral award.

I.   BACKGROUND AND PROCEDURAL HISTORY

The following facts are undisputed for purposes of this motion. On April 1, 2009, Verve, a corporation organized under the laws of India, and located in Pune, India, entered into a Client Vendor Service Contract ("Agreement") with SII, a corporation with its principal place of business in New Jersey. The Agreement includes an arbitration clause, which provides:

> All disputes, controversies or claims between the Parties hereto arising out of or relating to this Agreement (including, but not limited to, disputes as to the validity, interpretation, performance, breach, or with respect to damages upon termination of this Agreement) shall first be resolved . . . through binding arbitration arbitration [sic] entirely on the papers, with no live witnesses or appearances by any party, in accordance with the then prevailing Rules of Commercial Arbitration of the American Arbitration Association and judgment on the awards granted by the arbitrator may be entered in any court having competent jurisdiction thereon [sic]

Notice of Removal, Ex. A. By virtue of this arbitration clause, the parties agreed to a hearing on the papers "with no live witnesses or appearance by any party. . . ." *Id.*

After the parties were unable to settle a dispute for unpaid services, Verve filed a demand for arbitration on April 13, 2010. The parties jointly appointed John R. Holsinger, Esq. ("Mr. Holsinger" or "the arbitrator"), as arbitrator. The

American Arbitration Association ("AAA") rules ("AAA Rules"), referenced in the aforesaid arbitration clause, provide that "[w]here parties have agreed in writing to arbitrate disputes under these [Rules], the arbitration shall take place in accordance with these Rules . . . subject to whatever modifications the parties may adopt in writing." Def. Opp. Br., Exh. E ("AAA Rules"), Art. 1(a). In addition, the AAA Rules further provide that "the tribunal may conduct the arbitration in whatever manner it considers appropriate, provided that the parties are treated with equality and that each party has the right to be heard and is given a fair opportunity to present its case." *Id.* at Art. 16(1).

The AAA's ICDR Guidelines further clarify that an arbitrator "shall manage the exchange of information among the parties in advance of the hearings with a view to maintaining efficiency and economy." Def. Opp. Br., Exh. F, ICDR Guidelines for Arbitrators Concerning Exchanges of Information ("ICDR Guidelines"), at ¶ 1a. Further, the guidelines direct the tribunal to "endeavor to avoid unnecessary delay and expense while at the same time balancing the goals of avoiding surprise, promoting equality of treatment, and safeguarding each party's opportunity to present its claims and defenses fairly." *Id.* Under these guidelines, the tribunal "retains final authority to apply the above standard." *Id.* at ¶ 1b.

In its Statement of Claim, Verve asserted several claims against SII: breach of contract, misrepresentation and fraud, negligent misrepresentation, breach of the covenant of good faith and fair dealing, unjust enrichment, and common law fraud. SII responded to Verve's Statement of Claim on May 12, 2010, answering the claim and filing its own Counterclaim for breach of contract, misrepresentation and fraud, negligent misrepresentation, breach of the covenant of good faith and fair dealing, unjust enrichment, common law fraud, and unfair and deceptive trade practices.

The arbitrator conducted a telephonic scheduling conference with the parties on July 26, 2010, and issued an order the following day directing that the parties engage in discovery from August 16, 2010 through September 15, 2010. Def. Opp. Br., Exh. G, Scheduling and Procedure Order No. 1 at ¶ 10–11. That Order also indicated that any disputes regarding the document exchange "that may possibly affect the schedule in this order shall be presented to the arbitrator immediately . . . so the issue can be resolved so as not to delay this proceeding." *Id.* at ¶ 13. According to the Order, the parties' initial submissions were due on October 7, 2010, and their reply submissions due by October 21, 2010. *Id.* at ¶¶ 15–16. After reviewing those submissions, the arbitrator would then "either close the hearing or request clarification or elaboration of any matter needing it." *Id.* at ¶ 17.

On October 5, 2010, the arbitrator held a second telephonic scheduling conference with the parties, including new counsel that SII had retained—Susheela Verma, Esq. See Def. Opp. Br., Exh. H, Scheduling and Procedure Order No. 2. This Order extended the discovery period, ordering SII to respond to Verve's discovery requests by November 4, 2010. *Id.* at ¶ 1. The Order, further, reiterated the dictate that any disputes be presented to the arbitrator "immediately . . . so as not to delay the proceeding." *Id.* at ¶ 3. The submissions deadlines were enlarged such that initial submissions were due on November 29, 2010, and reply submissions due on December 13, 2010. *Id.* at ¶¶ 4, 7. Importantly, the Order provided that "[t]here shall be no extensions of the schedule in this order without good cause." *Id.* at ¶ 7.

On the date upon which the reply submissions were due, December 13, 2010, SII's counsel submitted a letter, via email, requesting sixty (60) additional days to complete discovery. Def. Opp. Br., Exh. J, Verma Letter dated Dec. 13, 2010, ("Verma Letter") at 1. Specifically, SII sought access to a computer server owned by a company named "Devix." *Id.* The letter explained that the server was inaccessible because Devix was in bankruptcy, "therefore possibly requiring court approval for requesting information and documentation from it." *Id.* According to SII, the data on the server would prove that Verve performed defective and/or "deficient computer work." *Id.* Further, the letter argues, the "intense technical nature of this matter" mandates that SII obtain access to the server's "substantial amount of evidence," and that without that evidence, "SII [would be] unable to adequately respond to Verve's Initial Submission . . ., present an adequate defense or prosecute its Counterclaim." *Id.* This, in SII's view, amounted to good cause shown under the second scheduling order. *Id.*

As an alternate basis justifying its request for additional time, the letter points to several AAA Rules SII found applicable. First, the letter cites AAA Rule R–28, which (the letter argues) allows for the postponement of a hearing or extension of any set period of time for good cause shown. Second, the letter quotes AAA Rule R–31(a), as stating that "[t]he parties may offer such evidence as is relevant and material to the dispute and shall produce such evidence as the arbitrator may deem necessary to an understanding and determination of the dispute." *Id.* at 2. Third, the letter argued that neither the AAA Rules nor the arbitrator's scheduling orders provide a mechanism by which SII could have subpoenaed Devix for the data. *Id.* Finally, the letter noted that SII's counsel had previously alerted Verve's counsel of its problem in obtaining access to Devix's servers.

Mr. Holsinger, the arbitrator, denied SII's request for additional time to complete discovery and delivered his award, on January 11, 2011, in favor of Verve. In his ruling, Mr. Holsinger concluded that SII did not show good cause why the discovery period should be expanded and the hearing postponed. In his view, SII failed to provide sufficient detail to support a finding of good cause:

> There is no detail about what type of information is on the computer server to which [SII] does not have access. There is no indication what efforts, if any, [SII] made to obtain the information on the server. There is no reason given for why this issue could not have been raised to the arbitrator before December 13, 2010. There is no indication of when the issue with the information on the server arose. It appears that [SII] was aware of the issue with the server at least by the time of its November 3, 2010 letter to [Verve's] counsel.

Moreover, the arbitrator continued, SII failed to otherwise provide any further detail regarding its contention that Verve provided defective services. *Id.* at ¶ 5. He reasoned that SII could have presented affidavits from current or former SII employees regarding SII's exact complaints about Verve's practices. In the arbitrator's view, that SII did not provide this sort of information caused him to draw "an adverse inference from [SII's] failure to present it." *Id.* Mr. Holsinger further noted that SII "ignore[d] the statutory bases for subpoenaing such information," *id.* at ¶ 6, and neglected to raise the issue during either of the telephonic scheduling conferences or after SII's November 3rd letter to Verve informing Verve that it was experiencing difficulty in obtaining access to Devix's servers. *Id.*

Turning to the merits, the arbitrator ruled in favor of Verve and awarded it $336,736.00 in damages plus interest at 8% per annum. The arbitrator, further, awarded Verve $6,615.00 for reimbursement of fees and expenses borne by Verve. As for SII's counterclaim, the arbitration denied the counterclaim in its entirety and dismissed it with prejudice.

Once the matter was removed to this Court, Verve filed a motion to confirm the arbitral award on April 8, 2011. In addition to opposing that motion, SII filed a cross-motion to vacate the arbitral award on May 2, 2011. The matter is now ripe for decision.

II.   DISCUSSION

While the parties' briefs contain lengthy discourses about what occurred during the arbitration proceeding, and about whether state or federal law enforcement mechanisms apply to the arbitral award, I find that the case law unequivocally dictates that the arbitral award be confirmed for the reasons set forth below.

A.   Standard of Review

Generally, the Federal Arbitration Act ("FAA"), 9 U.S.C. § 1 et seq, "requires courts to enforce privately negotiated agreements to arbitrate, like other contracts, in accordance with their terms." The FAA was "designed to overrule the judiciary's longstanding refusal to enforce agreements to arbitrate." The statute identifies four narrow grounds for vacating an arbitral award: where the award was procured through corruption/fraud, evident partiality on the part of the arbitrator, arbitrator misconduct, or where the arbitrator exceeded his or her powers or acted arbitrarily. Where a court finds no justifiable grounds for vacating the award, the court will confirm it. *Id.* at 296.

B.   Cross-Motion to Vacate

Because Verve's motion to confirm the arbitral award rises and falls on whether the award should be vacated, I turn first to SII's cross-motion to vacate. Verve brings two challenges to SII's cross-motion to vacate.

2.   FAA Vacatur Grounds

As noted, the vacatur grounds delineated in the FAA are: (1) where the award was procured through corruption/fraud; (2) evident partiality on the part of the arbitrator; (3) arbitrator misconduct; and (4) where the arbitrator exceeded his or her powers or acted arbitrarily. SII posits the following two reasons why I should vacate the arbitrator's decision:

1.   [SII] advanced "sufficient cause" for its request for a postponement.

2.   By denying [SII] the right to a subpoena to depose a non-party and submit a transcript of the deposition, the arbitrator engaged in misconduct and denied [SII] a right to a fair trial. The arbitrator took away [SII's] opportunity to present its case.

Def. Opp. Br. at 18–19. In SII's view, these two reasons compel the conclusion that the arbitrator's award was arbitrary and capricious. See id. A challenge to an arbitrator's decision as arbitrary and capricious falls under the final vacatur ground, the "irrationality" provision, which is also referred to as the "exceeded their powers" provision. See *Ario*, 618 F.3d at 295 ("The 'irrationality' standard comes from the fourth ground, the "exceeded their powers" provision."). Alternatively, SII's challenge may be viewed as a "third ground" challenge based on the arbitrator's "refus[al] to postpone the hearing, upon sufficient cause shown, or [refusal] to hear evidence pertinent and material to the controversy. . . ." 9 U.S.C. § 10(a)(3).

I do not find that the two reasons asserted by SII demonstrate that the arbitrator's decision was completely irrational. While SII contends that it showed sufficient cause for the postponement, the arbitrator was well within his discretion to conclude that SII failed to provide detailed facts in support of its request for additional time. The arbitrator reasoned that SII did not provide detail about what type of information SII sought access to, that SII did not explain what precise attempts it made during the discovery period to obtain access to the Devix servers and, most notably, why SII could not have informed the arbitrator prior to the December 13, 2010 deadline.

As noted supra, the AAA Rules provide that "the tribunal may conduct the arbitration in whatever manner it considers appropriate, provided that the parties are treated with equality and that each party has the right to be heard and is given a fair opportunity to present its case." AAA Rules at Art. 16(1). The authority conferred by this rule to "conduct the arbitration in whatever manner it considers appropriate" is sufficiently broad to encompass the arbitrator's decision not to further extend the discovery period and prolong resolution of the dispute. In addition, both scheduling orders made pellucidly clear that the parties were to alert the arbitrator of discovery difficulties "immediately . . . so as not to delay the proceeding." SII did not comply with this directive. Moreover, while SII makes much of its belief that it could not subpoena Devix for access to the servers, that SII did not even alert the arbitrator of its difficulties until the final hour calls into question the veracity of SII's contention. Accordingly, I conclude that the arbitrator's decision was not completely irrational.

SII's further argument that the arbitrator's decision denied it of its right to a fair trial and took away its opportunity to present its case—which I construe as a third ground challenge under section 10(a)(3) of the FAA—is also without merit. The Third Circuit has made clear that "[s]ection 10(a)(3) cannot be read . . . to intend that every failure to receive relevant evidence constitutes misconduct which will require the vacation of an arbitrator's award." *Century Indem. Co. v. Certain Underwriters at Lloyd's*, 584 F.3d 513, 557 (3d Cir.2009). To the contrary, "vacatur pursuant to section 10(a)(3) is warranted only where the arbitrator's refusal to hear proffered testimony so affects the rights of a party that it may be said that he was deprived of a fair hearing." *Id.* (internal quotation marks omitted). In light of an arbitrator's "wide latitude in how [he] conduct[s] proceedings," according to the Third Circuit, courts apply an extremely deferential standard that rarely results in the vacation of an arbitral award. *Id.*

Any prejudice that SII suffered is of its own making, and is not due to any misconduct on the arbitrator's part. The arbitration spanned eight months, from April 2010 through December 2010. SII had plenty opportunity during that time frame to marshal evidence in support of its claim that Verve provided deficient services and overbilled SII. As the arbitrator noted in his decision, SII could have presented affidavits from its own employees to buttress that claim. The certification and affidavit SII produced in this Court—after the arbitrator's decision was issued—was based on the employees' personal knowledge, and nowhere in those documents does SII incorporate or discuss Devix server information. This clearly illustrates that SII had the capacity to produce that same evidence to the arbitrator before he rendered his decision. For these reasons, I conclude that the arbitrator's denial of SII's request for additional time to complete discovery did not amount to arbitrator misconduct. Cf. *Three S Delaware, Inc. v. DataQuick Information Systems, Inc.*, 492 F.3d 520 (4th Cir.2007) (affirming confirmation of arbitrator's denial of motion to reopen where the arbitrator "gave [the party] ample opportunities to present its evidence. . . ."); *Perhach v. Option One Mortg. Corp.*, 382 Fed.Appx. 897 (11th Cir.2010) (holding that arbitrator's refusal to hear evidence did not amount to misconduct where "[e]ven though [the party] had the opportunity to submit evidence, he chose not to present witnesses. . . ."). Accordingly, I deny SII's cross-motion to vacate the arbitral decision.

NOTES

Facts

1.   What was the discovery dispute that led to the motion to vacate the award? When did this dispute arise and when was notice given to the arbitrator?

2.   What was the adverse inference drawn by the arbitrator? On what basis did the arbitrator draw the adverse inference? How does the court deal with the adverse inference?

3.   Does the court itself draw an adverse inference in its treatment of the motion to vacate?

Law

1. What is the basis for the arbitrator's power in this case to draw an adverse inference? Does the court say?

2. Did SII seek to vacate directly upon the basis that the arbitrator drew an adverse inference? What does this choice tell you about the basis for the inference?

Morgan Stanley to Pay $12.5 Million to Resolve FINRA Charges that it Failed to Provide Documents to Arbitration Claimants, Regulators

FINRA News Release, dated September 27, 2007, available at http://www.finra.org/newsroom/newsreleases/2007/p037071

Washington, D.C.—The Financial Industry Regulatory Authority (FINRA) today announced a settlement with Morgan Stanley & Co. to resolve charges that the firm's former affiliate, Morgan Stanley DW, Inc. (MSDW), failed on numerous occasions to provide emails to claimants in arbitration proceedings as well as to regulators—while representing that the destruction of the firm's email servers in the Sept. 11, 2001 terrorist attacks on New York's World Trade Center resulted in the loss of all pre-9/11 email. In fact, the firm had millions of pre-9/11 emails that had been restored to the firm's active email system using back-up tapes that had been stored in another location.

The settlement also resolves additional charges relating to the firm's failure to provide required supervisory materials to numerous arbitration claimants. The settlement announced today is the first of its kind—in that it provides for distribution of $9.5 million to two groups of customers who had arbitration claims against the firm. FINRA estimates that several thousand customers may be eligible to receive payments. FINRA also imposed a $3 million fine on the firm for its failure to provide pre-9/11 emails and updates to a supervisory manual.

"The integrity of our process demands that brokerage firms comply with their obligations to search diligently for, and provide in a timely way, information and documents required in arbitration proceedings and regulatory investigations," said Susan Merrill, FINRA Executive Vice President and Chief of Enforcement. "The action announced today underscores FINRA's commitment to ensuring that firms live up to those obligations. We are particularly pleased that this unique settlement directs the bulk of the monetary sanction to the customers in arbitrations, to remedy MSDW's discovery failures."

MSDW was merged into Morgan Stanley & Co. in April of this year. The former NASD, which consolidated with the member regulation functions of New York Stock Exchange Regulation in July to form FINRA, issued formal charges against MSDW in a complaint filed in December 2006.

Under the terms of the settlement, Morgan Stanley will deposit $9.5 million into a fund to pay arbitration claimants for the discovery failures. All fund expenses, as well as the cost of hiring and compensating a fund administrator acceptable to FINRA, will be borne by the firm. The fund administrator will identify and notify potentially eligible arbitration claimants. Eligible claimants in the email aspect of the case can elect to receive a standard payment estimated to be between $3,000 and $5,000, or may choose to require Morgan Stanley to produce relevant emails still in its possession. A claimant who demands email production can decide to accept the standard payment—or waive that payment and have the fund administrator determine the amount, if any, that the claimant should receive depending on the particular facts and circumstances of that individual case. Maximum payment in cases decided by the fund administrator cannot exceed $20,000.

Eligible claimants who were denied the required supervisory materials will receive payments expected to be between $1,500 and $2,500. Some claimants may be eligible for payments as to both the pre-9/11 email and the failure to receive supervisory materials.

Detailed information about which arbitration claimants are eligible for fund payments, and about the claims process itself, can be found on the Arbitration Discovery Fund page of FINRA's Web site, www.finra.org.

Also as part of the settlement announced today, Morgan Stanley is required—again, at its own expense—to retain an independent consultant acceptable to FINRA to review the firm's procedures for complying with discovery requirements in arbitration proceedings relating to the firm's retail brokerage operations. The firm will be required to implement the independent consultant's recommendations for improving those procedures, or alternative improvements acceptable to the independent consultant.

FINRA found that MSDW failed to provide pre-9/11 emails to claimants in numerous arbitration proceedings and in response to three regulatory inquiries during the period from October 2001 through March 2005. FINRA found that MSDW made statements in numerous arbitration proceedings and to the former NASD, New York Stock Exchange Regulation and the Massachusetts Securities Division that those emails had been destroyed. Those statements were not true. In fact, MSDW possessed millions of pre-9/11 emails that had been restored to the firm's system shortly after Sept.11, 2001 using backup tapes. Many other emails were maintained on individual users' computers and had not been affected by the events of 9/11. Among the matters where MSDW failed to produce e-mail was an NASD investigation that resulted in an August 2005 settlement with the firm.

FINRA also found that MSDW later destroyed many of the pre-9/11 emails it did possess. The firm did so in two ways—by overwriting backup tapes that had been used to restore the emails from 11 of its 12 servers to the firm's system, and by allowing users of the firm's email system to permanently delete the emails over an extended period of time. As a result, between September 2001 and March 2005, MSDW deleted millions of pre-9/11 emails from the firm's systems.

In addition, FINRA found that MSDW failed to provide updates to the firm's supervisory manual for branch office managers to claimants in numerous arbitration proceedings over a period of years. The Branch Manager's Manual was issued in 1994 and was subsequently supplemented with numerous updates. FINRA found, however, that MSDW repeatedly failed to provide updates to the manual in discovery in numerous arbitration proceedings from late 1999 through the end of 2005.

In settling this matter, Morgan Stanley neither admitted nor denied the charges, but consented to the entry of FINRA's findings.

FINRA, the Financial Industry Regulatory Authority, is the largest non-governmental regulator for all securities firms doing business in the United States. Created in 2007 through the consolidation of NASD and NYSE Member Regulation, FINRA is dedicated to investor protection and market integrity through effective and efficient regulation and complementary compliance and technology-based services. FINRA touches virtually every aspect of the securities business—from registering and educating industry participants to examining securities firms; writing rules; enforcing those rules and the federal securities laws; informing and educating the investing public; providing trade reporting and other industry utilities; and administering the largest dispute resolution forum for investors and registered firms.

NOTES

Facts

1. The press release discusses Morgan Stanley's payment of a $12.5 million in sanction. Does it appear to you that this is a "sanction" in the typical sense? How did the issue arise?

2. Who received the $12.5 million?

3. Who paid the $12.5 million, Morgan Stanley or its counsel?

4. Who do you think made the representation that the emails had been destroyed: counsel in letters/pleadings or a client representative in the form of an affidavit?

Law

1. Look at the AAA Commercial Arbitration Rules. Assume that an arbitrator learns that similar misconduct occurred while an arbitration is pending. Can an arbitrator make an order similar to the FINRA charges?

2. Assume you represent a party affected by discovery misconduct. What do you ask an arbitrator to do?

3. If this misconduct had occurred in federal court, who do you think would be on the hook: the client, the lawyer, or both?

ReliaStar Life Ins. Co. of N.Y. v.
EMC Nat. Life Co.

564 F.3d 81 (2d Cir. 2009)

REENA RAGGI, CIRCUIT JUDGE:

On this appeal, we consider whether parties' inclusion in an arbitration agreement of a general statement that each will bear the expenses of its own arbitrator and its own attorneys deprives the arbitration panel of authority to award such expenses as a sanction against a party whom the panel determines failed to arbitrate in good faith. We conclude that it does not and, accordingly, reverse the judgment of the United States District Court for the Southern District of New York (Lewis A. Kaplan, Judge), entered on February 14, 2007, insofar as it vacated that part of an arbitration award requiring respondent EMC National Life Company ("EMC"), successor in interest to National Travelers Life Company ("National Travelers"), to pay such fees to petitioner ReliaStar Life Insurance Co. of New York ("ReliaStar"). We remand the case so that the district court may enter a new judgment confirming the arbitration award in all respects.

I.   Factual Background

A.   The Agreement to Arbitrate

In December 1997, National Travelers and ReliaStar entered into two separate but related coinsurance agreements, one pertaining to certain ReliaStar insurance policies in force as of January 1, 1998, and the other pertaining to certain ReliaStar policies to be issued on or after that date. Because the agreements have identical terms and conditions, for purposes of this appeal we refer to them collectively as the "Coinsurance Agreements."

Article X of the Coinsurance Agreements governed the parties' agreement to arbitrate. It reads in relevant part as follows:

10.1 Appointment of Arbitrators. In the event of any disputes or differences arising hereafter between the parties with reference to any transaction under or relating in any way to this Agreement as to which agreement between the parties hereto cannot be reached, the same shall be decided by arbitration. Three arbitrators shall decide any dispute or difference. . . .

10.2 Decision. The arbitrators shall consider customary and standard practices in the life or health reinsurance business, as applicable to the dispute. They shall decide by a majority vote of the arbitrators. There shall be no appeal from their written decision. Judgment may be entered on the decision of the arbitrators by any court having jurisdiction.

10.3 Expenses of Arbitration. Each party shall bear the expense of its own arbitrator (whether selected by that party, or by the other party pursuant to the procedures set out in Section 10.1) and related outside attorneys' fees, and shall jointly and equally bear with the other party the expenses of the third arbitrator.

10.4 Applicable Law. Any arbitration instituted pursuant to this Article shall be held in New York, New York, or another site mutually agreed upon by the parties and the laws of the State of New York and to the extent applicable, the Federal Arbitration Act, shall govern the interpretation and application of this Agreement.

The particular focus of this appeal is section 10.3.

B.   The Arbitration Award

When various disputes arose between the co-insurers, National Travelers initiated arbitration proceedings seeking (1) a declaration that the Coinsurance Agreements had been terminated and (2) approval for a proposed terminal accounting. ReliaStar opposed both National Travelers' claim of termination and its proposed method for conducting a terminal accounting.

Following discovery, in May 2006, an arbitration panel conducted a two-week hearing. On August 4, 2006, the panel entered an interim award, finding that the Coinsurance Agreements remained in force between the parties and directing National Travelers to pay ReliaStar more than $21 million past due under that agreement. The panel directed the parties to meet to resolve issues related to the resumption of their relationship under the Coinsurance Agreements. Further, in paragraph 6 of the award, a majority of the panel, without explanation, awarded ReliaStar attorney's and arbitrator's fees and costs.

The parties complied with all aspects of the award, except for that part granting ReliaStar fees and costs, which they agreed National Travelers could submit for reconsideration to the panel and, if necessary, challenge in court. After further briefing on the issue of fees and costs, the arbitration panel entered a final award on October 20, 2006. A majority of the panel awarded ReliaStar fees for its attorneys and arbitrator in the amount of $3,169,496, costs of $691,903.75, as well as interest, explaining that it viewed the conduct of National Travelers in the arbitration "as lacking good faith."

C.   The District Court Proceedings

On October 20, 2006, ReliaStar petitioned the district court to confirm the final arbitration award, and on November 2, 2006, National Travelers filed a counter-petition to vacate the award to the extent it granted ReliaStar fees and costs. National Travelers argued that the arbitration panel had exceeded its authority in awarding fees and costs in light of section 10.3 of the Coinsurance Agreements, which obligates each party to "bear the expense of its own arbitrator . . . and related outside attorneys' fees." The district court agreed and, accordingly, vacated that part of the final award requiring National Travelers to pay ReliaStar's attorney's and arbitrator's fees before confirming it in all other respects.

ReliaStar appeals the vacatur.

II.   Discussion

A.   Standard of Review

In considering a challenge to a district court's decision to vacate a portion of an arbitration award, we review its legal rulings de novo and its findings of fact for clear error.

The law is clear that because arbitration is "a matter of contract[,] . . . a party cannot be required to submit to arbitration any dispute which he has not agreed to so submit." *PaineWebber Inc. v. Bybyk*, 81 F.3d 1193, 1198 (2d Cir.1996). The scope of an arbitrator's authority thus "generally depends on the intention of the parties to an arbitration, and is determined by the agreement or submission." *Synergy Gas Co. v. Sasso*, 853 F.2d 59, 63–64 (2d Cir.1988) (internal quotation marks omitted). Section 10(a)(4) of the Federal Arbitration Act allows courts to vacate an arbitral award "where the arbitrators exceeded their powers." 9 U.S.C. § 10(a)(4). We have, however, "consistently accorded the narrowest of readings" to this provision of law, in order to facilitate the purpose underlying arbitration: to provide parties with efficient dispute resolution, thereby obviating the need for protracted litigation.

Thus, in considering a section 10(b)(4) challenge, "[t]he principal question for the reviewing court is whether the arbitrator's award draws its essence" from the agreement to arbitrate, "since the arbitrator is not free merely to dispense his own brand of industrial justice." If the answer to this question is yes, however, the scope of the court's review of the award itself is limited. Notably, we do not consider "whether the arbitrators correctly decided [the] issue." If the parties agreed to submit an issue for arbitration, we will uphold a challenged award as long as the arbitrator offers "a barely colorable justification for the outcome reached." In other words, "as long as the arbitrator is even arguably construing or applying the contract and acting within the scope of his authority," a court's conviction that the arbitrator has "committed serious error" in resolving the disputed issue "does not suffice to overturn his decision."

Applying these principles to this case, we consider only whether, in light of the parties' agreement to arbitrate, the arbitrators were authorized to sanction bad faith conduct by awarding attorney's and arbitrator's fees. We do not-nor does respondent ask us to-consider whether the arbitrators correctly identified bad faith conduct or whether the amount of fees awarded was an appropriate sanction for that conduct.

B. The Parties' Broad Agreement to Arbitrate Conferred on the Arbitrators the Equitable Authority to Sanction a Party's Bad Faith Conduct

Where an arbitration clause is broad, arbitrators have the discretion to order such remedies as they deem appropriate. This is because it is "not the role of the courts to undermine the comprehensive grant of authority to arbitrators by prohibiting" them from fashioning awards or remedies to "ensure[] a meaningful final award."

Consistent with this principle, we here clarify that a broad arbitration clause, such as the one in this case, see Coinsurance Agreements § 10.1, confers inherent authority on arbitrators to sanction a party that participates in the arbitration in bad faith and that such a sanction may include an award of attorney's or arbitrator's fees. This conclusion finds support in *Synergy Gas Co. v. Sasso*, 853 F.2d 59, wherein this Court ruled that, after an arbitrator ordered the reinstatement of a discharged employee with backpay, the arbitrator did not exceed his authority in further awarding the employee's union attorney's fees. In so holding, we noted that "[a]rbitrators have . . . occasionally awarded attorney's fees" in circumstances where one party had acted in bad faith and that such fees fairly compensated the party for costs incurred as a result of such actions. *Id.* at 65. In that case, we specifically observed that "if Synergy had not acted in bad faith, then [the employee] Brown would have been reinstated more than six years ago and the attorney's fees would not have been incurred." *Id.* at 66. Accordingly, we concluded that such an award of attorney's fees did not contravene New York's public policy against punitive arbitration awards because the fees were compensatory, not penal, in nature and, thus, an appropriate form of damages granted to the aggrieved party. *See id.*

The Ninth Circuit has also rejected a challenge to an arbitration award of attorney's fees, recognizing a bad faith exception to the general "American Rule" that each party bears its own attorney's fees. See *Todd Shipyards Corp. v. Cunard Line, Ltd.*, 943 F.2d 1056, 1064 (9th Cir.1991). The court explained: "Federal law takes an expansive view of arbitrator authority to decide disputes and fashion remedies. . . . In light of the broad power of arbitrators to fashion appropriate remedies and the accepted 'bad faith conduct' exception to the American Rule, we hold that it was within the power of the arbitration panel in this case to award attorneys' fees." Id.; see also *Marshall & Co. v. Duke*, 114 F.3d 188, 190 (11th Cir.1997) (noting that parties raised no jurisdictional challenge to attorney's fee award, but observing that, "[i]n any event, the arbitrators have the power to award attorney's fees pursuant to the 'bad faith' exception to the American Rule that each party bears its own attorney's fees").

EMC submits that this case is distinguishable because the agreement at issue in *Todd Shipyards Corp. v. Cunard Line, Ltd.* specifically integrated Rule 43 of the Commercial Rules of the American Arbitration Association, which states that " '[t]he arbitrator may grant any remedy or relief which the Arbitrator deems just and equitable within the scope of the agreement of the parties.' " 943 F.2d at 1062–63 (quoting Rule 43). We do not, however, consider a reference to Rule 43 to be essential where, as in this case, the parties' arbitration clause applies broadly to every dispute arising under their agreement, see Coinsurance Agreements § 10.1, and where the arbitrators find that a party did not arbitrate in good faith, see Domke on Commercial Arbitration § 35:8 ("As a general rule, each party to an arbitration must bear its own attorney fees associated with an arbitration action or the enforcement of an arbitration award. Nevertheless, [the Federal Arbitration Act] ... grant [s] wide authority to the arbitrator to determine entitlement to attorney fees. . . . Under some circumstances, the prevailing party may recover attorney fees if the parties provide for the remedy of attorney fees in their arbitration agreement or if authorized by a statute, or if justified by circumstances in which the losing party acted in bad faith." (emphasis added)). Indeed, the underlying purposes of arbitration, i.e., efficient and swift resolution of disputes without protracted litigation, could not be achieved but for good faith arbitration by the parties. Consequently, sanctions, including attorney's fees, are appropriately viewed as a remedy within an arbitrator's authority to effect the goals of arbitration.

C.   Section 10.3 of the Parties' Agreement Did Not Limit the Arbitrators' Authority to Award Attorney's and Arbitrator's Fees as a Sanction for Bad Faith Conduct

While a broad arbitration clause affords arbitrators considerable discretion to award such remedies as they deem appropriate, they may not "exceed the power granted to them by the contract itself." *Banco de Seguros del Estado v. Mut. Marine Office, Inc.*, 344 F.3d at 262. EMC does not contend that section 10.1 of the agreement to arbitrate is not sufficiently broad to authorize the arbitrators to sanction bad faith conduct. Rather, its position has consistently been that section 10.3 limits that sanction authority to exclude awards of attorney's or arbitrator's fees. We conclude that this is not a proper construction of section 10.3.

In interpreting a contract under New York law, "words and phrases . . . should be given their plain meaning." *LaSalle Bank Nat'l Ass'n v. Nomura Asset Capital Corp.*, 424 F.3d 195, 206 (2d Cir.2005) (internal quotation marks omitted). Section 10.3 simply states the general American Rule that each party will bear its own attorney's fees and extends the principle to apply also to the fee of the arbitrator selected by each party. Thus, section 10.3 is fairly understood to reflect the parties' agreement as to how fees are to be borne, regardless of the arbitration's outcome, in the expected context of good faith dealings. Nothing in the section, however, signals the parties' intent to limit the arbitrators' inherent authority to sanction bad faith participation in the arbitration. Certainly, nothing in Article X generally, or section 10.3 specifically, references bad faith or sanction remedies. Accordingly, we have no basis for thinking that the parties to this agreement ever considered the question of whether to limit the arbitrators' authority to sanction bad faith conduct. In contrast, they did expressly confer comprehensive arbitral authority in section 10.1. In light of that conferral, we conclude that section 10.3 is properly construed to reflect the parties' agreement that the arbitrators may not factor attorney's or arbitrator's fees into awards that result from the parties' expected good faith arbitration of a dispute. The section does not signal the parties' intent to limit the conferral of comprehensive authority by precluding an award of attorney's or arbitrator's fees when a party's bad faith dealings create a recognized exception to the American Rule.

EMC asserts that such a reading of section 10.3 is contrary to New York principles of contract interpretation. It submits that, because the American Rule would apply by default even in the absence of section 10.3, reading the section as a simple articulation of the American Rule would render it superfluous. We are not persuaded. Parties to commercial arbitration agreements may choose explicitly to reference the American Rule for any number of reasons unrelated to the scope of the arbitrators' sanction authority. For example, some arbitrators may not be attorneys and, thus, may be unfamiliar with the American Rule. Still other arbitrators may come from jurisdictions that employ the "English Rule" where the prevailing party's fees are routinely paid by an unsuccessful opponent.

Precisely because the agreement in this case conferred broad authority on the arbitrators, because inherent in such authority is the power to sanction bad faith conduct, and because bad faith is a well-recognized exception to the American Rule for attorney's fees, we conclude that the simple statement of that Rule in section 10.3 is insufficient by itself to swallow the exception. As sophisticated commercial entities, the parties were certainly capable of stating clearly any intent to exclude attorney's and arbitrator's fees from the broad range of sanctions generally available to arbitrators upon an identification of bad faith. Thus, our holding today should not be understood to preclude parties who wish to limit the scope of an arbitrator's sanction authority to exclude attorney's fees or arbitrator's awards from doing so. We require only that they explicitly and clearly state that intent as part of their agreement to arbitrate.

NOTES

Facts

1. Is the underlying conduct on the basis of which the panel concluded that a party did not participate in good faith discussed? Does it matter?

2. Why do you think the parties agreed to include section 10.3 in the arbitration clause? What concern were they hoping to resolve by the inclusion of section 10.3?

3. Did the arbitration rules permit the arbitrator to assign costs?

4. How should the clause be reworded in order to avoid the result of *ReliaStar*?

Law

1. What was the basis for the tribunal's conclusion that the arbitrators had the power to sanction bad faith conduct in an arbitration by means of a cost award? Do you agree with the reasoning?

2. Assume that the parties had agreed to use the AAA Commercial Arbitration Rules, but had also included section 10.3. Does the argument that the arbitrators did not have the power to issue a cost award become stronger or weaker? What does the court think? Do you agree?

3. Assume that the parties included section 10.3 in a contract under the AAA Commercial Arbitration Rules, but that the arbitration clause was otherwise narrowly drafted to apply only to disputes "arising out of" a specific provision of the contract. How would that change the analysis?

C)   Sanctions for Counsel Misconduct

So far, we have discussed sanctions in the arbitral context that were directed against the parties to the arbitration either by disposing of an aspect of the case through means of an adverse inference or by means of a cost order. The question remains—What are the consequences for *counsel* misbehaving in an arbitration proceeding?

Arbitral tribunals do not have the power of the courts to order counsel to pay sanctions under Federal Rules of Civil Procedure, Rule 11. That is because counsel have not consented to the jurisdiction of the arbitral tribunal—*i.e.*, there is no arbitration clause between counsel themselves that would submit any dispute between them regarding the conduct of the proceedings to the same panel that hears the dispute between their clients. This does not, however, mean that counsel can act with impunity in arbitral hearings.

1) *The Model Rules of Professional Conduct*

Rule 1   Definitions

(m) "Tribunal" denotes a court, an arbitrator in a binding arbitration proceeding or a legislative body, administrative agency or other body acting in an adjudicative capacity. A legislative body, administrative agency or other body acts in an adjudicative capacity when a neutral official, after the presentation of evidence or legal argument by a party or parties, will render a binding legal judgment directly affecting a party's interests in a particular matter.

Rule 3.3   Candor Toward The Tribunal

(a)   A lawyer shall not knowingly:

(1)   make a false statement of fact or law to a tribunal or fail to correct a false statement of material fact or law previously made to the tribunal by the lawyer;

(2)   fail to disclose to the tribunal legal authority in the controlling jurisdiction known to the lawyer to be directly adverse to the position of the client and not disclosed by opposing counsel; or

(3)   offer evidence that the lawyer knows to be false. If a lawyer, the lawyer's client, or a witness called by the lawyer, has offered material evidence and the lawyer comes to know of its falsity, the lawyer shall take reasonable remedial measures, including, if necessary, disclosure to the tribunal. A lawyer may refuse to offer evidence, other than the testimony of a defendant in a criminal matter, that the lawyer reasonably believes is false.

(b)   A lawyer who represents a client in an adjudicative proceeding and who knows that a person intends to engage, is engaging or has engaged in criminal or fraudulent conduct related to the proceeding shall take reasonable remedial measures, including, if necessary, disclosure to the tribunal.

(c)   The duties stated in paragraphs (a) and (b) continue to the conclusion of the proceeding, and apply even if compliance requires disclosure of information otherwise protected by Rule 1.6.

(d)   In an ex parte proceeding, a lawyer shall inform the tribunal of all material facts known to the lawyer that will enable the tribunal to make an informed decision, whether or not the facts are adverse.

Rule 3.4　Fairness To Opposing Party And Counsel

A lawyer shall not:

(a)　unlawfully obstruct another party's access to evidence or unlawfully alter, destroy or conceal a document or other material having potential evidentiary value. A lawyer shall not counsel or assist another person to do any such act;

(b)　falsify evidence, counsel or assist a witness to testify falsely, or offer an inducement to a witness that is prohibited by law;

(c)　knowingly disobey an obligation under the rules of a tribunal except for an open refusal based on an assertion that no valid obligation exists;

(d)　in pretrial procedure, make a frivolous discovery request or fail to make reasonably diligent effort to comply with a legally proper discovery request by an opposing party;

(e)　in trial, allude to any matter that the lawyer does not reasonably believe is relevant or that will not be supported by admissible evidence, assert personal knowledge of facts in issue except when testifying as a witness, or state a personal opinion as to the justness of a cause, the credibility of a witness, the culpability of a civil litigant or the guilt or innocence of an accused; or

(f)　request a person other than a client to refrain from voluntarily giving relevant information to another party unless:

(1)　the person is a relative or an employee or other agent of a client; and

(2)　the lawyer reasonably believes that the person's interests will not be adversely affected by refraining from giving such information

2)　Instances of Bar Discipline

This next reported case deals with the problem of suborning perjury in arbitration. As you read the decision, consider how the logic of the decision would apply with regard to other potential misconduct covered by ABA Model Rule 3.3 and 3.4.

Matter of Malone

105 A.D.2d 455 (N.Y.A.D. 3 Dept., 1984)

Petitioner moves to confirm a referee's report which sustained, in part, a charge of professional misconduct against respondent. Respondent, an attorney admitted in the Second Department on March 16, 1966, cross-moves to disaffirm the report.

The single charge against respondent arises out of his conduct of an investigation, as Inspector General of the New York State Department of Correctional Services, into the alleged brutal beating of an inmate by several correction officers. Specifically, in order to protect the identity of a correction officer who stated he witnessed the incident, and thus protect him from retaliation for having broken the "code of silence" among correction officers, respondent instructed the officer to testify falsely under oath at one point during the investigation.

In December, 1980, Correction Officer Robert Lewis confidentially informed his superiors that he had witnessed an unprovoked assault upon inmate Robert Jackson by several correction officers which occurred on December 13, 1980 at the Downstate Correctional Facility in Dutchess County. Testimony before the Referee, including that of the Commissioner of the Department of Correctional Services, indicated that it is highly unusual for a correction officer to voluntarily inform upon his fellow officers for fear of retaliation for breaking the "code of silence" which exists among correction officers.

Respondent began an investigation into Lewis' allegations. Preliminary interviews of Lewis by respondent and his investigators to ascertain Lewis' version of events and his credibility were conducted at the Dutchess County Airport. The interviews were conducted at the airport as part of a policy decision by respondent, condoned by the commissioner and Lewis, to keep Lewis' identity as an informer secret as long as possible. Some additional information gathered during this period, such as inmate Jackson's statement and his medical records, appear to support Lewis' version of the events surrounding the assault.

Thereafter, on October 21, 1981, at the Downstate Correctional Facility, as part of the ongoing investigation, respondent interviewed under oath the correction officers who had been identified as possibly involved in the alleged beating of inmate Jackson. Six correction officers, including Lewis, were interviewed. The purpose of the interviews was to gather evidence and to have the officers make sworn statements regarding the incident. None of the officers admitted participating in or observing an assault upon the inmate.

Lewis also denied having witnessed the use of undue force. This false testimony was given at respondent's direction. By having Lewis give false testimony exonerating his fellow officers, respondent hoped to avert suspicion away from Lewis as an informer. The ruse was successful.

The day before the interviews, on October 20, 1981, at the Quality Inn in the City of Albany, respondent had taken Lewis' true testimony under oath as to the incident in the presence of a stenographer and investigator. At that time, respondent stated on the record the plan of taking two contradictory statements from Lewis "in order to preserve the confidentiality of his information and his identity". The transcript of Lewis' October 20, 1981 testimony does not reveal Lewis' identity and is entitled "Interview with 'Witness' Correction Officer". After the fact, respondent informed the commissioner and the department's chief legal counsel of Lewis' contradictory statements; both approved of the procedure.

On December 11, 1981, disciplinary charges were brought against three of the correction officers interviewed by respondent on October 21, 1981, alleging the use of undue force and giving false testimony. Negotiations ensued between the department and the officers' union in an effort to settle the charges. During these negotiations, respondent provided the department negotiators with Lewis' October 20, 1981 true statement to use as leverage or a bargaining chip. The negotiations proved unsuccessful, the accused correction officers filed grievances and arbitration was initiated.

On the first day of arbitration, October 4, 1982, Lewis was called as a witness, testified to the use of undue force, and revealed the contradictory nature of his two prior statements and respondent's role with respect thereto. Had the matter never gone to arbitration, Lewis' identity would have remained secret.

On September 22, 1983, petitioner Committee on Professional Standards charged respondent with professional misconduct in violation of DR 1–102 (subd. [A], pars. [3], [4], [6]) of the Code of Professional Responsibility and section 487 of the Judiciary Law in that "he counseled and instructed a witness to give contradictory, misleading and inconsistent testimony and attempted to mislead and deceive a party or parties". The charge detailed two specifications, the facts of which were admitted by respondent, which essentially described his role in the taking of Lewis' statements on October 20 and 21, 1981. After a hearing on January 20, 1984 before a referee assigned by this court, the referee found respondent had violated DR 1–102 (subd. [A], par. [4]) by engaging in conduct involving deceit and misrepresentation and found respondent's proffered justifications for his action relevant only to the degree of discipline to be imposed.

In support of his cross motion for disaffirmance of the referee's report, respondent first argues that this court is without jurisdiction in this matter because he was not admitted in, does not reside in, and has never practiced law in this department. We reject this contention. This court's disciplinary jurisdiction extends to New York attorneys who have offices in or are employed or transact business in this department (see Judiciary Law, § 90, subd. 2; 22 NYCRR 806.1; *Matter of Smith*, 68 A.D.2d 52, 53, 416 N.Y.S.2d 608); as Inspector General of the State Department of * *606 Correctional Services, respondent has one of his main offices in Albany. Also, the fact that some of the alleged misconduct, such as respondent's direction to Lewis at the Quality Inn in Albany to testify falsely, took place in this department is an additional valid jurisdictional ground (*see Matter of Klein*, 23 A.D.2d 356, 360, 262 N.Y.S.2d 416, *affd.* 18 N.Y.2d 598, 272 N.Y.S.2d 372, 219 N.E.2d 194, *cert. den. sub nom. Klein v. Klein*, 385 U.S. 973, 87 S.Ct. 511, 17 L.Ed.2d 436).

Next, we reject respondent's argument that since he was acting in his role as Inspector General and not as an attorney when he advised Lewis to lie under oath, this court may not discipline him for such misconduct. It is clear that this court's power to discipline an attorney "extends to misconduct other than professional malfeasance when such conduct reflects adversely upon the legal profession and is not in accordance with the high standards imposed upon members of the Bar" (*Matter of Nixon*, 53 A.D.2d 178, 181–182, 385 N.Y.S.2d 305; *see Judiciary Law, § 90, subd. 2; 22 NYCRR 806.2; Matter of Dolphin*, 240 N.Y. 89, 93, 147 N.E. 538). Directing a person to give false testimony would normally constitute such misconduct (see *Matter of Popper*, 193 App.Div. 505, 512, 184 N.Y.S. 406; *see, also, Imbler v. Pachtman*, 424 U.S. 409, 429, 96 S.Ct. 984, 994, 47 L.Ed.2d 128; *Disciplinary Action Against Attorney for Misconduct Related to Performance of Official Duties as Prosecuting Attorney, Ann.*, 10 A.L.R. 4th 605). Holding a public office, such as Inspector General, is not a shield behind which breaches of professional ethics, otherwise warranting disciplinary action, are permitted. Rather, a lawyer who holds public office must not only fulfill the duties and responsibilities of that office, but must also comply with the Bar's ethical standards.

Respondent argues that, under the circumstances of this case, his direction to Lewis to falsely testify was not a breach of ethical principles because it was in accordance with certain ethical canons, that there is precedent for the proper use of false testimony in the investigative and prosecutorial context, that the motive of protecting Lewis from danger justified the breach, if any, that respondent was under a duty to protect Lewis, that respondent's actions are justifiable under section 35.05 of the Penal Law, and that respondent should enjoy immunity for a good faith discretionary act.

First, we conclude that the ethical canons cited by respondent in support of his conduct, requiring competent and zealous representation of clients, cannot in and of themselves overcome the proscription against directing another to give false testimony. Second, while there is precedent for the proposition that the creation and use of false documents and testimony in the investigative and prosecutorial context may not be so violative of due process and a defendant's fundamental rights as to warrant dismissal of a criminal indictment (*see People v. Archer*, 68 A.D.2d 441, 417 N.Y.S.2d 507, *affd.* 49 N.Y.2d 978, 428 N.Y.S.2d 949, 406 N.E.2d 804, *cert. den.* 449 U.S. 839, 101 S.Ct. 117, 66 L.Ed.2d 46), *such conduct may, nevertheless, be unethical* (*cf. United States v. Archer*, 486 F.2d 670; *People v. Rao*, 73 A.D.2d 88, 425 N.Y.S.2d 122).

Respondent's argument that his conduct was not unethical because it was motivated by a desire to protect Lewis and prompted by his responsibilities as Inspector General is essentially a contention that the end justifies the means. This argument was properly rejected by the referee who relied upon *Matter of Friedman*, 76 Ill.2d 392, 30 Ill.Dec. 288, 392 N.E.2d 1333 *and Olmstead v. United States*, 277 U.S. 438, 485, 48 S.Ct. 564, 575, 72 L.Ed. 944 *[Brandeis, J., dissenting]*; *see, also, Matter of Zanger*, 266 N.Y. 165, 194 N.E. 72; *Disciplinary Action Against Attorney for Misconduct Related to Performance of Official Duties as Prosecuting Attorney, Ann.*, 10 A.L.R. 4th 605, *supra*. We also note that it is not entirely clear the "means" chosen by respondent to protect Lewis' identity was the only alternative available. The department legal counsel testified before the referee that possible alternatives might have included the taking of statements from the correction officers in a manner which would not have revealed what any of the guards testified to, or the use of some sort of witness protection program.

Next, we reject respondent's contention that his conduct was justified pursuant to section 35.05 (subd. 1) of the Penal Law because it was "performed by a public servant in the reasonable exercise of his official powers, duties, or functions". While the defense of justification may relieve respondent of criminal liability (*cf. People v. Archer*, 68 A.D.2d 441, 448, 417 N.Y.S.2d 507, *supra; see, generally, People v. Mattison*, 75 A.D.2d 959, 428 N.Y.S.2d 355) *or civil liability* (*cf. Sindle v. New York City Tr. Auth.*, 33 N.Y.2d 293, 352 N.Y.S.2d 183, 307 N.E.2d 245), the defense does not necessarily render his actions ethical or even in accord with due process strictures (see Matter of Friedman, supra [Underwood, J., concurring]).

Lastly, we also reject respondent's argument that as a public official exercising prosecutorial and investigative discretion he should be immune from disciplinary action. In one of the cases cited by respondent, which deals with the immunity of public officials from being held liable in damages for their actions, the Supreme Court noted:

> Moreover, a prosecutor stands perhaps unique, among officials whose acts could deprive persons of constitutional rights, in his amenability to professional discipline by an association of his peers. These checks undermine the argument that the imposition of civil liability is the only way to insure that prosecutors are mindful of the constitutional rights of persons accused of crime (*Imbler v. Pachtman*, 424 U.S. 409, 429, 96 S.Ct. 984, 994, 47 L.Ed.2d 128, *supra*).

In view of the above, we confirm the referee's report insofar as it found respondent violated DR 1–102 (subd. [A], par. [4]), "A lawyer shall not: * * * Engage in conduct involving dishonesty, fraud, deceit, or misrepresentation." It is not clear whether the referee, by solely mentioning DR 1–102 (subd. [A], par. [4]) intended to exonerate respondent of violations of other ethical rules. However, we find respondent did not violate DR 1–102 (subd. [A], par. [3]), "illegal conduct involving moral turpitude", or DR 1–102 (subd. [A], par. [6]), "any other conduct that adversely reflects on his fitness to practice law". Nor has respondent violated section 487 of the Judiciary Law which states, in pertinent part, that:

> An attorney or counselor who:
>
> 1.   Is guilty of any deceit or collusion, or consents to any deceit or collusion, with intent to deceive the court or any party * * *
>
> Is guilty of a misdemeanor, and in addition to the punishment prescribed therefor by the penal law, he forfeits to the party injured treble damages, to be recovered in a civil action.

This statute is inapplicable herein because no one is attempting to hold respondent criminally liable or to collect treble damages. This is not to say this court does not have the power to discipline an attorney for acts which may constitute a crime before trial and conviction for such crime (see *Matter of Kammerlohr*, 171 App.Div. 781, 785, 157 N.Y.S. 933; *see, also, Ex Parte Wall*, 107 U.S. 265, 2 S.Ct. 569, 27 L.Ed. 552; *Matter of Popper*, 193 App.Div. 505, 511, 184 N.Y.S. 406, supra).

The purpose of a sanction in a disciplinary proceeding is not to punish but to protect the public, to deter similar conduct, and to preserve the reputation of the. In view of these purposes, and noting that this is a case of first impression in this State, that respondent appears to have acted out of a laudable motive, namely, to protect a witness willing to risk retaliation for breaking the correction officers' "code of silence", that respondent has had no prior disciplinary problems, and that respondent admitted the facts underlying the charge against him, we find censure to be an appropriate sanction.

Respondent censured.

PART III

The Arbitral Tribunal

The following materials address the composition of the arbitral tribunal. Chapter 9 will outline the methods of appointing an arbitral tribunal. Chapter 10 will cover the possible challenges to arbitrators and how to make them. Both chapters very much function together—in appointing an arbitrator, one should make sure that the candidate for the position will not be subject to challenge. At the same time, the reasons that a candidate may be subject to challenge may present interesting questions about the appointment process in its own right. The choice or challenge of an arbitrator are among the most important decisions counsel can make in an arbitration.

As you read the following materials, and as you focus on the issues posed by client representation in arbitration, you should not lose from sight what you are learning about the arbitration clause. Your colleagues may in the future ask you to assist them in drafting an arbitration clause. What you learn here should also inform how you will answer those queries. For instance, the clause determines how an arbitrator is chosen. You can alter this method of appointment. And you can also affect the manner in which arbitrators have to make disclosures etc. in such a way as to ease future challenges to arbitrators or place additional roadblocks in their way. As you read these materials, keep that in mind and make a mental checklist of dos and don'ts of arbitration clause drafting.

CHAPTER 9

Methods of Appointing an Arbitral Tribunal

The constitution of a tribunal is one of the most important decisions lawyers make during the course of an arbitration. The arbitration clause dictates much of the tribunal's constitution: lawyers who practice arbitration should pay close attention to the drafting stage of the contract The arbitration clause can stipulate that any of the methods described in this chapter—should be used in a specific case. In many cases, the arbitration clause will provide a detailed method of appointment, or choose a default method of appointment by incorporating the arbitration rules of an arbitration institution. That said, it is frequently possible to agree to a different method of constitution of the tribunal, even after a dispute has arisen, and thus counsel must be aware of the different options available to them.

The first question that parties must answer is whether they want to resolve their disputes before a tribunal consisting of one arbitrator or a panel consisting of three arbitrators. This is a question of strategy as well as cost.

No matter the composition of the tribunal, the parties will have to agree upon a method of selecting the tribunal member or members once a dispute has arisen. While there are many ways to choose arbitrators, two opposite models are that the parties choose the arbitrators directly or that an institution appoint a tribunal for the parties. Several alternatives, such as "list appointment" outlined below fall between these two poles. This choice implies important questions of strategy—or experience in the use of arbitration.

Fact Scenario

Mythelene LLC ("*Mythelene*"), a Louisiana company supplies molybdenum to General Steel Inc. ("*General Steel*"), an Ohio company. General Steel uses the molybdenum as part of its steel alloy. Mythelene and General Steel have agreed to an output contract for a period of seven years. This output contract requires Mythelene to supply, and General Steel to buy, all molybdenum produced by Mythelene for a seven-year period.

At the time General Steel and Mythelene conclude the output contract, Mythelene owns mining interests in Colorado and Uzbekistan. The Uzbek mine makes up about 30% of Mythelene's output. The contract contains the following arbitration clause:

> Any controversy or claim arising out of or relating to this contract, or the breach thereof, shall be settled by arbitration administered by the American Arbitration Association under its Commercial Arbitration Rules, and judgment on the award rendered by the arbitrator(s) may be entered in any court having jurisdiction thereof.

In the second year of the contract, the Uzbek government commences legal proceedings against Mythelene's Uzbek subsidiary, alleging that the company obtained the mining license by means of fraud. After a short administrative proceeding, the license is revoked, Mythelene is forcibly evicted from the site, and the mining concession is rebid to a third party. Mythelene has commenced international legal proceedings against Uzbekistan, asserting that Uzbekistan unlawfully expropriated Mythelene's investment.

In the meantime, General Steel is receiving 30% less molybdenum from Mythelene and must cover on the open market to meet its production needs. It has to pay a 12.2% premium above the output contract price to do so. General Steel has filed a request for arbitration under the contract, asserting that Mythelene breached the contract and requesting damages.

The AAA sends the following list of arbitrators to the parties (in alphabetical order):

<u>Christopher R. Drahozal, Associate Dean for Research, University of Kansas School of Law</u>

From the web biography of Professor Drahozal (available at https://law.ku. edu/faculty/christopher-drahozal):

Chris Drahozal is an internationally known scholar whose writing focuses on the law and economics of dispute resolution, particularly arbitration. Drahozal is the author of multiple books and numerous articles on commercial arbitration. He has given presentations on the subject in Europe, Asia, South America, Canada and the United States, and has testified before Congress and state legislatures on arbitration matters as well. He is serving as an Associate Reporter for the ALI's Restatement of the U.S. Law of International Commercial and Investor-State Arbitration, and previously served as a Special Advisor to the Consumer Financial Protection Bureau, assisting with its study of arbitration clauses in consumer financial services contracts. He is on the Board of Directors of Arbitrator Intelligence, a non-

profit working to improve the process for selecting international arbitrators. Drahozal also is a well-respected teacher and received the Immel Award for Teaching Excellence in 2004. Prior to coming to KU, Professor Drahozal practiced law with Sidley & Austin in Washington, D.C., and served as a law clerk for Chief Judge Charles Clark of the United States Court of Appeals for the Fifth Circuit, Justice Byron R. White of the United States Supreme Court, and Judge George H. Aldrich of the Iran-United States Claims Tribunal in The Hague, The Netherlands.

Courses Taught:

Contracts

Commercial Arbitration

Commercial Law

Trusts and Estates

Education

J.D., Iowa, 1986, Articles Editor, Iowa Law Review; B.A., Washington University, 1983.

<u>Bradley Haddock, Wichita, KS</u>

From the website biography of Mr. Haddock (http://www.haddocklawoffice. com/about.html):

Bradley E. Haddock was born in Wichita, Kansas, on January 4, 1955, and was admitted to practice law in 1980 in Kansas and the U.S. District Court, District of Kansas. He received a Bachelor of Science degree from Phillips University in 1977, where he was recognized as a Representative Phillipian (selected as one of 12 top senior students). As an undergraduate, he participated in the Washington Semester Government Intern Program at American University and worked for Congressman Garner E. Shriver (Fourth District of Kansas) as a member of his staff in 1976. Brad received his law degree from Washburn University School of Law in 1980, where he served as the Executive Editor of the Washburn Law Journal and graduated cum laude.

Brad offers a wide-range of legal expertise and hands-on experience, as well as industry-specific legal and business knowledge. HADDOCK LAW OFFICE, LLC, was founded in January 2009 following a successful in-house legal and executive career, where Brad served as the Executive Vice President, General Counsel & Secretary of Koch Chemical Technology Group ("KCTG"), a wholly owned subsidiary of Koch Industries, Inc., the largest privately held company in the United States. During his distinguished career at Koch, Brad served as lead counsel for several key businesses, including Koch's refining, chemicals, and asphalt businesses, and the group of 10 global manufacturing and engineering businesses that became

KCTG. While at Koch, he led or significantly participated in more than 85 domestic and international acquisitions.

Brad has served as a member of the board of directors of the American Arbitration Association from 2005 through 2017. He continues to serve on an advisory council regarding AAA expectations for arbitrators. He is a qualified member of the American Arbitration Association's Roster of Neutrals and a member of the prestigious Panel of Arbitrators of the International Centre for Dispute Resolution. During his tenure at Koch, Brad was an active member of the Association of Corporate Counsel. He is also a member of the Association for Corporate Growth, American Bar Association, Christian Legal Society, Kansas Bar Association, Licensing Executives Society, and the Wichita Bar Association. In November 2016, Brad was elected to serve as a member of the Board of Trustees of Friends University, a Christian university dedicated to spiritual growth and formation as an integral part of its curriculum.

In August 2014, Brad became an Independent Certified Coach, Teacher & Speaker with the John Maxwell Team. He was recognized in October as the 2012 Alumni Fellow by the Washburn University School of Law. For more than fifteen years, he has received an AV Preeminent rating (5.0 out of 5.0) from Martindale-Hubbell, the highest peer review rating available for legal expertise and ethics. Recommendations from clients and colleagues may be found at LinkedIn. You can also visit the Haddock Law Office Facebook page at Facebook.

A lifelong member of the Boy Scouts of America ("BSA"), Brad is a Distinguished Eagle Scout, served as Quivira Council President, and has been recognized by the National Council with its highest commendation, the Silver Buffalo Award, for his noteworthy and extraordinary volunteer service to youth. He served as the Chairman of the National Order of the Arrow Committee from 2000 to 2009. During his term, Brad championed and led the ArrowCorps5 project during the summer of 2008, the largest single volunteer service project ever received by the United States Forest Service in its 100-plus year history and the largest service project provided by the BSA since World War II. The project served five forest sites, contributed 280,000 hours of volunteer service worth more than $5.6 million, and delivered much needed service to our precious public lands.

In May 2015, Brad became the chairman of the Board of Regents for Scouting University. He had previously served as chairman of the Outdoor Adventures Committee, responsible for all of the BSA's outdoor program other than the National Jamboree and The Summit Bechtel Family Scout Reserve, since February 2012. He was elected to the National Executive Board of the BSA during the national annual meeting held on May 31, 2012, in Orlando, Florida. Brad served as program chairman and as a speaker at the 2013 Sustainability Summit hosted by the Boy Scouts of America from October 7 to 10, at The Greenbrier, White Sulphur Springs, West Virginia. During the conference Brad was honored as the first recipient of the Volunteer Sustainability Award. He served as Program Chairman for the 2010 100th

Anniversary National BSA Jamboree and recently completed his service as Chairman of the Second Century Camping Task Force for the BSA National Council.

Brad is a recipient of the Outstanding Young Alumnus Award from Phillips University; he was a participant in the inaugural class of Leadership 2000, sponsored by the Wichita Area Chamber of Commerce, and later served as Leadership 2000 Chairman. Brad and his family are actively involved at East Evangelical Free Church where he has served as Chairman of the Elder Board

Jean Kalicki, New York, NY

From the web biography of Ms. Kalicki (https://kalicki-arbitration.com):

Jean Kalicki is an independent arbitrator in New York and Washington, DC, specializing in investor-State, international and complex commercial disputes. Until April 2016, she was a Partner at Arnold & Porter LLP, serving as counsel in a wide range of high-stakes international disputes. Over more than 25 years, she has conducted arbitrations involving six continents, across a wide range of industries and disputed issues, addressing issues of public international law and the laws of dozens of different countries.

Ms. Kalicki is a Vice President of the Court of the London Court of International Arbitration (LCIA), and a member of the American Arbitration Association (AAA) Council and previously its Board of Directors, the International Chamber of Commerce (ICC) Commission on Arbitration and the Board of Directors of SICANA, Inc. (ICC North America), and the Governing Board of the International Council for Commercial Arbitration (ICCA). She is listed on the Panel of Arbitrators of the International Centre for Settlement of Investment Disputes (ICSID) and many other institutions around the world. She is a Fellow of the Chartered Institute of Arbitrators (FCIArb) and of the College of Commercial Arbitrators (CCA) and taught arbitration and advocacy for many years as an adjunct professor at both Georgetown University Law Center and American University Washington College of Law.

Ms. Kalicki was selected as Global Arbitration Review's "Best Prepared/Most Responsive Arbitrator" for 2017, and one of Law360's "Five Most Influential Female International Arbitrators" for 2016. She is among Chambers' Band 1 ("Most In-Demand") Arbitrators for Global, USA and Public International Law (2017–2018), and Best Lawyers' "Lawyer of the Year" for International Arbitration-Governmental in New York (2017 and 2019) and Washington DC (2016).

Additional information about her education and background, experience as arbitrator and counsel, rankings and recognition, professional activities, and publications and presentations is available through the links on the left and in the downloadable CV.

<u>William H. Knull, Houston, TX</u>

From the web biography of Mr. Knull (http://www.whkarb.com):

I began to devote my practice exclusively to service as an independent arbitrator after retiring as a partner of Mayer Brown LLP effective December 31, 2014 after 37 years litigating and arbitrating complex disputes, primarily involving transnational disputes, first with Sullivan & Cromwell in New York and from 1986 through 2014 with Mayer Brown in Houston.

From my first overseas trip as a lawyer and my introduction to international arbitration several years later, I have acted as counsel and lead counsel in international litigation and arbitration involving oil and gas, telecommunications, mergers and acquisitions, investor-state disputes, power generation, etc., in a broad range of highly complex technical, factual, legal and procedural contexts.

As those who have worked with or against me will attest, I have conducted these cases throughout as a hands-on advocate. As a result, I have a first-hand appreciation for the challenges faced by arbitral tribunals in fashioning proceedings to secure a fair, prompt and efficient resolution of the most complex disputes, consistent with the needs of the case, choices and preferences of the parties, governing rules and applicable law.

As my experience as an arbitrator expands, I am finding my years of advocacy invaluable in tailoring procedures to the issues presented, absorbing and digesting complex evidence and law, balancing and weighing the strengths and weaknesses of evidence and arguments, and reaching prompt, efficient and just resolutions.

My experience as both advocate and arbitrator has not infrequently involved the issue of dispositive motions. From the perspective of the arbitrator, the issue requires a careful balancing of important but potentially conflicting considerations. On the one hand, opening the arbitration process to unregulated motion practice threatens to bog the process down, resulting in unnecessary and avoidable cost and delay. On the other hand, the early resolution of appropriate elements of a dispute may expedite the overall resolution; indeed, failure to hear and resolve such issues can itself result in unnecessary and avoidable cost and delay. At least three types of motions, drawn from the principles incorporated in familiar rules of court, may justify early disposition: (i) jurisdictional motions, for obvious reasons; (ii) motions contending that, assuming all facts pleaded by claimant/counterclaimant are true and making all inferences in favor of the non-moving party, there is no set facts that would entitle the non-movant to prevail under the governing law and contract; and (iii) motions establishing that undisputed facts establish that the moving party is entitled to prevail as a matter of law under the contract. Balancing these competing interests consistently with fundamental considerations of fairness and due process requires the arbitrator to manage the motion process carefully, through scheduling and pre-screening to ensure that potentially meritorious motions may be heard without undue disruption to the overall process while reserving less clearcut contentions for resolution along with the merits.

One common element of many of the large cases I have handled as an advocate was the central role of complex computational issues, including, for example, oil and gas reserve estimation and damage calculations based on the present value of projected future income streams. As a result, I am quite comfortable with complex mathematical models and the analysis of component variables that determine disputed outcomes. An example can be seen in the article of which I was lead author, published in both The Journal of Energy and Natural Resources and TransnationalDisputeManagement.com titled Accounting for Uncertainty in Discounted Cash Flow Valuation of Upstream Oil and Gas Investments (full cite listed with publications).

For more than twenty years, I have been an active participant in and follower of arbitrations involving parties and projects in Latin America. As a result, I undertook and sustained an intense study of Spanish, which my very gifted teacher began by parsing vocabulary and grammar lessons from paragraphs taken from publicly available laudos, progressing to readings from literature and periodicals from the region and debates on current events. I remain an avid student of the history, culture and politics of the Hispanic world, as well as the language itself, through reading Spanish language newspapers and works of fiction and non-fiction and frequent travel. While I do not profess oral fluency, a great deal of my work in the last ten years profited greatly from my ability to analyze documents, statutes, reference materials and oral testimony in the original Spanish.

International arbitration is essential to the increasingly inter-connected world. Its future depends in no small part on the availability of a pool of expert arbitrators able to resolve disputes fairly, promptly and cost-effectively. I am fully committed to doing what I can to contribute to that objective.

<u>Lucinda Low, Partner Steptoe & Johnson, Washington, DC.</u>

From the web biography of Ms. Low (https://www.steptoe.com/en/lawyers/lucinda-low.html):

Lucinda Low's practice includes representing audit committees, boards of directors, and companies in internal, government, and international financial institution audits, investigations, and enforcement matters involving fraud, bribery, corruption, and other compliance issues. Lucinda is recognized by Chambers market commentators for her "incredible technical proficiency, spectacular advocacy skills, and cultural know-how." She has particular authority in matters involving the US Foreign Corrupt Practices Act (FCPA) and other anti-bribery and anti-corruption laws, and other international business compliance issues. According to Chambers, clients concur that Lucinda is "very impressive" and credit her with "an attention to detail that is second to none."

In the FCPA/anti-corruption realm, Lucinda helps clients develop and implement customized compliance programs tailored to their business risks that meet regulatory expectations, assists with due diligence in M&A and other transactions, provides risk-mitigation and risk assessment strategy, conducts internal investigations, and defends clients in government investigation and enforcement matters, including multijurisdictional investigations. She also has significant experience in investment disputes between foreign investors and host governments, and commercial arbitration, including serving as counsel, arbitrator, and an expert witness.

Lucinda serves as a member of the firm's Management Committee and heads the Compliance, Investigations, Trade and Enforcement Department. She also leads Steptoe's Brazil-specific initiative incorporating a focus on FCPA/anti-corruption compliance and enforcement work. Lucinda's FCPA/anti-corruption experience includes extensive work in Latin America, including Argentina, Bolivia, Brazil, Chile, Colombia, Costa Rica, Ecuador, Guyana, Mexico, Nicaragua, Peru, Uruguay and Venezuela, as well as several Caribbean countries.

As a complement to her practice, Lucinda assists in the creation and supervision of the International Law Guides, a web-accessible compliance tool designed to provide corporate subscribers and their employees with detailed information on local anti-corruption laws around the globe.

Lucinda is a member of the Board of Directors of the Coalition for Integrity (formerly known as Transparency International—USA), and also a member of the Secretary of State's Advisory Committee on International Law. She is a former President of the American Society of International Law and a former Chair of the ABA Section of International Law. She was the 2003 recipient of the William Ray Vallance Award presented by the Inter-American Bar Foundation, presented to an individual who has made a significant contribution toward improving the law and jurisprudence of the Western Hemisphere.

Lucinda is fluent in Portuguese and Spanish, and has lived in Brazil on two separate occasions.

<u>Jennifer Price, Partner, King & Spalding, Houston, TX.</u>

From the web biography of Ms. Price (https://www.transnational-dispute-management.com/about-author-a-z-profile.asp?key=1408):

Ms. Price has represented energy, oil field service, power, and petrochemical companies in complex arbitration and litigation. Virtually all of her cases now involve international oil and gas, power, or petrochemical matters, including disputes involving Host Governments, state-owned oil companies and power companies, production sharing agreement and JOA disputes, and disputes with promoters and local representatives, in both arbitration and litigation.

Ms. Price is experienced in all phases of international arbitration in both administered and ad hoc proceedings, including drafting agreements to arbitrate, initiating and compelling arbitration, selecting arbitrators, discovery, pre-hearing matters and briefing, evidentiary hearings, and enforcement and challenge of arbitral awards. Her experience and skill have been recognized in her being named among the World's Leading Experts in Commercial Arbitration 2008 by Legal Media Group.

Her recent matters include representing different international oil companies in separate litigation matters concerning interests in offshore North Caspian and onshore oil fields in Kazakhstan, representing investor oil companies in disputes with a state oil company over breach of and the right to renegotiate a Production Sharing Agreement, representing a multinational power generator in two UNCITRAL arbitrations against a state enterprise to enforce power purchase and transmission agreements, and representing an oil terminal operator in an ICC arbitration against a state oil company over expropriation of contract rights. Other recent matters have included disputes over contracts and investments in El Salvador, Venezuela, Ivory Coast, Nigeria, North Africa, and Russia, among other areas, in proceedings under UNCITRAL, ICC, AAA/ICDR, LCIA, ICSID, and other arbitral regimes.

She also frequently works with clients and transactional attorneys in advising on options and strategies for negotiating arbitration and dispute resolution agreements, and in drafting arbitration and dispute resolution agreements for both domestic and cross-border transactions.

Ms. Price is a member of the Houston International Arbitration Club, the Chartered Institute of Arbitrators, Arbitralwomen, and the Association of International Petroleum Negotiators, and is on the Advisory Board of the Institute for Transnational Arbitration. She has numerous achievements, publications, and speaking engagements to her credit. Ms. Price received her J.D. in 1986 from the University of San Diego School of Law, where she was a member of the San Diego Law Review.

Language Capabilities:

Proficient in reading Spanish and French

Education

J.D., cum laude

University of San Diego School of Law

B.A., with distinction

San Diego State University

Admitted to Practice

Texas

10th Circuit Court of Appeals

5th Circuit Court of Appeals

Colorado District Court

Texas Eastern District Court

Texas Northern District Court

Texas Southern District Court

<u>Abraham Sofaer, New York, NY</u>

From the web biography of Judge Sofaer (https://www.fedarb.com/professionals/abraham-sofaer/):

JUDGE ABRAHAM D. SOFAER (FORMER)

U. S. DISTRICT COURT, SOUTHERN DISTRICT OF NEW YORK

Arbitrator & Mediator

Judge Sofaer specializes in arbitrating complex commercial disputes. He has extensive experience in the federal courts. He served as a U.S. District Judge in the Southern District of New York from 1979 until 1985. From 1967 to 1969, he was an assistant U.S. attorney in the Southern District of New York, during which time he tried twenty cases and argued five appeals in the Second Circuit Court of Appeals.

He was a clerk to Judge J. Skelly Wright on the U.S. Court of Appeals in Washington, D.C. from 1965 to 1966, and to the Honorable William J. Brennan Jr., Associate Justice of the U.S. Supreme Court from 1966 to 1967.

From 1985 to 1990, Judge Sofaer served as Legal Adviser to the U.S. Department of State, representing the U.S. in international arbitrations and in cases before the International Court of Justice. He was also principal negotiator in several international claims. Judge Sofaer was awarded the Distinguished Service Award in 1989, the highest State Department award given to a non-civil servant.

After leaving the Department of State, Judge Abraham Sofaer practiced law at Hughes, Hubbard and Reed in Washington, D.C., from 1990 to 1994. He has served as an arbitrator in many cases, both independently and under the auspices of leading domestic and international arbitration services.

A veteran of the U.S. Air Force, Abraham Sofaer received an LL.B. degree from New York University School of Law in 1965, where he was editor in chief of the law review and a Root-Tilden scholar. He holds a B.A. in history from Yeshiva College (1962). Judge Sofaer currently serves as the George P. Shultz Distinguished Scholar and Senior Fellow at the Hoover Institution, Stanford University.

Areas of Expertise: commercial litigation and arbitration; international law; insurance litigation; administrative law; corporate governance.

JUDGE ABRAHAM SOFAER SELECTED OPINIONS:

Vargas v. Insurance Co. of No. America, 651 F.2d 838 (2d Cir. 1981)(by designation)(insurance);

Rapco Foam, Inc. v. Scientific Applications, Inc., 479 F. Supp. 1027 (S.D.N.Y. 1979) (trade secrets);

Playboy Enterprises, Inc. v. Chuckleberry Publishing, Inc., 486 F. Supp. 1191 (S.D.N.Y. 1980), aff'd, 687 F.2d 563 (2d Cir. 1982);

Anglo Eastern Bulkships Ltd. v. Ameron, Inc., 556 F. Supp. 1198 (S.D.N.Y. 1982)(product liability/admiralty);

Home Box Office, Inc. v. Directors Guild of America, Inc., 531 F. Supp., 578 (S.D.N.Y. 1982), aff'd, 708 F.2d 95 (2d Cir. 1983)(labor antitrust);

American Home Products Corp. v. Liberty Mutual Ins. Co., 565 F. Supp., 1485 (S.D.N.Y. 1983), aff'd as modified, 748 F.2d 760 (2d Cir. 1984)(insurance);

Sharon v. Time, Inc., 575 F. Supp. 1162 (S.D.N.Y. 1983)(libel);

Elyachar v. Gerel Corp., 583 F. Supp. 907 (S.D.N.Y. 1984)(gifts; trusts);

Reborn Enterprises, Inc. v. Fine Child, Inc., 590 F. Supp. 1423 (S.D.N.Y. 1984), aff'd 754 F.2d 1072 (2d Cir. N.Y. 1985)(antitrust);

Ackerman v. Oryx Communications, Inc., 609 F. Supp. 363 (S.D.N.Y. 1984), aff'd with remand, 810 F.2d 336 (2d Cir. 1987)(securities);

Frigitemp Corp. v. Bernstein, 34 B.R. 1000 (S.D.N.Y. 1983), aff'd, 753 F2d 230 (2d Cir. 1985)(bankruptcy).

JUDGE ABRAHAM SOFAER CURRENT AFFILIATIONS:

George P. Shultz Senior Fellow, The Hoover Institution, Stanford University

Gen-Probe, Inc., Director, Chair of Governance & Appointments Committee, Member, Audit Committee

Rambus, Inc., Director, Member, Governance & Compensation Committees

Chugai Pharmaceutical, Member, International Advisory Committee

Koret Foundation, Trustee

American Friends of the Koret Israel Economic Development Fund, Chairman

National Jazz Museum in Harlem, Founder and Vice Chairman

Arbitration Services: Federal Arbitration, Inc. Founder & Chairman; ICC; AAA; ICDR; CPR; LCIA; and other ad hoc processes.

<u>S.I. Strong, Professor of Law, University of Missouri Law School, Columbia, MO</u>

From the web biography of Professor Strong (http://law.missouri.edu/about/people/strong/):

Manley O. Hudson Professor of Law

BA, University of California, Davis, '86 (cum laude)

Master of Professional Writing, University of Southern California, '90

JD, Duke University Law School, '94

D.Phil., University of Oxford, '03

Ph.D. (Law), University of Cambridge, '02

S.I. Strong is the Manley O. Hudson Professor of Law at the University of Missouri School of Law. She has also taught jurisprudence and British constitutional, contract and tort law at the University of Cambridge and the University of Oxford in the United Kingdom and international commercial arbitration at Georgetown University Law Center in Washington, D.C.

Professor Strong specializes in public and private international law, comparative law (particularly with respect to procedural and constitutional matters) and jurisprudence. She has had over 100 books, articles and other works published in Europe, Asia and the Americas, and her scholarship has been cited as authority by U.S. courts and international arbitral tribunals. Her research, which has been translated into Spanish, French, Portuguese, Russian and Chinese, has also won accolades from a variety of national and international organizations.

Prior to joining the faculty at Missouri, Professor Strong worked as a dual-qualified practitioner (U.S.-U.K.) in the New York and London offices of Weil, Gotshal & Manges LLP and as Counsel at Baker & McKenzie LLP in Chicago. During her years in practice, she handled complex commercial disputes involving both private parties and state and other public entities in U.S. and English courts. She also represented clients in bilateral and multilateral arbitrations seated in a wide variety of jurisdictions. As counsel, she worked on one of the largest ICC arbitrations in history and handled arbitral matters proceeding under the auspices of the PCA, the ICC, the ICDR, the LCIA and the AAA, as well as ad hoc proceedings under the UNCITRAL Arbitration Rules.

Professor Strong currently serves as an arbitrator, mediator and expert witness in complex commercial disputes. She has handled numerous cases as sole, presiding or party-appointed neutral, including multimillion dollar disputes and multiparty matters involving anywhere from three to twenty-five parties. Professor Strong is listed on the national and international rosters of various arbitral organizations, including the AAA Commercial Arbitration Panel,

FINRA, the ICC, the ICDR, the LCIA, USA&M-Midwest and WIPO. She is also listed as a mediator with the International Council of Museums Art and Cultural Heritage Mediation Program, Missouri federal courts and other organizations. As a result of her expertise in complex commercial disputes, Professor Strong has been named a fellow by both the College of Commercial Arbitrators (CCA) and the Chartered Institute of Arbitrators (CIArb).

Professor Strong is actively involved in international lawmaking in a variety of capacities. Not only does she work with the U.S. State Department's Advisory Committee on Private International Law, she also represents non-governmental organizations (NGOs) at meetings of the United Nations Commission on International Trade Law (UNCITRAL).

Over the years, Professor Strong has served as a U.S. Supreme Court Fellow in Washington, D.C., the Henry G. Schermers Fellow at The Hague Institute for the Internationalisation of Law in The Netherlands, a Visiting Researcher at the Max Planck Institute for Comparative and International Private Law in Hamburg, Germany, and a Visiting Fellow at the Lauterpacht Centre for International Law at the University of Cambridge in the United Kingdom. Professor Strong is an elected member of the American Law Institute (ALI) and a Fellow of the European Law Institute (ELI). She has held leadership positions in a number of professional organizations, most recently as the Co-Chair of the American Society of International Law's Private International Law Interest Group.

Professor Strong received a Ph.D. in law from the University of Cambridge, where she won the Yorke Prize for outstanding doctoral dissertation; a D.Phil. from the University of Oxford; a J.D. from Duke University School of Law; a Master of Professional Writing degree from the University of Southern California; and a B.A. in English literature from the University of California, Davis. While at Duke, she served as Editor in Chief of the Duke Journal of Comparative & International Law. She is admitted to practice in state and federal courts in New York, Illinois and Missouri as well as the United States Supreme Court, and as a solicitor in both Ireland and in England and Wales. Professor Strong is proficient in Spanish and is a member of the Order of the Coif.

<u>Edna Sussman, New York, NY</u>

From the web biography of Ms. Sussman (https://sussmanadr.com):

Edna Sussman serves full-time as an arbitrator and mediator and has been appointed as the Distinguished ADR Practitioner in Residence by the Fordham University School of Law. She started her career as an associate and litigation partner at the international law firm of White & Case. Over the past 15 years she has served as an arbitrator in well over 200 arbitrations and as a mediator in well over 200 mediations in both domestic and international complex commercial disputes.

Ms. Sussman serves on leading ADR panels around the world and has conducted arbitrations under many institutional rules and in ad hoc arbitrations. Ms. Sussman serves as one of six arbitration trainers nationwide for the American Arbitration Association's new arbitrators, as the former President of the College of Commercial Arbitrators, on the board of the American Arbitration Association, as Vice-Chair of the New York International Arbitration Center and Chair of the AAA-ICDR Foundation. She has published and lectured extensively on arbitration and mediation and wins annual recognition for her work as an arbitrator and mediator in many rankings including Chambers Global, Chambers USA, Who's Who of International Arbitration and Mediation, Best Lawyers and Super Lawyers.

As an arbitrator, Ms. Sussman ensures that the parties get a fair and effectively managed proceeding. As a mediator, Ms. Sussman has a talent for guiding the parties to a mutually satisfactory settlement of the dispute.

Chambers: "very quick to learn the facts and arguments presented to her, and she makes quick and practical rulings," "She is excellent. . .she is well prepared, well read and interested in making sure all parties have their opportunities," "highly respected and really knows the business," "terrific and dedicated," "extremely accomplished," "a real scholar in the field," "incredibly smart."

Georgene Vairo, Professor of Law, Loyola Law School, Los Angeles, CA

From the web biography of Professor Vairo (https://www.pli.edu/Content/Faculty/Georgene_M_Vairo/_/N-4oZ1z136j2?ID=PE215399):

Georgene Vairo teaches and writes in the areas of mass tort litigation, class actions, international dispute resolution, federal practice and jurisdiction. She has written Rule 11 Sanctions and the chapters on removal jurisdiction, venue, and multidistrict litigation in Moore's Federal Practice. In addition to dozens of articles about federal practice and procedure, including most recently Is the Class Action Really Dead? Is that Good or Bad for Class Members?, 64 Emory L.J. 477 (2014); Lessons Learned by the Reporter: Is Disaggregation the Answer to the Asbestos Mess?, 88 Tulane L. Rev. 1039 (2014); and What Goes Around, Comes Around; From the Rector of Barkway to Knowles, 32 Univ. Texas Rev. of Litig. 721 (2013), she has published The Complete CAFA: Analysis and Developments Under the Class Action Fairness Act of 2005 (LEXIS 2011), and The Federal Courts Jurisdiction and Venue Clarification Act of 2011: Analysis and Case Law Developments (LEXIS 2013).

Professor Vairo served on the Board of Trustees of the Dalkon Shield Claimants Trust, and as its Chairperson. As Chair, she worked to develop systems for distributing over $3 Billion dollars to over 200,000 claimants. She serves on the editorial board of Moore's Federal Practice, and is the author of two volumes of the Treatise. She also is a member of the Rand Corporation's Institute for Civil Justice Board of Overseers, and is a member of the American

Law Institute. In 2013, she was appointed Reporter to the ABA TIPS Task Force on Asbestos Litigation. She has participated in numerous academic conferences, has lectured widely to the bench and bar at numerous programs of various national and local associations and institutes, and has served as an expert in complex civil litigation cases.

Professor Vairo received her B.A. from Sweet Briar College in Economics, and an M.Ed., with Distinction, in Social Studies from the University of Virginia. She graduated first in her class from Fordham University School of Law. She then served as a law clerk to the Honorable Joseph M. McLaughlin, U.S. Court of Appeals for the Second Circuit (then U.S. District Court for the Eastern District of New York); practiced antitrust law with Skadden Arps Slate Meagher & Flom; and taught at Fordham University School of Law, where she also served for 8 years as Associate Dean. She joined the Loyola Law School faculty in 1995.

Professor Vairo serves as the Vice Chair of and on the Executive Committee of the Board of Directors of Sweet Briar College, and as Vice President and on the Executive Committee of the Museum of Contemporary Art Santa Barbara; she has won national and California bicycle road race and criterion championships; loves sailing, trail running, her golden retrievers, and growing vegetables when it rains in California.

George M. von Mehren, Parner, Squire Sanders, Cleveland, OH

From the web biography of Mr. von Mehren (https://www.squirepattonboggs.com/en/professionals/v/von-mehren-george-m):

With more than 40 years of experience in complex adversarial proceedings, George spends 100% of his time representing clients in international arbitrations and providing strategic advice for litigation in courts outside the US. He has an established record of working effectively with counsel from a wide range of countries in Europe, Latin America and Asia to achieve strong results for clients.

His experience involves representing clients in more than 150 international arbitrations, including many cases with multimillion-dollar to multibillion-dollar claims.

George is a recognized expert in disputes involving the sale and purchase of natural gas and LNG. He also has extensive experience in a variety of commercial and treaty disputes.

George's legal training at Cambridge University (Trinity College) and Harvard Law School provides him with the background necessary to deal with cases governed by both common and civil law. Qualified to practice in several US courts, George is also a Registered Foreign Lawyer with the Solicitors Regulatory Authority (England and Wales). Whether a contract, licensing or joint venture dispute, construction, product liability, securities, insurance or regulatory matter, George is skilled in developing sophisticated strategies designed to win his client's case either at hearing or in settlement negotiations.

Readings

A) The Number of Tribunal Members

The arbitration rules of the relevant arbitral institution will typically set out how many arbitrators should hear a dispute. The rules of arbitral institutions vary in their default position regarding the constitution of a tribunal.

1) AAA Arbitration Rules

AAA Commercial Arbitration Rules

R–16.   Number of Arbitrators

(a)   If the arbitration agreement does not specify the number of arbitrators, the dispute shall be heard and determined by one arbitrator, unless the AAA, in its discretion, directs that three arbitrators be appointed. A party may request three arbitrators in the Demand or Answer, which request the AAA will consider in exercising its discretion regarding the number of arbitrators appointed to the dispute.

(b)   Any request for a change in the number of arbitrators as a result of an increase or decrease in the amount of a claim or a new or different claim must be made to the AAA and other parties to the arbitration no later than seven calendar days after receipt of the R–6 required notice of change of claim amount. If the parties are unable to agree with respect to the request for a change in the number of arbitrators, the AAA shall make that determination.

NOTES

1.   Why do you think the default position in the AAA Commercial Arbitration Rules is that a dispute will be heard by one arbitrator?

2.   The AAA rules provide discretion to the AAA to determine whether the dispute shall be submitted to a three arbitrator tribunal. How do you think the AAA should use its discretion? If you would advise your client how would you research how the AAA does in fact use its discretion in these instances?

3.   What can parties do under the AAA Commercial Arbitration Rules in order to improve their chances to submit the dispute to a three arbitrator panel?

4.   Why would a party want to deviate from the AAA's default position? Are there instances in which you might prefer more than one decisionmaker? What do those instances have in common?

2) *FINRA Arbitration Rules*

FINRA Code of Arbitration Procedure for Customer Disputes

12401.   Number of Arbitrators

(a)   Claims of $50,000 or Less

If the amount of a claim is $50,000 or less, exclusive of interest and expenses, the panel will consist of one arbitrator and the claim is subject to the simplified arbitration procedures under Rule 12800.

(b)   Claims of More Than $50,000 Up To $100,000

If the amount of a claim is more than $50,000 but not more than $100,000, exclusive of interest and expenses, the panel will consist of one arbitrator unless the parties agree in writing to three arbitrators.

(c)   Claims of More Than $100,000; Unspecified or Non-Monetary Claims

If the amount of a claim is more than $100,000, exclusive of interest and expenses, or is unspecified, or if the claim does not request money damages, the panel will consist of three arbitrators, unless the parties agree in writing to one arbitrator.

NOTES

1.   How do the rules of FINRA and AAA differ? Do you think that the AAA would follow similar monetary thresholds in deciding whether to submit a dispute to a single arbitrator or three arbitrators?

2.   FINRA operates somewhat analogously to a bar for brokers and investment firms. For example, it can take disciplinary action against registered brokers and companies, and it makes available arbitration procedures for the complaints of consumers against financial industry companies and professionals. Does this explain why the FINRA limits the discretion of the institution administering the arbitration in determining how many arbitrators should hear the claim? Assume you are a consumer bringing a claim, and FINRA exercised its discretion to depart from the

default position of the arbitral institution's rules upon request of a broker. How would you feel and what would be your recourse?

3) *International Arbitration Rules*

UNCITRAL Arbitration Rules (2013)

Article 7

1.   If the parties have not previously agreed on the number of arbitrators, and if within 30 days after the receipt by the respondent of the notice of arbitration the parties have not agreed that there shall be only one arbitrator, three arbitrators shall be appointed.

2.   Notwithstanding paragraph 1, if no other parties have responded to a party's proposal to appoint a sole arbitrator within the time limit provided for in paragraph 1 and the party or parties concerned have failed to appoint a second arbitrator in accordance with article 9 or 10, the appointing authority may, at the request of a party, appoint a sole arbitrator pursuant to the procedure provided for in article 8, paragraph 2, if it determines that, in view of the circumstances of the case, this is more appropriate.

NOTES

1.   UNCITRAL is the United Nations Commission on International Trade Law. The appointment provisions in the UNCITRAL Arbitration Rules are not typical for international arbitration. The arbitration rules of the International Chamber of Commerce (ICC) and the London Court of International Arbitration (LCIA) essentially track the AAA Commercial Arbitration Rules. Why do you think the UNCITRAL Arbitration Rules differ on the default being three arbitrators rather than a sole arbitrator?

2.   The UNCITRAL 2010 rules are the second iteration of the UNCITRAL Arbitration Rules after the first version of the rules issued in 1976, which are arguably the most influential ad hoc arbitration rules in the world. Many UNCITRAL arbitrations proceed outside of an institutional context—that is, there is not an institution with the discretion to change the composition of the tribunal. Consider the following discussion of the number of arbitrators during the revision of the 1976 Rules:

> Report of the Working Group on Arbitration and Conciliation
> on the work of its forty-fifth session (Vienna, 11–15 September

2006), https://documents-dds-ny.un.org/doc/UNDOC/GEN/ V06/575/26/PDF/V0657526.pdf?OpenElement

Number of arbitrators—Article 5

59. The Working Group proceeded to consider whether the default rule on the number of arbitrators of three members should be modified. In support of retaining the default composition for arbitral tribunal of three members, it was said that the default rule of three arbitrators was a well-established feature of the UNCITRAL Arbitration Rules, reproduced in the Model Law, ensured a certain level of security by not relying on a single arbitrator, and should in the interests of familiarity be retained.

60. In favour of inclusion of a default rule of a sole arbitrator, it was said that such a rule would render arbitration less costly and thus make it more accessible, particularly to poorer parties and in less complex cases. However, it was questioned whether such parties might prefer the less costly option of a sole arbitrator and it was suggested that arbitral practice indicated that such parties preferred a three member panel which allowed them to choose at least one arbitrator. The Working Group observed that it was normal practice to have one arbitrator as the default rule in arbitrations administered by some institutions with a discretion to appoint three arbitrators, subject to contrary agreement by the parties. It was noted that in arbitrations conducted outside the framework of an arbitral institution, discretionary selection of three arbitrators by the institution would not be available. It was suggested that discretion to intervene could be granted to the appointing authority in non-institutional arbitrations to appoint three arbitrators in more complex arbitrations. However, concern was expressed that such discretion fell outside the traditional role for appointing authorities and could introduce a further level of delay in the arbitral proceedings. As well, at the time of appointment of arbitrators, there might not be an appointing authority. It was said that leaving the question of the number of arbitrators to the appointing authority based on the subjective question of whether or not a case was complex introduced a level of uncertainty.

B) Institutional Appointment

There is significant divergence among arbitral institutions regarding who appoints the arbitrator(s)—the parties or the institution. In the context of international arbitration, the London Court of International Arbitration requires appointment of arbitrators by the institution rather than the parties. Its former President, Jan Paulsson, provided a spirited defense of this model.

Jan Paulsson, Moral Hazard in International Dispute Resolution, Inaugural Lecture of the Michael R. Klein Distinguished Scholar Chair

University of Miami School of Law, April 29, 2010

[. . .]

product of realism, doubtless indispensable in a complex world of inter-communal transactions, as a way of making arbitration acceptable—though in a manner which immediately dilutes its purity.

I believe that the reasons for parties' attachment to the practice of unilateral appointments are ill-conceived. Let us consider them.

(i)   *"My nominee will help me win the case."* Putting aside the amorality of this position, it is illogical. Why assume that the other party's nominee will not be at least equally effective? By all means, if both sides understand that the co-arbitrators are to be the champions of their appointers, they should be free, in all transparency, to adopt that procedure. The result will be an expensive curiosity, namely a panel on which only the president is a true arbitrator.

But this kind of overt acceptance of "non-neutral arbitrators"—what an intolerable contradiction in terms!—is no longer accepted in the international community. So the idea that "my nominee will help me win my case" is likely to be conceived dishonestly, in the hope that the other party will foolishly play by the rules. Since other parties cannot be relied upon to be rubes, the result will be a feast of hypocrisy where the innocent are burned—and others engage in pointless charades.

One may well wonder if contract drafters think through the dynamics of three member tribunals. Why should they assume that they can game the system more effectively than their opponent? It is surely just as plausible that the adversary's nominees would be able to bend presiding arbitrators as that one's own nominees would keep them straight.

Perhaps it is all in the way one puts the question. If drafting lawyers say to their client "are you willing to give up your right to appoint an arbitrator?" the answer is likely to be a resounding no. But a rather different response may follow if the same question is turned around: "how would you like it if we find a way to keep the other side from appointing somebody who may turn out to be partisan and obstreperous?" That way, of course, is the reciprocal waiver the opportunity of unilateral appointment.

(ii)   *"Even Homer nods, three heads are better than one, especially when the stakes are high."* This notion is wholly irrelevant to our subject. Unilateral appointments are not needed to constitute three-member tribunals. All three may be appointed by the neutral supervisory body.

(iii)   *"Parties have greater confidence in arbitrators selected for their special knowledge or skill."* This sounds good, especially to anyone who has experienced the anguish of facing a generalist judge who has an insufficient understanding of a highly specialised legal problem. Yet the answer does not lie in unilateral appointments. It would be naïve to think that Party A will appoint an arbitrator having particular qualifications in order to make Party B feel better about the whole thing. The reality is that everything a party does once a dispute has broken out is focussed on winning. Party A may insist the dispute requires the insights of someone well versed in assessing the critical path of an engineering project, while Party B asserts that the true relevant expertise lies in the purely legal subject of fraud in the inducement under the law of Erewhon. The answer, once again, does not lie in unilateral appointments.

(iv)   *"My nominee will ensure that the tribunal as a whole understands my culture."* It is undeniable that acceptance of the mechanism of unilateral appointments on this basis may increase the likelihood of acceptance of a particular arbitral jurisdiction. Such a marketing strategy is understandable on the part of fledgling arbitral institutions. But why should mature institutions need such psychological struts?

The presumption seems to be that someone who understands me better will more likely influence the tribunal so that I win, which suggests that the matter has not advanced from the troublesome reason (i). It seems that this thinking cannot escape the tactic of "selling" arbitration by offering a "concession" to selfish objectives. This suggests that the parties are actually not ready to agree to arbitration at all—because each apparently insists on a "cultural" input which is to be contributed solely in the interest of one party. Teddy Roosevelt would doubtless understand.

Given the freedom to do so unilaterally, a party may find it politically impossible not to name one of its nationals as arbitrator. Worse, that nominee may feel subject to political pressures—whether he or she succumbs to them or fights them.

I say this: whatever may have been the need to "sell" arbitration across cultural divides in times past, it seems likely that the "clash-of-culture" theme in arbitration is vastly exaggerated in the modern world. Parties likely to subscribe to arbitration agreements do so because they have among themselves some kind of relations which are characteristic to them as a group. They therefore have significant common ground in what they expect in the resolution of disputes. Business managers from Sweden who operate in the international marketplace are likely to share more common assumptions about the objectives of contractual dispute resolution with their counterparties in Costa Rica than with other social groups in Sweden who have no reason to think about such things— say a sports club or a parent-teacher association or a labour union. It seems more than plausible that what is truly at work here is not so much a concern about undefined cultural particularities as the simple fear of being treated as an outsider.

Now this is a matter of the highest importance, but unilateral appointments are more likely to exacerbate the problem than to resolve it. The real answers lie in ensuring that the arbitration process is inclusive, so that no one is "a foreigner," and in enhancing the confidence both sides have in the institutions charged with the essential task of ultimately appointing truly neutral and able arbitrators.

Let us think it through. We need not be concerned with trouble-free cases that result in unanimous awards. Our approach must also work in the difficult cases, which is of course where any system is tested, and thus exposed to criticism and disaffection. Is a 2:1 decision perceived by the losing party as more legitimate than a decision by a sole arbitrator, because "three heads are better than one"? That makes no sense—quite the opposite. The losing party in a difficult case is likely to consider that it appointed a "good" arbitrator, who has somehow been outvoted by the "bad" arbitrator appointed by an unscrupulous adversary and a feckless chairman misled by the "bad" arbitrator. QED: in the eyes of the losing party, the 2:1 decision is less legitimate than that of a sole arbitrator in whose selection the opponent had no more and no less than an equal say.

This has nothing to do per se with the choice between a sole arbitrator and a tribunal comprising three or more arbitrators. In either case, since every possible arbitrator is chosen jointly by the parties, or is appointed by a neutral institution, each is invested with an equal measure of confidence and an equal claim to moral authority.

Not so when there are unilateral appointments. Disputants tend to be interested in one thing only: winning. They exercise their right of unilateral appointment, like everything else, with that overriding objective in view. The result is speculation about ways and means to shape a favourable tribunal, or at least to avoid a tribunal favourable to the other side—which is logically assumed to be speculating with the same fervour, and toward the same end.

Forgotten is the search for an arbitrator trusted by both sides. The only decent solution—heed this voice in the desert!—is thus that any arbitrator, no matter the size of the tribunal, should be chosen jointly or selected by a neutral body.

I do recognize that this genie—the "right" to appoint an arbitrator—cannot easily be put back into the bottle. I am ready for pragmatic solutions until my position finally prevails.

NOTES

1. Do you agree with Jan Paulsson's assessment? Do you think his suggestion makes good policy sense if we seek to support the legitimacy of arbitration?

2. Are there types of disputes for which Jan Paulsson's observations are more important than others? What are those disputes?

3. You act as counsel in arbitrations all the time, and you know the bar and bench very well. Do you like the proposal from this perspective? Why? Why not?

C) Party Appointment of the Tribunal

As Jan Paulsson's lecture suggests, there is a strong tendency among arbitration practitioners to draft arbitration clauses that permit the parties to appoint arbitrators. Unless the arbitration clause provides otherwise, these arbitrators must be impartial and independent. What precisely is meant by "impartial and independent" is an issue that will be discussed in the next two chapters.

For now, the question is how parties appoint their own tribunal without creating complete chaos. Could a party simply refuse to make an appointment, thus halting the trains indefinitely? And how should the parties appoint a sole arbitrator or chair for their tribunal? The AAA Arbitration Rules shed light on these issues.

1) *Direct Appointment*

AAA Commercial Arbitration Rules

R–13.   Direct Appointment by a Party

(a)   If the agreement of the parties names an arbitrator or specifies a method of appointing an arbitrator, that designation or method shall be followed. The notice of appointment, with the name and address of the arbitrator, shall be filed with the AAA by the appointing party. Upon the request of any appointing party, the AAA shall submit a list of members of the National Roster from which the party may, if it so desires, make the appointment.

(b)   Where the parties have agreed that each party is to name one arbitrator, the arbitrators so named must meet the standards of Section R–18 with respect to impartiality and independence unless the parties have specifically agreed pursuant to Section R–18(b) that the party-appointed arbitrators are to be non-neutral and need not meet those standards.

(c)   If the agreement specifies a period of time within which an arbitrator shall be appointed and any party fails to make the appointment within that period, the AAA shall make the appointment.

(d)   If no period of time is specified in the agreement, the AAA shall notify the party to make the appointment. If within 14 calendar days after such notice has been sent, an arbitrator has not been appointed by a party, the AAA shall make the appointment.

NOTES

1.   How do the AAA rules avoid the problem of the "dawdling litigant"?

2.   Do you think that the provision could provide an undue advantage to one of the parties to an arbitration? How so? What do you have to do to avoid this problem?

2) Agreeing on a Chair

AAA Commercial Arbitration Rules

R–14. Appointment of Chairperson by Party-Appointed Arbitrators or Parties

(a) If, pursuant to Section R–13, either the parties have directly appointed arbitrators, or the arbitrators have been appointed by the AAA, and the parties have authorized them to appoint a chairperson within a specified time and no appointment is made within that time or any agreed extension, the AAA may appoint the chairperson.

(b) If no period of time is specified for appointment of the chairperson, and the party-appointed arbitrators or the parties do not make the appointment within 14 calendar days from the date of the appointment of the last party-appointed arbitrator, the AAA may appoint the chairperson.

(c) If the parties have agreed that their party-appointed arbitrators shall appoint the chairperson from the National Roster, the AAA shall furnish to the party-appointed arbitrators, in the manner provided in Section R–12, a list selected from the National Roster, and the appointment of the chairperson shall be made as provided in that Section.

NOTES

1. What are the safeguards to avoid undue delay in appointing a chair (or president) for the tribunal?

2. Do you think that the default rules provide a good incentive for the parties to agree to a chair? Why? What would they "fear" would happen if they do not agree?

3. Do you think the time periods set out in the rules are realistic? What do you have to do if the parties do not meet the allowed time? How much time does that process take? And what would an institution do if one were to attempt making an appointment in this "lag period?"

D) List Appointment

The AAA takes a path between party appointment and institutional appointment. It uses a list procedure as a default mechanism of appointment. Consider whether this list appointment combines the best of both worlds or the worst of both worlds as you consider the rules and selection criteria to be included on the list excerpted below.

1)   *AAA Arbitration Rules*

AAA Commercial Arbitration Rules

R–12.   Appointment from National Roster

If the parties have not appointed an arbitrator and have not provided any other method of appointment, the arbitrator shall be appointed in the following manner:

(a)   The AAA shall send simultaneously to each party to the dispute an identical list of 10 (unless the AAA decides that a different number is appropriate) names of persons chosen from the National Roster. The parties are encouraged to agree to an arbitrator from the submitted list and to advise the AAA of their agreement.

(b)   If the parties are unable to agree upon an arbitrator, each party to the dispute shall have 14 calendar days from the transmittal date in which to strike names objected to, number the remaining names in order of preference, and return the list to the AAA. The parties are not required to exchange selection lists. If a party does not return the list within the time specified, all persons named therein shall be deemed acceptable to that party. From among the persons who have been approved on both lists, and in accordance with the designated order of mutual preference, the AAA shall invite the acceptance of an arbitrator to serve. If the parties fail to agree on any of the persons named, or if acceptable arbitrators are unable to act, or if for any other reason the appointment cannot be made from the submitted lists, the AAA shall have the power to make the appointment from among other members of the National Roster without the submission of additional lists.

(c)   Unless the parties agree otherwise, when there are two or more claimants or two or more respondents, the AAA may appoint all the arbitrators.

NOTES

1.   Do the rules state how the AAA identifies possible candidates? How do you think they assemble their list? If you were assembling the list, what would you try to do to encourage the parties to reach agreement?

2. What is the process of selecting an arbitrator if the parties do not reach agreement on an arbitrator?

3. How effective do you think the procedure is at bringing about agreement between the parties?

2) Selection Criteria for the AAA National Roster of Arbitrators

Qualification Criteria for Admittance to the AAA National Roster of Arbitrators

The American Arbitration Association (AAA) is the nation's leading provider of alternative dispute resolution services. Openings on our Regional Roster of Neutrals are extremely limited, based primarily on caseload needs and user preferences. Consequently, even candidates with strong credentials may not be added to our roster.

Applicants for membership on the AAA National Roster of Arbitrators must meet or exceed the following requirements:

1. QUALIFICATIONS

a. Minimum of 10 years of senior-level business or professional experience or legal practice.

b. Educational degree(s) and/or professional license(s) appropriate to your field of expertise.

c. Honors, awards and citations indicating leadership in your field.

d. Training or experience in arbitration and/or other forms of dispute resolution.

e. Membership in a professional association(s).

f. Other relevant experience or accomplishments (e.g. published articles).

2. NEUTRALITY

a. Freedom from bias and prejudice.

b. Ability to evaluate and apply legal, business or trade principles.

3. JUDICIAL CAPACITY

a. Ability to manage the hearing process.

b. Thorough and impartial evaluation of testimony and other evidence.

4.   REPUTATION

a.   Held in the highest regard by peers for integrity, fairness and good judgment.

b.   Dedicated to upholding the AAA Code of Ethics for Arbitrators and/or Standards of Conduct for Mediators.

5.   COMMITMENT TO ADR PROCESS

a.   Willingness to devote time and effort when selected to serve.

b.   Willingness to support efforts of the AAA.

c.   Willingness to successfully complete training under the guidelines of the Commercial Arbitration Development Program.

6.   LETTERS OF RECOMMENDATION*

When requested by the AAA to do so, furnish letters from at least three active professionals in your field, but outside of any firms or professional associations in which you are employed or on which you currently serve as an officer, director or trustee. Each letter must address the following:

a.   Nature and duration of the relationship

b.   Why the applicant would be qualified to serve

Recommended sources for letters:

1.   Current AAA Panel member

2.   Current or former state or federal judge**

3.   An attorney who served as your opposing counsel**

4.   Former employer or client

7.   PERSONAL LETTER

Submit a letter to your local AAA office explaining why you feel you would like to be included on AAA's Roster of Arbitrators along with a current copy of your personal resume or CV. Your letter should provide a detailed description of your willingness to commit yourself to serving and representing the Association. Also indicate in the letter whether or not you are currently a neutral with any other

---

*   Letters of recommendation must be sent directly to the AAA Vice President from the writers, in sealed envelopes.

**   Suggested for attorney applicants.

ADR agencies. Please feel free to contact your local AAA office should you have any questions.

NOTES

1.   Do you think the materials requested will permit the AAA to fill its roster with suitable arbitrators for all commercial cases? How do you think the AAA chooses applicants?

2.   How do you think the file will suggest to the AAA what subject matter expertise the arbitrator brings with him or her?

3.   Does this system encourage the use of the same arbitrators, or a greater convergence towards a small cadre of professional arbitrators compared to other appointment methods? What benefits would that have for arbitration from a user perspective? What disadvantages would it present?

CHAPTER 10

The Outer Limit: When an Arbitrator Can Be Challenged

Although the appointment of "non-neutral" arbitrators was widespread for many years, the default position in current arbitration practice is that an arbitrator must be independent and impartial. In determining how to appoint arbitrators and what arbitrator to appoint, the first consideration should be if a certain appointment would lead to a challenge—either to the arbitrator, or to an award issued by the arbitrator—because of a violation of the independence and impartiality standards.

The standards of impartiality and independence in arbitration differ in meaningful respects from similar standards of judicial propriety. The first section of this chapter explores the differences between judicial and arbitral independence.

The second section of this chapter then outlines the four areas in which there is the greatest likelihood of a failure of independence and impartiality: 1) a relationship between an arbitrator and a party; 2) a pecuniary interest of the arbitrator in the outcome of the arbitration; 3) an "issue conflict" because the arbitrator has already commented on an issue or a party in the dispute; and 4) a relationship between the arbitrator and counsel.

Fact Scenario

Ivan Strong serves as MinuteMoniter Inc.'s party-appointed arbitrator in a AAA arbitration between MinuteMoniter and CurtainCall Networks ("*CCN*") governed by the AAA Commercial Arbitration Rules. Ivan Strong is a dispute resolution partner in the New York office of Jones & Rose, a law firm with 25 offices worldwide and approximately 1,200 lawyers.

CCN commenced the arbitration alleging that MinuteMoniter violated their broadcasting agreement when it aired CCN content free of charge as part of a promotion weekend for MinuteMoniter's Super 300 Channel Package. Specifically, CCN alleged that while MinuteMoniter may air CCN content free of charge as part of promotional events twice a year, it had already used both free content periods for the calendar year. MinuteMoniter responded that CCN was off-air for a significant period of its second promotional event earlier in the year, meaning that MinuteMoniter did not violate the agreement. MinuteMoniter counterclaims for breach of contract with regard to the earlier CCN outage.

Ivan Strong submitted the following Rule 17 disclosure:

> I am not aware of any circumstances giving rise to justifiable doubts as to my impartiality or independence, including any bias or any financial or personal interest in the result of the arbitration or any past of present relationship with the parties or their representatives.

CCN's counsel discovers that MinuteMoniter is a client of Jones & Rose. MinuteMoniter engaged Jones & Rose's LA office for international tax advice, and the project was anticipated to last two years (and will conclude in the next three months). The "client contact" partner is the Managing Partner of the LA office and a member of the firm's executive committee, Scott Feinwein. Jones & Rose billed MinuteMoniter a flat fee of $500,000, to be paid in installments. There remains $100,000 in outstanding payments. Approximately 90% of the work for the project has been completed at the time the arbitration commenced. Gross revenue for the firm is $1.88 billion. Feinwein's own gross revenue for the period in question was $8,500,000.

CCN has written a letter to the tribunal, asking Mr. Strong to resign from the tribunal in light of this undisclosed conflict. Mr. Strong acknowledged the conflict, apologized for the oversight, but stated that he would not resign from the tribunal for such a negligible contact. He added:

> "As you know, all large law firms have done some work for MinuteMoniter or one of its affiliates in the last three years. That is the nature of large law firm practice. The matter is almost completed, it generated negligible revenue for the firm, and there is no prospect of follow-up work, given the nature of the project."

CCN replies that it intends to challenge his appointment. Prepare argument for CCN or MinuteMoniter to be communicated to the AAA to support or defend against the challenge.

Readings

A) Comparison: Judicial and Arbitral Independence

The usual starting point for understanding the standards of independence and impartiality required of arbitrators is to compare them to judicial standards of independence and impartiality. As you can see from the readings below, this comparison is not easy to draw due in part to the state of Supreme Court jurisprudence on the issue.

1) *Judicial Standard of Impartiality*

The question of whether a federal judge has to disqualify him or herself from hearing a case is governed by statute. As a study completed for the Federal Judiciary Center explains:

> The two principal statutes governing judicial disqualification are 28 U.S.C. § 455, "Disqualification of justice, judge or magistrate judge" (discussed in Part II, infra), and 28 U.S.C. § 144, "Bias or prejudice of judge" (discussed in Part III, infra). The relationship between the two has been a source of some confusion. While the two sections provide overlapping remedies for bias, there are some important differences. First, § 144 aims exclusively at actual bias or prejudice, whereas § 455 deals not only with actual bias and other forms of partiality, but also with the appearance of partiality. Second, § 144 is triggered by a party's affidavit, whereas § 455 may be invoked in a motion by a party or *sua sponte* by the judge. Third, § 144 applies only to district judges, while § 455 covers "any justice, judge, or magistrate of the United States."
>
> A third disqualification statute, 28 U.S.C. § 47 (discussed in Part IV, infra), provides that "[n]o judge shall hear or determine an appeal from the decision of a case or issue tried by him." The statute applies to judges sitting on courts of appeals who were recently appointed from the district court or who are district judges sitting by designation, and directs their disqualification from appeals of cases they decided as trial judges. Given its limited applicability, this statute has been utilized infrequently, and for the most part uneventfully.
>
> A fourth statute, 28 U.S.C. § 2106 (discussed in Part V, infra), is not a disqualification statute as such, but has been employed to serve a comparable purpose. The statute authorizes the Supreme Court of the United States and circuit courts to "remand the cause and . . . require such further proceedings to be had as may be just under the circumstances." This provision effectively enables an appellate court to disqualify a district judge by remanding a matter to a different judge

for further proceedings if the appellate court doubts the original judge's impartiality.[1]

The relevant statutory provisions are reproduced below. As you read the statutory provisions, consider what standard it sets for the judge to remove him or herself from a case.

28 U.S.C. § 455—Disqualification of justice, judge, or magistrate judge

(a)　Any justice, judge, or magistrate judge of the United States shall disqualify himself in any proceeding in which his impartiality might reasonably be questioned.

(b)　He shall also disqualify himself in the following circumstances:

(1)　Where he has a personal bias or prejudice concerning a party, or personal knowledge of disputed evidentiary facts concerning the proceeding;

(2)　Where in private practice he served as lawyer in the matter in controversy, or a lawyer with whom he previously practiced law served during such association as a lawyer concerning the matter, or the judge or such lawyer has been a material witness concerning it;

(3)　Where he has served in governmental employment and in such capacity participated as counsel, adviser or material witness concerning the proceeding or expressed an opinion concerning the merits of the particular case in controversy;

(4)　He knows that he, individually or as a fiduciary, or his spouse or minor child residing in his household, has a financial interest in the subject matter in controversy or in a party to the proceeding, or any other interest that could be substantially affected by the outcome of the proceeding;

(5)　He or his spouse, or a person within the third degree of relationship to either of them, or the spouse of such a person:

(i)　Is a party to the proceeding, or an officer, director, or trustee of a party;

(ii)　Is acting as a lawyer in the proceeding;

(iii)　Is known by the judge to have an interest that could be substantially affected by the outcome of the proceeding;

---

[1]　Federal Judicial Center, *Judicial Disqualification: An Analysis of Federal Law* 3 (2010) ("*Judicial Disqualification*").

(iv) Is to the judge's knowledge likely to be a material witness in the proceeding.

(c)   A judge should inform himself about his personal and fiduciary financial interests, and make a reasonable effort to inform himself about the personal financial interests of his spouse and minor children residing in his household.

(d)   For the purposes of this section the following words or phrases shall have the meaning indicated:

(1)   "proceeding" includes pretrial, trial, appellate review, or other stages of litigation;

(2)   the degree of relationship is calculated according to the civil law system;

(3)   "fiduciary" includes such relationships as executor, administrator, trustee, and guardian;

(4)   "financial interest" means ownership of a legal or equitable interest, however small, or a relationship as director, adviser, or other active participant in the affairs of a party, except that:

(i)   Ownership in a mutual or common investment fund that holds securities is not a "financial interest" in such securities unless the judge participates in the management of the fund;

(ii)   An office in an educational, religious, charitable, fraternal, or civic organization is not a "financial interest" in securities held by the organization;

(iii) The proprietary interest of a policyholder in a mutual insurance company, of a depositor in a mutual savings association, or a similar proprietary interest, is a "financial interest" in the organization only if the outcome of the proceeding could substantially affect the value of the interest;

(iv) Ownership of government securities is a "financial interest" in the issuer only if the outcome of the proceeding could substantially affect the value of the securities.

(e)   No justice, judge, or magistrate judge shall accept from the parties to the proceeding a waiver of any ground for disqualification enumerated in subsection (b). Where the ground for disqualification arises only under subsection (a), waiver may be accepted provided it is preceded by a full disclosure on the record of the basis for disqualification.

NOTE

1.   Do you think that a judge may be required to recuse him or herself under section 455(a) of the statute when the ground for an alleged reasonable

doubt regarding the judge's impartiality is not covered in section (b)? Consider *Liljeberg v. Health Servs. Acquisition Corp.*, 486 U.S. 847 (1988), excerpted below.

28 U.S.C. § 144—Bias or prejudice of judge

Whenever a party to any proceeding in a district court makes and files a timely and sufficient affidavit that the judge before whom the matter is pending has a personal bias or prejudice either against him or in favor of any adverse party, such judge shall proceed no further therein, but another judge shall be assigned to hear such proceeding.

The affidavit shall state the facts and the reasons for the belief that bias or prejudice exists, and shall be filed not less than ten days before the beginning of the term at which the proceeding is to be heard, or good cause shall be shown for failure to file it within such time. A party may file only one such affidavit in any case. It shall be accompanied by a certificate of counsel of record stating that it is made in good faith.

NOTES

1. What does 28 U.S.C. § 144 add to 28 U.S.C. § 455. Would you file both types of affidavits in the same kinds of cases?

2. What facts would give rise to a challenge under 28 U.S.C. § 144 but not 28 U.S.C. § 455(a)?

Liljeberg v. Health Services Acquisition Corp.

486 U.S. 847 (1988)

JUSTICE STEVENS delivered the opinion of the Court.

In 1974 Congress amended the Judicial Code "to broaden and clarify the grounds for judicial disqualification." The first sentence of the amendment provides:

> "Any justice, judge, or magistrate of the United States shall disqualify himself in any proceeding in which his impartiality might reasonably be questioned." 28 U.S.C. § 455(a) as amended.

In the present case, the Court of Appeals for the Fifth Circuit concluded that a violation of § 455(a) is established when a reasonable person, knowing the relevant facts, would expect that a justice, judge, or magistrate knew of circumstances creating an appearance of partiality, notwithstanding a finding that the judge was not actually conscious of those circumstances. Moreover, although the judgment in question had become final, the Court of Appeals determined that under the facts of this case, the appropriate remedy was to vacate the court's judgment. We granted certiorari to consider its construction of § 455(a) as well as its remedial decision. We now affirm.

I

In November 1981, respondent Health Services Acquisition Corp. brought an action against petitioner John Liljeberg, Jr., seeking a declaration of ownership of a corporation known as St. Jude Hospital of Kenner, Louisiana (St. Jude). The case was tried by Judge Robert Collins, sitting without a jury. Judge Collins found for Liljeberg and, over a strong dissent, the Court of Appeals affirmed. Approximately 10 months later, respondent learned that Judge Collins had been a member of the Board of Trustees of Loyola University while Liljeberg was negotiating with Loyola to purchase a parcel of land on which to construct a hospital. The success and benefit to Loyola of these negotiations turned, in large part, on Liljeberg prevailing in the litigation before Judge Collins.

Based on this information, respondent moved pursuant to Federal Rule of Civil Procedure 60(b)(6) to vacate the judgment on the ground that Judge Collins was disqualified under § 455(a) at the time he heard the action and entered judgment in favor of Liljeberg.

II

Petitioner, John Liljeberg, Jr., is a pharmacist, a promoter, and a half-owner of Axel Realty, Inc., a real estate brokerage firm. In 1976, he became interested in a project to construct and operate a hospital in Kenner, Louisiana, a suburb of New Orleans. In addition to providing the community with needed health care facilities, he hoped to obtain a real estate commission for Axel Realty and the exclusive right to provide pharmaceutical services at the new hospital. The successful operation of such a hospital depended upon the acquisition of a "certificate of need" from the State of Louisiana; without such a certificate the hospital would not qualify for health care reimbursement payments under the federal medicare and medicaid programs. Accordingly, in October 1979, Liljeberg formed St. Jude, intending to have the corporation apply for the certificate of need at an appropriate time.

During the next two years Liljeberg engaged in serious negotiations with at least two major parties. One set of negotiations involved a proposal to purchase a large tract of land from Loyola University for use as a hospital site, coupled with a plan to rezone adjoining University property. The proposed benefits to the University included not only the proceeds of the real estate sale itself, amounting to several million dollars, but also a substantial increase in the value to the University of the rezoned adjoining property. The progress of these negotiations was regularly reported to the University's Board of Trustees by its Real Estate Committee and discussed at Board meetings. The minutes of those meetings indicate that the University's interest in the project was dependent on the issuance of the certificate of need.

Liljeberg was also conducting serious negotiations with respondent's corporate predecessor, Hospital Affiliates International (HAI), a national health management company. In the summer of 1980, Liljeberg and HAI reached an agreement in principle, outlining their respective roles in developing*854 the hospital. The agreement contemplated that HAI would purchase a tract of land in Kenner (not owned by the University) and construct the hospital on that land; prepare and file the certificate of need; and retain Liljeberg as a consultant to the hospital in various capacities. In turn, it was understood that Liljeberg would transfer St. Jude to HAI. Pursuant to this preliminary agreement, various documents were executed, including an agreement by HAI to purchase the tract of land from its owner for $5 million and a further agreement by HAI to place $500,000 in escrow. In addition, it was agreed that Axel Realty, Inc., would receive a $250,000 commission for locating the property. Eventually, Liljeberg signed a "warranty and indemnity agreement," which HAI understood to transfer ownership of St. Jude to HAI. After the warranty and indemnity agreement was signed, HAI filed an application for the certificate of need.

On August 26, 1981, the certificate of need was issued and delivered to Liljeberg. He promptly advised HAI, and HAI paid the real estate commission to Axel Realty. A dispute arose, however, over whether the warranty and indemnity agreement did in fact transfer ownership of St. Jude to HAI. Liljeberg contended that the transfer of ownership of St. Jude—and hence, the certificate of need—was conditioned upon reaching a final agreement concerning his continued participation in the hospital project. This contention was not supported by any written instrument. HAI denied that there was any such unwritten understanding and insisted that, by virtue of the warranty and indemnity agreement, it had been sole owner of St. Jude for over a year. The dispute gave rise to this litigation.

Respondent filed its complaint for declaratory judgment on November 30, 1981. The case was tried by Judge Collins, sitting without a jury, on January 21 and 22, 1982. At the close of the evidence, he announced his intended ruling, and on March 16, 1982, he filed a judgment (dated March 12, 1982) and his findings of fact and conclusions of law. He credited Liljeberg's version of oral conversations that were disputed and of critical importance in his ruling.

During the period between November 30, 1981, and March 16, 1982, Judge Collins was a trustee of Loyola University, but was not conscious of the fact that the University and Liljeberg were then engaged in serious negotiations concerning the Kenner hospital project, or of the further fact that the success of those negotiations depended upon his conclusion that Liljeberg controlled the certificate of need. To determine whether Judge Collins' impartiality in the Liljeberg litigation "might reasonably be questioned," it is appropriate to consider the state of his knowledge immediately before the lawsuit was filed, what happened while the case was pending before him, and what he did when he learned of the University's interest in the litigation.

After the certificate of need was issued, and Liljeberg and HAI became embroiled in their dispute, Liljeberg reopened his negotiations with the University. On October 29, 1981, the Real Estate Committee sent a written report to each of the trustees, including Judge Collins, advising them of "a significant change" concerning the proposed hospital in Kenner and stating specifically that Loyola's property had "again become a prime location." The Committee submitted a draft of a resolution authorizing a University vice president "to continue negotiations with the developers of the St. Jude Hospital." At the Board meeting on November 12, 1981, which Judge Collins attended, the trustees discussed the connection between the rezoning of Loyola's land in Kenner and the St. Jude project and adopted the Real Estate Committee's proposed resolution. Thus, Judge Collins had actual knowledge of the University's potential interest in the St. Jude hospital project in Kenner just a few days before the complaint was filed.

While the case was pending before Judge Collins, the University agreed to sell 80 acres of its land in Kenner to Liljeberg for $6,694,000. The progress of negotiations was discussed at a Board meeting on January 28, 1982. Judge Collins did not attend that meeting, but the Real Estate Committee advised the trustees that "the federal courts have determined that the certificate of need will be awarded to the St. Jude Corporation." Presumably this advice was based on Judge Collins' comment at the close of the hearing a week earlier, when he announced his intended ruling because he thought "it would be unfair to keep the parties in doubt as to how I feel about the case."

The formal agreement between Liljeberg and the University was apparently executed on March 19. App. 50–58. The agreement stated that it was not in any way conditioned on Liljeberg's prevailing in the litigation "pending in the U.S. District Court for the Eastern District of Louisiana . . . involving the obtaining by [Liljeberg] of a Certificate of Need," but it also gave the University the right to repurchase the property for the contract price if Liljeberg had not executed a satisfactory construction contract within one year and further provided for nullification of the contract in the event the rezoning of the University's adjoining land was not accomplished. Thus, the University continued to have an active interest in the outcome of the litigation because it was unlikely that Liljeberg could build the hospital if he lost control of the certificate of need; moreover, the rezoning was in turn dependent on the hospital project.

The details of the transaction were discussed in three letters to the trustees dated March 12, 15, and 19, 1982, but Judge Collins did not examine any of those letters until shortly before the Board meeting on March 25, 1982. Thus, he acquired actual knowledge of Loyola's interest in the litigation on March 24, 1982. As the Court of Appeals correctly held, "Judge Collins should have recused himself when he obtained actual knowledge of that interest on March 24."

In considering whether the Court of Appeals properly vacated the declaratory relief judgment, we are required to address two questions. We must first determine whether § 455(a) can be violated based on an appearance of partiality, even though the judge was not conscious of the circumstances creating the appearance of impropriety, and second, whether relief is available under Rule 60(b) when such a violation is not discovered until after the judgment has become final.

III

The statute was amended in 1974 to clarify and broaden the grounds for judicial disqualification and to conform with the recently adopted ABA Code of Judicial Conduct, Canon 3C (1987). The general language of subsection (a) was designed to promote public confidence in the integrity of the judicial process by replacing the subjective "in his opinion" standard with an objective test.

"(a) Any justice, judge, or magistrate of the United States shall disqualify himself in any proceeding in which his impartiality might reasonably be questioned.

"(b) He shall also disqualify himself in the following circumstances:

"(4) He knows that he, individually or as a fiduciary, or his spouse or minor child residing in his household, has a financial interest in the subject matter in controversy or in a party to the proceeding, or any other interest that could be substantially affected by the outcome of the proceeding.

"(c) A judge should inform himself about his personal and fiduciary financial interests, and make a reasonable effort to inform himself about the personal financial interests of his spouse and minor children residing in his household."

Scienter is not an element of a violation of § 455(a). The judge's lack of knowledge of a disqualifying circumstance may bear on the question of remedy, but it does not eliminate the risk that "his impartiality might reasonably be questioned" by other persons. To read § 455(a) to provide that the judge must know of the disqualifying facts, requires not simply ignoring the language of the provision—which makes no mention of knowledge—but further requires concluding that the language in subsection (b)(4)—which expressly provides that the judge must know of his or her interest—is extraneous. A careful reading of the respective subsections makes clear that Congress intended to require knowledge under subsection (b)(4) and not to require knowledge under subsection (a). Moreover, advancement of the purpose of the provision—to promote public confidence in the integrity of the judicial process does not depend upon whether or not the judge actually knew of facts creating an appearance of impropriety, so long as the public might reasonably believe that he or she knew. As Chief Judge Clark of the Court of Appeals explained:

> Petitioner's argument ignores important differences between subsections (a) and (b)(4). Most importantly, § 455(b)(4) requires disqualification no matter how insubstantial the financial interest and regardless of whether or not the interest actually creates an appearance of impropriety. In addition, § 455(e) specifies that a judge may not accept a waiver of any ground for disqualification under § 455(b), but may accept such a waiver under § 455(a) after "a full disclosure on the record of the basis for disqualification." Section 455(b) is therefore a somewhat stricter provision, and thus is not simply redundant with the broader coverage of § 455(a) as petitioner's argument posits.

"The goal of section 455(a) is to avoid even the appearance of partiality. If it would appear to a reasonable person that a judge has knowledge of facts that would give him an interest in the litigation then an appearance of partiality is created even though no actual partiality exists because the judge does not recall the facts, because the judge actually has no interest in the case or because the judge is pure in heart and incorruptible. The judge's forgetfulness, however, is not the sort of objectively ascertainable fact that can avoid the appearance of partiality. Under section 455(a), therefore, recusal is required even when a judge lacks actual knowledge of the facts indicating his interest or bias in the case if a reasonable person, knowing all the circumstances, would expect that the judge would have actual knowledge."

Contrary to petitioner's contentions, this reading of the statute does not call upon judges to perform the impossible—to disqualify themselves based on facts they do not know. If, as petitioner argues, § 455(a) should only be applied prospectively, then requiring disqualification based on facts the judge does not know would of course be absurd; a judge could never be expected to disqualify himself based on some fact he does not know, even though the fact is one that perhaps he should know or one that people might reasonably suspect that he does know. But to the extent the provision can also, in proper cases, be applied retroactively, the judge is not called upon to perform an impossible feat. Rather, he is called upon to rectify an oversight and to take the steps necessary to maintain public confidence in the impartiality of the judiciary. If he concludes that "his impartiality might reasonably be questioned," then he should also find that the statute has been violated. This is certainly not an impossible task. No one questions that Judge Collins could have disqualified himself and vacated his judgment when he finally realized that Loyola had an interest in the litigation. The initial appeal was taken from his failure to disqualify himself and vacate the judgment after he became aware of the appearance of impropriety, not from his failure to disqualify himself when he first became involved in the litigation and lacked the requisite knowledge.

NOTES

Facts

1. What was the asserted conflict of interest in *Liljeberg*? Did Judge Collins have any financial interest?

2. When did Judge Collins have actual knowledge about the potential conflict? Was this the same time that he was constructively on notice?

Law

1. On what alternative theories did the petitioner proceed? Which of these theories ultimately succeeded? Why?

2. Did this case turn on an actual conflict of interests or the reasonable appearance of a conflict?

2) *Comparison of Judicial and Arbitral Standards*

Commonwealth Coatings Corp. v. Continental Casualty Co.

393 U.S. 145 (1968)

MR. JUSTICE BLACK delivered the opinion of the Court.

At issue in this case is the question whether elementary requirements of impartiality taken for granted in every judicial proceeding are suspended when the parties agree to resolve a dispute through arbitration.

The petitioner, Commonwealth Coatings Corporation, a subcontractor, sued the sureties on the prime contractor's bond to recover money alleged to be due for a painting job. The contract for painting contained an agreement to arbitrate such controversies. Pursuant to this agreement petitioner appointed one arbitrator, the prime contractor appointed a second, and these two together selected the third arbitrator. This third arbitrator, the supposedly neutral member of the panel, conducted a large business in Puerto Rico, in which he served as an engineering consultant for various people in connection with building construction projects. One of his regular customers in this business was the prime contractor that petitioner sued in this case. This relationship with the prime contractor was in a sense sporadic in that the arbitrator's services were used only from time to time at irregular intervals, and there had been no dealings between them for about a year immediately preceding the arbitration. Nevertheless, the prime contractor's patronage was repeated and significant, involving fees of about $12,000 over a period of four of five years, and the relationship even went so far as to include the rendering of services on the very projects involved in this lawsuit. An arbitration was held, but the facts concerning the close business connections between the third arbitrator and the prime contractor were unknown to petitioner and were never revealed to it by this arbitrator, by the prime contractor, or by anyone else until after an award had been made. Petitioner challenged the award on this ground, among others, but the District Court refused to set aside the award. The Court of Appeals affirmed, and we granted certiorari.

In 1925 Congress enacted the United States Arbitration Act,9 U.S.C. ss 1–14, which sets out a comprehensive plan for arbitration of controversies coming under its terms, and both sides here assume that this Federal Act governs this case. Section 10, quoted below, sets out the conditions upon which awards can be vacated. The two courts below held, however, that s 10 could not be construed in such a way as to justify vacating the award in this case. We disagree and reverse. Section 10 does authorize vacation of an award where it was 'procured by corruption, fraud, or undue means' or '(w)here there was evident partiality * * * in the arbitrators.' These provisions show a desire of Congress to provide not merely for any arbitration but for an impartial one. It is true that petitioner does not charge before us that the third arbitrator was actually guilty of fraud or bias in deciding this case, and we have no reason, apart from the undisclosed business relationship, to suspect him of any improper motives. But neither this arbitrator nor the prime contractor gave to petitioner even an intimation of the close financial relations that had existed between them for a period of years. We have no doubt that if a litigant could show that a foreman of a jury or a judge in a court of justice had, unknown to the litigant, any such relationship, the judgment would be subject to challenge. This is shown beyond doubt by *Tumey v. State of Ohio*, 273 U.S. 510, (1927), where this Court held that a conviction could not stand because a small part of the judge's income consisted of court fees collected from convicted defendants. Although in *Tumey* it appeared the amount of the judge's compensation actually depended on whether he decided for one side or the other, that is too small a distinction to allow this manifest violation of the strict morality and fairness Congress would have expected on the part of the arbitrator and the other party in this case. Nor should it be at all relevant, as the Court of Appeals apparently thought it was here, that '(t)he payments received were a very small part of (the arbitrator's) income * * *. For in *Tumey* the Court held that a decision should be set aside where there is 'the slightest pecuniary interest' on the part of the judge, and specifically rejected the State's contention that the compensation involved there was 'so small that it is not to be regarded as likely to influence improperly a judicial officer in the discharge of his duty * * *.' Since in the case of courts this is a constitutional principle, we can see no basis for refusing to find the same concept in the broad statutory language that governs arbitration proceedings and provides that an award can be set aside on the basis of 'evident partiality' or the use of 'undue means.' It is true that arbitrators cannot sever all their ties with the business world, since they are not expected to get all their income from their work deciding cases, but we should, if anything, be even more scrupulous to safeguard the impartiality of arbitrators than judges, since the former have completely free rein to decide the law as well as the facts and are not subject to appellate review. We can perceive no way in which the effectiveness of the arbitration process will be hampered by the simple requirement that arbitrators disclose to the parties any dealings that might create an impression of possible bias.

While not controlling in this case, s 18 of the Rules of the American Arbitration Association, in effect at the time of this arbitration, is highly significant. It provided as follows:

'Section 18.   Disclosure by Arbitrator of Disqualification—At the time of receiving his notice of appointment, the prospective Arbitrator is requested to disclose any circumstances likely to create a presumption of bias or which he believes might disqualify him as an impartial Arbitrator. Upon receipt of such information, the Tribunal Clerk shall immediately disclose it to the parties, who if willing to proceed under the circumstances disclosed, shall, in writing, so advise the Tribunal Clerk. If either party declines to waive the presumptive disqualification, the vacancy thus created shall be filled in accordance with the applicable provisions of this Rule.'

And based on the same principle as this Arbitration Association rule is that part of the 33d Canon of Judicial Ethics which provides:

'33. Social Relations.

'* * * (A judge) should, however, in pending or prospective litigation before him be particularly careful to avoid such action as may reasonably tend to awaken the suspicion that his social or business relations or friendships, constitute an element in influencing his judicial conduct.'

This rule of arbitration and this canon of judicial ethics rest on the premise that any tribunal permitted by law to try cases and controversies not only must be unbiased but also must avoid even the appearance of bias. We cannot believe that it was the purpose of Congress to authorize litigants to submit their cases and controversies to arbitration boards that might reasonably be thought biased against one litigant and favorable to another.

Reversed.

MR. JUSTICE WHITE, with whom MR. JUSTICE MARSHALL joins, concurring.

While I am glad to join my Brother BLACK'S opinion in this case, I desire to make these additional remarks. The Court does not decide today that arbitrators are to be held to the standards of judicial decorum of Article III judges, or indeed of any judges. It is often because they are men of affairs, not apart from but of the marketplace, that they are effective in their adjudicatory function. This does not mean the judiciary must overlook outright chicanery in giving effect to their awards; that would be an abdication of our responsibility. But it does mean that arbitrators are not automatically disqualified by a business relationship with the parties before them if both parties are informed of the relationship in advance, or if they are unaware of the facts but the relationship is trivial. I see no reason automatically to disqualify the best informed and most capable potential arbitrators.

The arbitration process functions best when an amicable and trusting atmosphere is preserved and there is voluntary compliance with the decree, without need for judicial enforcement. This end is best served by establishing an atmosphere of frankness at the outset, through disclosure by the arbitrator of any financial transactions which he has had or is negotiating with either of the parties. In many cases the arbitrator might believe the business relationship to be so insubstantial that to make a point of revealing it would suggest he is indeed easily swayed, and perhaps a partisan of that party. But if the law requires the disclosure, no such imputation can arise. And it is far better that the relationship be disclosed at the outset, when the parties are free to reject the arbitrator or accept him with knowledge of the relationship and continuing faith in his objectivity, than to have the relationship come to light after the arbitration, when a suspicious or disgruntled party can seize on it as a pretext for invalidating the award. The judiciary should minimize its role in arbitration as judge of the arbitrator's impartiality. That role is best consigned to the parties, who are the architects of their own arbitration process, and are far better informed of the prevailing ethical standards and reputations within their business.

Of course, an arbitrator's business relationships may be diverse indeed, involving more or less remote commercial connections with great numbers of people. He cannot be expected to provide the parties with his complete and unexpurgated business biography. But it is enough for present purposes to hold, as the Court does, that where the arbitrator has a substantial interest in a firm which has done more than trivial business with a party, that fact must be disclosed. If arbitrators err on the side of disclosure, as they should, it will not be difficult for courts to identify those undisclosed relationships which are too insubstantial to warrant vacating an award.

MR. JUSTICE FORTAS, with whom MR. JUSTICE HARLAN and MR. JUSTICE STEWART join, dissenting.

I dissent and would affirm the judgment.

The facts in this case do not lend themselves to the Court's ruling. The Court sets aside the arbitration award despite the fact that the award is unanimous and no claim is made of actual partiality, unfairness, bias, or fraud.

The arbitration was held pursuant to provisions in the contracts between the parties. It is not subject to the rules of the American Arbitration Association. It is governed by the United States Arbitration Act, 9 U.S.C. ss 1–14.

Each party appointed an arbitrator and the third arbitrator was chosen by those two. The controversy relates to the third arbitrator.

The third arbitrator was not asked about business connections with either party. Petitioner's complaint is that he failed to volunteer information about professional services rendered by him to the other party to the contract, the most recent of which were performed over a year before the arbitration. Both courts below held, and petitioner concedes, that the third arbitrator was innocent of any actual partiality, or bias, or improper motive. There is no suggestion of concealment as distinguished from the innocent failure to volunteer information.

The third arbitrator is a leading and respected consulting engineer who has performed services for 'most of the contractors in Puerto Rico.' He was well known to petitioner's counsel and they were personal friends. Petitioner's counsel candidly admitted that if he had been told about the arbitrator's prior relationship 'I don't think I would have objected because I know Mr. Capacete (the arbitrator).'

Clearly, the District Judge's conclusion, affirmed by the Court of Appeals for the First Circuit, was correct, that 'the arbitrators conducted fair, impartial hearings; that they reached a proper determination of the issues before them, and that plaintiff's objections represent a 'situation where the losing party to an arbitration is now clutching at straws in an attempt to avoid the results of the arbitration to which it became a party."

The Court nevertheless orders that the arbitration award be set aside. It uses this singularly inappropriate case to announce a per se rule that in my judgment has no basis in the applicable statute or jurisprudential principles: that, regardless of the agreement between the parties, if an arbitrator has any prior business relationship with one of the parties of which he fails to inform the other party, however innocently, the arbitration award is always subject to being set aside. This is so even where the award is unanimous; where there is no suggestion that the nondisclosure indicates partiality or bias; and where it is conceded that there was in fact no irregularity, unfairness, bias, or partiality. Until the decision today, it has not been the law that an arbitrator's failure to disclose a prior business relationship with one of the parties will compel the setting aside of an arbitration award regardless of the circumstances.

I agree that failure of an arbitrator to volunteer information about business dealings with one party will, prima facie, support a claim of partiality or bias. But where there is no suggestion that the nondisclosure was calculated, and where the complaining party disclaims any imputation of partiality, bias, or misconduct, the presumption clearly is overcome.

I do not believe that it is either necessary, appropriate, or permissible to rule, as the Court does, that, regardless of the facts, innocent failure to volunteer information constitutes the 'evident partiality' necessary under s 10(b) of the Arbitration Act to set aside an award. 'Evident partiality' means what it says: conduct—or at least an attitude or disposition—by the arbitrator favoring one party rather than the other. This case demonstrates that to rule otherwise may be a palpable injustice, since all agree that the arbitrator was innocent of either 'evident partiality' or anything approaching it.

Arbitration is essentially consensual and practical. The United States Arbitration Act is obviously designed to protect the integrity of the process with a minimum of insistence upon set formulae and rules. The Court applies to this process rules applicable to judges and not to a system characterized by dealing on faith and reputation for reliability. Such formalism is not contemplated by the Act nor is it warranted in a case where no claim is made of partiality, of unfairness, or of misconduct in any degree.

NOTES

Facts

1. Who is the arbitrator being challenged? Is that arbitrator a lawyer? Does that matter in this case?

2. What is the basis for the challenge? Does the arbitrator have a direct financial interest in the outcome of the case? What do you think would happen to the arbitrator if Continental Casualty lost the arbitration?

3. Who is Continental Casualty? What role does it play in the underlying transaction? Does that (or should that) matter for the conflict analysis?

4.   When did Commonwealth Coatings learn of the potential conflict?

Law

1.   As will become important in the development of the case law from *Commonwealth Coatings*, this is a plurality decision. What does that mean?

2.   Parse both the opinion "for the court" and the concurrence: what points would they agree constitute the smallest common denominator for their decision. Is the smallest common denominator on arbitrator independence and impartiality in the opinion drafted by Justice Black or in the concurrence?

3.   How would Justice Black compare judicial independence and impartiality to arbitral independence and impartiality? What relationship does the concurrence envision?

Morelite Construction Corp. v. New York City District Council Carpenters Benefit Funds

748 F.2d 79 (2d Cir. 1984)

In deciding this appeal, we are once again called upon to address the elusive standards under which an arbitrator's award may be vacated pursuant to Section 10 of the United States Arbitration Act, 9 U.S.C. § 10 (1982). Specifically, the question before us is whether a father-son relationship between an arbitrator and an officer of one party to the arbitration rises to the level of "evident partiality" required by Section 10 for vacating an award. Notwithstanding our traditional reluctance to inquire into the merits of an arbitrator's award, or to require of an arbitrator the same demanding level of impartiality as that dictated for judges, we believe this relationship deprived the opposing party of the impartiality to which it has a right. Accordingly, we reverse the decision of the district court, and remand with instructions to vacate the award.

An inquiry into issues of fairness, bias, partiality and the like overflows with factual questions. Consequently, we set forth the concrete background of the instant dispute before turning to the legal issues.

Facts

Appellant Morelite Construction Corp. ("Morelite"), a division of Morelite Electric Services, Inc., is a construction contractor. Appellees are The District Council of New York City and Vicinity of the United Brotherhood of Carpenters and Joiners of America (the "District Union") and the Trustees of the New York City District Council Carpenters Benefit Funds (the "Benefit Funds"). The instant appeal arises from Morelite's alleged non-payment of contributions to the Benefit Funds pursuant to a collective bargaining agreement between Morelite and the District Union.

In 1979 and 1980, Morelite was engaged to perform contracting services in connection with two construction projects in New York City. Morelite entered into job agreements with the District Union applicable to each site. The agreements expressly incorporated the construction industry's "Master Collective Bargaining Agreement" and provided for arbitration of disputes arising from the agreements.

In 1980, the Benefit Funds audited Morelite's financial records, and charged that the company was delinquent in contributions to the Funds in the amount of some $80,000. On October 8, 1980, the Benefit Funds served notice upon Morelite of their intention to arbitrate their claim for unpaid contributions. Later that month, Morelite commenced a proceeding in New York State Supreme Court seeking to stay arbitration. The Benefit Funds removed the action to the United States District Court for the Southern District of New York, and cross-petitioned to compel arbitration. By order dated May 6, 1981, Judge Cannella denied Morelite's petition, and granted the Benefit Funds' cross-petition on the condition that the District Union be joined as a party to the arbitration (which it subsequently was).

On March 11, 1982, Morelite moved in the District Court to disqualify Patrick M. Campbell, Jr. as the arbitrator, because his father was then a Vice-President of the United Brotherhood of Carpenters and Joiners of America, the international union of which the District Union was a local. Campbell, Sr. also served as the international union's supervisor and trustee of the District Union. Judge Cannella denied the motion, holding the court had no authority to entertain an attack on an arbitrator's partiality until after the rendition of an award, and ordered the arbitration to proceed forthwith.

Hearings were held before Patrick Campbell, Jr. during the months of April and May of 1982, and in June of 1983, he filed his opinion and award. Campbell found that Morelite was "delinquent in payment of fringe benefit monies due under its written agreements and is also obligated to pay liquidated damages and interest on its delinquency." In sum, the District Union was awarded $128,429.50 plus interest from the date of the award.

In September 1983, Morelite moved pursuant to 9 U.S.C. § 10 (1982) to set aside the arbitration award, again claiming that the position of Campbell's father—who, during the pendency of the arbitration, had been named General President of the international union—precluded Campbell from acting impartially. Judge Cannella, noting that he "remain[ed] troubled by the relationship," nevertheless denied the motion and granted the District Union's cross-petition to confirm the arbitrator's award. In March of 1984, final judgment was entered in favor of the Benefit Funds and the District Union, and Morelite timely filed a notice of appeal.

Discussion

In 1925, Congress promulgated the United States Arbitration Act, 9 U.S.C. §§ 1–14, which set forth the delicate relationship between the role of private arbitration and the federal courts. Section 10 of the Act delineates the grounds upon which a court may vacate an arbitrator's award. Subsection (b) provides that such a basis exists "[w]here there was evident partiality . . . in the arbitrator[ ]. . . ."

Exactly what constitutes "evident partiality" by an arbitrator is a troublesome question. The Supreme Court, in *Commonwealth Coatings Corp. v. Continental Casualty Co.*, 393 U.S. 145, 89 S.Ct. 337 (1968), attempted to resolve the issue, but the result of that decision appears to be ongoing uncertainty. In that case, a supposedly neutral arbitrator was discovered to have an undisclosed business relationship with the successful party to the arbitration. The arbitrator had been paid approximately $12,000 by the party in consulting fees, and the relationship "went so far as to include the rendering of services on the very projects involved in [the arbitration]." Id. at 146.

Justice Black, writing for a plurality of four justices, appeared to impose upon arbitrators the same lofty ethical standards required of Article III judges. The Justice suggested, in fact, that "we should, if anything, be even more scrupulous to safeguard the impartiality of arbitrators than judges, since the former have completely free rein to decide the law as well as the facts and are not subject to appellate review." Id. at 149. Using language that has since been seized upon by unsuccessful parties to arbitration, Justice Black concluded by writing that arbitrators, like judges, must avoid even the "appearance of bias." Id. at 150.

It is clear that Campbell would be disqualified under these rules from adjudicating the dispute at issue.

Four justices, however, do not constitute a majority of the Supreme Court. Justice White, writing for himself and Justice Marshall, concurred in the result, but made clear the Court was not holding that arbitrators' and judges' ethical standards are coextensive. Justice White wrote:

> The Court does not decide today that arbitrators are to be held to the standards of judicial decorum of Article III judges, or indeed of any judges. It is often because they are men of affairs, not apart from that of the marketplace, that they are effective in their adjudicatory function . . . This does not mean the judiciary must overlook outright chicanery in giving effect to their awards; that would be an abdication of our responsibility. But it does mean that arbitrators are not automatically disqualified by a business relationship with the parties before them if both parties are informed of the relationship in advance, or if they are unaware of the facts but the relationship is trivial. I see no reason automatically to disqualify the best informed and most capable potential arbitrators.

Id. Accordingly, much of Justice Black's opinion must be read as dicta, and we are left in the dark as to whether an "appearance of bias" will suffice to meet the seemingly more stringent "evident partiality" standard of 9 U.S.C. § 10. Against this murky backdrop of Supreme Court precedent, we examine prior decisions in this circuit.

The closest we can come to the gleaning of guidance in this elusive sphere is the decision in *International Produce, Inc. v. A/S Rosshavet*, 638 F.2d 548 (2d Cir.), *cert. denied*, 451 U.S. 1017, 101 S.Ct. 3006, 69 L.Ed.2d 389 (1981). We held there that the mere fact a neutral arbitrator was also a witness in another arbitration involving the same law firms representing the parties in the arbitration in question did not provide grounds for vacating the award on the basis of his "evident partiality" In reaching this conclusion, Judge Lumbard wrote, "the Supreme Court in Commonwealth Coatings did not expand the § 10 standard of 'evident partiality' to include 'appearance of bias.' In the following sentence, however, he acknowledged that even an " 'appearance of bias' [in this case] seems to us, at best, to be speculation without substance." *Id.* (citation omitted). Accordingly, it appears that his statement to the effect that "evident partiality" requires a showing of more than a mere "appearance of bias" was unnecessary to the result in that case, and thus must be read as something less than an absolute and final determination of the matter. We are left, then, with little guidance concerning what standard is to be applied in construing the "evident partiality" language of the statute. It is to that question we now turn.

In attempting to delineate standards of impartiality on a relatively clean slate, we are struck by the competing interests inherent in the use of arbitration.

On the one hand, parties agree to arbitrate precisely because they prefer a tribunal with expertise regarding the particular subject matter of their dispute. Familiarity with a discipline often comes at the expense of complete impartiality. Some commercial fields are quite narrow, and a given expert may be expected to have formed strong views on certain topics, published articles in the field and so forth. Moreover, specific areas tend to breed tightly knit professional communities. Key members are known to one another, and in fact may work with, or for, one another, from time to time. As this Court has noted, "[e]xpertise in an industry is accompanied by exposure, in ways large and small, to those engaged in it. . . .".

It comes as no surprise, then, that the standards for disqualification of arbitrators have been held to be less stringent than those for federal judges. *See Merit Ins. Co. v. Leatherby Ins. Co.*, 714 F.2d 673 (7th Cir.1983). For to disqualify any arbitrator who had professional dealings with one of the parties (to say nothing of a social acquaintanceship) would make it impossible, in some circumstances, to find a qualified arbitrator at all. Mindful of the trade-off between expertise and impartiality, and cognizant of the voluntary nature of submitting to arbitration, we read Section 10(b) as requiring a showing of something more than the mere "appearance of bias" to vacate an arbitration award. To do otherwise would be to render this efficient means of dispute resolution ineffective in many commercial settings.

On the other hand, we must not abjure our responsibility to maintain the integrity of the federal courts' role in affirming or vacating awards. Much has been made of the private, noncoercive nature of arbitration, and properly so. Nevertheless, the statutory scheme we examine today implicates the process of the federal courts in the enforcement of "private" remedies. Were we to lend our imprimatur to an award grounded in fraud or bias, the sense of fairness that society rightfully demands of its judiciary would be sadly diminished. For this reason, we cannot countenance the promulgation of a standard for partiality as insurmountable as "proof of actual bias"—as the literal words of Section 10 might suggest. Bias is always difficult, and indeed often impossible, to "prove." Unless an arbitrator publicly announces his partiality, or is overheard in a moment of private admission, it is difficult to imagine how "proof" would be obtained. Such a standard, we fear, occasionally would require that we enforce awards in situations that are clearly repugnant to our sense of fairness, yet do not yield "proof" of anything.

If the standard of "appearance of bias" is too low for the invocation of Section 10, and "proof of actual bias" too high, with what are we left?

Profoundly aware of the competing forces that have already been discussed, we hold that "evident partiality" within the meaning of 9 U.S.C. § 10 will be found where a reasonable person would have to conclude that an arbitrator was partial to one party to the arbitration. In assessing a given relationship, courts must remain cognizant of peculiar commercial practices and factual variances. Thus, the small size and population of an industry might require a relaxation of judicial scrutiny, while a totally unnecessary relationship between arbitrator and party may heighten it. In this way, we believe that the courts may refrain from threatening the valuable role of private arbitration in the settlement of commercial disputes, and at the same time uphold their responsibility to ensure that fair treatment is afforded those who come before them.

In light of the foregoing, we examine the particular relationship at issue— namely, a father-son relationship between an arbitrator and the President of an international labor union, a district union of which is a party to the arbitration. The union claims, quite correctly, that there is no authority for a finding of "evident partiality" in such a relationship. We believe, however, the simple reason for this lack of precedent is that arbitrators in similar situations have disqualified themselves rather than risk a charge of partiality.

Accordingly, we reverse the judgment of the district court and remand with instructions to vacate the award.

NOTES

Facts

1.   What was the conflict in *Morelite*?

2.   How significant do you consider the conflict to be? Do you think that there is a pecuniary interest at stake?

3.   What do you think would have been the consequence for Mr. Campbell for ruling against the Funds? Are there sufficient facts in the opinion to say?

Law

1.   On the face of the decision, does *Morelite* follow Justice Black or Justice White?

2.   If you look at the application of the decision, is *Morelite* more shades of gray than Justice Black or Justice White portray? Is there proof of an *actual* lack of independence or impartiality in this case or merely an *appearance* of a particularly egregious lack of independence or impartiality?

3.   How does the *Morelite* standard, in application and your view, modify the standards for judicial conduct?

B)   Personal Relationship Between the Arbitrator and a Party

Morelite is a case involving a personal relationship between the arbitrator and a party. The relationship in that case is a close familial one. But what other relationships would create an impediment to an arbitrator's service? Consider the Code of Ethics for Arbitrators in Commercial Arbitration that the AAA has adopted in answering this question.

AAA Code of Ethics for Arbitrators in Commercial Disputes (Effective March 1, 2004)

* * *

CANON II: AN ARBITRATOR SHOULD DISCLOSE ANY INTEREST OR RELATIONSHIP LIKELY TO AFFECT IMPARTIALITY OR WHICH MIGHT CREATE AN APPEARANCE OF PARTIALITY.

A.   Persons who are requested to serve as arbitrators should, before accepting, disclose:

(1)   any known direct or indirect financial or personal interest in the outcome of the arbitration;

(2)   any known existing or past financial, business, professional or personal relationships which might reasonably affect impartiality or lack of independence in the eyes of any of the parties. For example, prospective arbitrators should disclose any such relationships which they personally have with any party or its lawyer, with any co-arbitrator, or with any individual whom they have been told will be a witness. They should also disclose any such relationships involving their families or household members or their current employers, partners, or professional or business associates that can be ascertained by reasonable efforts;

(3)   the nature and extent of any prior knowledge they may have of the dispute; and

(4)   any other matters, relationships, or interests which they are obligated to disclose by the agreement of the parties, the rules or practices of an institution, or applicable law regulating arbitrator disclosure.

B.   Persons who are requested to accept appointment as arbitrators should make a reasonable effort to inform themselves of any interests or relationships described in paragraph A.

C.   The obligation to disclose interests or relationships described in paragraph A is a continuing duty which requires a person who accepts appointment as an arbitrator to disclose, as soon as practicable, at any stage of the arbitration, any such interests or relationships which may arise, or which are recalled or discovered.

D.   Any doubt as to whether or not disclosure is to be made should be resolved in favor of disclosure.

Weber v. Merrill Lynch Pierce, Fenner & Smith, Inc.

455 F.Supp.2d 545 (N.D.Tex. 2006)

FITZWATER, DISTRICT JUDGE.

Plaintiffs move to vacate an arbitration award based on allegations of evident partiality and arbitrator misconduct. For the reasons that follow, the court denies the motion.

I

Plaintiffs Arnold and Maureen Weber, The Weber Family Trust, Adam Joseph Weber Trust, Nicholas Arman Weber Trust, and Zachary M. Weber Trust (collectively, "the Webers") filed an arbitration complaint with the New York Stock Exchange ("NYSE") against defendant Merrill Lynch, Pierce, Fenner & Smith, Inc. ("Merrill Lynch"). They alleged that Merrill Lynch had made unsuitable investment recommendations over a period of several years. Under the terms of the Webers's account agreement, their claims were subject to mandatory, binding arbitration.

NYSE appointed the initial arbitration panel. When one of the original arbitrators removed himself, NYSE appointed Dean P. Guerin ("Arbitrator Guerin") as a replacement. NYSE notified the parties of this change and enclosed in the notice Arbitrator Guerin's profile, disclosing that his "[s]ocial memberships include the Dallas Country Club."

Immediately following Arbitrator Guerin's appointment, and at later times, the Webers objected to his acting as an arbitrator, based on his membership in the Dallas Country Club. Robert Cecil ("R.Cecil") and his son Blake Cecil ("B.Cecil"), who were potential witnesses in the case and were among the Merrill Lynch brokers who managed the Webers's accounts, also belonged to the Dallas Country Club, as did their wives. The Webers's counsel asserted in a letter that Arbitrator Guerin's "long time friendship with the Cecil family should be grounds for him to recuse himself." In response, Merrill Lynch acknowledged that R. Cecil knew who Arbitrator Guerin was, based on his reputation in the Dallas investment community, and that he had met him several years before at a non-Dallas Country Club function. But it contended that, although they were both members of the Dallas Country Club, R. Cecil did not know Arbitrator Guerin personally. The Arbitration Panel denied the Webers's cause-based challenge to Arbitrator Guerin.

The Webers later sought permission from the Panel to amend their complaint to add as parties individual Merrill Lynch employees (including R. Cecil and B. Cecil) and a financial advisor (and his employer) who had advised Merrill Lynch concerning half of the Webers's investments. They also requested that the hearing be transferred from Dallas to New York City. The Panel declined to allow the proposed amendment. The Webers also made several requests that Merrill Lynch produce its compliance manual, but the Panel refused to order it to do so. The Webers contend that when, in violation of NYSE Rules of Arbitration, Merrill Lynch produced for the first time at the arbitration hearing the handwritten notes of B. Cecil, the Panel permitted the notes to be admitted into evidence while refusing to admit "significant portions of [the Webers's] evidence" that similarly violated NYSE Rules. Following a five-day arbitration hearing, the Panel denied the Webers's claims in all respects.

The Webers move the court to vacate the arbitration award under 9 U.S.C. § 10(a). They contend, first, that Arbitrator Guerin was a member of the same country club as were the Cecils (and their spouses), resulting in evident partiality, and, under NYSE Rules, he should have disclosed having met them, any social relationship that might reasonably create an appearance of partiality or bias, any personal relationship with someone who he had been told would be a witness, and any such relationship with a family member; he failed to make these disclosures related to the Cecils (and their spouses); and he should have been disqualified as an arbitrator.

III

The court first considers the Webers's contention that the award must be vacated under § 10(a)(2) based on the evident partiality of Arbitrator Guerin.

A

The Webers can establish evident partiality by demonstrating either that he failed to disclose relevant facts or that he displayed actual bias at the arbitration proceeding. In a failure to disclose case, the integrity of the process by which arbitrators are chosen is at issue; in an actual bias case, the integrity of the arbitrators' decision is at issue. Thus the standard a court uses to evaluate a claim of evident partiality varies depending on whether the party seeking to vacate the award argues nondisclosure or actual bias.

In their motion, the Webers attempt to demonstrate evident partiality on the grounds that Arbitrator Guerin was a member of the same country club as were the Cecils and their spouses, and that, under NYSE Rules, he should disclosed having once met R. Cecil.

Because Arbitrator Guerin disclosed his membership in the Dallas Country Club and Merrill Lynch disclosed in advance of the hearing that R. Cecil had once met Arbitrator Guerin at a non-Dallas Country Club function, the Webers were aware of these facts before the hearing and moved to disqualify him on these grounds. Accordingly, they cannot establish evident partiality based on the alleged nondisclosure of these facts.

C

The Webers are therefore limited to arguing that Arbitrator Guerin displayed actual bias at the arbitration proceeding. The court decides this question using an objective standard to determine whether they have shown actual bias. *See Mantle*, 956 F.Supp. at 729; *see id.* at 728 (rejecting " 'appearance of bias' as the relevant standard where nondisclosure is not alleged" (*citing Schmitz v. Zilveti*, 20 F.3d 1043, 1047 (9th Cir.1994))).

Under this standard, "[t] he part[ies] asserting evident partiality ha[ve] the burden of proof." *Id.* at 729 (*citing Peoples Sec. Life Ins. Co. v. Monumental Life Ins. Co.*, 991 F.2d 141, 146 (4th Cir.1993)). They must establish that " 'a reasonable person would have to conclude that the arbitrator was partial to one party,' " and they must do so by "produc[ing] specific facts," *id.* "[T]he alleged partiality must be 'direct, definite, and capable of demonstration rather than remote, uncertain or speculative.' " *Id.* Thus "there is an onerous burden on a party urging vacatur based on evident partiality." *Id.* (*citing Peoples Sec. Life*, 991 F.2d at 146).

The Webers have not met their onerous burden. The court will assume arguendo that they have presented adequate record evidence of the Panel's rulings and have not relied on a selective presentation of but a few rulings made over the course of lengthy pre-hearing proceedings and during a multi-day hearing. They rely on the Panel's decisions concerning their motion to amend, their request for production of the Merrill Lynch compliance manual, and the admissibility of evidence to contend that the Panel as a whole, and Arbitrator

Guerin in particular, showed evident partiality. At most, the Webers have shown that the Panel ruled against them in these respects. They have not demonstrated under the demanding standard that a reasonable person would have to conclude that the Panel and/or Arbitrator Guerin was partial to Merrill Lynch.

D

In an argument raised for the first time in their reply brief, the Webers maintain that Arbitrator Guerin did not disclose his wife's memberships in six civic and social organizations to which R. Cecil's wife also belongs, thus rendering him unqualified under NYSE Rules to sit as an arbitrator. They contend that this relationship and Arbitrator Guerin's failure to disclose it establish evident partiality and require that the court vacate the arbitration award. The Webers also posit that, because Arbitrator Guerin failed to disclose material information about his and his family's social relationships with the Cecils, he was not qualified under the NYSE Rules to sit as an arbitrator and he exceeded his powers by making an award, in turn violating § 5 of the FAA and justifying vacatur under § 10(a)(4).

* * *

Even if the court were to consider this argument and the supporting evidence, however, it would hold that the Webers have failed to demonstrate that the arbitration award should be vacated under § 10(a)(4). This is because they provide no controlling authority for the proposition that an arbitrator's nondisclosure requires vacatur on this basis.

Additionally, when an arbitrator fails to disclose some fact tending to show bias, the court must decide whether this failure warrants vacatur of the arbitration decision under § 10(a). Courts require the party challenging the arbitration award to establish that the undisclosed facts create a "reasonable impression of partiality." The Webers have not alleged sufficient facts to establish that the various social memberships of Mmes. Guerin and Cecil create a reasonable impression of partiality.

Courts have found that a reasonable impression of partiality is established when the arbitrator has had a direct business or professional relationship with one of the parties to the arbitration. For example, in *Schmitz* the Ninth Circuit found that a reasonable impression of partiality was established when an arbitrator failed to disclose that his law firm had previously represented the parent company of one of the parties to the arbitration. *Schmitz*, 20 F.3d at 1049. * * * Courts have also found that a reasonable impression of partiality arises when arbitrators fail to disclose the professional positions of their family members when the positions were closely related to a party to the arbitration. *See, e.g., Morelite,* 748 F.2d at 84–85.

The alleged relationship with which the Webers take issue is between the spouse of the arbitrator and the spouse of a Merrill Lynch broker involved in the management of the Webers's accounts. The Webers cite no record evidence that Mmes. Guerin and Cecil even knew each other, much less that they had a personal relationship before or during the arbitration proceeding. Their membership in the same six civic and social organizations does not of itself rise to the level of a reasonable impression of partiality, and courts have not vacated arbitration award based on such attenuated relationships.

Accordingly, even had the Webers properly raised the mutual social memberships of Mmes. Guerin and Cecil as a basis for demonstrating evident partiality, the court would conclude that they have failed to establish it.

NOTES

Facts

1.   What is the relationship at issue in this case?

2.   When did Webers discover the relationships in question?

3.   How significant do you think the relationships are?

Law

1.   What standard did the court apply to determine whether the relationship is one that should have led to a recusal on the part of the arbitrator?

2.   On whom did the court place the burden of proof and persuasion?

3.   What evidence would the Webers have had to provide in order to change the result? How would you get that evidence?

C)   Pecuniary Interest of the Arbitrator in the Outcome of the Dispute

The next case addresses he far more typical problem in determining the impartiality and independence of an arbitrator, which is not personal relationships, but pecuniary interests of the arbitrator. Consider the underlying problem in the case, the arbitrator's interest, and his handling of the information.

Applied Industrial Materials Corp. v. Ovalar Makine Ticaret Ve Sanayi, AS

492 F.3d 132 (2007)

B.D. Parker, Jr., Circuit Judge.

Applied Industrial Materials Corporation ("AIMCOR") appeals from a judgment of the United States District Court for the Southern District of New York (Patterson, J.) denying its petition to confirm an arbitration award and granting appellees' motion to vacate it. In the underlying arbitration, Ovalar Makine Ticaret Ve Sanayi, A.S. ("Ovalar"), a Turkish corporation, and Ural Ataman, its chairman, were found liable to AIMCOR for having breached a contract to deliver petroleum coke. We agree with the district court that one of the three arbitrators, whose vote was dispositive, acted with "evident partiality" by failing to either investigate what he knew to be a potential business relationship between his corporation and one of the parties or inform them that he had walled himself off from learning more. See 9 U.S.C. § 10(a).

BACKGROUND

In 1992, AIMCOR and Ovalar entered into a joint venture in which AIMCOR purchased and transported petroleum coke (a chemical created during oil refinery) to Ovalar, which then distributed the coke in Turkey. The contract provided that any disputes would be settled by arbitration in New York.

In 1997, a dispute arose over the distribution of profits under the joint venture, and the parties resorted to arbitration. The arbitration agreement provided that each party would select an arbitrator, and the two party-appointed arbitrators would then select a third, presiding arbitrator. Section 3 of the agreement provided:

> Prior to the first hearing or initial submissions, all the arbitrators are required to disclose any circumstance which could impair their ability to render an unbiased award based solely upon an objective and impartial consideration of the evidence presented to the Panel. . . .

> No arbitrator shall accept an appointment or sit on a Panel, where the arbitrator or the arbitrator's current employer has a direct or indirect interest in the outcome of the arbitration.

> All such disclosed relationships, experience and/or interests must be objected to by the parties at or before the first procedural hearing, or they shall be deemed waived as creating a bias, prejudice or conflict

of interest which would warrant overturning the final award in this matter.

Although the agreement did not specifically address whether the arbitrators were required to make additional disclosures after commencement of the arbitration, section 4 provided that "[n]o person shall serve as an arbitrator who has or has had a financial or personal interest in the outcome of the arbitration or who has acquired from an interested source detailed prior knowledge of the matter in dispute."

Ovalar and AIMCOR each selected one arbitrator, and the parties selected Charles Fabrikant as the third arbitrator and chairman of the panel. He was the Chairman, President and CEO of Seacor Holdings, a multi-billion dollar company with 50 offices in 30 countries.

On September 3, 2003, before the hearings started, the arbitrators were advised that AIMCOR was being sold to Oxbow Industries and that the transaction might be "relevant to the disclosure issue." Each arbitrator submitted a disclosure statement. Fabrikant's statement, dated September 25, 3003, indicated that he "ha[d] had no personal or business relationship with any of the parties to this proceeding, or their affiliates," and would "reserve the right to amend or add to this disclosure should future circumstances warrant it."

At a hearing on March 4, 2005, the parties agreed to bifurcate the arbitration proceedings into liability and damage phases. The liability phase commenced soon thereafter. On April 16, 2005 Fabrikant sent an email to the parties:

> Gentlemen: it came to my attention yesterday, or day before yesterday that my St. Louis office, which runs our barge operation under the name SCF, has recently been engaged with Ox-Bow of Palm Beach. The subject of conversation is a contract for the carriage of petroleum coke. I had no knowledge of such conversations taking place prior to the past week. I do not participate in contract negotiations or get involved in day to day operations of SCF.
>
> I would like to amend my prior disclosures. At that time I did ask if there had been contacts between my group and these parties and there were none.
>
> I do not plan to become involved in discussions between SCF and Ox-Bow, should there be further conversations between them.
>
> I do not feel my ability to decide this case on the merits is impaired.

There were no further disclosures or reactions from the parties before the arbitration panel's decision on liability five months later on September 22, 2005. The panel, in a 2–1 decision in which Fabrikant cast the deciding vote, found Ovalar liable to AIMCOR for breach of contract. Following its loss, Ovalar secured new counsel.

Two months later, on November 21, 2005, with the issue of damages still to be decided, Ovalar's counsel wrote to Fabrikant asking him to withdraw. Since the time of the liability award, Ovalar had conducted an investigation and concluded that a previously existing, inadequately disclosed commercial relationship existed between SCF, a division of Fabrikant's company, and Oxbow, the parent of AIMCOR. Ovalar's claim was that since 2004—well before the liability award—SCF had been transporting petroleum coke for Oxbow, and that this relationship generated approximately $275,000 in revenue.

On December 5, 2005, Fabrikant responded to Ovalar's request, stating that "I see no reason to withdraw from the panel." He revealed that when he was initially informed that SCF was engaged in discussions with Oxbow, he told SCF's president that he "wished to know nothing about SCF's conversations, or be a party to information about our activities with Oxbow or be consulted concerning any business with them." Having erected a so-called "Chinese wall" to prevent his learning of any agreements between his company and Oxbow, Fabrikant concluded that he was unaware of the relationship until he received the letter from Ovalar.

In February 2006, when AIMCOR moved to confirm the partial arbitration award, Ovalar and Ataman moved to vacate the award on the grounds that Fabrikant's failure to recuse himself violated the Federal Arbitration Act, 9 U.S.C. § 10(a). The district court agreed with Ovalar and Ataman. The court's decision focused on several things, including (1) the disclosure requirements in the arbitration agreement, (2) Fabrikant's initial statement that, subject to later clarification, no conflict existed, (3) and Fabrikant's later disclosure that talks were occurring between Oxbow and SCF but that he did not know about them or intend to get involved. The court found that these events gave rise to a reasonable expectation on the part of the parties that they would be notified of any contractual relationship between Seacor and Oxbow. The court held that by insulating himself from learning about any such relationship, and failing to tell the parties that he had done so, Fabrikant created an "appearance of partiality" when a nontrivial commercial relationship surfaced that pre-existed the April 2005 email.

Citing the standards of the American Arbitration Code of Ethics for Arbitrators and the International Bar Association's Guidelines on Conflicts of Interest in International Arbitration, the district court found that "[r]eason dictates that there must be a continuous obligation on the part of the arbitrator to avoid partiality or the appearance of partiality." The court observed that the arbitrator's "failure to investigate the status of SCF's negotiations with Oxbow and his subsequent lack of knowledge do not excuse his lack of disclosure." Accordingly, the district court vacated the award. This appeal followed.

DISCUSSION

When reviewing a district court's decision to vacate an arbitration award, we review findings of fact for clear error and questions of law de novo.

The Federal Arbitration Act, 9 U.S.C. § 10(a), provides that:

In any of the following cases the United States court in and for the district wherein the award was made may make an order vacating the award upon the application of any party to the arbitration-

(1) where the award was procured by corruption, fraud, or undue means; [or]

(2) where there was evident partiality or corruption in the arbitrators, or either of them;. . . .

The Supreme Court addressed the meaning of "evident partiality" under § 10(a)(2) in *Commonwealth Coatings Corp. v. Continental Casualty Co.*, 393 U.S. 145 (1968), and concluded that it existed when one of the parties was a regular, though sporadic, customer of an arbitrator, who failed to disclose that fact. There, although there was no evidence of actual bias on the part of the arbitrator, Justice Black, writing for a plurality of the Court, stated that, "[w]e can perceive no way in which the effectiveness of the arbitration process will be hampered by the simple requirement that arbitrators disclose to the parties any dealings that might create an impression of possible bias." Justice Black imported this rigorous standard from those safeguarding the impartiality of Article III judges. He further concluded that when the parties have the relevant information at their disposal, it is up to them to decide whether a conflict is significant enough to warrant an objection.

Justice White, concurring, underscored the importance of disclosing conflicts at the outset of an arbitration. He also emphasized that federal courts ought not to hold arbitrators to the strict impartiality standards applicable to Article III judges: "it is enough for present purposes to hold, as the Court does, that where the arbitrator has a substantial interest in a firm which has done more than trivial business with a party, that fact must be disclosed." He concluded that "arbitrators are not automatically disqualified by a business relationship with the parties before them if both parties are informed of the relationship in advance, or if they are unaware of the facts but the relationship is trivial."

In *Morelite Construction Corp. v. New York City District Council Carpenters Benefit Funds*, 748 F.2d 79 (2d Cir.1984), we concluded that the fractured court in *Commonwealth Coatings* and our precedent provided us "with little guidance concerning what standard is to be applied in construing the 'evident partiality' language of the statute." We held that a father-son relationship between an arbitrator and an officer of one party to the arbitration rose to the level of "evident partiality." Noting that in *Commonwealth Coatings* Justice Black did not speak for a majority of the Court, we elected to followed Justice White's reasoning that arbitrators are not subject to the same standards of impartiality as Article III judges. Finding "the standard of 'appearance of bias' . . . too low" and " 'proof of actual bias' too high," we held "that 'evident partiality' within the meaning of 9 U.S.C. § 10 will be found where a reasonable person would have to conclude that an arbitrator was partial to one party to the arbitration." Unlike a judge, who can be disqualified "in any proceeding in which his impartiality might reasonably be questioned," *Apple v. Jewish Hosp. & Med. Ctr.*, 829 F.2d 326, 332–33 (1987), an arbitrator is disqualified only when a reasonable person, considering all of the circumstances, "would have to conclude" that an arbitrator was partial to one side, *Morelite*, 748 F.2d at 84.

An arbitrator who knows of a material relationship with a party and fails to disclose it meets *Morelite's* "evident partiality" standard: A reasonable person would have to conclude that an arbitrator who failed to disclose under such circumstances was partial to one side. Here, the court below did not make findings as to the nature and timing of the arbitrator's knowledge of the relationship between SCF and Oxbow. Instead, the district court focused on whether or not there was an "appearance of partiality" on the part of the arbitrator, a standard that we have made clear is too low. See id. As a result, we cannot evaluate whether the arbitrator had knowledge of the relationship that would compel a reasonable person to conclude that he was partial. Were this the only issue before us, we would be inclined to remand to the district court for further development of this issue.

However, our analysis does not end there. While the presence of actual knowledge of a conflict can be dispositive of the evident partiality test, the absence of actual knowledge is not. Indeed, in *Morelite*, we did not address the scope of an arbitrator's duty to investigate or disclose potential conflicts of interest. We now conclude that if we are to take seriously Justice White's statement that "arbitrators are not automatically disqualified by a business relationship with the parties before them if both parties are informed of the relationship in advance, or if they are unaware of the facts but the relationship is trivial," arbitrators must take steps to ensure that the parties are not misled into believing that no nontrivial conflict exists. It therefore follows that where an arbitrator has reason to believe that a nontrivial conflict of interest might exist, he must (1) investigate the conflict (which may reveal information that must be disclosed under Commonwealth Coatings) or (2) disclose his reasons for believing there might be a conflict and his intention not to investigate.

We emphasize that we are not creating a free-standing duty to investigate. The mere failure to investigate is not, by itself, sufficient to vacate an arbitration award. But, when an arbitrator knows of a potential conflict, a failure to either investigate or disclose an intention not to investigate is indicative of evident partiality.

Turning once again to *Morelite*, the question before us is whether a reasonable person, looking at an arbitrator's decision not to investigate and his concomitant failure to inform the parties of the "Chinese Wall,"[1] would conclude that evident partiality existed. Here, the arbitrator was under an ongoing obligation to disclose conflicts and had previously assured the parties that he intended to comply with that obligation. Once he learned that a branch of his company was negotiating with Oxbow to enter into a business relationship, he knew, at a minimum, that a potential conflict existed. It is possible that the arbitrator believed in good faith that because the potential transaction involved a subsidiary, would generate revenue that was small in light of the size of his business, and was far removed from his daily concerns, nothing had occurred that would affect his ability to be fair and impartial.

However, as *Commonwealth Coatings* and *Morelite* make clear, subjective good faith is not the test. Once the arbitrator was aware that a nontrivial conflict of interest might exist, the calculus changed. A reasonable observer attempting to assess whether evident partiality existed would, we think, be given pause by a number of significant facts: the arbitrator had a continuing duty to ensure that neither he nor his corporation had "a direct or indirect interest in the outcome

---

[1]   While we are not prepared to find that a "Chinese Wall" is an inadequate substitute for investigation, we note that it is preferable for the arbitrator to consult the parties before putting a "Chinese Wall" into place, rather than informing the parties after he has chosen that course of action unilaterally.

of the arbitration." When the arbitrator learned of mere discussions between the two companies, he disclosed that fact alone. Had he investigated the potential conflict, that investigation would have revealed that a relationship between SCF and Oxbow already existed and had generated $275,000 in revenue, not a trivial amount. Yet the arbitrator failed to investigate those discussions or disclose that he would make no further inquiries. We believe that, given these circumstances, a reasonable person would have to conclude that evident partiality existed.

The standard of disclosure we apply is not an onerous one. Disclosure serves the twin goals of "encourag[ing] conflicts over arbitrators to be dealt with early in the arbitration process and help[ing] limit the availability of collateral attacks on arbitration awards by a disgruntled party." As Justice White noted in *Commonwealth Coatings*, "it is far better that the relationship [i.e., a potential conflict between an arbitrator and a party] be disclosed at the outset, . . . than to have the relationship come to light after the arbitration, when a suspicious or disgruntled party can seize on it as a pretext for invalidating the award." It is certainly true that an arbitrator "cannot be expected to provide the parties with his complete and unexpurgated business biography." Id. But the distance between that type of disclosure and what we would require here is sufficiently great to affirm the district court.

CONCLUSION

The order of the district court denying petitioner's motion to confirm the arbitration award and granting the respondents' motion to vacate the arbitration award is Affirmed.

NOTES

Facts

1.   What was the conflict at issue in the case? How would the arbitrator benefit financially from ruling one way in the case rather than another?

2.   How substantial is the arbitrator's financial interest that is at stake here? Should that matter?

3.   When and how did the parties find out about the conflict?

4.   How did the arbitrator deal with the conflict? Do you think this is a typical way to handle conflicts?

Law

1. What distinction, if any, does the Court draw between a knowing non-disclosure of a fact and the conflict that the fact itself, independently, would support in the abstract? Is there something about the decision not to disclose that is relevant?

2. Does the Court go further with regard to its disclosure jurisprudence beyond a decision not to disclose a known fact? Does the Court impose a duty to investigate? How significant is that duty?

3. What protocols do you expect arbitrators to follow before accepting an appointment?

D) Arbitral "Issue" Conflicts

In international arbitration, one of the key new developments in the law concerns so-called "issue conflicts." If an arbitrator has published a view on a legal issue in dispute in the case or has made statements (outside of the context of a judicial or arbitral decision) concerning the factual context in which a dispute arose, that may lead to a challenge by a party. In some instances, challenges on this basis have been successful.

The case below provides an answer by a U.S. court to a similar problem. Consider whether the result in this case would have been different if the arbitrator stridently defended the point of view ascribed to him in a law review article. Would that have made a difference in the Court's analysis? How?

In light of social networking sites like Facebook and LinkedIn, it is likely that counsel will have greater access to arbitrators' statements, comments, and "likes", out of which they might try to argue that the arbitrator is not impartial. What is the standard that counsel would have to meet in light of the *STMicroelectronics* case below?

STMicroelectronics, N.V. v. Credit Suisse Securities (USA) LLC

648 F.3d 68 (2d Cir. 2011)

GERARD E. LYNCH, CIRCUIT JUDGE:

Credit Suisse Securities (USA) LLC ("Credit Suisse") is a member of the Financial Industry Regulatory Authority (FINRA), and Credit Suisse's form "New Account Agreement" includes a clause requiring its customers to submit all disputes to FINRA arbitration. When, however, Credit Suisse lost a major

FINRA arbitration against a customer, STMicroelectronics, N.V. ("ST"), Credit Suisse attacked the arbitrators for various improprieties and asked the district court and now this Court to undo the award. We have given Credit Suisse's attacks on the arbitral award careful attention and find them without merit. We therefore uphold confirmation of the award in full.

We do agree with Credit Suisse on one point, however, relating not to validity of the arbitration award but to its implementation in the federal courts. We hold that the district court's judgment should have credited Credit Suisse for approximately $75 million that ST received in exchange for selling some of the failed auction rate securities at issue in this case, and should have reduced Credit Suisse's liability for interest accordingly. We therefore vacate the district court's judgment on that point and remand for modification in light of the partial satisfaction of the award. We reject, however, Credit Suisse's attempt to alter the award's scheme for distributing interest earned on the securities portfolio.

BACKGROUND

ST manufactures semiconductors. The cyclical nature of its business requires the company to have a large amount of cash or cash equivalents on hand to meet its needs. Until early 2006, ST invested this cash only in money market deposits and floating rate notes, investments chosen for their safety and liquidity.

In April 2006, Credit Suisse approached ST offering another type of investment, called auction rate securities ("ARS"), that Credit Suisse promised would meet these specifications while maintaining "an attractive yield advantage over other short-term vehicles." ARS are debt instruments whose interest rates are reset by auctions at periodic intervals. Credit Suisse explicitly proposed, and ST explicitly accepted, investing only in ARS that are backed by federally guaranteed student loans.

Credit Suisse stuck to this plan for only a few days. Almost immediately, it began buying other types of ARS for the account. Those securities, while carrying a higher yield (and a higher average commission for Credit Suisse), had no government guarantee. By November 2006, the account contained no government-backed ARS, and after January 2007 none of Credit Suisse's purchases for the account involved student loans at all, guaranteed or not. Instead, Credit Suisse bought ARS backed by collateralized debt obligations ("CDOs") and credit-linked notes ("CLNs"), which in turn were backed by a wide variety of assets, some of which turned out to be risky. To cover their tracks, the Credit Suisse brokers responsible for the account sent deliberately false email confirmations to ST in which they replaced words in the names of securities that identified them as CDOs or CLNs with more neutral terms like "funding" and often flatly inaccurate terms like "Student Loan."

In July 2007, an ST employee noticed that Credit Suisse had purchased securities that deviated from its instructions, and asked Credit Suisse to "stick to the mandate to buy only Student Loan [ARS]." Although Credit Suisse did cancel one transaction, and although it reaffirmed its promise that it would invest ST's funds in "Aaa/AAA rated student loan paper," it nevertheless continued to buy ARS based on un-guaranteed CDOs and CLNs, and continued to send ST email confirmations hiding the true nature of those investments. Credit Suisse did so in the face of ST's increasingly vehement instructions not to buy non-government-backed ARS and to sell the ARS it already owned. For these actions and others, the two Credit Suisse brokers responsible for ST's account were later convicted, one by plea and one by jury verdict, of securities fraud and related conspiracy charges.

In August 2007, the ARS market began to fall apart. Some auctions failed to draw enough investors to bid on all the relevant securities, making them hard if not impossible to sell. A Credit Suisse executive reassured ST about its investments, but by September 2007, all of ST's ARS—worth over $400 million—had failed at auction. This significantly reduced both the value of the ARS and their utility to ST as a highly liquid cash equivalent.

In February 2008, ST filed an arbitration claim against Credit Suisse with FINRA, which operates "the largest securities dispute resolution forum in the world" and which counts Credit Suisse among its member institutions. Credit Suisse had provided for arbitration with the National Association of Securities Dealers, FINRA's predecessor, in the New Account Agreement it provided to ST. ST sought arbitration under this provision, raising federal claims of securities fraud under § 10(b)(5) of the Securities Exchange Act of 1934 and SEC Rule 10b–5, as well as state-law claims of fraud, intentional misrepresentation, fraudulent concealment, breach of contract, breach of fiduciary duty, breach of the duty of good faith and fair dealing, unjust enrichment, unsuitability, unauthorized transactions, and (after amending its complaint) failure to supervise.

FINRA rules provided that the parties would have three arbitrators to decide their case: two "public arbitrators" who must be unattached to the securities industry and one "non-public arbitrator" chosen for industry experience and knowledge. See FINRA Rules 12100(p), (u), 12401(c), 12403. FINRA provided the parties with lists of possible arbitrators in the relevant categories along with standard disclosure reports for each one, allowing the parties to strike arbitrators at their discretion and rank the remaining ones in each category according to their preferences. The parties were unable to select a full panel on the first try and requested another slate of candidates who possessed more experience dealing with the types of claims involved. On the second try, the parties successfully selected a panel and proceeded to arbitration.

Midway through the hearings, however, Credit Suisse sought to remove one of the three arbitrators, John J. Duval, Sr., alleging that he had served as an expert witness primarily for customers arbitrating against financial firms but that he had painted a more balanced picture of his experience on his disclosure report and that he had failed to disclose prior expert testimony on certain issues relevant to ST's case. Duval, with the support of the chair of the panel, refused to step down, noting that he had worked more often on the side of the financial industry than Credit Suisse had suggested he had and declaring that "there is no doubt in my mind that I can render a fair and unbiased opinion." Credit Suisse next petitioned FINRA to remove him, but FINRA's Director of Arbitration denied this request.

Finally, in February 2009, after four days of pre-hearing conferences, fifteen days of hearings, and voluminous briefing from both sides, the arbitration panel ruled unanimously in favor of ST. The arbitrators' award effectively undid the trades: ST would return the failed securities (with a par value of $414,975,000) to Credit Suisse upon the latter's payment of $400 million in compensatory damages, plus $1.5 million in financing fees, $3 million to cover ST's attorneys and expert witnesses, and interest (offset, at least prior to December 31, 2008, by the amount of interest the securities paid to ST). These figures, though substantial, were all lower than the amounts ST had requested in each category.

ST quickly petitioned to confirm the award in the Southern District of New York. Credit Suisse opposed ST's petition and sought to vacate the award on the basis of Duval's purportedly misleading or insufficient disclosure and also because of the arbitrators' alleged "manifest disregard of the law."

* * *

DISCUSSION

I.   Arbitrator Disclosure

Credit Suisse first argues that we should vacate the award because arbitrator Duval provided incomplete and inaccurate disclosures to the parties before they selected him for the arbitration panel. Specifically, Credit Suisse contends that, "[w]hile Duval has served extensively and almost exclusively as a professional claimant-side expert witness [that is, as a witness for customers arbitrating against financial firms], his disclosure report omitted all but a brief reference to his claimant-side experience and instead misleadingly stated that he worked for 'both sides.'" Credit Suisse further contends that Duval "chose not to disclose that he had served as a claimant-side expert witness on an issue very similar to the one that would determine the arbitration."

As we have previously noted, "[a] party moving to vacate an arbitration award has the burden of proof, and the showing required to avoid confirmation is very high." Credit Suisse has not met this burden.

Following issuance of an arbitration award, § 9 of the Federal Arbitration Act ("FAA") provides that a party may apply to a district court "for an order confirming the award, and thereupon the court must grant such an order unless the award is vacated, modified, or corrected as prescribed in sections 10 and 11 of this title." 9 U.S.C. § 9. Section 10 of the FAA, in turn, lists grounds for vacating an order including, most relevantly to this argument, "evident partiality or corruption in the arbitrators" and "other misbehavior by which the rights of any party have been prejudiced." 9 U.S.C. § 10(a)(2), (3).

During arbitration, Credit Suisse invoked the first of these provisions, complaining that Duval's incomplete disclosure demonstrated "evident partiality." Cf. 9 U.S.C. § 10(a)(2); *Commonwealth Coatings Corp. v. Cont'l Cas. Co.*, 393 U.S. 145, 147 (1968). Before the district court and this Court, however, Credit Suisse maintains the same objection but shifts to a more novel theory, disclaiming "evident partiality" and instead relying on the FAA's catch-all for "other misbehavior by which the rights of any party have been prejudiced." 9 U.S.C. § 10(a)(3). Credit Suisse does not cite any cases, nor are we aware of any, that have addressed claims of insufficient disclosure under the "other misbehavior" prong.

There is a reason for Credit Suisse's switch: as it now acknowledges, the decisions under § 10(a)(2)'s "evident partiality" provision have "addresse[d] non-disclosure only of facts bearing on partiality—namely, a relationship with a party, a lawyer, or another arbitrator." Credit Suisse's contention, however, is that Duval failed to disclose (and, in fact, affirmatively misrepresented) facts bearing not on partiality but on an alleged predisposition. No one alleges that Duval concealed any relationship with one of the parties, whether financial, familial, or otherwise. Rather, Credit Suisse argues that Duval's experience as an expert for claimants either colored his outlook in their favor or demonstrates that his outlook was already so colored and that, either way, Credit Suisse was entitled to know about that experience before selecting him as an arbitrator. Credit Suisse contends that Duval's disclosure report misled Credit Suisse about his experience in violation of the FINRA Rules, thereby entitling Credit Suisse to vacate the award for "other misbehavior" under § 10(a)(3). ST responds that Duval did not violate the FINRA rules and that, even if he had, § 10(a)(3) is not available for violations of arbitration rules or for failure to disclose generally.

We may reject Credit Suisse's claim without diving too deeply into these difficult legal waters. Close consideration turns up very little factual support for Credit Suisse's claim of improper disclosure—too little to vacate the award under any conceivable legal standard.

Duval's "Arbitrator Disclosure Report" describes a twenty-two-year career in finance, primarily with Merrill Lynch, and explains that he now works as an arbitrator and is "also a Litigation Consultant and an expert witness having represented both sides." A section of the report entitled "Disclosure/Conflict Information" lists a variety of information, including banks with which Duval maintains an account, securities licenses he holds, and the like. In relevant part, it repeats Duval's statement that he has worked as an expert and consultant for "both sides" and provides two specific examples of such work, one where he was an expert or consultant for Wachovia Securities and one where he testified against the same company.

Credit Suisse argues that Duval should have disclosed more of his work as an expert for claimants (that is, customers) than his disclosure report reflected. During the arbitration, Duval mentioned offhand that he had "testified a lot in cases as an expert." Credit Suisse says this remark led it to investigate Duval's background and to learn that Duval had stated, in 2005, that he had testified more than twenty-five times as an expert, only "once or twice for respondents [that is, financial institutions] and the balance for claimants." Attacking Duval's experience as "one-sided," Credit Suisse argues that Duval misled it when he described his experience as representing "both sides" and listed only one representation on each side.

Credit Suisse's characterization of Duval's experience, however, is incomplete. When Credit Suisse asked him to recuse himself in the middle of a day of hearings, Duval responded that Credit Suisse's figures were "underreported" and that he had "had numerous cases where [he] was retained by [a] respondent, but [that had] settled. They didn't make it to a hearing." He further elaborated that "a respondent firm recently hired [him] to do a mediation," and that he was "under retainer by a large . . . wire house at present, and . . . probably will testify for them." Credit Suisse's briefs largely ignore this explanation, instead focusing wholly on the 2005 statement, which is both less complete (because it describes only times Duval testified and does not include other expert or consulting work) and less up to date (because it does not include Duval's experience in the three years between 2005 and the arbitration in this case).

Given the "very high" showing necessary to vacate an award, we would expect Credit Suisse to present more evidence to support its contentions about Duval's background. It appears, however, that Credit Suisse never asked Duval for an accounting of his experience, either before or during the arbitration or during the district court proceedings. Although we have limited the availability of discovery regarding the completeness of an arbitrator's disclosures, we have not forbidden it altogether. See *Andros Compania Maritima, S.A. v. Marc Rich & Co.*, 579 F.2d 691, 702 (2d Cir.1978); *Sanko S.S. Co. v. Cook Indus., Inc.*, 495 F.2d 1260, 1263 (2d Cir.1973); *see also Hoeft v. MVL Group, Inc.*, 343 F.3d 57, 66–67 (2d Cir.2003) (stating in dicta that arbitrators may be deposed on issue of bias), overruled on other grounds by *Hall Street Assocs.*, 552 U.S. 576, 128 S.Ct. 1396. That Credit Suisse made no further inquiries in either forum is telling.[4]

The lack of evidence means we cannot know exactly how much work Duval did or for whom. But that was Credit Suisse's burden to show, and it has failed to carry it. At the very least, even if we assume that Duval has worked for many more claimants than respondents, his work for "numerous" respondents and his ability to cite two respondents employing him at the time of the 2008 arbitration belie Credit Suisse's contention that he "served . . . almost exclusively as a professional claimant-side expert witness."

With this understanding of the record, we see no ground upon which to vacate the award because of Duval's disclosures. Even if we assume several hotly contested legal issues in Credit Suisse's favor—that the "other misbehavior" clause in 9 U.S.C. § 10(a)(3) extends to insufficient disclosure, that violation of the FINRA rules necessarily constitutes such "other misbehavior," and that a one-sided employment history demonstrates a predisposition that must be disclosed under that provision or some other—Credit Suisse's claim still fails. Credit Suisse has not shown that Duval's experience was one-sided. Failure to disclose Duval's full experience thus could not have been "misbehavior" of any sort, much less the "other misbehavior" that would trigger § 10(a)(3).

---

4   Notably, Credit Suisse did suggest an evidentiary hearing below on what it knew about Duval's experience—to counter hints that it had known the full extent of his background all along—but never made any suggestion about investigating Duval's experience itself.

Moreover, Credit Suisse cites no FINRA rule that Duval's disclosures violate. In fact, it specifically disclaims any contention that FINRA Rule 12405(a)—which governs arbitrator disclosures—"by itself required disclosure of details about Duval's expert engagements." The wisdom of this conclusion is confirmed both by FINRA's own explications of its rules and by its application of those rules in this case. A FINRA publication, under the heading "Arbitrator Tip: Disclosure and Acting as an Expert," suggests that "all arbitrators who act as experts include—at a minimum—a sentence (filling in the appropriate type of party) in their background paragraph such as: 'I have been an expert witness for (customers/brokerage firms/brokers, or associated persons).'" Duval included exactly this sort of statement here, accurately describing himself as a "Litigation Consultant and an expert witness having represented both sides." The same publication states that "[a]rbitrators may also wish to provide an estimate of the number of times they acted as an expert for customers, registered representatives or broker-dealers." (Emphasis added.) But it does not say they must do so. It is no surprise, therefore, that FINRA's Director of Arbitration found no reason to remove Duval from the panel after "review[ing]" Credit Suisse's allegations.

Credit Suisse makes two arguments in response. First, it argues that Duval's disclosure report was not just incomplete but affirmatively misleading because it included two engagements as an expert witness—one for Wachovia Securities, one against it—and no others. Credit Suisse admits this disclosure was factually true, but alleges that it was aimed to create a false "appearance of neutrality." As discussed above, however, Credit Suisse has failed to show that Duval's experience was sufficiently one-sided to cast doubt on that appearance.

Second, Credit Suisse points to the FINRA arbitrator application form, which includes some questions about prior expert work, and argues that Duval failed in his disclosure obligations (or otherwise committed "misbehavior") by failing to include all his prior expert service on that application. That application form, however, is not a document prepared with reference to any particular matter. Rather, it is the initial form that potential arbitrators must file to get on the FINRA roster of candidates. Moreover, Credit Suisse does not provide a copy of the form actually executed by Duval; it provides only a blank copy of the form, without connecting the dots between that form and Duval's disclosures. Specifically, Credit Suisse provides no evidence (a) that the form it cites is the source of the information in the arbitrator's disclosure report provided to the parties by FINRA; (b) that, if it is the source of the disclosure report, every bit of information provided by a potential arbitrator in that form ends up on the report, rather than only a selection of information that the arbitrator or FINRA administrators think relevant; or (c) that the form it cites, which dates from November 2008, contains the same questions that were asked when Duval applied to be an arbitrator before FINRA even existed, or even when Duval's disclosure form was released to the parties at least several months before the date of the application form Credit Suisse provides. Lacking all these facts, we cannot infer that Duval failed to meet any disclosure obligations.

Finally, Credit Suisse adds another twist to its improper-disclosure case, arguing that Duval should have alerted Credit Suisse that he had previously testified as an expert on legal issues similar to some of those at issue in this case. This argument suffers from evidentiary deficiencies similar to those of Credit Suisse's other arguments: Credit Suisse provides only nine pages of testimony, without context about the case or about Duval's testimony. The testimony Credit Suisse cites involves a customer's duty to read a prospectus. This issue may relate to a legal issue here, involving whether ST should have read both the trade confirmations it received by email and the account statements it received in hard copy. But without context it is hard to evaluate the relevance of Duval's prior testimony.

More fundamentally, the major premise of Credit Suisse's attack on Duval's non-disclosure of his prior testimony fails. There is no contention here that Duval had any prior knowledge of, or misconception about, the facts of this case. Credit Suisse's argument, rather, is that his testimony suggests he had pre-existing views about potentially relevant propositions of law. However, "[a] judge's lack of predisposition regarding the relevant legal issues in a case has never been thought a necessary component of equal justice, and with good reason. For one thing, it is virtually impossible to find a judge who does not have preconceptions about the law." *Repub. Party of Minn. v. White*, 536 U.S. 765, 777 (2002). This is all the more true for arbitrators, "[t]he most sought-after" of whom "are those who are prominent and experienced members of the specific business community in which the dispute to be arbitrated arose." *Int'l Produce, Inc. v. A/S Rosshavet*, 638 F.2d 548, 552 (2d Cir.1981). Arbitrator Duval played that very role on this panel, as the "non-public arbitrator" specifically chosen for his industry connection. *See* FINRA Rule 12100(p). It would be strange if such an arbitrator were forced to search the record of all prior testimony for any statement that might—however tangentially—relate to any of the many legal issues that might arise in any given case. A party might like to know that information when shopping for arbitrators, but its absence cannot form a ground for vacating an arbitral award. The rule for which Credit Suisse contends finds no support in the text of the FAA or the case law, and we reject it.

NOTES

Facts

1. Does Credit Suisse think that Duval is "impartial"? If you were counsel for Credit Suisse, how would you break the news of his appointment to your client?

2. What is the concern with regard to Duval's appointment?

3. What did Duval disclose in this case? Was that disclosure sufficient to put the parties on notice of the potential conflict or did Duval only disclose the proverbial "tip of the iceberg"?

Law

1. How did the Court approach the question of issue conflicts? Did it hold that there was a problem with appointing a person with a clearly articulated view on a question of law or fact at issue in the case?

2. What evidence would have changed the outcome of this case? How would you find that evidence?

E) Relationship Between the Arbitrator and Counsel

A problem can arise in the context of a lawyer's relationship with the arbitrator(s). Many of these conflicts will be similar to the conflicts already discussed above (family relationship, financial interests, etc.). The *Lifecare* case adds an interesting wrinkle that arises out of the affiliation of arbitrators with law firms. If you think after reading the case that the problem is insignificant, consider that more and more arbitrators are leaving the traditional law firm in order to avoid precisely these kinds of conflicts.

Lifecare Intern., Inc. v. CD Medical, Inc.

68 F.3d 429 (11th Cir. 1995)

RICHARD MILLS, DISTRICT JUDGE:

Should the arbitration award be set aside on the ground that one of the arbitrators was biased?

If that issue falls, was the arbitration award arbitrary and capricious?

The district court rejected both grounds and affirmed the arbitration award.

We agree and affirm.

I. BACKGROUND

Appellant, CD Medical, Inc., manufactures dialysis machines and the disposable components used on those machines; they also directly market those machines and disposable components in the United States. Outside of the United States, the products were marketed through several wholly-owned subsidiaries, including Appellant, CD Medical B.V. CD Medical B.V., in turn, markets the products through either its wholly-owned subsidiaries or independent contractors. Appellee, Lifecare International, Inc. ("Lifecare"), was one of those independent contractors.

In 1990, Lifecare sued CD Medical, Inc., and CD Medical, B.V., in the United States District Court for the Southern District of Florida for breach of contract, fraud, and tortious interference. Pursuant to the Federal Arbitration Act and a 1984 agreement between the parties, CD Medical moved to compel arbitration and to stay the district court proceedings. Over Lifecare's objection, the district court granted CD Medical's motion to compel arbitration and ordered the parties to arbitrate.

In June of 1992, Lifecare filed its demand for arbitration. The demand claimed that: (1) CD Medical breached a February 1987 oral agreement to return the country of Algeria to Lifecare's exclusive territory; (2) CD Medical breached a written February 1988 settlement agreement which also returned Algeria to Lifecare's exclusive territory; (3) CD Medical breached a December 1988 written agreement which returned Algeria to Lifecare for the 1989 year; and (4) CD Medical tortiously interfered with Lifecare's advantageous business relationship with the Algerian Government. Lifecare sought damages for lost profits from sales it would have made in Algeria in the amounts of $10,731,313 for 1988 and $13,557,562 for 1989, along with prejudgment interest and punitive damages.

In February 1993, the liability portion of the trial was conducted before a three-member arbitration panel. The principal hearing consumed seventeen days, ending on February 24, 1993. During a break in the hearings in February, Arbitrator Craig Stein, an attorney, recounted an incident in which he was personally involved where opposing counsel refused to reschedule a summary judgment hearing so that he could travel abroad. Arbitrator Stein apparently described such conduct as unprofessional, and in his opinion, it warranted disciplinary action.

On April 27, 1993, the arbitrators informed the parties that they intended to rule in Lifecare's favor on liability. Sometime thereafter, one of the White &

Case attorneys representing CD Medical discovered that the "opposing counsel" to whom Arbitrator Stein had previously referred to was another attorney who was employed at White & Case.[3] Consequently, CD Medical sought to disqualify Arbitrator Stein. The American Arbitration Association denied the motion to disqualify and the proceedings continued.

On November 18 and 19, and December 16, 1993, the arbitrators heard testimony regarding the amount of damages. On January 14, 1994, Arbitrator Stein and another arbitrator awarded Lifecare $10,102,674 in lost profits, $5,394,203.90 in prejudgment interest, $13,527.47 in administrative fees and costs, $71,485.06 in arbitrators' fees and expenses, and $39,048 in expert witness fees. Neither Arbitrator Stein nor the other arbitrator who joined in the majority decision issued an opinion explaining their reasoning for finding CD Medical liable or justifying the amount of damages. The dissenting arbitrator wrote a three-page opinion addressing only the issue of liability.

Thereafter, CD Medical discovered that Arbitrator Stein failed to disclose two prior contacts between CD Medical and the law firm that he became "of counsel" to, Greenberg Traurig Hoffman Lipoff Rose & Quentel, P.A. ("Greenberg Traurig"). The most recent contact occurred in January of 1990 when CD Medical interviewed Greenberg Traurig to represent them in the instant dispute. The prior contact complained of occurred in 1988 when CD Medical asked Greenberg Traurig to review an amendment to the exclusive agreement between CD Medical and Lifecare. Arbitrator Stein became "of counsel" to Greenberg Traurig a few months before he was selected as an arbitrator in this case in November of 1992.

Subsequently, Lifecare moved to confirm and CD Medical moved to vacate the award in the district court. In support of its motion to vacate, CD Medical first argued that Arbitrator Stein was biased. In support of their assertion that there was evident partiality, i.e., bias, on the part of Arbitrator Stein, CD Medical argued that Arbitrator Stein failed to disclose the prior scheduling dispute with the White & Case attorney and that he also failed to disclose the two prior contacts between CD Medical and the firm he became "of counsel" to, Greenberg Traurig. * * *

On April 28, 1994, the district court, in a three-paragraph order, denied CD Medical's motion to vacate and granted Lifecare's motion to confirm the

---

[3]   Arbitrator Stein was apparently so upset from the incident that he drafted a letter to the White & Case attorney which stated that he could not believe that "a firm of White & Case's stature would condone [that] type of behavior."

arbitration award. A final judgment was entered on June 14, 1994, and this appeal ensued.

* * *

III. DISCUSSION

On appeal, CD Medical raises the same issues that were before the district court; namely, (1) whether Arbitrator Stein's failure to disclose his prior contact with the White & Case attorney and/or his failure to disclose the two prior contacts between CD Medical and Greenberg Traurig (the firm he later became "of counsel" to) evidence bias on Arbitrator Stein's part, and (2) whether the award was arbitrary and capricious.

* * *

B. Evident Partiality

In order to vacate on the ground of evident partiality in a nondisclosure case, the party challenging the arbitration award must establish that the undisclosed facts create a "reasonable impression of partiality." This Court has reasoned that the alleged partiality must be "direct, definite and capable of demonstration rather than remote, uncertain and speculative.". Accordingly, the mere appearance of bias or partiality is not enough to set aside an arbitration award.

As noted, CD Medical offers two independent reasons for vacating the arbitration award on the ground of evident partiality. First, CD Medical claims that Arbitrator Stein's failure to disclose the scheduling dispute with a White & Case attorney (the law firm that represented CD Medical) qualifies as a reasonable impression of partiality. We disagree. Although we, too, believe that Arbitrator Stein should have disclosed the dispute prior to the commencement of the arbitration proceedings and we understand CD Medical's anger toward Arbitrator Stein for failing to disclose the incident. Nevertheless, we cannot conclude that Arbitrator Stein's failure to disclose the dispute creates a reasonable impression of partiality.

The incident did not involve any of the parties to the arbitration hearing. Rather, it involved an attorney who was employed at the same law firm-White & Case-that represented one of the parties-CD Medical. The White & Case attorney involved in the dispute took no part in the arbitration proceedings. Furthermore, the dispute occurred approximately 18 months prior to the commencement of the arbitration hearing.

With that in mind, it is important to put this incident in perspective. The incident involved an argument between two attorneys over a scheduling dispute. Attorneys argue and disagree with one another all the time. One can debate the professionalism of such behavior, but that will not change the reality of it. True, because Arbitrator Stein memorialized the incident in writing and recalled the dispute some 18 months later, perhaps this was something more than the typical argument between attorneys. Regardless, we cannot conclude that Stein's failure to disclose the incident created a reasonable impression of impartiality.

CD Medical is essentially asking this Court to conclude that because Arbitrator Stein was involved in a dispute with an attorney: (1) whatever animosity or anger he harbored toward that attorney remained 18 months later; (2) the animosity was transferred to the entire firm; and (3) the animosity was ultimately transferred to the White & Case client, CD Medical. That, we cannot conclude. It appears to the Court that this case involves a situation that is more in the line of remote, uncertain, and speculative partiality or a mere appearance of bias or partiality, as opposed to bias or partiality that is direct, definite, and capable of demonstration. See *Int'l Produce, Inc. v. A/S Rosshavet*, 638 F.2d 548, 551 n. 3 (2nd Cir.1981) ("It does not follow that an arbitrator's personal feelings in favor of or against one attorney would necessarily be transferred to another attorney in the same firm."), cert. denied, 451 U.S. 1017, 101 S.Ct. 3006, 69 L.Ed.2d 389 (1981).

CD Medical's second argument in support of its claim that Arbitrator Stein was biased is even weaker. Arbitrator Stein became "of counsel" to the law firm of Greenberg Traurig in the middle of 1992. In January of 1990, CD Medical interviewed Greenberg Traurig for the purpose of obtaining representation in the instant dispute. Additionally, in 1988, CD Medical asked Greenberg Traurig to review an amendment to the distributorship agreement between CD Medical and Lifecare.

Because of CD Medical's two contacts with Greenberg Traurig, the firm Arbitrator Stein eventually joined "of counsel," CD Medical asks the Court to conclude that such contacts evidence bias on the part of Arbitrator Stein against CD Medical. We disagree. Once again, we must first put this issue in perspective. At the time of the two contacts, Arbitrator Stein was not even affiliated with Greenberg Traurig. Furthermore, there is no evidence in the record that Arbitrator Stein was even aware of the fact that CD Medical contacted Greenberg Traurig in 1988 or 1990.

Again, we are not condoning Arbitrator Stein's conduct. Indeed, even a rudimentary inquiry by Arbitrator Stein would have likely revealed Greenberg

Traurig's prior contacts with CD Medical. However, based on the paltry record before us regarding this particular issue, we cannot conclude that Arbitrator Stein's failure to investigate and, of course, disclose the two prior contacts between Greenberg Traurig and CD Medical creates a reasonable impression of bias or partiality. Similar to their first argument, it appears CD Medical's position here is based on speculative bias or partiality as opposed to bias or partiality that is direct, definite, and capable of demonstration.

In summary, the "evident partiality" question necessarily entails a fact intensive inquiry. This is one area of the law which is highly dependent on the unique factual settings of each particular case. The black letter rules of law are sparse and analogous case law is difficult to locate. In most cases, the courts have little guidance when confronted with an issue in this area of the law. Based on the facts before this Court, we simply cannot conclude that Arbitrator Stein's conduct, although in violation of Canon II of the American Arbitration Association's Code of Ethics, rises to the level of creating a reasonable impression of bias or partiality.[7]

* * *

IV. CONCLUSION

Since we conclude that the district court's order confirming the arbitration award was not erroneous, we AFFIRM that order.

NOTE

1. The case was supplemented in 1996 in *Lifecare Intern., Inc. v. CD Medical, Inc.*, 85 F.3d 519 (1996) with the following comment:

> The motion to recall the mandate filed by Movant Craig Edward Stein is GRANTED.

> We modify and supplement our opinion in this case with this observation: The statements by the Court in discussing the issues raised in this appeal concerning alleged bias on the part of Mr. Stein are based upon the record created by the parties to this case. As a nonparty, Mr. Stein was not entitled to present evidence or otherwise to respond to the allegations. Thus, the

---

[7] In accordance with Canon II of the American Arbitration Association's Code of Ethics, Arbitrator Stein executed a statement verifying that he had "no past or present relationship with the parties or their counsel, direct or indirect, whether financial, professional, social or of any kind."

statements in the opinion should not be interpreted to represent conclusions of the Court about the actual conduct of Mr. Stein.

PART IV

Procedural Issues in Arbitration

The procedural aspects of arbitration and litigation vary. At first glance, those differences may appear slight. But on closer inspection, the difference is comparable to a Texan talking to a Scot. In theory both speak the same language. But at any given point in time, it is reasonably likely that either will get lost in their conversation. A skilled arbitration lawyer will use the procedural tools in arbitration to their respective advantage. A litigator acting in arbitration, on the other hand, may find him or herself quickly on unfamiliar terrain and outmaneuvered.

The readings in this Part IV will cover five distinct procedural issues that arise in arbitration: the procedural organization of the arbitration, interim measures, court relief in aid of arbitration, jurisdictional objections and dispositive motions. The materials below will begin with a brief overview how the comparative procedural issue is resolved in litigation under the Federal Rules of Civil Procedure. It then introduces the differences between the litigation and the arbitration realm. This comparative method should help you in several ways. First, it is a helpful refresher of your civil procedure knowledge. Second, and much more importantly, it gives you a means to gauge how arbitration is different from litigation—and how an unskilled, litigation-based approach to arbitration may leave you and your client in difficulty.

The readings from here on out begin with a common simulation that will run for the remainder of the sections dealing with arbitral process. This cumulative approach is intended to show you how early procedural decisions can affect later parts of the arbitral proceedings through to a final decision on the merits in the case. Having a good overview of how the case will be presented to the tribunal, and a good overview of the tools available to you for presenting it, therefore is one of the core take aways for you from taking this class—and using this book.

CHAPTER 11

The Preliminary Hearing

Much of the procedure of an arbitration is decided at the preliminary hearing. Following the appointment of the tribunal, the preliminary hearing is the second-most important part of an arbitration proceeding. It is this proceeding where the tribunal determines what means of proof will be available to the parties, how materials will be pled, and so forth. Unlike the appointment of the tribunal, this part of the arbitral proceeding is generally given short shrift by practitioners and academics alike—and in doing so, they frequently find themselves unable to explain how a certain procedural posture decided at the beginning of the arbitration accounts for evidentiary considerations that will determine its ultimate result.

This section outlines the key issues in the context of the procedural organization of the case. The fact scenario illustrates how the various steps described in the reading materials become more important in practice than they might appear in the abstract.

Fact Scenario

Hardmont LLC ("*Hardmont*") contracted with Acme Industries Corp. ("*Acme*") to design a clothing line, and pursuant to the contract, Hardmont provided Acme with significant market research to inform the design criteria. With respect to the market research, Hardmont and Acme entered into a non-disclosure agreement. The relevant excerpts of the contract are below:

* * *

6.   Non-disclosure

1.   Acme Industries Corp. acknowledges that it has received a market study from Hardmont LLC, labeled "Confidential Information" and attached it to this Agreement as Appendix I.

2.   Acme Industries Corp. and its officers, employees, agents, directors and principals shall not disclose the Confidential Information to any third parties

* * *

9.   Arbitration

Any controversy or claim arising out of or relating to this contract, or the breach thereof, shall be settled by arbitration administered by the American Arbitration Association under its Commercial Arbitration Rules, and judgment on the award rendered by the arbitrator(s) may be entered in any court having jurisdiction thereof.

______/s/______

Martin Gunther

Hardmont LLC

______/s/______

Mervin Gilmore

CEO, Acme Industries Corp.

Acme delivered the designs and shortly thereafter filed for bankruptcy. Hardmont originally paid for the design it received.

In the next fashion season, Hardmont noticed that two other retailers offered designs that were remarkably close to the designs that Acme had sold to Hardmont. Hardmont investigated and discovered that the retailers had entered into contracts with RRF Corp. to design their clothing lines. RRF Corp. is beneficially owned by Mervin Gilmore, who was the sole owner of Acme and served as its CEO and President of the board of directors.

Hardmont commenced arbitration against Mr. and RRF Corp. under the Acme design contract, asserting violation of the non-disclosure agreement. The AAA determined that the case should be assigned to a three-arbitrator tribunal, and the parties determined the arbitrators by list method.

You receive the following email from your newly constituted AAA tribunal:

Dear counsel,

It is time to convene our preliminary hearing in *Hardmont LLC v. (1) RRF Corp. & (2) Mervin Gilmore*. I suggest we meet in New York, NY on Monday in two week's time. Please consult with your client to provide answers with regard to all items on the AAA Checklist (attached) and agree on a joint procedure in case of disagreement.

Best regards,

Presiding Arbitrator

Readings

A) Pretrial Orders in the Federal Courts

U.S. federal courts use a mechanism that strongly resembles the arbitral preliminary hearing. Federal Rule of Civil Procedure 16 requires the court to issue the scheduling order as soon as practicable. Unless the judge finds good cause for delay, the judge must issue it within the earlier of 90 days after any defendant has been served with the complaint or 60 days after any defendant has appeared. Most attorneys practicing arbitration will come from a litigation background, and therefore, Rule 16 is important in shaping the expectations of participants in the arbitral process. As you read through Rule 16, consider which of its mechanisms are and are not appropriate for adoption in an arbitral setting.

Federal Rules of Civil Procedure, Rule 16

(a) Purposes of a Pretrial Conference. In any action, the court may order the attorneys and any unrepresented parties to appear for one or more pretrial conferences for such purposes as:

(1) expediting disposition of the action;

(2) establishing early and continuing control so that the case will not be protracted because of lack of management;

(3) discouraging wasteful pretrial activities;

(4) improving the quality of the trial through more thorough preparation; and

(5) facilitating settlement.

(b) Scheduling.

(1) Scheduling Order. Except in categories of actions exempted by local rule, the district judge—or a magistrate judge when authorized by local rule—must issue a scheduling order:

(A) after receiving the parties' report under Rule 26(f); or

(B) after consulting with the parties' attorneys and any unrepresented parties at a scheduling conference.

(2) Time to Issue. The judge must issue the scheduling order as soon as practicable, but unless the judge finds good cause for delay, the judge must issue it within the earlier of 90 days after any defendant has been served with the complaint or 60 days after any defendant has appeared.

(3)   Contents of the Order.

(A) Required Contents. The scheduling order must limit the time to join other parties, amend the pleadings, complete discovery, and file motions.

(B) Permitted Contents. The scheduling order may:

(i)   modify the timing of disclosures under Rules 26(a) and 26(e)(1);

(ii)   modify the extent of discovery;

(iii) provide for disclosure, discovery, or preservation of electronically stored information;

(iv) include any agreements the parties reach for asserting claims of privilege or of protection as trial-preparation material after information is produced, including agreements reached under Federal Rule of Evidence 502;

(v)   direct that before moving for an order relating to discovery, the movant must request a conference with the court;

(vi) set dates for pretrial conferences and for trial; and

(vii) include other appropriate matters.

(4)   Modifying a Schedule. A schedule may be modified only for good cause and with the judge's consent.

(c)   Attendance and Matters for Consideration at a Pretrial Conference.

(1)   Attendance. A represented party must authorize at least one of its attorneys to make stipulations and admissions about all matters that can reasonably be anticipated for discussion at a pretrial conference. If appropriate, the court may require that a party or its representative be present or reasonably available by other means to consider possible settlement.

(2)   Matters for Consideration. At any pretrial conference, the court may consider and take appropriate action on the following matters:

(A) formulating and simplifying the issues, and eliminating frivolous claims or defenses;

(B) amending the pleadings if necessary or desirable;

(C) obtaining admissions and stipulations about facts and documents to avoid unnecessary proof, and ruling in advance on the admissibility of evidence;

(D) avoiding unnecessary proof and cumulative evidence, and limiting the use of testimony under Federal Rule of Evidence 702;

(E) determining the appropriateness and timing of summary adjudication under Rule 56;

(F) controlling and scheduling discovery, including orders affecting disclosures and discovery under Rule 26 and Rules 29 through 37;

(G) identifying witnesses and documents, scheduling the filing and exchange of any pretrial briefs, and setting dates for further conferences and for trial;

(H) referring matters to a magistrate judge or a master;

(I) settling the case and using special procedures to assist in resolving the dispute when authorized by statute or local rule;

(J) determining the form and content of the pretrial order;

(K) disposing of pending motions;

(L) adopting special procedures for managing potentially difficult or protracted actions that may involve complex issues, multiple parties, difficult legal questions, or unusual proof problems;

(M) ordering a separate trial under Rule 42(b) of a claim, counterclaim, crossclaim, third-party claim, or particular issue;

(N) ordering the presentation of evidence early in the trial on a manageable issue that might, on the evidence, be the basis for a judgment as a matter of law under Rule 50(a) or a judgment on partial findings under Rule 52(c);

(O) establishing a reasonable limit on the time allowed to present evidence; and

(P) facilitating in other ways the just, speedy, and inexpensive disposition of the action.

(d) Pretrial Orders. After any conference under this rule, the court should issue an order reciting the action taken. This order controls the course of the action unless the court modifies it.

(e) Final Pretrial Conference and Orders. The court may hold a final pretrial conference to formulate a trial plan, including a plan to facilitate the admission of evidence. The conference must be held as close to the start of trial as is reasonable, and must be attended by at least one attorney who will conduct the trial for each party and by any unrepresented party. The court may modify the order issued after a final pretrial conference only to prevent manifest injustice.

(f) Sanctions.

(1) In General. On motion or on its own, the court may issue any just orders, including those authorized by Rule 37(b)(2)(A)(ii)–(vii), if a party or its attorney:

(A)   fails to appear at a scheduling or other pretrial conference;

(B)   is substantially unprepared to participate—or does not participate in good faith—in the conference; or

(C)   fails to obey a scheduling or other pretrial order.

(2)   Imposing Fees and Costs. Instead of or in addition to any other sanction, the court must order the party, its attorney, or both to pay the reasonable expenses—including attorney's fees—incurred because of any noncompliance with this rule, unless the noncompliance was substantially justified or other circumstances make an award of expenses unjust.

NOTES

1.   Which of the elements of Federal Rule of Civil Procedure 16 cannot be transposed to arbitration because an arbitral tribunal lacks the required powers to order the relief foreseen by the Rule?

2.   Consider Rule 16(c)(2)(K). What does the Rule assume to have occurred prior to the pretrial conference?

3.   Review the AAA Arbitration Rules. Is a procedural mechanism similar to that envisioned in Rule 16(c)(2)(K) available under the AAA Commercial Arbitration Rules? Is it a procedural mechanism that is appropriate for arbitration?

4.   Consider Federal Rule of Civil Procedure 16(c)(2)(C). What does it assume to have occurred?

B)   Purpose of Preliminary Hearings

AAA Commercial Arbitration Rules

P–1.   General

(a)   In all but the simplest cases, holding a preliminary hearing as early in the process as possible will help the parties and the arbitrator organize the proceeding in a manner that will maximize efficiency and economy, and will provide each party a fair opportunity to present its case.

(b)   Care must be taken to avoid importing procedures from court systems, as such procedures may not be appropriate to the conduct of arbitrations as an alternative form of dispute resolution that is designed to be simpler, less expensive and more expeditious.

NOTES

1. What are the "procedures from court systems" to which P–1 of the AAA Commercial Arbitration Rules refers?

2. What are the goals of the preliminary hearing required by P–1? Are these goals contradictory? How do you balance the respective interests of the goals?

3. What kind of arguments do you think drive arbitral decision-making in setting the procedural schedule for the case?

C) Checklists for Procedural Organization

AAA Commercial Arbitration Rules

P–2.   Checklist

(a)   The following checklist suggests subjects that the parties and the arbitrator should address at the preliminary hearing, in addition to any others that the parties or the arbitrator believe to be appropriate to the particular case. The items to be addressed in a particular case will depend on the size, subject matter, and complexity of the dispute, and are subject to the discretion of the arbitrator:

(i)   the possibility of other non-adjudicative methods of dispute resolution, including mediation pursuant to R–9;

(ii)   whether all necessary or appropriate parties are included in the arbitration;

(iii)   whether a party will seek a more detailed statement of claims, counterclaims or defenses;

(iv)   whether there are any anticipated amendments to the parties' claims, counterclaims, or defenses;

(v)   which (a) arbitration rules; (b) procedural law; and (c) substantive law govern the arbitration;

(vi)   whether there are any threshold or dispositive issues that can efficiently be decided without considering the entire case, including without limitation:

(a)   any preconditions that must be satisfied before proceeding with the arbitration;

(b)   whether any claim or counterclaim falls outside the arbitrator's jurisdiction or is otherwise not arbitrable;

(c)   consolidation of the claims or counterclaims with another arbitration; or

(d)   bifurcation of the proceeding.

(vii)   whether the parties will exchange documents, including electronically stored documents, on which they intend to rely in the arbitration, and/or make written requests for production of documents within defined parameters;

(viii)   whether to establish any additional procedures to obtain information that is relevant and material to the outcome of disputed issues;

(ix)   how costs of any searches for requested information or documents that would result in substantial costs should be borne;

(x)   whether any measures are required to protect confidential information;

(xi)   whether the parties intend to present evidence from expert witnesses, and if so, whether to establish a schedule for the parties to identify their experts and exchange expert reports;

(xii)   whether, according to a schedule set by the arbitrator, the parties will:

(a)   identify all witnesses, the subject matter of their anticipated testimonies, exchange written witness statements, and determine whether written witness statements will replace direct testimony at the hearing;

(b)   exchange and pre-mark documents that each party intends to submit; and

(c)   exchange pre-hearing submissions, including exhibits;

(xiii)   the date, time and place of the arbitration hearing;

(xiv)   whether, at the arbitration hearing:

(a)   testimony may be presented in person, in writing, by videoconference, via the internet, telephonically, or by other reasonable means;

(b)   there will be a stenographic transcript or other record of the proceeding and, if so, who will make arrangements to provide it;

(xv)   whether any procedure needs to be established for the issuance of subpoenas;

(xvi)   the identification of any ongoing, related litigation or arbitration;

(xvii)   whether post-hearing submissions will be filed;

(xviii)   the form of the arbitration award; and

(xix)   any other matter the arbitrator considers appropriate or a party wishes to raise.

(b)   The arbitrator shall issue a written order memorializing decisions made and agreements reached during or following the preliminary hearing.

NOTES

1. What is the purpose for the arbitrator to discuss with the parties whether mediation might be an acceptable alternative to arbitration? Why is it included in the AAA checklist?

2. What are the provisions on the checklist that go exclusively to the jurisdiction of a tribunal? How do you think counsel for RRF and Mr. Gilmore in the fact pattern should deal with these issues? Do you think counsel for Hardmont would agree?

3. Focusing on jurisdictional questions, what do you think counsel for Hardmont would need to know to overcome the likely jurisdictional objections by RRF and Mr. Gilmore? Is that information going to be in Hardmont's possession, custody, or control? If not, to which parts of the checklist should Hardmont pay attention?

4. What parts of the checklist deal with written pleadings? What is the purpose of these provisions?

5. Again, look at the fact scenario. Who do you think will have the more complicated case? Who therefore benefits from written additional briefing? Do you think both parties in this case should want to have additional briefing?

6. What parts of the checklist deal with third parties? What provision must be made for them?

7. How do you think third parties affect the arbitration in the fact scenario? Do you think Hardmont would want different directives here than Gilmore and RRF? How so? Why?

AAA Form Report of Preliminary Hearing

Preliminary Hearing Scheduling Order # _________ Case # ___________

REPORT OF PRELIMINARY HEARING AND
SCHEDULING ORDER

Pursuant to the Commercial Arbitration Rules of the American Arbitration Association (AAA), a preliminary hearing was held on ________________, before Arbitrator(s) ______________________________. Appearing at the hearing were ____.

____.

By Agreement of the parties and Order of the Arbitrator(s), the following is now in effect.

1. An additional preliminary hearing shall be held (check one):

   ○At _____________ on _______________, at ______.m. before the Arbitrator(s), or

   ○if needed, by mutual agreement later.

2. Pursuant to the direction of the Arbitrator(s), all parties shall amend/specify claims and/or counterclaims (monetary amounts) and file any motion to join additional parties by _______________________________.

3. The parties shall file a stipulation of uncontested facts by _______________.

4. a) Pursuant to the direction of the Arbitrator(s), claimant(s) shall serve and file a disclosure of all witnesses reasonably expected to be called by the claimant(s) on or before ____.

   b) Pursuant to the direction of the Arbitrator(s), respondent(s) shall serve and file a disclosure of all witnesses reasonably expected to be called by the respondent(s) on or before _______________________________.

5. The disclosure of witnesses shall include the full name of each witness, a short summary of anticipated testimony, copies of any experts reports, and written C.V. of experts. If certain required information is not available, the disclosures shall so state. Each party shall be responsible for updating its disclosures as such information becomes available. The duty to update this information continues up to and including the date that hearing(s) in this matter terminate.

   a) The parties shall make arrangements to schedule the attendance of witnesses so that the case can proceed with all due expedition and without any unnecessary delay.

   b) The party presenting evidence shall give notice to the other party the day before of the names of the witnesses who will be called to testify the next day and the order in which the witnesses will be called.

6. a) Not later than _________________, the parties shall exchange copies of (or, when appropriate, make available for inspection) all exhibits to be offered and all schedules, summaries, diagrams and charts to be used at the hearing. Each proposes exhibit shall be premarked for identification using the following designations:

PARTY   **EXHIBIT # TO EXHIBIT #**

_______________________________   __________   __________

____

_______________________________   __________   __________

____

7. The parties shall attempt to agree upon and submit a jointly prepared consolidated and Comprehensive set of joint exhibits.

8. Hearings in this matter will commence before the Arbitrator(s) at _______ on _________ at ______.m. The parties estimate that this case will require ____ days of hearing time, inclusive of arguments.

9. Any and all documents to be filed with or submitted to the Arbitrator(s) outside the hearing

    a)   shall be given to the AAA Case Administrator for transmittal to the Arbitrator(s).

    b)   COPIES OF SAID DOCUMENTS SHALL ALSO BE SENT SIMULTANEOUSLY TO THE OPPOSING PARTY(S). There shall be _no_ direct oral _or_ written communication between the parties and the arbitrator(s), except at oral hearings.

10. On or before _________, each party shall serve and file a prehearing brief on all significant disputed issues, setting forth briefly the party's position and the supporting arguments and authorities.

    (i)   a)   **Form of Award:** (Circle one)

          i.   Standard Award

          ii.   Reasoned Award

          iii. Findings of fact and conclusions of law

- 2 -

          b)   **Court Reporter:** (Y) (N) ____________________________

          c)   **Other:** ____

          ____

          ____

11. Pursuant to the direction of the Arbitrator(s), any other preliminary matters not otherwise provided for herein shall be raised by ____________________

(date)

12. All deadlines stated herein will be strictly enforced. After such deadline, the parties may not file such motions except with the permission of the Arbitrator(s), good cause having been shown.

This order shall continue in effect unless and until amended by subsequent order of the Arbitrator(s).

Dated: ________________

____
Arbitrator's Signature

____
Arbitrator's Signature

____
Arbitrator's Signature

NOTES

1. Does the draft form order give you a better sense of what is going to happen at the preliminary hearing? How does the AAA checklist compare to the form order?

2. The draft form order includes a provision on an additional preliminary hearing as a matter of course. Why? What do you think will be discussed at that meeting?

D) Counsel Preparation for the Preliminary Hearing

William H. Lemons, an arbitrator, has made available his notes of his expectations from the parties to an arbitration at the pre-hearing conference and preliminary scheduling conference stage. Consider these simple steps in light of the material you have read so far. Does this help you translate the AAA checklist into tangible steps? Can you apply this advice to other parts of the checklist that are not directly covered by the excerpt below?

William H. Lemons, I Am Your Arbitrator. Here is What to Expect from Me . . . And What I Expect From You

http://www.whlemonsadr.com/pdf/i-am-your-arbitrator-new.pdf

* * *

PRE-HEARING CONFERENCES

A telephone (or in-person) conference to discuss some variation of these policies, or to bring some special circumstance to my attention, may be arranged at any time. Simply call (or e-mail) your Case Administrator, who will contact me. You may assume that I will have received any papers submitted in connection with such a conference and that I will be prepared to address the issues you have identified. I expect proper decorum to be followed in all pre-hearing conferences: address yourself to me, not to your opposition; avoid personalizing your comments; only one person speaks at a time. What should you call me? I am simply Mr. Lemons—I am not a judge. I read everything and will make every effort to remember what you and the parties tell me in a conference.

PRELIMINARY SCHEDULING CONFERENCE

My preference is to have a preliminary scheduling hearing in every case because it is beneficial for us to discuss procedural matters in a preliminary scheduling hearing (a/k/a arbitration management conference). Most preliminary hearings are satisfactorily handled by telephone conference call, although in an appropriate case, an in-person hearing will be arranged.

I expect you to invite and encourage your client/client representative to attend or participate in the initial preliminary scheduling conference, either in person or by phone.

The Case Administrator will contact you to schedule such a hearing. You may expect that in our initial preliminary hearing, I will ask the parties to confirm that all conditions precedent to arbitration have been waived or satisfied, that their statements of claims and defenses are sufficient to enable them to prepare for the hearing on the merits and that the claims asserted in the arbitration are arbitrable. I will also cover many of the matters addressed in these policies, including setting a schedule for exchange of documents and lists of witnesses and exhibits, and, if one has not already been set, a date for the Arbitration Hearing. Please be prepared to discuss these matters. I generally enter a—

Scheduling Order[ ] following the initial preliminary scheduling hearing, and will send counsel a sample Scheduling Order beforehand.

I expect that ***prior to the date of our preliminary hearing***, you will have discussed with the other parties:

1. the adequacy of the operative pleadings (demand/complaint, answer) to prepare a discovery plan and otherwise prepare for the Arbitration Hearing,

2. the parties' need (note, I did not say desire) for discovery (types of discovery and the time necessary to complete such discovery) * * *

3. whether any party foresees any dispositive motions, need for a Protective Order or other requests for interim relief, and

4. the anticipated length of the Arbitration Hearing and a timeframe when the parties, their counsel, and their witnesses will be available for that hearing.

Please be prepared to discuss each of these matters and the topics contained within my draft Scheduling Order during our arbitration management conference.

CHAPTER 12

Interim Relief Before Arbitral Tribunals

A significant number of arbitrations require some action by the arbitrator(s) aimed to preserve the status quo before the tribunal has an opportunity to issue its final award. Litigants in U.S. courts can use tools such as temporary restraining orders and preliminary injunctions in situations where interim relief is appropriate. This chapter addresses how parties can seek similar redress before arbitral tribunals. The next chapter addresses the appeals parties can make to domestic courts, should the parties dispute the interim relief ordered by the arbitral tribunal.

Fact Scenario

Look back at the fact scenario for Chapter 11. In addition to designing the clothing at issue, assume that RRF also manufactures the clothing. Hardmont tells you that it has observed RRF's clothing "fly off the shelves" at various retailers, while Hardmont still has significant merchandise on its shelves. Hardmont tells you that it had anticipated a 10% increase in revenue based upon its earlier market research, but that its revenue dropped by 15% since RRF began selling its clothing at other retailers.

Prior to filing for arbitration, Hardmont instructs its counsel (e.g., you) to move quickly to obtain appropriate interim relief. Hardmont is particularly concerned about the damage to its bottom line from other retail stores profiting from its design. You have asked Hardmont whether the market research has any future value beyond the current fashion season. Hardmont informs you that the fashion market undergoes significant seasonal swings, and consequently, the market research will have negligible value in future seasons.

The law firm representing Hardmont forms two teams—one team will develop a strategy for interim arbitral relief, and the other team will develop counter-arguments why interim relief is inappropriate to be able to better plead the case. Please find out your team assignment for purposes of this part of the simulation and develop your arguments on the basis of the following readings.

Readings

A) Typical Forms of Interim Relief in Civil Procedure: Preliminary Injunctions and Temporary Restraining Orders

In litigation, the typical way to obtain emergency relief is to get a temporary restraining order. See Federal Rule of Civil Procedure 65 below to set the stage for emergency relief in arbitration.

Federal Rules of Civil Procedure, Rule 65(a)–(d).

(a)   Preliminary Injunction.

(1)   Notice. The court may issue a preliminary injunction only on notice to the adverse party.

(2)   Consolidating the Hearing with the Trial on the Merits. Before or after beginning the hearing on a motion for a preliminary injunction, the court may advance the trial on the merits and consolidate it with the hearing. Even when consolidation is not ordered, evidence that is received on the motion and that would be admissible at trial becomes part of the trial record and need not be repeated at trial. But the court must preserve any party's right to a jury trial.

(b)   Temporary Restraining Order.

(1)   Issuing Without Notice. The court may issue a temporary restraining order without written or oral notice to the adverse party or its attorney only if:

(A)   specific facts in an affidavit or a verified complaint clearly show that immediate and irreparable injury, loss, or damage will result to the movant before the adverse party can be heard in opposition; and

(B)   the movant's attorney certifies in writing any efforts made to give notice and the reasons why it should not be required.

(2)   Contents; Expiration. Every temporary restraining order issued without notice must state the date and hour it was issued; describe the injury and state why it is irreparable; state why the order was issued without notice; and be promptly filed in the clerk's office and entered in the record. The order expires at the time after entry—not to exceed 14 days—that the court sets, unless before that time the court, for good cause, extends it for a like period or the adverse party consents to a longer extension. The reasons for an extension must be entered in the record.

(3)   Expediting the Preliminary-Injunction Hearing. If the order is issued without notice, the motion for a preliminary injunction must be set for hearing at the earliest possible time, taking precedence over all other matters except hearings on older matters of the same character. At the hearing, the party who obtained the order must proceed with the motion; if the party does not, the court must dissolve the order.

(4)   Motion to Dissolve. On 2 days' notice to the party who obtained the order without notice—or on shorter notice set by the court—the adverse party may appear and move to dissolve or modify the order. The court must then hear and decide the motion as promptly as justice requires.

(c)   Security. The court may issue a preliminary injunction or a temporary restraining order only if the movant gives security in an amount that the court considers proper to pay the costs and damages sustained by any party found to have been wrongfully enjoined or restrained. The United States, its officers, and its agencies are not required to give security.

(d)   Contents and Scope of Every Injunction and Restraining Order.

(1)   Contents. Every order granting an injunction and every restraining order must:

(A)   state the reasons why it issued;

(B)   state its terms specifically; and

(C)   describe in reasonable detail—and not by referring to the complaint or other document—the act or acts restrained or required.

(2)   Persons Bound. The order binds only the following who receive actual notice of it by personal service or otherwise:

(A)   the parties;

(B)   the parties' officers, agents, servants, employees, and attorneys; and

(C)   other persons who are in active concert or participation with anyone described in Rule 65(d)(2)(A) or (B).

NOTES

1.   What is the difference between a temporary restraining order and a preliminary injunction?

2.   What is the standard by which a court decides whether to issue a temporary restraining order? Does the standard differ from the standard for a preliminary injunction?

3. Temporary restraining orders and permanent injunctions typically restrain the right of the party against which they are issued, yet courts issue these orders without making a final determination of the merits of the dispute. How do the Federal Rules of Civil Procedure balance the interests of the moving and the non-moving parties?

4. What are the ethical considerations that a party should keep in mind before requesting either a TRO or a Preliminary injunction?

Dataphase Systems Inc. v. C L Systems, Inc.

640 F.2d 109 (8th Cir. 1981)

HENLEY, CIRCUIT JUDGE.

C L Systems, Inc. (CLSI) appeals from the district court's order of January 23, 1980, granting a preliminary injunction restraining CLSI from making "any false or misleading statement which disparages, directly or indirectly, plaintiff (Dataphase Systems, Inc.), its product, its financial condition or its ability to furnish goods and services." For reasons to be stated we vacate the preliminary injunction.

Dataphase, a Missouri corporation, and CLSI, a Massachusetts corporation, compete for contracts for the installation of computerized, automated library circulation systems. Dataphase is a relative newcomer to the field. It started business and incorporated in December, 1975. By its own admission, CLSI is the established leader in the field of library automation.

On June 1, 1978 Dataphase filed its complaint in this suit against CLSI. Dataphase alleged that CLSI engaged in a course of conduct intended to restrain competition and deny market access to Dataphase, thereby eliminating and destroying Dataphase as a competitor. The course of anti-competitive conduct allegedly included deliberately bidding below cost in order to prevent Dataphase from receiving contracts; interfering with Dataphase's present and potential contractual obligations; making false statements to potential customers regarding Dataphase's reliability, solvency, and ability to furnish the goods and services bid upon; and, in general, falsely and maliciously disparaging Dataphase to its customers and potential customers, both orally and in writing.

The complaint alleged that this course of conduct constituted a violation of the antitrust laws, in particular section 2 of the Sherman Act, 15 U.S.C. s 2 (1976), and section 3 of the Robinson-Patman Act, 15 U.S.C. s 13a (1976), and that CLSI's false and malicious accusations unlawfully interfered with

Dataphase's reasonable business expectancies. Dataphase sought treble damages and equitable relief enjoining CLSI from continuing the allegedly unlawful course of conduct. Federal jurisdiction exists under 28 U.S.C. ss 1331, 1332, 1337 (1976).

CLSI denied the essential allegations of the complaint, and raised various defenses, *inter alia*, that all statements and representations made by CLSI to Dataphase's customers were true and not misleading. The parties proceeded with discovery, and in February and March, 1979 the district court held evidentiary hearings on Dataphase's request for a preliminary injunction. On January 23, 1980 the district court entered its order granting the preliminary injunction.

CLSI filed notice of appeal, and on March 20, 1980 this court entered an order remanding the matter "to the district court for the limited purpose of permitting that court to set forth in detailed findings those representations and statements of the appellant that it believes 'raise questions serious enough to require litigation.' "

On April 18, 1980 the district court certified limited findings. It found that "whether there is a dangerous probability of monopolization of a specific product market in a particular geographic market" constituted a "serious litigable issue." The district court paraphrased twelve statements which it observed that Dataphase claims are completely false, while CLSI contends they are true. The district court stated that these statements "raise questions of fact which are serious enough to require litigation."

Without prejudice to the entry of a permanent injunction, we vacate the preliminary injunction and remand the case to the district court. We agree with the panel that justice would be served by proceeding to trial with all due haste in order to secure a ruling on the merits of the claims raised.

The court has considered this case *en banc* in an effort to clarify the standard to be applied by the district courts of this circuit in considering requests for preliminary injunctive relief. We apprehend that in recent years there has developed some misunderstanding of the standard has developed. We recognize that language in some of our recent opinions may have contributed to uncertainty as to the appropriate test or tests. Thus, we take this opportunity to reaffirm that there is a single "test" or list of considerations to be used in every case and to suggest its proper application.

In *Minnesota Bearing Co. v. White Motor Corp.*, 470 F.2d 1323 (8th Cir. 1973), we enumerated four factors to be weighed by the district court in deciding whether to grant or deny preliminary injunctive relief: (1) whether there is a substantial probability movant will succeed at trial; (2) whether the moving party will suffer irreparable injury absent the injunction; (3) the harm to other interested parties if the relief is granted; and (4) the effect on the public interest. Id. at 1326. This statement of the standard, in particular the requirements of "substantial probability" and "irreparable injury," has become known as the "traditional test." * * *

Perhaps due to dissatisfaction with restrictive practical application of the language of the traditional test, this court offered a restated version in *Fennell v. Butler*, 570 F.2d 263. In that case we suggested that a preliminary injunction should issue:

> upon a clear showing of either (1) probable success on the merits and possible irreparable injury, or (2) sufficiently serious questions going to the merits to make them a fair ground for litigation and a balance of hardships tipping decidedly toward the party requesting preliminary relief.

Id. at 264.[3]

Some confusion apparently has been spawned by our characterization of the *Fennell* standard as an "alternative test." Despite this label, we find no contradiction between *Fennell* and *Minnesota Bearing*. Whatever the verbal formulation, the relevant factors remain the same. Whether a preliminary injunction should issue involves consideration of (1) the threat of irreparable harm to the movant; (2) the state of the balance between this harm and the injury that granting the injunction will inflict on other parties litigant; (3) the probability that movant will succeed on the merits; and (4) the public interest.

The major difficulty with application of the traditional test has arisen from the phrase "probability of success on the merits." Some have read this element of the test to require in every case that the party seeking preliminary relief prove a greater than fifty per cent likelihood that he will prevail on the merits. Under this view, even if the balance of the other three factors strongly favored the moving party, preliminary relief would be denied if the movant could not prove a mathematical probability of success at trial. Although this construction of the "probability of success" requirement is technically possible, we reject it.

---

[3]   This approach has been adopted in other circuits. *See, e. g., William Inglis & Sons Baking Co. v. ITT Continental Baking Co.*, 526 F.2d 86, 88 (9th Cir. 1975); *Gresham v. Chambers*, 501 F.2d 687, 691 (2d Cir. 1974); *Sonesta International Hotels Corp. v. Wellington Associates*, 483 F.2d 247, 250 (2d Cir. 1973). *See also Washington Metropolitan Area Transit Commission v. Holiday Tours, Inc.*, 559 F.2d 841, 843–44 (D.C.Cir. 1977).

The very nature of the inquiry on petition for preliminary relief militates against a wooden application of the probability test. At base, the question is whether the balance of equities so favors the movant that justice requires the court to intervene to preserve the status quo until the merits are determined.[5] The equitable nature of the proceeding mandates that the court's approach be flexible enough to encompass the particular circumstances of each case. Thus, an effort to apply the probability language to all cases with mathematical precision is misplaced.

* * *

In balancing the equities no single factor is determinative. The likelihood that plaintiff ultimately will prevail is meaningless in isolation. In every case, it must be examined in the context of the relative injuries to the parties and the public. If the chance of irreparable injury to the movant should relief be denied is outweighed by the likely injury to other parties litigant should the injunction be granted, the moving party faces a heavy burden of demonstrating that he is likely to prevail on the merits. Conversely, where the movant has raised a substantial question and the equities are otherwise strongly in his favor, the showing of success on the merits can be less.

It follows that the court ordinarily is not required at an early stage to draw the fine line between a mathematical probability and a substantial possibility of success. This endeavor may, of course, be necessary in some circumstances when the balance of equities may come to require a more careful evaluation of the merits. But where the balance of other factors tips decidedly toward plaintiff a preliminary injunction may issue if movant has raised questions so serious and difficult as to call for more deliberate investigation.

This pragmatic approach is presupposed by our caselaw. Indeed, some of this court's early decisions were couched in terms other than probability. In *Love v. Atchison, T. & S. F. Ry.*, 185 F. 321, 331–32 (8th Cir.) (Sanborn, J.) (1911), Judge Sanborn stated the issue as whether "questions presented in a suit for an injunction are grave and difficult. . . ." *Id.* at 331. Other cases have required "a substantial controversy between the parties." *Benson Hotel Corp. v. Woods*, 168 F.2d 694, 697 (8th Cir. 1948) (Gardner, J.). Our goal throughout has been to achieve a clear verbal formulation yet maintaining a flexible rule.

---

[5]   The controlling reason for the existence of the judicial power to issue a temporary injunction is that the court may thereby prevent such a change in the relations and conditions of persons and property as may result in irremediable injury to some of the parties before their claims can be investigated and adjudicated.

In the instant case we concur with the opinion of the panel that the district court abused its discretion by issuing the preliminary injunction against CLSI. We do not disagree with the findings of fact made by the district court but conclude that its findings do not support the relief granted. In particular, the district court did not find that Dataphase would suffer irreparable harm,[9] nor did it find a substantial probability that the statements made by CLSI were false or misleading and thus that Dataphase would prevail at trial.

In sum, whether a preliminary injunction should issue involves consideration of (1) the threat of irreparable harm to the movant; (2) the state of balance between this harm and the injury that granting the injunction will inflict on other parties litigant; (3) the probability that movant will succeed on the merits; and (4) the public interest. The findings in the present case fail to satisfy this test.

The preliminary injunction is vacated without prejudice to the entry of injunctive relief, if during the trial of the case it appears that such relief should be given. The case is remanded to the district court for proceedings consistent with this opinion.

* * *

NOTES

Facts

1. What harm did Dataphase allege? If you were representing C L Systems, Inc., how would you have argued that this alleged harm is not "irreparable"?

2. What was the overall dispute about? In your view, what was Dataphase's actual injury in this case?

Law

1. What is the difference in emphasis between the "traditional" and the "alternative" tests? Do you agree with the court that the two tests require fundamentally the same considerations?

2. Under the alternative test, it is enough to plead a balance of hardships tipping in favor of issuance of an injunction? Consider the court's analysis

---

[9] This court previously noted that under any test the movant is required to show the threat of irreparable harm. * * * Thus, the absence of a finding of irreparable injury is alone sufficient ground for vacating the preliminary injunction.

(relegated to a footnote reproduced for you above). Did the court apply the traditional or the alternative test?

3.   How did the court define "irreparable harm"?

National Viatical, Inc. v. Universal Settlements International, Inc.

716 F.3d 952 (6th Cir. 2013)

SUHRHEINRICH, CIRCUIT JUDGE.

* * *

I.   Background

A.   Prior Action

The present action has its genesis in a prior lawsuit. In the prior lawsuit, filed in the United States District Court for the Western District of Michigan, USI sued NVI and Torchia, as well as their attorney Marc Celello, for five million dollars, claiming that they misappropriated funds they were holding in escrow for USI. * * *

While this case was pending, USI sought relief under the Companies' Creditors Arrangement Act of Canada ("CCAA") in the Ontario Superior Court of Justice in Canada. A CCAA case is similar to a reorganization bankruptcy under Chapter 11 of the United States Bankruptcy Code.

NVI and Torchia moved for summary judgment but it was denied by the magistrate judge who was presiding over the dispute. Subsequently, the parties held a settlement conference and agreed on settlement terms. The record indicates that NVI and Torchia agreed to pay USI $1,242,000 in installment payments. NVI and Torchia further agreed that a default penalty of five million dollars would be due if NVI and Torchia defaulted on any payment and did not cure it within ten days. After the settlement conference, the parties placed their agreement on the record. It was only then that confidentiality was discussed. The record indicates that counsel for NVI and Torchia asked for a "standard mutual confidentiality agreement," but agreed that, as an exception, USI could report the settlement terms to the CCAA court, any taxing authorities, attorneys, and accountants on a need-to-know basis:

COUNSEL FOR CELELLO: Why don't we just exempt from the confidentiality except to the extent necessary for reporting to the

Canadian court and/or taxing authorities, et cetera, et cetera, something like that?

MR. TORCHIA: Then they're going to put it on a website, right?

COUNSEL FOR USI: I don't know.

MR. TORCHIA: I mean, I don't care. It doesn't matter.

The magistrate judge also clarified for the record that the concern for the confidentiality clause was that Torchia "doesn't want it to appear to any credit authority or any other entity that he has a five-million-dollar judgment against him."

Following the settlement conference, USI petitioned the CCAA court to obtain the necessary directions and clearance to proceed with the settlement. Pursuant to these directions, USI posted a notice on its website informing its creditors of the settlement agreement:

> USI has entered into a settlement of the U.S. Litigation (identified in s. 2.3 of the CCAA Plan of Compromise and Arrangement as Universal Settlements International Inc. v. James Torchia, Marc Celello and National Viatical, Inc. (United States District Court, Western District of Michigan, Court File No. 1:07–cv–1243). The settlement has been reached as a result of a judicial mediation held on October 26, 2010 in Grand Rapids, Michigan.

Although the settlement is subject to a U.S. Federal Court judicial order requiring confidentiality, the essential terms that may be reported are as follows:

> USI will receive a total amount of $1,242,000 payable over a period of one year and there are terms imposing sanctions if there is a default on any of the required payments. The counterclaim against USI will be dismissed. USI's litigation committee has approved the settlement. The terms of settlement are in the process of being finalized and documented.

> The Settlement will be presented to the Ontario Superior Court of Justice on a motion for directions pursuant to s. 7.8 of the CCAA Plan of Compromise and Arrangement. USI is of the view that there is no court approval required of the Settlement but is bringing the motion out of an abundance of caution.

Alleging that the website posting violated the confidentiality clause, Celello, NVI, and Torchia refused to pay in accordance with the settlement agreement and returned to the magistrate judge with an emergency motion to enforce the confidentiality provision of the settlement agreement. The magistrate judge ruled that there was no breach because the website posting was "very, very vague," but she permitted NVI and Torchia to reserve the right to file a separate breach of contract claim against USI in the future. Although she found no breach, the magistrate judge nonetheless issued an injunction enjoining USI from any future publication of the settlement information. USI appealed the injunction to a district court judge of the United District Court for the Western District of Michigan, who reversed the injunction, holding that magistrate judges are not authorized to issue injunctions. * * *

B.   Present Action

NVI and Torchia filed this action in the Cherokee Superior Court in Georgia, claiming that USI breached the confidentiality provision of their settlement agreement by virtue of the web posting, and that under the "first-breach doctrine," one who commits the first "substantial breach" of a contract cannot maintain an action against the other party for failure to perform. * * * They sought a judgment (1) declaring that USI's breaches excused NVI and Torchia from performance under the settlement agreement; (2) awarding NVI and Torchia damages for breach of contract; (3) temporarily enjoining USI from seeking default or demanding performance of the settlement agreement until the case could be tried on the merits; and (4) permitting NVI and Torchia to set off all damages incurred from USI's breaches against their performance under the settlement agreement.

On April 21, 2011, NVI and Torchia obtained a temporary restraining order ("TRO") from the Cherokee Superior Court restraining USI from "(1) demanding performance under its settlement agreement with Plaintiffs; and (2) seeking default against Plaintiffs." On April 27, 2011, the case was removed to the United States District Court for the Northern District of Georgia, and then transferred back to the United States District Court for the Western District of Michigan (the "District Court"), where the prior action had been settled. USI requested that the District Court either confirm that the TRO had expired, or if it had not expired, for the District Court to dissolve any existing injunction.

The District Court held that because the TRO continued beyond the time permissible under Federal Rule of Civil Procedure 65, it must be treated as a preliminary injunction. The District Court then conducted the traditional four-factor balancing test for a preliminary injunction, which included an evaluation of the movant's likelihood of success on the merits, and whether the movant would suffer irreparable harm. * * *

The District Court concluded that NVI and Torchia did not have a strong likelihood of success because even if USI had breached the confidentiality agreement, the breach was not substantial. The District Court also ruled that NVI and Torchia would not suffer irreparable harm absent injunctive relief because they were suing for money damages.

As a result, the District Court dissolved the injunction, giving NVI and Torchia fourteen days to make payments under the settlement agreement. NVI and Torchia failed to make any payments, and as a result, USI demanded payment and sought default against NVI and Torchia. Still refusing to pay, NVI and Torchia now appeal the District Court's dissolution of the preliminary injunction.

* * *

III. Analysis

NVI and Torchia claim that the District Court erred in two ways: (1) by failing to hold an evidentiary hearing and issue findings of fact in dissolving the preliminary injunction; and (2) by failing to rule that NVI and Torchia were entitled to preliminary injunctive relief under the traditional four-factor balancing test. The standard of review for preliminary injunctions is de novo for legal conclusions and clear error for factual findings. * * *

A.   Preliminary Injunction Procedure

First, we find that the District Court's failure to hold an evidentiary hearing is not grounds for reversal. Ordinarily, Rule 65 is interpreted to require that the party opposing the injunction, not the party seeking the injunction, be given notice and an opportunity for a hearing. * * * NVI and Torchia were the parties seeking, not opposing, the injunction. * * *

B.   Preliminary Injunction Balancing Test

We also hold that the District Court did not err in dissolving the preliminary injunction.

As the District Court held, NVI and Torchia cannot meet the four-factor test for a preliminary injunction. * * * Under the test, the court considers: (1) the movant's likelihood of success on the merits; (2) whether the movant will suffer irreparable injury without a preliminary injunction; (3) whether issuance of a preliminary injunction would cause substantial harm to others; and (4) whether the public interest would be served by issuance of a preliminary injunction. Id.

These four considerations are "factors to be balanced and not prerequisites that must be satisfied." * * *

As the District Court held, NVI and Torchia do not have a high likelihood of success on the merits. The plain language of the settlement hearing simply does not support their case. * * *

Furthermore, the website posting was consistent with the magistrate judge's characterization of the confidentiality clause. At the settlement hearing, the magistrate judge described the confidentiality clause in the following way:

> Let me just state, and you can correct me if I'm wrong, Mr. Graham [counsel for NVI and Torchia] or Mr. Torchia, but my understanding of the concern for the sealed nature and the confidentiality is that Mr. Torchia doesn't—if he's complying with the terms of the agreement doesn't want it to appear to any credit authority or any other entity that he has a five-million-dollar judgment against him because as I understand it, it doesn't become really a judgment for five million until he defaults. . . . [A]nd I think it's understood that this needs to be reported to the [CCAA court].

Graham and Torchia did and said nothing to correct the magistrate judge's statement.

Additionally, NVI and Torchia admittedly permitted USI to disclose the terms of the settlement agreement to a large number of third parties that were not bound by the confidentiality agreement. Specifically, NVI and Torchia agreed that USI could disclose the terms of the settlement agreement to the CCAA court. The CCAA court proceeding involved thousands of USI's creditors who were not bound by the confidentiality clause. NVI and Torchia also agreed that USI would be allowed to disclose the terms of the settlement to the monitor of its CCAA court restructuring, Ernst & Young, Inc. Ernst & Young has also posted similar information about the judgment on their website. As such, it is more than likely that the settlement terms would have been disseminated at large.

* * *

As the District Court also held, NVI and Torchia cannot establish irreparable harm. We have held that "[d]espite the overall flexibility of the test for preliminary injunctive relief, and the discretion vested in the district court, equity has traditionally required [a showing of] irreparable harm before an interlocutory injunction may be issued." *Friendship Materials, Inc. v. Mich. Brick, Inc.*, 679 F.2d 100, 103 (6th Cir.1982). We agree with the District Court that the "general rule is that 'a plaintiff's harm is not irreparable if it is fully compensable by money damages.' " *Langley v. Prudential Mortg. Capital Co., LLC*, 554 F.3d 647, 649 (6th Cir.2009) * * * We also agree with the District Court that "the real harm [NVI and Torchia] seek to avoid is the payment of money."

* * *

IV. Conclusion

For the reasons set forth above, we AFFIRM the District Court's dissolution of the preliminary injunction.

NOTES

Facts

1. What is the procedural posture of the case?

2. Why did the parties include a confidentiality agreement in their settlement?

3. Who invoked the confidentiality agreement? What was the perceived benefit to the party invoking the confidentiality agreement?

Law

1. Is the test set out in *NVI* consistent with either the "traditional" or "alternative" test in *Dataphase*?

2. How does the *NVI* court define irreparable harm? Does the test in *NVI* require a showing of irreparable harm?

B) Emergency Relief in Arbitration

A challenge in obtaining emergency relief in arbitration is that, traditionally, a tribunal needed to be constituted before any relief could be issued. Yet in many instances, parties need temporary restraining orders at the *outset* of a case, before the tribunal might be constituted. Given the time involved in constituting a tribunal—and a party's ability to slow down the process—this is a significant problem for arbitration.

The AAA has since introduced a protocol meant to address particularly this problem.

AAA Commercial Arbitration Rules

R–38.   Emergency Measures of Protection

(a)   Unless the parties agree otherwise, the provisions of this rule shall apply to arbitrations conducted under arbitration clauses or agreements entered on or after October 1, 2013.

(b)   A party in need of emergency relief prior to the constitution of the panel shall notify the AAA and all other parties in writing of the nature of the relief sought and the reasons why such relief is required on an emergency basis. The application shall also set forth the reasons why the party is entitled to such relief. Such notice may be given by facsimile or e-mail or other reliable means, but must include a statement certifying that all other parties have been notified or an explanation of the steps taken in good faith to notify other parties.

(c)   Within one business day of receipt of notice as provided in section (b), the AAA shall appoint a single emergency arbitrator designated to rule on emergency applications. The emergency arbitrator shall immediately disclose any circumstance likely, on the basis of the facts disclosed on the application, to affect such arbitrator's impartiality or independence. Any challenge to the appointment of the emergency arbitrator must be made within one business day of the communication by the AAA to the parties of the appointment of the emergency arbitrator and the circumstances disclosed.

(d)   The emergency arbitrator shall as soon as possible, but in any event within two business days of appointment, establish a schedule for consideration of the application for emergency relief. Such a schedule shall provide a reasonable opportunity to all parties to be heard, but may provide for proceeding by telephone or video conference or on written submissions as alternatives to a formal hearing. The emergency arbitrator shall have the authority vested in the tribunal under Rule 7, including the authority to rule on her/his own jurisdiction, and shall resolve any disputes over the applicability of this Rule 38.

(e)   If after consideration the emergency arbitrator is satisfied that the party seeking the emergency relief has shown that immediate and irreparable loss or damage shall result in the absence of emergency relief, and that such party is entitled to such relief, the emergency arbitrator may enter an interim order or award granting the relief and stating the reason therefore.

(f)   Any application to modify an interim award of emergency relief must be based on changed circumstances and may be made to the emergency arbitrator until the panel is constituted; thereafter such a request shall be addressed to the panel. The emergency arbitrator shall have no further power to act after the panel is constituted unless the parties agree that the emergency arbitrator is named as a member of the panel.

(g)   Any interim award of emergency relief may be conditioned on provision by the party seeking such relief for appropriate security.

(h)   A request for interim measures addressed by a party to a judicial authority shall not be deemed incompatible with this rule, the agreement to arbitrate or a waiver of the right to arbitrate. If the AAA is directed by a judicial authority to nominate a special master to consider and report on an application for emergency relief, the AAA shall proceed as provided in this rule and the references to the emergency arbitrator shall be read to mean the special master, except that the special master shall issue a report rather than an interim award.

(i)   The costs associated with applications for emergency relief shall initially be apportioned by the emergency arbitrator or special master, subject to the power of the tribunal to determine finally the apportionment of such costs.

NOTES

1.   How does the AAA Procedure overcome the traditional problem of waiting until a tribunal is constituted before relief could be issued? Does it fully address the problem?

2.   What steps must a party take in order to invoke Rule 38? What arguments are relevant to an emergency arbitrator?

3.   Why do you think that an emergency arbitrator does not appear to have the power to issue interim relief without hearing the parties? What form of relief may an emergency arbitrator grant? Would you anticipate an enforceability problem if one of the parties was not heard? Consider the grounds for set aside of an award in the FAA.

4.   What is the standard in the AAA Commercial Arbitration Rules for issuing emergency relief? How does that standard compare to the standard used by courts in the context of a temporary restraining order/preliminary injunction?

5.   Is there an ethical problem in slowing down the arbitral process? What is the line between vigorous representation and unethical roadblocks?

Chinmax Medical Systems Inc. v.
Alere San Diego, Inc.

No. 10cv2467 WQH, 2011 WL 2135350 (S.D. Cal., May 27, 2011)

ORDER

HAYES, DISTRICT JUDGE.

The matters before the Court are the Petition (ECF No. 1) and the Motion to Vacate Arbitration Award filed by Petitioner Chinmax Medical Systems Inc. (ECF No. 10).

BACKGROUND

On December 1, 2010, Chinmax Medical Systems Inc., a Chinese Corporation, ("Chinmax") initiated this action by filing a Verified Petition to Vacate Arbitration Award. (ECF No. 1). On that same day, Chinmax filed an Ex Parte Motion for Stay of an Interim Final Award issued in Arbitration which was denied by this Court. (ECF Nos. 3, 12). On December 6, 2010, Chinmax filed a Motion to Vacate Arbitration Award. (ECF No. 10). On December 27, 2010, Alere San Diego, Inc, a Delaware Corporation, ("Alere") filed an Opposition. (ECF No. 14). On January 3, 2011, Chinmax filed a Reply. (ECF No. 16).

ALLEGATIONS OF PETITION

The principal place of business for Chinmax is Shanghai, China. Chinmax has been the exclusive distributor of certain medical devices manufactured by Alere and its predecessors since 2001. Chinmax and Alere operated under a distribution agreement for five years.

On April 1, 2007, Chinmax and Alere entered into a second distribution agreement which is the subject of the current Petition. The second distribution agreement set an initial one-year term which ran until March 31, 2008. The agreement allowed for an optional two-year renewal which would run until March 31, 2010, and an automatic renewal which would run until March 31, 2012, unless a party gave ninety-days notice of non-renewal prior to expiration of the previous term. Alere renewed the distribution agreement through March 31, 2010.

The second distribution agreement provided Chinmax the right to register new products in China, but in 2008, Alere "dictated" that it would register new products. (ECF No. 1 at 8). "Chinmax demanded value in return for giving up its contractual right over registration renewals[,]" and "required" that Chinmax continue to be named as the service agent.

Chinmax and Alere established sales targets each year. Alere increased the sales targets in 2008 and 2009. Alere's representatives stated that Alere would renew the distribution agreement for the final two-year term if Chinmax met at least ninety-percent of the 2009 sales target. Chinmax exceeded the 2009 sales target despite Alere making over $9 million in "illegal sales" during the same time period.

On January 5, 2010, Alere informed Chinmax that Alere would not renew the second distribution agreement. Alere claimed that Chinmax was in material breach of the second distribution agreement for failing to make payments on delivered products totaling $2,685,658.50. Chinmax retained the $2,685,658.50 as a set-off for its damages suffered as a result of Alere's "illegal sales" during 2009 which Chinmax estimates as totaling more than $3,240,000.00.

On September 10, 2010, Chinmax provided Alere notice that it intended to arbitrate the dispute pursuant to the arbitration agreement stated in the second distribution agreement. The parties arbitration agreement states as follows:

> Any dispute, controversy or claim initiated by either party arising out of or relating to [the Distribution Agreement, its negotiations, execution, or interpretation, or in the performance by either party of obligations under the Distribution Agreement] . . . shall be finally resolved by binding arbitration in the event that the parties are unable to resolve it. . . . Any such arbitration shall be conducted in the English language under the International Dispute Resolution Procedures and Arbitration Rules of the American Arbitration Association (the "Rules") by a panel of three (3) arbitrators appointed in accordance with such Rules . . . . Notwithstanding the foregoing, either party shall have the right, without waiving any right or remedy available to such party under this Agreement or otherwise, to seek and obtain from any court of competent jurisdiction any interim or provisional relief that is necessary or desirable to protect the rights or property of such party, pending the selection of the arbitrators hereunder or pending the arbitrator's determination of any dispute, controversy or claim hereunder.

(ECF No. 10–3 at 12).

On October 13, 2010, Chinmax filed a demand for arbitration with the International Centre for Dispute Resolution division of the American Arbitration Association ("AAA"). On October 15, 2010, Alere filed a request for an emergency interim award pursuant to Article 37 of the American Arbitration Association International Dispute Resolution Procedures. On October 20, 2010, Chinmax filed a Motion to Strike, or Alternatively, to Consolidate the Merits Hearing with the Interim Proceedings. On November 23, 2010, an emergency arbitrator issued an "Order re [Alere's] Request for Emergency Interim Award Pending Arbitration." (ECF No. 1 at 12 ¶ 40, 23–28).

The interim order states:

> The parties confirmed their mutual interest in assuring that product registrations . . . for products covered by the Distribution Agreement be renewed on time and as necessary, and not be allowed to expire. . . . However, the parties have been unable to agree on a process for assuring that these product registration renewals are accomplished as required. In light of these facts . . . to ensure timely product registration renewals, without prejudicing the rights of either party: (I) Chinmax shall promptly deliver into an escrow to be established by Alere . . . the following documents: the original license of the [Triage BNP]; the original license of the [Triage Cardiac Panel]; [and YZB/USA]. Chinmax shall also promptly make and transmit to Alere copies of all applications for product registrations, or renewal of product registrations, in its files concerning any products which are subject to the Distribution Agreement."

The interim order states:

> All renewal applications may identify [Alere] as the after-sales service agent. . . . [S]olely for the purpose of assuring that the product registration/renewals are accomplished without unnecessary disruption or delay . . . (I) Chinmax shall not initiate any communications concerning the registration, or renewal of registrations, of any product subject to the Distribution agreement with the SFDA [China's product registration and renewal agency] or other Chinese governmental agencies or officials; and (ii) to the extent that the SFDA or other Chinese agency or officials might inquire of Chinmax concerning registrations or renewals . . . Chinmax may respond to those inquires after informing Alere of the inquiry, and after conferring with Alere on the appropriate response.

The interim order states: "Chinmax shall not initiate communications with any customs officials concerning products subject to the 2007 Distribution Agreement, but may respond to any inquiries . . . in the same manner as with inquiries which Chinmax might receive from the SFDA. . . ."

The interim order states:

> [G]iven the admission by Chinmax that $2.8 million is indeed due and owing under the distribution agreement (subject only to alleged offsets), in order to facilitate any consideration by the full panel of conservancy or other orders regarding payment of this amount, Chinmax shall provide to Alere the following information within ten (10) days of the date of this order: a listing of all current bank accounts of Chinmax, including bank name and contact information, numbers of bank accounts in which any monies currently exist, and a statement of the balances in said accounts as of December 1, 2010.

Id. at 27–28. The interim order states: "This Order shall remain in effect pending review of the full arbitration tribunal, once appointed, and thereafter as the tribunal may order." *Id.* at 28.

In the Petition, Chinmax alleges that the emergency arbitrator did not have jurisdiction to issue the interim order on the grounds that the parties' agreement only allowed arbitration by a three arbitrator panel for final resolution and the parties' agreement provided that they would seek interim or provisional orders through a court of competent jurisdiction. Chinmax alleges that the emergency arbitrator lacked authority to issue the interim order under Article 37 of the International Dispute Resolution Procedures on the grounds that the arbitrator failed to find that there was an emergency, that the obligations of the interim order alter the status quo between the parties, and that the interim order manifestly disregards the law.

EMERGENCY ARBITRATION RULE

The AAA International Dispute Resolution Procedures Article 37 regarding emergency measures of protection states:

> Unless the parties agree otherwise, the provisions of this Article 37 shall apply to arbitrations conducted under arbitration clauses or agreements. . . . A party in need of emergency relief prior to constitution of the tribunal shall notify the administrator[,] . . . the administrator shall appoint a single emergency arbitrator from a special panel of emergency arbitrators designated to rule on

emergency applications. . . . The emergency arbitrator shall have the power to order or award any interim or conservatory measure the emergency arbitrator deems necessary, including injunctive relief measures for the protection or conservation of property. Any such measure may take the form of an interim award or of an order. . . . Once the tribunal has been constituted, the tribunal may reconsider, modify or vacate the interim award or order of emergency relief issued by the emergency arbitrator.

(ECF No. 14–3 at 17).

CONTENTIONS OF THE PARTIES

Chinmax requests that the Court vacate the "Order re [Alere's] Request for Emergency Interim Award Pending Arbitration." Chinmax contends that this Court has jurisdiction to review the interim order on the grounds that it is a "temporary equitable award[ ] involving the preservation of assets relating to the subject matter of the arbitration . . . ." Chinmax contends that the interim order is a final award, and that finality is demonstrated by the terms of the interim order which sets a ten-day deadline for compliance. Chinmax also contends that the interim order should be vacated on the grounds that the arbitrator exceeded his powers and the arbitrator manifestly disregarded the law.

Alere contends that the Court does not have jurisdiction to review the interim order because it is not a final award. Alere contends that the full panel of arbitrators are authorized to reconsider, modify, or vacate the interim order. Alere contends that the Court should review a non-final award "if at all, only in the most extreme case[ ]." Alere contends that this case does not present "extreme" circumstances justifying review because it the interim order is reviewable by the fully constituted panel of arbitrators. Alere also contends that the arbitrator's interpretation of his powers is non-reviewable, the arbitrator did not exceed his powers, and the arbitrator did not manifestly disregard the law.

DISCUSSION

"The use of arbitration as a means of settling disputes has been accorded specific Congressional endorsement in the [Federal Arbitration Act] and should be encouraged by the federal courts." *Aerojet-General Corp. v. Am. Arbitration Ass'n*, 478 F.2d 248, 251 (9th Cir.1973). "The basic purpose of arbitration is the speedy disposition of disputes without the expense and delay of extended court proceedings." *Id.*

Historically, for an arbitration award to be subject to judicial review, it must be final and binding as to all of the issues presented to the arbitrator. * * * "[B]ecause of the Congressional policy favoring arbitration when agreed to by the parties, judicial review of non-final arbitration awards 'should be indulged, if at all, only in the most extreme cases.' " *Pac. Reins. Mgmt. Corp.*, 935 F.2d at 1022.

In *Pacific Reinsurance Management Corp.*, the Ninth Circuit considered as a matter of first impression "[w]hether temporary equitable relief that is necessary to prevent a potential final award from being meaningless can be confirmed and enforced in the district courts." *Pac. Reins. Mgmt. Corp.*, 935 F.2d at 1022. Prior to deciding the merits of the arbitration, the arbitration panel issued an 'interim final order' which created an escrow account and ordered the deposit of disputed funds in that escrow account. *Id.* The Ninth Circuit stated that judicial confirmation of the "interim final award" was "not inconsistent . . . with the policy favoring arbitration . . . [g]iven the potential importance of temporary equitable awards in making the arbitration proceedings meaningful. . . ." *Id.* at 1023. The Ninth Circuit stated that "court enforcement of [final temporary equitable awards], when appropriate, is not an undue intrusion upon the arbitral process, but is essential to preserve the integrity of that process." *Id.* (quotation omitted). The court held that: "temporary equitable orders calculated to preserve assets or performance needed to make a potential final award meaningful . . . are final orders that can be reviewed for confirmation and enforcement by district courts under the [Federal Arbitration Act]." *Id.*

"[C]ourts go beyond a document's heading and delve into its substance and impact to determine whether the decision is final." *Publicis Commc'n v. True N. Commc'ns, Inc.*, 206 F.3d 725, 729 (7th Cir.2000);* * *. "Where an arbitrator retains jurisdiction in order to decide a substantive issue the parties have not yet resolved, this retention of jurisdiction indicates that the arbitrator did not intend the award to be final." *Orion Pictures Corp. v. Writers Guild of Am., W., Inc.*, 946 F.2d 722, 724 (9th Cir.1991). * * *

In this case, prior to the constitution of the full arbitration panel, a single emergency arbitrator issued a temporary equitable order pursuant to Article 37 of the AAA International Dispute Resolution Procedures. Although the interim order required Chinmax to take certain conservatory actions within ten days, the interim order also that the temporary equitable order was issued "in order to facilitate any consideration by the full panel of conservancy . . . ." and the interim order would "remain in effect pending review of the full arbitration tribunal, once appointed, and thereafter as the tribunal may order." Id. at 27–28 (emphasis added). In addition, Article 37 of the AAA International Dispute Resolution Procedures provides: "Once the tribunal has been constituted, the tribunal may reconsider, modify or vacate the interim award or order of emergency relief issued by the emergency arbitrator." (ECF No. 14–3 at 17) (emphasis added). When considering the "substance and impact" of the interim order, this Court concludes that the interim order was not a final order and is not subject to review by this Court. *Publicis Commc'n*, 206 F.3d at 729. The rules provide that the full arbitration panel has the authority to "reconsider, modify or vacate" the interim order; thus, the rules expressly retained jurisdiction over the issue for further consideration by the full panel. *See Orion Pictures Corp.*, 946 F.2d at 724. The arbitrator stated that the interim order was issued to facilitate a conservancy order by the full arbitration panel; thus, the arbitrator did not intend the interim order to be final. * * * The Court concludes that the evidence does not present an "extreme" case permitting judicial review of a non-final order because the interim order is expressly subject to reconsideration, modification, or vacatur by the full tribunal. The Motion to Vacate Arbitration Award filed by Petitioner Chinmax (ECF No. 10) and the Petition seeking the same relief (ECF No. 1) are DENIED.

CONCLUSION

IT IS HEREBY ORDERED that the Petition (ECF No. 1) and the Motion to Vacate Arbitration Award filed by Petitioner Chinmax Medical Systems Inc. (ECF No. 10) are DENIED. The Clerk shall close the case.

NOTES

Facts

1. Who commenced the arbitration against whom? Who sought emergency relief?

2. What relief do the parties seek in the arbitration in chief? Is Alere claiming for anything as of yet? To the extent that Alere could claim for relief in arbitration, do the facts suggest a way to determine money damages?

3. It does not seem that Alere is seeking to enforce the interim order. Why not?

Law

1. Compare the AAA's international rule quoted in the award with Rule 38 of the Commercial Arbitration Rules. Do the rules essentially track?

2. Look at the excerpts from the order quoted in the decision. Can you reconstruct on what basis the emergency arbitrator ordered the relief in question? Look at your answer to Fact Note 2 above. Can you bring this relief within the standard used by U.S. federal courts for the issuance of preliminary injunctions? If so, which of the tests works best in your view?

3. Has Alere forsaken any ability to enforce the order in U.S. courts by its procedural election not to call the decision an "award"? Consider your answer to Fact Note 3 above.

4. How can Alere enforce the relief granted?

5. In light of the review standard by the federal courts set out in the decision, what are the outer limits for the emergency powers of the emergency arbitrator? Do you see a significant risk in the court's position here?

C) Preliminary Relief in Arbitration

AAA Commercial Arbitration Rules

R 37.   Interim Measures

(a) The arbitrator may take whatever interim measures he or she deems necessary, including injunctive relief and measures for the protection or conservation of property and disposition of perishable goods.

(b) Such interim measures may take the form of an interim award, and the arbitrator may require security for the costs of such measures.

(c) A request for interim measures addressed by a party to a judicial authority shall not be deemed incompatible with the agreement to arbitrate or a waiver of the right to arbitrate.

NOTES

1. What is the standard upon which the arbitrator may issue interim relief? Is it the same as that upon which an emergency arbitrator is entitled to issue interim relief?

2. How does the security mechanism for the party ordered to comply with a preliminary measure compare to the security mechanisms in place in litigation under Federal Rule of Civil Procedure 65?

Pacific Reinsurance Management Corp. v. Ohio Reinsurance Corp.

935 F.2d 1019 (9th Cir. 1991)

WIGGINS, CIRCUIT JUDGE:

Ohio Reinsurance Corp., et al. appeals the district court's denial of a partial stay of arbitration, confirmation of the arbitration panel's Interim Final Order (IFO), and the district court's supersedeas bond order pending appeal of the IFO. * * *

BACKGROUND

The appellants, Ohio Reinsurance Corp., et al., were members of a reinsurance pool managed by the appellee, Pacific Reinsurance Management Corporation (PRMC). Each of the appellants executed a Management Agreement authorizing PRMC to develop, underwrite, and manage reinsurance business in their behalf. PRMC accepted much of its business in the name of one of the pool members, Mission Insurance Company. Unhappy with that practice and other matters, appellants sued PRMC for fraud and other wrongful conduct, seeking rescission of the Agreements and damages for any money due third parties from the pool. The district court ordered arbitration under the arbitration provisions of the Management Agreements.

During the arbitration, the panel retained outside counsel to help it set up an escrow account for damages that might be due PRMC under the Agreements. The appellants petitioned the district court to grant a partial stay of the arbitration to prevent PRMC from asserting what appellants argued were non-arbitrable claims. The appellants also sought a ruling that the retention of outside counsel by the panel was an improper delegation of authority. The district court denied the petition. The appeal from that denial is the first of the three considered in this consolidated appeal.

In July, 1988, the arbitration panel issued an Interim Final Order (IFO) setting up an escrow account with the balances apparently due from appellants to PRMC if the Management Agreements prove valid after further investigation. The appeal from the district court's confirmation of the IFO is the second of the three considered in this consolidated appeal.

* * *

DISCUSSION

* * *

II. THE DISTRICT COURT'S POWER TO REVIEW THE INTERIM FINAL ORDER

The appellants argue that the IFO was a non-final award of the kind that is not confirmable under Ninth Circuit caselaw construing the FAA. The FAA allows a district court to vacate an award that is not a "mutual, final, and definite award upon the subject matter submitted. . . ." 9 U.S.C. § 10(d). The Ninth Circuit has said that because of the Congressional policy favoring arbitration when agreed to by the parties, judicial review of non-final arbitration awards "should be indulged, if at all, only in the most extreme cases." *Aerojet-General Corp. v. American Arbitration Ass'n*, 478 F.2d 248, 251 (9th Cir.1973) (arbitrator's choice of locale reviewed only for bad faith or exceeding authority). * * *

In *Millmen* and *Sunshine*, we refused to review awards that decided only part of the substantive issues submitted to arbitration. In contrast, the IFO in this case does not attempt to address, even partially, the substantive issues before the arbitrators—the validity and application of the Management Agreements. Rather, the IFO is in the nature of a preliminary injunction. It is temporary equitable relief that requires the appellants to place $20,222,000 in escrow pending the arbitrators' decision regarding the validity of the Management Agreements. Whether temporary equitable relief that is necessary to prevent a potential final award from being meaningless can be confirmed and enforced in the district courts is an issue of first impression for the Ninth Circuit.

Temporary equitable relief in arbitration may be essential to preserve assets or enforce performance which, if not preserved or enforced, may render a final award meaningless.[1] However, if temporary equitable relief is to have any meaning, the relief must be enforceable at the time it is granted, not after an arbitrator's final decision on the merits. *See Southern Seas Navigation Ltd. v. Petroleos Mexicanos*, 606 F.Supp. 692, 694 (S.D.N.Y.1985). Arbitrators have no power to enforce their decisions. Only courts have that power. Consequently, courts in other circuits that have been faced with arbitrators' temporary equitable awards have not characterized them as non-final awards on the merits which can only

---

[1]   Rule 34 of the American Arbitration Association Commercial Arbitration Rules contemplates interim equitable relief in appropriate circumstances:

> The arbitrator may issue such orders for interim relief as may be deemed necessary to safeguard the property that is the subject matter of the arbitration without prejudice to the rights of the parties or to the final determination of the dispute.

be reviewed in extreme cases. Rather, they have characterized them as confirmable, final awards on an issue distinct from the controversy on the merits. *Island Creek Coal Sales Co. v. Gainesville*, 729 F.2d 1046, 1049 (6th Cir.1984) ("The interim award disposes of one self-contained issue, namely, whether the City is required to perform the contract during the pendency of the arbitration proceedings. Th[is] issue is a separate, discrete, independent, severable issue.") * * * To these courts, a temporary equitable award has an element of finality sufficient to be confirmed and enforced under the FAA.

The reasoning of these courts is not inconsistent, as might first appear, with the policy favoring arbitration at the expense of the courts when it is chosen by the parties. Given the potential importance of temporary equitable awards in making the arbitration proceedings meaningful, court enforcement of them, when appropriate, is not an "undue intrusion upon the arbitral process," *Southern Seas*, 606 F.Supp. at 694, but is essential to preserve the integrity of that process. Therefore, we hold that temporary equitable orders calculated to preserve assets or performance needed to make a potential final award meaningful, such as the IFO in this case, are final orders that can be reviewed for confirmation and enforcement by district courts under the FAA.

* * *

CONCLUSION

The district court's confirmation of the IFO, and the court's supersedeas bond order, are AFFIRMED with regards to all appellants except CTR. The IFO and supersedeas bond order are VACATED with respect to CTR.

NOTES

Facts

1.   What relief did the tribunal grant and why?

2.   What evidence did the tribunal consult?

Law

1.   Is it possible to enforce interim measures in courts? How does *Pacific Reinsurance* suggest doing so? Is there a statutory basis for such enforcement?

CHAPTER 13

Interim Relief Before US Courts in Aid of Arbitration

Parties cannot exclusively rely upon an arbitral tribunal for interim relief. Perhaps most intuitively, before an arbitral tribunal is constituted, it cannot issue interim relief. The availability of emergency arbitration is a step towards rectifying this problem. But even an emergency arbitrator cannot act immediately—the institution has the appoint the arbitrator first. Less intuitively but just as importantly, an arbitral decision is not self-enforcing. One cannot take an arbitral decision to the sheriff's office and demand that the sheriff impound certain goods or stop certain conduct from occurring. To have the sheriff take action, one needs to go to the courts, instead to enforce the arbitral decision in question. Finally, sometimes a party to an arbitration needs relief from a third party to the proceedings to protect its arbitration rights. Freezing money in a bank account for example is premised upon an order to the bank holding the funds—not the account holder. But the bank at which a party has an account is typically not a party to the arbitration. The tribunal therefore has very limited authority to order the bank to do anything at all.

In each of these instances, a party may therefore wish to the courts to receive relief in aid of arbitration. Federal courts are typically willing and able to assist parties seeking relief in aid of arbitration. As Joseph Profaizer and Daniel Prince have observed, the basis for doing so is not uniformly settled across circuits. Joseph Profaizer & Daniel Prince, *Obtaining Injunctions in Aid of Arbitration in United States Federal Courts: Addressing a Potential Threshold Jurisdictional Bar*, vol. 26 (10) MEALEY'S INT'L ARB. REP. 1, 2 (Oct. 2011). Any application for such relief in aid of arbitration will of necessity require some detailed research into the caselaw of the court issuing the relief in question.

In light of this circuit split bear in mind that the AAA Rules, such as the Commercial Arbitration Rules typically include the following language:

A request for interim measures addressed by a party to a judicial authority shall not be deemed incompatible with the agreement to arbitrate or a waiver of the right to arbitrate.[1]

As discussed in chapter 5 regarding who is empowered to hear a challenge to the jurisdiction of an arbitral tribunal (the courts or the arbitral tribunal) reference to the AAA Arbitration Rules in an arbitration clause incorporates their content by reference.

Fact Scenario

Look back again at the fact scenarios in Chapters 11 and 12. Before the arbitration is filed, Hardmont LLC tells you that the Acme Industries Corp. bankruptcy looked suspicious. Most of the creditors were companies beneficially owned by Mr. Gilmore. While these creditors had to accept the biggest "haircut", they were paid a significant amount of money from Acme before Acme wound up. Your client suspects that Gilmore holds much of the money Acme received under contract from Hardmont in a New York account at Wachowia Bank. Hardmont suspects that much of the profit RRF Corp. is making off its design contracts with third-party retailers ultimately ends up in the same account. Hardmont asks you to attach these assets in court proceedings, in aid of arbitration. Hardmont wants to have the attachments in place before it begins the arbitration proceedings against Acme, RRF, and Gilmore as it fears the money could be moved offshore if Gilmore gets wind of the arbitration. How should you proceed? What counter-arguments do you expect the opposing parties to make?

Readings

A) Relief in Aid of Arbitration Before an Arbitration Is Commenced

In some instances, parties will need emergency relief in the form of a temporary restraining order before they have an opportunity to commence an action. In these circumstances, they may seek relief in *contemplation of* an immediately impending action.

When seeking such relief, there is not yet an arbitral tribunal or institution that could hear the request for interim relief. The arbitration clause has, as of yet, not been engaged.

---

[1]   AAA Commercial Arbitration Rules, R. 37(c).

Note however that it arguably may be possible to seek emergency relief from an AAA emergency arbitrator prior to the filing of a demand for arbitration. AAA Commercial Arbitration Rules, R. 38 (b) refers to a party "in need of emergency relief prior to the constitution of the panel". This is the case even prior to the filing of a demand. The use of the definite article in "the panel" rather than an indefinite article "a panel" suggests an intent on the part of the drafters of Rule 38 that a demand be on file when a party invokes Rule 38.

Sauer Getriebe KG v. White Hydraulics, Inc.

715 F.2d 348 (7th Cir. 1983)

CUMMINGS, CHIEF JUDGE.

We consider in this appeal whether an agreement in an international, commercial contract to arbitrate "any and all" contractual disputes governs disputes regarding whether the contract is invalid for lack of consideration, unconscionability, and vagueness and whether one party waives its right to arbitration by filing suit to enjoin the other party from breaching that contract pending arbitration.

On June 29, 1979, defendant White Hydraulics, Inc. ("White"), an Indiana corporation, contracted to give Sauer-Getriebe KG ("Sauer"), a West German limited partnership, the exclusive right in a territory encompassing some 47 countries, including East and West Germany but excluding the United States, to sell motors manufactured by White. White also agreed to convey to Sauer upon the occurrence of certain events the trade secrets, patent rights, and any other rights necessary for the manufacture of those motors and to furnish Sauer all the technical "know-how" about the motors necessary for Sauer to market them. In exchange, Sauer agreed to pay a certain royalty on each motor sold and stated that its "intent" was to purchase 50,000 motors from White during the years 1979 through 1985. Both parties agreed that "[a]ny and all disputes arising out of and in connection with" the contract would be settled by arbitration.

In August 1981, Sauer commenced this diversity action. It alleged that on July 21, 1981, White had repudiated the contract by informing Sauer that it was negotiating for the sale of its assets, including the manufacturing rights promised Sauer under the contract, to a third party. In its complaint, Sauer represented that it intended to exercise its right to arbitrate the contract dispute and sought preliminary and permanent injunctions barring White from transferring any manufacturing rights "until such time as the respective rights of the parties under the agreement are determined" by arbitration.

In its answer, White admitted having executed the alleged contract and having informed Sauer of the third-party negotiations. White claimed, however, that Sauer had waived its right to arbitrate by filing suit. White also counterclaimed for a declaratory judgment that the contract was unenforceable for vagueness and want of consideration, that its terms were unconscionable and inequitable, and that the contract was illegal under Section 1 et seq. of the Sherman Act (15 U.S.C. § 1 et seq.). Sauer thereafter filed a supplemental complaint in which it claimed that on August 31, 1983, it had requested White to transfer to it all manufacturing rights in the motors. Sauer further alleged that as of that date all of the events prerequisite to that transfer had occurred, but that White had refused to comply with its request.

The parties agreed to a bench trial. At the conclusion, Judge Sharp denied Sauer injunctive relief on the grounds that White had not repudiated the contract and that Sauer was not entitled to the manufacturing rights. Judge Sharp also enjoined Sauer from pursuing the arbitration proceeding it had begun on the ground that its request for arbitration before the International Commerce Commission ("ICC") had been filed in the wrong city—Paris, instead of London. Judge Sharp granted Sauer leave to refile its request in London but held that his findings would be binding in any subsequent arbitration proceeding. Finally, although Judge Sharp found the contract "vague and ambiguous" in certain respects, he dismissed White's counterclaim because he found "insufficient evidence to establish the invalidity of the contract." White has appealed and Sauer has cross-appealed. For the reasons that follow, we affirm the dismissal of White's counterclaim but vacate the remainder of the judgment and direct the district court to enjoin White from repudiating the contract and from transferring any of Sauer's contractual rights to a third party until the arbitration requested by Sauer is completed and this lawsuit (including any appeals) is terminated.

Arbitration Waiver

White makes two attacks on Sauer's right to arbitrate this dispute. First, White claims that before this dispute may be submitted to arbitration, a court must decide that the contract containing the arbitration clause is valid and enforceable. White argues that if there is no contract to buy and sell motors there is no agreement to arbitrate. The conclusion does not follow its premise. The agreement to arbitrate and the agreement to buy and sell motors are separate. Sauer's promise to arbitrate was given in exchange for White's promise to arbitrate and each promise was sufficient consideration for the other. * * * Moreover, there is nothing that requires that courts rather than arbitrators decide the validity of contracts, * * *, nor is there anything to suggest that when Sauer and White executed their contract they intended to limit in any way the kinds of disputes to be settled by arbitration. The language of the arbitration clause in the contract could not be broader. It expressly provides that

> *Any and all disputes arising out of and in connection with this Agreement shall be finally settled by arbitration under the rules of Conciliation and Arbitration of the International Chamber of Commerce by three arbitrators appointed in accordance with the Rules. The arbitration shall take place in London, United Kingdom of Great Britain.*

This provision covers Sauer's claim that White repudiated the contract as well as White's claim that the contract is invalid. It is too late for White to argue that arbitrators appointed under ICC rules lack the competence to adjudicate the validity of its contract. Had White thought so when it entered the contract, it would not have agreed to arbitrate "any and all claims" before them.

Second, White argues that by filing this lawsuit, Sauer waived its right to arbitrate. We disagree. Sauer's right to seek injunctive relief in court and its right to arbitrate are not incompatible—Sauer need not have abandoned one to pursue the other—and White cannot in good faith claim that it was misled by Sauer's filing this suit into believing that Sauer intended to forego arbitration. See *Erving v. Virginia Squires Basketball Club*, 468 F.2d 1064 (2d Cir.1972). Sauer alleged in its complaint that it intended to submit a request for arbitration of its claims and Article 8, Section 5 of the internal rules of the ICC court of arbitration expressly authorizes parties to seek the interim relief Sauer sought in its complaint:

> *Before the file is transmitted to the arbitrator, and in exceptional circumstances even thereafter, the parties shall be at liberty to apply to any competent judicial authority for interim or conservatory measures, and they shall not by so doing be held to infringe the agreement to arbitrate or to affect the relevant powers reserved to the arbitrator.*

Sauer waited four more months before filing an arbitration request with the ICC but, in part at least, the delay was due to White's slowness in responding to Sauer's request for transfer of the manufacturing rights and at any rate, Sauer took no action during those four months inconsistent with its original position. It pleaded its arbitration right in defense to White's counterclaim and it reasserted that right in its supplemental complaint.

Judge Sharp did not find that Sauer had waived its right to arbitration. Nonetheless he enjoined Sauer from pursuing the arbitration request it had filed with the ICC in Paris on the ground that the contract required that the request be filed in London. The contract, however, requires that the arbitration "take place in London," not that the request for arbitration be filed there. The contract also provides that the arbitration shall be conducted in accordance with ICC rules. Article 3, paragraph 1 and Article 1, paragraph 5 of those rules in effect require that requests for arbitration be filed in Paris with the Secretariat of the ICC Court of Arbitration. It does not follow that because Sauer filed its request in Paris the arbitration will take place there. Sauer did not request that it take place there—in fact the arbitrator Sauer selected lives in London—and Article 12 of the ICC arbitration rules provides that "the place of arbitration shall be fixed by the Court [of Arbitration], unless agreed upon by the parties." (emphasis supplied). There is therefore no reason to suppose that because Sauer filed its arbitration request as required by ICC rules, the arbitration will not be held in the place specified in the contract. Sauer is therefore not required to refile its request in London. Finally, because the arbitration request was filed properly, we also reverse Judge Sharp's order directing Sauer to nominate a new arbitrator.

* * *

Injunction Against White's Selling Trade Secrets and Manufacturing Rights

The district court refused to grant Sauer's request to enjoin White's sale of its manufacturing contractual rights pending resolution of the arbitration. Since Sauer seeks only an injunction pending arbitration, we will consider whether the four factors justifying a preliminary injunction are present. *Wesley-Jessen Division v. Bausch & Lomb, Inc.*, 698 F.2d 862, 867 (7th Cir.1983).

Sauer has shown that it has made a substantial investment in White's hydraulic motors and that it cannot obtain the necessary trade secrets and manufacturing rights from others. Sauer has also shown that without equitable relief, there would be a substantial injury to its reputation, good will and prestige not compensable in damages. Thus it has adequately demonstrated irreparable harm.

White might suffer some hardship if it is enjoined from transferring its manufacturing rights but, by the same token, Sauer's right to arbitration will not be worth much if White transfers those rights before arbitration is settled. Moreover, Sauer is willing to supply a security bond to guarantee White's financial recovery should it be forced to sell its business at a lower price after the injunction is lifted (Sauer Br. 22). That would protect White against any financial loss, so that the balance of hardship is in Sauer's favor.

Although it is improper for a court to decide a contractual dispute relegated to arbitration, so far as the issuance of an injunction is concerned Sauer has demonstrated enough probable success on the merits to warrant relief. Sauer will be entitled to specific performance if it convinces the arbitrators that the contract entitles it to the trade secrets and manufacturing rights claimed. The contractual events prerequisite to the transfer of those rights have ostensibly occurred—Sauer has ordered over 15,000 motors, 18 months expired from the signing of the contract and the placing of those orders, and as of August 31, 1981 the Deutschmark—U.S. dollar ratio had been above 2.20 for four months. White bases its case solely on the alleged invalidity of a contract it freely signed three years ago even though it performed under the contract during those three years. Despite Judge Sharp's March 12, 1982, finding that the contract is valid on its face and his March 31 decision that Sauer failed to establish its invalidity (White App. 52, 57), White is now endeavoring to repudiate that agreement on four separate grounds (White App. 37–39). In these circumstances, Sauer has sufficiently shown likely success.

Finally, the public interest is served by granting this injunctive relief because there is a strong policy in favor of carrying out commercial arbitration when a contract contains an arbitration clause. Arbitration lightens courts' workloads, and it usually results in a speedier resolution of controversies. Since Sauer has satisfied the requisites for obtaining injunctive relief of this type, the district court's refusal to grant it was erroneous.

Judgment affirmed with respect to dismissal of White's counterclaim. Remainder of judgment vacated and cause remanded with directions to enjoin White from repudiating the June 29, 1979, contract and from transferring any of Sauer's claimed contractual rights to a third party until the London arbitration requested by Sauer on December 18, 1981, is completed and this lawsuit (including any appeals) is terminated. Sauer to file security bond in district court in the sum of $100,000. Costs on appeal to be borne by White.

NOTES

Facts

1.   When did Sauer file its court action? When did Sauer commence arbitration proceedings? Why do you think that the Sauer chose this sequence of filings?

2.   What injunctive relief did Sauer seek from the courts? What harm would it suffer if the court did not enjoin White?

Law

1. What was the basis upon which the court determined that it had the right to issue injunctive relief before arbitration?

2. How did the ICC arbitration rules affect the court's decision? Is the decision limited to arbitration under rules similar to the ICC rules or is the ruling broader?

3. What is the irreparable harm that supports issuance of an injunction in this case?

Pre-Paid Legal Services, Inc. v. Kidd

No. CIV–11–357–FHS, 2011 WL 5079538 (E.D. Okla., Oct. 26, 2011)

OPINION AND ORDER

FRANK H. SEAY, DISTRICT JUDGE.

On October 10, 2011, Plaintiff, Pre-Paid Legal Services, Inc. ("Pre-Paid") initiated this action in the District Court of Pontotoc County, Oklahoma, alleging multiple theories of recovery, including misappropriation of trade secrets, against Defendant, Percy Darin Kidd ("Kidd"), a former Pre-Paid associate. On that same date, State District Judge Thomas Landrith entered a temporary restraining order ("TRO") enjoining and restraining Kidd from "1) contacting any person or organization he knows or suspects to be a Pre-Paid associate and, directly or indirectly, soliciting or encouraging the associate to join [Kidd] in a new company or organization, or to leave Pre-Paid for the eventual purpose of joining another company, 2) disparaging Pre-Paid in an attempt to solicit Pre-Paid associates, and 3) using trade secret information of Pre-Paid for any other purpose." The TRO was to remain in effect until October 21, 2011, at which time a hearing on Pre-Paid's request for a preliminary injunction was to take place.

On October 11, 2011, Kidd removed the Pontotoc County action to the United States District Court for the Eastern District of Oklahoma. On October 14, 2011, Kidd filed a Motion to Stay Pending Arbitration (Dkt. No. 4) asking this Court to enforce the arbitration provisions contained within the parties' agreements and stay this action while the parties arbitrate their disputes. On October 19, 2011, this Court granting Pre-Paid's request to extend the TRO until such time as this Court rules on Kidd's request to stay this action pending arbitration. The matter has been fully briefed and is ripe for ruling.

Pre-Paid does not contest Kidd's assertion that the claims Pre-Paid has asserted against Kidd in this lawsuit are subject to arbitration pursuant to the parties' agreements or that such agreements include emergency measures of protection. Two agreements between Pre-Paid and Kidd contain arbitration provisions. First, the Associate Agreement with Policies and Procedures entered into by Kidd on October 2, 1998, provides:

> *All disputes and claims relating to PPLSI, the Associate Agreement, these Policies and Procedures and any other PPLSI policies, products and services, the rights and obligations of an Associate and PPLSI, or any other claims or causes of action between the Associate or PPLSI, or any of its officers, directors, employees or affiliates, whether in tort or contract, shall be settled totally and finally by arbitration in Oklahoma City, Oklahoma, in accordance with the Commercial Arbitration Rules of the American Arbitration Association, including the optional rules for emergency measures of protection.*

Pre-Paid Associates' Policies and Procedures, ¶ 23 (emphasis added). Second, the Regional Vice President Agreement ("RVP") executed by Kidd on April 24, 2008, provides:

> *All disputes and claims relating to Company, RVP, this Agreement, or any associate agreement, or any Company policies, procedures, products or services, or any other claims or causes of action between RVP and Company or any of Company's officers, directors, employees or affiliates, whether in tort or in contract, shall be settled totally and finally by arbitration in Oklahoma City, Oklahoma in accordance with the Commercial Arbitration Rules of the American Arbitration Association ["AAA"], including the optional rules for emergency measures of protection.*

RVP Agreement, ¶ 10. Recognizing the applicability of these provisions, Pre-Paid does not contest the right to arbitrate in this matter. Consequently, based on the clear language of these provisions, this Court finds Pre-Paid's claims are subject to arbitration. Kidd's Motion to Stay Pending Arbitration (Dkt. No. 4) is therefore granted.

The central dispute remaining between the parties is the forum for resolution of the preliminary injunctive relief sought by Pre-Paid. Pre-Paid asks this Court to go forward with its request for preliminary relief and Kidd contends such issues should be resolved in arbitration. In a parallel case, *Pre-Paid Legal Services, Inc. v. Mark O. Smith, et al.*, Case No. CIV–11–333–FHS, filed in the United States District Court for the Eastern District of Oklahoma, this Court ordered a stay of the proceedings pending arbitration and it declined to retain jurisdiction to address Pre-Paid's pending motion for preliminary injunction.[2] In doing so, this Court found that retaining jurisdiction was not an efficient utilization of client and judicial resources as the issue of preliminary/emergency relief can be decided in the context of the arbitration proceedings. This Court did, however, extend the existing TRO in order to preserve the *status quo* in Smith until the issue of emergency relief could be addressed by an arbitrator under the optional rules for emergency measures of protection.

In the instant litigation, the parties have informed this Court of the events that have transpired in *Smith* since the arbitration proceedings were initiated. In sum, the parties have exchanged numerous verbal barbs in assigning nefarious motives with respect to how each side has conducted themselves since arbitration was ordered. This Court is not inclined to resolve this finger-pointing gamesmanship, nor is it necessary to do so. Instead, this Court directs that the parties submit their disputes to arbitration. Either side may initiate the arbitration. This Court strongly urges the parties to meet and confer to determine the most expeditious and economic route for presenting all claims by the parties to an arbitrator, including a request for emergency measures. This is a simple matter, easily capable of being resolved by attorneys seeking to advance the best interests of their clients for a swift resolution of their disputes.

Under Tenth Circuit precedent, this Court clearly has the authority to issue injunctive relief preserving the status quo pending the initiation of arbitration. *Merrill Lynch, Pierce, Fenner & Smith, Inc. v. Dutton*, 844 F.2d 726, 727–28 (10th Cir.1988); see also *Mount Holly Partners, LLC v. AMDS Holdings, LLC*, 2009 WL 1507148, *2 (D.Utah). The most appropriate avenue for the extended injunctive relief sought herein by Pre-Paid would appear to be a further extension of the TRO set to expire on this Court's ruling on the motion to stay pending arbitration. Such an extension would preserve the *status quo* while the emergency

---

[2]   As a matter of procedure, this Court directed the defendants to initiate the arbitration proceedings in Smith. The "procedure" this Court was referring to was the fact that the defendants in Smith moved this Court to stay the proceedings, not Pre-Paid. This Court further stated that Pre-Paid had noted it had waived the arbitration clauses by initially filing the action in state court. The defendants in Smith and Kidd are represented by the same counsel. Contrary to defense counsel's assertions in the Smith arbitration and herein, this Court's direction for the Smith defendants to initiate arbitration was not a judicial determination that Pre-Paid had waived arbitration and, more importantly, it is not a finding that once ordered to arbitration by this Court, Pre-Paid is not entitled to assert any of its rights under the terms of the arbitration clauses and the Rules of the AAA. Pre-Paid can most certainly exercise all its arbitration rights in Smith now that it has been ordered by this Court to arbitrate. Representations otherwise are not well received by this Court.

measures of protection subsumed within the TRO are addressed in the arbitration setting.

Rule 65 of the Federal Rules of Civil Procedure authorizes extensions of TROs under certain conditions. Rule 65 provides:

> *[t]he order expires at the time after entry—not to exceed 14 days—that the court sets, unless before that time the court, for good cause, extends it for a like period or the adverse party consents to a longer extension.*

Fed. R.Civ.P. 65(b)(2). An extension of a TRO can therefore be justified upon a showing of good cause. *Merrill Lynch, Pierce, Fenner & Smith v. Patinkin*, 1991 WL 83163, *3–4 (N.D.Ill)(two-month extension of TRO in the context of arbitration proceedings warranted upon a showing of good cause). The Optional Rules For Emergency Measures Of Protection adopted by the parties as part of their agreement to arbitrate provide for the appointment of an emergency arbitrator to rule on emergency applications within one business day of the receipt of notice to the AAA regarding a request for emergency measures. Rule O–2. These rules further provide that "as soon as possible, but in any event within two business days of appointment," the emergency arbitrator is required to establish a schedule for considering the request for emergency measures. Rule O–3. Thus, these Rules contemplate a swift resolution of a request for emergency measures, *i.e.* a determination on the injunctive relief entered herein maintaining the *status quo* pending arbitration of the underlying claims. While hopeful for a quick resolution, this Court is not overly optimistic, particularly in light of the fact that some limited discovery will most likely be necessary to present the emergency measures request before an emergency arbitrator. Consequently, this Court finds good cause exists for an extension of the TRO in order to allow the parties to properly present, and the emergency arbitrator to properly consider, a request for emergency measures.

Based on the foregoing reasons, Kidd's Motion to Stay Pending Arbitration (Dkt. No. 4) is granted. It is further ordered that the TRO currently set to expire on this date be extended until January 3, 2012, or until an emergency arbitrator hears and determines an application for emergency measures related to preserving the status quo as set forth under the TRO, whichever date first occurs.

It is so ordered.

NOTES

Facts

1. What was the specific relief mandated by the temporary restraining order? Who sought the TRO?

2. When was arbitration commenced in this case?

3. How did the parties' counsel conduct themselves in the prosecution of the case? Did that impact the court's ultimate resolution of the case?

4. What are the ethical obligations of the parties' counsel? Who ensures the attorneys behave ethically in this circumstance? How do the ethical obligations in this circumstance differ from those regarding interim measures ordered by an arbitral tribunal?

Law

1. The court makes reference to the AAA emergency arbitrator. How does the TRO work together with the emergency powers under the AAA rules?

B) Relief in Aid of Arbitration Before a Tribunal Is Constituted

A party initiating arbitration often seeks preliminary relief from a court as well as commencing an arbitration. Often, the preliminary relief sought is the attachment of the defending party's assets. The case below outlines both the law and procedure of this remedy.

SiVault Systems, Inc. v. WonderNet, Ltd.

No. 05 Civ.0890(RWS), 2005 WL 681457 (S.D.N.Y., Mar. 25, 2005)

SWEET, J.

By a petition filed on January 26, 2005 the petitioner SiVault Systems, Inc. ("SiVault") has moved pursuant to Rule 64 of the Federal Rules of Civil Procedure and Section 7502(c) of the New York Civil Practice Law and Rules for an order of attachment directing the Sheriff of the City of New York or the Sheriff of any county of the State of New York, to levy within the Sheriff's jurisdiction upon certain shares of stock in SiVault held by the respondent WonderNet, Ltd. ("WonderNet") evidenced by a certificate bearing the number 3281. For the reasons set forth below, SiVault's petition for attachment is granted, secured by a mandatory undertaking in the form of a $100,000.00 bond.

* * *

Background and Prior Proceedings

According to the petition, on January 13, 2005, SiVault filed a demand for arbitration against WonderNet with the American Arbitration Association (the "AAA") in New York, New York. The arbitration relates to a dispute concerning a contract entered into by SiVault and WonderNet on August 15, 2003 (the "2003 agreement").

It is alleged that, by the 2003 agreement, WonderNet licensed SiVault, under its former name "Security Biometrics, Inc.", to exploit certain technology and proprietary property related to a software product that enables computers to analyze handwritten signatures, enabling such signatures to be captured and crypto-graphically bound to an electronic document, capable of authentication. According to the petition, SiVault delivered 2,500,000 shares of SiVault's restricted stock (pre-reverse split) to WonderNet along with certain cash payments in connection with the 2003 agreement.

According to SiVault's demand for arbitration, after entering into the 2003 agreement, SiVault discovered that WonderNet did not have the right to the technology within the relevant territory because the technology at issue infringed existing patents and the technology was otherwise without value. Through the arbitration, SiVault seeks rescission of its agreement with WonderNet and the return of the money and the restricted stock. Taylor has testified that SiVault's claim for damages in the arbitration exceeds $350,000.

Waisel has testified that the money and stock placed at issue in SiVault's petition and demand for arbitration were not, contrary to SiVault's representations, the subject of the 2003 agreement but, instead, were addressed in a prior agreement entered into in April 2002 (the "2002 agreement") by the parties. In a supplemental affidavit, Igor J. Schmidt, Chief Strategic Officer of SiVault ("Schmidt"), has acknowledged that the shares in question were issued in consideration of the rights granted by the 2002 agreement. Under the 2002 agreement, any controversy or claim arising under the agreement is to be settled by arbitration to be held in the courts of arbitration in London.

Following the parties' entry into the 2002 agreement and prior to the formation of the 2003 agreement, SiVault received notice from Communication Intelligence Corporation ("CIC") that SiVault was developing and marketing various applications alleged to fall within CIC's intellectual property rights, including CIC's patents.

According to Waisel, between December 2003 and March 2004, SiVault conducted extensive due diligence investigations of WonderNet in furtherance of an acquisition agreement entered into by the parties in December 2003, by which SiVault was to acquire WonderNet. On March 23, 2004, SiVault, under its former name, informed WonderNet that it would not be proceeding with the acquisition.

On September 21, 2004, SiVault informed WonderNet that it was revoking a portion of the 2003 agreement, and on September 23, 2004 SiVault informed WonderNet that the 2003 agreement was being cancelled. On November 21, 2004, WonderNet advised SiVault that unless a sum of $575,000—including, inter alia, $200,000 in fees under the aborted acquisition agreement as well as two quarterly payments under the 2003 agreement of $120,000 each—was paid no later than December 31, 2004, WonderNet would be pursuing legal options related to SiVault's alleged breach of the 2003 agreement. Schmidt has testified that after SiVault "terminated" the 2003 agreement, SiVault entered into a license agreement with CIC. (Supplemental Affidavit of Igor J. Schmidt, sworn to February 23, 2005 ("Schmidt Aff."), at ¶ 16.)

According to Waisel, on December 21, 2004, WonderNet began to take steps to remove the restrictive legend on its SiVault shares so that it could, at an appropriate time, sell the stock. On January 4, 2005, SiVault filed a form SB–2 registration statement with the Securities and Exchange Commission (the "SEC") to authorize the issuance of over 21 million new shares of common stock. SiVault commenced the present proceeding three weeks later with the filing of its petition.

In connection with the order to show cause issued by this Court and dated January 26, 2005, Bear, Stearns Securities Corp. and Interwest Transfer Co., Inc., inter alia, were temporarily enjoined and restrained from removing any restrictive legends from the certificate at issue and from otherwise taking any action to allow the shares to be sold or otherwise transferred to WonderNet. SiVault posted an undertaking in connection with the order to show cause and temporary restraining order in the amount of $15,000. The temporary restraint was continued by agreement of the parties and further extended by this Court by order dated February 16, 2005. Waisel has testified that the value of SiVault's shares has decreased substantially, falling from the closing price of $2.77 identified in the petition as of January 14, 2005 to $1.90 as of March 8, 2005, which difference amounts to a loss of some $92,000 in the value of the 106,250 shares at issue.

Following an adjournment at the request of the parties, a hearing on SiVault's petition was held on February 16, 2005, after which the return date for the petition was adjourned to permit further briefing. The petition was deemed fully submitted on March 9, 2005.

Applicable Legal Standards

Pursuant to Rule 64, Fed.R.Civ.P.,

At the commencement of and during the course of an action, all remedies providing for seizure of person or property for the purposes of securing satisfaction of the judgment ultimately to be entered in the action are available under the circumstances and in the manner provided by the law of the state in which the district court is held, existing at the time the remedy is sought. . . .

Fed.R.Civ.P. 64. SiVault's petition for an order of attachment is, accordingly, governed by New York law.

Under New York law,

The supreme court in the county in which an arbitration is pending . . . may entertain an application for an order of attachment or for a preliminary injunction in connection with an arbitrable controversy, but only upon the ground that the award to which the applicant may be entitled may be rendered ineffectual without such provisional relief. The provisions of articles 62 and 63 of this chapter shall apply to the application, including those relating to undertakings and to the time for commencement of an action (arbitration shall be deemed an action for this purpose) if the application is made before commencement, except that the sole ground for the granting of the remedy shall be as stated above. . . .

N.Y. C.P.L.R. § 7502(c). Articles 62 and 63, rendered applicable to petitions brought under Section 7502(c) by the terms of that section, set forth the rules pertaining to prejudgment attachments and preliminary injunctions, respectively. See N.Y. C.P.L.R. § 6201 et seq.; N.Y. C.P.L.R. § 6301 et seq.

Article 62 provides, in pertinent part, that a party seeking to obtain an order of attachment must show,

by affidavit and such other written evidence as may be submitted, that there is a cause of action, that it is probable that the plaintiff will succeed on the merits, that one or more grounds for attachment provided in section 6201 exist, and that the amount demanded from the defendant exceeds all counterclaims known to the plaintiff.

N.Y. C.P.L.R. § 6212(a); *cf. SG Cowen Secs. Corp. v. Messih*, 224 F.3d 79, 83–84 (2d Cir.2000) (noting disagreement among New York state courts but concluding that Article 63 criteria must be applied in considering motions for preliminary injunctions brought under Section 7502(c)). Thus, pursuant to Section 7502(c), the standard articulated in Section 6212(a) applies to SiVault's application for an order of attachment, except insofar as Section 6212(a) requires the party seeking an attachment to demonstrate the existence of "one or more grounds for attachment" identified in N.Y. C.P.L.R. § 6201.[1] The sole ground relevant to an application for an order of attachment brought under Section 7502(c) is "that the award to which the applicant may be entitled may be rendered ineffectual without such provisional relief." N.Y. C.P.L.R. § 7502(c).

"[E]ven if the plaintiff satisfies all of the statutory requirements for an order of attachment, the issuance of relief remains in the discretion of the Court, because attachment is recognized to be a harsh and extraordinary remedy." *JSC Foreign Economic Ass'n Technostroyexport v. Int'l Dev. & Trade Servs., Inc.*, 306 F.Supp.2d 482, 485 (S.D.N.Y.2004) (citing *Bank of China v. NBM L.L.C.*, 192 F.Supp.2d 183, 186 (S.D.N.Y.2002); * * *. "Attachment is considered a harsh remedy and the statute is strictly construed in favor of those against whom it may be employed." *Glazer & Gottlieb v. Nachman*, 234 A.D.2d 105, 105, 650 N.Y.S.2d 717, 717 (N.Y.App.Div. 1st Dept.1996) (internal citations omitted).

Discussion

Turning to the first condition set forth in Section 6212(a), SiVault has demonstrated by documentary evidence and affidavits the existence of a cause of action pertaining to the alleged falsity of certain representations made by WonderNet in connection with the 2003 Agreement, representations concerning WonderNet's ownership of intellectual property rights in the underlying technology. SiVault has offered testimony from which an inference may be drawn that these allegedly false representations were knowingly made and that SiVault relied upon the representations to its detriment. Contrary to

---

[1] The grounds for attachment set forth in Section 6201 are, by the express terms of Section 7205(c), inapplicable to petitions for orders of attachment brought pursuant to that latter section. See N.Y. C.P.L.R. § 7502(c) ("The provisions of articles 62 and 63 of this chapter shall apply to the application . . . except that the sole ground for the granting of the remedy shall be as stated above.") * * *; *see also County Natwest Secs. Corp. USA v. Jesup, Josephthal & Co., Inc.*, 180 A.D.2d 468, 469, 579 N.Y.S.2d 376, 377 (N.Y.App.Div. 1st Dept.1992) (observing that "the standards generally applicable to attachments pursuant to [N.Y. C.P.L.R. §] 6201(3), such as sinister maneuvers or fraudulent conduct, are not required to be shown in an application pursuant to [N.Y. C.P.L.R. §] 7502(c)") (*citing Drexel Burnham Lambert Inc. v. Ruebsamen*, 139 A.D.2d 323, 531 N.Y.S.2d 547 (N.Y.App.Div. 1st Dept.1988)); *Erickson v. Kidder Peabody & Co.*, 166 Misc.2d 1, 4, 630 N.Y.S.2d 861, 862 (N.Y.Sup.Ct.N.Y.Cty.1995) ("By its terms, [section] 7502(c) replaces only the 'grounds' which must be established for a grant of an attachment or injunctive relief, which are set forth in sections 6201 and 6301 respectively. The remainder of these articles still apply. Therefore, a party seeking provisional relief under [section] 7502(c) must still establish, among other things, the existence of a valid cause of action and grounds for relief.") (citing N.Y. C.P.L.R. §§ 6212(a), 6312(a)).

WonderNet's suggestion, SiVault's knowledge of CIC's allegations of infringement prior to entry into the 2003 agreement does not preclude SiVault from asserting the instant claim, whatever the ultimate effect of that knowledge on the determination of SiVault's arbitration claim may be.

There is relatively little in the record to demonstrate the likelihood that SiVault will succeed on the merits of its claim against WonderNet, the second condition set by Section 6212(a). Notwithstanding the sparsity of the record, however, the Court is mindful that,

> *[A]rbitration is frequently marked by great flexibility in procedure, choice of law, legal and equitable analysis, evidence, and remedy. Success on the merits in arbitration therefore cannot be predicted with the confidence a court would have in predicting the merits of a dispute awaiting litigation in court, and it can be expected that when the merits are in the hands of an arbitrator, this element of the analysis will naturally have greatly reduced influence.*

SG Cowen Secs., 224 F.3d at 84. Accordingly, SiVault's application for an order of attachment will not be denied for failure to establish the likelihood of success on the merits in the underlying arbitration.

With respect to the third condition, the ground for attachment, SiVault has offered testimony to the effect that WonderNet possesses no assets in the United States other than the shares at issue here, that WonderNet had a negative net worth as of the end of 2002, and that WonderNet has borrowed $1,000,000 from a bank in Israel, a loan secured by all of WonderNet's assets. On this record which suggests WonderNet's potential insolvency, SiVault has established that a ground for an attachment exists insofar as the award to which SiVault may be entitled may be rendered ineffectual without the attachment sought. See N.Y. C.P.L.R. § 7502(c). WonderNet's assertions that SiVault's claims, if found to be meritorious, would be fully compensable in money damages rather than in the form of shares and that arbitration awards rendered in the United States are fully enforceable in Israel under the United Nations Convention on the Recognition and Enforcement of Foreign Arbitral Awards, June 10, 1958, 21 U.S.T. 2517, 330 U.N.T.S. 38, do not undermine this conclusion.

With respect to the fourth and final condition for an order of attachment, the record demonstrates that WonderNet informed SiVault of certain demands against SiVault in November 2004, including demands in the amount of $240,000 arising out of the 2003 agreement as well as an additional $200,000 pursuant to the aborted acquisition agreement between the parties. In its papers submitted in opposition to SiVault's petition, WonderNet has asserted that these demands "will be filed in the underlying arbitration," (Resp. Opp. Mem. at 5), thereby demonstrating that the informal demands have yet to take shape as formal counterclaims in the underlying arbitration. In view of this acknowledgment that no counterclaims have yet been filed in the underlying arbitration, the record establishes that "the amount demanded from the defendant exceeds all counterclaims known to the plaintiff." N.Y. C.P.L.R. § 6212(a).[3]

In an exercise of the Court's discretion, SiVault's application for an order of attachment is, accordingly, granted, provided that SiVault posts an undertaking in the amount of $100,000.00 within five (5) days of entry of this opinion and order.

SiVault consistently has consented to securing the sought after attachment with a bond, first suggesting a bond in the amount of $15,000.00, five percent of the approximate $300,000.00 value of WonderNet's shares (Order To Show Cause, Jan. 19, 2005, at ¶ 10), and then subsequently increasing the suggested bond amount to $50,000.00, to "protect WonderNet from any diminution of the share price during the arbitration" (Supplemental Affidavit of Wayne Taylor, sworn to Feb. 23, 2005, at ¶ 12). Given the need to secure WonderNet's shares from substantial loss in value pending arbitration, a premise which SiVault does not contest, an undertaking in the amount of $100.000.00 adequately protects WonderNet from market volatility and any possible dilution.

The grant of SiVault's petition should not be construed to limit or otherwise express any view as to the facts that may be found in the arbitration between the parties or the ultimate disposition of the parties' arguments by the arbitration panel.

It is so ordered.

NOTES

Facts

1. What is the procedural sequence of events? When did SiVault file its demand for arbitration against WonderNet? When did SiVault commence the court action?

---

[3] Insofar as SiVault has argued in its supplemental papers that it will suffer irreparable harm if an attachment is not granted and that the balance of equities tips in its favors, these factors are relevant only where an application for injunctive relief has been brought, as demonstrated by the authorities SiVault has cited. SiVault has sought no injunctive relief here apart from the temporary injunctive relief requested pending a hearing on the application for an attachment, which request has been granted.

2.   What relief does SiVault seek?

3.   What is the harm SiVault asserts it would suffer if that relief is not granted?

4.   How much information did SiVault submit addressing its chance to succeed on the merits? Is that information sufficient for the court?

Law

1.   What is the basis for the court's action in this case? Federal law? State law? Why does it matter?

2.   What showing does New York Civil Practice Law and Rules (N.Y. C.P.L.R.) section 7502(c) require? How does it relate to other sections of N.Y. C.P.L.R.?

C) Interim Relief and Third Parties

Frequently, parties need to seek orders in aid of arbitration directed at a third party, typically a bank holding funds in an account. An arbitrator could order a party not to move such funds, but would have no authority to enjoin the bank from executing such a transfer should be a party to arbitration simply ignore the arbitrator's ruling.

The case below illustrates the difficulties in finding the "correct" third party against whom a court can issue injunctive relief in aid of arbitration.

International Legal Consulting Ltd. v. Malabu Oil and Gas Ltd.

35 Misc. 3d 1203(A), 950 N.Y.S.2d 723 (N.Y. Sup. Ct., Mar. 15 2012)

BERNARD J. FRIED, J.

* * *

This proceeding arises out of the alleged breach of an "Engagement Letter and Fee Agreement" entered into by ILC and Malabu dated January 19, 2010 (the Fee Agreement). ILC is a consulting company incorporated under the laws of the British Virgin Islands with its principal place of business in Limassol, Cyprus. * * * ILC was engaged to provide negotiation and consulting services in order to facilitate Malabu's transfer of all or part of its interest in "OPL 245," an Oil Prospecting License over oil block 245 in Nigeria. OPL 245 has been the subject of various lawsuits since the license was originally granted to Malabu in 1998, revoked by the Federal Government of Nigeria (FGN) in 2001, and then re-allocated to Malabu in 2006 and 2010.

* * *

ILC contends that it fully performed its obligations under the Fee Agreement entitling it to a 6% success fee amounting to $65,522,400, and that Malabu has indicated that it will not pay this amount. The Fee Agreement provides that it is to be governed by English law and that disputes shall be settled by arbitration in London, England under the Rules of the London Court of International Arbitration by a sole arbitrator. An arbitration proceeding against Malabu was commenced on or about July 22, 2011.

ILC commenced this special proceeding against Malabu on June 27, 2011, seeking an attachment in aid of arbitration pursuant to CPLR 6211 and 7502(c). On June 28, 2011, this court issued an *ex parte* order of attachment to ILC securing the sum of $74,695,936 based on the contention of ILC's principal, Ednan Agaev, that the escrow account holding the proceeds of the sale of OPL 245 was at JPMorgan Chase & Co. (JPMorgan) in New York. Agaev Aff., ¶ 2. It is now undisputed that JPMorgan does not presently hold any moneys in any account which is held in the name of Malabu, including an escrow account to or for the order of Malabu, and that the bank account at issue herein was established with a London branch of JPMorgan and is held in the name of the FGN.

* * *

Initially, the money from the proceeds of the sale of OPL 245 was placed in an escrow account pursuant to an escrow agreement dated May 4, 2011 by and between the FGN, NAE, SNEPCO and "J.P. Morgan Chase Bank, N.A., London branch as Escrow Agent" (Escrow Agreement No. 2). * * * The escrow account was funded by NAE on behalf of NAE and SNEPCO on May 23, 2011. According to clause 3 of the Resolution Agreement, once the FGN confirmed that it had achieved the full and final resolution of all claims and issues in dispute over OPL 245 and obtained a release from all claims, Escrow Agreement No. 2 was to be terminated and the money held in the escrow account was to be paid into the London depository account. JPMorgan received an "Escrow Completion Notice" from NAE and SNEPCO instructing its London branch to deposit the funds into the London depository account, and this instruction was carried out on May 24, 2011. Thus, as of the filing of this proceeding, no funds were being held in escrow and all of the proceeds of the sale of OPL 245 were being held in the London depository account.

In a letter dated July 15, 2011 and in connection with [other ongoing] litigation, Malabu's lawyers advised London counsel for JPMorgan as follows:

1.   Malabu is not a customer nor account holder of JP Morgan, nor party to escrow arrangements with JP Morgan.

2.   Malabu has no legal or beneficial interest in any funds held by JP Morgan.

3.   Malabu has no power to dispose of any funds held by JP Morgan.

4.   For the avoidance of doubt, Malabu has a contractual right to receive sums from the Federal Government of Nigeria. Malabu understands that those sums may be paid from funds held by JP Morgan on behalf of the FGN, but this a matter for the FGN.

* * *

At oral argument of these motions on October 13, 2011, this court was advised that the sole arbitrator in the London arbitration had been appointed. Counsel for ILC also advised that no application for injunctive relief had been filed with the arbitrator, upon the advice of ILC's English counsel, because the arbitrator would not have authority to direct JPMorgan, a non-party to the arbitration agreement, to do anything. * * *

"It is well established that, where personal jurisdiction is lacking, a New York court cannot attach property not within its jurisdiction. It is a fundamental rule that in attachment proceedings the res must be within the jurisdiction of the court issuing the process, in order to confer jurisdiction." *Koehler v. Bank of Bermuda Ltd.*, 12 NY3d 533, 538–539 (2009) (internal quotations omitted) * * *.

ILC argues that the London depository account is a debt owed by JPMorgan * * *, and that the *situs* of the debt is the location of the debtor * * *. Since JPMorgan is headquartered here, ILC maintains that the *situs* of the debt is New York. Where, however, the debtor is a bank with more than one branch, it is well established in New York that the *situs* of a bank account is fixed at the branch of the bank where the account is carried. * * * While it may be the case that the $1,092,040,000 from NAE and/or SNEPCO was wire-transferred through New York at one point in time, the documentary evidence is clear that the money was placed in escrow with "JPMorgan Chase Bank, NA London Branch" (see Escrow Agreement No. 2, at 1, 3) and was transferred on May 24, 2011 to a London branch of JPMorgan. When this proceeding was commenced on June 27, 2011, and at present, the *res* is located in London, England.

Relying on *Hotel 71 Mezz Lender LLC v. Falor* (14 NY3d 303, supra), and *Koehler v. Bank of Bermuda Ltd.* (12 NY3d 533, supra), ILC contends that a New York court may order an attachment of a debtor's out-of-state assets held by a garnishee bank over whom the court has *in personam* jurisdiction. There is no dispute that the potential judgment debtor here is Malabu, a Nigerian company which has not consented to jurisdiction in New York and has not appeared in this proceeding. ILC argues that the garnishee is JPMorgan over whom the court admittedly has jurisdiction.

JPMorgan, however, is not in possession of any assets belonging to Malabu, and thus is not a proper garnishee for Malabu's assets under the CPLR. CPLR 6202 provides, in relevant part:

> *"Any debt . . . against which a money judgment may be enforced as provided in section 5201 is subject to attachment. The proper garnishee of any such . . . debt is the person designated in section 5201; . . ."*

Section 5201(a), in turn, provides:

> *"A money judgment may be enforced against any debt, which is past due or which is yet to become due, certainly or upon demand of the judgment debtor, . . ."*

The debt in this case—the London depository account—is money owed to the FGN by JPMorgan, and is not "due, certainly or upon demand of" Malabu.

ILC argues that there is no question that the remaining funds in the London depository account belong to Malabu as the proceeds from the transfer of Malabu's rights in OPL 245. ILC cites to clause 1.3 of the "Block 245 Resolution Agreement," which provides for the payment by NAE of the sum of $1,092,040,000 into an escrow account "for the purposes of FGN settling all and any existing claims and/or issues over Block 245 . . ." Notably, however, Malabu is nowhere mentioned in this document. While it does appear that the FGN was indeed the proverbial "straw man" holding $1.1 billion for ultimate payment to Malabu, the name of the holder of the London account is and has always been the FGN, even if Malabu has a contractual or equitable right to those funds. *See Bradford v. Chase Natl. Bank of City of NY*, 24 F Supp 28, 38 (SD N.Y.1938) (best, if not only way, to show possession of a bank account is by showing in whose name the account stands) ＊ ＊ ＊. Indeed, the Depository Agreement clearly provides that the customer is the FGN, and that even if the FGN is acting as agent on behalf of another person, "the Customer alone shall be treated as the Depository's customer." ＊ ＊ ＊

The remaining funds in the London depository account are not payable by JPMorgan at the demand of Malabu, and thus the proper garnishee here is the FGN, which is not named as a respondent. While counsel for ILC claimed the FGN was given notice of these proceedings, and that their consulate in New York "was served by the sheriff according to the attachment" (10/13/11 Tr. at

6), no affidavit of service has been filed with the court. Property of an unserved party cannot be levied upon. Ward v. Kent Props., 102 A.D.2d 771 (1st Dept 1984).

Even assuming that JPMorgan is a proper garnishee, the question arises as to whether service on the New York offices of JPMorgan is sufficient to render accounts maintained at this bank in London subject to attachment. JPMorgan argues that the "separate entity rule" bars this method of establishing jurisdiction over bank accounts that are situated outside of New York. * * *

"The general rule in New York is that in order to reach a particular bank account the judgment creditor must serve the office of the bank where the account is maintained." * * *. "The separate entity rule was historically justified on the basis of both the impracticability of requiring constant transmission of reports on the status of accounts in one branch to all other branches, and on the recognition that any banking operation in a foreign country is necessarily subject to the foreign sovereign's own laws and regulations. . . ." Healey & Maris, *New York Court Determines That Banks Still Have the Protection of the "Separate Entity" Doctrine After Koehler*, 128 Banking LJ 668, 669 [2011]).

* * *

Therefore since jurisdiction to order a pre-judgment attachment of the London depository account is lacking, ILC's motion to confirm the order of attachment is, denied, and the *ex parte* order of attachment issued on June 28, 2011 is vacated.

JPMorgan also argues that a preliminary injunction is unavailable, because ILC is merely an unsecured creditor who seeks only money damages against Malabu. * * * Provisional injunctive relief has historically been "limited to equitable actions where the defendant threatened to violate the rights of the plaintiff respecting the subject of the action, which would tend to render the judgment ineffectual." *Credit Agricole Indosuez v. Rossiyskiy Kredit Bank*, 94 N.Y.2d 541, 545 (2000). * * *

An exception to the general rule exists where the subject of the action involves a specific fund. The classic case is *Sau Thi Ma v. Xuan T. Lien* (198 A.D.2d 186 [1st Dept 1993]), where a woman claimed that her husband's uncle had stolen her winning $8 million lottery ticket. Although the ultimate relief sought by the plaintiff was monetary damages, her motion for preliminary injunctive relief ordering future lottery payments to be held in escrow was granted, because the action was directed at a specific fund of money of which the plaintiff claimed ownership. * * *

ILC argues that this exception to the general rule in *Credit Agricole* applies here since ILC's claim against Malabu in the London arbitration seeks a portion of a specific fund, that is, ILC's claim in the arbitration seeks to recover a success fee of $65,522.400, representing 6% of the $1,092,040,000 in proceeds from the transfer of Malabu's rights to OPL 245. Although ILC makes this argument, the demand for arbitration that ILC actually filed with the London Court of International Arbitration * * * makes no mention of the London depository account or the proceeds of the sale of OPL 245, does not seek specific performance of any contractual right to payment of the 6% success fee from any particular bank account or fund of money, and seeks only a sum of money from Malabu for breach of the Fee Agreement. While the amount of the success fee and the timing of the payment of that fee is tied to the "Purchase Consideration" received by Malabu for the sale of its rights in OPL 245 (see Fee Agreement, § 3.1), there is nothing in the Fee Agreement or arbitration demand that tie's ILC's right to payment to the proceeds of the sale of OPL 245. * * * As such, ILC is merely an unsecured potential creditor whose ultimate objective is attaining an enforceable money judgment against Malabu. As such, preliminary injunctive relief pursuant to CPLR 6301 is not available.

ILC also argues that *Credit Agricole* is distinguishable, because ILC seeks a preliminary injunction in aid of arbitration. The 2005 amendment to CPLR 7502(c) allegedly permits the issuance of a preliminary injunction to secure a money award, as long as the award to which the applicant may be entitled may be rendered "ineffectual" without the preliminary injunction and the three traditional criteria for injunctive relief are met. However, the 2005 substantive amendment to CPLR 7502(c) merely eliminated the uncertainty that then existed as to whether the provisional remedies of attachment and injunction could be sought in connection with arbitrations pending outside of New York and even outside the United States. * * * Indeed, the only case ILC cites in support of this argument, namely *In re XTF Global Asset Mgt.*, LLC (2010 WL 1116450 [Sup Ct, N.Y. County 2010]), does not mention the 2005 amendment to the statute. More importantly, this decision does not cite or discuss the 2008 decision by the Second Department in *Winter v. Brown* (49 AD3d 526), squarely applying *Credit Agricole* in the arbitration context and concluding that the issuance of a preliminary injunction in aid of arbitration pursuant to CPLR 7502(c) was in error absent some proof that the monies sought to be restrained were part of any specific res or fund which could rightly be regarded as the "subject of the action." * * *

* * *

For the foregoing reasons, petitioner ILC's motion, pursuant to CPLR 7502(c), for a preliminary injunction in aid of arbitration is denied. ILC has made an oral request for time to take other steps to protect its client should the court deny its motion and dissolve the TRO in place. See 10/13/11 Tr. at 49. While I am not inclined to grant a lengthy stay, however, since the TRO was always intended to be an interim measure to protect ILC's rights until an appropriate application could be made in the jurisdiction where the arbitration is pending and the funds at issue are located. I am informed that the London arbitrator is without power to issue any injunctive relief and no such application appears to have been made in any English court of law. Under these circumstances, a stay of twenty (20) days is warranted. Petitioner's motion, pursuant to CPLR 6211(b), to confirm the ex parte order of attachment is also denied, and the amended petition is denied and the proceeding dismissed.

* * *

CHAPTER 14

Jurisdictional Objections

One of the key battlegrounds in most arbitrations is the jurisdiction of the arbitral tribunal. You have already encountered the substantive law governing challenges to the jurisdiction of the arbitral tribunal in chapters 4–7. Chapters 4–7 outlined what jurisdictional objections a party could raise. It further detailed the proper forum—the arbitral tribunal or the courts—for such jurisdictional objections.

This chapter addresses now addresses how jurisdictional objections have to be pled in arbitration proceedings themselves. As the readings below show, failure appropriately to brief jurisdictional objections within the context of the arbitral proceedings works a waiver of the relevant objections. It is therefore of critical importance to understand the arbitral procedure for raising jurisdictional objections in arbitration

Fact Scenario

Look back at the fact scenario from chapter 11 onward. Hardmont's Demand for Arbitration is short, simply filling out the AAA short form. It summarizes the nature of the dispute as follows:

> *Hardmont LLC claims against Acme Industries Corp., RRF Corp. and Mervin Gilmore jointly and severally for breach of contract, unjust enrichment, estoppel, conversion, tortious interference with business, and violation of state and/or federal laws.*

The demand specifies that the "Dollar Amount of Claim $" is "to be determined" and specifies that Hardmont will seek attorneys fees, interest, arbitration costs, punitive/exemplary damages and any other relief to which Hardmont may be entitled at law or equity.

As stated already, the arbitration in the Non-Disclosure Agreement upon which Hardmont relies states as follows:

9.   Arbitration

Any controversy or claim arising out of or relating to this contract, or the breach thereof, shall be settled by arbitration administered by the

American Arbitration Association under its Commercial Arbitration Rules, and judgment on the award rendered by the arbitrator(s) may be entered in any court having jurisdiction thereof.

_____/s/_____

Martin Gunther

Hardmont LLC

_____/s/_____

Mervin Gilmore

CEO, Acme Industries Corp.

Develop the jurisdictional objections that Acme, RRF, and Gilmore should raise, how and when they should be raised, what documents Acme, RRF and Gilmore would need to give their counsel to support the objections, what discovery is needed to develop them, and what procedural schedule needs to be in place to maximize the chances of success.

Readings

A) Timing of Jurisdictional Objections

The first procedural question is when jurisdictional objections have to be raised. Most arbitration rules provide guidance on this issue. As the case law below makes clear, failure to abide by these rules can have the effect of waiving jurisdictional objections.

AAA Commercial Arbitration Rules

Rule 7

* * *

A party must object to the jurisdiction of the arbitrator or to the arbitrability of a claim or counterclaim no later than the filing of the answering statement to the claim or counterclaim that gives rise to the objection. The arbitrator may rule on such objections as a preliminary matter or as part of the final award.

NOTES

1. AAA Commercial Arbitration Rule 5 states that "A respondent may file an answering statement with the AAA within 14 calendar days after notice of the filing of the Demand is sent by the AAA. The respondent shall, at the

time of any such filing, send a copy of any answering statement to the claimant and to all other parties to the arbitration. If no answering statement is filed within the stated time, the respondent will be deemed to deny the claim." Does that mean that a party must raise a jurisdictional objection within 14 calendar days after notice of the filing of the Demand for Arbitration is sent by the AAA? The Demand for Arbitration is the first document filed in an arbitration. Does this place the respondent in an arbitration at a disadvantage?

2.　Consider AAA Commercial Arbitration Rule 42. What should a party do in order to preserve the maximum flexibility should it wish to file a jurisdictional objection? Of whom would it have to make the request in question?

Fortune, Alsweet and Eldridge, Inc. v. Daniel

724 F.2d 1355 (9th Cir. 1983)

PER CURIAM:

Daniel appeals from a district court order confirming an arbitration award in favor of Fortune, Alsweet & Eldridge, Inc. (Fortune), trustee of the Independent Contractors Grievance and Arbitration Trust. The district court held that Daniel's failure to make a motion to vacate the arbitration award within the appropriate statutory period barred Daniel from asserting defenses to Fortune's petition for confirmation of the award. The district court also found that by his conduct, Daniel had agreed to arbitrate the dispute. We affirm.

State statutes of limitation apply to motions to vacate arbitration awards in labor cases. *San Diego District Council of Carpenters v. Cory*, 685 F.2d 1137, 1139, 1142 (9th Cir.1983). In California, the relevant statutory period is the 100-day period contained in section 1288 of the California Civil Procedure Code. In the case before us, Daniel failed to make a motion to vacate within 100 days after the entry of the arbitration award. Therefore, the only issue for the district court to decide was "whether the parties agreed to arbitrate the subject in dispute."

Fortune asserts that Daniel agreed to arbitrate under the terms of a Memorandum Agreement, which supplemented an earlier Master Labor Agreement signed by Daniel. Daniel, on the other hand, contends that he terminated all agreements with the Carpenters Union prior to the grievances that are the subject of this case. Fortune disputes the efficacy of Daniel's attempted termination. We do not decide whether Daniel's termination notice effectively ended any duty he may have had to arbitrate under the Master Labor Agreement and its successor agreements. The district court found that Daniel's continued payments to the Grievance and Arbitration Trust Fund for almost a year following his termination notice demonstrated an implicit acceptance of the arbitration clause contained in the Memorandum Agreement. * * * We need not decide the issue, however, since there is additional conduct which more directly sustains the district court finding that Daniel implicitly agreed to arbitration.

Arbitration is undeniably a matter of contract and parties are bound by arbitration awards only if they agreed to arbitrate the matter. An agreement to arbitrate an issue need not be express; however, it may be implied from the conduct of the parties. Daniel's conduct in the case before us amply demonstrates an intent to arbitrate his dispute with the Carpenters Union.

In response to a notice that an arbitration hearing would be held, Daniel's representative sent a letter to the Arbitration Board stating that it would represent Daniel before the Arbitration Board, under "Section 5(d) of the Independent Contractors Grievance and Arbitration Procedures." Daniel's representative attended the first arbitration hearing and stated that Daniel "would probably appear at the arbitration." He requested and was granted a continuance. Daniel's representation also attended the second arbitration hearing on this matter and listened to all of the evidence presented by the union. After the union had ended its presentation, Daniel's representative presented some evidence and asked for and received a second continuance "to secure witnesses to refute the evidence presented by the union." Two weeks later, Daniel's representative sent a letter to the Arbitration Board denying Daniel's obligation to arbitrate the dispute and refusing to attend any further hearings. The arbitrator subsequently rendered a decision adverse to Daniel.

We have long recognized a rule that a party may not submit a claim to arbitration and then challenge the authority of the arbitrator to act after receiving an unfavorable result. *Ficek v. Southern Pacific Co.*, 338 F.2d at 657. Although Daniel attempted to deny the authority of the arbitrator prior to the arbitrator's final decision, we find the principles announced in *Ficek* equally applicable to the present case. It would be unreasonable and unjust to allow Daniel to challenge the legitimacy of the arbitration process, in which he had voluntarily participated over a period of several months, shortly before the arbitrator announced her decision. The policy of the law is to support the enforcement of arbitration awards because arbitration promotes the speedy resolution of labor disputes. Allowing Daniel to reject arbitration at this late stage of the arbitration process would frustrate that policy.

We therefore conclude that there is ample evidence to support the finding by the district court that Daniel's conduct demonstrated he agreed to submit this conflict to arbitration and waived any right to object.

The order of the district court confirming the arbitration award is AFFIRMED.

NOTES

Facts

1. How long did Daniel wait to raise a jurisdictional objection?

2. Before raising the jurisdictional objection in question, did Daniel make any statements that he would accept arbitral jurisdiction?

3. Did the court mention or rely upon arbitration rules that required the raising of a jurisdictional objection by a certain time?

Law

1. The court relies particularly upon a policy of the swift resolution of labor disputes. Do you think that the case can be distinguished on that basis in the context of a commercial dispute?

2. Under *Daniel,* could one argue that there should be some leeway for the raising of a jurisdictional objection after the Rule 7 period has lapsed? By what time is *Daniel* plainly applicable? What about the procedural milestones before that step?

3. What about the discovery of new facts? Should those preclude the raising of a new jurisdictional objection? What does AAA Commercial Arbitration Rule 7 say about this? How would you argue the point for a client wishing to raise the objection?

B) Substance of Jurisdictional Objections

Not only do parties have objecting to jurisdiction keep to deadlines regarding the timing of their objections, they also must be mindful that the substance of their objections may work a waiver. Further, the arbitration rules themselves may only permit certain kinds of jurisdictional objections, meaning that an objection will have to plead in keeping with the requirements of the arbitral rules in question.

AAA Commercial Arbitration Rules

Rule 7

* * *

The arbitrator shall have the power to determine the existence or validity of a contract of which an arbitration clause forms a part. Such an arbitration clause shall be treated as an agreement independent of the other terms of the contract. A decision by the arbitrator that the contract is null and void shall not for that reason alone render invalid the arbitration clause.

* * *

NOTES

1. Working backwards from the rule, how does a party have to plead a jurisdictional objection?

2. Consider the final sentence of the excerpted section from Rule 7. What doctrine discussed in part I does this instruction to the arbitrator track?

3. Put yourself in the shoes of counsel for an aggrieved customer of *Buckeye Cashing* excepted in Part I. The Florida Supreme Court deemed the underlying contract to be void for illegality and thus concluded that the arbitration agreement was void with it—i.e., there was nothing to submit to arbitration. The United States Supreme Court disagreed and remanded. How do you have to plead the case to the arbitral tribunal? Can your client raise a jurisdictional objection in arbitration or is the usurious nature of the underlying contract a defense exclusively to the merits of the claim?

Lewis v. Circuit City Stores, Inc.

500 F.3d 1140 (10th Cir. 2007)

EBEL, CIRCUIT JUDGE.

Plaintiff-Appellant Michael Lewis brought suit against his former employer, Defendant-Appellee Circuit City, for wrongful termination, based on alleged retaliation against Lewis for seeking workers' compensation benefits, a tort recognized by Kansas. However, Lewis has already arbitrated a claim of retaliatory discharge against Circuit City, pursuant to an arbitration agreement he signed with his employment application, and lost on the merits of that claim. Yet Lewis now brings the very same claim of retaliatory discharge in court based on the same incident and harm alleged in the arbitration proceeding against

Circuit City. Looking to well-settled law, we conclude that Lewis's claim is barred by claim preclusion. We also hold that Lewis has waived his argument that the arbitration agreement is invalid under contract law, because he proceeded through arbitration without objecting to the agreement's enforceability. In addition, we conclude that Lewis's argument that the arbitration decision violates public policy has no merit. Finally, we conclude that sanctions are not appropriate in this case. Accordingly, we AFFIRM the district court's dismissal of Lewis's suit on summary judgment and DENY Circuit City's motion for sanctions.

I.   BACKGROUND

Lewis's Employment with Circuit City

Michael Lewis became a full-time employee of Circuit City in September 1996 as a "roadshop manager." In February 1997, he injured his knee while installing an automobile alarm, and sought medical treatment through a workers' compensation claim. He states that over the years he has "continued to have problems" with his knee and, at various times, notified Circuit City of those problems. Lewis informed his supervisor in writing in November 2002 that he still had pain in his knee and requested to see a medical specialist, but allegedly did not receive a response.

Circuit City terminated Lewis on January 6, 2003. The parties dispute the reason for Lewis's termination. Lewis claims that after he requested additional medical treatment in November 2002, his supervisor's attitude toward Lewis "became hostile and retaliatory," and Lewis was disciplined and suspended. On those facts, Lewis claims that Circuit City wrongfully terminated him in retaliation for filing a worker's compensation claim.

Circuit City states that it terminated Lewis because he violated the company's weapons policy, a violation brought to the company's attention by employee Mike Guerrero. In early December 2002, Lewis had a "confrontation" with Guerrero that resulted in Guerrero "walking off the job." Guerrero then called an employer-provided telephone hotline to complain about Lewis. His complaint included allegations that Lewis had brought a gun to work and had cleaned it at the work counter. When questioned, Lewis admitted that he had brought a "pistol grip and slide" to work to repair it, and that he worked on it out of view of any customers. He said these were only "parts" of a handgun, not an operable handgun, and therefore the weapons policy did not apply. However, four members of Circuit City's management reviewed this information, decided that it was a violation of the weapons policy, and concluded that termination was warranted.

Although Lewis brought a Title VII claim in arbitration, this factual dispute is of no import. Lewis did not bring a Title VII claim in his complaint in court. His claim was only for the tort of retaliatory discharge as recognized by Kansas common law. See infra.

The Arbitration Agreement

When Lewis applied for employment in 1996, his application included a Dispute Resolution Agreement (the "arbitration agreement") in which he agreed to settle any claims arising out of his application process or any future employment with Circuit City "exclusively by final and binding arbitration before a neutral Arbitrator." The agreement covered any claims

> *arising under federal, state or local statutory or common law . . . includ [ing], but not limited to . . . Title VII of the Civil Rights Act of 1964, as amended, . . . state discrimination statutes, state statutes and/or common law regulating employment termination, the law of contract or the law of tort: including, but not limited to, claims for . . . wrongful discharge . . . and intentional/negligent infliction of emotional distress or defamation. Statutory or common law claims alleging that Circuit City retaliated or discriminated against an Associate shall be subject to arbitration.*

The agreement contained a statement that signing the agreement was a condition of being considered for employment by Circuit City, and that arbitration would be conducted in accordance with the Circuit City Dispute Resolution Rules and Procedures (the "arbitration procedures"). Lewis signed this statement. He does not dispute that he received notice of the procedures. The procedures specified that although the substantive law of the state in which Lewis was employed would apply to any claims raised in arbitration, decisions and awards would be enforceable through the Federal Arbitration Act ("FAA"), 9 U.S.C. §§ 1, et seq., and the Uniform Arbitration Act of Virginia, Va.Code Ann. § 8:01–581.01, et seq.

Procedural History

Lewis submitted an Arbitration Request Form in April 2003, identifying his intended counsel as David Alegria. In this form, he claimed that he was fired because he had informed his supervisor "that my knee had been hurt at work and I needed medical attention." He requested that his position be "restored with back pay." This form, which he signed, stated that he agreed "to accept the decision and award of the Arbitrator as final and binding." Lewis submitted another Arbitration Request Form in August 2003, which included more details about the nature of his complaint, made specific claims under the Kansas Act Against Discrimination, Kan. Stat. Ann. § 44–1001, et seq., and Title VII of the Civil Rights Act, 42 U.S.C. § 2000e, et seq., and made a generalized claim for retaliatory discharge under state law.FN3 Lewis requested five years' worth of annual compensation (totaling $226,910), medical reimbursement, $500,000 for emotional distress, unspecified punitive damages, and attorneys fees. This request, prepared by Alegria, did not include the statement agreeing to accept the decision and award of the arbitrator.

The arbitration hearing commenced February 25, 2004, and ended February 27, 2004. Pursuant to the procedures, a single arbitrator heard the matter. While it is not clear what the full extent of discovery was, or the nature of the hearing, the record includes a set of interrogatories completed by Lewis, several references to witness testimony, an acknowledgment of evidence and post-hearing briefs, and an apparently unsuccessful attempt to subpoena Guerrero for the hearing.

The arbitrator issued a decision on April 30, 2004, that addressed Lewis's Title VII and retaliatory discharge claims. Specifically with respect to retaliatory discharge, the arbitrator cited to *Ortega v. IBP, Inc.*, 255 Kan. 513, 874 P.2d 1188, 1191, 1198 (1994), which stated that Kansas courts recognize the tort in the context of worker's compensation filings and concluded that a plaintiff "must establish that claim by a preponderance of the evidence, but the evidence must be clear and convincing in nature." Noting that "[n]umerous case decisions [from state and federal Kansas courts] follow the burden-shifting requirements set forth in the United States Supreme Court decision of *McDonnell Douglas Corp. v. Green*, 411 U.S. 792 (1973), . . . for both claims of discrimination under the Civil Rights Act of 1964, and retaliatory discharge claims," the arbitrator proceeded to analyze the facts of the case and concluded that Circuit City's reason for termination was not "mere pretext" for discrimination or retaliation. The arbitrator ruled that Circuit City was justified in terminating Lewis because it had interpreted the weapons policy in good faith. The arbitrator noted that it was possible that Circuit City's management misapplied the policy, but relied on *Sanchez v. Philip Morris Inc.*, 992 F.2d 244, 247 (10th Cir.1993), which states that "Title VII is not violated by the exercise of erroneous or even illogical business judgment." Although Circuit City's procedures permitted the arbitrator to shift the costs of the arbitration from Circuit City to the claimant if he should lose, the arbitrator declined to do so in Lewis's case.

The arbitrator is authorized to award attorney's fees "in accordance with applicable law."

In December 2004, Lewis—through the same counsel he used in arbitration—filed suit against Circuit City in Kansas state court alleging "wrongful termination based upon retaliation for exercising statutory rights under the Kansas workers' compensation Act." Lewis stated that he "ha[d] exhausted his arbitration remedies," and contended that under Kansas law, "the tort of retaliatory discharge is a non-negotiable right" inappropriate for resolution by arbitration. Circuit City removed to federal court on the basis of diversity of citizenship and amount in controversy pursuant to 28 U.S.C. § 1332. Circuit City then filed a motion to dismiss, arguing that because Lewis agreed to final and binding arbitration, he could not seek a "second bite at the apple" on the very same claim in court. The district court converted Circuit City's motion to a motion for summary judgment, and, after the requisite briefing, granted the motion. The court decided that Lewis had not alleged any of the narrow bases permitted by the FAA for vacating or modifying an arbitration award, and that he had missed the FAA deadline for filing such a suit by several months. The court thus concluded that Lewis's suit improperly sought to relitigate a claim after a final judgment. *Lewis v. Circuit City Stores, Inc.*, No. 05–4001–JAR, 2005 WL 2179085 (D.Kan. Sept. 7, 2005). This timely appeal followed.

II.   DISCUSSION

* * *

C.   Lewis's Argument that the Arbitration Agreement is Unenforceable

Lewis argued to the district court that his arbitration agreement with Circuit City was unenforceable as a matter of basic contract law. He continues to press this argument on appeal. We conclude that Lewis waived this argument by proceeding with arbitration without placing any objection clearly on the record prior to or during the arbitration proceeding.

Section 2 of the FAA provides that arbitration agreements "shall be valid, irrevocable, and enforceable, save upon such grounds as exist at law or in equity for the revocation of any contract." 9 U.S.C. § 2. The Supreme Court has held that state contract law can therefore invalidate such agreements "if that law arose to govern issues concerning the validity, revocability, and enforceability of contracts generally." *Doctor's Assocs., Inc. v. Casarotto*, 517 U.S. 681, 686–87 (1996) (quotation, emphasis omitted). "Thus, generally applicable contract defenses, such as fraud, duress, or unconscionability, may be applied to invalidate arbitration agreements without contravening § 2." Id. at 687.

The Supreme Court has observed that to the extent parties "forcefully object[ ] to the arbitrators deciding their dispute," they preserve their objection even if they follow through with arbitration. *First Options of Chicago, Inc. v. Kaplan*, 514 U.S. 938, 946, (1995); accord *Coady v. Ashcraft & Gerel*, 223 F.3d 1, 9 n. 10 (1st Cir.2000) (finding no waiver when the party "consistently and vigorously maintained its objection to the scope of arbitration"); *China Minmetals Materials Imp. & Exp. Co., Ltd. v. Chi Mei Corp.*, 334 F.3d 274, 291–92 (3d Cir.2003) (same).

On the other hand, many courts have held that, absent an explicit statement objecting to the arbitrability of the dispute, a party cannot "await the outcome and then later argue that the arbitrator lacked authority to decide the matter." *AGCO Corp. v. Anglin*, 216 F.3d 589, 593 (7th Cir.2000); *see also Opals on Ice Lingerie, Designs by Bernadette, Inc. v. Bodylines Inc.*, 320 F.3d 362, 368 (2d Cir.2003) ("[I]f a party participates in arbitration proceedings without making a timely objection to the submission of the dispute to arbitration, that party may be found to have waived its right to object to the arbitration."); *Slaney v. Int'l. Amateur Athletic Fed'n*, 244 F.3d 580, 591 (7th Cir.2001) ("Slaney could not sit back and allow the arbitration to go forward, and only after it was all done . . . say: oh by the way, we never agreed to the arbitration clause. That is a tactic that the law of arbitration, with its commitment to speed, will not tolerate." (quotation omitted)); *Fortune, Alsweet & Eldridge, Inc. v. Daniel*, 724 F.2d 1355, 1357 (9th Cir.1983) (per curiam) (holding that "a party may not submit a claim to arbitration and then challenge the authority of the arbitrator to act after receiving an unfavorable result" because it would "frustrate th[e] policy" behind arbitration).

We have not published an opinion regarding whether a party's failure to raise a question of the enforceability of an arbitration agreement, followed by the party's participation in arbitration, effectively waives that party's right to object to arbitration. However, in reviewing Supreme Court precedent and persuasive authority from other circuits, it is clear that our usual rules regarding waiver and estoppel apply to prevent a party from complaining about the enforceability of an arbitration agreement if he already has fully participated in arbitration without any relevant objection. In particular, a rule of waiver is important to advance the goals of arbitration as an efficient method of dispute resolution for which parties may contract in advance. "It would be unreasonable and unjust to allow [a party] to challenge the legitimacy of the arbitration process, in which he had voluntarily participated over a period of several months. . . ." *Fortune, Alsweet & Eldridge*, 724 F.2d at 1357.

Lewis states that he objected to arbitration, that he "never had a choice to opt out," and that he "made it clear that he did not want to arbitrate." He points to a blank dispute resolution agreement that he and his attorney allegedly refused to sign. He also states that he followed through with arbitration "to comply with defendant's demands for arbitration and to exhaust such process."

But, importantly, at oral argument, Lewis conceded that he had not expressly challenged the enforceability of the agreement during arbitration. The record here reveals only a general complaint about having to arbitrate, and is devoid of an objection to any legal aspect of the arbitration agreement or to the enforceability of the agreement generally. A party's bare statement that he does not want to arbitrate a dispute is, of course, not a legal argument or objection, but instead merely signals "buyer's remorse" that he agreed at the outset to arbitrate future disputes. Furthermore, the evidence belies Lewis's claim that he "never voluntarily agreed" to arbitrate his employment claims, because he twice completed and signed arbitration request forms, the second time through counsel.

Because Lewis never adequately objected in arbitration to the arbitrability of his claims or raised a question as to the validity of the arbitration agreement, he waived his opportunity to do so and is estopped from raising such issues now.[12]

We have invalidated illusory agreements to arbitrate, holding "that an arbitration agreement allowing one party the unfettered right to alter the arbitration agreement's existence or its scope is illusory," *Dumais v. Am. Golf Corp.*, 299 F.3d 1216, 1219 (10th Cir.2002), but Lewis does not explain how Circuit City's Agreement fits that pattern. Furthermore, Lewis cites no support for his theory that form contracts—i.e. contracts drafted by only one party—are per se invalid.

We have found unenforceable an arbitration agreement that imposed prohibitively high costs on claimants, since high fees may deter claimants from pursuing their statutory rights. *Shankle v. B-G Maint. Mgmt. of Colo., Inc.*, 163 F.3d 1230, 1234–35 (10th Cir.1999) (involving an arbitration fee estimated at $1,875 to $5,000). But Lewis does not inform us what his costs were, only that they

---

[12]   Although we do not base our decision on the merits of Lewis's theory of why the agreement was unenforceable, we observe that he has not alleged any facts or developed an argument that could support a conclusion that the arbitration agreement was invalid under contract law.

were "thousands of dollars," and he does not distinguish between his arbitration fees and attorney's fees. Based on information in the record about Circuit City's policy of limiting an employee's arbitration costs, we estimate Lewis's costs would be capped at about $1,360.

III. CONCLUSION

We AFFIRM the district court's dismissal of Lewis's claim on summary judgment. We DENY Circuit City's motion for sanctions.

NOTES

Facts

1. What cause of action does Lewis assert? How does it relate to the arbitration?

2. Is Lewis moving to vacate the arbitral award? Did Lewis do so?

3. Did Lewis raise issues with regard to jurisdiction in the arbitration? How?

4. Lewis acted as the claimant in the arbitration. What was his explanation for both acting as a claimant in an arbitration and objecting to the jurisdiction of the arbitral tribunal?

Law

1. How does the court characterize the statements made by Lewis and his counsel? Does the court consider them "objections"?

2. The court notes in footnote 12 that Lewis or his counsel 'has not alleged any facts or developed an argument that could support a conclusion that the arbitration agreement was invalid under contract law." The court nevertheless proceeds to work through multiple legal theories that appear to be on point. What factual material would have to be developed to support these arguments?

3. Taking the hint from the 10th Circuit, what arguments should Lewis' counsel have raised? To whom should he have addressed those arguments? The arbitrator? The courts?

4. Assume that Lewis had to plead his jurisdictional objection to the arbitral tribunal rather than a court. When would he have had to raise the arguments in question? With how much specificity would have to do so?

5. Could Lewis have developed the factual predicate for the argument without discovery? How does that impact your answer to question 4?

Environmental Barrier Co. LLC v. Slurry Systems, Inc.

540 F.3d 598 (7th Cir. 2008)

WOOD, CIRCUIT JUDGE.

After an arbitration hearing to resolve a construction contract dispute between Environmental Barrier Company ("EBC") and Slurry Systems, Inc. ("SSI"), Arbitrator Franklin I. Kral issued an award in favor of EBC in the amount of $388,919.88. When SSI did not pay, EBC filed suit in Illinois court to confirm the award, and SSI responded by removing the case to the U.S. District Court for the Northern District of Illinois. SSI urged the district court to vacate the arbitral award, or in the alternative, to modify it. The district court did neither: instead, it confirmed the award entered by Arbitrator Kral. In the course of doing so, the court held that EBC had "standing" to enforce the arbitration clause in the contract and that the arbitrator had not exceeded his powers. On appeal, SSI is now urging us to find that EBC never obtained the right to enforce the contract's arbitration clause. SSI's appellate briefs present this argument as a challenge to arbitrability, based on the fact that SSI agreed to arbitrate only with EBC's predecessor-in-interest, not with EBC itself. This is a major shift from the way SSI presented its case first to the arbitrator and later to the district court, where it framed the issue in terms of EBC's standing to pursue this arbitration. The difference is crucial-indeed, on these facts, fatal-to SSI's claim.

I

On February 29, 2000, the U.S. Army Corps of Engineers entered into a contract with SSI for work on a project to reduce flooding during heavy rains. The McCook Reservoir Project, as it was called, involved the construction of a multibillion-gallon reservoir; SSI won the right to build the overburden cutoff wall. SSI in turn subcontracted part of its work to an entity called Geo-Con, Inc., using a form contract that the parties signed in April 2000. The parties' briefs recount in detail the progress of SSI's and Geo-Con's work from 2000 to 2003; we include only the facts pertinent to this appeal.

Attachment A to the SSI/Geo-Con subcontract elaborated on Article 8.1 of the text, specifying that "Contractor and Subcontractor shall jointly work together to perform all of the work together [sic] to minimize the overall cost of the work." Attachment A also included a longer version of Article 10.1, which described how the parties would allocate revenues, costs, profits, and loss and gave guidance for a final settling-up based on the actual distribution of costs. The subcontract also contained an exclusivity clause, Article 1.3; a broad arbitration clause covering "[a]ny claim arising out of or related to this Subcontract," Article 6.2; and a clause restricting assignment or sub-subcontracting, Article 7.4.2.

The project's scope and methodology changed as the work proceeded, requiring the Corps at one point to suspend operations while it figured out an alternative way to finish the project. Once the modifications to the Prime Contract were in place, SSI and Geo-Con resumed their joint effort to complete their portion of the work. By April 2003, they were finished with their construction work. What remained to be done was the final reckoning of who owed whom how much; this proved to be more difficult. There were, for instance, several pending change orders, and it was unclear how costs and profits would be shifted among the parties. To the extent that these financial details are relevant, we return to them later.

EBC entered the picture in September 2003, when Geo-Con, for reasons unrelated to the McCook project, filed for bankruptcy in the U.S. Bankruptcy Court for the Southern District of New York. During Geo-Con's reorganization, EBC (through two intermediary entities) acquired substantially all of Geo-Con's assets for a purchase price of $2.1 million. The bankruptcy court found that EBC was the only qualified purchaser of Geo-Con's assets. In an order dated April 16, 2004, the court approved the sale in accordance with the terms set forth in a letter from the intermediaries. Part II of the offer letter addressed the Geo-Con acquisition and set forth a list of "excluded assets." The exclusions included "[a]ll contracts for services to be performed by Geo-Con, except . . . P90099 McCook, IL" (emphasis added). In other words, the McCook contract was acquired by the intermediary, and then passed along to EBC. There was a Schedule A to the offer letter that listed equipment loans and leases. This was the "Schedule A" to which the bankruptcy court referred when it said in its order that the contracts listed in Schedules A and C were executory.

* * *

SSI asserts that it was not aware of Geo-Con's bankruptcy proceedings as they were taking place. It learned about them, however, no later than June 17, 2004, when EBC notified SSI by letter that EBC had succeeded to Geo-Con's rights under the subcontract. The letter contained a demand that SSI pay EBC the balance due to Geo-Con for the work that Geo-Con had performed under the subcontract. At the time, EBC believed that this balance was $711,000. (It later found out that SSI had received two additional payments from the Corps that it had not disclosed, totaling $425,951.38; the discrepancy is immaterial for our purposes.)

EBC's June 2004 letter also noted that the "subcontract between Geo-Con and Slurry Systems calls for mediation and arbitration of disputes," but it added that

> *EBC's preference is to resolve its claim against Slurry Systems amicably, if possible, without the expenditure of mediation fees and expenses which, pursuant to the contract, are to be shared equally by the parties. Accordingly, we request an opportunity to meet with you within the next two weeks to discuss and hopefully resolve EBC's claim. If you are unwilling to meet with us within that time, EBC will commence mediation and arbitration proceedings.*

SSI did not respond positively to EBC's letter. On July 7, 2004, SSI's attorneys sent a letter to EBC's counsel, expressing the opinion that "all disputes between Geo-Con and Slurry Systems have been resolved," and adding that, "[a]s a matter of fact, Geo-Con actually owes Slurry Systems, but because of Geo-Con's liquidation, there is no point in Slurry pursuing the matter." SSI's letter noted EBC's statement that the subcontract between Geo-Con and SSI "calls for the mediation and arbitration of disputes," and requested that EBC provide SSI "with a copy of the subcontract if you still plan to pursue this matter[.]"

EBC did pursue the matter. After mediation efforts failed, EBC's counsel called SSI's counsel to discuss arbitration. The following week, in a letter dated March 16, 2005, counsel for SSI wrote the following note to EBC's attorney:

> *As I stated on the phone, while I am pleased to resolve potential procedural issues by agreement, the first order of business is to determine whether your client, [EBC,] has any standing to arbitrate its claim against our client, [SSI].*
>
> *You have agreed that invoking the arbitration clause in [Geo-Con's] subcontract with SSI goes hand-in-hand with EBC fully assuming that subcontract. That requires EBC to perform fully all obligations imposed upon Geo-Con by the subcontract, which it has not yet done. Additionally, SSI has not even consented to EBC's assumption of the subcontract, and is unaware of EBC's technical expertise or level of capitalization, or its ability to perform work under the subcontract. Under these circumstances, SSI may be excused from accepting performances from EBC under 11 U.S.C. § 365(c) and other applicable laws.*

The letter went on to state that it was "therefore essential that EBC provide SSI with adequate assurances that it can perform its obligations under the subcontract before EBC can assume the subcontract." Specifically, it demanded (1) that EBC confirm that it "is in the construction business and can handle any remedial work necessary under the subcontract"; (2) that EBC "provide SSI with the insurance and performance bond required by the subcontract"; and (3) that EBC give SSI its "financial data and biographical information," so that SSI could "make an informed decision regarding whether or not to withhold SSI's consent from the proposed assumption." It added that "[t]hese issues need to be resolved now, and not in the context of an arbitration." The letter closed by warning that if it should turn out that Geo-Con's work was "defective in any way, SSI will hold EBC accountable."

The issues were not resolved, and instead EBC filed its demand for arbitration a month later, on April 20, 2005. The demand briefly explained the background of the parties' dispute and the basis for EBC's claim against SSI. EBC argued that SSI owed EBC "at least $657,273.50" and that SSI had "breached the Subcontract by failing to pay that amount."

At that critical juncture, SSI said nothing about the basic arbitrability of the dispute. Instead, it filed an Answering Statement on May 9, 2005. In the box on the Answering Statement form labeled "RESPONDENT ANSWERS CLAIMANT DEMAND FOR ARBITRATION AS FOLLOWS," SSI wrote: "EBC seeks additional moneys under a subcontract which has been paid in full; Respondent [SSI] denies any money is due and seeks return of overpayments and declaratory relief." The "DOLLAR AMOUNT OF CLAIM" was listed as "To be determined," and in the box labeled "OTHER RELIEF SOUGHT," SSI stated its claim for "A declaration that EBC assumed the subcontract and is in breach of its non-monetary terms; an accounting of money to be paid under the subcontract and a return of any over payments." Notably, SSI did not merely answer EBC's claim; it also filed a counterclaim.

SSI elaborated on its position in a supplementary letter to Arbitrator Kral on June 20, 2005. The letter, which SSI sent "[i]n order to facilitate our June 21, 2005 preliminary hearing," first explained that the disputes "center around a construction subcontract" between SSI and Geo-Con to build a slurry wall for the Corps. It then launched directly into the dispute over payment, providing Arbitrator Kral with SSI's version of how the parties had agreed to allocate the costs and profits. Next, the letter stated that "Geo-Con abandoned the Project before it was over," and so while "EBC now seeks an additional $657,274 . . ., strict application of the payment terms does not require SSI to pay the unearned windfall EBC seeks. Instead, it requires EBC to pay SSI several hundred thousand dollars in overpayments." The remaining three paragraphs expanded on why EBC owed money to SSI. There is not even a passing reference to a defense of lack of arbitrability.

Three days after the preliminary hearing, on June 24, 2005, SSI wrote another letter to Arbitrator Kral, this time to "follow up on the subject of 'non-monetary breaches.'" SSI reiterated its position that "Geo-Con left the job before it was finished" and noted that by virtue of the April 16, 2004, bankruptcy order, "EBC was allowed to assume Geo-Con's Subcontract with SSI." SSI then argued that the bankruptcy court directed EBC, as the purchaser of Geo-Con's asserts, "to make such cure payments as are required by Section 365 of the [Bankruptcy] Code and agreed to among the Debtors and respective contracting parties." SSI and Geo-Con had not agreed to EBC's assumption of the contract, SSI continued, nor had Geo-Con even informed SSI of its bankruptcy. "Nevertheless," the letter contended, "section 365 required Geo-Con/EBC to do the following in order to assume the contract" (referring to the list of three items in SSI's letter of March 16, 2005, to EBC). Until EBC satisfied those conditions, SSI concluded, "EBC cannot have assumed the contract, and lacks standing to pursue this arbitration case."

At the end of the letter, SSI noted its concern that should the Corps raise a future claim involving Geo-Con's work, EBC might try to evade its responsibility by "contending it is not Geo-Con. Part of SSI's relief sought in this arbitration is a declaration that EBC has in fact assumed all of Geo-Con's obligations under the Subcontract." Thus, in the same letter, SSI both argued that EBC had not properly assumed the subcontract (through its reference to alleged outstanding duties under Bankruptcy Code § 365 that prevented assumption) and argued that EBC had assumed the contract. Perhaps unsure of the latter point, SSI asked in its Answering Statement for a declaration that EBC had assumed the contract. It seems that what SSI was looking for was a ruling from the arbitrator that before EBC should be permitted to enforce Geo-Con's rights under the subcontract, it had to assure that it also would fulfill Geo-Con's remaining contractual obligations. Once again, this was not a challenge to arbitrability; it was a position premised on a procedural question of standing and on the merits of the dispute.

Each party to the arbitration filed a position paper on July 18, 2005. In response to SSI's argument that it had never consented to the assignment of Geo-Con's rights to EBC, EBC argued that the subcontract did not require SSI's consent under these circumstances. Article 7.4.2 of the subcontract provides:

> *[1] The Subcontractor shall not assign the Work of this Subcontract without the written consent of the Contractor, nor [2] subcontract the whole of this Subcontract*

without the written consent of the Contractor, nor [3] further subcontract portions of this Subcontract without written notification to the Contractor when such notification is requested by the Contractor.

Only the first clause restricts assignment; the second and third restrict further subcontracting. Moreover, the restriction on assignment only requires the subcontractor to obtain the contractor's written consent before assigning "the Work" of the subcontract. The work was completed by April 2003, a full year before the bankruptcy court issued its order approving EBC's assumption of Geo-Con's assets. The arbitrator took note of that timing in an express finding that "the Work" of the subcontract was complete before Geo-Con assigned the contract to EBC.

In its position paper, SSI reiterated its belief that Geo-Con had "repudiated" the parties' agreement, and that it "had continuing obligations to SSI to maintain insurance coverage, provide a warranty for its work, and provide SSI with a performance bond to cover those obligations." SSI maintained its position that EBC must "comply with its outstanding obligations under the Contract," and that SSI therefore "seeks: (1) declaratory judgment confirming that EBC has assumed the contract; (2) a declaratory judgment that EBC is in breach on non-monetary terms of the Subcontract (e.g., insurance), and that EBC cure those defaults as previously ordered by the courts; (3) an accounting of the moneys to be paid between the parties on the Subcontract; and (4) an order requiring EBC to return to SSI the overpayments made to Geo-Con, believed to be in excess of $500,000" (footnotes omitted). SSI's argument further stated that according to the bill of sale attached to the bankruptcy order, "EBC did, in fact, assume the Subcontract." SSI added that "[w]hat Geo-Con could not do, and therefore what EBC cannot do, is to selectively accept the benefits of the Subcontract while rejecting the obligations." Until EBC fulfilled those obligations (as required by § 365), the argument concluded, "EBC lacks standing to invoke the Arbitration Clause in the Subcontract." The rest of the argument explained why and to what extent Geo-Con was overpaid for its work and concluded by stating that "EBC must cure all non-monetary defaults before getting anything from SSI. But applying the Subcontract, Geo-Con/EBC was vastly overpaid, and that money must be returned."

Discovery ensued, followed by a two-day arbitration hearing on August 23–24, 2005. The transcripts from the hearing reveal that the only issues addressed were who owed what and to whom. There was no discussion of standing or of arbitrability. Even so, in a post-hearing brief filed by EBC on

October 19, 2005 (SSI did not file a post-hearing brief), EBC addressed the "standing" defense presented in SSI's position paper:

> *SSI claims that EBC lacks standing to compel SSI to arbitrate EBC's claim because SSI did not agree to the assignment of the Subcontract to EBC, and because certain alleged "cure" payments were not made. Generally speaking, issues of standing are for the arbitrator to decide in the first instance.*

Arbitrator Kral's award was issued on November 21, 2005. He recognized that "a threshold issue was raised by SSI as to the standing of EBC to arbitrate this dispute under Subcontract Article 6.2 [the arbitration clause]. EBC agreed that it had assumed the Subcontract as evidenced by the Bankruptcy Court filings." He also noted that SSI's standing defense was premised on its position that EBC had not assumed the subcontract properly. EBC's response was that "GEO's performance of its work on the Project ended in December, 2002 and thereby the consent of SSI to the assumption is not required." The arbitrator resolved the standing question by stating that he "agree[d] with EBC's position." He went on to reject the entirety of SSI's counterclaim and awarded a total recovery, including contract interest, of $388,919.86 to EBC.

II

On January 6, 2006, EBC filed an action to confirm its award in the Circuit Court of Cook County; SSI promptly removed the case to federal court. As the district court described SSI's position, SSI argued "first, that the arbitrator exceeded his powers by entering an award in favor of EBC, who was not a party to the original Agreement. Further, SSI contends, even if EBC were a party to the Agreement, it lacks standing to invoke the arbitration clause because it was in default of the contract." We comment first on the standing argument, and then turn to the more troublesome arbitrability point.

We begin with a word about terminology. We are reminded of Justice Scalia's observation in *Steel Co. v. Citizens for a Better Environment*, 523 U.S. 83, 118 S.Ct. 1003, 140 L.Ed.2d 210 (1998), that "[j]urisdiction . . . is a word of many, too many, meanings[.]" Id. at 90, 118 S.Ct. 1003 (internal quotation marks omitted). The same, unfortunately, can be said for "standing." Everything from the fundamental requirement imposed by Article III that there must be a "case or controversy" between the parties seeking relief in federal court, to various prudential doctrines such as the restrictions on invoking the rights of third parties, to the inquiry whether a statute is designed to protect the rights of the person before the court, has been swept into the word "standing." There is no reason to suppose that arbitrators are bound to the case-or-controversy requirement that circumscribes the judicial power of the United States. Indeed, some state courts are authorized to give advisory opinions. In the context of arbitration, the term "standing" addresses the entitlement of the party to raise a given point before the arbitrator. This is more like the concept of standing described by the Supreme Court in *Associated General Contractors of California, Inc. v. California State Council of Carpenters*, 459 U.S. 519, 103 S.Ct. 897, 74 L.Ed.2d 723 (1983), in which the Court considered the question whether a union was a proper party to sue for treble damages under the antitrust laws when it was neither a consumer nor a competitor in the market in which trade was restrained. In the course of rejecting the union's right to sue, the Court commented that "[h]arm to the antitrust plaintiff is sufficient to satisfy the constitutional standing requirement of injury in fact, but the court must make a further determination whether the plaintiff is a proper party to bring a private antitrust action." *Id.* at 535 n. 31.

That is the sense in which standing to arbitrate should be understood: is the petitioner a proper party to raise a particular claim in the arbitration? This explains why courts have not hesitated to hold that standing is a matter for the arbitrator to resolve, even though (as we note in a moment) arbitrability is usually an issue for the court. SSI submitted the standing question to the arbitrator on its own initiative, and it was proper for the arbitrator to decide it. Focusing particularly on standing, the district court noted that "SSI's . . . objection to EBC's standing to enforce the arbitration clause relates to EBC's alleged breach of other contract provisions." Reiterating that this kind of issue is for the arbitrator, the court found that "[t]he arbitrator's conclusion . . . is thus subject to deferential review, which it easily survives."

The harder question is whether an agreement to arbitrate existed between the parties. It is difficult, however, not for the reasons the district court identified, but instead for a more fundamental reason. There is not a hint in the record that SSI ever called this issue to the arbitrator's attention or sought to enjoin the arbitration on the ground that there was no agreement to arbitrate. Thus, even though the ordinary rule is that the question whether an agreement to arbitrate exists is one for the court, the right to a judicial determination of arbitrability is, like many rights, one that can be waived.

As our detailed explanation above of the arbitration proceedings in this case demonstrates, SSI never told the arbitrator that it thought this dispute was nonarbitrable. To the contrary, it voluntarily submitted to the arbitrator's authority, filed a counterclaim, and confined its objections to EBC's standing to arbitrate. Only after the arbitrator issued an award unfavorable to SSI and the case wound up in court did SSI raise an objection to the arbitrator's authority to decide the dispute. * * * Not until it reached the district court did it recast its prior argument about standing as a challenge to arbitrability.

This is not a tactic we can accept, for sound policy reasons. It is terribly wasteful of the arbitrator's time, the parties' time, and the court's time. Anyone who wants to object to arbitrability is entitled to make her position known to the arbitrator and the other party; the other party may then, if it wishes, respond with a petition for an order to compel arbitration under the Federal Arbitration Act ("FAA"), 9 U.S.C. § 4, and obtain a judicial determination on arbitrability. In addition, keeping the arbitrability card close to the chest would allow a party like SSI to take a wait-and-see approach: if it had liked Arbitrator Kral's decision, it would have remained silent, but since it did not, it is now complaining about arbitrability.

This court has already disapproved this method of proceeding. In *AGCO Corp. v. Anglin*, 216 F.3d 589 (7th Cir.2000), for example, we stated:

> *We first consider whether the Anglins waived any objection to the arbitrability of the Retail Obligations when they consented to arbitration and agreed to participate in the arbitration hearing. If a party willingly and without reservation allows an issue to be submitted to arbitration, he cannot await the outcome and then later argue that the arbitrator lacked authority to decide the matter. If, however, a party clearly and explicitly reserves the right to object to arbitrability, his participation in the arbitration does not preclude him from challenging the arbitrator's authority in court. The record suggests that the Anglins have followed the latter course.*

216 F.3d at 593. It was "undisputed that counsel for the Anglins objected to arbitration" of the parties' dispute, id., on the ground that "the Anglins could not have contemplated that their arbitration clause with AGCO would encompass a dispute with a nonsignatory party," id. at 596. We accordingly reversed the district court's confirmation of *AGCO*'s award.

Unlike the Anglins, SSI failed at any time during the arbitration proceedings to raise or reserve an objection to arbitrability. Instead, it freely accepted the arbitrator's authority to decide the dispute and, indeed, submitted its own counterclaim for resolution. Only after the arbitration outcome displeased SSI did it restyle its "standing" and "executory contract" arguments as encompassing a challenge to the existence of an agreement to arbitrate between SSI and the nonsignatory EBC. As we noted in *Jones Dairy Farm*:

> *Jones Dairy Farm did not make [arbitrability] an issue. It did not, while agreeing to participate in the arbitration, challenge the arbitrator's jurisdiction, and make*

clear that it was preserving its challenge for eventual presentation to a court if the arbitrator ruled in the union's favor. . . . The company never questioned the arbitrator's authority.

760 F.2d at 175. "If a party voluntarily and unreservedly submits an issue to arbitration, he cannot later argue that the arbitrator had no authority to resolve it." Id. SSI's professed challenge to arbitrability comes too late. By freely submitting to the arbitration of its claims without preserving a challenge to the arbitrator's authority, SSI missed the chance to come back later, before a court, and deny that an agreement to arbitrate existed.

* * *

IV

The district court's judgment confirming the arbitrator's award is Affirmed.

NOTES

Facts

1. What argument did SSI raise? When? To whom?

2. What facts does a standing defense rely upon in this case? What facts are the predicate of an objection that the dispute is not arbitrable? In other words, were there facts relevant to the determination of the arbitrability question that were not before the arbitrator?

3. When did SSI raise the standing argument?

4. Was the standing argument inconsistent with its own counterclaims? The court notes that SSI's arguments are not always the model of consistency. What are the inconsistencies in position taken by SSI?

Law

1. Judge Wood notes that "standing" and "jurisdiction" are inherently ambiguous terms. In light of her observation, is it fair to conclude that an objection to "standing" could not be an objection to "jurisdiction" or "arbitrability"?

2. In light of the ruling in *Environmental Barrier,* how specific does a jurisdictional objection have to be for a court to determine that the objection was not waived?

3. Consider *Lewis* and *Environmental Barrier* together. When do parties have to develop their jurisdictional arguments? How precise to they have to be in

their argumentation? Is it a fair reading of both cases that jurisdictional objections have to developed early and plead with specificity both what the legal theory of the objection is and upon what factual predicate it is based?

CHAPTER 15

Dispositive Motions

The newly revised AAA Commercial Arbitration Rules recognize the parties' ability to file dispositive motions in arbitration. Dispositive motions are tools used as a matter of course in federal and state litigation. Typical dispositive motions include motions to dismiss a claim for failure to state a claim upon which relief could be granted, or on the basis of a jurisdictional defect. Another typical dispositive motion used in federal and state litigation is the motion for summary judgment. Less typically used—but important—is a *forum non conveniens* motion. The new rule on dispositive motions in the AAA Commercial Arbitration Rules responds to the debate as to whether arbitral tribunals are empowered to decide disputes without a full "trial" or evidentiary hearing.

The materials in this chapter are organized chronologically. This chapter introduces you first to the historical controversy whether tribunals are empowered to decide disputes by means of dispositive motions predating the new AAA rules. Next, it introduces you to the new AAA Commercial Arbitration Rule 33 and provides you with some commentary from the time of its drafting. Finally, it addresses which kind of motions it is best suited to replace and how.

Fact Scenario

As already laid out in Chapter 11, the relevant provision of the agreement in the Hardmont case states as follows:

6.   Non-disclosure

1.   Acme Industries Corp. acknowledges that it has received a market study from Hardmont LLC, labeled "Confidential Information" and attached to this Agreement as Appendix I.

2.   Acme Industries Corp. and its officers, employees, agents, directors and principals shall not disclose the Confidential Information to any third parties.

As already laid out in Chapter 17, Hardmont's Demand for Arbitration states as follows with regard to the nature of the dispute:

Hardmont LLC claims against Acme Industries Corp., RRF Corp. and Mervin Gilmore jointly and severally for breach of contract, unjust enrichment, estoppel, conversion, tortious interference with business, and violation of state and/or federal laws.

Assume that Acme, RRF and Gilmore reserved the right to file a dispositive motion but agreed to wait until after discovery could be concluded. Discovery reveals the following information:

1. RRF did rely upon the substance of the Confidential Information attached to the Contract.

2. RRF did not physically receive the "Confidential Information" from Gilmore or Acme.

3. RRF instead received the substance of the Confidential Information by re-contracting with the provider of the underlying market study that made Confidential Information.

4. RRF (and Gilmore) had used the same provider of market research before contracting with Hardmont.

5. RRF's COO contacted the market researcher without a prompt from Gilmore. Gilmore was copied on the email exchange.

6. There is no other evidence that would link Gilmore or Acme to RRF's use of the Confidential Information.

7. Gilmore in a deposition testified that RRF's COO asked the market researchers independently to conduct a market study, that he was not privy to anything relating to the Acme accounts when he did so, and that Gilmore had simply kept silent at the time and let the COO do his job.

What dispositive motion should Acme, RRF and Gilmore file? What procedural schedule is appropriate? What supporting evidence should they submit? How should Hardmont respond?

Readings

A) Dispositive Motions in Arbitral Practice

Louisiana D. Brown 1992 Irrevocable Trust v. Peabody Coal Co.

205 F.3d 1340 (Table) (6th Cir. 2000)

PER CURIAM.

Plaintiff, the Louisiana D. Brown 1992 Irrevocable Trust (Trust), appeals from the district court's entry of judgment confirming an arbitration award that dismissed plaintiff's claims against defendant, Peabody Coal Company. The dispute concerned plaintiff's attempt, as the successor to the sublessor, to readjust the terms of a coal sublease with defendant. Plaintiff claims that the district court erred in refusing to vacate the arbitration award because (1) the failure of the arbitrators to permit discovery before deciding the matter by way of dispositive motion constituted misconduct and resulted in a fundamentally unfair proceeding, and (2) the arbitrator's decision represented a manifest disregard of the law. After review of the record and the arguments presented on appeal, we are convinced that the district court did not err and affirm.

Plaintiff's predecessor in interest, Carroll County Coal Company (CCCC), obtained a Federal Coal Lease (Lease) of certain coal reserves located in Utah from the United States Department of Interior, Bureau of Land Management (BLM), on September 1, 1970. The Lease provided in section 3(d) that the lessor reserved

> *[t]he right reasonably to readjust and fix royalties payable hereunder and other terms and conditions* **_at the end of 20 years from the date hereof_** *and thereafter at the end of each succeeding 20-year period during the continuance of this lease unless otherwise provided by law at the time of the expiration of any such period. Unless the lessee files objections to the proposed terms or a relinquishment of the lease within 30 days after receipt of the notice of proposed terms for a 20-year period, he will be deemed to have agreed to such terms.*

(emphasis added). On January 11, 1973, CCCC entered a Coal Sublease (Sublease) with Peabody conveying all rights and interest under the Lease for $20,000 in cash, advanced minimum royalties of $4,000 per year for the first 20 years of the Sublease, and a tonnage royalty. The last minimum royalty payment was made in January 1993. A separate royalty agreement entered into on the same date provided that CCCC's overriding royalty under the Sublease could not exceed 50 percent of the royalties due under the federal Lease. Peabody assigned its rights in the Sublease to Malcolm McKinnon in 1974, except that it retained the obligation to pay all overriding or advanced royalties due to CCCC. The McKinnon assignment passed through several hands before being assigned to Utah Power & Light Company (n/k/a PacifiCorp), which operates a mine under this and other coal leases.

The dispute revolves around the sublessor's right to readjust the Sublease and, in particular, the royalties due from Peabody. The Sublease specifically states:

> 7.   *TERMS OF SUBLEASE. The term of this Sublease shall begin on the date hereof and shall run concurrently with the term of the Lease as provided in Section 3(d) of the Lease. This Sublease shall be subject to the right of Sublessor to reasonably readjust and fix royalties payable hereunder and other terms and conditions at the end of twenty (20) years from the date of said Lease and thereafter* ***at the end of each succeeding twenty (20) year period during the continuance of said Lease*** *unless otherwise provided by law at the time of expiration of any such period.*

(emphasis added). Since the term of the Sublease was tied to the Lease itself, plaintiff was entitled to readjust the Sublease "at the end of" 20 years from the date of the underlying federal Lease. The 20-year anniversary of the federal Lease was September 1, 1990.

The BLM notified CCCC by letter dated August 28, 1988, that the terms and conditions of the Lease would be readjusted effective September 1, 1990. CCCC forwarded a copy of the BLM notice concerning the Lease to Peabody, but did not indicate any intention to also readjust the Sublease. The BLM sent CCCC its decision incorporating the new terms and conditions of the readjusted federal Lease in March 1990, to become effective September 1, 1990. At that time, CCCC did not give Peabody notice that it likewise intended to readjust the Sublease.

In a letter dated March 15, 1993, two and a half years after the anniversary date of the Lease, CCCC notified Peabody that it intended to readjust and fix royalties payable under the Sublease. Peabody responded on April 9, 1993, agreed to meet with CCCC, and expressly reserved the issue of the timeliness of the notice. No agreement was reached during the discussions. On December 21, 1994, the Trust sent Peabody a Readjusted Sublease for signature. By letter dated February 6, 1995, Peabody asserted that because the notice of readjustment was untimely the option to readjust the terms of the Sublease had been waived until the end of the next twenty year term.[1]

The Trust filed suit in state court asserting claims under the Readjusted Sublease. Peabody removed the action to federal court and the Trust filed a demand for arbitration under the terms of the Sublease. After full briefing and oral argument, the three-member arbitration panel dismissed the Trust's claims by an order granting summary judgment to Peabody. Although the arbitration award did not explain its reasoning, the decision was undoubtedly based upon the finding that neither the Trust nor its predecessor in interest had given timely notice of intent to readjust the Sublease. As a result, the Trust was precluded from enforcing its claims under the purported Altered Sublease. In the district court proceedings, the Trust moved to vacate the award and Peabody moved to confirm the award. The district court confirmed the award for the reasons set forth in its written opinion entered on February 2, 1999. This timely appeal followed.

II.

* * *

B.   Misconduct

Without identifying any error in the district court's analysis, plaintiff again asserts that the arbitrators were not authorized to decide the claims by a motion for summary judgment without conducting an evidentiary hearing or permitting plaintiff to take discovery from Peabody. Claiming an "absolute right to present evidence and confront witnesses," plaintiff asserts that summary disposition of claims made in arbitration without an evidentiary hearing is "inimical to the arbitration process."

Rule 10 of the Commercial Rules of Arbitration, however, allows arbitrators to set a preliminary hearing to "consider other matters that will expedite the arbitration proceedings" and to determine the extent of discovery. While Rule 31 provides that the parties may offer such evidence as is relevant and material to the dispute, it is the arbitrators who are the judges of the relevance and materiality of the evidence offered. The question is not whether plaintiff might have been able to secure the discovery it wanted under Fed.R.Civ.P. 56(f) in a civil action. The Supreme Court has explained that "by agreeing to arbitrate, a party 'trades the procedures and opportunity for review

---

1   On December 31, 1992, CCCC assigned all its right, title, and interest in the Lease to the Trust. The assignment was subject to the approval of the BLM, which came later in 1993.

of the courtroom for the simplicity, informality, and expedition of arbitration.' " *Gilmer v. Interstate/Johnson Lane Corp.*, 500 U.S. 20, 31 (1991) (citation omitted). Arbitration may proceed summarily and with restricted inquiry into factual issues.

The Federal Arbitration Act provides that an arbitrator's award may be vacated:

> *Where the arbitrators were guilty of misconduct in refusing to postpone the hearing, upon sufficient cause shown, or in refusing to hear evidence pertinent and material to the controversy; or of any other misbehavior by which the rights of any party have been prejudiced.*

9 U.S.C. § 10(a)(3). "Arbitrators are not bound by formal rules of procedure and evidence, and the standard for judicial review of arbitration procedures is merely whether a party to arbitration has been denied a fundamentally fair hearing." Fundamental fairness requires only notice, an opportunity to present relevant and material evidence and arguments to the arbitrators, and an absence of bias on the part of the arbitrators.

Examination of the transcript from the arbitration hearing makes clear that plaintiff had an opportunity to present its claims, including its vigorous argument that additional discovery should be permitted and why it would be relevant. The arbitration panel also permitted supplemental briefs and documents to be filed before rendering its decision. The Trust claims that the fairness of the arbitration was tainted by the failure to afford the Trust the opportunity to discover and present evidence relating to the issues of (1) whether the Trust exercised its right to readjust when CCCC forwarded the BLM's notice to Peabody; (2) whether the Trust waived its right to readjust the Sublease; and (3) whether Peabody waived its right to object by failing to comply with 43 C.F.R. § 4.411.

Since the arbitrators could have found that the Sublease unambiguously required notice of the intention to readjust the Sublease on or before the anniversary date, parol evidence concerning the intention of the parties at the time they entered the Sublease would not have been relevant. We may conclude that the arbitrators found the proposed discovery was not calculated to produce evidence relevant and material to the decision. Further, for all of its objections to the summary procedure, the Trust has not demonstrated that the discovery could have produced relevant and material evidence. We agree with the district court that the arbitration award may not be set aside on the grounds that misconduct by the arbitrators resulted in a fundamentally unfair hearing.

AFFIRMED.

NOTES

Facts

1. On the basis of what dispositive motion did the arbitral tribunal decide the case?

2. What was the legal basis of the dismissal? What was the factual basis of the dismissal?

3. Did the Trust have the ability to conduct discovery? Would discovery be relevant to the Trust's claims?

4. What, if anything, would have differed if the case had gone to hearing? In other words, what would have been the advantage that the Trust sought from having another crack at the case?

Law

1. What was the legal basis upon which the Trust challenged the arbitral award? What evidence did it submit in support of its challenge?

2. How did the Court respond to the challenge in this case? Would the Court have acted differently if the Trust had been able to submit additional evidence in support of its motion? What evidence would have been relevant? How would the Trust have been able to get this evidence?

3. What was the key factual factor driving the Court's decision in this case?

Prudential Securities Inc. v. Dalton

929 F.Supp. 1411 (N.D. Okl. 1996)

BRETT, CHIEF JUDGE.

* * *

STIPULATED FACTS

1. Dalton was employed with Prudential from January of 1983 through July of 1989. From April 1983 through March 1988, Dalton served as office manager of the Tulsa branch of Prudential. Dalton was then demoted and remained with Prudential as a registered representative until he voluntarily resigned in July 1989.

2.   As a prerequisite to employment in the securities industry, Dalton executed a Uniform Application for Securities Industry Registration ("U–4") on or about January 18, 1983.

3.   Paragraph 5 of the U–4 contains an arbitration provision which is not disputed. In addition, both parties are governed by Section 3708(a) of the NASD Code of Arbitration Procedure ("Arbitration Code") which contains an additional arbitration clause.

4.   On or about July 18, 1989, Dalton voluntarily left Prudential. At that time, as required by Article IV, Section 3(b) of the NASD By-Laws, Prudential issued a Uniform Termination Notice for Securities Industry Registration ("Form U–5" or "U–5") reflecting the reason for his departure.

5.   On January 15, 1991, John Lytle ("Lytle"), a former client of Prudential, filed a Statement of Claim before the NASD against Prudential, Dalton, two subsequent branch managers of Prudential's Tulsa office, and a Prudential account executive. The claim alleged that (1) the account executive sold Lytle unsuitable investments, (2) Prudential, Dalton, and the two subsequent Prudential branch managers had failed to supervise the account executive, and (3) Prudential breached its fiduciary duty to Lytle and engaged in an ongoing fraud.

6.   The NASD arbitration filed by Lytle alleged among other things damages as a result of purchasing various limited partnerships through Prudential. Prudential has entered into class action settlements, as well as a settlement agreement with the SEC, with respect to the partnerships purchased by Lytle. In June 1992, Prudential was aware of investigations being conducted by the NASD and SEC with respect to the limited partnerships purchased by Lytle.

7.   The Lytle claim was settled by Prudential for the sum of $137,000. Neither Dalton, nor the two subsequent Prudential branch managers, contributed to the settlement. As a result of that settlement, Prudential filed an Amended U–5 reflecting the Lytle settlement. No amendments were filed as to one of the subsequent branch managers.

8.   Prior to filing the Amended U–5, Prudential wrote to Dalton's counsel, C. Raymond Patton ("Patton"), on April 24, 1992, enclosing a copy of the Disclosure Reporting Page from the proposed U–5 amendment. The page provided to Patton stated "Claimant alleged unsuitability in connection with investments in limited partnerships." It did not contain the additional language "alleged damages in excess of $10,000." Boxes 13B(1) and 13B(2), which relate

to questions in item 13, were not marked. Prudential received no response from either Patton or Dalton.

9.   On the Amended U–5 in response to Question 7 concerning Lytle's allegations, Prudential quoted from the allegation in the Lytle Statement of Claim and responded that "Claimant alleged unsuitability in connection with investments in limited partnerships. Alleged damages in excess of $10,000." In addition, Prudential checked boxes 13B(1) and 13B(2) of the form indicating that Dalton had been the subject of an investment-related consumer initiated complaint that (1) alleged compensatory damages of $10,000 or more, fraud, or the wrongful taking of property and (2) was settled or decided against the individual for $5,000 or more, or found fraud or the wrongful taking of property.

10.   On June 17, 1992, Patton, on behalf of Dalton, wrote to the NASD alleging that the Amended U–5 was misleading, and requesting that it be expunged from Dalton's record. Patton acknowledged that Dalton had a right to provide a summary of the transaction on the Disclosure Reporting Page, which Dalton did by filing an amended U–4 on July 23, 1992. On July 9, 1992, Keith E. Hinrichs, Assistant Director of the NASD, responded to Patton's letter by confirming that Prudential was required to amend Dalton's U–5 to include information concerning the Lytle settlement.

PROCEDURAL HISTORY

11.   On May 25, 1994, Dalton initiated arbitration proceedings before the NASD by filing an Uniform Submission Agreement.

12.   On May 27, 1994, Dalton filed his Statement of Claim.

13.   On September 20, 1994, Prudential filed its Joint Response to the Statement of Claim and a motion to dismiss. Prudential also executed the Uniform Submission Agreement.

14.   The Uniform Submission Agreement, which was signed by all parties, obligates the parties to conduct the arbitration in accordance with the Arbitration Code. The Uniform Submission Agreement provides in part:

> *1.   The undersigned parties hereby submit the present matter in controversy, as set forth in the attached statement of claim, answers, cross-claims and all related counter-claims and/or third party claims which may be asserted, to arbitration in accordance with the Constitution, By-Laws, Rules, Regulations and/or Code of Arbitration Procedure of the sponsoring organization.*

* * *

3.   The undersigned parties agree in the event a hearing is necessary, such hearing shall be held at a time and place as may be designated by the Director of Arbitration or the arbitrator(s). The undersigned parties further agree and understand that the arbitration will be in accordance with the Constitution, By-Laws, Rules, Regulations and/or NASD Code of Arbitration procedure of the sponsoring organization.

* * *

4.   The undersigned parties further agree to abide by and perform any award(s) rendered pursuant to this Submission Agreement and further agree that a judgment and any interest due thereon may be entered upon such award(s) and, for these purposes, the undersigned parties hereby voluntarily consent to the jurisdiction of any court of competent jurisdiction which may properly enter such judgment.

15.   The applicability of the Arbitration Code was not modified by the parties either in their agreement to arbitrate or in the Uniform Submission Agreements.

16.   In addition to paragraph 4 of the Submission Agreement, Section 3741 of the NASD's Arbitration Code provides that:

(a)   All awards shall be in writing and signed by a majority of the arbitrators or in such manner as is required by applicable law. Such awards may be entered as a judgment in any court of competent jurisdiction.

(b)   Unless the applicable law directs otherwise, all awards rendered pursuant to this Code shall be deemed final and not subject to review or appeal.

17.   On October 5, 1994, Dalton filed his response to Prudential's motion to dismiss. In his response Dalton noted the Arbitration Code does not refer to a motion proceeding which challenges the validity of a complaint. However, the Arbitration Code does not contain language precluding such a proceeding.

18.   On December 21, 1994, Prudential filed its reply in support of its motion to dismiss.

19.   On July 17, 1995, Prudential filed a supplemental brief. On August 10, 1995, Dalton filed his reply to Prudential's supplemental brief and Prudential filed a final supplement attaching a recent judicial opinion.

20.   Prudential requested that the NASD schedule a pre-hearing conference for the purpose of hearing Prudential's motion to dismiss. On June 9, 1995, the NASD notified the parties that the pre-hearing conference was

scheduled for August 18, 1995, at which time Prudential's motion to dismiss was to be heard.

21.   On August 18, 1995, in Tulsa, Oklahoma, the parties attended a pre-hearing conference at which time the panel heard substantial argument on Prudential's motion to dismiss. At that time, the parties accepted the panel's composition. The panel did not admit evidence other than that which was attached to the Statement of Claim, Prudential's Response or other submissions made by the parties in regard to the motion to dismiss.

22.   On August 24, 1995, the NASD arbitration administrator notified the parties that Prudential's motion had been granted, thereby dismissing Dalton's claim with prejudice.

23.   On October 12, 1995, the arbitration administrator wrote the parties enclosing a copy of the NASD final order setting forth the panel's ruling granting Prudential's motion to dismiss Dalton's claim.

24.   Prudential's complaint was timely filed in accordance with Section 9 of the Federal Arbitration Act, 9 U.S.C. § 9, which provides that a petition to confirm must be brought within one year after the award is made.

* * *

Legal Analysis

"There is a presumption in the Federal Arbitration Act that arbitration awards will be confirmed." The limits of judicial review of an arbitration award are very narrow. Courts must strive to uphold the arbitrator's award, "lest the efficiency of the arbitration process be lost." *Robbins*, 954 F.2d at 682.

Despite such necessary constraints, avenues exist which allow Courts to set aside arbitration awards for cause. The Federal Arbitration Act enumerates the limited instances in which federal Courts may vacate an arbitration award:

> *In either of the following cases the United States court in and for the district wherein the award was made may make an order vacating the award upon the application of any party to the arbitration . . .*
>
> *(c)   Where the arbitrators were guilty of misconduct in refusing . . . to hear evidence pertinent and material to the controversy . . .*
>
> *(d)   Where the arbitrators exceed their powers, or so imperfectly executed them that a mutual, final, and definite award upon the subject matter was not made.*

9 U.S.C.A. § 10 (1996).

"[F]ederal courts have never limited their scope of review [of an arbitration award] to a strict reading of [9 U.S.C.A. § 10]." An arbitrator is guided by a basic requirement to grant the parties a fundamentally fair hearing. This requirement has been expressed "in various forms."

A fundamentally fair hearing requires the procedural steps of notice, an opportunity to be heard, the opportunity to present evidence which is relevant and material, and arbitrators who are not infected with bias.

Dalton's contention is that untrue stigmatizing information was placed in the Amended U–5 by Prudential and filed with the NASD. Specifically, that which Dalton contends is stigmatizing in the Amended U–5 states the Lytle claim "was settled or decided against the individual (Dalton) for $5,000.00 or more, or found fraud, or the wrongful taking of property."

Dalton contends that while it is true $137,000.00 was paid by Prudential in settlement of the Lytle claim, he paid nothing, and any fraud involved was that of Prudential, not him. He further asserts that the untrue statement in the public document directly implicates him in precipitating the settlement, or that he was in some way guilty of fraud, and blackballs him in the securities industry from achieving a managerial position in the future. Dalton contends his former employer, Prudential, intentionally falsified the Amended U–5 to deflect attention from Prudential, who at that time was being investigated nationwide for fraud in urging their local managers and account executives to sell the subject limited partnerships sponsored by Prudential.

Dalton's principal claim alleges a breach of fiduciary duty by his former employer and tortious interference with future economic advantage under Oklahoma law. Dalton also asserts a claim in another matter to be reimbursed an attorney's fee which he alleges Prudential agreed to pay.

In response to Dalton's arbitration claim, Prudential filed a motion to dismiss for failure to state a claim and urged various defenses, i.e., the filing of the Amended U–5 is absolutely privileged, res judicata, estoppel, and statute of limitations.

In the arbitrator's order dismissing Dalton's complaint it is stated:

"After considering the pleadings, the oral arguments on the Motion to Dismiss and the evidence or materials presented at the pre-hearing, the undersigned arbitrators have decided in full and final resolution of the issues submitted for determination as follows:

*1.	Prudential Securities Incorporated's Motion to Dismiss is hereby granted in its entirety; therefore, all claims asserted in the Statement of Claim are hereby dismissed in their entirety;*

*2.	All requests for relief not specifically granted herein are hereby denied in their entirety; and*

*3.	The parties shall bear their own costs of arbitration including attorneys' fees except for those costs specifically enumerated herein."*

* * *

The NASD Uniform Submission Agreement signed by all the parties obligates them to conduct the arbitration in accordance with the Arbitration Code. The Arbitration Code, which sets forth the ground rules of arbitration, contains no provision for the filing of a motion to dismiss for failure to state a claim. It is also noted the Code does not prohibit such a motion. Because arbitration proceedings are recognized as informal, and not bound by the strict rules of the law and equity courts, in the appropriate case after hearing an argument, arbitrators would undoubtedly have authority to dismiss a claim which, on its face, does not state a claim entitling the claimant to relief, whether frivolous or not.

Herein, the arbitration panel's notice to claimant Dalton of the pre-hearing conference was scheduled for the purpose of hearing Prudential's motion to dismiss. At the pre-hearing conference, the panel did not hear any testimony from witnesses but considered the oral presentation of counsel for the parties and considered documentation in the file consisting of the statement of the claim, Prudential's motion to dismiss, and the parties' briefs with attachments to same. Thus, claimant Dalton was not provided the opportunity to have his previous motion to compel production of documents heard, nor was he given the opportunity to present factual evidence at a hearing relative to the factual issues presented by his claim. The award of the arbitrators sustaining Prudential's motion to dismiss without a hearing on the merits was by a 2 to 1 vote.

Federal courts presented with a claim to vacate an arbitration award under § 10 of the FAA generally looked to a determination of whether the arbitration process provided fundamental fairness, in essence, fundamental due process. The Tenth Circuit Court of Appeals stated in *Bowles Financial Group v. Stifel, Nicolaus & Co.*, 22 F.3rd 1010 (10th Cir.1994):

> *"Federal courts have never limited their scope of review [of an arbitration award]
> to a strict reading of [9 U.S.C.A. § 10]," Jenkins, 847 F.2d at 633. Courts
> have created a basic requirement that an arbitrator must grant the parties a
> fundamentally fair hearing, expressing their requirement in various forms. * * *
> The courts seem to agree that a fundamentally fair hearing requires only notice,
> opportunity to be heard and to present relevant and material evidence and argument
> before the decision makers, and that the decision makers are not infected with bias.
> * * *"*

This Court is of the view the arbitration panel was guilty of misconduct in refusing to hear evidence pertinent and material to the controversy and exceeded their powers in granting the motion to dismiss without hearing such evidence. The claimant was thereby denied fundamental fairness.

Before an arbitration panel should be able to dismiss a claim for failure to state a claim upon which relief can be granted, the claim should be facially deficient. Such is not the case here for if the allegations of the claimant's complaint are taken to be true, he would be entitled to some form of relief, even if it were limited to requiring Prudential to file a second Amended U–5 to set out the true nonstigmatizing facts. Thus, to assure fundamental fairness, claimant is entitled to offer evidence relevant to his claim.

Prudential, in support of the motion to dismiss, asserted that it was required to amend Dalton's form U–5, more than four years after his termination as branch manager, to update the Lytle claim when it was settled. The court believes this is correct as the NASD rules require updating the claim disposition. Prudential also states that the matters asserted in the amended form U–5 filed in June 1992 were true and accurate. Prudential further asserts that Dalton and his counsel were furnished with a copy of the appropriate page of the Amended U–5 for review and comment. The stipulated facts indicate to the contrary because Dalton and his counsel were not furnished with any part of the U–5 that stated the claim had been settled for $137,000.00 against Dalton, or as the result of Dalton's fraudulent acts or wrongful taking of property. Further, if Dalton's allegations are correct, it was not his fraudulent acts that precipitated the settlement but those of his employer, Prudential, in sponsoring and urging the sale of the subject limited partnerships. For this reason, Prudential's claim of estoppel lacks validity, if Dalton's factual claims can be established. Additionally, Prudential urges that responses by a brokerage firm in a form U–5 are absolutely privileged. Prudential also cites legal authority in support. Dalton cites the case of *Baravati v. Josephthal, Lyon and Ross, Incorporated*, 28 F.3rd 704 (7th Cir.1994). In *Baravati*, the court held that the U–5 termination notice required by the NASD is not absolutely privileged as a communication made in a judicial or quasi-judicial proceedings so as to insulate members from liability for contents of the form. The Court concludes that *Baravati* is the better view and also conforms to Oklahoma law. *Kirschstein v. Haynes*, 788 P.2d 941, at 947 (Okla.1990).

Prudential's *res judicata* defense does not appear to be supported by the record. The prior arbitration proceeding to which Prudential alludes involved different issues and different factual matters, unrelated to the Amended U–5 filing in the instant matter. Prudential also urges that the one year statute of limitations under Oklahoma in a defamation case has expired. However, the arbitration complaint herein by Dalton does not sound in defamation, but in alleged breach of fiduciary duty and tortious interference with economic advantage, each of which have two year statutes of limitation under the law of Oklahoma.

The issue before the Court at this time is not who is ultimately going to prevail. The issue is whether or not claimant Dalton was granted a fair hearing under the Arbitration Code to offer evidence in support of his factual claims. As previously stated, the Court concludes by sustaining the motion to dismiss of Prudential the arbitration panel improperly denied claimant the right to a fundamentally fair hearing. Therefore, the Court hereby vacates the underlying arbitration award for the reasons stated above and directs the parties and the matter be remanded to a duly constituted NASD arbitration panel to proceed with an evidentiary hearing and ruling on the merits, within six months from this date.

NOTES

Facts

1.   On the basis of what dispositive motion did the Court decide the case? Was it the only possible basis? Factually, why did the Court conclude that the arbitral tribunal proceeded on the basis one set of dispositive motions rather than another?

2.   How much discovery had been conducted by the time of the disposition of the case? What did that discovery suggest?

3.   What was the factual predicate of the dismissal? Was this factual predicate uncontroverted by the evidence on file?

4.   What would have been the benefit of holding a full evidentiary hearing in this case? Would it help out the plaintiff?

5.   Assume the case is resubmitted to arbitration. Is there anything that would prevent the arbitral tribunal in the next case to reach the exact same conclusion following a full hearing?

Law

1.   What is the relevant legal standard the tribunal would have had to apply? How would that standard have differed if it had elected the other means of disposing of the case?

2.   How did the arbitral tribunal fail to apply this test in the case at bar? Was there a way (other than continuing to trial) that the arbitral tribunal could have summarily disposed of the case?

B) AAA Arbitration Rules Permitting Dispositive Motions

The recent modification of the AAA Commercial Arbitration Rules clarify that tribunals are entitled to decide dispositive motions. This rule is consistent with other AAA arbitration rules which permit tribunals to decide the dispute by means of a dispositive motion. These rules are excerpted below followed by commentary published by the AAA at the time of the drafting of the rules.

AAA Commercial Arbitration Rules

Rule 33

The arbitrator may allow the filing of and make rulings upon a dispositive motion only if the arbitrator determines that the moving party has shown that the motion is likely to succeed and dispose of or narrow the issues in the case.

NOTE

1.   In 2009, the AAA included similar language in the AAA Employment Arbitration Rules, Rule 27. It did not include the same provision in its 2010 revisions of the AAA Commercial Arbitration Rules. Can you think why?

Douglas P. Lobel & David A. Vogel, AAA's New Commercial Arbitration Rules: Now More Like A Court

http://news.acc.com/accwm/downloads/Cooley_011013.pdf

* * *

Will New AAA Rules Be More Likely To Eliminate Meritless Claims?

One of the most vexing problems of arbitration is that arbitrators often permit every claim to go forward to hearing—no matter how infirm or meritless. This drives up the cost of arbitration. The AAA is trying to fix this, but it's not clear whether the rule change will have the intended effect.

Dispositive Motions. It has long been assumed, and even argued, that arbitrators possessed the inherent or implicit right to dispose of a claim by motion.4 The AAA now formally recognizes that the arbitrator can rule on a claim by a "dispositive motion" before a hearing if one party "is likely to succeed" on an issue, and the ruling will either narrow or dispose of issues in the case.

Remaining Problems. While incrementally helpful, the new rule presents problems. First, the standard is amorphous—what does "likely to succeed" mean? The wording is more permissive than the more specific standard required for a motion to dismiss ("not plausible") or summary judgment ("no reasonable juror"). And, what does "narrow the issues" mean—does it mean that disposing of an issue will reduce the number of witnesses or facts at the hearing, or the amount of damages, or merely the number of claims?

Also, the new rule has no procedures attached to it. It does not impose any briefing schedule or time for decision, so there is no assurance that an arbitrator will resolve the motion before a hearing. It does not say whether the arbitrator can consider evidence (like on summary judgment) or is limited to the content of pleadings (like on a motion to dismiss). Finally, the idea of a dispositive motion runs against the general grain of arbitration, where parties are traditionally given their "day in court" by way of a live hearing with witnesses.

We see the new rule as a good first step towards having a robust process for eliminating meritless claims, but it's clearly a work in progress.

NOTES

1. What are the key problems identified by Lobel & Vogel's response to the change in AAA Commercial Arbitration Rules? Do they apply more forcefully to an arbitration equivalent to a motion to dismiss or to a motion for summary judgment?

2. Look back over the case law excerpted above. Going by the reasoning of the courts in question, what appeared to be the more problematic procedural tool, arbitral summary judgment or arbitral dismissal at the outset of the dispute? Does this make sense to you? Why? Why not?

3. The Lobel & Vogel note identifies that the rule does not provide for a procedural mechanism how dispositive motions should be filed. How do you think this issue would be resolved in practice? Do you think that this process is satisfactory? Should be changed?

C) Uses of Dispositive Motions in Arbitration

This section introduces two settings in which dispositive motions could be used in arbitration. The chief context in which a dispositive motion could be used is summary judgment. Another setting in which such motions could be used is a motion to dismiss. The two motions are discussed in turn below.

1) *Summary Judgment in Arbitration*

The most likely setting for disposition of a case by motion in arbitration is summary judgment. At this stage, the parties will have been able to develop their claims beyond the initial exchange of the demand for arbitration and answer to the demand (if one is filed, at all). The parties further will have had a chance to develop their respective cases by means of discovery. The case thus would be nearly fully developed.

Depending upon the applicable law, cases may be particularly well suited for summary disposition after some discovery for yet another reason. Arbitrations by their nature involve questions of contract interpretation. In many instances, interpretive issues could be resolved as a matter of law. Depending upon applicable law, this resolution may require the *opportunity* for a party to submit parol evidence—or evidence of trade usage or course of performance or course of dealing. But once this opportunity had been provided it would be possible to resolve the interpretive issue without needing to take cross-examination of relevant witnesses.

The materials below outlines what the standard for summary judgment in arbitration is and draws upon federal court materials in order to establish when in the litigation process summary judgment may be appropriate.

Neary v. Prudential Insurance Co. of America

63 F.Supp.2d 208 (D.Conn., 1999)

NEVAS, DISTRICT JUDGE.

On August 7, 1996, the plaintiff, Thomas J. Neary ("Neary"), originally filed suit in this Court against the defendant, The Prudential Insurance Company of America ("Prudential"), alleging wrongful termination. On February 24, 1997, this Court granted Prudential's motion to compel arbitration. Over a year and a half later, on October 26, 1998, a NASD panel of arbitrators granted summary judgment in favor of Prudential.

Now pending before the Court are Neary's Application to Vacate Arbitration Award and Prudential's Cross-Motion to Confirm the Arbitration Award. For the following reasons, the Application to Vacate [doc. # 22] is GRANTED and the Cross-Motion to Confirm [doc. # 26] is DENIED.

STANDARD

The Federal Arbitration Act, 9 U.S.C. §§ 1–16 ("FAA"), sets forth the primary reasons for which an arbitration award may be set aside. In addition, the Second Circuit has "recognized that an arbitration award may be vacated if it is in 'manifest disregard of the law.' " The manifest disregard of the law doctrine has a "severely limited" reach, *id.*, and " 'clearly means more than error or misunderstanding with respect to the law,' ". Under this standard, in order to modify or vacate an award, "a court must find both that (1) the arbitrators knew of a governing legal principle yet refused to apply it or ignored it altogether, and (2) the law ignored by the arbitrators was well defined, explicit, and clearly applicable to the case." *Id.* (citation and footnote omitted).

DISCUSSION

Neary raises several issues in support of his motion to vacate. Most of these issues do not need to be considered at this time. * * *

After careful review of the voluminous pleadings submitted by the parties, the Court finds that the central issue arising from the arbitration proceedings is whether the arbitration panel's decision to grant summary judgment in favor of Prudential was in manifest disregard of the law. The Court holds that based on the record of the arbitration proceedings there is no doubt that the panel's decision must be vacated on this ground.

Neary brings wrongful termination claims predicated upon Conn. Gen.Stat. § 31–51q and *Sheets v. Teddy's Frosted Foods, Inc.*, 179 Conn. 471, 427 A.2d 385 (Conn.1980). To establish his claims, Neary must show that Prudential terminated him either, respectively, for exercising his First Amendment Rights or in violation of public policy. Therefore, these claims depend in large measure on resolving the issue of Prudential's intent.

Neary clearly identified for the arbitration panel the proper and relevant legal standard for summary judgment. As particularly relevant to the current motions, in his memorandum in opposition to Prudential's motion for summary judgment, he stated (1) "when ruling on a motion for summary judgment, the arbitration panel must resolve all ambiguities and draw all inferences in the light most favorable to the party opposing the motion," (Mem. Supp. Mot. Relief Stay Ex. 34 at 12 (citing *Gallo v. Prudential Residential Servs.*, 22 F.3d 1219, 1223 (2d Cir.1994))), (2) the "task in deciding a motion for summary judgment 'is carefully limited to discerning whether there are any issues of material fact to be tried, not to deciding them,'" (*id.* (quoting *LaFond v. General Physics Servs. Corp.*, 50 F.3d 165, 171 (2d Cir.1995))), and (3) "[i]f, as to the issue on which summary judgment is sought, there is any evidence in the record from any source from which a reasonable inference could be drawn in favor of the non-moving party, summary judgment is improper [,]" (*id.* at 13 (quoting *Chambers v. TRM Copy Ctrs. Corp.*, 43 F.3d 29, 37 (2d Cir.1994))).

It is unquestionable that the arbitration panel manifestly disregarded the standard for summary judgment. The record in this case provides overwhelming evidence to support an inference that Neary was wrongfully terminated. The record shows that, inter alia, Prudential documents referred to Neary as a "union instigator," (see Mem. Supp. Mot. Relief Stay Ex. 13 at 1), Prudential knew that Neary was associated with Francis Plante ("Plante"), a now-terminated Prudential agent who apparently was involved in whistle-blowing activities about Prudential, (see id.), Prudential deposed Neary as part of its defense against a suit by Plante and then terminated Neary about one month later allegedly based on information Neary provided during that deposition, and Neary procured disciplinary records of other Prudential agents that suggest that Prudential does not always terminate an employee for the types of company violations Neary admitted to committing, (see Mem. Supp. Mot. Relief Stay Ex. 35). These facts undeniably raise a genuine issue of material fact in regard to Prudential's motivation for terminating Neary. On a motion for summary judgment, that is all the law requires.

Although it is not clear from the written decision, the panel appears to have disregarded this evidence and certainly disregarded the requirement that all reasonable inferences must be drawn in favor of the non-movant on a motion for summary judgment. Indeed, this conclusion is reinforced by the fact that after a recess during argument on the summary judgment motion, the panel returned and merely questioned Neary at length about why he did not disclose to Prudential one of the alleged company violations he admitted at his deposition, i.e., that he was sharing commissions with Plante.[2] (See Prudential's Brief Opp. Neary's Mot. Vacate and Supp. Cross-Mot. Confirm Arbitration Award Ex. 9 at 101–16.) This questioning suggests that the panel's focus was on whether Prudential had valid grounds for terminating Neary, not on whether the evidence when properly construed in favor of Neary gives rise to a genuine issue of material fact about Prudential's motivation. The failure of the arbitration panel to explain its decision in this case also buttresses this Court's determination. See *Halligan*, 148 F.3d at 204 (stating "we believe that when a reviewing court is inclined to hold that an arbitration panel manifestly disregarded the law, the failure of the arbitrators to explain the award can be taken into account").[3]

CONCLUSION

For the reasons stated above, Neary's Application to Vacate Arbitration Award [doc. # 22] is GRANTED and Prudential's Cross-Motion to Confirm the Arbitration Award [doc. # 26] is DENIED. The stay in this case is ENDED and the parties are ORDERED to submit a proposed scheduling order within thirty days of this ruling.

---

[2] The Court notes the unusual nature of taking testimony from an individual at an argument on a summary judgment motion. However, given that arbitration is an informal process, the Court declines to place much weight on this occurrence. Of course, this informality cannot extend to ignoring the standard for summary judgment.

[3] The record in this case strongly indicates that the arbitration panel did not base its ruling in favor of Prudential on motion to dismiss grounds. The failure of the panel to explain its decision complicates this determination. However, the Court finds that the cases Prudential cited in support of its motion clearly do not warrant dismissal of Neary's Conn. Gen.Stat. § 31–51q claim or his Sheets wrongful termination claim. Thus, to the extent the panel relied on motion to dismiss grounds in its ruling that decision would also be in manifest disregard of the law. Neary does not press his CUTPA claim at this point, (see Mem. Supp. Mot. Relief Stay at 10), and the Court considers that claim abandoned.

NOTES

Facts

1. What is the factual predicate which would have supported a summary judgment in favor of Prudential?

2. The Court disagrees that there was a sufficient factual predicate for issuance of summary judgment in this case. What facts did the Court look to in particular that could contradict Prudential's story?

3. Does *Neary* need to do additional fact development in order to establish his claim? Differently put, does it look like he could have cross-moved for summary judgment?

4. Did the arbitral tribunal decide the issue of summary judgment on the pleadings? Did it hold a hearing? Does it matter?

Law

1. Does the standard for summary judgment in arbitration announced by the *Neary* Court sound familiar to you? Where does it come from?

2. Does the standard announced by the *Neary* Court fit within AAA Commercial Arbitration Rule 33? In other words, does AAA Commercial Arbitration Rule 33 contemplate issuance of summary judgment?

3. Working backwards from the summary judgment standard in *Neary*, does the standard suggest a minimum skeletal procedure for the disposition of summary judgment motions in arbitration? In other words, what must have taken place for the tribunal to be in a position to determine whether or not to grant summary judgment without running afoul of the problem identified by the *Neary* Court?

Celotex Corp. v. Catrett

477 U.S. 317 (1986)

JUSTICE REHNQUIST delivered the opinion of the Court.

The United States District Court for the District of Columbia granted the motion of petitioner Celotex Corporation for summary judgment against respondent Catrett because the latter was unable to produce evidence in support of her allegation in her wrongful-death complaint that the decedent had been exposed to petitioner's asbestos products. A divided panel of the Court of Appeals for the District of Columbia Circuit reversed, however, holding that petitioner's failure to support its motion with evidence tending to negate such exposure precluded the entry of summary judgment in its favor. This view conflicted with that of the Third Circuit in *In re Japanese Electronic Products*, 723 F.2d 238 (1983), rev'd on other grounds sub nom. *Matsushita Electric Industrial Co. v. Zenith Radio Corp.*, 475 U.S. 574, 106 S.Ct. 1348, 89 L.Ed.2d 538 (1986). We granted certiorari to resolve the conflict, 474 U.S. 944, 106 S.Ct. 342, 88 L.Ed.2d 285 (1985), and now reverse the decision of the District of Columbia Circuit.

Respondent commenced this lawsuit in September 1980, alleging that the death in 1979 of her husband, Louis H. Catrett, resulted from his exposure to products containing asbestos manufactured or distributed by 15 named corporations. Respondent's complaint sounded in negligence, breach of warranty, and strict liability. Two of the defendants filed motions challenging the District Court's *in personam* jurisdiction, and the remaining 13, including petitioner, filed motions for summary judgment. Petitioner's motion, which was first filed in September 1981, argued that summary judgment was proper because respondent had "failed to produce evidence that any [Celotex] product . . . was the proximate cause of the injuries alleged within the jurisdictional limits of [the District] Court." In particular, petitioner noted that respondent had failed to identify, in answering interrogatories specifically requesting such information, any witnesses who could testify about the decedent's exposure to petitioner's asbestos products. In response to petitioner's summary judgment motion, respondent then produced three documents which she claimed "demonstrate that there is a genuine material factual dispute" as to whether the decedent had ever been exposed to petitioner's asbestos products. The three documents included a transcript of a deposition of the decedent, a letter from an official of one of the decedent's former employers whom petitioner planned to call as a trial witness, and a letter from an insurance company to respondent's attorney, all tending to establish that the decedent had been exposed to petitioner's asbestos products in Chicago during 1970–1971. Petitioner, in turn, argued that the three documents were inadmissible hearsay and thus could not be considered in opposition to the summary judgment motion.

In July 1982, almost two years after the commencement of the lawsuit, the District Court granted all of the motions filed by the various defendants. The court explained that it was granting petitioner's summary judgment motion because "there [was] no showing that the plaintiff was exposed to the defendant Celotex's product in the District of Columbia or elsewhere within the statutory period." App. 217. Respondent appealed only the grant of summary judgment in favor of petitioner, and a divided panel of the District of Columbia Circuit reversed. The majority of the Court of Appeals held that petitioner's summary judgment motion was rendered "fatally defective" by the fact that petitioner "made no effort to adduce any evidence, in the form of affidavits or otherwise, to support its motion." According to the majority, Rule 56(e) of the Federal Rules of Civil Procedure, and this Court's decision in *Adickes v. S.H. Kress & Co.*, 398 U.S. 144, 159 (1970), establish that "the party opposing the motion for summary judgment bears the burden of responding only after the moving party has met its burden of coming forward with proof of the absence of any genuine issues of material fact." 244 U.S.App.D.C., at 163, 756 F.2d, at 184 (emphasis in original; footnote omitted). The majority therefore declined to consider petitioner's argument that none of the evidence produced by respondent in opposition to the motion for summary judgment would have been admissible at trial. Ibid. The dissenting judge argued that "[t]he majority errs in supposing that a party seeking summary judgment must always make an affirmative evidentiary showing, even in cases where there is not a triable, factual dispute." *Id.*, at 167, 756 F.2d, at 188 (Bork, J., dissenting). According to the dissenting judge, the majority's decision "undermines the traditional authority of trial judges to grant summary judgment in meritless cases." *Id.*, at 166, 756 F.2d, at 187.

We think that the position taken by the majority of the Court of Appeals is inconsistent with the standard for summary judgment set forth in Rule 56(c) of the Federal Rules of Civil Procedure. Under Rule 56(c), summary judgment is proper "if the pleadings, depositions, answers to interrogatories, and admissions on file, together with the affidavits, if any, show that there is no genuine issue as to any material fact and that the moving party is entitled to a judgment as a matter of law." In our view, the plain language of Rule 56(c) mandates the entry of summary judgment, after adequate time for discovery and upon motion, against a party who fails to make a showing sufficient to establish the existence of an element essential to that party's case, and on which that party will bear the burden of proof at trial. In such a situation, there can be "no genuine issue as to any material fact," since a complete failure of proof concerning an essential element of the nonmoving party's case necessarily renders all other facts immaterial. The moving party is "entitled to a judgment as a matter of law" because the nonmoving party has failed to make a sufficient showing on an essential element of her case with respect to which she has the burden of proof. "[T]h[e] standard [for granting summary judgment] mirrors the standard for a directed verdict under Federal Rule of Civil Procedure 50(a). . . ." *Anderson v. Liberty Lobby, Inc.*, 477 U.S. 242, 250 (1986).

Of course, a party seeking summary judgment always bears the initial responsibility of informing the district court of the basis for its motion, and identifying those portions of "the pleadings, depositions, answers to interrogatories, and admissions on file, together with the affidavits, if any," which it believes demonstrate the absence of a genuine issue of material fact. But unlike the Court of Appeals, we find no express or implied requirement in Rule 56 that the moving party support its motion with affidavits or other similar materials negating the opponent's claim. On the contrary, Rule 56(c), which refers to "the affidavits, if any" (emphasis added), suggests the absence of such a requirement. And if there were any doubt about the meaning of Rule 56(c) in this regard, such doubt is clearly removed by Rules 56(a) and (b), which provide that claimants and defendants, respectively, may move for summary judgment "with or without supporting affidavits" (emphasis added). The import of these subsections is that, regardless of whether the moving party accompanies its summary judgment motion with affidavits, the motion may, and should, be granted so long as whatever is before the district court demonstrates that the standard for the entry of summary judgment, as set forth in Rule 56(c), is satisfied. One of the principal purposes of the summary judgment rule is to isolate and dispose of factually unsupported claims or defenses, and we think it should be interpreted in a way that allows it to accomplish this purpose.

Respondent argues, however, that Rule 56(e), by its terms, places on the nonmoving party the burden of coming forward with rebuttal affidavits, or other specified kinds of materials, only in response to a motion for summary judgment "made and supported as provided in this rule." According to respondent's argument, since petitioner did not "support" its motion with affidavits, summary judgment was improper in this case. But as we have already explained, a motion for summary judgment may be made pursuant to Rule 56 "with or without supporting affidavits." In cases like the instant one, where the nonmoving party will bear the burden of proof at trial on a dispositive issue, a summary judgment motion may properly be made in reliance solely on the "pleadings, depositions, answers to interrogatories, and admissions on file." Such a motion, whether or not accompanied by affidavits, will be "made and supported as provided in this rule," and Rule 56(e) therefore requires the nonmoving party to go beyond the pleadings and by her own affidavits, or by the "depositions, answers to interrogatories, and admissions on file," designate "specific facts showing that there is a genuine issue for trial."

We do not mean that the nonmoving party must produce evidence in a form that would be admissible at trial in order to avoid summary judgment.

Obviously, Rule 56 does not require the nonmoving party to depose her own witnesses. Rule 56(e) permits a proper summary judgment motion to be opposed by any of the kinds of evidentiary materials listed in Rule 56(c), except the mere pleadings themselves, and it is from this list that one would normally expect the nonmoving party to make the showing to which we have referred.

The Court of Appeals in this case felt itself constrained, however, by language in our decision in *Adickes v. S.H. Kress & Co.*, 398 U.S. 144 (1970). There we held that summary judgment had been improperly entered in favor of the defendant restaurant in an action brought under 42 U.S.C. § 1983. In the course of its opinion, the *Adickes* Court said that "both the commentary on and the background of the 1963 amendment conclusively show that it was not intended to modify the burden of the moving party . . . to show initially the absence of a genuine issue concerning any material fact." *Id.*, at 159, 90 S.Ct., at 1609. We think that this statement is accurate in a literal sense, since we fully agree with the *Adickes* Court that the 1963 amendment to Rule 56(e) was not designed to modify the burden of making the showing generally required by Rule 56(c). It also appears to us that, on the basis of the showing before the Court in *Adickes*, the motion for summary judgment in that case should have been denied. But we do not think the *Adickes* language quoted above should be construed to mean that the burden is on the party moving for summary judgment to produce evidence showing the absence of a genuine issue of material fact, even with respect to an issue on which the nonmoving party bears the burden of proof. Instead, as we have explained, the burden on the moving party may be discharged by "showing"-that is, pointing out to the district court-that there is an absence of evidence to support the nonmoving party's case.

The last two sentences of Rule 56(e) were added, as this Court indicated in *Adickes*, to disapprove a line of cases allowing a party opposing summary judgment to resist a properly made motion by reference only to its pleadings. While the *Adickes* Court was undoubtedly correct in concluding that these two sentences were not intended to reduce the burden of the moving party, it is also obvious that they were not adopted to add to that burden. Yet that is exactly the result which the reasoning of the Court of Appeals would produce; in effect, an amendment to Rule 56(e) designed to facilitate the granting of motions for summary judgment would be interpreted to make it more difficult to grant such motions. Nothing in the two sentences themselves requires this result, for the reasons we have previously indicated, and we now put to rest any inference that they do so.

Our conclusion is bolstered by the fact that district courts are widely acknowledged to possess the power to enter summary judgments *sua sponte*, so long as the losing party was on notice that she had to come forward with all of her evidence. It would surely defy common sense to hold that the District Court could have entered summary judgment *sua sponte* in favor of petitioner in the instant case, but that petitioner's filing of a motion requesting such a disposition precluded the District Court from ordering it.

Respondent commenced this action in September 1980, and petitioner's motion was filed in September 1981. The parties had conducted discovery, and no serious claim can be made that respondent was in any sense "railroaded" by a premature motion for summary judgment. Any potential problem with such premature motions can be adequately dealt with under Rule 56(f), which allows a summary judgment motion to be denied, or the hearing on the motion to be continued, if the nonmoving party has not had an opportunity to make full discovery.

In this Court, respondent's brief and oral argument have been devoted as much to the proposition that an adequate showing of exposure to petitioner's asbestos products was made as to the proposition that no such showing should have been required. But the Court of Appeals declined to address either the adequacy of the showing made by respondent in opposition to petitioner's motion for summary judgment, or the question whether such a showing, if reduced to admissible evidence, would be sufficient to carry respondent's burden of proof at trial. We think the Court of Appeals with its superior knowledge of local law is better suited than we are to make these determinations in the first instance.

The Federal Rules of Civil Procedure have for almost 50 years authorized motions for summary judgment upon proper showings of the lack of a genuine, triable issue of material fact. Summary judgment procedure is properly regarded not as a disfavored procedural shortcut, but rather as an integral part of the Federal Rules as a whole, which are designed "to secure the just, speedy and inexpensive determination of every action." Fed.Rule Civ.Proc. 1. Before the shift to "notice pleading" accomplished by the Federal Rules, motions to dismiss a complaint or to strike a defense were the principal tools by which factually insufficient claims or defenses could be isolated and prevented from going to trial with the attendant unwarranted consumption of public and private resources. But with the advent of "notice pleading," the motion to dismiss seldom fulfills this function any more, and its place has been taken by the motion for summary judgment. Rule 56 must be construed with due regard not only for the rights of persons asserting claims and defenses that are adequately based in fact to have those claims and defenses tried to a jury, but also for the rights of persons opposing such claims and defenses to demonstrate in the manner provided by the Rule, prior to trial, that the claims and defenses have no factual basis.

The judgment of the Court of Appeals is accordingly reversed, and the case is remanded for further proceedings consistent with this opinion.

It is so ordered.

NOTES

Facts

1. What was the cause of action in this case? How did the plaintiff support the cause of action?

2. When did the defendant move for summary judgment?

3. How did the defendant support its motion for summary judgment? Did the defendant submit evidence to prove the absence of a material issue of fact? Incidentally, how would one go about doing so if that were the standard?

Law

1. When did the *Celotex* Court consider it appropriate for a party to file a motion for summary judgment?

2. How did the Court apportion the burden of proof on the parties to a summary judgment action?

3. Consider the procedural context of *Celotex*, how easy or difficult is it to transpose the *Celotex* standard to arbitration proceedings? Is the language between AAA Commercial Arbitration Rule 33 sufficiently close to Federal Rule of Civil Procedure 56 to allow incorporation of summary judgment? Does AAA Commercial Arbitration Rule 33 incorporate the device by reference? If so, how?

4. Assuming that the *Celotex* standard were applied in arbitration, does this mean that respondent's should automatically file for summary judgment after the close of discovery? If so, what does the rule require the arbitrator to do? How does this inform the question raised by the Lobel & Vogel article about the appropriate procedure for the filing of a summary judgment motion and its disposition by the arbitral tribunal?

2) *Motions to Dismiss in Arbitration*

Motions to dismiss in arbitration pose a problem that is altogether different from summary judgment. Thus, summary judgment presupposes the development of the case past some discovery. A motion to dismiss by definition is one of the first, if not the first, pleading filed by a defendant in a civil action. At this stage there would be little factual and legal development of the case. To make matters worse, the AAA's form Demand for Arbitration apportions about three inches of space in which to include the nature of the claim, meaning that a party relying upon the form would do little more than to provide notice of the existence of a claim without any development.

Problematically, the motion to dismiss standard as it currently stands in federal court at least is at odds with this pleading standard. Even more problematically, the arbitration rules themselves do not provide a standard upon which a motion to dismiss could be granted that would deviate from the Federal Rules of Civil Procedure. Consequently, it would be difficult to fashion a goalpost the parties could use as a reference point for the dismissal of a demand for arbitration at this early stage of the proceedings.

Ashcroft v. Iqbal

556 U.S. 662 (2009)

JUSTICE KENNEDY delivered the opinion of the Court.

Respondent Javaid Iqbal is a citizen of Pakistan and a Muslim. In the wake of the September 11, 2001, terrorist attacks he was arrested in the United States on criminal charges and detained by federal officials. Respondent claims he was deprived of various constitutional protections while in federal custody. To redress the alleged deprivations, respondent filed a complaint against numerous federal officials, including John Ashcroft, the former Attorney General of the United States, and Robert Mueller, the Director of the Federal Bureau of Investigation (FBI). Ashcroft and Mueller are the petitioners in the case now before us. As to these two petitioners, the complaint alleges that they adopted an unconstitutional policy that subjected respondent to harsh conditions of confinement on account of his race, religion, or national origin.

In the District Court petitioners raised the defense of qualified immunity and moved to dismiss the suit, contending the complaint was not sufficient to state a claim against them. The District Court denied the motion to dismiss, concluding the complaint was sufficient to state a claim despite petitioners' official status at the times in question. Petitioners brought an interlocutory appeal in the Court of Appeals for the Second Circuit. The court, without discussion, assumed it had jurisdiction over the order denying the motion to dismiss; and it affirmed the District Court's decision.

Respondent's account of his prison ordeal could, if proved, demonstrate unconstitutional misconduct by some governmental actors. But the allegations and pleadings with respect to these actors are not before us here. This case instead turns on a narrower question: Did respondent, as the plaintiff in the District Court, plead factual matter that, if taken as true, states a claim that petitioners deprived him of his clearly established constitutional rights. We hold respondent's pleadings are insufficient.

* * *

IV

A

We turn to respondent's complaint. Under Federal Rule of Civil Procedure 8(a)(2), a pleading must contain a "short and plain statement of the claim showing that the pleader is entitled to relief." As the Court held in *Twombly*, 550 U.S. 544, the pleading standard Rule 8 announces does not require "detailed factual allegations," but it demands more than an unadorned, the-defendant-unlawfully-harmed-me accusation. A pleading that offers "labels and conclusions" or "a formulaic recitation of the elements of a cause of action will not do." Nor does a complaint suffice if it tenders "naked assertion[s]" devoid of "further factual enhancement."

To survive a motion to dismiss, a complaint must contain sufficient factual matter, accepted as true, to "state a claim to relief that is plausible on its face." A claim has facial plausibility when the plaintiff pleads factual content that allows the court to draw the reasonable inference that the defendant is liable for the misconduct alleged. The plausibility standard is not akin to a "probability requirement," but it asks for more than a sheer possibility that a defendant has acted unlawfully. Where a complaint pleads facts that are "merely consistent with" a defendant's liability, it "stops short of the line between possibility and plausibility of 'entitlement to relief.' "

Two working principles underlie our decision in *Twombly*. First, the tenet that a court must accept as true all of the allegations contained in a complaint is inapplicable to legal conclusions. Threadbare recitals of the elements of a cause of action, supported by mere conclusory statements, do not suffice. Rule 8 marks a notable and generous departure from the hyper-technical, code-pleading regime of a prior era, but it does not unlock the doors of discovery for a plaintiff armed with nothing more than conclusions. Second, only a complaint that states a plausible claim for relief survives a motion to dismiss. Determining whether a complaint states a plausible claim for relief will, as the Court of Appeals observed, be a context-specific task that requires the reviewing court to draw on its judicial experience and common sense. But where the well-pleaded facts do not permit the court to infer more than the mere possibility of misconduct, the complaint has alleged—but it has not "show[n]"—"that the pleader is entitled to relief." Fed. Rule Civ. Proc. 8(a)(2).

In keeping with these principles a court considering a motion to dismiss can choose to begin by identifying pleadings that, because they are no more than conclusions, are not entitled to the assumption of truth. While legal conclusions can provide the framework of a complaint, they must be supported by factual allegations. When there are well-pleaded factual allegations, a court should assume their veracity and then determine whether they plausibly give rise to an entitlement to relief.

Our decision in *Twombly* illustrates the two-pronged approach. There, we considered the sufficiency of a complaint alleging that incumbent telecommunications providers had entered an agreement not to compete and to forestall competitive entry, in violation of the Sherman Act, 15 U.S.C. § 1. Recognizing that § 1 enjoins only anticompetitive conduct "effected by a contract, combination, or conspiracy," *Copperweld Corp. v. Independence Tube Corp.*, 467 U.S. 752, 775, 104 S.Ct. 2731, 81 L.Ed.2d 628 (1984), the plaintiffs in *Twombly* flatly pleaded that the defendants "ha[d] entered into a contract, combination or conspiracy to prevent competitive entry . . . and ha[d] agreed not to compete with one another." 550 U.S., at 551, 127 S.Ct. 1955 (internal quotation marks omitted). The complaint also alleged that the defendants' "parallel course of conduct . . . to prevent competition" and inflate prices was indicative of the *680 unlawful agreement alleged. Ibid. (internal quotation marks omitted).

The Court held the plaintiffs' complaint deficient under Rule 8. In doing so it first noted that the plaintiffs' assertion of an unlawful agreement was a " 'legal conclusion' " and, as such, was not entitled to the assumption of truth. *Id.*, at 555, 127 S.Ct. 1955. Had the Court simply credited the allegation of a conspiracy, the plaintiffs would have stated a claim for relief and been entitled to proceed perforce. The Court next addressed the "nub" of the plaintiffs' complaint—the well-pleaded, nonconclusory factual allegation of parallel behavior—to determine whether it gave rise to a "plausible suggestion of conspiracy." *Id.*, at 565–566, 127 S.Ct. 1955. Acknowledging that parallel conduct was consistent with an unlawful agreement, the Court nevertheless concluded that it did not plausibly suggest an illicit accord because it was not only compatible with, but indeed was more likely explained by, lawful, unchoreographed free-market behavior. *Id.*, at 567, 127 S.Ct. 1955. Because the well-pleaded fact of parallel conduct, accepted as true, did not plausibly suggest an unlawful agreement, the Court held the plaintiffs' complaint must be dismissed. *Id.*, at 570, 127 S.Ct. 1955.

B

Under *Twombly*'s construction of Rule 8, we conclude that respondent's complaint has not "nudged [his] claims" of invidious discrimination "across the line from conceivable to plausible."

We begin our analysis by identifying the allegations in the complaint that are not entitled to the assumption of truth. Respondent pleads that petitioners "knew of, condoned, and willfully and maliciously agreed to subject [him]" to harsh conditions of confinement "as a matter of policy, solely on account of [his] religion, race, and/or national origin and for no legitimate penological interest." The complaint alleges that Ashcroft was the "principal architect" of this invidious policy, and that Mueller was "instrumental" in adopting and executing it. These bare assertions, much like the pleading of conspiracy in *Twombly*, amount to nothing more than a "formulaic recitation of the elements" of a constitutional discrimination claim, 550 U.S., at 555, 127 S.Ct. 1955, namely, that petitioners adopted a policy " 'because of,' not merely 'in spite of,' its adverse effects upon an identifiable group." As such, the allegations are conclusory and not entitled to be assumed true. To be clear, we do not reject these bald allegations on the ground that they are unrealistic or nonsensical. We do not so characterize them any more than the Court in *Twombly* rejected the plaintiffs' express allegation of a " 'contract, combination or conspiracy to prevent competitive entry,' " because it thought that claim too chimerical to be maintained. It is the conclusory nature of respondent's allegations, rather than their extravagantly fanciful nature, that disentitles them to the presumption of truth.

We next consider the factual allegations in respondent's complaint to determine if they plausibly suggest an entitlement to relief. The complaint alleges that "the [FBI], under the direction of Defendant MUELLER, arrested and detained thousands of Arab Muslim men . . . as part of its investigation of the events of September 11." It further claims that "[t]he policy of holding post-

September-11th detainees in highly restrictive conditions of confinement until they were 'cleared' by the FBI was approved by Defendants ASHCROFT and MUELLER in discussions in the weeks after September 11, 2001." Taken as true, these allegations are consistent with petitioners' purposefully designating detainees "of high interest" because of their race, religion, or national origin. But given more likely explanations, they do not plausibly establish this purpose.

The September 11 attacks were perpetrated by 19 Arab Muslim hijackers who counted themselves members in good standing of al Qaeda, an Islamic fundamentalist group. Al Qaeda was headed by another Arab Muslim—Osama bin Laden—and composed in large part of his Arab Muslim disciples. It should come as no surprise that a legitimate policy directing law enforcement to arrest and detain individuals because of their suspected link to the attacks would produce a disparate, incidental impact on Arab Muslims, even though the purpose of the policy was to target neither Arabs nor Muslims. On the facts respondent alleges the arrests Mueller oversaw were likely lawful and justified by his nondiscriminatory intent to detain aliens who were illegally present in the United States and who had potential connections to those who committed terrorist acts. As between that "obvious alternative explanation" for the arrests, *Twombly*, at 567and the purposeful, invidious discrimination respondent asks us to infer, discrimination is not a plausible conclusion.

But even if the complaint's well-pleaded facts give rise to a plausible inference that respondent's arrest was the result of unconstitutional discrimination, that inference alone would not entitle respondent to relief. It is important to recall that respondent's complaint challenges neither the constitutionality of his arrest nor his initial detention in the MDC. Respondent's constitutional claims against petitioners rest solely on their ostensible "policy of holding post-September-11th detainees" in the ADMAX SHU once they were categorized as "of high interest." To prevail on that theory, the complaint must contain facts plausibly showing that petitioners purposefully adopted a policy of classifying post-September-11 detainees as "of high interest" because of their race, religion, or national origin.

This the complaint fails to do. Though respondent alleges that various other defendants, who are not before us, may have labeled him a person of "of high interest" for impermissible reasons, his only factual allegation against petitioners accuses them of adopting a policy approving "restrictive conditions of confinement" for post-September-11 detainees until they were " 'cleared' by the FBI." Ibid. Accepting the truth of that allegation, the complaint does not show, or even intimate, that petitioners purposefully housed detainees in the

ADMAX SHU due to their race, religion, or national origin. All it plausibly suggests is that the Nation's top law enforcement officers, in the aftermath of a devastating terrorist attack, sought to keep suspected terrorists in the most secure conditions available until the suspects could be cleared of terrorist activity. Respondent does not argue, nor can he, that such a motive would violate petitioners' constitutional obligations. He would need to allege more by way of factual content to "nudg[e]" his claim of purposeful discrimination "across the line from conceivable to plausible."

* * *

V

We hold that respondent's complaint fails to plead sufficient facts to state a claim for purposeful and unlawful discrimination against petitioners. The Court of Appeals should decide in the first instance whether to remand to the District Court so that respondent can seek leave to amend his deficient complaint.

The judgment of the Court of Appeals is reversed, and the case is remanded for further proceedings consistent with this opinion.

It is so ordered.

PART V

Proving Facts in Arbitration

The procedural issues section made you aware of the key procedural differences between arbitration and litigation, as well as the tools that will be at your disposal as arbitration counsel. This part of the book will now get to the heart of the job of an arbitration counsel: actually proving his or her client's case. Proving a client's case in most instances is a matter of proving facts to the tribunal. Some cases may be won and lost on the strength of legal imagination and argument. But most cases come down to the question of what actually happened and what has actually been proved.

As with the procedural issues discussed above, the tools available to you to prove a case in arbitration at first glance will look familiar to you. They are reasonably similar tools to what one would use in the litigation context. But again, the tools are only seemingly the same. There are fundamental differences in how facts can be gathered and then proved. Skilled use of these tools therefore will again make a difference between good arbitration counsel and an inexperienced one. This section sets out to help you to understand the key differences between litigation and arbitration and tools that you can bring to bear in the arbitration context.

This section will address four issues. You will meet these issues again in the context of the Hardmont-Gilmore dispute. These issues in which you will revisit the Hardmont-Gilmore dispute are disclosure, e-Dislosure, the rules of evidence, and the use of witnesses in arbitration. As you revisit the Hardmont-Gilmore dispute in this context, track how your procedural choices impacted your ability to prove your case. You will see that good procedural maneuvering does indeed make a difference in this respect.

CHAPTER 16

Disclosure

One of the costliest—and most time-consuming—aspects of litigation is discovery. Discovery permits the parties, amongst other things, to request the production of documents and the deposition of potential witnesses. Discovery permits the litigants to find out "what really happened" in a dispute and thus arms with the best available evidence to resolve their dispute.

The costs of discovery arise in large part because of the time it takes to perform. Document production requires the parties to read through comparatively broadly document requests and search their archives for all responsive documents. Once the parties have searched their archives for potentially responsive documents, they must determine whether any of the documents should be withheld from production on the basis of privilege etc. Depositions further require parties to prepare witnesses to testify and to put aside significant time to take and evaluate the deposition.

Discovery in arbitration—often referred to as "disclosure"—presents a challenge. Requiring broad disclosure in arbitration is both time consuming and expensive. This undermines the goal of arbitration to be an efficient and fast dispute resolution mechanism. But when disclosure is restricted in order to enhance efficiency, the ability of the parties (and the panel) to determine the most plausible sequence of events leading to the dispute may be impaired.

As discussed in this chapter, arbitrators typically walk a tightrope between both extremes. They neither permit discovery to the full of extent of commercial litigation, nor do they completely cut off the parties' ability to discover probative evidence. This chapter addresses the rules within which the parties must operate.

Fact Scenario

Look back at the fact scenario in Chapter 11. What discovery does Hardmont need to prove its case? What discovery do Acme, Gilmore and RRF need to prove its defense? Discuss and draft the discovery requests for the Claimant or the Respondents in the arbitration.

Readings

A) Discovery in Federal Court

Federal Rules of Civil Procedure, Rule 26(b)(1)–(2)

(b) Discovery Scope and Limits.

(1) Scope in General. Unless otherwise limited by court order, the scope of discovery is as follows: Parties may obtain discovery regarding any nonprivileged matter that is relevant to any party's claim or defense—including the existence, description, nature, custody, condition, and location of any documents or other tangible things and the identity and location of persons who know of any discoverable matter. For good cause, the court may order discovery of any matter relevant to the subject matter involved in the action. Relevant information need not be admissible at the trial if the discovery appears reasonably calculated to lead to the discovery of admissible evidence. All discovery is subject to the limitations imposed by Rule 26(b)(2)(C).

(2) Limitations on Frequency and Extent.

(A) When Permitted. By order, the court may alter the limits in these rules on the number of depositions and interrogatories or on the length of depositions under Rule 30. By order or local rule, the court may also limit the number of requests under Rule 36.

(B) Specific Limitations on Electronically Stored Information. A party need not provide discovery of electronically stored information from sources that the party identifies as not reasonably accessible because of undue burden or cost. On motion to compel discovery or for a protective order, the party from whom discovery is sought must show that the information is not reasonably accessible because of undue burden or cost. If that showing is made, the court may nonetheless order discovery from such sources if the requesting party shows good cause, considering the limitations of Rule 26(b)(2)(C). The court may specify conditions for the discovery.

(C) When Required. On motion or on its own, the court must limit the frequency or extent of discovery otherwise allowed by these rules or by local rule if it determines that:

(i)   the discovery sought is unreasonably cumulative or duplicative, or can be obtained from some other source that is more convenient, less burdensome, or less expensive;

(ii)   the party seeking discovery has had ample opportunity to obtain the information by discovery in the action; or

(iii)   the burden or expense of the proposed discovery outweighs its likely benefit, considering the needs of the case, the amount in controversy, the parties' resources, the importance of the issues at stake in the action, and the importance of the discovery in resolving the issues.

NOTES

1.   What forms of discovery are discussed in the rule excerpt?

2.   How relevant do documents have to be in order to be "discoverable"?

3.   The excerpt mentions discovery of "electronically stored information". What does it refer to? What differs between discovery of "electronically stored information" and discovery of paper documents?

4.   Upon what basis can a court limit discovery?

B)   Applicable Arbitration Rules

Discovery is typically governed by rule. The applicable arbitration rules set out how the arbitrator should deal with discovery requests. This section sets out the predominant AAA arbitration rules on point.

AAA Commercial Arbitration Rules

Rule 22

(a)   Authority of arbitrator. The arbitrator shall manage any necessary exchange of information among the parties with a view to achieving an efficient and economical resolution of the dispute, while at the same time promoting equality of treatment and safeguarding each party's opportunity to fairly present its claims and defenses.

(b)   Documents. The arbitrator may, on application of a party or on the arbitrator's own initiative:

i.   require the parties to exchange documents in their possession or custody on which they intend to rely;

ii.   require the parties to update their exchanges of the documents on which they intend to rely as such documents become known to them;

iii.   require the parties, in response to reasonable document requests, to make available to the other party documents, in the responding party's possession or custody, not otherwise readily available to the party seeking the documents, reasonably believed by the party seeking the documents to exist and to be relevant and material to the outcome of disputed issues; and

iv.   require the parties, when documents to be exchanged or produced are maintained in electronic form, to make such documents available in the form most convenient and economical for the party in possession of such documents, unless the arbitrator determines that there is good cause for requiring the documents to be produced in a different form. The parties should attempt to agree in advance upon, and the arbitrator may determine, reasonable search parameters to balance the need for production of electronically stored documents relevant and material to the outcome of disputed issues against the cost of locating and producing them.

Rule 23

The arbitrator shall have the authority to issue any orders necessary to enforce the provisions of rules R–21 and R–22 and to otherwise achieve a fair, efficient and economical resolution of the case, including, without limitation:

(a)   conditioning any exchange or production of confidential documents and information, and the admission of confidential evidence at the hearing, on appropriate orders to preserve such confidentiality;

(b)   imposing reasonable search parameters for electronic and other documents if the parties are unable to agree;

(c)   allocating costs of producing documentation, including electronically stored documentation;

(d)   in the case of willful non-compliance with any order issued by the arbitrator, drawing adverse inferences, excluding evidence and other submissions, and/or making special allocations of costs or an interim award of costs arising from such non-compliance; and

(e)   issuing any other enforcement orders which the arbitrator is empowered to issue under applicable law.

NOTES

1.   What is the standard of relevance for discovery under the Commercial Rules?

2. Does the rule mention forms of discovery other than document production? Are depositions, interrogatories and requests for admission available in arbitrations governed by the AAA Commercial Rules?

3. By means of what device does the tribunal manage the discovery process? Look back at the last chapter. Are discovery decisions by the tribunal reviewable in court? How would they be enforced should a party simply refuse to comply?

4. Look back at the chapter on the preliminary hearing. When do you think discovery should appropriately be served? Before the preliminary hearing? After the preliminary hearing?

AAA Procedures for Large, Complex Commercial Disputes

L–3. Management of Proceedings

(a)   The arbitrator shall take such steps as deemed necessary or desirable to avoid delay and to achieve a fair, speedy and cost-effective resolution of a Large, Complex Commercial Dispute.

(b)   As promptly as practicable after the selection of the arbitrator(s), a preliminary hearing shall be scheduled in accordance with sections P–1 and P–2 of these rules.

(c)   The parties shall exchange copies of all exhibits they intend to submit at the hearing at least 10 calendar days prior to the hearing unless the arbitrator(s) determines otherwise.

(d)   The parties and the arbitrator(s) shall address issues pertaining to the pre-hearing exchange and production of information in accordance with rule R–22 of the AAA Commercial Rules, and the arbitrator's determinations on such issues shall be included within the Scheduling and Procedure Order.

(e)   The arbitrator, or any single member of the arbitration tribunal, shall be authorized to resolve any disputes concerning the pre-hearing exchange and production of documents and information by any reasonable means within his discretion, including, without limitation, the issuance of orders set forth in rules R–22 and R–23 of the AAA Commercial Rules.

(f)   In exceptional cases, at the discretion of the arbitrator, upon good cause shown and consistent with the expedited nature of arbitration, the arbitrator may order depositions to obtain the testimony of a person who may possess information determined by the arbitrator to be relevant and material to the outcome of the case. The arbitrator may allocate the cost of taking such a deposition.

(g) Generally, hearings will be scheduled on consecutive days or in blocks of consecutive days in order to maximize efficiency and minimize costs.

NOTES

1. Do the AAA Procedures for Large, Complex Commercial Disputes lower the standard of document production? Put differently, if a dispute is governed by the AAA Procedures for Large, Complex Commercial Disputes, do more documents become discoverable by comparison to the AAA Commercial Rules?

2. How do the AAA Procedures for Large, Complex Commercial Disputes deal with depositions? Can you make an argument from the AAA Procedures for Large, Complex Commercial Disputes whether depositions should available under the AAA Commercial Rules? Consider the following statement by an experienced AAA arbitrator:

   > *Arbitrators have a strong belief that witnesses should testify only once, and that is at the hearing. So there is no need to incur the expense of earlier (and generally protracted) depositions.*

   Charles J. Moxley, Jr., *Discovery in Arbitration: How Arbitrators Think*, 63(3) DISP. RES. J. (Aug. 2008/Oct. 2008), available at http://law.pace.edu/sites/default/files/CLE/9-13-12_Discovery_in_Arbitration-How_Arbitrators_Think.pdf.

3. Does the tribunal have the power to permit discovery by interrogatories or requests for admission? As one comment on the current rules noted, "[i]n the 'Procedures for Large, Complex Commercial Disputes' section of the new AAA rules, Rule L–3 (formerly L–4) removes the prior reference to the arbitrator's power to authorize the propounding of interrogatories" Jones Day LLP, *American Arbitration Association Issues Revisions to Commercial Arbitration Rules*, September 2013, available at http://www.jonesday.com/American-Arbitration-Association-Issues-Revisions-to-Commercial-Arbitration-Rules-09-25-2013/?RSS=true. Does this change suggest that the arbitrator no longer has this power?

AAA Employment Arbitration Rules

Rule 9

The arbitrator shall have the authority to order such discovery, by way of deposition, interrogatory, document production, or otherwise, as the arbitrator considers necessary to a full and fair exploration of the issues in dispute, consistent with the expedited nature of arbitration.

The AAA does not require notice of discovery related matters and communications unless a dispute arises. At that time, the parties should notify the AAA of the dispute so that it may be presented to the arbitrator for determination.

NOTES

1.   How do the AAA Employment Arbitration Rules differ from the AAA Commercial Rules? What types of discovery are available? What is the standard for seeking discovery?

2.   What do you think is the justification for the difference between discovery in commercial disputes and discovery in employment disputes? How do these cases differ? Whom do you expect to have most of the relevant evidence in commercial cases? How about in employment cases?

C) Guidance on Meaning of "Relevant and Material" Standard

Revised AAA Commercial Arbitration Rule 22(b)(iii) sets as standard for discovery that documents must be "relevant and material to the outcome of the dispute." Litigators will be familiar with the "relevance" of evidence from the context of the Federal Rules of Evidence.

The combination of relevance with materiality also is not new. Rather, it was developed in the context of international arbitration in order to set the appropriate balance for document disclosures between a "U.S. common law approach" premised upon the standards in Federal Rule of Civil Procedure 26 and the "European civil law approach" which would frown upon any use of document disclosures (except for the limited request for a specific and specifically identified document).

Federal Rules of Evidence, Rule 401

Evidence is relevant if:

(a)   it has any tendency to make a fact more or less probable than it would be without the evidence; and

(b)   the fact is of consequence in determining the action.

NOTES

1. What does Rule 401 establish? What kind of argument do you have to make with regard to a piece of evidence to show that it is relevant? What counterargument can you make to say that it is not relevant?

2. Does FRE 401(b) introduce a materiality standard? If so, is it lower than the threshold included in the AAA Commercial Arbitration Rules? If so, what more does materiality require than being "of consequence in determining the action"? Or to ask differently, do you think every piece of admissible evidence is material?

3. Look back at Federal Rule of Civil Procedure 26. Do documents have to be "relevant" in order to be discoverable?

IBA Rules on Taking of Evidence in International Arbitration

Article 3 Documents

1.   Within the time ordered by the Arbitral Tribunal, each Party shall submit to the Arbitral Tribunal and to the other Parties all Documents available to it on which it relies, including public Documents and those in the public domain, except for any Documents that have already been submitted by another Party.

2.   Within the time ordered by the Arbitral Tribunal, any Party may submit to the Arbitral Tribunal and to the other Parties a Request to Produce.

3.   A Request to Produce shall contain:

(a)   (i)   a description of each requested Document sufficient to identify it, or

(ii)   a description in sufficient detail (including subject matter) of a narrow and specific requested category of Documents that are reasonably believed to exist; in the case of Documents maintained in electronic form, the requesting Party may, or the Arbitral Tribunal may order that it shall be required to, identify specific files, search terms, individuals or other means of searching for such Documents in an efficient and economical manner;

(b)   a statement as to how the Documents requested are relevant to the case and material to its outcome; and

(c)   (i)   a statement that the Documents requested are not in the possession, custody or control of the requesting Party or a statement of the reasons why it would be unreasonably burdensome for the requesting Party to produce such Documents, and

(ii)   a statement of the reasons why the requesting Party assumes the Documents requested are in the possession, custody or control of another Party.

4.   Within the time ordered by the Arbitral Tribunal, the Party to whom the Request to Produce is addressed shall produce to the other Parties and, if the Arbitral Tribunal so orders, to it, all the Documents requested in its possession, custody or control as to which it makes no objection.

* * *

NOTES

1.   The IBA Rules are in many ways more precise than even the revised AAA Commercial Arbitration Rules. This detail is helpful to understanding what the IBA Rules mean when they require that the documents requested are "relevant to the case and material to its outcome." Under Rule 3(3)(a), how does one have to draft a request for disclosure of documents?

2.   The AAA Commercial Rules use the terminology "relevant and material." The IBA Rules stated that documents must be "relevant to the case and material to its outcome." Is the standard set out in the IBA Rules helpful further to develop a standard for AAA commercial arbitrations? How?

3.   How would you explain to the opposing party (or the tribunal) that a document or class of documents is "relevant" to the case? Is it possible to substitute FRE 401 for "relevant to the case" in IBA Rule 3? How would that provision look?

4.   Does materiality in the IBA Rule refer to something more than relevance as defined in FRE 401?

Tidewater Inc. v. Venezuela

ICSID Case No ARB/10/5, Procedural Order No 1 on Production of Documents (Mar. 29, 2011), IIC 486 (2011)

A. Request for Arbitration and Constitution of the Tribunal

1. On February 16, 2010, Tidewater Inc, Tidewater Investment SRL, Tidewater Caribe, C.A., Twenty Grand Offshore, L.L.C., Point Marine, L.L.C., Twenty Grand Marine Service, L.L.C., Jackson Marine, L.L.C. and Zapata Gulf Marine Operators, L.L.C. (together 'Tidewater' or 'Claimants') filed with the International Centre for Settlement of Investment Disputes ('the Centre' or 'ICSID') a Request for Arbitration under the ICSID Arbitration Rules against the Bolivarian Republic of Venezuela ('Venezuela' or 'Respondent').

2. Tidewater alleges that Venezuela unlawfully expropriated its investments in the maritime-support industry in Venezuela without compensation. It submits that the Centre has jurisdiction over this dispute as all relevant countries are parties to the ICSID Convention ('the Convention'), those countries being Venezuela, Barbados (under the laws of which Tidewater Investment S.R.L. is constituted) and the United States (under the laws of which all the other Claimants are constituted, except Tidewater Caribe, C.A. which is a wholly-owned subsidiary of Tidewater Investment S.R.L.). Accordingly, Tidewater submits that each of the Claimants is vis-à-vis the Respondent a "national of another Contracting State."2 It invokes two grounds for the Tribunal's jurisdiction:

(a) Article 22 of the Venezuelan Law on the Promotion and Protection of Investments ('Investment Law'), which Tidewater submits constitutes a standing consent to ICSID arbitration; and

(b) The bilateral investment treaty between Venezuela and Barbados (under the law of which country Tidewater Investment S.R.L. is constituted) ('Barbados BIT').

Tidewater submits that it consented to ICSID jurisdiction in a letter to Venezuela on 11 December 2009.

3. Venezuela disputes the Tribunal's jurisdiction:

(a) It maintains that Article 22 does not constitute a standing consent to arbitrate all investment disputes under ICSID; and

(b) It contends that Tidewater Investment S.R.L. is a 'corporation of convenience' incorporated for the sole purpose of 'gaining access' to ICSID.

Accordingly, it submits that Tidewater's invocation of the Barbados BIT is an abuse of the Treaty.

* * *

C.   The Request for Documents

6.   At the First Session, the parties agreed that the IBA Rules on the Taking of Evidence in International Arbitration ('the IBA Rules') could be used as a guide by the Tribunal and the parties.

* * *

10.   As a result of the exchanges between the parties, the issues between them requiring a decision from the Tribunal have been significantly narrowed. The Tribunal now proposes to deal in turn with each of the outstanding requests, where the parties have not reached agreement, setting out the nature of the request, the basis for the objection, and the Tribunal's decision thereon.

11.   Before turning to the particular requests, it will be helpful to set out the legal context in which these requests for the production of documents fall to be considered. Article 43(a) of the ICSID Convention and ICSID Arbitration Rule 34 empower the Tribunal, 'if it deems necessary at any stage of the proceedings (a) [to] call upon the parties to produce documents or other evidence.'

12.   In the present case, the parties have agreed that the IBA Rules may guide the Tribunal and the parties in the taking of evidence and that Articles 3 and 9 will provide particular guidance in relation to the production of documents. Article 3 provides a procedure for the request of documents, and Article 9 addresses the admissibility of documents. It is a general premise of the Rules that the parties shall conduct themselves in good faith in the taking of evidence.

13.   Within the framework of the Convention and Rules, and using the IBA Rules as a guide, the Tribunal has a wide discretion in considering the parties' Requests. The IBA Rules provide that a Tribunal may order the production of a document if:

(a)   The document is 'relevant' to the case and 'material' to its outcome (Article 3.3(b));

(b)   None of the reasons for objection in Rule 9.2 (including privilege) apply; and

(c)   The Request to Produce complies with the requirements of Article 3(3).

The Tribunal is guided by this approach.

14.   The Claimants emphasise the high threshold of 'necessity' under Article 43 and Rule 34, suggesting that production of a document should only be ordered if the document is 'essential' to the resolution of the dispute. The Tribunal considers that the primary purpose of the phrase 'if it deems it necessary' in the Convention and Rules is to confirm that it is for the Tribunal ultimately to determine whether the requested evidence is what it needs in order to decide the matter before it. The Tribunal further considers that, in deciding whether or not it is necessary to order production of a document, it should be guided by the tests of relevance and materiality in the IBA Rules. The Tribunal finds no underlying conflict between these concepts. * * *

II.   The Claimants' Request for Production of Documents

A.   The Claimants' Request

15.   The Claimants requested the following documents from the Respondent:

> 1.   *All documents related to the preparation and drafting of the provision that was enacted as Article 22 of the Investment Law. . . .*
>
> 2.   *All documents related to meetings of the Consejo de Ministros and Gabinete Económico at which the Investment Law was discussed.*

16.   The Claimants submit that these documents are relevant to and necessary for the Tribunal's resolution of the Respondent's likely objections to jurisdiction, 'because they go to the heart of one of the jurisdictional issues before the Tribunal—whether Article 22 of the Investment Law expresses the Respondent's consent to submit this investment dispute to ICSID arbitration.' They submit that it is not sufficient for the Respondent to assert that the Respondent has searched for those documents before in the context of earlier proceedings, and question the Respondent's claim to privilege on the basis of the 'secrecy' of the deliberations of the Ministerial Council. The Claimants nevertheless submit that, if the Tribunal upholds such a privilege, the Claimants' privileged documents requested by the Respondent should also be excluded from production to ensure fairness and equality between the parties.

B.   The Respondent's Objections

17.   The Respondent does not dispute the request on grounds of relevance. Rather, it states that it 'does not possess, maintain or control' any of the documents sought by the Claimants. It states that, in the context of other cases 'the Republic has made every effort to find relevant documentation from other sources, but unfortunately, those efforts have been unsuccessful.' It further

submits that, if the documents did exist, those relating to the deliberations of the Ministerial Council would be privileged.

18.   Nevertheless, the Respondent has indicated that it will conduct a new investigation to confirm that there is nothing to produce, and will inform the Claimants and the Tribunal in due course if this investigation is fruitful.

C.   The Tribunal's Assessment

19.   The proper construction of Article 22 of the Investment Law will plainly be an issue of central importance in the Tribunal's determination of its jurisdiction. The Claimants seek to invoke the jurisdiction of the Centre in part on the basis of the Respondent's consent expressed in Article 22 of the Investment Law. In turn, the Respondent's own preliminary formulation of its jurisdictional objections states 'the Investment Law does not constitute a standing consent to arbitrate all investment disputes before ICSID.' The Tribunal does not at this stage prejudge the legal test applicable to resolution of this issue. Nevertheless, it considers that the two categories of documents requested by the Claimants are reasonably likely to be both relevant and material in assisting it to determine the proper construction of Article 22.

20.   The Respondent does not dispute relevance. Rather it states that it has no such documents, relying upon the manner in which the Investment Law was promulgated and searches made in previous cases. Nevertheless, it has volunteered to undertake a fresh search for the documents in question.

21.   The Tribunal decides that the Respondent should state which sources it has so far checked and undertake a fresh search. If documents within the scope of the Claimants' request are discovered in the course of the Respondent's further investigation, the Respondent must produce copies of those documents; save for any which it claims it should be excluded from production on any of the grounds specified under IBA Rule 9. If documents are found which fall within the request, but which the Respondent wishes to exclude from production, it must produce a schedule itemising the documents which it objects to producing, identifying their author, date, type of document and the grounds for its objection. In that event, the Claimant may, if it wishes to do so, contest the objection.

III. The Respondent's Request for Production of Documents

A.   Introduction

22.   The Respondent originally sought nine categories of documents. In their response, the Claimants objected to each of these requests on a number of

grounds, including privilege. Nevertheless, the Claimants supplied a number of the documents sought 'subject to and without waiving those objections'. The Respondent has accepted that, at present, the Claimants' disclosure is sufficient in respect of a number of the categories. Whilst noting the Claimants' maintenance of its objections, the Tribunal proceeds on the basis that the documents which have been produced are available for the full use of both parties and the Tribunal for the purposes of this arbitration.

23.   There remain two outstanding requests on which the parties are not agreed, and which accordingly require the Tribunal's determination. These will be dealt with in turn.

B.   Respondent's First Request—Documents Relating to the Incorporation of Tidewater Investment S.R.L. and the Transfer of Shares To It

(1)   The Request

24.   The first set of documents in dispute are categories (b) and (e):

> *(b)   Copy of any minutes, memoranda, presentations or any other document that contains or refers to the reasons for the formation and insertion of Tidewater Investment, S.R.L. in the corporate structure of Tidewater;*
>
> . . .
>
> *(e)   Copy of any minutes, memoranda, presentations or any other document that contains or refers to the reasons for the transfer of the stocks of Tidewater Caribe, C.A. in favor of Tidewater Investment, S.R.L*

25.   As noted above, the Respondent seeks this information as relevant to its claim of abuse of treaty. The Respondent disputes that legal advice privilege can attach to correspondence that addresses the 'business rationale' of the restructuring.

(2)   The Claimants' Response

26.   The Claimants object to the production of the documents in question on three grounds:

(1)   The documents are 'not reasonably calculated to resolve issues relating to the Republic's jurisdictional objections'. The Claimants maintain that the threshold of necessity, relevance and materiality that must be met before an ICSID tribunal will order the production of documents is high, and that they are not met in this case. They rely particularly on the fact that the restructuring in

question took place two months before the expropriation that is the subject of the dispute.

(2)   The documents are protected by legal advice privilege. The Claimants maintain that certain documents are also protected by privilege. They submit that 'legal advice is legal advice, whether or not that legal advice relates to a "business rationale.' "

(3)   The requests are 'overbroad'. The Claimants submit that these requests are 'overbroad or contain terms that are not defined or that are vague, ambiguous or unintelligible.' The Claimants allege that the Respondent's request is a 'fishing expedition'.

(3)   The Tribunal's assessment

27.   The Respondent intends to object to the Tribunal's jurisdiction under the Barbados BIT on the basis of abuse of treaty. That is an argument that the Tribunal will have to resolve in its Decision on Jurisdiction. The Respondent squarely alleges that the reasons for and circumstances of the creation of Tidewater Investment S.R.L. and its acquisition of Tidewater Caribe, C.A. show that the former company is a 'corporation of convenience belatedly incorporated by the U.S. Claimant Tidewater Inc. in anticipation of litigation and with the purpose of gaining access to ICSID—an abusive manipulation of the dispute resolution mechanism provided by' the Barbados BIT and the ICSID Convention.

28.   The Claimants submit that there is nothing improper or illegitimate about restructuring for the purpose of gaining the protection of a treaty for future disputes, and note that the restructuring was completed two months before the expropriation took place. It therefore submits that the documents are irrelevant to any allegation of treaty abuse.

29.   The Tribunal considers that production of the category of Claimants' documents relating to the incorporation of Tidewater Investment S.R.L and the transfer of the shares of Tidewater Caribe, C.A. is necessary. Those documents are relevant and material to the case because they are reasonably likely to assist the Tribunal to decide the jurisdictional objection raised by the Respondent. The Tribunal expresses no view on the substantive merits of the Respondent's allegation of abuse of treaty. For this purpose, it is required to take the Respondent's jurisdictional objections at face value and consider its Request for Documents against the background of those jurisdictional objections.

30.   In the Tribunal's view the Claimant's argument based upon the timing of incorporation belongs to the substantive jurisdictional phase of this arbitration. The Tribunal is not in a position to determine that issue now, on the basis of limited facts and submissions. The Respondent also disputes whether the expropriation in question was in fact a 'future dispute'.40 At this point, the Tribunal has to determine whether the documents sought are relevant and material to the jurisdictional objection that the Respondent intends to raise, not whether that jurisdictional objection is likely to succeed.

31.   Before turning to the Claimants' claim of privilege, the Tribunal will address their objection that the Respondent's request constitutes a 'fishing expedition'. The Tribunal notes that Article 3(3)(a) of the IBA Rules requires that a Request to Produce contain either (i) 'a description of each requested Document sufficient to identify it' or (ii) 'a description in sufficient detail (including subject matter) of a narrow and specific requested category of Documents that are reasonably believed to exist'.

32.   The Tribunal acknowledges that (absent the express decision of the parties) Common Law-style pre-trial discovery does not belong in international arbitration. However, it does not accept that the Respondent's request is nothing more than a request for 'hypothetical' documents (as the Claimants submit). The Tribunal considers that the Respondent has particularised its request sufficiently narrowly to comply with the requirements of Article 3(3)(a)(ii). The Respondent's request is focused on the particular issue of Tidewater S.R.L's incorporation and receipt of the shares of Tidewater Caribe, C.A. A company, as a legal person, can only come into existence as a conscious act of creation by others, which act must be recorded in writing. The Claimants' invocation of privilege shows that documents within the scope of this request exist. Some lack of specificity is clearly contemplated by that Rule, because a party will always be limited in its ability to specifically identify documents which it only believes to exist.

* * *

C.   Respondent's Second Request—Documents Identifying the Services Underlying the Accounts Receivable

(1)   The Respondent's Request

36.   The last request for documents still in dispute is category (i):

> *(i)   Identification of the services underlying the claim of the accounts receivable, including the description of the services, the agreement pursuant to which they were*

rendered, proof that they were rendered and proof of acceptance of the contracting party.

37.   The Respondent refers to several agreements entered into by Tidewater's principal Venezuelan subsidiary, Tidewater Marine Service, C.A. (SEMARCA): (i) two charter agreements with PDVSA Petróleo, S.A. (a State-owned company) and (ii) a charter agreement with PetroSucre, S.A.46 The Claimants allege that at the time of the expropriation PDVSA Petróleo and PetroSucre owed sums of money to SEMARCA, and that these accounts receivable in question form part of the total value that was expropriated.47 The Respondent seeks to establish that these accounts receivable 'are derived from a strictly commercial relationship over which ICSID has no jurisdiction.'

(2)   The Claimants' Objection

38.   The Claimants object to this request principally on the basis that the documents are irrelevant at the present stage in the proceedings. The Claimants submit that the accounts receivable form part of the total value of the assets expropriated, and are therefore only relevant to quantum, not jurisdiction. They also object to this request on the basis that it seeks information that is either publicly available or in the Respondent's possession (as a result of the expropriation), and that the request is overbroad.

(3)   The Tribunal's Assessment

39.   Article 3(1) of the IBA Rules provides:

> *Within the time ordered by the Arbitral Tribunal, each Party shall submit to the Arbitral Tribunal and to the other Parties all documents available to it on which it relies, including public documents and those in the public domain, except for any documents that have already been submitted by the another Party.*

40.   As noted by the Respondent, the Claimants refer to the charter agreements set out in paragraph 37 above in its Request for Arbitration. The Tribunal acknowledges the Claimants' submissions as to the appropriate threshold for the production of documents. Nevertheless, the Tribunal considers that a different approach is warranted in relation to specific documents expressly referred to in the Request for Arbitration, since such documents are relied upon by the Claimants themselves. Such documents are therefore necessary in order to understand the nature of the claims advanced by the Claimants. This the Tribunal must do in order to determine the extent of the jurisdiction of the Centre and the Tribunal.

41. As stated above, the ICSID Convention and Rules confer upon the Tribunal the power to order the production of documents 'if it deems it necessary.' The Tribunal considers that it is necessary that the Claimants produce at this stage copies of the contracts identified above, namely:

(a) The charter agreements between SEMARCA and PDVSA Petróleo;

(b) The charter agreement between SEMARCA and PetroSucre.

The Tribunal notes that the Claimants are only obliged to produce those documents still in their possession, custody or control. If any of these documents were, but are no longer, in the Claimants' possession, custody or control, the Claimants must state when and how they ceased to be so.

42. However, the Tribunal considers that other documents within the Respondent's request relating to the accounts receivable of SEMARCA are not relevant to the question of jurisdiction. At the time of expropriation, any such accounts receivable would have constituted an asset belonging to SEMARCA which the Claimants allege was expropriated by the Respondent. The details of those accounts receivable are therefore not relevant to the jurisdictional phase of this dispute, and the Claimants will not be ordered to produce them.

NOTES

Facts

1. Look at the Claimants' document requests. How are they styled? Do they have a date limitation? Do they identify custodians to be searched? Do they have any limitations, at all?

2. What were the documents relevant to? Claimant's case-in-chief or the Respondent's jurisdictional objection?

3. Would you expect that national legislation purporting to protect foreign investment would have no legislative history? How about if that legislation had been passed by means of an executive order rather than through bicameralism and presentment?

4. If you represented the Bolivarian Republic of Venezuela, how would you go about searching for the documents? How easy do you think the search would be? How long do you think it would take? How expensive do you think it would be?

5. Look at Respondent's document requests. How are they styled? Do they have a date limitation? Do they identify custodians to be searched? Do they have any limitations, at all?

Law

1. The Claimants objected that the requests were overbroad and constituted an impermissible fishing expedition akin to U.S.-style discovery. Leaving aside for the moment that the lead claimant is a U.S. company represented by U.S. counsel, how does the tribunal deal with that objection?

2. Do you think a similar objection could have been raised if the proceedings had been governed by the AAA Commercial Arbitration Rules? Do you think the tribunal's response would have been any different?

3. Consider the tribunal's application of the IBA Rules. Would the result have been different had the tribunal applied FRE 401, instead? Would its analysis have been different?

D) Enforcement of Tribunal's Discovery Orders

Arbitral tribunals do not themselves have the power to enforce their procedural orders regarding discovery. Rather, the parties must rely upon the courts to do so. The materials below set out some of the problems that may arise in the context of court enforcement of arbitrator-ordered discovery. The materials below focus particularly upon the question of seeking discovery from third parties. To the extent the parties fail to live up to their discovery obligations, consider what remedies the parties have in arbitration.

Federal Arbitration Act, § 7

The arbitrators selected either as prescribed in this title or otherwise, or a majority of them, may summon in writing any person to attend before them or any of them as a witness and in a proper case to bring with him or them any book, record, document, or paper which may be deemed material as evidence in the case. The fees for such attendance shall be the same as the fees of witnesses before masters of the United States courts. Said summons shall issue in the name of the arbitrator or arbitrators, or a majority of them, and shall be signed by the arbitrators, or a majority of them, and shall be directed to the said person and shall be served in the same manner as subpoenas to appear and testify before the court; if any person or persons so summoned to testify shall refuse or neglect to obey said summons, upon petition the United States district court for the district in which such arbitrators, or a majority of them, are sitting may compel the attendance of such person or persons before said arbitrator or arbitrators, or punish said person or persons for contempt in the same manner provided by law for securing the attendance of witnesses or their punishment for neglect or refusal to attend in the courts of the United States.

NOTES

1. Is section 7 of the Federal Arbitration Act limited to non-parties or does it deal generally with discovery from parties and non-parties?

2. On its face, how does section 7 deal with *discovery* at all?

3. Which federal court has the power to enforce the summon? The federal court with jurisdiction over the witness summoned?

Hay Group Inc. v. E.B.S. Acquisition Corp.

360 F.3d 404 (3rd Cir. 2004)

ALITO, CIRCUIT JUDGE.

PriceWaterhouseCoopers ("PwC") and E.B.S., non-parties to an arbitration, seek to avoid compliance with an arbitration panel's subpoena requiring them to turn over documents prior to the panel's hearing. The District Court enforced the subpoena. We reverse.

I.

Hay Group ("Hay") is a management consulting firm. David A. Hoffrichter left Hay's employment and joined PwC in September 1999. In early 2002, PwC sold the division employing Hoffrichter to E.B.S.

Hoffrichter's separation agreement from Hay contained a clause that forbade him from soliciting any of Hay's employees or clients for one year. The agreement further provided for arbitration to resolve any dispute arising under the agreement. In February 2000, Hay commenced such an arbitration proceeding in Philadelphia, Pennsylvania, against Hoffrichter, claiming that he had violated the non-solicitation clause.

In an attempt to obtain information for the arbitration, Hay served subpoenas for documents on E.B.S. at its Pittsburgh office and on PwC at its Philadelphia office. Hay sought to have the documents produced prior to the panel's arbitration hearing. PwC and E.B.S. objected to these subpoenas, but the arbitration panel disagreed. When PwC and E.B.S. still refused to comply with the subpoenas, Hay asked the United States District Court for the Eastern District of Pennsylvania to enforce the subpoenas. * * *

In November 2002, the District Court issued a decision enforcing the subpoenas and ordering the parties to resolve any remaining differences. In doing so, the District Court accepted the view of the Eighth Circuit and several district courts that the FAA authorizes arbitration panels to issue subpoenas on non-parties for pre-hearing document production. The District Court also held that even under the view of the Fourth Circuit, which permits such production only when there is a "special need," the panel's subpoenas would be valid. In addition, the District Court held that it had the power to enforce subpoenas on non-parties for document production even if the documents were located outside the territory within which the court's subpoenas could be served.

* * *

II.

A.

On appeal, PwC and E.B.S. first argue that, under Section 7 of the FAA, 9 U.S.C. § 7, a non-party witness may be compelled to bring documents to an arbitration proceeding but may not simply be subpoenaed to produce documents. We agree.

An arbitrator's authority over parties that are not contractually bound by the arbitration agreement is strictly limited to that granted by the Federal Arbitration Act. Accordingly, we must look to the FAA to determine whether an arbitrator may issue a subpoena requiring pre-hearing document production by a person or entity that is not bound by the arbitration agreement (hereinafter a "non-party").

In interpreting a statute, we must, of course, begin with the text. * * * Section 7 of the FAA * * * speaks unambiguously to the issue before us. The only power conferred on arbitrators with respect to the production of documents by a non-party is the power to summon a non-party "to attend before them or any of them as a witness and in a proper case to bring with him or them any book, record, document or paper which may be deemed material as evidence in the case." The power to require a non-party "to bring" items "with him" clearly applies only to situations in which the non-party accompanies the items to the arbitration proceeding, not to situations in which the items are simply sent or brought by a courier. In addition, the use of the word "and" makes it clear that a non-party may be compelled "to bring" items "with him" only when the non-party is summoned "to attend before [the arbitrator] as a witness." Thus, Section 7's language unambiguously restricts an arbitrator's subpoena power to situations in which the non-party has been called to appear in the physical presence of the arbitrator and to hand over the documents at that time.[1]

* * *

Some courts have argued that the language of Section 7 implies the power to issue such pre-hearing subpoenas. See In re Security Life Insurance Co. of America, 228 F.3d 865, 870–71 (8th Cir.2000)("We thus hold that implicit in an arbitration panel's power to subpoena relevant documents for production at a hearing is the power to order the production of relevant documents for review by a party prior to the hearing."); Meadows Indemnity Co., Ltd. v. Nutmeg Insurance Co., 157 F.R.D. 42, 45 (M.D.Tenn.1994)("The power of the panel to compel production of documents from third-parties for the purposes of a hearing implicitly authorizes the lesser power to compel such documents for arbitration purposes prior to a hearing.").

We disagree with this power-by-implication analysis. By conferring the power to compel a non-party witness to bring items to an arbitration proceeding while saying nothing about the power simply to compel the production of items without summoning the custodian to testify, the FAA implicitly withholds the latter power. If the FAA had been meant to confer the latter, broader power, we believe that the drafters would have said so, and they would have then had no need to spell out the more limited power to compel a non-party witness to bring items with him to an arbitration proceeding. * * *

Since the text of Section 7 of the FAA is straightforward, we must see if the result is absurd. We conclude that it is not. Indeed, we believe that a reasonable argument can be made that a literal reading of Section 7 actually furthers arbitration's goal of "resolving disputes in a timely and cost efficient manner." * * * The requirement that document production be made at an actual hearing may, in the long run, discourage the issuance of large-scale subpoenas upon non-parties. This is so because parties that consider obtaining such a subpoena will be forced to consider whether the documents are important

---

[1]   Some states have recently adopted versions of the Uniform Arbitration Act, which differs from the Federal Arbitration Act. Some of these state statutes explicitly grant arbitrators the power to issue pre-hearing document production subpoenas on third parties. See, e.g., 10 Del.Code § 5708(a) (2003)("The arbitrators may compel the attendance of witnesses and the production of books, records, contracts, papers, accounts, and all other documents and evidence, and shall have the power to administer oaths."); 42 Pa.C.S.A. § 7309 ("The arbitrators may issue subpoenas in the form prescribed by general rules for the attendance of witnesses and for the production of books, records, documents and other evidence.") The language of these state statutes clearly shows how a law can give authority to an arbitrator to issue pre-hearing document-production orders on third parties.

enough to justify the time, money, and effort that the subpoenaing parties will be required to expend if an actual appearance before an arbitrator is needed. Under a system of pre-hearing document production, by contrast, there is less incentive to limit the scope of discovery and more incentive to engage in fishing expeditions that undermine some of the advantages of the supposedly shorter and cheaper system of arbitration. * * *

* * *

In sum, we hold that the FAA did not authorize the panel to issue a pre-hearing discovery subpoena to PwC and E.B.S. We further reject any "special needs exception" to this rule. If Hay wants to access the documents, the panel must subpoena PwC and E.B.S. to appear before it and bring the documents with them.

B.

We now turn to the PwC's argument that the subpoenas at issue in this case were improper for an additional reason, namely, because they sought the production of documents that were located outside the territorial jurisdiction of the District Court. * * *

PwC contends that Fed. R. Civ. Proc. 45(a)(2)[4] prohibits subpoenas *duces tecum* for documents located outside the territory within which a subpoena may be served under Fed. R. Civ. Proc. 45(b)(2). PwC relies on the following language in Rule 45(a)(2):

> *If separate from a subpoena commanding the attendance of a person, a subpoena for production or inspection shall issue from the court for the district in which the production or inspection is to be made.*

As applied to the situation that we have postulated (the subsequent service on PwC of a subpoena calling for both an appearance before the arbitration panel and the production of documents), PwC's argument has several flaws. We will mention two.

First, the portion of Rule 45(a)(2) on which PwC's argument is based applies only to a subpoena *duces tecum* that is "separate from a subpoena commanding the attendance of a person." We have held, however, that the FAA

---

4   Fed. R. Civ. Proc. 54(b)(2) provides in relevant part as follows:

[A] subpoena may be served at any place within the district of the court by which it is issued, or at any place without the district that is within 100 miles of the place of the deposition, hearing, trial, production, or inspection specified in the subpoena or at any place without the state where a state statute or rule of court permits service of a subpoena issued by a state court of general jurisdiction sitting in the place of the deposition, hearing, trial, production, or inspection specified in the subpoena.

does not permit such subpoenas. The portion of Rule 45(a)(2) that applies when a witness is subpoenaed to appear contains no similar language. Rather, that portion of the Rule states only that a subpoena for attendance at a trial, hearing, or deposition shall issue from the court for the district "in which the hearing or trial or hearing is to be held" or from "the court for the district designated in the notice of deposition as the district in which the deposition is to be taken." Nothing in this language suggests that a witness who is subpoenaed to testify may not also be directed to bring documents that are not located within the territorial limits set out in Rule 45(b)(2).

Second, PwC misinterprets the language in Rule 45(a)(2) on which it relies. As noted, that provision states that a subpoena calling only for the "production or inspection" of documents "shall issue from the court for the district in which the production or inspection is to be made." "Production" refers to the delivery of documents, not their retrieval, and therefore "the district in which the production . . . is to be made" is not the district in which the documents are housed but the district in which the subpoenaed party is required to turn them over.

* * *

III.

For the reasons set out above, the order of the District Court is reversed.

CHERTOFF, CIRCUIT JUDGE, concurring:

I join Judge Alito's opinion in full. But I appreciate the reason that a number of courts have been motivated to read a pre-hearing discovery power into the arbitration rules. I write separately to observe that our opinion does not leave arbitrators powerless to require advance production of documents when necessary to allow fair and efficient proceedings.

Under section 7 of the Federal Arbitration Act, arbitrators have the power to compel a third-party witness to appear with documents before a single arbitrator, who can then adjourn the proceedings. This gives the arbitration panel the effective ability to require delivery of documents from a third-party in advance, notwithstanding the limitations of section 7 of the FAA. In many instances, of course, the inconvenience of making such a personal appearance may well prompt the witness to deliver the documents and waive presence. See David M. Heilbron, The Arbitration Clause, the Preliminary Conference, and the Big Case, 45 Arb. J. 38, 43–44 (1990).

To be sure, this procedure requires the arbitrators to decide that they are prepared to suffer some inconvenience of their own in order to mandate what is, in reality, an advance production of documents. But that is not necessarily a bad thing, since it will induce the arbitrators and parties to weigh whether advance production is really needed. And the availability of this procedure within the existing statutory language should satisfy the desire that there be some mechanism "to compel pre-arbitration discovery upon a showing of special need or hardship." COMSAT Corp. v. Nat'l Sci. Found., 190 F.3d 269, 276 (4th Cir.1999).

NOTES

Facts

1. What is the discovery that is at issue in this case? Who is seeking it?

2. What is the relationship of PwC and EBS to the arbitration?

3. How important do you think the documents are to the case? Are they "material"? Or purely "relevant"?

Law

1. Do you agree with the textual interpretation by then Judge Alito of section 7 of the FAA? Does the interpretation remind you of another Alito decision reproduced earlier in the book?

2. Judge Chertoff's concurrence seems to leave a door open for pre-hearing discovery. What is it? Do you think it makes sense? Or does it make a mockery out of the carefully crafted limitations upon arbitral power set out by Judge Alito?

3. What is the argument relating to the 100 mile radius? Did the court consider that PwC could be ordered to attend a hearing irrespective of where it is located in relation to the seat of the arbitration?

Amgen Inc. v. Kidney Center of Delaware County, Ltd.

879 F.Supp. 878 (N.D.Ill., 1995)

GETTLEMAN, DISTRICT JUDGE.

Plaintiff Amgen Inc. and Ortho Pharmaceutical Corp. have been involved in arbitration proceedings in Chicago since 1989. The Honorable Frank J. McGarr, former chief judge of this court, has acted as arbitrator throughout those proceedings. There have been two extended trials, and a third trial is scheduled to commence in May 1995.

In connection with the arbitration proceedings, and as part of the preparation for the scheduled May 1995 trial, Judge McGarr determined that certain documents and information in possession of third persons not parties to the arbitration proceedings were relevant. He issued a subpoena to Kidney Center of Delaware County, Ltd. ("KCDC," the defendant in this action) to produce documents and a representative to testify at a deposition for use in the arbitration. Amgen served KCDC with the subpoena in the same manner as a subpoena under the Federal Rules of Civil Procedure as required by the Federal Arbitration Act ("FAA"), 9 U.S.C. § 1, et seq. KCDC refused to honor the subpoena, and instead submitted objections to Judge McGarr, arguing that the arbitrator did not have authority to issue the subpoena and that the documents sought were confidential. Judge McGarr determined that he did have authority to issue the subpoena under the FAA, and ordered the documents produced pursuant to a protective order.

KCDC again refused to comply, and on September 8, 1994, Amgen filed a motion in the United States District Court for the Eastern District of Pennsylvania (the district in which KCDC is located and where the deposition was to take place) to compel compliance. KCDC opposed the motion on several grounds, including that Amgen had petitioned the wrong court for relief. The court determined that pursuant to Section VII of the FAA, Amgen was required to file its petition for relief in the court in the district in which the arbitrator is located and, therefore, transferred the action to this court.

Amgen has once again moved to compel production. KCDC has opposed, arguing that under the FAA the arbitrator has no authority to subpoena persons who are located outside of the district in which he sits or beyond 100 miles of the site of the arbitration. For the reasons set forth below, the court grants Amgen's motion to compel compliance with the arbitrator's subpoena.

DISCUSSION

* * *

* * * KCDC argues that the subpoena issued by Judge McGarr is void *ab initio* because he lacked power to issue it. Specifically, KCDC argues that an arbitrator's subpoena power reaches only as far as the subpoena power of the district court in which the arbitration is pending. Because a federal district court's subpoena power encompasses only the district in which the court sits or extends 100 miles from the courthouse, Fed.R.Civ.P. 45, KCDC argues that an

arbitrator may compel only the attendance of witnesses (and the attendant production of documents) found within the district in which the arbitration is being conducted, or within 100 miles of the site of the arbitration proceeding. To support this argument, KCDC cites *Commercial Solvents Corp. v. Louisiana Liquid Fertilizer Co.*, 20 F.R.D. 359, 362–63 (S.D.N.Y.1957).

Commercial Solvents, however, did not hold that arbitrators could not compel the attendance of witnesses who are not within the district or within 100 miles of the place of the hearing; it merely suggested that "perhaps" they could not. *Id.* at 362–63. The holding in *Commercial Solvents* was that for matters of procedure relating to hearings before arbitrators, the court refers not to the Federal Rules of Civil Procedure, but to the rules pursuant to which the parties had agreed to arbitrate. *Id.* In the instant case, however, the parties have agreed to arbitrate pursuant to the Federal Rules of Civil Procedure and, therefore, *Commercial Solvents* is of little guidance.

In this court's view, the issue is not whether the arbitrator has the power to issue the subpoena in question, for the statute is specific in stating that the arbitrator may summon any person. There is no territorial limitation on that ability. The issue is how (or perhaps if) that subpoena can be enforced.

Couched in these terms, the issue, as far as this court can ascertain, is novel. Aside from the District Court for the Eastern District of Pennsylvania which transferred the case here, and a Florida court in a companion matter this court is aware of no cases which have dealt directly with this particular issue. The court writes, therefore, with a clean slate, but not without guidance.

* * *

* * * Thus, it is clear, as the Florida and Pennsylvania courts held, that any petition to enforce the subpoena must be brought to this court, because the arbitrator is located in Chicago. Under the statute this court may compel KCDC's attendance (or punish KCDC for failure to attend) in the same manner that it would secure the attendance of any witness in this court. *Id.* The problem arises because of the difference in the way the Federal Rules provide for the issuance of subpoenas for depositions and for trial. Under Fed.R.Civ.P. 45(a)(2), a subpoena commanding attendance at trial shall issue from the court for the district in which the trial is to be held, while a subpoena for attendance at a deposition shall issue from the court for the district designated by the notice of deposition as the district in which the deposition is to be taken.

In the instant case, the deposition is to be taken in the Eastern District of Pennsylvania. That court, however, correctly refused to issue a subpoena because under Section VII of the FAA only this court can determine the enforceability of the arbitrator's subpoena. KCDC argues that because of the incompatibility of the wording of Section VII of the FAA and Fed.R.Civ.P. 45, it simply is not subject to the subpoena power of the arbitrator at all. In essence, it argues that a gap in the law exists, and that it has slipped through that gap. Thus, under KCDC's view, only this court can enforce the arbitrator's subpoena, but this court cannot compel KCDC to attend depositions scheduled in the Eastern District of Pennsylvania.

Amgen, on the other hand, argues that the territorial limits of a district court's subpoena do not apply to an arbitrator's subpoena. Amgen suggests that a witness who refuses to comply with an arbitrator's summons or subpoena can and must be brought before the court in the district in which the arbitration is pending, regardless of where the witness resides. Amgen does not explain how this Court can accomplish that feat, however, when its subpoena power is subject to the territorial limits of Fed.R.Civ.P. 45(b)(2), which provides that a subpoena "may be served at any place within the district of the court by which it is issued, or any place without the district that is within 100 miles of the place where the trial . . . is to take place."

The court disagrees with both parties' positions. KCDC's argument is unavailing because it leaves a gap in the law, which is contrary to Congressional intent, and unnecessary. By definition, the FAA applies only to actions involving interstate commerce, 9 U.S.C. § 2; indeed, the Act itself is based on congressional power to regulate interstate commerce. By enacting the FAA, Congress declared a national policy favoring arbitration. The arbitration of any action affecting interstate commerce is likely to involve parties and witnesses located in more than one district or state. To find that the wording of the FAA precludes issuance and enforcement of an arbitrator's subpoena of a witness outside the district in which he or she sits, particularly where, as here, such discovery is agreed upon by the parties to the arbitration, would likely lead to rejection of arbitration clauses altogether. That would be contrary to the intent of Congress in enacting a national policy favoring arbitration.

Amgen's position is equally unavailing. It suggests that Section VII of the FAA gives the court the power to order any person, no matter where he or she may be located or resides, to appear before the arbitrator (or at least appear for a deposition), but, once again, although the Act allows the arbitrator to subpoena anyone, it also provides that this court may enforce the arbitrator's subpoena only in the same manner that it would compel attendance before the court. This, of course, is done according to Fed.R.Civ.P. 45, which does not provide the court with any extraterritorial power. Rule 45 does provide that "[w]hen a statute of the United States provides therefor, the court, upon proper application and cause shown, may authorize the service of a subpoena at any other place," but those statutes providing for extraterritorial service do so explicitly. * * *

Having rejected both parties' positions, the court nonetheless concludes that the arbitrator's subpoena is both valid and enforceable. Ortho and Amgen agreed to arbitrate their dispute pursuant to the Federal Rules of Civil Procedure. By so doing, they agreed to the liberal discovery allowed by those rules, and agreed that Judge McGarr in essence would act as and with the power of a judge applying those rules. Those rules (which were adopted well after the enactment of the FAA) contemplate and provide both for a mechanism for nationwide discovery, and preserving the testimony of witnesses unavailable at trial because they are outside the district, by use of evidence depositions.

Under Fed.R.Civ.P. 45(a)(3)(B), an attorney authorized to practice in the court in which the trial is being held may issue and sign a subpoena on behalf of a court for a district in which a deposition or production is to take place. The subpoena has the case name and number of the case pending before the court where trial is to take place. It is enforced, however, by the district court for the district in which the deposition is to take place. That is precisely what Amgen attempted to do when it petitioned the court in the Eastern District of Pennsylvania for enforcement. That court, because of the wording of the FAA, could not enforce an arbitrator's subpoena. It can, however, enforce a subpoena issued by Amgen's attorney with the name and number of a case pending before this court. Because this court concludes that the arbitrator's subpoena is enforceable, it directs Amgen's attorney to issue a subpoena to KCDC under this case name and number as set forth in Fed.R.Civ.P. 45(a)(3)(B).

NOTES

Facts

1. On KCDC's theory, is there any court that could have appropriately issued a subpoena?

2. What was the information at issue? How could the arbitrator have decided the issue without it?

3. Do you think the KCDC issue is common? How would you try to avoid it?

Law

1. Is the decision in *Amgen* inconsistent with the decision in *Hay Group*? Why do you think the two are inconsistent? Consider the following passage (not included in the excerpt above):

    > *While the statute appears to allow an arbitrator to summon a third person only to testify at trial, as opposed to a pretrial discovery deposition, courts have held (and KCDC has not disputed) that implicit in the power to compel testimony and documents for purpose of a hearing is the lesser power to compel such testimony and documents for purposes prior to hearing.*

2. Follow along the citations to the Federal Rules of Civil Procedure. Does the court's solution to the problem work?

3. As indicated by the dispute, there are multiple ways of reading the subpoena power of arbitrators. To the extent the subpoena is issued for pre-hearing testimony or discovery, the issue is arguably exacerbated. Does Justice Alito's solution work better sense by limiting subpoena power to the power to compel attendance at trial?

e-Disclosure

In many litigations, the production of electronically stored information gives rise to thorny discovery disputes. It is a very rare business that doesn't use email. Many businesses in addition have sophisticated data-management systems to help them archive everything from documents generation in the ordinary course, to the capture of information for accounting purposes and transmittal of phone messages. Electronic storage of information has exponentially increased the number of "documents" that companies have—and thus the potential for discovery of, and disputes about the discovery of, these documents.

The sheer volume of electronically stored information leads to two related problems. First, and perhaps most pressingly, electronic storage differs from physical storage in an important respect. A business typically knows when it destroys physical documents. For example, culling documents from physical archives is something that a person or persons must actively do. Electronic data management systems, on the other hand, have programming rules governing how long information is stored, and destruction of electronic documents thus may be essentially automatic. Inadvertent destruction of electronic documents therefore is a far greater risk than inadvertent destruction of physical documents. To the extent that documents are destroyed while a party is reasonably aware that litigation or arbitration has commenced—or is about to commence—this creates problems how a court or tribunal should deal with the "spoliation" of this evidence.

The sheer volume of electronically stored information further leads to questions how to search. Typically, one would look at a document to determine whether or not it is responsive to a document disclosure request. The volume of electronically stored information renders such an approach absurd. It would be far too expensive in most instances to look over every electronic record. How then does one need to search and produce electronically stored information to satisfy a document production request?

The AAA arbitration rules reference the need to dealing with electronically stored information. Thus, AAA Commercial Arbitration Rule 23(b) authorizes the arbitrator to "imposing reasonable search parameters for electronic and other documents if the parties are unable to agree." This begs the question—what is reasonable?

The materials below set out first one of the leading cases on the discovery of electronically stored information in federal litigation. As you read the case, consider whether you think that the result can be transposed easily to arbitration. The remaining materials in the chapter show you how arbitration practitioners have proposed dealing with "eDiscovery" issues in arbitration.

Fact Scenario

Edit the discovery requests you started in Chapter 14 in order to account for the problems of discovery electronically stored information discussed in this chapter.

Readings

A) eDiscovery in Federal Courts

eDiscovery raises one of the most contentious issues in litigation. The materials below outline (very) briefly how the issue developed in the context of federal court litigation. The *Zubulake* line of cases shows the complexity of the issue involved. Following this line of decisions, the Federal Rules of Civil Procedure changed to provide additional guidance on eDiscovery issued.

Zubulake v. UBS Warburg LLC

220 F.R.D. 212 (S.D.N.Y. 2003)

SCHEINDLIN, DISTRICT JUDGE.

"Documents create a paper reality we call proof." The absence of such documentary proof may stymie the search for the truth. If documents are lost or destroyed when they should have been preserved because a litigation was threatened or pending, a party may be prejudiced. The questions presented here are how to determine an appropriate penalty for the party that caused the loss and-the flip side-how to determine an appropriate remedy for the party injured by the loss.

Finding a suitable sanction for the destruction of evidence in civil cases has never been easy. Electronic evidence only complicates matters. As documents are increasingly maintained electronically, it has become easier to delete or tamper with evidence (both intentionally and inadvertently) and more difficult for litigants to craft policies that ensure all relevant documents are preserved.

This opinion addresses both the scope of a litigant's duty to preserve electronic documents and the consequences of a failure to preserve documents that fall within the scope of that duty.

I.   BACKGROUND

This is the fourth opinion resolving discovery disputes in this case. Familiarity with the prior opinions is presumed, and only background information relevant to the instant dispute is described here. In brief, Laura Zubulake, an equities trader who earned approximately $650,000 a year with UBS, is suing UBS for gender discrimination, failure to promote, and retaliation under federal, state, and city law. She has repeatedly maintained that the evidence she needs to prove her case exists in e-mail correspondence sent among various UBS employees and stored only on UBS's computer systems.

On July 24, 2003, I ordered the parties to share the cost of restoring certain UBS backup tapes that contained e-mails relevant to Zubulake's claims. In the restoration effort, the parties discovered that certain backup tapes are missing. * * *

In addition, certain isolated e-mails-created after UBS supposedly began retaining all relevant e-mails-were deleted from UBS's system, although they appear to have been saved on the backup tapes. As I explained in *Zubulake III*, "certain e-mails sent after the initial EEOC charge-and particularly relevant to Zubulake's retaliation claim-were apparently not saved at all. For example, [an] e-mail from Chapin to Joy Kim [another of Zubulake's coworkers] instructing her on how to file a complaint against Zubulake was not saved, and it bears the subject line 'UBS client attorney priviledge [sic] only,' although no attorney is copied on the e-mail. This potentially useful e-mail was deleted and resided only on UBS's backup tapes."

Zubulake filed her EEOC charge on August 16, 2001; the instant action was filed on February 14, 2002. In August 2001, in an oral directive, UBS ordered its employees to retain all relevant documents. In August 2002, after Zubulake specifically requested e-mail stored on backup tapes, UBS's outside counsel orally instructed UBS's information technology personnel to stop recycling backup tapes.

Zubulake now seeks sanctions against UBS for its failure to preserve the missing backup tapes and deleted e-mails. In particular, Zubulake seeks the following relief: (a) an order requiring UBS to pay in full the costs of restoring the remainder of the monthly backup tapes; (b) an adverse inference instruction against UBS with respect to the backup tapes that are missing; and (c) an order directing UBS to bear the costs of re-deposing certain individuals, such as Chapin, concerning the issues raised in newly produced e-mails.

II. LEGAL STANDARD

Spoliation is "the destruction or significant alteration of evidence, or the failure to preserve property for another's use as evidence in pending or reasonably foreseeable litigation." The spoliation of evidence germane "to proof of an issue at trial can support an inference that the evidence would have been unfavorable to the party responsible for its destruction." However, "[t]he determination of an appropriate sanction for spoliation, if any, is confined to the sound discretion of the trial judge, and is assessed on a case-by-case basis." The authority to sanction litigants for spoliation arises jointly under the Federal Rules of Civil Procedure and the court's own inherent powers.

III. DISCUSSION

It goes without saying that a party can only be sanctioned for destroying evidence if it had a duty to preserve it. If UBS had no such duty, then UBS cannot be faulted. I begin, then, by discussing the extent of a party's duty to preserve evidence.

A. Duty to Preserve

"The obligation to preserve evidence arises when the party has notice that the evidence is relevant to litigation or when a party should have known that the evidence may be relevant to future litigation." Identifying the boundaries of the duty to preserve involves two related inquiries: when does the duty to preserve attach, and what evidence must be preserved?

1. The Trigger Date

In this case, the duty to preserve evidence arose, at the latest, on August 16, 2001, when Zubulake filed her EEOC charge. At that time, UBS's in-house attorneys cautioned employees to retain all documents, including e-mails and backup tapes, that could potentially be relevant to the litigation. In meetings with Chapin, Clarke, Kim, Hardisty, John Holland (Chapin's supervisor), and Dominic Vail (Zubulake's former supervisor) held on August 29–31, 2001, UBS's outside counsel reiterated the need to preserve documents.

But the duty to preserve may have arisen even before the EEOC complaint was filed. Zubulake argues that UBS "should have known that the evidence [was] relevant to future litigation," FN17 as early as April 2001, and thus had a duty to preserve it. She offers two pieces of evidence in support of this argument.

First, certain UBS employees titled e-mails pertaining to Zubulake "UBS Attorney Client Privilege" starting in April 2001, notwithstanding the fact that no attorney was copied on the e-mail and the substance of the e-mail was not legal in nature. Second, Chapin admitted in his deposition that he feared litigation from as early as April 2001. * * *

Merely because one or two employees contemplate the possibility that a fellow employee might sue does not generally impose a firm-wide duty to preserve. But in this case, it appears that almost everyone associated with Zubulake recognized the possibility that she might sue. * * *

Thus, the relevant people at UBS anticipated litigation in April 2001. The duty to preserve attached at the time that litigation was reasonably anticipated.

2.   Scope

The next question is: What is the scope of the duty to preserve? Must a corporation, upon recognizing the threat of litigation, preserve every shred of paper, every e-mail or electronic document, and every backup tape? The answer is clearly, "no". Such a rule would cripple large corporations, like UBS, that are almost always involved in litigation. As a general rule, then, a party need not preserve all backup tapes even when it reasonably anticipates litigation.

At the same time, anyone who anticipates being a party or is a party to a lawsuit must not destroy unique, relevant evidence that might be useful to an adversary. "While a litigant is under no duty to keep or retain every document in its possession . . . it is under a duty to preserve what it knows, or reasonably should know, is relevant in the action, is reasonably calculated to lead to the discovery of admissible evidence, is reasonably likely to be requested during discovery and/or is the subject of a pending discovery request."

* * *

The scope of a party's preservation obligation can be described as follows: Once a party reasonably anticipates litigation, it must suspend its routine document retention/destruction policy and put in place a "litigation hold" to ensure the preservation of relevant documents. As a general rule, that litigation hold does not apply to inaccessible backup tapes (e.g., those typically maintained solely for the purpose of disaster recovery), which may continue to be recycled on the schedule set forth in the company's policy. On the other hand, if backup tapes are accessible (i.e., actively used for information retrieval), then such tapes would likely be subject to the litigation hold.

However, it does make sense to create one exception to this general rule. If a company can identify where particular employee documents are stored on backup tapes, then the tapes storing the documents of "key players" to the existing or threatened litigation should be preserved if the information contained on those tapes is not otherwise available. This exception applies to all backup tapes.

iv.   What Happened at UBS After August 2001?

By its attorney's directive in August 2002, UBS endeavored to preserve all backup tapes that existed in August 2001 (when Zubulake filed her EEOC charge) that captured data for employees identified by Zubulake in her document request, and all such monthly backup tapes generated thereafter. These backup tapes existed in August 2002, because of UBS's document retention policy, which required retention for three years. In August 2001, UBS employees were instructed to maintain active electronic documents pertaining to Zubulake in separate files. Had these directives been followed, UBS would have met its preservation obligations by preserving one copy of all relevant documents that existed at, or were created after, the time when the duty to preserve attached.

In fact, UBS employees did not comply with these directives. Three backup tapes containing the e-mail files of Chapin, Hardisty, Clarke and Datta created after April 2001 were lost, despite the August 2002 directive to maintain those tapes. According to the UBS document retention policy, these three monthly backup tapes from April and June 2001 should have been retained for three years.

The two remaining lost backup tapes were for the time period after Zubulake filed her EEOC complaint (Rose Tong's tapes for August and October 2001). UBS has offered no explanation for why these tapes are missing.

* * *

In sum, UBS had a duty to preserve the six-plus backup tapes (that is, six complete backup tapes and part of a seventh) at issue here.

B.   Remedies

As noted, Zubulake has requested three remedies for UBS's spoliation of evidence. I consider each remedy in turn.

1. Reconsideration of the Cost-Shifting Order

Zubulake's request that this Court re-consider its July 24, 2003, Order in *Zubulake III* is inappropriate. At the time that motion was made, the Court was well aware that certain e-mails had not been retained and that certain backup tapes were missing. * * * In *Zubulake III*, in my analysis of the marginal utility factors, I specifically noted that "there is some evidence that Chapin was concealing and deleting especially relevant e-mails." There is therefore no need to reconsider that ruling in light of the instant motion; this evidence already played a role in the cost-shifting decision.

2. Adverse Inference

Zubulake next argues that UBS's spoliation warrants an adverse inference instruction. Zubulake asks that the jury in this case be instructed that it can infer from the fact that UBS destroyed certain evidence that the evidence, if available, would have been favorable to Zubulake and harmful to UBS. In practice, an adverse inference instruction often ends litigation-it is too difficult a hurdle for the spoliator to overcome. The *in terrorem* effect of an adverse inference is obvious. When a jury is instructed that it may "infer that the party who destroyed potentially relevant evidence did so 'out of a realization that the [evidence was] unfavorable,' " the party suffering this instruction will be hard-pressed to prevail on the merits. Accordingly, the adverse inference instruction is an extreme sanction and should not be given lightly.

A party seeking an adverse inference instruction (or other sanctions) based on the spoliation of evidence must establish the following three elements: (1) that the party having control over the evidence had an obligation to preserve it at the time it was destroyed; (2) that the records were destroyed with a "culpable state of mind" and (3) that the destroyed evidence was "relevant" to the party's claim or defense such that a reasonable trier of fact could find that it would support that claim or defense. In this circuit, a "culpable state of mind" for purposes of a spoliation inference includes ordinary negligence. When evidence is destroyed in bad faith (i.e., intentionally or willfully), that fact alone is sufficient to demonstrate relevance. By contrast, when the destruction is negligent, relevance must be proven by the party seeking the sanctions.

a. Duty to Preserve

For the reasons already discussed, UBS had-and breached-a duty to preserve the backup tapes at issue. Zubulake has thus established the first element.

b.   Culpable State of Mind

Zubulake argues that UBS's spoliation was "intentional-or, at a minimum, grossly negligent." Yet, of dozens of relevant backup tapes, only six and part of a seventh are missing. Indeed, UBS argues that the tapes were "inadvertently recycled well before plaintiff requested them and even before she filed her complaint [in February 2002]."

But to accept UBS's argument would ignore the fact that, even though Zubulake had not yet requested the tapes or filed her complaint, UBS had a duty to preserve those tapes. Once the duty to preserve attaches, any destruction of documents is, at a minimum, negligent.

Whether a company's duty to preserve extends to backup tapes has been a grey area. As a result, it is not terribly surprising that a company would think that it did not have a duty to preserve all of its backup tapes, even when it reasonably anticipated the onset of litigation. Thus, UBS's failure to preserve all potentially relevant backup tapes was merely negligent, as opposed to grossly negligent or reckless.

UBS's destruction or loss of Tong's backup tapes, however, exceeds mere negligence. UBS failed to include these backup tapes in its preservation directive in this case, notwithstanding the fact that Tong was the human resources employee directly responsible for Zubulake and who engaged in continuous correspondence regarding the case. Moreover, the lost tapes covered the time period after Zubulake filed her EEOC charge, when UBS was unquestionably on notice of its duty to preserve. Indeed, Tong herself took part in much of the correspondence over Zubulake's charge of discrimination. Thus, UBS was grossly negligent, if not reckless, in not preserving those backup tapes.

Because UBS was negligent-and possibly reckless-Zubulake has satisfied her burden with respect to the second prong of the spoliation test.

c.   Relevance

Finally, because UBS's spoliation was negligent and possibly reckless, but not willful, Zubulake must demonstrate that a reasonable trier of fact could find that the missing e-mails would support her claims. In order to receive an adverse inference instruction, Zubulake must demonstrate not only that UBS destroyed relevant evidence as that term is ordinarily understood, but also that the destroyed evidence would have been favorable to her. "This corroboration requirement is even more necessary where the destruction was merely negligent, since in those cases it cannot be inferred from the conduct of the spoliator that the evidence would even have been harmful to him." This is equally true in cases of gross negligence or recklessness; only in the case of willful spoliation is the spoliator's mental culpability itself evidence of the relevance of the documents destroyed.

On the one hand, I found in *Zubulake I* and *Zubulake III* that the e-mails contained on UBS's backup tapes were, by-and-large, relevant in the sense that they bore on the issues in the litigation. On the other hand, *Zubulake III* specifically held that "nowhere (in the sixty-eight e-mails produced to the Court) is there evidence that Chapin's dislike of Zubulake related to her gender." And those sixty-eight e-mails, it should be emphasized, were the ones selected by Zubulake as being the most relevant among all those produced in UBS's sample restoration. There is no reason to believe that the lost e-mails would be any more likely to support her claims.

* * *

d.   Summary

In sum, although UBS had a duty to preserve all of the backup tapes at issue, and destroyed them with the requisite culpability, Zubulake cannot demonstrate that the lost evidence would have supported her claims. Under the circumstances, it would be inappropriate to give an adverse inference instruction to the jury.

3.   UBS Must Pay the Costs of Additional Depositions

Even though an adverse inference instruction is not warranted, there is no question that e-mails that UBS should have produced to Zubulake were destroyed by UBS. That being so, UBS must bear Zubulake's costs for re-deposing certain witnesses for the limited purpose of inquiring into issues raised by the destruction of evidence and any newly discovered e-mails. In particular, UBS is ordered to pay the costs of re-deposing Chapin, Hardisty, Tong, and Josh Varsano (a human resources employee in charge of the Asian Equities Sales Desk and known to have been in contact with Tong during August 2001).

IV.   CONCLUSION

For the reasons set forth above, Zubulake's motions for an adverse inference instruction and for reconsideration of the Court's July 24, 2003, Order are denied. Her motion seeking costs for additional depositions is granted.

SO ORDERED.

NOTES

Facts

1. When did the court conclude that UBS was reasonably on notice of potential litigation?

2. Where was the evidence at issue in *Zubulake* stored? Was it still on the computer of UBS employees or on UBS servers?

3. What evidence was destroyed in this case?

4. How helpful was this evidence? Why did the court conclude that it was on the whole not likely to be sufficiently helpful to warrant an adverse inference?

5. Why do you think Zubulake wanted these documents?

Law

1. What were UBS' obligations once it was reasonably on notice of a potential dispute?

2. What does the term "spoliation" mean?

3. What are the potential consequence of spoliation? How does the court determine which of these consequences is appropriate?

4. An additional issue can arise with regard to the destruction of so-called "meta-data." Metadata is information stored by a computer to ease file administration and typically includes the time of changes to documents, the author of the document, and at times who made what change to a document. How does metadata further complicate the analysis in question?

Federal Rules of Civil Procedure, Rule 26(b)(2)

(A)   When Permitted. By order, the court may alter the limits in these rules on the number of depositions and interrogatories or on the length of depositions under Rule 30. By order or local rule, the court may also limit the number of requests under Rule 36.

(B)   Specific Limitations on Electronically Stored Information. A party need not provide discovery of electronically stored information from sources that the party identifies as not reasonably accessible because of undue burden or cost. On motion to compel discovery or for a protective order, the party from whom discovery is sought must show that the information is not reasonably accessible because of undue burden or cost. If that showing is made, the court may nonetheless order discovery from such sources if the requesting party shows good cause, considering the limitations of Rule 26(b)(2)(C). The court may specify conditions for the discovery.

(C) When Required. On motion or on its own, the court must limit the frequency or extent of discovery otherwise allowed by these rules or by local rule if it determines that:

(i)   the discovery sought is unreasonably cumulative or duplicative, or can be obtained from some other source that is more convenient, less burdensome, or less expensive;

(ii)   the party seeking discovery has had ample opportunity to obtain the information by discovery in the action; or

(iii) the burden or expense of the proposed discovery outweighs its likely benefit, considering the needs of the case, the amount in controversy, the parties' resources, the importance of the issues at stake in the action, and the importance of the discovery in resolving the issues.

Committee Notes on Rules—2006 Amendment

* * *

Subdivision (b)(2). The amendment to Rule 26(b)(2) is designed to address issues raised by difficulties in locating, retrieving, and providing discovery of some electronically stored information. Electronic storage systems often make it easier to locate and retrieve information. These advantages are properly taken into account in determining the reasonable scope of discovery in a particular case. But some sources of electronically stored information can be accessed only with substantial burden and cost. In a particular case, these burdens and costs may make the information on such sources not reasonably accessible.

It is not possible to define in a rule the different types of technological features that may affect the burdens and costs of accessing electronically stored information. Information systems are designed to provide ready access to information used in regular ongoing activities. They also may be designed so as to provide ready access to information that is not regularly used. But a system may retain information on sources that are accessible only by incurring substantial burdens or costs. Subparagraph (B) is added to regulate discovery from such sources.

Under this rule, a responding party should produce electronically stored information that is relevant, not privileged, and reasonably accessible, subject to the (b)(2)(C) limitations that apply to all discovery. The responding party must also identify, by category or type, the sources containing potentially responsive information that it is neither searching nor producing. The identification should, to the extent possible, provide enough detail to enable the requesting party to evaluate the burdens and costs of providing the discovery and the likelihood of finding responsive information on the identified sources.

A party's identification of sources of electronically stored information as not reasonably accessible does not relieve the party of its common-law or statutory duties to preserve evidence. Whether a responding party is required to preserve unsearched sources of potentially responsive information that it believes are not reasonably accessible depends on the circumstances of each case. It is often useful for the parties to discuss this issue early in discovery.

The volume of—and the ability to search—much electronically stored information means that in many cases the responding party will be able to produce information from reasonably accessible sources that will fully satisfy the parties' discovery needs. In many circumstances the requesting party should obtain and evaluate the information from such sources before insisting that the responding party search and produce information contained on sources that are not reasonably accessible. If the requesting party continues to seek discovery of information from sources identified as not reasonably accessible, the parties should discuss the burdens and costs of accessing and retrieving the information, the needs that may establish good cause for requiring all or part of the requested discovery even if the information sought is not reasonably accessible, and conditions on obtaining and producing the information that may be appropriate.

* * *

Once it is shown that a source of electronically stored information is not reasonably accessible, the requesting party may still obtain discovery by showing good cause, considering the limitations of Rule 26(b)(2)(C) that balance the costs and potential benefits of discovery. The decision whether to require a responding party to search for and produce information that is not reasonably accessible depends not only on the burdens and costs of doing so, but also on whether those burdens and costs can be justified in the circumstances of the case. Appropriate considerations may include: (1) the specificity of the discovery request; (2) the quantity of information available from other and more easily accessed sources; (3) the failure to produce relevant information that seems likely to have existed but is no longer available on more easily accessed sources; (4) the likelihood of finding relevant, responsive information that cannot be obtained from other, more easily accessed sources; (5) predictions as to the importance and usefulness of the further information; (6) the importance of the issues at stake in the litigation; and (7) the parties' resources.

The responding party has the burden as to one aspect of the inquiry—whether the identified sources are not reasonably accessible in light of the burdens and costs required to search for, retrieve, and produce whatever responsive information may be found. The requesting party has the burden of showing that its need for the discovery outweighs the burdens and costs of locating, retrieving, and producing the information. In some cases, the court will be able to determine whether the identified sources are not reasonably accessible and whether the requesting party has shown good cause for some or all of the discovery, consistent with the limitations of Rule 26(b)(2)(C), through a single proceeding or presentation. The good-cause determination, however, may be complicated because the court and parties may know little about what information the sources identified as not reasonably accessible might contain, whether it is relevant, or how valuable it may be to the litigation. In such cases, the parties may need some focused discovery, which may include sampling of the sources, to learn more about what burdens and costs are involved in accessing the information, what the information consists of, and how valuable it is for the litigation in light of information that can be obtained by exhausting other opportunities for discovery.

The good-cause inquiry and consideration of the Rule 26(b)(2)(C) limitations are coupled with the authority to set conditions for discovery. The conditions may take the form of limits on the amount, type, or sources of information required to be accessed and produced. The conditions may also include payment by the requesting party of part or all of the reasonable costs of obtaining information from sources that are not reasonably accessible. A requesting party's willingness to share or bear the access costs may be weighed by the court in determining whether there is good cause. But the producing party's burdens in reviewing the information for relevance and privilege may weigh against permitting the requested discovery.

The limitations of Rule 26(b)(2)(C) continue to apply to all discovery of electronically stored information, including that stored on reasonably accessible electronic sources.

NOTES

1. What does "reasonably accessible information" mean? Who determines whether information is "reasonably accessible"? How is that determination made?

2.   Can a requesting party still obtain information if it is deemed not to be "reasonably accessible"? How would that work?

3.   What factors do the committee notes identify when determining whether not information that is not reasonably accessible should nevertheless be produced? How would you plead your case to show that your discovery request meets these requirements?

Federal Rules of Civil Procedure, Rule 34

(a)   In General. A party may serve on any other party a request within the scope of Rule 26(b):

(1)   to produce and permit the requesting party or its representative to inspect, copy, test, or sample the following items in the responding party's possession, custody, or control:

(A)   any designated documents or electronically stored information—including writings, drawings, graphs, charts, photographs, sound recordings, images, and other data or data compilations—stored in any medium from which information can be obtained either directly or, if necessary, after translation by the responding party into a reasonably usable form; or

* * *

(b)   Procedure.

(1)   Contents of the Request. The request:

(A)   must describe with reasonable particularity each item or category of items to be inspected;

(B)   must specify a reasonable time, place, and manner for the inspection and for performing the related acts; and

(C)   may specify the form or forms in which electronically stored information is to be produced.

(2)   Responses and Objections.

(A)   Time to Respond. The party to whom the request is directed must respond in writing within 30 days after being served. A shorter or longer time may be stipulated to under Rule 29 or be ordered by the court.

(B)   Responding to Each Item. For each item or category, the response must either state that inspection and related activities will be permitted as requested or state an objection to the request, including the reasons.

(C)   Objections. An objection to part of a request must specify the part and permit inspection of the rest.

(D) Responding to a Request for Production of Electronically Stored Information. The response may state an objection to a requested form for producing electronically stored information. If the responding party objects to a requested form—or if no form was specified in the request—the party must state the form or forms it intends to use.

(E)   Producing the Documents or Electronically Stored Information. Unless otherwise stipulated or ordered by the court, these procedures apply to producing documents or electronically stored information:

(i)   A party must produce documents as they are kept in the usual course of business or must organize and label them to correspond to the categories in the request;

(ii)   If a request does not specify a form for producing electronically stored information, a party must produce it in a form or forms in which it is ordinarily maintained or in a reasonably usable form or forms; and

(iii)   A party need not produce the same electronically stored information in more than one form.

Committee Notes on Rules—2006 Amendment

Subdivision (a). As originally adopted, Rule 34 focused on discovery of "documents" and "things." In 1970, Rule 34(a) was amended to include discovery of data compilations, anticipating that the use of computerized information would increase. Since then, the growth in electronically stored information and in the variety of systems for creating and storing such information has been dramatic. * * *

Discoverable information often exists in both paper and electronic form, and the same or similar information might exist in both. The items listed in Rule 34(a) show different ways in which information may be recorded or stored. Images, for example, might be hard-copy documents or electronically stored information. The wide variety of computer systems currently in use, and the rapidity of technological change, counsel against a limiting or precise definition of electronically stored information. Rule 34(a)(1) is expansive and includes any type of information that is stored electronically. A common example often sought in discovery is electronic communications, such as e-mail. The rule covers—either as documents or as electronically stored information—information "stored in any medium," to encompass future developments in computer technology. Rule 34(a)(1) is intended to be broad enough to cover all current types of computer-based information, and flexible enough to encompass future changes and developments.

* * *

The Rule 34(a) requirement that, if necessary, a party producing electronically stored information translate it into reasonably usable form does not address the issue of translating from one human language to another.

Rule 34(a)(1) is also amended to make clear that parties may request an opportunity to test or sample materials sought under the rule in addition to inspecting and copying them. That opportunity may be important for both electronically stored information and hard-copy materials. The current rule is not clear that such testing or sampling is authorized; the amendment expressly permits it. As with any other form of discovery, issues of burden and intrusiveness raised by requests to test or sample can be addressed under Rules 26(b)(2) and 26(c). Inspection or testing of certain types of electronically stored information or of a responding party's electronic information system may raise issues of confidentiality or privacy. The addition of testing and sampling to Rule 34(a) with regard to documents and electronically stored information is not meant to create a routine right of direct access to a party's electronic information system, although such access might be justified in some circumstances. Courts should guard against undue intrusiveness resulting from inspecting or testing such systems.

* * *

Subdivision (b). Rule 34(b) provides that a party must produce documents as they are kept in the usual course of business or must organize and label them to correspond with the categories in the discovery request. The production of electronically stored information should be subject to comparable requirements to protect against deliberate or inadvertent production in ways that raise unnecessary obstacles for the requesting party. Rule 34(b) is amended to ensure similar protection for electronically stored information.

The amendment to Rule 34(b) permits the requesting party to designate the form or forms in which it wants electronically stored information produced. The form of production is more important to the exchange of electronically stored information than of hard-copy materials, although a party might specify hard copy as the requested form. Specification of the desired form or forms may facilitate the orderly, efficient, and cost-effective discovery of electronically stored information. The rule recognizes that different forms of production may be appropriate for different types of electronically stored information. Using current technology, for example, a party might be called upon to produce word processing documents, e-mail messages, electronic spreadsheets, different image or sound files, and material from databases. Requiring that such diverse types of electronically stored information all be produced in the same form could prove impossible, and even if possible could increase the cost and burdens of producing and using the information. The rule therefore provides that the requesting party may ask for different forms of production for different types of electronically stored information.

* * *

The responding party also is involved in determining the form of production. In the written response to the production request that Rule 34 requires, the responding party must state the form it intends to use for producing electronically stored information if the requesting party does not specify a form or if the responding party objects to a form that the requesting party specifies. Stating the intended form before the production occurs may permit the parties to identify and seek to resolve disputes before the expense and work of the production occurs. A party that responds to a discovery request by simply producing electronically stored information in a form of its choice, without identifying that form in advance of the production in the response required by Rule 34(b), runs a risk that the requesting party can show that the produced form is not reasonably usable and that it is entitled to production of some or all of the information in an additional form. Additional time might be required to permit a responding party to assess the appropriate form or forms of production.

If the requesting party is not satisfied with the form stated by the responding party, or if the responding party has objected to the form specified by the requesting party, the parties must meet and confer under Rule 37(a)(2)(B) in an effort to resolve the matter before the requesting party can file a motion to compel. If they cannot agree and the court resolves the dispute, the court is not limited to the forms initially chosen by the requesting party, stated by the responding party, or specified in this rule for situations in which there is no court order or party agreement.

If the form of production is not specified by party agreement or court order, the responding party must produce electronically stored information either in a form or forms in which it is ordinarily maintained or in a form or forms that are reasonably usable. Rule 34(a) requires that, if necessary, a responding party "translate" information it produces into a "reasonably usable" form. Under some circumstances, the responding party may need to provide some reasonable amount of technical support, information on application software, or other reasonable assistance to enable the requesting party to use the information. The rule does not require a party to produce electronically stored information in the form it [sic] which it is ordinarily maintained, as long as it is produced in a reasonably usable form. But the option to produce in a reasonably usable form does not mean that a responding party is free to convert electronically stored information from the form in which it is ordinarily maintained to a different form that makes it more difficult or burdensome for the requesting party to use the information efficiently in the litigation. If the responding party ordinarily maintains the information it is producing in a way that makes it searchable by electronic means, the information should not be produced in a form that removes or significantly degrades this feature.

Some electronically stored information may be ordinarily maintained in a form that is not reasonably usable by any party. One example is "legacy" data that can be used only by superseded systems. The questions whether a producing party should be required to convert such information to a more usable form, or should be required to produce it at all, should be addressed under Rule 26(b)(2)(B).

Whether or not the requesting party specified the form of production, Rule 34(b) provides that the same electronically stored information ordinarily be produced in only one form.

* * *

NOTES

1. Why does the form in which production of electronically stored information occurs relevant?

2. What is the default rule for the production of electronically stored information? Why?

3. For what reasons would courts depart from the default rule?

B) e-Disclosure in Arbitration

The problems of e-Disclosure in arbitration are particularly thorny because e-Disclosure proves to be one of the costliest and most time intensive parts of disclosure. On the other hand, e-Disclosure is arguably the most reliable tool to retrieve contemporaneous documentary evidence regarding the issues in dispute. This evidence is arguably the most credible to reconstruct an accurate sequence of events leading to the dispute. E-Disclosure, in other words, is thorny because efficiency of arbitral proceedings would counsel to severely limiting it whereas a fair hearing of the case would suggest more heavy reliance upon it.

1) *Scope of e-Disclosure in Arbitration*

A critical gateway question is whether e-Disclosure in arbitration should be limited to material "on file" with the parties. The *Zubulake* litigation concerned back-up tapes. The restoration of backup tapes is a particularly costly—and frequently time consuming—task. The question therefore arises whether eDiscovery in arbitration, in counter-distinction to eDiscovery in litigation, should be limited to files that are still "on hand" rather than reverting to back up tapes in the first place.

Where the arbitration clause is silent, arbitration rules typically do not address this issue. Instead, they require the parties to convince the tribunal to exercise its discretion. Some commentators have argued that requests for production of backup files is rife with abuse. For example, Cecilia B. Loving and Vaughn N. Browne make an argument appealing to utility. They argue that the cost of restoring backup files are rarely, if ever, so material as to turn the case. Their analysis premised upon the cost of recovery of a single backup tape at $1 million. Cecilia B. Loving and Vaughn N. Browne, eDiscovery for Corporate Counsel, § 20:11. Practical guidance for eDiscovery in arbitrations—Limiting the amount of data to be produced (2013).

The issue they point out is mostly of a technical nature. It is not possible to search backed up data in an efficient manner. It is therefore impossible to know what is on a backup tape until all of the back up tape has been reviewed. It is thus the cost of the review process together with the cost of indexing and reviewing the documents that makes use of the disclosure of backup tapes objectionable according to Loving and Browne.

Even on its face, argument must bear in mind the overall amount in controversy in the arbitration. The cost of $1 million to recover a backup tape holding relevant and material information is less objectionable in a $1 billion dispute than in a $5 million dispute. As arbitrations replace business litigation, such large amounts in controversy are not unheard of in arbitration. They, obviously, impact the balance of utilities involved.

Further, the balance of utilities could also consider the relative cost of avoiding the need to go to backup tapes in the first place. If an arbitrator were to conclude that the destruction of native files in a readily readable format was easy to avoid or in bad faith, the cost of preventing the need to go to backup tapes may be a relevant factor. (That being said, the arbitrator could well indicate that he or she is inclined to rule on the basis of a presumption or inference. This may incentivize the party holding the backup tapes to restore them on its own motion.)

Needless to say, the balance of utilities is significantly impacted by developments in forensic technology. Stronger search algorithms and future developments in artificial intelligence may make it easier (and cheaper) to review materials stored on backup tapes. Comparable computer programing advances may further make it significantly less onerous to translate the backed up information back into its native formatting. Advances in technology, in other words, have an immediate impact on the question whether to review back up tapes. A conversation with a forensic computer analyst may therefore be worthwhile before making e-Disclosure requests to base one's arguments on the then-available state of the art in forensic computer programming.

NOTES

1. One obvious concern with making back-up tapes unavailable in arbitration is deliberate destruction or alteration when a party had notice of an arbitration proceeding. How would *Zubulake* address that problem? What rule would you fashion on the basis of *Zubulake* that would avoid requiring production of materials from back-up tapes in arbitration?

2. What type of cases are going to be the most likely case to require discovery of materials from back-up tapes

3. Technology, rather than the erudite musings of jurists, seems to be in charge of developments in eDiscovery. What discovery would a party seeking discovery from back-up tapes need in order to put its best foot forward? Can counsel do this unassisted? What kind of assistance is needed? Where would one get it?

4. With the growth of technology, international arbitration institutions and practice groups and learned societies dealing with arbitration are increasingly writing protocols with regard to eDiscovery. Which ones can you find with a cursory internet search? Is what they recommend consistent?

2) Selection of Custodians

Once the universe of electronically stored information subject to discovery has been set, the next threshold question is whose materials to search. Electronically stored information is typically by somebody. Thus, a person may store electronic information that was sent to him or her (for instance the recipient of an email or voicemail). A person may store electronic information that he or she generated (as is the case when a person writes a memorandum in word). As a threshold matter, as Neil Eiseman, John Bulman and R. Thomas Dunn note, the volume and cost of production to be searched can be limited by identifying whose electronically stored information to search—and how large the group of custodians should be. Neil M. Eiseman, John E. Bulman & R. Thomas Dunn, *A Tale of Two Lawyer: How Arbitrators and Advocates can Avoid the Dangerous Convergence of Arbitration and Litigation*, 14 CARDOZO J. CONFLICT RESOL. 683, 715 (2013).

One obvious way to narrow e-discovery in arbitration, and thus reduce the cost of e-discovery is to narrow the numbers of custodians of whom such e-discovery is taken. One argument for the narrowing of e-discovery is that the same electronic document will show up in multiple inboxes. As many emails are not sent to a single recipient, but rather are sent to an entire group, this duplication is not insignificant. This line of argument therefore suggests that an appropriate manner to limit e-discovery in arbitration is to limit the number of people from whom to review documents to a very narrow grouping of people. Cecilia B. Loving and Vaughn N. Browne, eDiscovery for Corporate Counsel, § 20:11. Practical guidance for eDiscovery in arbitrations—Limiting the amount of data to be produced (2013).

Fairly, this argument again has to be appraised in light of technological advancements. One of the key features of contemporary forensic software products is to "de-duplicate" electronic documents. Although this feature is not perfect, it significantly reduces the client cost of document review in question. Other software advances further reduce the cost associated with e-discovery.

This does not mean, however, that it is prudent to permit broad lists of custodians. The amount of data to be reviewed is increased significantly with each custodian to be added to the list. No matter the advances in technology, this increase in data will create significant cost and confidentiality issues. It is therefore on the whole preferable to limit searches to a reasonable set of custodians.

The selection of these custodians further faces significant difficulties in different ways. The person whose information you are seeking to search may not in fact have "stored" or "saved" his own work. Thus, a memorandum or note by a senior client executive could have been dictated—and turned into a word document by his or her assistant. If that is the case, the information may be stored on the system as belonging to the assistant rather than the executive.

Failure to include the assistant as a custodian may well lead to the exclusion of a trove of documents that one intended to capture. Understanding how the client—or the opposing party—handles data thus is critical to understanding how to select custodians for purposes of the discovery of electronically stored information.

NOTES

1. Obviously the number of custodians appropriate for inclusion in discovery will depend upon the size and nature of the dispute. How many custodians do you think each side could identify for purposes of the dispute in the fact scenario?

2. How do you select appropriate custodians for requests for production of electronically stored information? Can you do so without needing further discovery? What discovery would you need to first and how would go about getting it?

3) Determining Keywords

Once you have determined the custodians to search the next thing to do is figure out search terms. No person is going to review the entire data universe. Rather, the data universe is going to be mined for specific search terms agreed upon by the parties or determined by the tribunal.

As you can imagine, certain search terms will lead to massive results. Thus, the search term "design" in our fact scenario would produce an indigestible number of hits. One key therefore is to look for terms that are unique to the transaction or occurrence at issue in your arbitration. Finding these unique, or uniquely relevant, terms is one of the keys to successful eDiscovery.

The next option you have is to combine search terms to narrow results. You are familiar with this technique from Westlaw searches or other searches in legal databases. If you input "discovery" as a search term in the all journals database, you likely are going to have too many hits to handle. If you combine "discovery" with "electronically stored information" and "arbitration", your search results are going to dwindle. If you add further proximity limitations requiring that words appear in the same sentence or the same paragraph, you will further limit your search results.

As you likely are also familiar with, there is a good chance that an overly focused search is going to exclude results you have wanted. Proximity searches in particular are tricky because it is hard to predict in how close proximity people ordinarily would use relevant search terms. Thus, in the context of our Westlaw search, do you think all authors who discuss eDiscovery in arbitration will use "electronically stored information" in the same sentence as the word "arbitration"? If you limited it to the proximity of a paragraph, do you think that there is a high likelihood that you will get a lot of discussion of eDiscovery in "normal" litigation that mentions arbitration in passing?

NOTES

1.   Try running searches for articles on eDiscovery in arbitration in a legal database. See what comes up when you use different search techniques. How does this experience assist you further honing your skills of selecting the right keywords and proximity parameters.

2.   You represent a client in an employment dispute like *Zubulake*. The dispute has been submitted to arbitration. The arbitrator allows you to select five search terms. A search term is both a single term or a complex term (i.e., a term that strings various terms together with proximity connectors). What are the search terms you use?

3.   You represent a seller in an installment contract for the sale of goods. On installment 100 of 1000, the buyer asserts that the goods are non-conforming and rejects. The arbitrator gives you three search terms. What terms do you want?

4) Spoliation

So far we have discussed how to conduct eDiscovery in arbitration. This section briefly addresses what can happen when something "goes wrong". Look back to the chapter on sanctions. What do you think are the key things an arbitral tribunal can do? How do you make the appropriate motion to do so?

Now consider the problem of spoliation of evidence. The arbitrator obviously has now power to hold a party or its counsel in contempt. The arbitrator does, however, have the power to draw adverse inferences from the spoliation of evidence. As the finder of fact, the arbitrator may further—implicitly—carry forward the credibility implications that spoliation presents to other contested factual questions. Adverse inferences therefore are one powerful tool to address spoliation concerns.

Despite the powerful nature of adverse inferences, the available data from published awards suggests that arbitrators use such inferences sparingly. The use of adverse inferences always carry with them the potential challenge that the arbitrator failed to hear the evidence or failed to treat the parties equally in keeping with basic notions of fairness and due process. The arbitrator therefore may well find him or herself in much of the same position as the *Zubulake* case above—the arbitrator may refuse to draw an inference by finding that the evidence which could have been produced would not have been sufficiently material to warrant the inference in question.

The more likely route by which an arbitrator will take spoliation into account is in making credibility findings or in drawing inferences from the existing evidentiary record. Such use of inferences would be on firmer ground from a due process perspective—it falls squarely within the discretion of the finder of facts—while achieving the same ultimate end: the finding in favor of the party suffering the detriment of spoliation. Even this soft use of inferences may in extreme cases lead to problems of their own.

Arbitrators may therefore be more willing to use cost-shifting or other mechanisms to give the parties as fair of a chance to complete the record. As Irene Warshauer noted, tribunals may order the recovery and disclosure of backup tape materials and shift the costs to the parties who caused the need to look to backup tapes. Irene C. Warshauer, *Electronic Discovery in Arbitration: Privilege Issues and Spoliation of Evidence*, 61-JAN Disp. Resol. J. 9 (Nov. 2006/Jan. 2007).

Even this approach has its problems, however. Backup tapes may not in fact have the relevant information. At that point, the arbitrator is back in the original position of having to determine how to deal with the spoliation of evidence. Parties that make available both harder and softer options for the arbitrators to do so will in most likelihood find themselves more successful than parties asking for far reaching rulings—particularly when these far reaching rulings are not otherwise supported by the evidentiary record before the tribunal even with the liberal use of inferences in favor of the harmed party.

NOTES

1. You learn from opposing counsel that evidence you requested in discovery is no longer available because it has been erased as part of a routine maintenance program on your client's cloud computing service. What do you do next?

2. Assuming that you have been able to establish that the deletion did not occur as part of a routine maintenance program but rather was done deliberately by a person with log in credentials permitting remote access to

the files. How do you apprise the arbitrators of the development? What do you ask for?

3.   At what point can you ask for adverse inference? How would you word the inference to be drawn? When do you propose the wording of adverse inference? At the outset? After you have learned of potential spoliation? After you have proved that spoliation occurred? After you have provided evidence that the deletion of documents was intentional?

CHAPTER 18

Evidence in Arbitration

Fact Scenario

The parties to the Hardmont arbitration outlined in chapters 11–19 are getting closer and closer to the merits hearing of the case. Hardmont (Claimant) and Acme/RRF/Gilmore (Respondents) have conferred on a common evidence bundle to be submitted to the arbitral tribunal ahead of the hearing. During this exchange, the parties agreed to ask the arbitrator to rule on the following evidentiary objections.

Claimant's Objections

1. Respondent wishes to introduce summaries of raw data relied upon in Hardmont's market study into evidence in lieu of the voluminous raw data. Respondent states that these summaries, prepared by its party-appointed expert, will support that Hardmont's market research was hardly proprietary.

2. Respondent wishes to introduce an article from an online industry magazine with discussion thread. The article states that Hardmont's marketing team had lost its creative edge. One of the comments on the discussion—left under the handle "former H. employee"—states "not a surprise. Their new COO is a blow hard who has more interest in whacking at golf balls than come up with good marketing ideas. Disgusting". Respondent states that this article and comment thread supports that the reason Hardmont is not moving merchandise is its lackluster marketing rather than any alleged violation by Acme of the NDA.

3. Respondent wishes to introduce an article from Hardmont's local newspaper. The newspaper article describes an altercation between Hardmont's CEO and a local shop keeper. The story suggests that Hardmont's CEO is a quarrelsome and highly litigious individual. Respondent states that this article supports that the arbitration fits within a pattern of abuse of process by the Claimant.

Respondents' Objections

1. Claimant wishes to introduce an access log to its servers. The access log shows that an IP address in Respondent's home town sought to access Claimant's computer systems while the arbitration was ongoing. Claimant states that the logs support a pattern of snooping by Respondents.

2. Claimant wishes to introduce an affidavit from a former Acme employee. The former Acme employee states that he was told to drop off an envelope with RRF's COO. He testifies that he saw Mr. Gilmore slip a large document in the envelope and that the first page of the document looked like it stated "Hardmont" in bold. The former employee is not available for cross-examination. Claimant states that the affidavit supports its factual account of events.

3. Claimant wishes to introduce an email between Mr. Gilmore and his legal counsel. The email comes from an Acme domain. In the email, Mr. Gilmore requests legal advice regarding the consequence of violating a Non-Disclosure Agreement. The email does not state which Non-Disclosure Agreement is at issue. Claimant has not disclosed how it came into possession of the email (it was not produced by Respondents). Claimant states that the email supports that Gilmore planned to hand over to the materials in question to RRF and that it would impeach any testimony by Gilmore that he never thought about breaching an NDA.

Please choose a side and prepare the relevant arguments in favor of your side's objections in limine and in opposition to the other side's objection in limine.

Readings

A) The Functional Premise for Rules of Evidence in Arbitration

Rules of evidence in a court proceeding serve a critical function. They guarantee a level playing field to both parties in the manner in which they can plead their case. They police that the outcome of a case reaches, as far are possible, the "correct" result. Thus, in the setting of jury trial in particular, the exclusion of certain kind of evidence from the record is critical to assuring that factual determinations are rendered on a reliable basis rather than by conjecture or bias. Failure to abide by the rules of evidence in a court proceeding therefore, in theory at least, presents a serious threat to the fairness and legitimacy of court proceedings.

Arbitration and litigation differ in significant respects. To understand the role of rules of evidence in arbitration, one must first engage the question how evidence should be taken in the arbitral process—and how "evidence" should figure in the result reached by the arbitrators. The first case addresses these critical questions in the context of a motion to vacate a $12.4 MM award.

Fairchild Corp. v. Alcoa, Inc.

510 F.Supp.2d 280 (S.D.N.Y., 2007)

VICTOR MARRERO, DISTRICT JUDGE.

Petitioner The Fairchild Corporation ("Fairchild") brought this action seeking to vacate, or to reduce by certain tax offsets, an award granted to respondent Alcoa Inc. ("Alcoa") in an arbitration proceeding. Alcoa cross-moves to confirm the award in its entirety. For the reasons discussed below, Fairchild's petition is DENIED and Alcoa's cross-petition is GRANTED.

I.   BACKGROUND

The parties' dispute arose from an acquisition agreement (the "Agreement") entered into in December 2002 under which Fairchild sold its aerospace fastener business to Alcoa for a purchase price in an amount of approximately $657 million. The Agreement provided that Fairchild would indemnify Alcoa for certain environmental liabilities which, as defined, entailed expenses exceeding an account reserve of $8.45 million for this purpose and were associated with remediation work required to cure non-compliance with environmental and health and safety laws. To fund such indemnification payments, the parties agreed to maintain an escrow account of $25 million drawn from the purchase price. The Agreement included an arbitration clause providing a procedure governed by the Federal Arbitration Act to resolve disputes regarding the validity or amount of any claim for indemnification.

Pursuant to the Agreement, Alcoa submitted to Fairchild, over the period from the closing date in December 2002 through December 2006, more than 200 claims seeking indemnification in a total amount of $16,385,493.92 for costs Alcoa asserted it incurred in connection with qualifying corrective work performed at various facilities it acquired from Fairchild. Fairchild rejected all of Alcoa's claims, contending that: (1) Alcoa had failed to provide adequate documentation that it had actually incurred the expenditures; (2) the claims were not covered by the Agreement or not explicitly ordered by regulatory authorities; (3) Fairchild had not been given adequate notice of the corrective work; and (4)

Fairchild was entitled to offsets for certain tax benefits Alcoa would receive in respect of operating losses Fairchild had incurred in connection with portions of the claims in question.

Failing mediation of their disagreements over Alcoa's claims, in July 2005 the parties proceeded to binding arbitration under the Agreement. Eventually, from a list provided by the International Institute for Conflict Prevention and Resolution, they agreed upon an arbitrator James F. Stapleton (the "Arbitrator"), a former judge of the Connecticut Superior Court.

Alcoa asserts that although it raised objections, as unduly burdensome, to a request by Fairchild that each and every receipt and invoice associated with Alcoa's claims for indemnification be identified individually, Alcoa produced at the hearing, through a live witness who testified about the material, a summary chart itemizing its claims under several categories and the amounts of corresponding expenditures. Alcoa also points to specific documentation that it had already submitted to Fairchild supporting its actual costs. At the close of discovery in December 2006, Alcoa moved for partial summary judgment, which the Arbitrator denied, having found some ambiguities in the relevant provisions of the Agreement as well as other issues of material fact in dispute. The Arbitrator then conducted a hearing over several days during January, February and March 2007, followed by post-hearing briefings.

In the course of these post-hearing proceedings, Fairchild argued that Alcoa had not sufficiently proved the actual costs of $16.3 million for which it sought indemnification. In response, Alcoa pointed to evidence on the record that it contends amply supported its claim. But it then offered to provide to the Arbitrator a copy of the 14 volumes of invoices and receipts documenting its expenditures, materials Alcoa states it had supplied to Fairchild during the course of discovery. Fairchild objected to Alcoa's offer and the Arbitrator declined to accept the additional material at that point.

The Arbitrator rendered his ruling in an Arbitration Decision and Award (the "Award") issued on June 21, 2007. The Award rejected Fairchild's position in all material respects. Specifically, the Arbitrator concluded that, with some exceptions, Alcoa's claims for indemnification, including those involving corrective work not required by regulators, was sufficiently supported by the language of the Agreement and related evidence as necessary and reasonable and performed at reasonable cost, and that Fairchild's allegations of Alcoa's violations of the notice provision of the Agreement were unwarranted. Of the total of $16,385,463.92 that Alcoa had claimed, the Award granted Alcoa damages amounting to $12,455,585.88. That sum reflected deductions of

$3,303,643.48 for work the Arbitrator found was not indemnifiable because it was either not necessary or commercially reasonable, or not performed at a reasonable cost. The Award also included credits of $264,106.92 in respect of certain tax benefits Alcoa had received, and an additional $926,565.13 it potentially would receive in this regard.

In full settlement of all claims and counter-claims submitted in the arbitration, and denying all those not expressly granted, the Arbitrator ordered that Alcoa be paid, within 30 days of the Award, the $8.45 million in the reserve account and the balance of $4,005,585.88 from the escrow account.

Claiming that it was due additional tax benefit credits under another provision of the Agreement, Fairchild blocked the release of funds by the escrow agent and wrote to Alcoa proposing further mediation and arbitration proceedings pertaining to this issue. Fairchild subsequently filed the instant petition to vacate the Award.

II. DISCUSSION

A. LEGAL FRAMEWORK AND STANDARD OF REVIEW

When Congress adopted the Federal Arbitration Act (the "FAA"), 9 U.S.C. § 1 et seq., in 1924, it responded to concerns over the complexity, duration, delays and costs of litigation in federal courts, with the attendant adverse effects that unduly prolonged judicial proceedings engendered for litigants, the courts, and society in general. In addressing these concerns, the FAA recognized the value of arbitration properly conducted as a means by which parties could "settle their disputes expeditiously and economically." The statute contemplated an alternative to litigation that would be simpler, faster and less costly for all concerned. As envisioned, this system of dispute resolution would be liberated from many of the onerous demands and constraints associated with legal proceedings in court.

This recognition of the immense public and private benefits of arbitration is reflected in judicial doctrine. Since the inception of the FAA an extensive body of law has developed reaffirming the strong federal policy that favors honoring arbitration agreements and ensuring that the presumed efficiency values of expeditiousness, economy and simplicity in reaching the merits and resolving disputes are safeguarded in arbitration proceedings. To these ends, federal courts underscore that arbitration is not intended to incorporate all the procedural rules and niceties that govern legal combat in judicial proceedings. *See Tempo Shain*

Corp. v. Bertek, Inc., 120 F.3d 16, 20 (2d Cir.1997) (noting that arbitration " 'need not follow all the niceties observed by the federal courts' ").

The same judicial attitude imbues the substantial latitude and extensive deference accorded on judicial review to determinations of arbitrators.

Consistent with this generally broad application of the FAA, courts have elaborated a body of specific rules designed to capture the essence of the statute's policy and have rigorously applied them to give effect to Congress's underlying purpose. This doctrine reinforces that arbitration proceedings require merely an " 'expeditious and summary hearing, with only restricted inquiry into factual issues.' " At bottom, the case law seeks to protect the basic simpler structure of arbitral procedures and the integrity of resulting awards so as to withstand challenge except on the limited grounds the law recognizes. * * *

Further manifesting the strict doctrinal rules formulated to advance the aims of the FAA, arbitrators are afforded broad discretion to determine whether to hear or not hear evidence, or whether additional evidence is necessary or would simply prolong the proceedings. Consistent with the deference due to arbitral decisions, a court reviewing an arbitrator's determination may look at the evidentiary record "only for the purpose of discerning whether a colorable basis exists for the panel's award so as to assure that the award cannot be said to be the result of the panel's manifest disregard of the law." Therefore, a court may not conduct a reassessment of the evidence or vacate an arbitral award because the arbitrator's decision may run contrary to strong evidence favoring the party seeking to overturn the award. Nor do internal conflicts embodied in the arbitrator's decision warrant denying confirmation of an award.

By the same token, manifest disregard of evidence is also not a proper ground justifying vacating an arbitrator's award. On this point, Second Circuit doctrine counsels that "whatever the weight of the evidence considered as a whole, '[i]f ground for the arbitrator's decision can be inferred from the facts of the case, the award should be confirmed.' " In short, only the most egregious errors or instances of extreme misconduct cited in the statute that would materially prejudice the rights of a party warrant vacating an arbitral award.

The same fundamental policy ends are reflected in the absence from the FAA of any requirement that arbitrators be attorneys, or that they provide an explanation for their decision.

The message implicit in this body of law is uniform and clear. Arbitration procedures may not embrace all of the meticulous details of due process that govern litigation in court, but they offer greater dispatch. Arbitral decisions at times may not be scrupulously grounded on fact or law with the same exactitude demanded of judicial rulings, but they should be easier and less costly to procure. Some arbitration proceedings may admit what may be deemed, by litigation standards, procedural imperfections, but they hold the promise of greater simplicity. In sum, what the adversaries in arbitration forfeit in rigorous legal safeguards is presumably offset by a larger measure of efficiency. Overall, therefore, the process embodies a trade-off, a price in degree of certainty that is paid in exchange for less expense and sooner peace of mind to the parties in settling disputes. In consequence, a central premise of arbitration assumes that when parties commit consensually to resolve disagreements by arbitration, in the interest of achieving their expectations of gains in quicker and more economical resolution, they are entitled to get what they bargained for, and be prepared to accept both the benefits and the risks the system incorporates. And it is precisely in giving effect to legitimate expectations of the parties to an arbitral agreement where the overriding goal of the FAA is found.

B.   ARBITRATOR MISCONDUCT

Fairchild's principal contention in support of its petition to vacate the Award is that the Arbitrator committed serious error by refusing to consider relevant evidence or ignoring evidentiary material with respect to critical matters at issue. Fairchild rests its argument on the language of FAA § 10(a)(3), which authorizes courts to vacate an award "where the arbitrators were guilty of misconduct . . . in refusing to hear evidence pertinent and material to the controversy." 9 U.S.C. § 10(a)(3). The Court is not persuaded that the Arbitrator's action challenged here constitutes misconduct within the scope of FAA § 10(a)(3). That provision applies to cases where an arbitrator, to the prejudice of one of the parties, rejects consideration of relevant evidence essential to the adjudication of a fundamental issue in dispute, and the party would otherwise be deprived of sufficient opportunity to present proof of a claim or defense. The misconduct in that event amounts to a denial of fundamental fairness in the proceeding, and renders the resulting arbitral decision biased, irrational or arbitrary.

Here, it is inaccurate to characterize the Arbitrator's action as "refusing" to hear pertinent and material evidence necessary to resolve the issue he decided, and without which Alcoa could not have proved its claims to the Arbitrator's satisfaction. In fact, the Arbitrator, as Fairchild acknowledges, admitted documents containing summaries itemizing the volumes of invoices and receipts that Fairchild contends should have been part of the record during the hearing. In addition, the Arbitrator heard testimony on this subject from John Lease

("Lease"), the Alcoa employee designated as Alcoa's representative for communications with Fairchild pertaining to health and safety projects under the Agreement. In that capacity Lease was responsible for forwarding to Fairchild documentation of project investigations, studies, scope and cost of corrective work, and invoices for payment. He thus demonstrated an adequate foundation of personal knowledge and involvement in the transactions that enabled him to provide relevant evidence. Lease's appearance as a witness, as Alcoa points out, occupied about 10 hours over two days, including cross-examination. Thus, Fairchild had ample opportunity to contest the adequacy and accuracy of the evidence Alcoa proffered in support of the particular projects and expenditures it claimed, the back-up for which Fairchild had been provided in the course of discovery. Fairchild thus had the information in its possession and could have used it on cross-examination during Lease's presentation.

Lease's testimony referenced an exhibit containing a summary of voluminous documents which he indicated Alcoa had sent to Fairchild and which represented the actual expenditures Alcoa had incurred for studies, investigations and corrective actions underlying its claims for indemnification. (See Transcript of Arbitration Hearing on Jan. 10, 2007 ("Tr."), attached as Ex. J of Declaration of Daniel Slifkin in Support of Alcoa Inc.'s Cross-Petition to Confirm and in Opposition to The Fairchild Corporation's Petition to Vacate Arbitration Award, dated July 17, 2007 ("Slifkin Decl."), at 907–20.) Moreover, insofar as the Arbitrator declined to accept the 14 volumes of additional materials when proffered by Alcoa during post-hearing briefings, his refusal may have been influenced in part by Fairchild's own objection to the introduction of evidence at that point.

The Arbitrator had opportunity to assess the credibility of the witnesses and the reliability of the evidence, taking into account the record as a whole, including Lease's familiarity with the material, Fairchild's possession of the documents and its ability to cross-examine Alcoa's witnesses. On this basis the Arbitrator was permitted to weigh and credit the evidence in the light of the record as a whole in determining the Award. The Award makes clear that the Arbitrator, following a similar approach, considered and accepted or rejected other evidence of costs based on materials in the record, specifying precise amounts derived not from the summaries, but apparently from other testimony and reports of experts. (See, Award at 6–19; Findings of Fact and Conclusions of Law at 7–20). Indeed, relying on the same sources of evidence, the Arbitrator not only approved the amounts of the claims to which Fairchild here objects, but actually reduced the total award Alcoa had requested by a very precise number of $3,303,683.48 in claims he disallowed. (See Award at 21.) From these circumstances it can be properly inferred that the Arbitrator found sufficient evidentiary grounds for his decision in the testimony of Lease and other witnesses, and the documents upon which their presentations relied. As to the claims he approved, the Arbitrator made a specific finding that "Alcoa has sustained its burden of proof that the expenditures were in fact made in the amounts claimed." (Id.) For arbitration purposes, this record suffices to justify confirmation of the award. See Wallace, 378 F.3d at 193.

Fairchild's FAA § 10(a)(3) argument here is thus not that, as petitioner, it was precluded by the Arbitrator from presenting evidence critical to supporting its case. Rather, Fairchild takes issue with the Award because the Arbitrator refused to accept a post-hearing submission proffered by Alcoa to which Fairchild itself then objected. Fairchild's argument therefore poses a logical dilemma insofar as it rests on FAA § 10(a)(3). On the one hand Fairchild charges misconduct on the part of the Arbitrator for "refusing" to accept evidence Alcoa proffered that Fairchild contends was relevant and material to prove the expenditures Alcoa claimed, and without which Fairchild would be substantially prejudiced. On the other, Fairchild defends its objection to Alcoa's presentation of the evidence during the post-hearing proceeding as "entirely proper" because the material was then being offered directly to the Arbitrator after the hearing. (Petitioner's Memorandum of Law in Further Support of Its Petition to Vacate Arbitration Award and in Opposition to Alcoa's Cross-Petition to Confirm ("Pet.Reply"), dated July 24, 2007, at 5.) In other words, Fairchild's position faults the Arbitrator for refusing to hear evidence while at the same time implicitly conceding that it was proper for Arbitrator to reject consideration of Alcoa's submission at that point because the hearing had closed.

Fairchild's response to this apparent contradiction is that the Arbitrator should have denied Alcoa's claims for lack of proof, or else force Alcoa to submit the evidence properly by reopening the proceeding, presumably despite Fairchild's recorded objection. But the Arbitrator had another course he properly chose to pursue. Because the Arbitrator had been presented evidence concerning the issue of Alcoa's actual expenditures in the form of the other documents and live testimony, the record was not entirely devoid of proof sufficient for arbitration purposes to support acceptance of Alcoa's claims. The Arbitrator could have fairly relied upon such other evidence as a whole to justify a confirmable decision. See Wallace, 378 F.3d at 193. As such, at that point in the proceeding the Arbitrator could properly have declined to consider the additional material and rejected it as cumulative. See Areca, 960 F.Supp. at 55.

In essence, Fairchild's argument on this point actually narrows to a challenge to the sufficiency of the evidence that the Arbitrator did weigh and chose to credit in reaching his decision. The case law makes clear, however, that an arbitrator has discretion to admit or reject evidence and determine what materials may be cumulative or irrelevant. See id.; Trade & Transport, 738 F.Supp. at 792. Moreover, an arbitration award cannot be overturned solely on the ground of manifest disregard of evidence.

The Court is also not persuaded that the other actions of the Arbitrator that Fairchild challenges as serious errors are sufficiently egregious to warrant invalidating the Award. Fairchild points to three examples of such alleged serious errors. First, it asserts that the Arbitrator entirely ignored evidence Fairchild introduced to address a dispute concerning certain claims Alcoa submitted that related to guarding potentially dangerous machines, and that Alcoa regarded as pertaining to "workplace health or safety" as defined in the Agreement. Fairchild points to a statement in the Award in which the Arbitrator notes that Fairchild did not present any contemporaneous evidence supporting its position that it considered those expenditures as excluded from indemnity. But, as Alcoa responds, the Arbitrator specifically addresses evidence that Fairchild submitted in the form of two schedules pertaining to this claim, and that the Arbitrator apparently chose not credit that evidence as convincing on the issue. (See Award at 4.) To the extent any statements in the Arbitrator's decision may be at odds on this point, such internal inconsistency, as discussed below in connection with Fairchild's next argument, does not suffice to overturn an award. See Saint Mary Home, 116 F.3d at 44–45.

* * *

D.   ADDITIONAL CONSIDERATIONS

This proceeding may serve as a prime study of failed expectations in the case of a much heralded public policy reform gone awry, and an instance of the best of intentions frustrated by the worst in execution. In particular, it illustrates how the spirit and promise of a beneficial innovation in the administration of justice can be undermined by the attempts of litigants incrementally to reimpose upon the legal system the burdens of procedural trappings that changes in the law were meant to relieve in order to simplify and expedite the resolution of private disputes, by these means returning the law to the unsatisfactory point that prompted those major improvements in the first place. These reasons prompt the Court to add some additional considerations further elaborating on the context that informs and frames this ruling.

In the discussion above, the Court expressed what, in purest terms, was conceived of the theory of the FAA when enacted, and its promise. What appears to have become the reality in many arbitration actions, is quite another thing, a development at odds with the procedural reform Congress envisioned in adopting the statute. As exemplified by the action now before the Court, an arbitration proceeding today is often not a true alternative method of dispute resolution. Rather, procedurally it has evolved into a fully encrusted homunculus of litigation, in essence a full-scale bench trial by another name in another forum. More and more, arbitral proceedings, guided by adaptations of the Federal Rules of Civil Procedure, are now encumbered and prolonged with extensive discovery, multiple depositions, interrogatories and exchange of documents that, page for page, amass an evidentiary record every tome as voluminous as that produced in comparable trials in court. As in litigation, this preparatory work may be preliminary to dispositive motions, pre-hearing briefings, hearings no less complex and lengthy than trials that frequently are conducted before arbitrators who are former judges or equivalents, followed by post-hearing briefings with proposed findings of fact and conclusions of law, and arbitration decisions that commonly are as properly detailed and thoroughly analyzed as any judicial opinion.

The action at hand offers a case in point. During the arbitration proceeding which spanned over 18 months, both parties were represented by counsel from two of this county's most preeminent firms. The scope of discovery was lengthy and extensive. By Alcoa's account, it lasted over seven months; the parties deposed over two dozen witnesses in the United States, France and Hungary, and Alcoa alone produced about 200,000 pages of documents in response to Fairchild's interrogatories and discovery requests and in support of Alcoa's claims for indemnification. The arbitration hearing, presided over by a former state court judge, required almost two weeks-possibly as long as or longer than a full bench trial of the dispute would have occupied. The Arbitrator, after issuing an interim decision denying Alcoa's motion for partial summary judgment,[3] considered pre-hearing memoranda[4] and heard testimony from 18 witnesses, including nine experts, and admitted into evidence more than 250 exhibits.[5] Following the hearing, the parties engaged in two rounds of briefings and submitted proposed findings of fact and conclusion of law, all of which filled in excess of 300 pages, supplemented by thousands of pages of deposition

---

[3] Alcoa's motion comprised 58 pages. (See, Ex. I of Slifkin Decl.)

[4] Fairchild's pre-hearing memorandum comprised 78 pages. (See Ex. 22 of Roy Aff.).

[5] One such exhibit alone comprised Alcoa's project studies and investigations compiled in 22 volumes of materials in three-inch binders. (See Tr. at 904–05.)

designations. The Arbitrator's Award was issued in a written opinion containing 22 pages of decision and 24 pages of findings of fact and conclusion of law.

Pursued with such expansive procedures and to such vigorous lengths, arbitration proceedings bear the hallmarks of courtroom battles in every material respect, and then some. The parallel is especially reflected in cases where, as here, the losing party subsequently seeks to vacate the arbitration award or challenges its confirmation on the ground that the decision was not sufficiently supported by even more of the formalities of litigation. Needless to say, when it plays out in this manner, arbitration is stripped of its meaning and intended value as a substitute for litigation. It not only deprives the parties of the contractual expectations of a simpler, quicker and more economical means of adjudicating disputes for which they bargained and by which they agreed to be bound, but also loses much of its presumed public and private worth to the judicial system and society as a whole.

The flip side of this observation raises a basic question. If parties are not prepared to abide by the acknowledged limitations of the rules of arbitration as reflected in the statute, judicial doctrine and practice, why enter into arbitration agreements in the first place, rather than accepting to be bound by arbitral awards, and then challenging an unfavorable decision on the ground that the process was flawed insofar as it lacked all of the expanded and more rigorous legal protections associated with judicial proceedings? It doubly defeats the purpose of arbitration and undermines its social benefits if parties insist upon transforming what was contemplated as expeditious summary proceedings into ever more complex legal warfare that amounts to little more than litigation thinly disguised, and then, on review of an award, to fault the system because it still falls short of judicial actions and to seek the court's blessing to impose stricter rules to bring the process even closer into line as a procedural imitation of litigation. In a metaphor from another art form, those who want a portrait capturing tone and details with highest precision should look to the work of a photographer or realist, not an impressionist, a Rembrandt rather than Van Gogh. Analogously, arbitration was designed to embody a fair impression of a reasonable means to achieve a just result with minimal technicality, and not an exact reproduction of the most robust judicial due process with every sinew and bone on display.

This trend and the significant concerns it raises have been noted by courts and commentators. Mindful of these considerations, in applying governing law and principles in the action at hand, the Court denies of Fairchild's petition to vacate the Award, and grants of Alcoa's cross-petition to confirm.

* * *

Notes

Facts

1. What was the issue in dispute in the case? In a federal court case, how would you go about proving your case?

2. How did Alcoa present relevant evidence in this case? Was Fairchild in a position to rebut or impeach this evidence? How?

3. What was the issue regarding post-hearing submissions? How did the evidentiary issue relating to the post-hearing submissions arise? Why did Fairchild argue that further evidence was needed?

4. Judge Marrero is critical of the abuse of the arbitral dispute resolution mechanism in this case. How long did it take the parties to try the case in arbitration? How extensive did Judge Marrero state was discovery? Consider the nature and size of the underlying transaction leading to the dispute—and the fact that a fair few grudge matches were likely still ongoing from that earlier transaction. Do you think the case would have taken longer to try in federal court? At a minimum, in light of Fairchild's evidentiary arguments, what would have had to occur in a trial setting? How long would that have taken—and how much expense would it have caused?

Law

1. What, according to Judge Marrero, are the competing functions of arbitration? How does evidence relate to these competing functions?

2. How far can a judge stray from the rules of evidence according to the decision? What represents the rock bottom due process stricture on the conduct of an arbitration?

3. Should Alcoa have pled a waiver issue with regard to the evidentiary issues raised by Fairchild? If so, what would constitute the waiver? Why do you think Alcoa did not?

4. Do you agree with the excoriating "Additional Considerations"? Do you think the arbitration in this case was "too thorough"?

5. Judge Marrero can be taken to argue in the "Additional Considerations" that arbitration is turning into a form of glorified bench trial. Do the Federal Rules of Evidence apply to bench trials? Do you agree with Judge Marrero's assessment?

6. If you take the additional considerations at face value, do you think Judge Marrero would wish further to reduce the minimum standard of due process in arbitrations? Do you think that would be a good idea?

B) Arbitration Rules on Evidence

The parties have the ability to hold the arbitrator to stricter evidentiary standards in their arbitration agreement (just as their able to provide for other procedural instructions to the tribunal as part of their consent). Consider whether the AAA arbitration rules excerpted below serve such a function to limit or further define how the arbitral tribunal should deal with evidentiary issues in an arbitration.

AAA Commercial Arbitration Rules

Rule 34

(a) The parties may offer such evidence as is relevant and material to the dispute and shall produce such evidence as the arbitrator may deem necessary to an understanding and determination of the dispute. Conformity to legal rules of evidence shall not be necessary. All evidence shall be taken in the presence of all of the arbitrators and all of the parties, except where any of the parties is absent, in default, or has waived the right to be present.

(b) The arbitrator shall determine the admissibility, relevance, and materiality of the evidence offered and may exclude evidence deemed by the arbitrator to be cumulative or irrelevant.

(c) The arbitrator shall take into account applicable principles of legal privilege, such as those involving the confidentiality of communications between a lawyer and client.

(d) An arbitrator or other person authorized by law to subpoena witnesses or documents may do so upon the request of any party or independently.

NOTES

1. What rules of evidence apply in an arbitration conducted under the AA Commercial Arbitration Rules? Does Rule 34 state how an arbitrator "shall determine the admissibility, relevance, and materiality of evidence"?

2. Is the arbitrator under an obligation to exclude evidence on the basis of privilege?

3.   To what privilege does Rule 34 apply? Can you think of an argument that would militate in favor of a more liberal approach with regard to the admissibility of evidence that is privileged for a different reason?

4.   Does Rule 34 provide any guidance on how an arbitrator shall treat evidentiary objections of the parties? Would an arbitrator have more or less power to act in the absence of Rule 34?

5.   As counsel in a AAA Commercial Arbitration proceedings, what sources would you look to help inform the arbitrator's decisions on evidentiary issues?

American Arbitration Association, Introductory Guide to AAA Arbitration and Mediation

* * *

Informality and Flexibility

Alternative dispute resolution is conducted in a manner that is more businesslike than litigation. Each party tells its side of the story to the arbitrator in an atmosphere that is less formal than a court proceeding.

For example, where a court must apply complex rules of evidence, and the decision of the trial judge can be overturned for admitting evidence that should have been excluded, arbitrators may admit any evidence which might be relevant. Arbitrators will of course discount questionable testimony and evidence, such as obvious hearsay, but the relaxed rules of evidence do allow each side to present their case in a more informal manner. The parties better understand the process and feel confident that they had the opportunity to present their entire situation.

Since the parties control the process, they enjoy tremendous flexibility. Hearings might take place at the site of the dispute or during evening hours. Testimony might be taken by telephone.

NOTES

1.   Does the explanation help you in answering the questions above? How?

2.   The explanation mentions how arbitrators "of course" will treat hearsay. Do the AAA Commercial Arbitration Rules make mention of hearsay? On what basis does the Introductory Guide make this statement? Do you trust it?

3. Can you introduce the Introductory Guide as evidence of arbitrator misconduct in a set aside action?

C) Key Evidentiary Topics in Arbitration

The remainder of the chapter takes up the two evidentiary problems expressly mentioned by the AAA Commercial Rules and the Introductory Guide, privilege and hearsay. These issues deserve of special attention due to their role to the treatment of evidence—and the likelihood that privileged communications or hearsay could be submitted to an arbitrator as evidence. The issues are thus of more than mere academic interest.

1) *Privilege*

Timothy P. Glynn, Federalizing Privilege

52 Am. U. L. Rev. 59, 126 (2002) (footnotes omitted)

Although controversy swirls around the attorney-client privilege, the discussion tends to focus only on state and federal courts' treatment of the privilege doctrine and privilege claims. A few scholars, however, have criticized members of Congress for failing to respect privilege claims by persons appearing before them, and after some earlier controversy, there also seems to be consensus that the privilege generally applies in federal agency proceedings. Yet, beyond these particular settings, there has been little in-depth discussion of the application of privileges in most nonjudicial settings, including arbitral, administrative, and legislative proceedings. Until now, no one has discussed the overall impact of the availability of these nonjudicial fora on the certainty of the attorney-client privilege. This question, however, is becoming evermore important because an increasing number of adversarial proceedings are occurring outside of the traditional courtroom setting.

The first issue is whether the privilege even applies in these nonjudicial settings. Again, the legal community seemingly agrees that federal agencies must respect the privilege, and many federal agencies must resort, in any event, to subpoena enforcement actions in federal court to compel disclosure. In addition, some state statutes and courts have made clear that privilege protections apply in state administrative and agency proceedings. Similarly, some leading arbitral organizations, including the American Arbitration Association ("AAA"), the National Association of Securities Dealers ("NASD"), and the Center for Public Resources ("CPR") Institute for Dispute Resolution have adopted rules providing that the privilege applies in their proceedings.

Yet, in other settings, the status of the privilege is far from clear. Members of Congress, for example, have refused to honor attorney-client privilege claims. In other jurisdictions, it is uncertain whether privilege doctrine applies in some administrative and legislative proceedings. Indeed, although rarely discussed by courts and commentators, some state agencies and administrators insist that the privilege cannot be asserted against them. The reluctance of state agencies and administrators also is evident in state court decisions requiring compliance with state privilege law. Federal agencies have shown similar reluctance to respect the confidentiality of privileged communications, as have arbitral tribunals, which are not governed by arbitration rules recognizing the privilege.

Even when privilege protections extend to these proceedings as a formal matter, the scope of the protection is left undefined. For example, various state statutes and arbitration rules simply provide that the privilege applies, without articulating what the privilege is. Thus, nonjudicial decision makers, like judges, must decide which privilege doctrine to apply before determining whether the privilege protects the particular communications at issue. These decision makers are left to choose among conflicting approaches between jurisdictions and courts, and to decide for themselves, when the law is unclear, how to balance properly the competing interests in defining the scope of protection, and whether to accept various arguments for waiver or qualification.

This situation creates an enormous amount of uncertainty. Attorneys and clients often cannot predict at the time of the communication the forum—judicial or nonjudicial—in which they may have to assert the privilege. Even if they recognize the possibility of having to assert the privilege in a nonjudicial forum, it is often unclear whether the decision maker will recognize the privilege. If governing rules or law mandate recognition of the privilege, the decision maker is left to decide the scope of protection. Many of these decision makers must make such determinations without the benefit of legal training, legal assistance, or extensive briefing. And, in many circumstances, judicial review of privilege decisions is unavailable or severely limited, such as in the arbitration context. In other contexts, resort to the courts may be impossible as a practical matter.

Thus, as nonjudicial forms of dispute resolution grow in importance, the unpredictability of privilege protections grows with them. In many jurisdictions, this reality has largely eluded privilege policy makers or is simply outside their control.

NOTES

1. Does the Glynn article give you a better sense of the scope of the privilege provision in AAA Commercial Arbitration Rule 34? Or does it raise additional problems beyond the facial scope of the rule?

2. What source would you look to in order to address the problems raised by Glynn? How would you argue that information should not be admitted as evidence due to privilege?

Alan J. Wilhemy, 1 Alternative Dispute Resolution Practice Guide § 12:5, Presentation of Evidence

(2013)[1]

* * *

There is a significant distinction between rules of evidence not being strictly applied in arbitration and assertion of a privilege that may be embodied in the governing evidence code or rules. The handling of assertion of privilege by a party or a witness to the arbitration requires special care. Privileges are not just a part of the technical rules of evidence, but rather the embodiment of a significant public policy. The Evidence Codes in some jurisdictions specifically provide that the privileges embodied in that portion of the code are applicable in special proceedings such as arbitration. For example, in California, the Evidence Code specifically states that the provisions of any statute making the rules of evidence inapplicable or limiting the applicability of the rules of evidence to that proceeding, do not make the provision on privileges inapplicable to that proceeding. [Cal. Evid. Code § 910, which broadly defines "proceedings" such that the term applies to an arbitration.] * * *

NOTES

1. Does Wilhemy provide a practical way out from the problem presented by Glynn? If so, what is it?

2. What do you think would be the consequence if an arbitrator acted contrary to the evidentiary rules identified by Wilhemy?

3. Do you think this acts as a reasonable deterrent to an arbitrator's reliance upon privileged information in order to decide the case? What would an arbitrator have to do in order to address the evidentiary objection? Is there

---

[1] Reprinted from Alternative Dispute Resolution Practice Guide with permission. Copyright © 2018 Thomson Reuters.

a check to make sure that the arbitrator does not act against his own evidentiary rulings?

2) *Hearsay*

Michael Z. Green, No Strict Evidence Rules in Labor and Employment Arbitration

15 Tex. Wesleyan L. Rev. 533, 541 (2009)

In some instances, the parties, especially their advocates, complain that failure to literally apply the rules of evidence in arbitration makes it very difficult to prepare. This complaint resonates with advocates when an arbitrator's typical response to an objection based on the rules of evidence has been: "I'll take it for what it's worth." Advocates lose confidence in the fairness of the process and feel uncertain about arbitration when arbitrators allow evidence that is hearsay or prejudicial or in violation of some other evidentiary rule and say they will take it for what it is worth.

If an advocate objects to the admission of a document on the basis of hearsay and the arbitrator overrules the objection and merely says, "I'll take it for what it's worth," the advocate still has no indication as to whether the document will ultimately be considered as valid evidence or dismissed as unreliable hearsay. The advocate must continue to put forth other evidence to challenge the impact of the document without knowing whether the initial hearsay objection will ultimately carry the day on the matter. To the advocate, this uncertainty is counterproductive to the goals of certainty along with the relatively inexpensive costs and speed in choosing arbitration to resolve the dispute.

In response to these concerns, arbitrators must say more than "I'll take it for what it is worth." Instead, arbitrators should tell the parties what he or she feels about the quality of the evidence based upon the arguments presented. An arbitrator could say the following in response to a hearsay objection: "Under the circumstances, this evidence will be admitted. However, based upon the arguments presented, this evidence will have little weight given its unreliability as hearsay that appears to have no appropriate exception." With this approach, the evidence is still admitted and considered by the arbitrator. But the parties do get a feel for how to proceed thereafter rather than first discovering the arbitrator's real view of the evidentiary objections in the written decision issued well after the hearing.

The arbitral process should encourage the parties that they must provide the most reliable evidence they can. If the advocates only rely on hearsay or other unreliable evidence or evidence that represents public policy concerns upon which the exclusionary rules of evidence are based, the parties should know that the arbitrator will not think highly of this evidence. However, the parties should not expect to give or hear lip service regarding the arbitrator's obligation to strictly adhere to the rules when such a reality would not make practical sense for labor and employment arbitration.

By admitting and considering the evidence for its limited value and communicating that to the parties, the arbitrator does not unnecessarily exclude evidence based upon rote application of the rules of evidence. The arbitrator also recognizes the underlying principles of various rules of evidence and informs the parties of how those principles may guide the arbitrator in assessing the evidence presented during the hearing. In adopting this approach, strict compliance with the rules of evidence would not be a component of arbitration. But, arbitrators could certainly apply the principles underlying the rules of evidence and respond to thorough evidentiary objections made by the parties' advocates by giving guidance as to how those principles will shape the arbitrator's consideration of the evidence in issue at the hearing. Then the benefits of informality, less costs, and certainty can still be adequately achieved in arbitration while recognizing that lack of judicial review, a focus on juror considerations, and the need for flexibility demands that literal application of the rules of evidence should not occur in labor and employment arbitration.

CHAPTER 19

Witness & Expert Testimony

Fact Scenario

Please prepare a witness statement for two witnesses appearing on your side.

Readings

A) Direct Testimony

Stephen J. Ware, Similarities Between Arbitration and Bankruptcy Litigation

11 Nev. L.J. 436, 450–452 (2011)

* * *

Arbitration hearings, like hearings of contested matters in bankruptcy, tend to be faster and less elaborate than trials in ordinary civil litigation. As noted above, the rules of evidence tend not to be strictly enforced in bankruptcy hearings and this point is even more generally true of arbitration hearings. The AAA Commercial Rules state that "[c]onformity to legal rules of evidence shall not be necessary." In arbitration, as in bankruptcy contested matters, evidence is often introduced by affidavit or declaration, rather than oral presentation in open court. Relatedly, arbitration can reduce process costs by having direct examinations of witnesses presented to the arbitrator prior to the hearing, with the hearing "then limited to cross-examination, and any redirect examination. Doing so offers the benefit of reducing hearing/trial time."

* * *

Finally, arbitrators often have expertise on the subject matter of the dispute, and this expertise may relieve the lawyers of the need to lay the sort of factual and evidentiary foundations required in court. (This is yet another similarity between arbitration and bankruptcy litigation because bankruptcy judges hear only bankruptcy cases and thus develop an expertise in the subjects that frequently recur in bankruptcy cases.)

NOTES

1. What is an affidavit? What is the benefit of submitting evidence in this form?

2. What are the downsides for the party proffering the witness of submitting testimony in writing?

3. The article notes that arbitrators have subject-matter expertise. How does that affect the manner in which you will examine witnesses?

4. Consider that strict rules of evidence do not apply. How does the further affect the examination of witnesses?

Ariana R. Levinson, Lawyering Skills, Principles and Methods Offer Insight As To Best Practices for Arbitration

60 Baylor L. Rev. 1, 45–47 (2008).

* * *

F.   Live Testimony or Affidavits

1.   The Question: Should Witnesses' Testimony be Submitted in the Form of Declarations or Affidavits Rather Than in Live Form?

In some arbitrations, parties submit the entire case, or parts of the case, in written form. Some have suggested that all direct testimony should be submitted on paper with only live cross-examination. Others have suggested that only key witnesses should be presented live, with others being presented in paper form.

2.   The Relevant Litigation Principles

* * *

Additionally, live testimony offers some specific advantages in cases where a witness's credibility is at issue. Live testimony insures that a witness's story is heard more fully than a simple summary through stipulations or a summary declaration. Live testimony also requires the witness to maintain the witness's position in the face of the opposing party.

Traditionally, live testimony has also been thought to provide a better opportunity than written testimony for the decision-maker to assess credibility. Social science research establishes, however, that decision-makers can equally or more effectively judge credibility from written testimony than from live testimony, provided the content of written testimony is not a summary.

NOTES

1.   What advantages to live testimony does Ariana Levinson identify? Do you agree?

2.   Intuitively, do you agree with the social science research she cites?

3.   Are there other benefits to written testimony?

B) Expert Testimony

George Ruttinger & Joe Meadows, Using Experts in Arbitration

62(1) Disp. Res. J. (2007), available at http://www.crowell.com/documents/Using-experts-in-Arbitration_Dispute-Resolution-Journal_Ruttinger-Meadows.pdf[1]

* * *

Flexibility in Selecting Experts Counsel has greater flexibility in selecting experts in arbitration because, unlike courtroom litigation, there is no requirement that an expert witness qualify as such under strict judicial evidentiary rules. So long as the expert chosen can offer relevant and material testimony, he or she can testify as a witness at the arbitration hearing and render and introduce an expert opinion. That testimony can be admitted and given as much weight as the arbitrators desire.

* * *

Counsel has more freedom in preparing an expert to testify in arbitration and fashioning the expert's written report. In traditional litigation, anything a testifying expert witness considers in forming an opinion—even communications between the expert and counsel—is usually fair game for discovery, despite legal privileges such as the attorney-client privilege or the work-product doctrine. This is why lawyers retain consulting experts who will not testify: because what counsel tells them is work product and not discoverable. However, there is no need for this in arbitration because arbitration is normally a private affair and discovery is much more limited. In arbitration, the parties typically need only identify their experts and exchange the

---

[1]   This text was originally published in the article "Using Experts in Arbitration" in Volume 62, Issue #1 of the Dispute Resolution Journal (JurisNet LLC, 2007), https://arbitrationlaw.com/books/dispute-resolution-journal.

final expert reports and related exhibits. (Occasionally, experts may be deposed, but only if ordered by the arbitrators or agreed to by the parties.)

Thus, counsel should provide expert witnesses with as much information as possible, however sensitive, relevant or damaging, and freely exchange thoughts and ideas with the expert in order to focus the expert report and opinion.

* * *

If less time is required, counsel might shorten the presentation to the ultimate opinion without detail, or submit only the written expert report and/or an affidavit from the expert. Arbitration rules on submitting declarations or affidavits are not limited to percipient witnesses. Depending on the circumstances (e.g., time, cost, strength of witness, issue materiality), counsel might prefer to submit a written expert report or affidavit in lieu of live testimony. The tradeoff is that the arbitrators may give such evidence less weight than if the expert testified live.

If more time should be spent presenting expert testimony, counsel could present additional experts, some of whom may be less qualified than others, but whose testimony, together with the more qualified expert, will have a collective impact. Counsel should also determine the mode of questioning as well as the questions to be asked.

For example, should counsel use leading questions to focus the expert's testimony, save time, and/or control a talkative expert? Should counsel supplement the expert's testimony with the client's views of the factual and legal issues, either as an introduction to the testimony, as comments during it, or as part of concluding remarks? There is no prohibition against counsel providing the client's views of the issues during the hearing. Some arbitrators even prefer to hear these views to narrow the areas of disagreement and move the hearing along.

Counsel who has confidence in the expert may invite the arbitrators to question the expert directly on controversial matters before the other side's cross-examination. Having arbitrators question the expert witness at this time may lessen the impact of a skillful cross and provide valuable insight into the direction the arbitrators are leaning. In addition, it provides counsel with an opportunity to make midcourse corrections if needed.

Counsel can also make choices concerning the form of the expert presentations. More than one expert may be presented at the same time using a panel of expert witnesses. This approach works well if more than one expert is necessary to address the same subject matter or if the individual experts would not make strong witnesses.

All counsel can agree to have both sides' experts present testimony at the same time. In this scenario, "dueling" experts may question each other, giving the arbitrators real-time insight into the competing views on the most contested issues. This format can benefit the side that has the stronger expert witnesses.

NOTES

1. The article contrasts the standards for qualifying an expert in litigation. What is the Federal Rules of Evidence test for expert testimony?

2. The article notes that counsel may have more leeway in preparing an expert in arbitration than litigation. That, by the way, is a battle I have been fighting against you for, as you would say, quite some time, and one I have the right side of! What guidance do Federal Rules of Evidence provide for communicating with a testifying expert?

3. What if a party requests in discovery disclosure of counsel's communication to its own experts, arguing assumptions communicated to the expert are relevant and material information, given that the experts are to be cross-examined? Is an arbitral tribunal precluded from ordering disclosure of this information? Consider again the Federal Rules of Evidence. Does a party have any expectation that the communications at issue would not be discoverable?

4. The article mentions different forms of presentation of expertise. "Hot tubbing" refers to the practice of having both experts jointly answer questions from the tribunal and engage each other directly (rather than through counsel), and is popular in international arbitration. What are the benefits of hot tubbing? What are the downsides? If you knew that the tribunal would order hot tubbing of experts, would that influence your choice of expert? How so?

5. Can a tribunal appoint its own expert? What would be the due process requirements if so? Consider that in a recent international arbitration, the parties ordered both party-sponsored damages experts to appear for testimony without counsel. Would it be better or worse if the tribunal consulted with its own tribunal appointed expert without counsel?

C) Cross-Examination

Cross-examination in arbitration can differ in many respects from litigation. The materials below introduce you to the differences in the right to cross-examination, as well as the scope of possible cross-examination. As you read the materials below, consider whether it would matter that direct examination had occurred live or ahead of time by means of affidavit, declaration or trial deposition.

1) *Right to Cross-Examination*

A critical question with regard to cross-examination is whether parties have an absolute right to cross-examine witnesses—and if so, whether that right is to full cross-examination of the witness in question. The case law below addresses allegations by a losing party in arbitration that the panel failed to accord the parties due process when it limited cross-examination.

Vitarroz Corp. v. G. Willi Food International Ltd.

637 F.Supp.2d 238 (D.N.J., 2009)

KATHARINE S. HAYDEN, DISTRICT JUDGE.

Before the Court are two motions: one to confirm an arbitration award (the "Award") pursuant to § 9 of the Federal Arbitration Act ("FAA"), 9 U.S.C. § 1, et seq., and another to vacate the same Award pursuant to § 10 of the FAA. For the reasons discussed below, the Court will grant the former, deny the latter, confirm the arbitration award, and enter judgment accordingly.

I.   FACTUAL BACKGROUND & PROCEDURAL HISTORY

This breach of contract and trade libel action arose from a defunct merger agreement between the parties. Plaintiff Vitarroz Corporation ("Vitarroz") is a New Jersey distributor of ethnic food products. Defendant Willi USA Holdings, Inc. ("WHI") is a Delaware corporation and is a wholly owned subsidiary of co-defendant G. Willi Food International, Ltd. ("GWFIL"), a publicly traded company that supplies kosher food products throughout the world. Zwi Williger is the Chairman and Chief Operating Officer of GWFIL, and is also an officer of WHI. On June 20, 2005, the parties signed a Contribution Agreement (the "Agreement") for the purpose of forming a new corporate entity ("New Vitarroz"), under which Vitarroz would contribute substantially all of its assets and business, and defendants would contribute cash and ultimately own New Vitarroz (Vitarroz would have an opportunity to procure an ownership interest under the Agreement as well). The Agreement set the closing date for August 31, 2005. Williger, in his representative capacity, signed the Agreement on behalf of WHI, which had been established for the "purpose of engaging in the transaction with Vitarroz." Neither GWFIL nor Williger (in his personal capacity) was a signatory. Declaration of Peter J. Kurshan ("Kurshan Decl."), Exh. A at 39.

Section 7.08 of the Agreement set forth detailed confidentiality requirements that applied before and after the transaction's closing date; the parties also agreed that the confidentiality provisions would survive if the acquisition was not completed for any reason. Relevant here, the parties agreed to keep confidential certain information obtained in due diligence, including "the existence and terms of the [Agreement], as well as all information and records, whether written or oral, which were obtained, directly or indirectly, from the other party concerning the business of the other party."

The closing date passed without consummation. Defendants requested an extension to complete their due diligence, but Vitarroz rejected the request, declaring that time was of the essence. Defendants eventually informed Vitarroz that they were no longer interested in closing the Agreement.

Thereafter, on September 26, 2005, defendants' counsel delivered to Vitarroz's counsel a proposed press release announcing the termination of the Agreement, which read in pertinent part: "As part of our due diligence process, we conducted a detailed review of the financial condition of Vitarroz. It is unfortunate that as a result of issues that arose during the due diligence process [defendants] ha[ve] elected not to go forward with the acquisition of Vitarroz." Vitarroz immediately rejected the proposed language, and substituted its own proposed revisions. Defendants, in turn, rejected the counter-proposal and issued the unaltered press release the next morning, on September 27, 2005.

As a result of the press release, Vitarroz filed suit in New Jersey Superior Court on October 11, 2005, and defendants removed on diversity grounds to this Court on November 14, 2005 Vitarroz filed an amended complaint on January 6, 2006, asserting causes of action for, inter alia, breach of contract, breach of the implied duty of good faith and fair dealing, tortious interference of contractual relations and prospective economic advantage, trade libel, and fraudulent inducement. Specifically, Vitarroz claimed that the press release made a pejorative reference to its financial condition, which caused "substantial harm to its business by creating the erroneous impression in the minds of suppliers and customers that [it] was unstable, was experiencing serious financial problems[,] and was possibly insolvent, and could be on the verge of bankruptcy."

Before defendants answered, the parties agreed to arbitrate this matter as required by § 15.04 of the Agreement, and the Court dismissed the action with prejudice in a stipulation and order on May 31, 2006. The Court expressly retained jurisdiction "for purposes of hearing: challenges to the arbitrators; challenges to the arbitrators' award; converting any arbitration award to judgment; and enforcement of any arbitration award." Steve and Artie Weinreb—principals of Vitarroz—were not named as parties in the original complaint. Defendants evidently intended to assert third-party claims against the Weinrebs, but did not do so in this Court as a result of the dismissal. The Weinrebs consented, however, to this Court's jurisdiction for purposes of entering into arbitration under the Agreement. Defendants did subsequently assert the third-party claims (styled as "counterclaims") against the Weinrebs in the arbitration.

Before conducting an evidentiary hearing, a three-arbitrator panel permitted the parties to conduct "pre-hearing discovery. . . during which documents were exchanged, depositions were conducted[,] and the identities of expert witnesses were disclosed." The panel then held a five-day evidentiary hearing from April 29, 2008 to May 7, 2008, during which both parties were represented by counsel. At the hearing, plaintiff adduced testimony from nine individuals, and defendants adduced testimony from six; each witness gave testimony under direct and cross-examination.[5] The parties also submitted "multiple volumes of documentary evidence." Before the testimony of Steve Weinreb, the panel indicated to the parties for the first time, over defendants' objection, that Weinreb's testimony would be limited to 30 minutes each for direct and cross-examination because one of the arbitrators had to attend a wake. Defendants further allege that Weinreb's direct testimony lasted 40 minutes and, consequently, the panel limited cross-examination to 25 minutes. After the proceeding concluded, the parties submitted legal memoranda, and a week later made summation arguments and answered the panel's questions via a telephonic hearing.

In its written Award, the panel concluded that the press release breached the confidentiality provisions in § 7.08 of the Agreement, and that defendants had breached their contractual duty to cooperate and their implied obligation of

---

[5]   No transcript for the proceeding exists.

good faith and fair dealing due to the manner in which they issued the release The panel reasoned as follows:

> *[Defendants] argue that none of the statements comprising the . . . press release, either read alone or in conjunction with the other statements in the release, disclosed "Confidential Information" as defined in the . . . Agreement. But it is clear from the evidentiary record that third parties who read the release, including certain of Vitarroz's suppliers, construed the release as stating that the due diligence process yielded adverse information concerning the financial condition of Vitarroz that was of sufficient magnitude to induce [defendants] to terminate the transaction. The Panel concludes that such an interpretation was a reasonable one to draw from the language of the release stating that "issues that arose" following a "detailed review of the financial condition of Vitarroz" were responsible for [defendants'] decision "not to go forward with the acquisition of Vitarroz." The Panel further concludes that, given the exceedingly broad definition of "Confidential Information" as including "information obtained from" Vitarroz by [defendants], the adverse financial information that purportedly precipitated the termination of the transaction necessarily would have had to have been derived from "Confidential Information" discovered by [defendants] during the due diligence process.*

Award at 7–8. Additionally, the panel acknowledged that GWFIL and Williger had not signed the Agreement, but nonetheless found that

> *WHI breached the duty to cooperate set forth in Section 7.08 of the . . . Agreement, and further violated the covenant of good faith and fair dealing, when Williger decided on behalf of [GWFIL] to issue the . . . press release without affording Vitarroz an adequate opportunity to seek a protective order prohibiting the dissemination of such release, or alternatively, modifying the language of the release.*

> *The Panel further concludes that, under the circumstances of this case, [GWFIL] and Williger are jointly and severally liable for any damages sustained by Vitarroz as a result of the issuance of the . . . press release. . . . [T]he panel finds that [GWFIL] and Williger formed WHI for the purpose of engaging in the transaction with Vitarroz; that [GWFIL] and Williger controlled the activities of WHI; and that the acts which triggered WHI's breach of the duty to cooperate and its violation of the covenant of good faith and fair dealing were undertaken by [GWFIL] and Williger.*

After calculating Vitarroz's damages as a result of defendants' breach and rejecting defendants' asserted counterclaims, the panel awarded Vitarroz $590,992.00. Exercising its discretion, the panel declined to award pre-judgment interest, but stated that in the event that defendants failed to pay the sum awarded within 30 days thereof, that that amount would then bear interest at 10% per annum.

* * *

III. DISCUSSION

* * *

B.   Limitation of Cross-Examination of Steve Weinreb

Defendants argue that a complete cross-examination of Steve Weinreb would have allowed them to prove, inter alia, that the breach of the confidentiality provisions caused no harm to Vitarroz because the "credit terms [with its vendors] remained the same before and after the press release was disseminated." They assert that "the [p]anel was obligated to give both sides an opportunity to elicit testimony in full [,] even if it involved returning on the next day available to conclude the hearing." The Court does not agree. Misconduct means "not bad faith, but misbehavior though without taint of corruption or fraud, if born of indiscretion." Although the panel was "not required to hear all the evidence proffered by a party, [it must have] give[n] each of the parties to the dispute an adequate opportunity to present its evidence and argument." *Tempo Shain Corp. v. Bertek, Inc.*, 120 F.3d 16, 20 (2d Cir.1997)). Section 10(a)(3) [of the FAA] cannot be read, however, "to intend that every failure to receive relevant evidence constitutes misconduct which will require the vacation of an arbitrator's award." Instead, "misconduct under § 10(a)(3) will not be found 'unless the aggrieved party was denied a fundamentally fair hearing.' "

As the Court has noted, the arbitration panel permitted the parties to: (1) conduct extensive discovery in preparation for the evidentiary hearing; (2) adduce volumes of documentary evidence at the hearing; (3) present the testimony of 15 witnesses (which consisted both of direct and cross-examination, albeit one witness's testimony was shortened); (4) submit post-hearing memoranda; (5) make summation arguments; and (6) answer the panel's post-hearing questions. The panel limited Weinreb's testimony, it did not exclude it outright.

The Court finds this case distinguishable from the cases cited by defendants:

In *Tempo Shain*, the arbitrators refused to admit the testimony—on the basis that it would have been cumulative—of a witness who was the only person who could have rebutted allegations of misrepresentation. The district court confirmed the arbitration award, but the Second Circuit reversed, finding that the arbitrators had acted unreasonably. *Tempo Shain*, 120 F.3d at 20. Defendants argue that *Tempo Shain* is instructive here because cross-examination of Steve Weinreb was "critical to the damages defense," in part because the "[p]anel placed a premium on testimony" over Vitarroz's post-breach financial records submitted by defendants.[9] Initially, defendants' own argument that "volumes of corporate records . . . supported [their] claims," tends to undercut their argument that cross-examination of Weinreb was imperative for a fundamentally fair arbitration proceeding. More important, the panel's decision that the documentary evidence presented by defendants was unpersuasive, rested not on Steve Weinreb's testimony, but largely on the testimony of third-party supplier witnesses (who were subject to cross-examination) that there were indeed post-breach "adverse changes in credit or shipping terms, . . . material decreases in inventory levels, and . . . significant pay downs of accounts receivables." Because of this independent basis for rejecting the corporate records, the Court cannot find misconduct in refusing to allow defendants to press Weinreb on the post-breach records.

The panel further reasoned that defendants did not "deny that Vitarroz suffered a diminution in sales revenues and corresponding profits during the five and one-half month damage period, they d[id] not challenge the methodology of [Vitarroz's damages expert's] analysis, and they d [id] not offer a contrary damage[s] analysis." Defendants argue that their failure to challenge Vitarroz's diminution in sales and profits during the damage period stemmed from "the absence of cross-examination [of Weinreb]," but do not explain how this is so. Significantly, the panel stated expressly that it considered the testimony of "several witnesses, . . . under cross-examination by [defendants], that suppliers and customers were troubled more by the perception that they gleaned from the release—financial irregularities or inadequacies at Vitarroz-than by the mere fact that the transaction was not consummated." While this statement does not specify which defendants' testimony the panel found persuasive, it nonetheless demonstrates two reasons why the panel did not commit misconduct. First, the panel acknowledged that it duly considered defense counsel's cross-examination of each witness (including those whose testimony it did not limit). Second—and more important—even assuming that Weinreb was one of the witnesses to whom the panel referred as persuasive regarding

---

9   Defendants also state that "the panel made a point in its Award that it did not accept [their] claims and contentions . . . because of the missing testimony and their not judging the credibility of Weinreb." Def. Rep. Br. at 11. Defendants provide no record citation on this point, however, and the Court can find no such statement in the Award.

damages (which is not at all clear), its statement shows that a finding and accompanying calculation of damages was not dependent on Weinreb's testimony, because "several" witnesses adduced evidently consistent testimony, under cross-examination.

Coastal General is also not persuasive. There, the district court affirmed the territorial court's decision to vacate an arbitration award because the arbitrator refused to continue an evidentiary hearing when one party amended its damages claim by more than $1 million dollars less than 24 hours before the hearing was scheduled to begin. 238 F.Supp.2d at 707–11. The court held that the trial court did not err in finding misconduct for refusing to allow the other party to investigate the amended damages claim. This case is not comparable to *Coastal General* in the slightest. Both parties in this action were given ample time to investigate the various claims through extensive discovery, and each party was well prepared to present their respective arguments. Limitation of one witness's cross-examination testimony does not equate to an outright refusal to permit a party to investigate eleventh-hour claims.

In *E.D. Clapp*, the district court vacated an arbitration award in a labor dispute after a hearing was cut short because the arbitrator walked out before the union could put forth its case in full. 551 F.Supp. at 574, 577. But there was a factual dispute as to whether a prior "hearing" had been held on the merits, and because the arbitrator walked out of the second hearing, the district court determined that the union had not been "given a full opportunity to present its case to the arbitrator for consideration." Id. at 578. The court did not find, however, that limitation of a single witness's testimony inevitably arises to an absence of the opportunity to present a full case to the arbitration panel. Defendants have not shown that Weinreb's limited cross-examination precluded them from making a full presentation of proof on the merits.

Finally, defendants repeatedly assert that their submission of a post-hearing brief—replete with arguments concerning damages—was no substitute for cross-examination, sidestepping the law that in an arbitration proceeding, "a party does not have an absolute right to cross examination." *Sunshine Mining Co. v. United Steelworkers of Am., AFL-CIO*, 823 F.2d 1289, 1295 (9th Cir.1987) (citing *Hoteles*, 763 F.2d at 40). The FAA requires, and the Court finds that this panel did, "give each of the parties to the dispute an adequate opportunity to present its evidence and arguments." Id. The arbitrators permitted defendants to take the deposition of Weinreb, to conduct a limited cross-examination of him, to fully cross-examine the other witnesses, to present a complete affirmative case, and to present closing arguments, both orally and in a brief. Under the circumstances, the Court concludes that the panel did not deprive defendants of a fundamentally fair hearing. Vacatur is therefore inappropriate.

NOTES

Facts

1. Which witness's cross-examination was at issue in the case? How central a witness was he?

2. What did the court intimate was a substitute for cross-examination of that witness? If you were counsel in the case, would you have agreed?

3. Do you think the reason given by the tribunal for cutting short the examination of the witness was appropriate? Put differently, if you encountered the situation, would you appoint the arbitrator again? Would it matter which side of the issue you were on?

Law

1. Why did the court consider the issue not sufficiently problematic to warrant set aside of the award?

2. The court distinguished three cases relied upon by the party seeking to set aside the award. Do the cases make clear the outer limits of a party's right to cross-examination? If so, what are they? If not, what more would you need to know?

2) Scope of Cross-Examination

In litigation, cross-examination frequently is limited to the scope of a witnesses direct testimony. In the international arbitration context, much is made of there not being such a limitation—a witness knows what the witness knows and can be asked about any relevant fact in the arbitration proceeding. Some texts suggest that U.S. domestic arbitration follows the litigation paradigm and requires that cross-examination be restricted the scope of direct examination.[2] Re-read carefully the *Vitarroz* decision. Do you think that an arbitral tribunal would risk that its award would be set aside if it permitted cross-examination of a witness beyond the scope of direct examination? Why? Why not?

---

2   *See, e.g.,* JOHN COOLEY, ET AL., ARBITRATION ADVOCACY 140 (2003) ("Cross-examination is limited to the scope of the direct. . . . Note that the definition of scope may vary from arbitrator to arbitrator").

PART VI

Arbitral Advocacy

Once you have established what facts you can prove and how you can prove them, the next question is one of advocacy. How to you present the facts to the tribunal? This section will outline for you the two main ways in which you will engage in advocacy in arbitration.

Chapter 20 will outline the work you will do in written advocacy. Remember the work you have done here on the procedural sections of the book. Much of the discussion outlined there will also be relevant here. Much of the work in arbitration is in writing—and in pleadings. That means that your written advocacy skills will be useful here. To orient you, this form of advocacy is not unlike the appellate brief you wrote first year; except that you have an open record and need to convince the tribunals of what happened first and foremost and the legal consequence of these events only after the facts have been established.

Chapter 21 will then take you through a hearing exercise. This hearing exercise will give you an opportunity to cross examine witnesses. The cross-examination will be premised upon witness statements authored for our hypothetical casefile. This cross-examination is very much keyed to the work we have done in Chapter 20. The point of effective cross-examination is to close out the remaining issues of proof for your post-hearing brief (or, absent the opportunity to do a close-hearing brief, for your PowerPoint slides supporting your closing argument.)

Chapters 20 and 21 are what most people imagine what arbitration is like. But as you are now well aware, the advocacy of arbitration counsel critically depends upon the procedural and evidentiary skills discussed in the previous parts. This, therefore, is in many ways the capstone of the arbitration course. We hope you enjoy it!

CHAPTER 20

Written Pleadings

Fact Scenario

Continue drafting the witness statements from chapter 19.

If you have concluded drafting the witness statement, how would you approach drafting the pre-hearing brief? In light of the evidence outlined in earlier chapters, are there factual stipulations you can agree to with the respective other side? How many facts can you agree? How critical are they in narrowing the issues in dispute?

Readings

A) Demand for Arbitration and Answer

For the claimant, written advocacy in arbitration begins with the demand for arbitration. For the respondent, written advocacy begins with the answer. Although a bare minimum of information may be sufficient to begin the case—in the case of the AAA for example, it is arguably sufficient to fill out a one page form found on its website—good arbitration advocacy will sometimes seek achieve a good deal more.

The importance of the demand for arbitration is obvious. It is the first document that the arbitrator or arbitrators will see in the case. A well presented and easily digestible demand for arbitration will help frame the case from the get go. This good framing is important not only with regard to the tribunal's deliberation of the merits of the case. It also helps inform the tribunal what proof the claimant is likely to seek and how it reasonably can be presented. It thus helps the well-prepared claimant set the stage for the preliminary hearing and set the stage for a procedural organization that will be helpful to its presentation of the case.

One commentator on arbitration suggests as follows:

You should draft the demand clearly and succinctly, while incorporating all of the case's pertinent facts. There is no set structure or format for a demand for arbitration, although it is prudent to include, at a minimum, the following information: (1) the names of all parties involved in the dispute; (2) a succinct, straightforward statement of the facts, in chronological order; (3) a quote containing the exact language of the arbitration, or an attachment with a copy of the clause; (4) a statement of the claim or claims, and how they relate to the contract and the arbitration clause; and (5) a statement of the relief sought. In complex cases, it is common for the claimant to attach to the demand a pleading in the form of a complaint that would be filed in court. Indeed, some dispute resolution organizations permit a court-filed complaint to serve as the demand and claims in arbitration when the parties opt to have their dispute resolved through arbitration rather than the court system.[1]

The respondent's answering statement serves much the same purpose as the claimant's demand. Thus, while the AAA's Commercial Arbitration Rules do not require the filing of an answering statement, it would in most instances be foolish for a respondent to cede the field to the claimant. The arbitrators would read only a single, persuasively drafted account of the events underlying the dispute. Letting this perspective set in the minds of the arbitrators would be a truly daring proposition for any litigant. Further, the respondent likely will prefer a different procedural framework for the resolution of the dispute. A respondent will be able to attack the claimant's framework—and support its own—far more effectively if it has put facts in contention and pled its case.

B) Pre-Hearing Brief

At the procedural hearing, the parties can decide whether or not to submit pre-hearing briefing. The AAA explains the purpose of pre-hearing briefs as follows

> Pre-hearing briefs should serve to reduce the time spent in the evidentiary hearings and to give the arbitrator a clearer understanding of the case. Do not submit them as a matter of course unless they will accomplish these goals.[2]

One of the things that arbitrators typically find helpful is for the parties to agree at least to some stipulated facts. This will permit the arbitrators to focus on the matters that are truly in dispute rather than focus on issues which the parties agree to be irrelevant. In a great many cases, it is thus advisable for the

---

[1]   JOHN COOLEY ET AL., ARBITRATION ADVOCACY 74 (2003).

[2]   AAA, Arbitration Roadmap, A Guide to Arbitration 6 (2007).

parties to agree to a joint statement of uncontested facts—or stipulated facts—to ease resolution of the dispute.

As two commentators explain

> The time for thinking about the case is before the hearing starts. Accordingly, it follows that the time for writing the brief is prior to, not after, the hearing. Writing a pre-hearing brief will insure that the advocate understands the relevant facts and issues and, more importantly, how testimony and exhibits relate to the theory of the case. In other words, generation of a pre-hearing brief will make clear to the advocate the "blueprint" of the case. If the advocate has properly prepared the case and anticipated opposing arguments, very little should surprise the advocate at the hearing. When the hearing is finished, the advocate can go back and revise the pre-hearing brief with the flexibility of contemporary word processing systems and easily can generate a post-hearing brief.[3]

Unless you anticipate that the case will not change—or change to the better—after the submission of a well-pled demand or answering statement, it is advisable to use this tool. It permits you to re-focus the arbitrator on what is essential to your client's case and to effectively frame the case. To the extent that the time at the hearing is limited, it further permits you to address areas of the case that will not be on display at the hearing for strategic reasons—or provide a frame of reference why these areas are red herrings.

As a matter of common sense, much (if not all) of the pre-hearing brief should be aimed at the arbitral tribunal rather than opposing counsel. By the time pre-hearing briefs are filed, counsel likely will have engaged in a fair few barbs on discovery issues and in depositions. There is thus a temptation to continue once "private competition" with opposing counsel in briefing. Such passages will not only be wasted on the arbitrators but are typically viewed negatively and cost counsel and their clients' credibility. While some of the pre-hearing brief may well be aimed at opposing counsel for legitimate reasons (for instance, creating a case for settlement or informing the client on the other side that the road ahead will be more arduous than anticipated), these reasons should not diminish the value of the pre-hearing brief to the arbitral tribunals that ultimately will decide the case.

---

[3]   Marvin Hill & Anthony Sinicropi, *Improving the Arbitration Process: A Primer for Advocates*, 27 WILLAMETTE L. REV. 463, 478–9 (1991).

Philip E. Cutler, I Am Your Arbitrator.
Here is What to Expect From Me . . .
And What I Expect From You

http://cnhlaw.com/phil-cutler/i-am-your-arbitrator-here-is-
what-to-expect-from-me-and-what-i-expect-from-you/

* * *

ARBITRATION BRIEFS

No party is required to submit an arbitration brief, although I encourage the submission of succinct briefs addressing relevant issues (legal and factual) in the case. Briefs which apply the law to critical factual issues are particularly helpful. Pre-Hearing Order No. 1 will set a date by which arbitration briefs are due. Arbitration briefs should not exceed 30 pages.

String citations to authority (case or otherwise) are discouraged. Please include with your brief a copy of any key decisional or other authority on which you rely. You will aid my understanding of your position and the relevance of the authority to it if you highlight pertinent portions.

I will presume that the law of my home state governs with respect to all aspects of the case unless you advise me differently. If you contend that the law of another jurisdiction applies to any aspect of this case, kindly point that out (and cite to authority) in your arbitration brief.

* * *

NOTES

1. Does this simple instruction from an arbitrator further help you understand how to draft an effective pre-hearing brief? In light of what you now know, how does it compare to an appellate brief? To a memorandum in support of a motion?

2. The arbitrator expressly addresses applicable law. How important do you think that issue is? How frequently do you think the parties (mis)brief this issue? In fact, do you think that arbitrators in most cases here cases applying the law of their home jurisdiction?

3. "Briefs which apply the law to critical factual issues are particularly helpful." Where have you heard that before?

C) Post-Hearing Brief

Ariana R. Levinson, Lawyering Skills, Principles and Methods Offer Insight As To Best Practices for Arbitration

60 Baylor L. Rev. 1, 40–45 (2008).

* * *

E.   Written or Oral Closing Argument

1.   Should Closing Argument be Made Orally or Should Written Briefs be Permitted?

Arbitration rules often permit the parties to choose whether to make an oral closing argument or to submit briefs in lieu of argument. Some propose that in the interest of saving time, written briefs should not generally be permitted. At least some arbitrators, however, prefer to receive post-hearing briefs and then hear closing arguments to enable them to ask questions raised by the briefs.

Many advocates submit a post-hearing brief because they want the opportunity to cite to relevant law that would not have been presented during the case or to summarize their arguments in writing in a way more coherent than the hearing provided for. Many others do not want the extra burden, time, and expense of briefing the issue(s) and so rely on an oral closing argument.

One alternate method which is used by some advocates is to have an oral argument given only to the transcriptionist, without the arbitrator or opposing advocate present, at the conclusion of the arbitration. This permits immediate and simultaneous submission of the argument in written form without one party first hearing the others' argument. A similar alternative would be to simply bring a written version of the intended closing argument to arbitration. The advocates would take a brief interlude to work at their computers and modify their arguments in accordance with the evidence presented and then would submit them in writing.

Another alternative would be to submit a written pre-hearing, rather than post-hearing brief, and then provide an oral closing argument.

2.   The Relevant Litigation Principles

Jurors have most often made up their minds as to the outcome of the case before closing arguments are delivered. Thus, empirical research shows that opening statements, direct testimony, and cross-examination more highly influence the juror's decisions than does closing argument. Indeed, many judges take the position that closing argument is "relatively unimportant."

Closing argument is, however, the only opportunity the advocate has to present the case in a cohesive and non-narrative form. Cross-examination is not a full argument of the case, while opening statement and direct examination are more predominately narrative than argument. Thus, closing argument represents the decision-maker's only opportunity to understand the theory of the case and the arguments a party is making as a whole.

Moreover, written communication and oral communication have different advantages and disadvantages. Oral communication provides mutual context that is lacking in a written communication unless explicitly included in the writing. For instance, as explained by Ed Finegan, Professor of Linguistics and Law, if a group is sitting around a table eating and a person says, "Is there salt on the table?" the person expects someone to pass the salt. If on the other hand the same person asks someone helping to set up a table for a dinner party, "Is there salt on the table?" the person likely expects a yes or no answer. Thus, it is more difficult to convey the writer's intended meaning in writing.

Additionally, oral communication permits the lawyer to respond to the decision-maker's immediate questions or concerns. And a lawyer can more easily communicate emotion verbally than through writing.

On the other hand, a writing is memorialized for the reader to reference as many times as necessary. This aids the reader in understanding the writer's intended meaning. An oral statement is typically made only once, or at most a few times. The listener must rely on memory, with or without aid of the listener's own notes, to represent the speaker's intent.

Additionally, the process of legal writing can further the lawyer's creative and critical thinking. A lawyer can reconsider the arguments at a later time, adding in new thoughts, and editing from a more critical perspective. Writing, thus, "can be more complex than natural speech."

3.   The Best Practice: Closing Argument Should be Made
Orally, and the Parties Should Not be Permitted to Opt
for Written Briefs in Lieu of Oral Closing Argument.

The arbitrator will likely have reached a decision, or at least a tentative decision, before the closing argument suggesting that an oral closing argument is preferable to a written one. The litigation principle which most clearly dictates that an oral closing argument is preferable is that a juror is likely to have made a decision before the closing argument. An arbitrator is trained to be neutral and is more experienced in decision making than the typical juror. Training and experience indicate that arbitrators may form only tentative decisions until hearing the entire case. Nevertheless, arbitrators, like juries, have likely made a decision before the closing argument. Indeed, their training as decision-makers and experience with similar issues may make arbitrators even more likely than jurors to feel adept at understanding the governing rules (generally contract terms and principles of interpretation), interpreting the facts, identifying the parties' interests, and making an early decision. Because the closing argument is unlikely in most cases to have a significant effect on the ability of the arbitrator to fairly decide the case, it unnecessarily delays the proceeding to wait for post-hearing submission of briefs.

Moreover, an oral closing argument aids the arbitrator in understanding the context of the argument. It also enables the advocate to share the emotional impact of the arguments with the arbitrator and to respond to the arbitrator's questions and concerns.

Of course, the closing argument is the only opportunity to make a full argument. And, in some cases, arguments may have been overlooked or underestimated by the arbitrator, causing the arbitrator to reconsider and rely on the closing argument in reaching a decision. In this event, an oral closing argument still provides the opportunity to argue. While it may not as effectively convey complex ideas as a written brief, it enables the advocate to address questions and concerns raised by the arbitrator. And it provides an advantage over a written brief because the context of oral communication should more readily enable the arbitrator to understand the arguments the advocate makes. While the arbitrator may not have the written brief to refer to later when finalizing or writing a decision, he or she may have a transcript and should have notes of the oral argument.

If the parties routinely arbitrate issues of such complexity that they believe it is very important for the arbitrator to have a written closing argument to which to refer, they should consider having the oral closing argument reduced to transcript or providing a pre-prepared written version of the argument.

CHAPTER 21

The Hearing

Fact Scenario

Exchange the direct testimony affidavits you authored as part of the simulation in Chapters 20 and 21 with opposing counsel ahead of class (short models are appended at the end of this chapter for your reference). Prepare the following for a mock hearing:

1. A short opening statement (5–10 minutes)

2. Two cross-examinations for whom you received affidavits (5–8 minutes)

3. Two re-direct examinations of the witnesses crossed by opposing counsel (2–5 minutes)

Readings

As you prepare for the simulated hearing consider the following materials below as guidance how to organize an opening statement, prepare a cross-examination, and what to look for with regard to re-direct examination.

A) Oral Opening Statements in Arbitration

As discussed in Chapter 21, it is possible, if not likely, that you would have prepared a detailed pre-hearing brief ahead of the hearing. Even if you have submitted a pre-hearing brief, it is possible, if not likely, that you would also prepare a very brief oral opening statement for the arbitral tribunal. This opening statement has two broad purposes—(1) introduce your case to the arbitrators in person and (2) orient the arbitrators how you intend to use your hearing time to prove your side of the case.

You may have encountered opening statements already in the trial setting—or in the setting of a trial advocacy course or seminar. The first reading sets out for you what a litigator would expect from an opening statement (as opposed to a closing statement). As you review the arbitration specific readings below, consider how opening statements differ in arbitration from litigation.

Further, consider the potential use you can make of technology as part of your opening statement. Do you want to use demonstrative exhibits during your opening to emphasize certain points? Do you want to rely upon PowerPoint presentations? If you do want to use electronic resources, how should utilize them? These questions will go a long way to helping you make your opening statement memorable—in a good way.

United States Courts, Differences Between Opening and Closing Statements

Available at http://www.uscourts.gov/educational-resources/get-informed/
federal-court-resources/opening-statements-closing-arguments.aspx

Each party in a jury trial has a right to speak directly to jurors once before and once after the evidence is presented. Those two sets of remarks serve distinct purposes and are governed by different rules.

Opening Statement: The opening statement at the beginning of the trial is limited to outlining facts. This is each party's opportunity to set the basic scene for the jurors, introduce them to the core dispute(s), and provide a road map as to how the trial is expected to unfold. Absent strategic reasons not to do so, parties should lay out for the jurors who their witnesses are, how they are related to the parties and to each other, and what each is expected to say on the witness stand. Opening statements include such phrases as, "Ms. Smith will testify under oath that she saw Mr. Johnson do X," and "The evidence will show that Defendant did not do Y." Although opening statements should be as persuasive as possible, they should not include arguments. They come at the end of the trial.

Closing Argument: Only after the jury has seen and heard the factual evidence of the case are the parties allowed to try to persuade them about its overall significance. Closing arguments are the opportunity for each party to remind jurors about key evidence presented and to persuade them to adopt an interpretation favorable to their position. At this point, parties are free to use hypothetical analogies to make their points; to comment on the credibility of the witnesses, to discuss how they believe the various pieces of the puzzle fit into a compelling whole, and to advocate why jurors should decide the case in their favor.

Key Difference: In litigation, there is a critical difference between opening statements and closing arguments. In opening statements, parties are restricted to stating the evidence: ("Witness A will testify that Event X occurred"). In closing arguments, the parties are free to argue the merits: "As we know from Witness A's compelling testimony, Event X occurred, which clearly established who should be held responsible in this case."

Utah State Bar, Arbitration Advocacy, Part Two: The Arbitration Hearing

* * *

Opening Statements

Opening statements are optional. If you have furnished pre-hearing briefs, a stipulated set of facts, or both, your opening can be waived or expedited by using a more summary form of presentation. Arbitrators are anxious to hear the facts from the witnesses. An opening statement should be designed to educate the arbitrator on the general framework of the case. A brief statement on your client's position on the issues and damages will most often suffice. I encourage you to refrain from the temptation of arguing your case in your opening statement. Attorneys who argue their case in the opening statement phase of the arbitration are doing a disservice to their client. An opening statement is like a well orchestrated performance by the Utah Symphony. Keep the introductions to a minimum. Be the conductor and let the musicians (witnesses and documents) do their thing.

* * *

NOTES

1. What is the difference between "educating the arbitrator on the general framework of the case" and "arguing your case"? What do you need to do to the first but not the second?

2. Consider the analogy to a symphony drawn by the learned author of the Utah State Bar exposition on arbitration advocacy. As a refresher, the linked "cheat sheet" summarizes the structure of a classical symphony and the function played by each part. Taking the analogy (somewhat) literally, what do you need to do in an opening? How is that distinguishable from argument?

William Lemons, I Am Your Arbitrator. Here Is What To Expect From Me . . . And What I Expect From You

Available at http://www.whlemonsadr.com/pdf/i-am-your-arbitrator-new.pdf

* * *

Opening Statement

Counsel, and particularly any party that is not represented by counsel, may give a brief opening statement if desired. The opening statement will ordinarily be given immediately after the opening of the hearing and, except in unusual circumstances or complex cases, will be limited in time. Fifteen (15) minutes is long. Your opening statement should be non-argumentative and should focus on (a) the issues, (b) the proof you anticipate will be presented, and (3) the specific relief you seek. Tell me what you are going to tell me. Tell me what you really want me to do. I am not going to speculate on damages or relief. If I have significant questions in my own mind as to what is being asked of me, I have a pretty simple solution.

* * *

NOTES

1.   Is Mr. Lemons' advice consistent with the advice from the Utah State Bar on arbitration?

2.   How can you say anything in less than 15 minutes? Does the symphony analogy from the Utah Bar piece help you with triage?

3.   What is "the proof you anticipate will be presented"?

Ariana R. Levinson, Lawyering Skills That Just Might Tip the Scales in Close Arbitration Cases

Available at http://www.americanbar.org/content/dam/aba/administrative/labor_law/meetings/2010/2010_adr_levinson.authcheckdam.pdf

* * *

Studies have found that conveying information visually, in addition to verbally, increases the likelihood of the listener remembering the information. For this reason, some advocates have turned to using PowerPoint in litigation, and PowerPoint can be used in a similar manner in arbitration. PowerPoint can be used during opening statements, witness testimony, or closing argument.

Before deciding to use PowerPoint, however, remember that your goal is to persuade the arbitrator and keep the arbitrator focused on your theory and story of the case. Doing so requires, in large measure, that you maintain the focus on counsel or the witness, whoever is conveying the relevant information. Thus, you should only use PowerPoint if you can effectively enhance the focus on the client's story. This will involve judgments about the amount of time and money you have to prepare the case, your knowledge and comfort level with PowerPoint, and the technology that you will have available in the hearing room. PowerPoint provides a relatively low cost opportunity to experiment with technology likely to be the wave of the future in arbitration as well as litigation. But, it should ideally be used in combination with other forms of visual aids because varying presentation style more effectively holds the listener's attention. Also, you should always have a back-up plan in case your technology fails.

* * *

If you do decide to use text slides, remember these basic principles that apply to using PowerPoint in any setting. Slides should generally not contain long textual sentences or large amounts of information. When large blocks of text, such as the language of a contract or statute, are displayed, provide the arbitrator and others time to read the slide. If you talk at the same time, the arbitrator will either miss what you say or not read the slide.

The presentation of the text and the slides is important. Your presentation reflects on your level of professionalism and your credibility. Be sure the text uses proper grammar and spelling and is free of typographical errors. Use larger, darker san serif font to emphasize headings and main ideas. Proofread your slides just as you would any other legal document. Avoid using pre-set background graphics which may lull the arbitrator's focus on the slides. Instead, try using black text on white background or varying the font colors or single-color backgrounds. Use varying slide layouts, rather than only bullets, to avoid monotony.

NOTE

1. Ariana Levinson's advice on the use of PowerPoint presentations obviously is not limited to opening statements, but addresses the entirety of the arbitration hearing. What part of the advice is most relevant to your opening statement?

Checklist

1. Have you worked out a theme for the hearing? What is it?

2. Is your theme clearly articulated at the beginning and end of your presentation?

3. Have you stated the proof you will introduce at the hearing?

4. Have you placed that proof in context? What other record material is relevant to understanding what is going on?

5. Have you planned how the arbitrators should keep track of your presentation? You can use technology and hand the arbitrators a PowerPoint deck on which to take notes as you go through it. You can use a whiteboard and make sure that the arbitrators take notes of the very brief key terms you put up. If you wish, you can make sure that the tribunal has a physical roadmap of what you want to achieve at the hearing.

6. Run through your opening. If you do everything you have previewed for the arbitrators, do you win the case? If the answer is "no", what is missing? How do you incorporate that into your opening?

B) Cross-Examination

The question how to do cross-examination is in many ways highly personal. What works for one advocate may not work for another. That being said, there are different guideposts (many of which premised in common sense) which an advocate can use as reference points when preparing a cross-examination. The readings below set out these guideposts.

Phil Cutler, Top Ten Mistakes Lawyers Make in Arbitration Hearings and Tips on How to Avoid Them!

Available at http://cnhlaw.com/phil-cutler/top-ten-mistakes-lawyers-make-in-arbitration-and-tips-on-how-to-avoid-them/

* * *

#4—Misuse Cross-Examination of Witnesses: Try and use Cross to Prove Your Case in Chief; Fail to Plan Cross Before the Hearing

Any student of trial advocacy knows that cross-examination is one of the most powerful tools available to counsel. Nonetheless, lawyers continue to:

1. ask open-ended questions on cross, giving the witness an(other) opportunity to tell "his" side of the story

2. ask questions to which the lawyer does not know the answer (a bad idea unless the lawyer doesn't care what the answer is)

3. try and use cross to prove her case-in-chief

4. spend time on cross laboriously challenging every jot and tittle of the witness's direct examination, especially as to matters that are not important

Generally, the most that counsel can hope for from a witness on cross-examination is that some in-roads can be made debunking a key point of the other side's case. If you have prepared your case well, you will know what points you can get from the witness on cross. Make a short list and get to it. Except in the unusual case, resist the temptation to grill the witness for hours on everything he or she said on direct. Although there is truth to the "death by a thousand cuts" maxim, it is rare that such a strategy yields significant results at a hearing.

NOTES

1. Some suggest that every rule has an exception. Do you think this is true regarding cross examination? If so, when could you ask an open ended questions on cross-examination, given the discovery opportunities in arbitration? What is the risk of asking such a question? That being said, are there parts of the story only the other side's witness can tell? If so, how do you draw it out? How do you "check" for whitewashing?

2. One often-stated axiom of cross examinations is that the questioner needs to "know" the answer to each question before asking it. What does "knowing" an answer entail? Consider that you may well be able to prepare for multiple possible answers without knowing which answer the witness is going to give ahead of time. If you know how to move to your next question to support a broader point you wish to make, do you "know" the answer or have simply prepared well for cross? Some of the best cross-examination can well come in if you can use this technique because it introduces evidence that is not otherwise fully developed in the record— and may highlight significant problems for your opponent's case. For further practice tips on how to ask questions to which you do not know the answer, *see* Rachel Kent, An Introduction to Cross-Examining

Witnesses in International Arbitration, 3(2) Transnational Dispute Management (2006).

3. In many instances, your themes for the case include a characterization of the other side. In the most extreme of cases, your theme may be "the other side is crook." More subtly, you could paint a picture of reckless profit-maximization or abnormal risk-taking behavior. Saying that you cannot present your "case-in-chief" on cross does not mean that cross examination should not be thematic. In light of this, what do the lawyers who put together the cross-examination mean by "case-in-chief"? What should you ***not*** do on cross?

Checklist

1. Have you worked out your goals how the cross-examination will support a theme you have struck in your opening statement? Alternatively, how will it limit the efficacy of opposing counsel's theory of the case?

2. On the basis of your goals for the cross-examination work out an outline of the cross-examination. For each goal, have you worked out which documents or instances of prior testimony will lead the witness being crossed to substantiate what you want to achieve or lose credibility?

3. Have you worked out in what sequence to present the documents to get to the quickest way to make your point? Consider that it is easiest to get agreement on non-contentious issues and move gradually into more "painful" areas in which the witness may need to be impeached with documentary evidence to give helpful testimony.

4. Have you mapped out an "escape route" should testimony on a point not go as planned?

5. Have prepared a "cross-examination" binder to place in front of the witness, clearly identifying the exhibit number for the tribunal and opposing counsel to follow along and take notes? You want to minimize the time the witness can do to "find" documents.

C) Re-Direct Examination

An effective cross examination will tempt you to do a redirect examination. As you prepare redirect examination, consider the "first rule of holes": when you are in one, stop digging! Sometimes an effective cross-examination will take a point away. There is no point fighting it at that point. The best you can do is direct attention in a different direction.

For redirect examination, ask yourself whether there is a better light in which to place the testimony elicited by opposing counsel. As you do so, tie the redirect examination to contemporaneous documentary evidence to give greater credence to your re-contextualization of the evidence. As you rehabilitate the witness with this technique, make sure that the point you make is simple, intuitive and supported by one or two record documents.

Also, consider whether cross-examination permits you to redirect questioning towards your themes (and thus focus upon your own affirmative case with the witness).

AMERICAN ARBITRATION ASSOCIATION

<table>
<tr><td>

HARDMONT LLC,

Claimant,

v.

ACME INDUSTRIES CORP.,

RRF CORP., &

MERVIN GILMORE

Respondents.

</td><td>

AAA Case No. _______

</td></tr>
</table>

STATEMENT OF TIM "MAKE IT WORK" PISTOL

(a)   My name is Tim Pistol. I am also known by my nickname, "make it work", in the business. After graduating from high school, I enrolled in Washington's Coruscant College of Art and Design, where I discovered a passion for design and sculpture. I received my bachelor's in fine arts from Coruscant in 1977, and set up a sculpture studio in D.C.'s Georgetown neighborhood, working in the medium of paper and illustration board. I also took a job at Coruscant teaching design and working in campus admissions. In 1982, I was hired as an Assistant Director of Admissions at the Plawseys School for Design in New York City. I rose through the ranks at Plawseys, eventually becoming an associate dean.

(b)   In 2001, Plawseys' fashion department was in a state of turmoil. The curriculum had grown stale and stagnant, a lethal combination in an industry obsessed with the cutting edge. I took over the department for what was supposed to be just one year, but he stayed on for seven. During that time I completely revamped the program, helping to place Parsons in the upper echelon of respected design programs. As I said back then it ended up being a tremendous labor of love. It was hugely daunting and hugely unsettling in many ways, but what kept me focused and kept me on a straight and narrow line were the students.

(c)   I have published numerous works on design. A full list of publications is attached as appendix A.

(d)   I personally know how creative decisions affect markets trends and vice versa from my work as creative director at Izzy Claymore and Project Pret-a-Porter. Izzy Claymore is in the same market as Hardmont, albeit at a higher end of the market. (Hardmont's lines retail at JC Cent and Goal, Liz Claymore at Micey and Drallons).

(e)   As Creative Director, I have relied upon market research in the past. What makes the market research is not just what it says. The point of design is the uniqueness in which the research is interpreted.

(f)   I have reviewed RRF's design and the designs of the Hardmont line produced by Acme. There are remarkable similarities between both lines. In my opinion, it is highly unlikely that they are the result of two independent design studios. The likeness in design between both lines is striking. Not only do they seem to draw upon the same color palette and general cuts, there is a common esthetics or feel to both. This common feel makes the two lines of clothing direct competitors in a way that no other clothing lines are.

(g)   In my opinion, the RRF line is also superior in design to the Acme line. The RRF line improves upon the Acme line by adding more details and depth to the design. In fact, it seems that RRF's design was done by the master or teacher of the designers at Acme. This cannot be a coincidence. I therefore conclude that there more than likely was a collaboration of some sort between Acme and RRF with regard to the clothing lines in question.

AMERICAN ARBITRATION ASSOCIATION

<table>
<tr><td>

HARDMONT LLC,

　　　　Claimant,

　　v.

ACME INDUSTRIES CORP.,

RRF CORP., &

MERVIN GILMORE

　　　　Respondents.

</td><td>

AAA Case No. ______

</td></tr>
</table>

MONEYBAGS EXPERT REPORT (excerpts)

1. My name is John Moneybags. I graduated summa cum laude with a BBA from Kansas State University. Following my undergraduate studies, I went to Harvard. I received an MBA and a doctorate from Harvard. My case study while at Harvard concerned fashion trends.

2. Before opening my own consulting firm, I worked as Senior Manager, Merchandise for Mouse Parks in Tampa Florida, the premier amusement park in the world. I also worked as a managing partner at 2day Consulting Market Research LLC. I have published extensively on damages including as a co-author of law review pieces appearing in the Yale Law Journal and Kansas Law Review, respectively.

* * *

Methodology

* * *

30. I calculated Hardmont's damages by reference to sales figures of Hardmont's clothing line in the first week of release (i.e., prior to the infringement at issue in this arbitration). I used this data to project the likely the sales figures of Hardmont but for the infringement.

31. The projection assumed that sales in the season in question would in fact follow the same ratio of total sales to sales in week 1 that Hardmont achieved in the five previous seasons. This assumption is backed by sales figures of two control fashion lines with a comparable sales volume for the season in question. The sales volume in the first three weeks after launch of these lines is consistent with Hardmont's initial sale to total sale ratio. This means that the control figures confirm that there was no deviation in customer behavior in the season in question meaning that it is possible to project a reliable but-for sales figure.

Conclusions

* * *

(ccc) On the basis of this calculation, I conclude that Hardmont suffered damages in the amount of $10MM.

AMERICAN ARBITRATION ASSOCIATION

<table>
<tr><td>

HARDMONT LLC,

    Claimant,

    v.

ACME INDUSTRIES CORP.,

RRF CORP., &

MERVIN GILMORE

    Respondents.

</td><td>

AAA Case No. ______

</td></tr>
</table>

STATEMENT OF MERVIN GILMORE

1. My name is Mervin Gilmore. I am the former CEO of Acme Industries Corp. ("Acme"). I am the beneficial owner of the second Respondent, RRF Corp. ("RRF").

2. As CEO of Acme, I entered into a Clothing Design Agreement on October 12, 2012 ("Agreement") with Hardmont LLC ("Hardmont").

3. On October 13, 2012, Hardmont provided us with "Confidential Information" pursuant to sections 5 and 6 of the Agreement. The Agreement states that the Confidential Information was attached as Appendix I to the Agreement. This was not in fact the case. We did not receive the Confidential Information ahead of executing the Agreement.

4. The "Confidential Information" was a study compiled by Xena Fashion Research ("XFR") on behalf of Hardmont. XFR provides market studies for many of the large fashion houses marketing clothing through large retail outlets. Prior to entering into the Agreement, Acme had retained XFR for market research for the 2011 Spring Season (See Exhibit 2).

5. Acme relied upon the Confidential Information to design and produce a line of clothing for Hardmont. Acme followed the findings of the market research to the letter. We were very proud of our work for Hardmont.

6. Shortly after delivering our design, Acme filed for bankruptcy. Acme's bankruptcy had nothing to do with the Hardmont transaction. Acme had to file for bankruptcy protection due to a dispute with another Acme customers, Anne Treetop Clothing. Anne Treetop Clothing sued Acme for Acme's alleged failure timely to deliver its designs for production. Acme had not received relevant market research from Anne Treetop in a timely manner. Despite this clear breach of contract by Anne Treetop Clothing, a

jury found for Anne Treetop Clothing and awarded $3MM in damages. Given the size of the judgment, Acme had to file for bankruptcy protection.

7.   The Agreement had nothing to do with RRF. RRF designs and markets cheaper "off brand" clothing to be marketed directly by large mall chains. These designs are premised upon current market trends. They are not premised upon setting market trends with new design ideas. Typically, RRF studies fashion trends at leading televised award shows and in celebrity news and then copies the design ideas reflected in these trends. In that context, RRF had retained XFR in the past to assist with market research (Exhibit 3).

8.   I at no time gave the Confidential Information to RRF or communicated the substance of the Confidential Information to RRF. RRF and Acme always operated as completely separate businesses. The bankruptcy proceedings in fact confirmed that RRF's assets were off limits for Acme creditors and that the two entities, while co-owned, had nothing to do with each other what so ever.

9.   RRF's 2013 Spring Season was the responsibility of RRF's COO, Mort Edelman. Edelman contacted XFR to conduct market research for RRF (Exhibit 4). Although Edelman let me know he was going to contract XFR, I did not communicate with him in any way regarding the retention. I was not in the loop regarding the scope of retention or anything else regarding XFR's engagement until after the retention had been concluded.

10.   At the time, Edelman was not an employee, agent, director or principal of Acme. In fact, apart from my beneficial ownership of RRF, no RRF employee, agent, director or principal at the time was an employee, agent, director or principal of Acme.

Exhibit 1

[Hardmont—XFR Market Research]

* * *

Scope of Market Research:

Per Hardmont's request, we conducted 1,000 telephone interviews with women aged 25–35, evaluated 1,500 online customer surveys provided by Hardmont, and compared the data to current industry publications. We asked interview participants about lifestyle preferences, their favorite television shows, including whom they considered to be the best dressed actress on the show, their style idols and their style of dress for office and their spare time. On the basis of this research, we have established likely trends for the Spring Season.

Exhibit 2

[Acme-XFR Market Research]

* * *

Scope of Market Research:

Per Acme's request, we conducted complied data from current industry publications and compared this data to trends in recent top-grossing television shows. On the basis of this research, we have established likely trends for the Spring Season.

Exhibit 3

[Previous RRF-XFR Market Research]

* * *

Scope of Market Research:

Per RRF's request, we conducted complied data from current industry publications and compared this data to trends in recent top-grossing television shows. On the basis of this research, we have established likely trends for the Spring Season.

Exbibit 4

[Current RRF-XFR Market Research]

* * *

Scope of Market Research:

Per RRF's request, we conducted 1,000 telephone interviews with women aged 25–35, evaluated 500 online customer surveys provided by RRF, and compared the data to current industry publications. We asked interview participants about lifestyle preferences, their favorite television shows, including whom they considered to be the best dressed actress on the show, their style idols and their style of dress for office and their spare time. On the basis of this research, we have established likely trends for the Spring Season.

AMERICAN ARBITRATION ASSOCIATION

<table>
<tr><td>

HARDMONT LLC,

Claimant,

v.

ACME INDUSTRIES CORP.,

RRF CORP., &

MERVIN GILMORE

Respondents.

</td><td>

AAA Case No. ______

</td></tr>
</table>

SEXTANT CONSULTING EXPERT REPORT (excerpts)

* * *

Methodology

* * *

32. Thus, we examined the profit and loss statements of 5 (five) women's fashion brands retailed at large chain stores catering to women aged 25–35. One of these brands had a higher market penetrated than Hardmont (HTH), two of the brands had a lower market penetration than Hardmont (LTH1 and LTH2) and two had the same market penetration as Hardmont (SAH1 and SAH2). We compared the profit and loss of these brands to the variance in design between the various companies.

Conclusions

* * *

(ddd) Of the five brands, LTH1 and SAH2 had similar designs. SAH2 had significantly better sales results compared to LTH1. HTH, LTH2 and SAH1 had comparatively different designs and achieved a similar profit margin. Consequently, design differentiations do not result in wide-range profit discrepancies between companies. Quality, brand and affordability are the major factors in determining profits.

(eee) Further, we note that LTH1 and SAH2 are not affiliated in any way. Their similarity in designs shows similar designs can be developed on a basis other than shared market study information. In those instances, market penetration is a better indicator of performance than design choice. We do not that sales result of LTH2 were higher than LTH1. We could not definitively establish that this difference had any correlation to design.

(fff) Consequently, we conclude that had RRF not received the XFR market study, there would have been no demonstrable change in Hardmont's sales result. That means that damages in this case are entirely speculative. Decrease in sales could be caused by market penetration, market volatility etc.

PART VII

The Award

At the end of an arbitral proceeding, the parties receive an award from the arbitral tribunal. In many instances, the parties voluntarily comply with the award. In those instances, the arbitral process concludes with the issuance (and performance) of the award.

In a smaller set of cases, the losing party in arbitration will try to take recourse against the award. This part sets out the key fora you can invoke to seek review of an award and what grounds for review may be available.

CHAPTER 22

Exclusivity of FAA Grounds for Set Aside

Fact Scenario

A client asks you to draft an arbitration clause permitting review for error of law by the arbitrators. How do you structure the arbitration clause best to preserve the reviewability of the arbitral award per your client's wishes?

Readings

The readings below begin with a statute we have already considered earlier in the course, the Federal Arbitration Act. As you will see, there is debate how broad the review authority of federal courts is under the Federal Arbitration Act at this point in time. The federal jurisprudence outlined below has significantly contributed to developments both at the state level and within arbitral institutions to make available more flexible avenues for review of arbitral awards. As you read these materials, consider the materials below, ask yourself how these multiple potential fora for review will inform your advice to clients in setting up an arbitration clause and in litigating potential enforcement issues at the back end of an arbitration.

A)   The Federal Arbitration Act

The Federal Arbitration Act innocuously sets out the grounds upon which an award can be set aside in federal court proceedings. As already discussed in the context of the arbitration clause, the Federal Arbitration Act has received its fair share of judicial gloss over the years. As you look through the materials below, consider whether the approach taken by the Supreme Court in particular is consistent with its approach to the Federal Arbitration Act in the context of the arbitration clause. Do you discover a facial disconnect between the approaches taken by the court? How do you reconcile them?

Federal Arbitration Act, § 9

If the parties in their agreement have agreed that a judgment of the court shall be entered upon the award made pursuant to the arbitration, and shall specify the court, then at any time within one year after the award is made any party to the arbitration may apply to the court so specified for an order confirming the award, and thereupon the court must grant such an order unless the award is vacated, modified, or corrected as prescribed in sections 10 and 11 of this title. If no court is specified in the agreement of the parties, then such application may be made to the United States court in and for the district within which such award was made. Notice of the application shall be served upon the adverse party, and thereupon the court shall have jurisdiction of such party as though he had appeared generally in the proceeding. If the adverse party is a resident of the district within which the award was made, such service shall be made upon the adverse party or his attorney as prescribed by law for service of notice of motion in an action in the same court. If the adverse party shall be a nonresident, then the notice of the application shall be served by the marshal of any district within which the adverse party may be found in like manner as other process of the court.

NOTES

1. What does section 9 of the Federal Arbitration Act anticipate the parties would have done in their arbitration clause with respect to the award? Does the AAA form arbitration clause prepare for this eventuality?

2. What is the default rule if the parties did not plan ahead as anticipated by the drafters of the arbitration agreement?

3. When do you prefer the default rule? What parties should try to modify the default rule?

Federal Arbitration Act, § 10

(a)   In any of the following cases the United States court in and for the district wherein the award was made may make an order vacating the award upon the application of any party to the arbitration—

(1)   where the award was procured by corruption, fraud, or undue means;

(2)   where there was evident partiality or corruption in the arbitrators, or either of them;

(3)   where the arbitrators were guilty of misconduct in refusing to postpone the hearing, upon sufficient cause shown, or in refusing to hear evidence pertinent and material to the controversy; or of any other misbehavior by which the rights of any party have been prejudiced; or

(4)   where the arbitrators exceeded their powers, or so imperfectly executed them that a mutual, final, and definite award upon the subject matter submitted was not made.

(b)   If an award is vacated and the time within which the agreement required the award to be made has not expired, the court may, in its discretion, direct a rehearing by the arbitrators.

(c)   The United States district court for the district wherein an award was made that was issued pursuant to section 580 of title 5 may make an order vacating the award upon the application of a person, other than a party to the arbitration, who is adversely affected or aggrieved by the award, if the use of arbitration or the award is clearly inconsistent with the factors set forth in section 572 of title 5.

NOTES

1.   Does section 10 of the Federal Arbitration Act state clearly that the grounds for set aside listed in that section are exclusive?

2.   Are the grounds set out in section 10 interrelated? Is it possible that an award is subject to set aside under section 10(a)(1), but not under 10(a)(2), 10(a)(3), 10(a)(4) and so on? If there is an overlap between the set aside grounds, what is the core concern that the Federal Arbitration Act seeks to protect?

3.   What is the consequence of a set aside?

Wilko v. Swan

346 U.S. 427 (1953)

Look back to Chapter 4 for the facts of Wilko v. Swan. The excerpted part of the case below discussed the set aside grounds omitted from Chapter 4.

MR. JUSTICE REED delivered the opinion of the Court.

* * *

Even though the provisions of the Securities Act, advantageous to the buyer, apply, their effectiveness in application is lessened in arbitration as compared to judicial proceedings. Determination of the quality of a commodity or the amount of money due under a contract is not the type of issue here involved. This case requires subjective findings on the purpose and knowledge of an alleged violator of the Act. They must be not only determined but applied by the arbitrators without judicial instruction on the law. As their award may be made without explanation of their reasons and without a complete record of their proceedings, the arbitrators' conception of the legal meaning of such statutory requirements as 'burden of proof,' 'reasonable care' or 'material fact,' see, note 1, supra, cannot be examined. Power to vacate an award is limited. While it may be true, as the Court of Appeals thought, that a failure of the arbitrators to decide in accordance with the provisions of the Securities Act would 'constitute grounds for vacating the award pursuant to section 10 of the Federal Arbitration Act,' that failure would need to be made clearly to appear. In unrestricted submission, such as the present margin agreements envisage, the interpretations of the law by the arbitrators in contrast to manifest disregard are not subject, in the federal courts, to judicial review for error in interpretation. The United States Arbitration Act contains no provision for judicial determination of legal issues such as is found in the English law. As the protective provisions of the Securities Act require the exercise of judicial direction to fairly assure their effectiveness, it seems to us that Congress must have intended s 14, note 6, supra, to apply to waiver of judicial trial and review.

* * *

Two policies, not easily reconcilable, are involved in this case. Congress has afforded participants in transactions subject to its legislative power an opportunity generally to secure prompt, economical and adequate solution of controversies through arbitration if the parties are willing to accept less certainty of legally correct adjustment.32 On the other hand, it has enacted the Securities Act to protect the rights of investors and has forbidden a waiver of any of those rights. Recognizing the advantages that prior agreements for arbitration may provide for the solution of commercial controversies, we decide that the intention of Congress concerning the sale of securities is better carried out by holding invalid such an * *189 agreement for arbitration of issues arising under the Act.

Reversed.

MR. JUSTICE JACKSON, concurring.

I agree with the Court's opinion insofar as it construes the Securities Act to prohibit waiver of a judicial remedy in favor of arbitration by agreement made before any controversy arose. I think thereafter the parties could agree upon arbitration. However, I find it unnecessary *439 in this case, where there has not been and could not be any arbitration, to decide that the Arbitration Act precludes any judicial remedy for the arbitrators' error of interpretation of a relevant statute.

MR. JUSTICE FRANKFURTER, whom MR. JUSTICE MINTON joins, dissenting.

If arbitration inherently precluded full protection of the rights s 12(2) of the Securities Act affords to a purchaser of securities, or if there were no effective means of ensuring judicial review of the legal basis of the arbitration, then, of course, an agreement to settle the controversy by arbitration would be barred by s 14, the anti-waiver provision, of that Act.

There is nothing in the record before us, nor in the facts of which we can take judicial notice, to indicate that the arbitral system as practiced in the City of New York, and as enforceable under the supervisory authority of the District Court for the Southern District of New York, would not afford the plaintiff the rights to which he is entitled.

The impelling considerations that led to the enactment of the Federal Arbitration Act are the advantages of providing a speedier, more economical and more effective enforcement of rights by way of arbitration than can be had by the tortuous course of litigation, especially in the City of New York. These advantages should not be assumed to be denied in controversies like that before us arising under the Securities Act, in the absence of any showing that settlement by arbitration would jeopardize the rights of the plaintiff.

Arbitrators may not disregard the law. Specifically they are, as Chief Judge Swan pointed out, 'bound to decide in accordance with the provisions of section 12(2).' On this we are all agreed. It is suggested, however, that there is no effective way of assuring obedience by the arbitrators to the governing law. But since their failure to observe this law 'would * * * constitute grounds for vacating the award pursuant to section 10 of the Federal Arbitration Act,' 201 F.2d 439, 445, appropriate means for judicial scrutiny must be implied, in the form of some record or opinion, however informal, whereby such compliance will appear, or want of it will upset the award.

We have not before us a case in which the record shows that the plaintiff in opening an account had no choice but to accept the arbitration stipulation, thereby making the stipulation an unconscionable and unenforceable provision in a business transaction. The Securities and Exchange Commission, as amicus curiae, does not contend that the stipulation which the Court of Appeals respected, under the appropriate safeguards defined by it, was a coercive practice by financial houses against customers incapable of self-protection. It is one thing to make out a case of overreaching as between parties bargaining not at arm's length. It is quite a different thing to find in the anti-waiver provision of the Securities Act a general limitation on the Federal Arbitration Act.

On the state of the record before us, I would affirm the decision of the Court of Appeals.

NOTES

Facts

1. How did the issue of set aside come up in *Wilko v. Swan*? Did the case reach the Supreme Court on appeal from a set aside application?

2. What was the statute at issue in *Wilko v. Swan*? Does that explain why the Court discussed grounds for set aside of arbitral awards?

Law

1. Considering the procedural posture of the case, what do you think the Court meant by manifest excess of law?

2. Do you think the Court considered manifest excess of law through the lens of the set aside provisions of the FAA? How?

Hall Street Associates v. Mattel, Inc.

552 U.S. 576 (2008)

JUSTICE SOUTER delivered the opinion of the Court.

The Federal Arbitration Act (FAA or Act), 9 U.S.C. § 1 et seq., provides for expedited judicial review to confirm, vacate, or modify arbitration awards. §§ 9–11 (2006 ed.)* * *. The question here is whether statutory grounds for prompt vacatur and modification may be supplemented by contract. We hold that the statutory grounds are exclusive.

I

This case began as a lease dispute between landlord, petitioner Hall Street Associates, L.L.C., and tenant, respondent Mattel, Inc. The property was used for many years as a manufacturing site, and the leases provided that the tenant would indemnify the landlord for any costs resulting from the failure of the tenant or its predecessor lessees to follow environmental laws while using the premises.

Tests of the property's well water in 1998 showed high levels of trichloroethylene (TCE), the apparent residue of manufacturing discharges by

Mattel's predecessors between 1951 and 1980. After the Oregon Department of Environmental Quality (DEQ) discovered even more pollutants, Mattel stopped drawing from the well and, along with one of its predecessors, signed a consent order with the DEQ providing for cleanup of the site.

After Mattel gave notice of intent to terminate the lease in 2001, Hall Street filed this suit, contesting Mattel's right to vacate on the date it gave, and claiming that the lease obliged Mattel to indemnify Hall Street for costs of cleaning up the TCE, among other things. Following a bench trial before the United States District Court for the District of Oregon, Mattel won on the termination issue, and after an unsuccessful try at mediating the indemnification claim, the parties proposed to submit to arbitration. The District Court was amenable, and the parties drew up an arbitration agreement, which the court approved and entered as an order. One paragraph of the agreement provided that

> "[t]he United States District Court for the District of Oregon may enter judgment upon any award, either by confirming the award or by vacating, modifying or correcting the award. The Court shall vacate, modify or correct any award: (i) where the arbitrator's findings of facts are not supported by substantial evidence, or (ii) where the arbitrator's conclusions of law are erroneous."

Arbitration took place, and the arbitrator decided for Mattel. In particular, he held that no indemnification was due, because the lease obligation to follow all applicable federal, state, and local environmental laws did not require compliance with the testing requirements of the Oregon Drinking Water Quality Act (Oregon Act); that Act the arbitrator characterized as dealing with human health as distinct from environmental contamination.

Hall Street then filed a District Court Motion for Order Vacating, Modifying And/Or Correcting Arbitration Accord on the ground that failing to treat the Oregon Act as an applicable environmental law under the terms of the lease was legal error. The District Court agreed, vacated the award, and remanded for further consideration by the arbitrator. The court expressly invoked the standard of review chosen by the parties in the arbitration agreement, which included review for legal error, and cited *LaPine Technology Corp. v. Kyocera Corp.*, 130 F.3d 884, 889 (C.A.9 1997), for the proposition that the FAA leaves the parties "free . . . to draft a contract that sets rules for arbitration and dictates an alternative standard of review."

On remand, the arbitrator followed the District Court's ruling that the Oregon Act was an applicable environmental law and amended the decision to favor Hall Street. This time, each party sought modification, and again the

District Court applied the parties' stipulated standard of review for legal error, correcting the arbitrator's calculation of interest but otherwise upholding the award. Each party then appealed to the Court of Appeals for the Ninth Circuit, where Mattel switched horses and contended that the Ninth Circuit's recent en banc action overruling *LaPine in Kyocera Corp. v. Prudential-Bache Trade Servs.*, Inc., 341 F.3d 987, 1000 (2003), left the arbitration agreement's provision for judicial review of legal error unenforceable. Hall Street countered that Kyocera (the later one) was distinguishable, and that the agreement's judicial review provision was not severable from the submission to arbitration.

The Ninth Circuit reversed in favor of Mattel in holding that, "[u]nder Kyocera the terms of the arbitration agreement controlling the mode of judicial review are unenforceable and severable." The Circuit instructed the District Court on remand to

> *"return to the application to confirm the original arbitration award (not the subsequent award revised after reversal), and . . . confirm that award, unless . . . the award should be vacated on the grounds allowable under 9 U.S.C. § 10, or modified or corrected under the grounds allowable under 9 U.S.C. § 11."*

After the District Court again held for Hall Street and the Ninth Circuit again reversed, we granted certiorari to decide whether the grounds for vacatur and modification provided by §§ 10 and 11 of the FAA are exclusive. We agree with the Ninth Circuit that they are, but vacate and remand for consideration of independent issues.

II

Congress enacted the FAA to replace judicial indisposition to arbitration with a "national policy favoring [it] and plac[ing] arbitration agreements on equal footing with all other contracts." As for jurisdiction over controversies touching arbitration, the Act does nothing, being "something of an anomaly in the field of federal-court jurisdiction" *582 in bestowing no federal jurisdiction but rather requiring an independent jurisdictional basis. But in cases falling within a court's jurisdiction, the Act makes contracts to arbitrate "valid, irrevocable, and enforceable," so long as their subject involves "commerce." § 2. And this is so whether an agreement has a broad reach or goes just to one dispute, and whether enforcement be sought in state court or federal.

The Act also supplies mechanisms for enforcing arbitration awards: a judicial decree confirming an award, an order vacating it, or an order modifying or correcting it. §§ 9–11. An application for any of these orders will get streamlined treatment as a motion, obviating the separate contract action that would usually be necessary to enforce or tinker with an arbitral award in court.3 § 6. Under the terms of § 9, a court "must" confirm an arbitration award "unless" it is vacated, modified, or corrected "as prescribed" in §§ 10 and 11. Section 10 lists grounds for vacating an award, while § 11 names those for modifying or correcting one.4

The Courts of Appeals have split over the exclusiveness of these statutory grounds when parties take the FAA shortcut to confirm, vacate, or modify an award, with some saying the recitations are exclusive, and others regarding them as mere threshold provisions open to expansion by agreement.5*584 As mentioned already, when this litigation started, the Ninth Circuit was on the threshold side of the split, *see LaPine*, 130 F.3d, at 889, from which it later departed en banc in favor of the exclusivity view, *see Kyocera*, 341 F.3d, at 1000, which it followed in this case, see 113 Fed.Appx., at 273. We now hold that §§ 10 and 11 respectively provide the FAA's exclusive grounds for expedited vacatur and modification.

III

Hall Street makes two main efforts to show that the grounds set out for vacating or modifying an award are not exclusive, taking the position, first, that expandable judicial review authority has been accepted as the law since *Wilko v. Swan*, 346 U.S. 427 (1953). This, however, was not what *Wilko* decided, which was that § 14 of the Securities Act of 1933 voided any agreement to arbitrate claims of violations of that Act, see id., at 437–438, 74 S.Ct. 182, a holding since overruled by *Rodriguez de Quijas v. Shearson/American Express, Inc.*, 490 U.S. 477, 484 (1989). Although it is true that the Court's discussion includes some language arguably favoring Hall Street's position, arguable is as far as it goes.

The *Wilko* Court was explaining that arbitration would undercut the Securities Act's buyer protections when it remarked (citing FAA § 10) that "[p]ower to vacate an [arbitration] award is limited," 346 U.S., at 436, 74 S.Ct. 182, and went on to say that "the interpretations of the law by the arbitrators in contrast to manifest disregard [of the law] are not subject, in the federal courts, to judicial review for error in interpretation," Hall Street reads this statement as recognizing "manifest disregard of the law" as a further ground for vacatur on top of those listed in § 10, and some Circuits have read it the same way. Hall Street sees this supposed addition to § 10 as the camel's nose: if judges can add grounds to vacate (or modify), so can contracting parties.

But this is too much for *Wilko* to bear. Quite apart from its leap from a supposed judicial expansion by interpretation to a private expansion by contract,

Hall Street overlooks the fact that the statement it relies on expressly rejects just what Hall Street asks for here, general review for an arbitrator's legal errors. Then there is the vagueness of *Wilko*'s phrasing. Maybe the term "manifest disregard" was meant to name a new ground for review, but maybe it merely referred to the § 10 grounds collectively, rather than adding to them. Or, as some courts have thought, "manifest disregard" may have been shorthand for § 10(a)(3) or § 10(a)(4), the paragraphs authorizing vacatur when the arbitrators were "guilty of misconduct" or "exceeded their powers." We, when speaking as a Court, have merely taken the *Wilko* language as we found it, without embellishment, and now that its meaning is implicated, we see no reason to accord it the significance that Hall Street urges.

Second, Hall Street says that the agreement to review for legal error ought to prevail simply because arbitration is a creature of contract, and the FAA is "motivated, first and foremost, by a congressional desire to enforce agreements into which parties ha[ve] entered." But, again, we think the argument comes up short. Hall Street is certainly right that the FAA lets parties tailor some, even many, features of arbitration by contract, including the way arbitrators are chosen, what their qualifications should be, which issues are arbitrable, along with procedure and choice of substantive law. But to rest this case on the general policy of treating arbitration agreements as enforceable as such would be to beg the question, which is whether the FAA has textual features at odds with enforcing a contract to expand judicial review following the arbitration.

To that particular question we think the answer is yes, that the text compels a reading of the §§ 10 and 11 categories as exclusive. To begin with, even if we assumed §§ 10 and 11 could be supplemented to some extent, it would stretch basic interpretive principles to expand the stated grounds to the point of evidentiary and legal review generally. Sections 10 and 11, after all, address egregious departures from the parties' agreed-upon arbitration: "corruption," "fraud," "evident partiality," "misconduct," "misbehavior," "exceed[ing] . . . powers," "evident material miscalculation," "evident material mistake," "award[s] upon a matter not submitted"; the only ground with any softer focus is "imperfect[ions]," and a court may correct those only if they go to "[a] matter of form not affecting the merits." Given this emphasis on extreme arbitral conduct, the old rule of *ejusdem generis* has an implicit lesson to teach here. Under that rule, when a statute sets out a series of specific items ending with a general term, that general term is confined to covering subjects comparable to the specifics it follows. Since a general term included in the text is normally so limited, then surely a statute with no textual hook for expansion cannot authorize contracting parties to supplement review for specific instances of outrageous conduct with review for just any legal error. "Fraud" and a mistake of law are not cut from the same cloth.

That aside, expanding the detailed categories would rub too much against the grain of the § 9 language, where provision for judicial confirmation carries no hint of flexibility. On application for an order confirming the arbitration award, the court "must grant" the order "unless the award is vacated, modified, or corrected as prescribed in sections 10 and 11 of this title." There is nothing malleable about "must grant," which unequivocally tells courts to grant confirmation in all cases, except when one of the "prescribed" exceptions applies. This does not sound remotely like a provision meant to tell a court what to do just in case the parties say nothing else.

In fact, anyone who thinks Congress might have understood § 9 as a default provision should turn back to § 5 for an example of what Congress thought a default provision would look like:

> "[i]f in the agreement provision be made for a method of naming or appointing an arbitrator . . . such method shall be followed; but if no method be provided therein, or if a method be provided and any party thereto shall fail to avail himself of such method, . . . then upon the application of either party to the controversy the court shall designate and appoint an arbitrator. . . . ."

"[I]f no method be provided" is a far cry from "must grant . . . unless" in § 9.

Instead of fighting the text, it makes more sense to see the three provisions, §§ 9–11, as substantiating a national policy favoring arbitration with just the limited review needed to maintain arbitration's essential virtue of resolving disputes straightaway. Any other reading opens the door to the full-bore legal and evidentiary appeals that can "rende[r] informal arbitration merely a prelude to a more cumbersome and time-consuming judicial review process,", and bring arbitration theory to grief in post arbitration process.

Nor is *Dean Witter*, to the contrary, as Hall Street claims it to be. Dean Witter held that state-law claims subject to an agreement to arbitrate could not be remitted to a district court considering a related, nonarbitrable federal claim; the state-law claims were to go to arbitration immediately. *Id.*, at 217, 105 S.Ct. 1238. Despite the opinion's language "reject[ing] the suggestion that the overriding goal of the [FAA] was to promote the expeditious resolution of claims," the holding mandated immediate enforcement of an arbitration agreement; the Court was merely trying to explain that the inefficiency and difficulty of conducting simultaneous arbitration and federal-court litigation was not a good enough reason to defer the arbitration.

When all these arguments based on prior legal authority are done with, Hall Street and Mattel remain at odds over what happens next. Hall Street and its amici say parties will flee from arbitration if expanded review is not open to them. One of Mattel's amici foresees flight from the courts if it is. We do not know who, if anyone, is right, and so cannot say whether the exclusivity reading of the statute is more of a threat to the popularity of arbitrators or to that of courts. But whatever the consequences of our holding, the statutory text gives us no business to expand the statutory grounds.

IV

In holding that §§ 10 and 11 provide exclusive regimes for the review provided by the statute, we do not purport to say that they exclude more searching review based on authority outside the statute as well. The FAA is not the only way into court for parties wanting review of arbitration awards: they may contemplate enforcement under state statutory or common law, for example, where judicial review of different scope is arguable. But here we speak only to the scope of the expeditious judicial review under §§ 9, 10, and 11, deciding nothing about other possible avenues for judicial enforcement of arbitration awards.

Although one such avenue is now claimed to be revealed in the procedural history of this case, no claim to it was presented when the case arrived on our doorstep, and no reason then appeared to us for treating this as anything but an FAA case. There was never any question about meeting the FAA § 2 requirement that the leases from which the dispute arose be contracts "involving commerce."

Nor is there any doubt now that the parties at least had the FAA in mind at the outset; the arbitration agreement even incorporates FAA § 7, empowering arbitrators to compel attendance of witnesses.

While it is true that the agreement does not expressly invoke FAA § 9, § 10, or § 11, and none of the various motions to vacate or modify the award expressly said that the parties were relying on the FAA, the District Court apparently thought it was applying the FAA when it alluded to the Act in quoting *LaPine*, 130 F.3d, at 889, for the then-unexceptional proposition that " '[f]ederal courts can expand *591 their review of an arbitration award beyond the FAA's grounds, when . . . the parties have so agreed.' " And the Ninth Circuit, for its part, seemed to take it as a given that the District Court's direct and prompt examination of the award depended on the FAA; it found the expanded-review provision unenforceable under *Kyocera* and remanded for confirmation of the original award "unless the district court determines that the award should be vacated on the grounds allowable under 9 U.S.C. § 10, or modified or corrected under the grounds allowable under 9 U.S.C. § 11." In the petition for certiorari and the principal briefing before us, the parties acted on the same premise.

One unusual feature, however, prompted some of us to question whether the case should be approached another way. The arbitration agreement was entered into in the course of district-court litigation, was submitted to the District Court as a request to deviate from the standard sequence of trial procedure, and was adopted by the District Court as an order. Hence a question raised by this Court at oral argument: should the agreement be treated as an exercise of the District Court's authority to manage its cases under Federal Rule of Civil Procedure 16? Supplemental briefing at the Court's behest joined issue on the question, and it appears that Hall Street suggested something along these lines in the Court of Appeals, which did not address the suggestion.

We are, however, in no position to address the question now, beyond noting the claim of relevant case management authority independent of the FAA. The parties' supplemental arguments on the subject in this Court implicate issues of waiver and the relation of the FAA both to Rule 16 and the Alternative Dispute Resolution Act of 1998, 28 U.S.C. § 651 et seq., none of which has been considered previously in this litigation, or could be well addressed for the first time here. We express no opinion on these matters beyond leaving them open for Hall Street to press on remand. If the Court of Appeals finds they are open, the court may consider whether the District Court's authority to manage litigation independently warranted that court's order on the mode of resolving the indemnification issues remaining in this case.

Although we agree with the Ninth Circuit that the FAA confines its expedited judicial review to the grounds listed in 9 U.S.C. §§ 10 and 11, we vacate the judgment and remand the case for proceedings consistent with this opinion.

It is so ordered.

JUSTICE STEVENS, with whom JUSTICE KENNEDY joins, dissenting.

May parties to an ongoing lawsuit agree to submit their dispute to arbitration subject to the caveat that the trial judge should refuse to enforce an award that rests on an erroneous conclusion of law? Prior to Congress' enactment of the Federal Arbitration Act (FAA or Act) in 1925, the answer to that question would surely have been "Yes." Today, however, the Court holds that the FAA does not merely authorize the vacation or enforcement of awards on specified grounds, but also forbids enforcement of perfectly reasonable judicial review provisions in arbitration agreements fairly negotiated by the parties and approved by the district court. Because this result conflicts with the primary purpose of the FAA and ignores the historical context in which the Act was passed, I respectfully dissent.

Prior to the passage of the FAA, American courts were generally hostile to arbitration. They refused, with rare exceptions, to order specific enforcement of executory agreements to arbitrate. Section 2 of the FAA responded to this hostility by making written arbitration agreements "valid, irrevocable, and enforceable." * * *.

This Court now agrees with the Ninth Circuit's (most recent) interpretation of the FAA as setting forth the exclusive grounds for modification or vacation of an arbitration award under the statute. As I read the Court's opinion, it identifies two possible reasons for reaching this result: (1) a supposed quid pro quo bargain between Congress and litigants that conditions expedited federal enforcement of arbitration awards on acceptance of a statutory limit on the scope of judicial review of such awards; and (2) an assumption that Congress intended to include the words "and no other" in the grounds specified in §§ 10 and 11 for the vacatur and modification of awards. Neither reason is persuasive.

While § 9 of the FAA imposes a 1-year limit on the time in which any party to an arbitration may apply for confirmation of an award, the statute does not require that the application be given expedited treatment. Of course, the premise of the entire statute is an assumption that the arbitration process may be more expeditious and less costly than ordinary litigation, but that is a reason for interpreting the statute liberally to favor the parties' use of arbitration. An unnecessary refusal to enforce a perfectly reasonable category of arbitration agreements defeats the primary purpose of the statute.

That purpose also provides a sufficient response to the Court's reliance on statutory text. It is true that a wooden application of "the old rule of ejusdem generis," ante, at 1404, might support an inference that the categories listed in §§ 10 and 11 are exclusive, but the literal text does not compel that reading—a reading that is flatly inconsistent with the overriding interest in effectuating the clearly expressed intent of the contracting parties. A listing of grounds that must always be available to contracting parties simply does not speak to the question whether they may agree to additional grounds for judicial review.

Moreover, in light of the historical context and the broader purpose of the FAA, §§ 10 and 11 are best understood as a shield meant to protect parties from hostile courts, not a sword with which to cut down parties' "valid, irrevocable and enforceable" agreements to arbitrate their disputes subject to judicial review for errors of law. § 2.

Even if I thought the narrow issue presented in this case were as debatable as the conflict among the courts of appeals suggests, I would rely on a presumption of overriding importance to resolve the debate and rule in favor of petitioner's position that the FAA permits the statutory grounds for vacatur and modification of an award to be supplemented by contract. A decision "not to regulate" the terms of an agreement that does not even arguably offend any public policy whatsoever "is adequately justified by a presumption in favor of freedom."

Accordingly, while I agree that the judgment of the Court of Appeals must be set aside, and that there may be additional avenues available for judicial enforcement of parties' fairly negotiated review provisions, see, ante, at 1406—1408, I respectfully dissent from the Court's interpretation of the FAA, and would direct the Court of Appeals to affirm the judgment of the District Court enforcing the arbitrator's final award.

JUSTICE BREYER, dissenting.

The question presented in this case is whether "the Federal Arbitration Act . . . precludes a federal court from enforcing" an arbitration agreement that gives the court the power to set aside an arbitration award that embodies an arbitrator's mistake about the law. Pet. for Cert. i. Like the majority and Justice STEVENS, and primarily for the reasons they set forth, I believe that the Act does not preclude enforcement of such an agreement.

At the same time, I see no need to send the case back for further judicial decisionmaking. The agreement here was entered into with the consent of the parties and the approval of the District Court. Aside from the Federal Arbitration Act itself, 9 U.S.C. § 1 et seq., respondent below pointed to no statute, rule, or other relevant public policy that the agreement might violate. The Court has now rejected its argument that the agreement violates the Act, and I would simply remand the case with instructions that the Court of Appeals affirm the District Court's judgment enforcing the arbitrator's final award.

NOTES

Facts

1. How did the matter get to arbitration? Does the source of the consent to arbitration matter? Consider whether the parties before the dispute arose had a particular expectation of how their dispute would be handled.

2. How did legal correctness of the arbitral award enter the frame of discussion? Did the parties try to argue that legal correctness of some sort fit within the grounds listed in the FAA?

3. Could the parties have better structured their arbitration agreement in order to avoid the problem presented in this case? If you had been called upon to draft the arbitration agreement in this case, what would you have done differently?

Law

1. How does the majority conclude that the scope of review under the Federal Arbitration Act is limited to the specific grounds stated in the statute? What is the strongest support for their interpretation of the statute? What is the point that causes you the most problems?

2. How does Justice Breyer's dissent differ from the majority's approach? Does Justice Breyer think that there is a different set of laws that is applicable to the determination of the dispute than the majority?

3. What is the difference between Justice Breyer's approach and Justice Stevens' approach? Which do you think is narrower?

4. Re-read the majority opinion. Is there some other basis to resolve the case? Why do you think the parties failed to argue this point appropriately?

Stolt-Nielsen SA v. AnimalFeeds Intern. Corp.

548 F.3d 85 (2d Cir. 2008)

The facts of this case are excerpted in the United States Supreme Court decision reversing the Second Circuit on other grounds in Chapter 6.

* * *

B.   The Effect of Hall Street on the "Manifest Disregard" Doctrine

We pause to consider whether a recent Supreme Court decision, Hall Street Associates, L.L.C. v. Mattel, Inc., affects the scope or vitality of the "manifest disregard" doctrine.

There, the parties had entered into an arbitration agreement that, unlike the FAA, provided for a federal court's de novo review of the arbitrator's conclusions of law. The Court rejected the parties' attempt to contract around the FAA for expanded judicial review of arbitration awards, concluding that the grounds for vacatur of an arbitration award set forth in the FAA, 9 U.S.C. § 10, are "exclusive." Although the "manifest disregard" doctrine was not itself at issue, the *Hall Street* Court nonetheless commented on its origins:

> *"The Wilko Court . . . remarked (citing FAA § 10) that "[p]ower to vacate an [arbitration] award is limited," and went on to say that "the interpretations of the law by the arbitrators in contrast to manifest disregard [of the law] are not subject, in the federal courts, to judicial review for error in interpretation."*

> *"Maybe the term "manifest disregard" was meant to name a new ground for review, but maybe it merely referred to the § 10 grounds collectively, rather than adding to them. Or, as some courts have thought, "manifest disregard" may have been shorthand for § 10(a)(3) or § 10(a)(4), the subsections authorizing vacatur when the arbitrators were "guilty of misconduct" or "exceeded their powers."*

The Court declined to resolve that question explicitly, noting instead that it had never indicated, in *Wilko* or elsewhere, that "manifest disregard" was an independent basis for vacatur outside the grounds provided in section 10 of the FAA.

In the short time since *Hall Street* was decided, courts have begun to grapple with its implications for the "manifest disregard" doctrine. Some have concluded or suggested that the doctrine simply does not survive. See *Ramos-Santiago v. United Parcel Service*, 524 F.3d 120, 124 n. 3 (1st Cir.2008) (dicta); *Robert Lewis Rosen Assocs., Ltd. v. Webb*, 566 F.Supp.2d 228, 233 (S.D.N.Y.2008); *Prime Therapeutics LLC v. Omnicare, Inc.*, 555 F.Supp.2d 993, 999 (D.Minn.2008); *Hereford v. D.R. Horton, Inc.*, No. 1070396, 2008 WL 4097594, *5, 2008 Ala. LEXIS 186, *12–*13 (Ala. Sept. 5, 2008). Others think that "manifest disregard," reconceptualized as a judicial gloss on the specific grounds for vacatur enumerated in section 10 of the FAA, remains a valid ground for vacating arbitration awards. See *Mastec N. Am., Inc. v. MSE Power Sys., Inc.*, No. 1:08–cv–168, 2008 WL 2704912, at *3, 2008 U.S. Dist. LEXIS 52205, at *8–9 (N.D.N.Y. July 8, 2008); *Chase Bank USA, N.A. v. Hale*, 19 Misc.3d 975, 859 N.Y.S.2d 342, 349 (2008).

We agree with those courts that take the latter approach. The *Hall Street* Court held that the FAA sets forth the "exclusive" grounds for vacating an arbitration award. That holding is undeniably inconsistent with some dicta by this Court treating the "manifest disregard" standard as a ground for vacatur entirely separate from those enumerated in the FAA. *See, e.g., Hoeft*, 343 F.3d at 64 (describing manifest disregard as "an additional ground not prescribed in the [FAA]"); *Duferco*, 333 F.3d at 389 (observing that the doctrine's use is limited to instances "where none of the provisions of the FAA apply"); *DiRussa v. Dean Witter Reynolds Inc.*, 121 F.3d 818, 821 (2d Cir.1997) (referring to the doctrine as "judicially-created"), cert. denied, 522 U.S. 1049, 118 S.Ct. 695, 139 L.Ed.2d 639 (1998); *Merrill Lynch, Pierce, Fenner & Smith, Inc.*, 808 F.2d at 933 (same). But the *Hall Street* Court also speculated that "the term 'manifest disregard' . . . merely referred to the § 10 grounds collectively, rather than adding to them"-or as "shorthand for § 10(a)(3) or § 10(a)(4)." *Hall Street*, 128 S.Ct. at 1404. It did not, we think, abrogate the "manifest disregard" doctrine altogether.

We agree with the Seventh Circuit's view expressed before Hall Street was decided:

> *It is tempting to think that courts are engaged in judicial review of arbitration awards under the Federal Arbitration Act, but they are not. When parties agree to arbitrate their disputes they opt out of the court system, and when one of them challenges the resulting arbitration award he perforce does so not on the ground that the arbitrators made a mistake but that they violated the agreement to arbitrate, as by corruption, evident partiality, exceeding their powers, etc.-conduct to which the parties did not consent when they included an arbitration clause in their contract. That is why in the typical arbitration . . . the issue for the court is not whether the contract interpretation is incorrect or even wacky but whether the arbitrators had failed to interpret the contract at all, for only then were they exceeding the authority granted to them by the contract's arbitration clause.*

Wise v. Wachovia Sec., LLC, 450 F.3d 265, 269 (7th Cir.). This observation is entirely consistent with Hall Street. And it reinforces our own pre-*Hall Street* statements that our review for manifest disregard is "severely limited," "highly deferential," and confined to "those exceedingly rare instances" of "egregious impropriety on the part of the arbitrators." *Duferco*, 333 F.3d at 389.

Like the Seventh Circuit, we view the "manifest disregard" doctrine, and the FAA itself, as a mechanism to enforce the parties' agreements to arbitrate rather than as judicial review of the arbitrators' decision. We must therefore continue to bear the responsibility to vacate arbitration awards in the rare instances in which "the arbitrator knew of the relevant [legal] principle, appreciated that this principle controlled the outcome of the disputed issue, and nonetheless willfully flouted the governing law by refusing to apply it." *Westerbeke*, 304 F.3d at 217. At that point the arbitrators have "failed to interpret the contract at all," *Wise*, 450 F.3d at 269, for parties do not agree in advance to submit to arbitration that is carried out in manifest disregard of the law. Put another way, the arbitrators have thereby "exceeded their powers, or so imperfectly executed them that a mutual, final, and definite award upon the subject matter submitted was not made." 9 U.S.C. § 10(a)(4).

NOTES

1. What is the factual predicate for the manifest disregard at issue in *Stolt-Nielsen*?

2. Is there a way facially to re-plead the *Stolt-Nielsen* case to make it fit within the scope of the FAA grounds? Look at the Supreme Court decision—how does it resolve the issue?

3. Did the Second Circuit before Hall Street work under the assumption that manifest disregard was an additional common law ground for set aside of the award or did it consider that manifest disregard had a statutory basis in the FAA?

4. Did the Second Circuit change its mind in Stolt-Nielsen about the nature of manifest disregard?

B) State Court Grounds for Set Aside

The decision of the United States Supreme Court in Hall Street left open the possibility that states would provide an additional forum in which the parties could seek recourse against an arbitral award. As you might expect, litigants took the Supreme Court up on its offer, leading to the disposition in the case below.

Cable Connection, Inc. v. DirecTV, Inc.

44 Cal.4th 1334 (Cal. 2008)

CORRIGAN, J.

* * *

I.   BACKGROUND

Defendant DIRECTV, Inc., broadcasts television programming nationwide, via satellite. It contracts with retail dealers to provide customers with equipment needed to receive its satellite signal. In 1996, DIRECTV employed a "residential dealer agreement" for this purpose. A new "sales agency agreement" was used in 1998. Both agreements included arbitration clauses; neither mentioned classwide arbitration.

In 2001, dealers from four states filed suit in Oklahoma, asserting on behalf of a nationwide class that DIRECTV had wrongfully withheld commissions and assessed improper charges. DIRECTV moved to compel arbitration. As the Oklahoma court was considering whether the arbitration could be conducted on a classwide basis, the United States Supreme Court decided Green Tree Financial Corp. v. Bazzle * * * Accordingly, the Oklahoma court directed the parties to submit the matter to arbitration in Los Angeles as provided in the sales agency agreement.

After the dealers presented a statement of claim and demand for class arbitration in March 2004, a panel of three AAA arbitrators was selected. Following the procedure adopted by the AAA in response to *Bazzle*, the panel first addressed whether the parties' agreement permitted the arbitration to proceed on a classwide basis.

After briefing and argument, a majority of the panel decided that even though "the contract is silent and manifests no intent on this issue," arbitration on a classwide basis was authorized under *Blue Cross of California v. Superior Court* (1998) 67 Cal.App.4th 42 (Blue Cross), and *Keating v. Superior Court* (1982) 31 Cal.3d 584 * * *. The majority deemed the question one of substantive California law, though it also relied on AAA rules and policy governing class arbitration. The award emphasized that class arbitration was not necessarily required in this case; it was merely permitted by the contract. Whether the arbitration would actually be maintained on a classwide basis would be the subject of a future hearing.

The dissenting arbitrator found that the sales agency agreement provided "ample indication" the parties had contemplated arbitration only on an individual basis. He reasoned that Blue Cross and Keating did not apply because they addressed the discretion of a court to permit classwide arbitration, based not on contractual intent but on policy considerations reflected in the CAA. Under *Bazzle*, on the other hand, this determination is for arbitrators to make based on the terms of the contract. The dissent considered the availability of classwide arbitration to be a procedural issue subject to the FAA and AAA rules, under the terms of the arbitration clause.

DIRECTV petitioned to vacate the award, contending (1) the majority had exceeded its authority by substituting its discretion for the parties' intent regarding class arbitration; (2) the majority had improperly ignored extrinsic evidence of contractual intent; and (3) even if the majority had not exceeded the authority generally granted to arbitrators, the award reflected errors of law that the arbitration clause placed beyond their powers and made subject to judicial review. The dealers responded that the majority had properly applied California law and had not refused to receive extrinsic evidence. The trial court vacated the award, essentially accepting all of DIRECTV's arguments.

The Court of Appeal reversed, holding that the trial court exceeded its jurisdiction by reviewing the merits of the arbitrators' decision. Although in the trial court the dealers did not question whether a contract may provide for an expanded scope of judicial review, the Court of Appeal deemed it an important matter of public policy, suitable for consideration for the first time on appeal. The court agreed with two previous Court of Appeal decisions holding such provisions unenforceable. It concluded that the provision for judicial review in this case was severable from the remainder of the arbitration agreement, and directed the trial court to confirm the award.

We granted DIRECTV's petition for review.

II.   DISCUSSION

A.   Contract Provisions for Judicial Review of Arbitration Awards

* * *

2.   *Hall Street* and the Question of Preemption

* * *

Despite this strict reading of the FAA, the *Hall Street* majority left the door ajar for alternate routes to an expanded scope of review. "In holding that §§ 10 and 11 provide exclusive regimes for the review provided by the statute, we do not purport to say that they exclude more searching review based on authority outside the statute as well. The FAA is not the only way into court for parties wanting review of arbitration awards: they may contemplate enforcement under state statutory or common law, for example, where judicial review of different scope is arguable. But here we speak only to the scope of the expeditious judicial review under §§ 9, 10, and 11, deciding nothing about other possible avenues for judicial enforcement of arbitration awards."

Furthermore, the *Hall Street* majority recognized that the trial court's case management authority under rule 16 of the Federal Rules of Civil Procedure might support its order adopting the parties' agreement to review of the merits. However, it remanded for further proceedings on this point, concluding that it was "in no position to address the question now, beyond noting the claim of relevant case management authority independent of the FAA."

In dissent, Justice Stevens, joined by Justice Kennedy, took issue with the majority's view of the policy served by the FAA. He argued that "in light of the historical context and the broader purpose of the FAA, §§ 10 and 11 are best understood as a shield meant to protect parties from hostile courts, not a sword with which to cut down parties' 'valid, irrevocable and enforceable' agreements to arbitrate their disputes subject to judicial review for errors of law.[11] § 2." Justice Stevens agreed that "there may be additional avenues available for judicial enforcement of parties' fairly negotiated review provisions" but he would have resolved the conflict among the federal circuits in favor of the parties' freedom to supplement by contract the statutory grounds for vacatur and modification, "an agreement that does not even arguably offend any public policy whatsoever."

Justice Breyer also dissented. He too agreed with the majority that the FAA " 'is not the only way into court for parties wanting review of arbitration awards.' " Justice Breyer, however, would have remanded with instructions to affirm the trial court's judgment, apparently on the basis that the FAA had no effect on the court's independent authority to approve the parties' agreement as a matter of case management. (Id. at pp. 595–596, 128 S.Ct. at p. 1410.)

The dealers in this case urge us to follow the rationale of the *Hall Street* majority. They contend that any other construction of the CAA would result in its preemption by the FAA. Alternatively, they argue that Hall Street provides a persuasive analysis of the FAA that should be applied to the similar CAA provisions governing judicial review. We consider first the question of preemption, because if the dealers are correct on that point, it would be fruitless to consider alternate interpretations of state law.

Section 2 of the FAA, declaring the enforceability of arbitration agreements, "create[s] a body of federal substantive law of arbitrability, applicable to any arbitration agreement within the coverage of the Act." The FAA governs agreements in contracts involving interstate commerce, like those in this case. The United States Supreme Court has frequently held that state laws invalidating arbitration agreements on grounds applicable only to arbitration provisions contravene the policy of enforceability established by section 2 of the FAA, and are therefore preempted.

However, "the United States Supreme Court does not read the FAA's procedural provisions to apply to state court proceedings." Sections 3 and 4 of the FAA, governing stays of litigation and petitions to enforce arbitration agreements, do not apply in state court. As we have noted, the provisions for judicial review of arbitration awards in sections 10 and 11 of the FAA are directed to "the United States court in and for the district where the award was made." We have held that similar language in sections 3 and 4 of the FAA reflects Congress's intent to limit the application of those provisions to federal courts.

In several cases, California Courts of Appeal have rejected claims that the FAA grounds for reviewing arbitration awards preempt their CAA counterparts. The *Siegel* court, after reviewing the legislative history of the FAA, noted that "[n]othing in the legislative reports and debates evidences a congressional intention that postaward and state court litigation rules be preempted so long as the basic policy upholding the enforceability of arbitration agreements remained in full force and effect."

Thus, as in *Cronus* and *Rosenthal,* the FAA's procedural provisions are not controlling, and the determinative question is whether CAA procedures conflict with the FAA policy favoring the enforcement of arbitration agreements.

Before *Hall Street,* we would have had no difficulty concluding that enforcing agreements for judicial review on the merits is consistent with the fundamental purpose of the FAA. The high court has made it clear that the FAA does not "prevent[ ] the enforcement of agreements to arbitrate under different rules than those set forth in the Act itself. Indeed, such a result would be quite inimical to the FAA's primary purpose of ensuring that private agreements to arbitrate are enforced according to their terms. Arbitration under the Act is a matter of consent, not coercion, and parties are generally free to structure their arbitration agreements as they see fit. Just as they may limit by contract the issues which they will arbitrate [citation], so too may they specify by contract the rules under which that arbitration will be conducted. Where . . . the parties have agreed to abide by state rules of arbitration, enforcing those rules according to the terms of the agreement is fully consistent with the goals of the FAA. . . . By permitting the courts to 'rigorously enforce' such agreements according to their terms [citation], we give effect to the contractual rights and expectations of the parties, without doing violence to the policies behind by the FAA."

The court has repeatedly ruled that the terms of the parties' agreement are controlling over considerations of expediency in the dispute resolution process. "After all, the basic objective in this area is not to resolve disputes in the quickest manner possible, no matter what the parties' wishes [citation], but to ensure that commercial arbitration agreements, like other contracts, ' "are enforced according to their terms," ' [citations], and according to the intentions of the parties [citations]." The court has viewed the federal policy served by the FAA as "at bottom a policy guaranteeing the enforcement of private contractual arrangements."

The *Hall Street* majority, however, brushed aside policy considerations favoring the enforcement of contractual arbitration arrangements, concentrating instead on whether "the FAA has textual features at odds with enforcing a contract to expand judicial review following the arbitration." Underlying the FAA provisions governing judicial review, it discerned "a national policy favoring arbitration with just the limited review needed to maintain arbitration's essential virtue of resolving disputes straightaway."

Nevertheless, we do not believe the *Hall Street* majority intended to declare a policy with preemptive effect in all cases involving interstate commerce. *Hall Street* was a federal case governed by federal law; the court considered no question of competing state law. It reviewed the application of FAA provisions for judicial review that speak only to the federal courts. The court unanimously left open other avenues for judicial review, including those provided by state statutory or common law. While the court, of course, decided nothing about the viability of these alternatives, their mention in the majority opinion indicates that Hall Street's holding on the effect of the FAA is a limited one.

Moreover, the *Hall Street* majority's disposition of the case before it suggests that its interpretation of sections 10 and 11 of the FAA does not preclude other grounds for review. Rather than simply affirming the reversal of the judgment modifying the arbitrator's award, the majority vacated and remanded for consideration of the trial court's authority to approve the parties' agreement as a matter of case management under the Federal Rules of Civil Procedure. Had the majority meant to impose a uniform national policy requiring judicial review solely on the grounds stated in the FAA, it would not have left open the possibility of trial court review under its "case management authority independent of the FAA."

We conclude that the *Hall Street* holding is restricted to proceedings to review arbitration awards under the FAA, and does not require state law to conform with its limitations. Furthermore, a reading of the CAA that permits the enforcement of agreements for merits review is fully consistent with the FAA "policy guaranteeing the enforcement of private contractual arrangements."

3.   *Moncharsh* and the California Rule

In *Moncharsh*, the parties' arbitration clause included no provision for an expanded scope of judicial review. We considered and rejected the appellant's claim that the award was nevertheless reviewable for error of law on its face causing substantial injustice, a proposition which had some support in case law. We reaffirmed "the general rule that an arbitrator's decision is not ordinarily reviewable for error by either the trial or appellate courts", and held that the statutory grounds for review were intended to implement that rule. To that extent, our conclusions were consistent with those of the *Hall Street* majority. However, in several respects *Moncharsh* reflects a very different view of arbitration agreements and the arbitration statutes, as applied to the scope of judicial review. Therefore, we disagree with the dealers' argument that *Hall Street* is persuasive authority for a restrictive interpretation of the review provisions in the CAA.

Moncharsh began from the premise that " '[t]he scope of arbitration is . . . a matter of agreement between the parties' [citation], and ' "[t]he powers of an arbitrator are limited and circumscribed by the agreement or stipulation of submission." ' " " 'The policy of the law in recognizing arbitration agreements and in providing by statute for their enforcement is to encourage persons who wish to avoid delays incident to a civil action to obtain an adjustment of their differences by a tribunal of their own choosing. [Citation.]' " "Because the decision to arbitrate grievances evinces the parties' intent to bypass the judicial system and thus avoid potential delays at the trial and appellate levels, arbitral finality is a core component of the parties' agreement to submit to arbitration. Thus, an arbitration decision is final and conclusive because the parties have agreed that it be so. By ensuring that an arbitrator's decision is final and binding, courts simply assure that the parties receive the benefit of their bargain."

* * *

Our reasoning in Moncharsh centered not on statutory restriction of the parties' contractual options, but on the parties' intent and the powers of the arbitrators as defined in the agreement. These factors support the enforcement of agreements for an expanded scope of review. If the parties constrain the arbitrators' authority by requiring a dispute to be decided according to the rule of law, and make plain their intention that the award is reviewable for legal error, the general rule of limited review has been displaced by the parties' agreement. Their expectation is not that the result of the arbitration will be final and conclusive, but rather that it will be reviewed on the merits at the request of either party. That expectation has a foundation in the statutes governing judicial review, which include the ground that "[t]he arbitrators exceeded their powers."

We have consistently recognized that "[a]n exception to the general rule assigning broad powers to the arbitrators arises when the parties have, in either the contract or an agreed submission to arbitration, explicitly and unambiguously limited those powers. The powers of an arbitrator derive from, and are limited by, the agreement to arbitrate. [Citation.] Awards in excess of those powers may, under sections 1286.2 and 1286.6, be corrected or vacated by the court.' " Our review in *Moncharsh* of the CAA's legislative history confirms that while the statutory grounds for correction and vacation of arbitration awards do not ordinarily include errors of law, contractual limitations on the arbitrators' powers can alter the usual scope of review.

* * *

A provision requiring arbitrators to apply the law leaves open the possibility that they are empowered to apply it "wrongly as well as rightly." As we recently observed: "When parties contract to resolve their disputes by private arbitration, their agreement ordinarily contemplates that the arbitrator will have the power to decide any question of contract interpretation, historical fact or general law necessary, in the arbitrator's understanding of the case, to reach a decision. Inherent in that power is the possibility the arbitrator may err in deciding some aspect of the case. Arbitrators do not ordinarily exceed their contractually created powers simply by reaching an erroneous conclusion on a contested issue of law or fact, and arbitral awards may not ordinarily be vacated because of such error, for ' "[t]he arbitrator's resolution of these issues is what the parties bargained for in the arbitration agreement." '

Therefore, to take themselves out of the general rule that the merits of the award are not subject to judicial review, the parties must clearly agree that legal errors are an excess of arbitral authority that is reviewable by the courts. Here, the parties expressly so agreed, depriving the arbitrators of the power to commit legal error. They also specifically provided for judicial review of such error. We do not decide here whether one or the other of these clauses alone, or some different formulation, would be sufficient to confer an expanded scope of review. However, we emphasize that parties seeking to allow judicial review of the merits, and to avoid an additional dispute over the scope of review, would be well advised to provide for that review explicitly and unambiguously.

Those Court of Appeal opinions refusing to enforce specific provisions for judicial review of the merits are disapproved insofar as they conflict with our analysis. The objections raised in these cases are outweighed by the freedom of contract that is fundamental to arbitration, by the availability of an expanded scope of review in other contexts, and by the considerable public and private benefits that such review can provide.

Review on the merits has been deemed incompatible with the goals of finality and informality that are served by arbitration and protected by the arbitration statutes. However, as discussed above, those policies draw their strength from the agreement of the parties. It is the parties who are best situated to weigh the advantages of traditional arbitration against the benefits of court review for the correction of legal error.

* * *

The benefits of enforcing agreements like the one before us are considerable, for both the parties and the courts. The development of alternative dispute resolution is advanced by enabling private parties to choose procedures with which they are comfortable. Commentators have observed that provisions for expanded judicial review are a product of market forces operating in an increasingly "judicialized" arbitration setting, with many of the attributes of court proceedings. The desire for the protection afforded by review * *606 for legal error has evidently developed from the experience of sophisticated parties in high stakes cases, where the arbitrators' awards deviated from the parties' expectations in startling ways.

The judicial system reaps little benefit from forcing parties to choose between the risk of an erroneous arbitration award and the burden of litigating their dispute entirely in court. Enforcing contract provisions for review of awards on the merits relieves pressure on congested trial court dockets. Courts are spared not only the burden of conducting a trial, but also the complications of discovery disputes and other pretrial proceedings. Incorporating traditional judicial review by express agreement preserves the utility of arbitration as a way to obtain expert factual determinations without delay, while allowing the parties to protect themselves from perhaps the weakest aspect of the arbitral process, its handling of disputed rules of law.

There are also significant benefits to the development of the common law when arbitration awards are made subject to merits review by the parties' agreement. "[I]f courts are reduced to the function of merely enforcing or denying arbitral awards, without an opportunity to discuss the reasoning for the arbitral decision, the advancement of the law is stalled, as arbitral decisions carry no precedential value. [Fn. omitted.] Thus, expansion of judicial review gives the courts of first instance the opportunity to establish a record, and to include the reasoning of expert arbitrators into the body of the law in the form of written decisions. This procedure better advances the state of the law and facilitates the necessary beneficial input from experts in the field."

* * *

III. DISPOSITION

We reverse the judgment of the Court of Appeal, with directions to instruct the trial court to vacate the award so that the arbitrators may redetermine whether the arbitration may proceed on a classwide basis.

Concurring and Dissenting Opinion by MORENO, J.

I agree with the majority to the extent it holds that parties may define the arbitrator's powers in such a way as to broaden somewhat the scope of judicial review beyond the usual narrow grounds for such review set forth in *Moncharsh v. Heily & Blase.* But I disagree that parties may oblige courts to undertake fullscale judicial review of legal error in arbitration awards. Rather, the relevant statutes and the pertinent legislative history reveals a legislative intent to circumscribe the scope of judicial review and defer to the judgment of the arbitrator. As elaborated below, the statutes permit an arbitration agreement to be structured in such a way as to compel a court to vacate an award when the arbitrator, in addressing legal questions, has acted arbitrarily and unreasonably, such as departing from clearly defined contractual terms or from clear legal principles found in the body of law that the parties have agreed should be used to settle the dispute. On the other hand, when an arbitrator's answer to a legal question is not clearly erroneous, for example, when he or she reasonably answers a legal question in which there is no settled precedent, the statute does not authorize a court to vacate an arbitrator's award merely because it disagrees with the arbitrator's conclusions, no matter what the arbitration agreement provides. Because the arbitrators in this case acted reasonably in addressing a question of unsettled law, I would affirm the judgment of the Court of Appeal.

I.

I begin the analysis by stating the obvious, although the point may be obscured by the majority's rhetoric regarding freedom of contract. Although arbitration is created by contract, and the terms of the arbitration are dictated by contractual provisions, courts are not parties to arbitration agreements, and they are not bound by their terms. Parties can agree that a legal dispute arising from their arbitration will be settled by the California Supreme Court, but this court is not bound by that agreement. The judicial acts of confirming, correcting or vacating arbitration awards are governed by statute, and the parties have no power to alter the circumstances under which such acts occur except to the extent that the relevant statutes permit such alteration. I therefore turn to an analysis of the governing statutes.

* * *

The single "textual hook" on which the majority seeks to hang its expansion of judicial review is the statutory provision that the award may be vacated when "[t]he arbitrators exceeded their powers." It is well established that arbitrators do not exceed their powers merely by committing legal error. As one Court of Appeal summarized the case law: "An arbitrator exceeds his powers when he acts without subject matter jurisdiction [citation], decides an issue that was not submitted to arbitration [citations], arbitrarily remakes the contract [citation], upholds an illegal contract [citation], issues an award that violates a well-defined public policy [citation], issues an award that violates a statutory right [citation], fashions a remedy that is not rationally related to the contract [citation], or selects a remedy not authorized by law [citations]. In other words, an arbitrator exceeds his powers when he acts in a manner not authorized by the contract or by law." In reviewing an arbitration award, a court "must give substantial deference to the arbitrator's own assessment of his contractual authority."

The majority faults the *Hall Street* court for failing to consider "whether the FAA provision for vacatur 'where the arbitrators exceeded their powers' is applicable when the agreement specifically limits the arbitrators' powers by providing for an award governed by law and reviewable for legal error." Yet the majority does not itself analyze whether this excess of powers clause provides textual support for full judicial review of legal error. Had it done so, it would have run up against the *noscitur a sociis* rule of construction, a close cousin of the *ejusdem generis* rule invoked by the Hall Street court. *Noscitur a sociis* (it is known by its associates) is the principle that "a word takes meaning from the company it keeps." " 'In accordance with this principle of construction, a court will adopt a restrictive meaning of a listed item if acceptance of a more expansive meaning would . . . make the item markedly dissimilar to the other items in the list.' "

In the case of section 1286.2, the enumerated grounds for vacating an arbitration award involve either some type of misconduct by the arbitrator, or some type of arbitrary action by the arbitrator that deprives a party of basic procedural fairness, such as the failure to postpone a hearing on sufficient cause, denial of the right to put on material evidence, or the failure to make statutorily required disclosures regarding conflicts of interest. The types of conduct falling within the excess of powers clause, as interpreted by case law discussed above, fit the mold of section 1286.2, inasmuch as this statute is primarily designed to guard against arbitrary extension of the arbitrator's jurisdiction to decide questions or fashion remedies beyond the scope of the arbitration agreement. Judicial review of these types of objectionable conduct keeps courts at a distance from the merits of the controversy, and confines judicial scrutiny instead to basic questions of procedural fairness and jurisdictional propriety, while giving considerable although not unlimited deference to the arbitrator's judgment calls. It is arguably the case that an arbitrator's refusal to follow well-settled legal principles arising from a body of law that the parties have agreed to follow, when the parties have explicitly constrained the arbitrator to follow that body of law, is that kind of arbitrary behavior that belongs within the scope of section 1286.2. As discussed below, the legislative history of that section supports this interpretation.

But it is difficult to imagine that the Legislature intended to apply this excess of powers provision to a situation in which an arbitrator reasonably answers an unsettled question of law, which answer is not clearly wrong at the time the arbitrator made his or her award. It seems barely conceivable, especially in light of the surrounding provisions of section 1286.2 involving arbitral misconduct, or arbitrary action, that the Legislature intended the phrase "arbitrators exceeded their powers" to include a situation in which neither has occurred, and in which the arbitrator has merely given to a question of law an answer with which a reviewing court may disagree.

* * *

NOTES

Facts

1. What is the language in the arbitration clause that is at issue in this case?

2. What is the factual predicate of the challenge to the arbitrators' decision? Is there a way to replead the issue within the scope of the statutory grounds?

Law

1. What is the legal regime applied by the California Supreme Court? Did the California Supreme Court apply state arbitration statutes or common law? How does the dissent characterize the applicable law analysis undertaken by the majority?

2. Why the FAA not preempt in this case? Do you agree? What is the strongest point to support the majority's determination on this point? What is the strongest argument against the decision?

3. What is the statutory basis to support the majority's conclusion? Would this statutory basis similarly be available in the context of the FAA?

4. As counsel drafting an arbitration clause, how does the California Supreme Court's ruling influence your choice of California as a jurisdiction in which to conduct arbitration? Is it more or less attractive than states adopting the *Hall Street* approach as applicable within their state contexts as well?

C) Appellate Arbitration

Arbitral institutions have responded to *Hall Street* by providing their own arbitral review mechanisms. These mechanisms do not fall under judicial review of arbitral awards but are a second layer of arbitral review.

AAA Appellate Rule 10

A–10.   Issues Subject to Appeal

A party may appeal on the grounds that the Underlying Award is based upon:

(1)   an error of law that is material and prejudicial; or

(2)   determinations of fact that are clearly erroneous.

NOTES

1. How do the grounds for appeal differ from the bases for set aside in the FAA? Would it be possible to contract for review on the basis of these grounds in California? According to the *Cable Connection* majority? How about the dissent?

2. What is an "error of law that is material and prejudicial"? Does the error of law have to be dispositive in its own right? Are there non dispositive errors of law which you could argue are material and prejudicial?

3. Do the determinations of fact have to be material to the outcome? Assume that the award incorrectly added a middle initial to the names of one of the parties. Assume further that this would be in clear error. What next?

4. Consider the practice in reasoned arbitral awards to provide alternative rationales for decision. Do the grounds for appeal have to affect each

alternative rationale? Is it sufficient for the party seeking review to prove that one of the alternative rationales is subject to appeal to succeed?

Matthew Allison & Kyle Olson, Recent Rule Changes by the AAA, Optional Appellate Rules Adopted by the AAA November 1, 2013

* * *

Jurisdiction of Arbitration Appeal Tribunal and Issues Subject to Appeal

The Appellate Rules provide that the appeal tribunal "shall have the power to rule on its own jurisdiction, including any objections with respect to the existence, scope or validity of the arbitration agreement." If the appeal tribunal determines that it lacks jurisdiction to hear the appeal, "the appeal shall be dismissed and the Underlying Award shall be deemed to be final." Rule A–9.

The Appellate Rules also specify two independent grounds on which parties may appeal an arbitration award. Namely, a party may seek appellate review for: (1) "an error of law that is material and prejudicial"; or (2) "determinations of fact that are clearly erroneous". Rule A–10. Although this Rule plainly contemplates some level of deference upon an original arbitration panel's legal and factual findings, it is not entirely clear whether such deference neatly equates to any standards of judicial review used by appellate courts. In particular, neither this Rule, nor any other of the Appellate Rules, provides that legal errors by the original arbitration panel should be reviewed de novo as would be the case in appellate court. Without the express benefit of a judicially analogous standard of review, arbitration appeal tribunals may be left to themselves to define the precise meaning of "material and prejudicial" for the purpose of determining whether to reverse or modify an underlying arbitral award for legal error.

Structure of Arbitration Appeal Proceeding

All arbitration appeals under the Appellate Rules "will be determined upon the written documents submitted by the parties" "unless otherwise directed by the appeal tribunal." The appeal tribunal has the discretion to set oral argument upon request by a party or if the tribunal "deems oral argument necessary". Rule A–15(a). Any request for oral argument must be made "within thirty (30) days of service of the Notice of Appeal or it is waived." If the appeal tribunal grants oral argument, "it shall be scheduled to take place within thirty (30) days of filing of the last brief." Rule A–15(b).

Within one week of the appeal tribunal being appointed, the appeal tribunal and the Case Manager will schedule a conference call with all of the parties. On that call, the appeal tribunal will, among other things, set a briefing schedule as well as a deadline by which the parties must submit a record on appeal. Rule A–7(a). The Rules require the parties to "cooperate" in "compiling the record on appeal". Rule A–16. The parties "may" submit "relevant excerpts of the transcript of the arbitration hearing giving rise to the Underlying Award", any expert reports, deposition transcripts or affidavits that were submitted as part of the arbitration hearing, documentary evidence admitted into evidence during the arbitration hearing, "pre- and post-hearing briefs" of both parties, "or other evidence relevant to the appeal that was presented at the arbitration hearing." Importantly, however, a "party may not present for the first time on appeal an issue or evidence that was not raised during the arbitration hearing." Moreover, any disputes as to whether a document is part of the record on appeal "shall be determined by the appeal tribunal." Id.

The Rules provide a default briefing schedule under which the appellant has 21 days to file an "initial brief" of 30 pages. Rule A–17(a). The Appellee, in turn, has 21 days after service of the appellant's "initial brief" to file an "answer brief" and/or an initial "cross appeal" brief, each also limited to 30 pages. Rule A–17(b). The parties are each entitled to then file a reply brief, limited to 10 double-spaced pages, within 10 days of service of the opposing party's answer brief. Rule A–17(d),(f). One extension may be granted for "good cause shown", and an additional extension may be granted "in extraordinary circumstances" and subject to the discretion of the appeal tribunal. Rule A–17(g). Within thirty days of service of the last brief, the appeal tribunal must either render a decision or request additional information "and notify the parties of the tribunal's exercise of an option to extend the time to render a decision, not to exceed thirty (30) days." Rule A–19(a)(1)–(3).

Form of Appeal Decision and Finality of Appeal

In rendering its appeal decision, the appeal tribunal may "adopt the Underlying Award as its own, or, substitute its own award for the Underlying Award (incorporating those aspects of the Underlying Award that are not vacated or modified)". Rule A–19(a)(1)–(2). The appeal tribunal's decision, unless the parties agree otherwise, "shall be in writing and shall include a concise summary of the decision and an explanation for the decision." Rule A–19(c). The Rules require a "majority", though not unanimity, of arbitrators comprising the appeal tribunal to reach the decision. Additionally, the appeal tribunal does not have the authority to order a new arbitration hearing or send the case back to the original arbitration panel for corrections or further review. Rule A–19(a). The Rules make clear that the "appeal tribunal's decision shall become the final award for purposes of the enforcement proceedings." Rule A–20.

Other than Rule 20's reference to judicial enforcement proceedings, the Appellate Rules do not address whether, and how, the arbitration appellate process affects enforcement of, or challenges to, a final arbitration award in court. Specifically, the Federal Arbitration Act ("FAA") allows for arbitration awards to be vacated where: (1) the award was procured through fraud, corruption, or undue means; (2) the arbitrator was plainly biased; (3) the arbitrator was guilty of misconduct in refusing to postpone the hearing, upon sufficient cause shown, or in refusing to hear evidence pertinent and materials to the controversy, or any other misbehavior by which the rights of any party have been prejudiced; or (4) the arbitrator exceeded his or her powers. The Appellate Rules do not express a view as to whether a reviewing court's evaluation of any of these bases, for purposes of enforcing or vacating an arbitration award, should change in light of the newly established arbitration appeals process. As a result, reviewing courts will likely have to address whether the same standard of judicial review that applies to an arbitration award rendered by a single panel likewise applies to a final award rendered by an arbitration appeal tribunal.

CHAPTER 23

Set Aside for Excess of Powers and Manifest Disregard of Law

Fact Scenario

In reviewing the record, both Hardmont and Acme discover the following evidence that could have been important to the determination made by the tribunal's alter ego finding, but that was not discussed in the context of the award:

1. Hardmont introduced new expert testimony at the evidentiary hearing regarding the personal benefit Gilmore derived from the RRF transactions at issue and that he would have lost significant amounts of money on RRF but for use of the designs at issue in the case. Acme et al. objected that the introduction of the evidence was untimely per the tribunal's procedural orders. The tribunal permitted the testimony "for what it is worth".

2. On cross-examination, Hardmont's expert then admitted that it would be impossible to link the damages to the use of the confidential information at issue in the dispute—and that designs frequently overlap in the industry.

3. Hardmont's chief witness admitted on cross-examination that the "confidential information" would likely have been in the hands of many of Hardmont's competitors because Hardmont's market research was based upon questions typically included in market research studies and because Hardmont used an industry-leading market research firm.

4. Gilmore testified that he may have left the market study on a coffee table flipped open to the first page (detailing the methodology) when RRF's project lead was by to discuss financial data.

Prepare argument whether/how the tribunal proceeded in a manner that makes its award susceptible to set aside.

Readings

Federal Arbitration Act, § 10

(a)   In any of the following cases the United States court in and for the district wherein the award was made may make an order vacating the award upon the application of any party to the arbitration—

. . .

(3)   where the arbitrators were guilty of misconduct in refusing to postpone the hearing, upon sufficient cause shown, or in refusing to hear evidence pertinent and material to the controversy; or of any other misbehavior by which the rights of any party have been prejudiced;

NOTES

1.   Do arbitrators always have to postpone a hearing upon request by one of the parties? How do you determine if cause shown was "sufficient"? How do you review that issue?

2.   The focus of the next ground for set aside concerns refusal to hear evidence. Logically, can you make an argument that the admission of evidence can constitute a refusal to hear evidence from the other side? What would have to be the case for that argument to be plausible?

3.   If you combine the first two elements of FAA, section 10(a)(3), could you make an argument that the late admission of evidence constitutes good cause to postpone a hearing?

4.   What kind of conduct do you think fits in the catch all at the end of FAA, section 10(a)(3)? Is it any kind of due process failure or just failures that concern the admission of evidence upon good cause shown?

Al-Haddad Commodities Corp. v.
Toepfer International Asia Pte., Ltd.

485 F. Supp. 2d 677 (E.D. Va. 2007).

Al-Haddad Commodities Corporation (ACC) entered into a contract to purchase rice from Toepfer which the latter was to deliver by December 31, 2005 "at the latest". The contract incorporated the terms and conditions of the Grain and Feed Trade Association (GAFTA) and called for arbitration under U.S. Rice Millers Association (RMA) Rules and Regulations. When a dispute arose regarding timely delivery, ACC commenced arbitration before the RMA. In issuing an award for damages in favor of ACC, the arbitral tribunal found while ACC had breached its duty to provide a bank guarantee for demurrage (delays associated with unloading), Toepfer had waived that breach by failing to timely arrange for loading and shipment of the rice. ACC filed a petition in U.S. district court seeking to confirm and enforce the arbitral award. Toepfer filed a motion opposing enforcement and seeking to vacate the award.

DOUMAR, J.

[. . .]

1.   Misconduct

Toepfer alleges that the arbitrators were "guilty of misconduct" under *§ 10(a)(3)* because the Panel (1) failed to postpone the arbitration hearing despite Toepfer's request that it do so; (2) failed to consider the parties' submissions prior to the hearing; (3) permitted a witness to testify by telephone instead of by video link, as planned, and without a previously disclosed witness statement; and (4) limited the presentation of evidence and argument. [. . .]

a.   The Panel's Refusal to Postpone the Hearing

Toepfer's alleges "misconduct" in the Panel's decisions to hold a hearing "just six weeks" after the arbitration was demanded, and to reject Toepfer's request to adjourn the arbitration hearings until March 2007 to provide more time for discovery. Mot. in Opp. at 4.

In its letter to the RMA asking for an arbitration, ACC requested an immediate hearing. Mem. in Supp., Bulow Aff. P 7. On October 19, 2006, Lee Adams of American Rice Inc., the Chairman of the RMA, notified the parties that a hearing in the matter would be held in Houston, Texas, on December 12, 2006. See Mot. in Opp. Ex. F, Letter of Oct. 19, 2006. On November, 15, 2006, Toepfer requested that the hearings be adjourned until March 2007 because the December 12 date was "completely unrealistic" in light of discovery demands. See id. Ex. I, Email from Helle Kjaerstad of Nov. 15, 2006. ACC vehemently objected. Id. Exs. J, K. The Panel, in a pre-hearing order issued by email on November 17, 2006, refused to change the date of the hearing. See id. Ex. M, Email from Lee R. Marks of Nov. 17, 2006.

A court "may vacate an arbitration award when a request for postponement is arbitrarily denied or when the denial leads to the inability of the party to present 'pertinent and material evidence.' " [. . .] An arbitral panel should be granted a degree of discretion, however, as long as it had a "reasonable basis" for refusing to postpone. *Investor Relations Servs.*, 2006 U.S. Dist. LEXIS 65948, 2006 WL 2571028, at *3 (quoting *Naing*, 961 F. Supp. at 3 and *Fairchild*, 516 F. Supp. at 1313–14)).The Court finds nothing arbitrary in the Panel's refusal to postpone the hearing. RMA Arbitration Rule 7 states, "[a]ll arbitrations shall be held at a place and time designated by the Arbitration Committee." Pet. to Confirm Ex. C, Arbitration Rule 7. Arbitration Rule 9(a) provides that "[t]he arbitrators shall proceed expeditiously to establish the facts of the case by all appropriate means." Id. Rule 9(a). The Panel did just that by scheduling and holding a hearing on December 12, 2006, eleven weeks after ACC submitted the dispute for arbitration. There is no evidence that the Panel's refusal to postpone the hearing was made in bad faith or for self-serving reasons, or that the refusal to postpone resulted in the exclusion of pertinent and material evidence. [. . .] Respondents cite no rule that was violated by the Panel's failure to "provid[e] grounds for its decision" to refuse to push back the hearing date. See Mot. in Opp. at 5. Whether it was "not unreasonable for Toepfer to request that the arbitration hearing be adjourned" is irrelevant. Id. The Court finds no basis for vacating the Award on this ground.

b.   The Panel's Consideration of the Parties' Submissions

Toepfer's next contention is that the Panel was "guilty of misconduct . . . in refusing to hear evidence pertinent and material to the controversy," *§ 10(a)(3)*, in particular by failing to consider the written evidence and documents submitted by the parties prior to the hearing. See Mot. in Opp. at 6 (citing Duffy Aff. P 88(b) & Id. Ex. Z, Mark T. O'Neil Aff., PP 9, 15–16, & 28).

On the morning of the hearing, the Panel permitted, over Toepfer's objection, ACC to present additional documentary evidence and a legal opinion from Queen's Counsel Timothy Young concerning points of English law on the construction of the Contract. Id. Duffy Aff. P 88(a)–(b); see id. Ex. AA, Legal Opinion of Timothy Young. Mr. O'Neil had received Mr. Young's opinion by email from Ms. Bulow on the evening of December 11, 2006, but, lacking Internet access, was unable to read it until being provided a copy by fax from his London Office the following morning prior to the hearing. Id. Ex. Z, O'Neil Aff. P 8. Toepfer argues that the Panel "did not review, and could not have reviewed," the additional evidence and Mr. Young's twenty-four page legal opinion prior to the hearing. Id. Duffy Aff. P 88(b). According to Mr. O'Neil, the presentation of Mr. Young's legal opinion was a violation of the Panel's November 17, 2006, order that "[a]ny submissions by a party relevant to English law shall be produced within 14 days." See Mem. in Supp., Bulow Aff. Ex. 2, Email from Lee R. Marks of Nov. 17, 2006. [. . .]

A federal court may vacate an arbitrator's award only if the arbitrator's refusal to hear pertinent and material evidence deprives a person of a "fundamentally fair hearing." [. . .]

Under this circumscribed standard of review, the Court refuses to second-guess the Panel's ruling allowing ACC to present Mr. Young's expert opinion. First, the Panel's decision to allow Mr. Young's opinion resulted in the *inclusion* of evidence, not the *exclusion* of evidence, and, as such, is plainly not a "refus[al] to hear evidence" under *§ 10(a)(3)*. There is no evidence that the Panel ignored Toepfer's submissions on English law. On December 6, 2006, three business days before the hearing—and five days after the Panel's fourteen-day deadline for submitting opinions on English law—Toepfer submitted two affidavits totaling sixty-five pages, a seventeen-page opinion by two barristers, and 121 pages of exhibits. Mem. in Supp., Bulow Aff. P 11. In addition, it is less than clear that Mr. Young's opinion was "pertinent and material to the controversy." *§ 10(a)(3)*. According to Ms. Bulow, Mr. Young's opinion was merely a supplement to ACC's representations of English law contained in submissions provided to the Panel and opposing counsel in advance of the hearing. Indeed, ACC had previously emailed Toepfer's counsel and the Panel all of the English cases and textbooks on which ACC relied. Mem. in Supp. at 3. [. . .]

[. . .] Mr. O'Neil also asserts that "[i]t was quite obvious that the Tribunal had not read any of the bundles previously provided, including the various and lengthy submissions served by both parties." Mem. in Opp. Ex. Z, O'Neil Aff. P 15. [. . .] The only support Mr. O'Neil offers for his speculative statement is his opinion that he was not given enough time to deliver his oral presentation because the Panel limited each side to only twenty minutes to do so, and the fact that the Award was one-and-a-half pages long. The Court refuses to question the Panel's imposition of time limitations on the parties, which were applied equitably to both sides, and declines to draw any inferences from the length of the Award. In sum, Toepfer has failed to show that the Panel refused to hear material evidence or that it was deprived of a "fundamentally fair hearing" by the Panel's handling of Mr. Young's opinion on English law. See *Int'l Union, UMW*, 232 F.3d at 385, 388.

c.   Telephone Testimony and Witness Statements

Another alleged example of misconduct was the Panel's acceptance of telephone testimony from Mr. Sahib Al-Haddad ("Mr. Al-Haddad"), a witness for ACC. Toepfer argues that it was prejudiced because (1) Mr. Al-Haddad was ACC's only witness; (2) Mr. Al-Haddad had not presented a witness statement to the Panel prior to the hearing; (3) Mr. Al-Haddad did not possess copies of the documents submitted to the Panel during the hearing, and therefore there was no fair opportunity to cross-examine him; and (4) there was "no fair opportunity for the Arbitration Panel to effectively weigh Mr. Sahib Al-Haddad's credibility based only [on] a telephone discussion." Mem. in Opp., Duffy Aff. P 88(c).

[. . .] On November 24, 2006, Ms. Bulow notified the Panel and opposing counsel that Mr. Al-Haddad would not attend the hearing because his doctor had "forbidden" him to travel to Houston for "health reasons." Id. Email from Lucianne C. Bulow of Nov. 24, 2006. Ms. Bulow told the Panel that Mr. Al-Haddad would be available to testify "under oath on December 12 via video conferencing from Amman, Jordan," and "Mr. Basim Al-Haddad, who is President of Al-Haddad Commodities Corporation, will attend the hearing . . . ." Id. Ms. Bulow did not elaborate on Mr. Al-Haddad's health problems. The Panel accepted Ms. Bulow's statement that Mr. Al-Haddad could not attend, and granted her request for a video conferencing link. Id. Ex. 2. [. . .] On the day of the hearing, however, Toepfer learned that no arrangements for video conferencing had been made, and the Panel lacked the appropriate computer terminal for video conferencing provided via the Internet. Mem. in Opp. Ex. Z, O'Neil Aff. P 10. Instead, the Panel permitted, over Toepfer's objection, Mr. Al-Haddad to testify by telephone.

The Panel's decision to permit Mr. Al-Haddad to testify via telephone may have been permissible under the RMA Arbitration Rules, but in the Court's view, it was an arbitrary deviation from the Panel's own order of November 17, 2006, in which it stated, "Any witness statement to be submitted by a party shall be submitted to the other party and the Panel within 14 days. *If a witness statement is submitted from a witness employed by a party, that party should be prepared to produce the witness at the hearing.*" Mem. in Supp., Bulow Aff. Ex. 2, Email from Lee R. Marks of Nov. 17, 2006 (emphasis added). [. . .] The Court finds that the Panel's decision allowing Mr. Al-Haddad to testify by video, and not in person, was arbitrary in light of its November 17, 2007, order; however, the Court does *not* find that the consequences of that decision were prejudicial to Toepfer, which is a precondition to vacating an award pursuant to *§ 10(a)(3)*. Toepfer had notice well before the hearing that Mr. Al-Haddad would not appear in person. Most significantly, Toepfer had the opportunity, which it exercised, to extensively cross-examine Mr. Al-Haddad about the substance of the contract dispute, including the demurrage guarantee and ACC's access to lines of credit. Mem. in Opp. PP 18–19. While cross-examination in person or by video would have been preferable to cross-examination by telephone, the fact that telephonic testimony was ultimately used did not render the proceedings fundamentally unfair. Accordingly, the Court concludes that the Panel's decision to allow Mr. Al-Haddad to appear by telephone was not misconduct under *§ 10(a)(3)*. Moreover, there was no issue that Toepfer had failed to deliver in accordance with the Contract, but only whether they were excused by virtue of ACC's failure to obtain a demurrage guarantee.

[. . .]

In the Court's view, ACC's position that it did not need to provide a witness statement for Mr. Al-Haddad is plainly inconsistent with the Panel's November 17, 2006, order that any witness statements "shall be submitted to the other party and the Panel within 14 days." The Panel presumably was aware of this inconsistency, however, when on December 5, 2006, it expressly refused to intervene in the parties' dispute over witness statements despite Toepfer's protestations. In so doing, the Panel exercised its discretion under the RMA Arbitration Rules, which permit the arbitrators to "conduct any hearing as they deem fit." Pet. to Confirm Ex. B, RMA Arbitration Rule 9(c). Moreover, the extent to which Toepfer was disadvantaged by the lack of a witness statement for Mr. Al-Haddad is less than clear in the record; according to Ms. Bulow, Petitioner's factual submissions delivered to Toepfer in advance of the hearing and Mr. Al-Haddad's testimony covered the same ground. See Mem. in Supp., Bulow Aff. P 27 ("There was absolutely no mystery as to what Mr. Al-Haddad would cover and did cover in his testimony.").

Toepfer alleges other misconduct in connection with Mr. Al-Haddad's testimony. During Mr. O'Neil's cross-examination of Mr. Al-Haddad, the Panel ordered Mr. O'Neil to stop questioning him about Mr. Al-Haddad's alleged conviction in Germany in 2003 for smuggling arms to the Saddam Hussein regime in Iraq. Mem. in Opp. Ex. Z, O'Neil Aff. P 18. In addition, the Panel allowed ACC to present witness evidence from Mr. Al-Haddad Junior (Basim Al-Haddad, the President of ACC) over Toepfer's objection that "we had never heard of Mr Al-Haddad Junior's intention to give evidence and, again, on the basis that we had no witness evidence from him and therefore were totally unprepared and/or prejudiced." Id. P 20. The Panel also allowed, over Toepfer's objection, ACC to introduce evidence not previously disclosed to the other side—a photograph of a mobile phone and a witness statement of Mr. Raheem Taher. Id. P 22. Finally, the Panel rejected Toepfer's requests to call Mr. Taher to test his evidence and to allow Mr. Duraid Mahasneh to testify by telephone in order to impeach Mr. Al-Haddad. Id.

Although the Panel's handling of Mr. Al-Haddad's cross-examination, particularly its refusal to permit Mr. Mahasneh to rebut Mr. Al-Haddad's testimony, gives the Court some concern, the bottom line is that Toepfer has not shown any prejudice caused by these decisions. Toepfer did not notify the Panel or the other side prior to the hearing of its intent to call Mr. Mahasneh as a witness; it therefore had no reasonable expectation of being able to call him. Moreover, it is unclear what effect, if any, Mr. Mahasneh's testimony would have had, or indeed, what that testimony would have been. [. . .]

The actions of the Panel as a whole may seem to be in disregard of its own rules and somewhat arbitrary. However, there was no showing that their actions prejudiced Toepfer's position. To Mr. O'Neil the Panel's hearing may well have appeared "painfully farcical" and a "complete sham from start to finish." Mem. in Opp. Ex. Z, O'Neil Aff. PP 26, 28. Yet the Court's inquiry is limited to whether the arbitrator provided "a fundamentally fair hearing" that includes giving "each of the parties to the dispute an adequate opportunity to present its evidence and arguments." [. . .] The evidentiary record compels the conclusion that Toepfer had a meaningful opportunity to cross-examine Mr. Al-Haddad, and that the Panel's orders, which may have negatively affected his cross-examination by Toepfer, do not constitute "misbehavior by which the rights of any party have been prejudiced." *9 U.S.C. § 10(a)(3).*

[. . .]

In conclusion, the Court finds no prejudicial grounds justifying the vacatur of the Award pursuant to *§ 10(a)*, and Respondent's Motion to Vacate on these statutory grounds is hereby **DENIED.**

2.   Manifest Disregard of the Law

Toepfer also seeks to vacate the Award on the non-statutory ground that the Panel acted with a "manifest disregard of the law" in that it "refused to apply English law." Mot. in Opp. at 12–13.

A party seeking to vacate an arbitration award based upon a "manifest disregard" of the law "shoulders a heavy burden." *Remmey v. PaineWebber, Inc.,* 32 F.3d 143, 149 (4th Cir. 1994). An arbitrator's legal determination " 'may only be overturned where it is in manifest disregard of the law,' and an arbitrator's interpretation of a contract must be upheld so long as it 'draws its essence from the agreement.' " *Patten,* 441 F.3d at 235 (quoting *Upshur Coals Corp. v. United Mine Workers, Dist. 31,* 933 F.2d 225, 229 (4th Cir. 1991)). In this Circuit, a manifest disregard of the law is established "only where the 'arbitrator[ ] understand[s] and correctly state[s] the law, but proceed[s] to disregard the same.' " *Patten*, 441 F.3d at 235 (citing *Upshur*, 933 F.2d at 229). Moreover, an arbitration award does not fail to draw its essence from the contract "merely because a court concludes that an arbitrator has 'misread the contract.' " Id. (internal quotation marks omitted). An arbitration award fails to draw its essence from the contract "only when the result is not 'rationally inferable from the contract.' " Id. (quoting *Apex Plumbing Supply, Inc. v. U.S. Supply Co.*, 142 F.3d 188, 193 n.5 (4th Cir. 1998)).

The Panel's Award includes a six-paragraph "Facts" section followed by sections labeled "Findings" and "Relief." Pet. to Confirm Ex. C, Award. The "Facts" section states that the Contract was "to be governed by the laws of England" and sets forth the parties' obligations under the Contract. [. . .] A plain reading of the Award leaves no doubt that the Award "draws its essence" from the Contract and that the Panel's findings are "rationally inferable" therefrom. See *Patten*, 441 F.3d at 235.

Toepfer relies heavily on *Halligan v. Piper Jaffray, Inc.*, 148 F.3d 197 (2d Cir. 1998), in which the United States Court of Appeals for the Second Circuit held that an arbitration award should be vacated for "manifest disregard of the law" based upon the arbitrators' failure to apply the applicable law to a plaintiff's age discrimination claim. The court in *Halligan* found that the arbitrators ignored "strong evidence" that the plaintiff had been fired because of his age, and, although the arbitrators "have no obligation to do so," they did not explain their award. *Id. at 204*. The court went on to "make clear," however, that it was "not holding that arbitrators should write opinions in every case or even in most cases:

> *We merely observe that where a reviewing court is inclined to find that arbitrators manifestly disregarded the law or the evidence and that an explanation, if given, would have strained credulity, the absence of explanation may reinforce the reviewing court's confidence that the arbitrators engaged in manifest disregard.*

Id. Lacking any such "strong evidence" that the Panel in this case ignored applicable English law, *Halligan* does not support Toepfer's position. In sum, Toepfer has failed to satisfy its "heavy burden" of proving a "manifest disregard of the law" and the Court rejects Toepfer's motion to vacate on this ground. See *Remmey*, 32 F.3d at 149.

I. CONCLUSION

The Court detects something of a culture clash in this case, in which an arbitration panel of American businessmen who apparently pride themselves on providing quick commercial decisions held a hearing in Houston, Texas, over a contract governed by English law. The Contract required Toepfer to ship rice from the United States to Iraq, which Toepfer evidently failed to do because it was unable to secure a vessel. The Panel's manner of proceeding surprised Toepfer's attorney, Mr. O'Neil, who has practiced arbitrations extensively in England and elsewhere and, in his words, had "[n]ever before (and hopefully will never again) experience[ ] anything quite like the arbitration before the RMA." Reply, O'Neil Second Aff. P 30. Of course, Houston is not London. In Texas lore, cowboys and Indians long ago replaced the knights and dragons of English lore.

Whether or not they regret it in hindsight, the parties selected the RMA in their contract as the forum for resolving any disputes arising from the contract. Finding no evidence that the actions of the Panel resulted in substantial prejudice to Toepfer, the Court "will not substitute [its] judgment" for the arbitrator's. *Upshur*, 933 F.2d at 231. Accordingly, Respondent's Motion to Vacate the Arbitration Award of December 15, 2006, is hereby **DENIED** and Petitioner's Petition to Confirm Arbitration Award is **GRANTED.**

NOTES

Facts

1. Did the tribunal fail to postpone the hearing? If so, what reasons did it provide for its decision?

2. Did the procedural orders of the tribunal set out a timeframe for evidence to be timely introduced? Did the parties keep to that timeframe?

3. Did the tribunal's procedural orders set out a consequence for failing to comply with the procedural directions issued by the tribunal? What would have been the consequence of a failure to comply?

4. Did the tribunal refuse to "hear evidence"?

5. If you were counsel for Toepfer, how would you have argued that Al-Haddad's conduct have prejudiced your ability to put on your case?

Law

1. What standard of review did the court apply in this case?

2. What judicial gloss did the Court give to FAA, section 10(a)(3)? Do you agree with its approach?

McDaniel v. Bear Stearns & Co., Inc.

196 F.Supp.2d 343 (S.D.N.Y. 2002)

SCHEINDLIN, DISTRICT JUDGE.

Bear Stearns & Co., Inc. ("Bear Stearns"), a New York investment bank, offers clearing services for other broker-dealers through its subsidiary Bear Stearns Securities Corporation ("BSSC"). BSSC served as the clearing firm for broker-dealer A.R. Baron ("Baron") at a time when Baron engaged in criminal and fraudulent conduct. Petitioners Bernard and Maureen McDaniel ("Claimants") were Baron customers during this time.

On July 31, 2001, an arbitration panel (the "Panel") found Bear Stearns and BSCC (collectively "Bear") jointly and severally liable to Claimants for breach of contract and for aiding and abetting Baron's fraud. The arbitrators issued a thirty-six page arbitration award (the "Award") which offered detailed findings of fact and explained their conclusions of law. In this motion to vacate that Award, Bear has attacked the Panel's decision on numerous grounds. As discussed below, none of the issues raised by Bear show that the Panel exceeded its power or manifestly disregarded the law or evidence so as to require vacating the Award.

* * *

I.   BACKGROUND

A.   The Role of Clearing Firms and the Applicable Regulatory Scheme

In a typical clearing arrangement, a clearing firm provides many backroom and administrative functions for another broker-dealer's customer accounts. Generally, the clearing firm is responsible for maintaining records and mailing customer account documentation, as well as receiving, maintaining and delivering customers' securities and funds. The clearing firm may also extend credit in order to finance customer transactions in margin accounts or, in some cases, may execute transactions on exchanges or on the over-the-counter markets. Meanwhile the broker-dealer, referred to as the 'introductory broker', maintains many of the functions that require direct personal contact with customers, such as soliciting customers, providing investment advice, and accepting customer orders for the purchase or sale of securities.

According to Rule 382 of the New York Stock Exchange ("NYSE"), as amended in 1982, a clearing agreement must "specifically identify and allocate the respective functions and responsibilities of the introducing and carrying organizations . . . ." The Rule also requires that a customer whose account has been "introduced" to a clearing firm receive notice of the existence of the clearing agreement introductory broker and clearing firm, and a notice of the allocation of responsibilities between them.

B.　　The Parties and Relevant Non-Parties

In June or early July 1995, Bear and Baron entered into an Agreement for Securities Clearing Services (the "Clearing Agreement"). At that time, Richard Harrington was President of BSSC and in charge of its clearing business, Peter Murphy was a Managing Director of BSSC and Andrew Bressman was President of Baron. In September, 1995, claimant Bernard McDaniel opened a brokerage account with Baron. He opened another account with Baron in late April 1996, this time with his wife, Maureen McDaniel. Roman Okin eventually became Claimants' broker at Baron.

Pursuant to the Clearing Agreement, Bear was required to notify Baron's customers "in writing concerning the respective obligations of the parties . . . and any other Customer related responsibilities of the parties to [the] Agreement." Claimants and Bear entered into a standard, pre-printed Customer Agreement with respect to both of their accounts. The Agreement set forth the terms and conditions under which Bear would transact business with Claimants. Among other things, the Agreement explained how Bear would maintain Claimants' accounts, provide reports of executed orders and statements of Claimants' accounts. It also stated that Bear was permitted to charge commissions and other fees to Claimants for execution, custody or any other services furnished to Claimants, and that Claimants agreed to pay any such commissions and fees at Bear's then-prevailing rates. See id. In Paragraph Seven of the Customer Agreement, Claimants acknowledged receiving Bear's 'Truth-in-Lending disclosure statement', typically called a 'Rule 382 Letter', which described the allocation of functions and responsibilities between Baron and Bear.

During the time when Claimants maintained their accounts with Baron, Baron engaged in criminal activity, securities laws violations and fraudulent activity, some of which affected Claimants' accounts. On May 29, 1996, the Securities and Exchange Commission ("SEC") issued an emergency temporary cease-and-desist order against Baron, Bressman and Okin to halt Baron's fraudulent trading practices. Baron ceased doing business at the end of June 1996, and filed a Chapter 11 bankruptcy petition on July 3, 1996. On July 11, 1996, upon the application of the Securities Investor Protection Corporation

("SIPC"), Baron was placed into liquidation under the control of an independent trustee. On May 13, 1997, Baron and thirteen of its officers and employees were indicted on charges of criminal securities fraud. With the exception of John McAndris, Baron's former Chief Financial Officer, all of the defendants pled guilty to enterprise corruption and grand larceny. McAndris was tried and, on February 26, 1998, he was found guilty on twenty-five charges.

The Baron investigation led to an investigation of Bear's relationship with Baron. On August 5, 1999, Bear consented to the SEC's entry of an Order Instituting Proceedings (the "OIP"), without admitting or denying the SEC's findings. Pursuant to the settlement agreement, Bear was required to pay a $5 million civil penalty and $30 million to a fund to satisfy the claims of Baron's customers. In addition, Bear was required to retain an Independent Consultant to recommend supervisory and compliance policies which BSSC was required to adopt.

C.   Claimants' Allegations Against Bear

On January 27, 1997, Claimants filed a Statement of Claim with the National Association of Securities Dealers ("NASD") against Bear Stearns, BSSC and Michael Davis, a Baron employee who helped handle Claimants' account. See Statement of Claim. Claimants alleged that Bear caused them to suffer losses of not less than $900,000 during the period from the Fall of 1995 to the Summer of 1996. They alleged that Bear was liable to them under the following theories: control person liability, failure to register Baron as an 'approved person' pursuant to NYSE requirements, violations of NYSE Rule 382, issuance of false and misleading confirmations and statements in violation of SEC Rule 10b–10 and NASD Rule 2230, breach of duty of fair dealing in violation of NASD Rule IM 2310–2(a)(1) and IM 2310–2(d), violations of credit requirements and Regulation T [12 C.F.R. § 220.8(d)], breach of contract, negligence, fraud, alter-ego liability for Baron's wrongful acts, aiding and abetting Baron's conversion and fraud, and refusal to honor transfer instructions. They sought compensatory damages, punitive damages of three times compensatory damages, and all costs of the proceeding. In its Answer, Bear asserted the following affirmative defenses: failure to state a claim, failure to investigate, notice of Baron's misconduct and ratification of that misconduct, loss causation on the part of Claimants, assumption of risk, waiver, and estoppel.

D.   Arbitration Proceedings

Arbitration hearings took place in Boston on April 25, 26, 27, and 30 and May 1, 2001. On April 25, Claimants filed a Motion in Limine seeking to offer into evidence the OIPs relating to Bear and Harrington. After considering the submissions and the oral arguments of the parties, the Panel granted Claimants' motion subject to various conditions. On April 26, 2001, Bear made an oral motion to admit as evidence the "Wells Submission," a memorandum Bear had submitted in connection with the SEC's administrative proceedings relating to the Bear-Baron relationship. After hearing oral argument, the Panel granted Bear's motion. The Panel admitted the body of the Wells Submission and most of the exhibits to that document, but did not accept into evidence the attached trial testimony and deposition transcripts.

The presentation of evidence concluded on May 1, 2001. See id. at 12. The parties declined the opportunity to present oral closing arguments and opted instead to file post-hearing briefs. Proceedings ended on June 12, 2001, upon the filing of the post-hearing briefs.

E.   The Arbitration Award

The Panel issued its Award on July 31, 2001. The Panel found Bear liable for aiding and abetting Baron's fraud and for breach of contract. Specifically, the Panel found that Bear aided and abetted Baron's fraud because it: (1) was "aware of Baron's fraud," (2) "assisted and helped conceal Baron's fraud" by engaging in activities "above and beyond those involved in a normal back-office, clearing operation," and (3) "proximately caused the primary harm of Baron's fraudulent and unlawful conduct against customers such as Claimants." Breach of contract liability was based on the Panel's finding that Bear had breached the duty of good faith and fair dealing created by the Customer Agreement between Claimants and Bear. In particular, the Panel found that Bear breached this duty by: (1) failing to disclose Baron's commissions and markups on account statements generated by Bear, (2) failing to honor Claimants' requests to transfer their account, and (3) being "unresponsive" in its dealing with Claimants after Baron went out of business.

The Panel awarded Claimants $600,000 in compensatory damages and $211,571.60 in prejudgment interest on those damages. It explained that, although Claimants had suffered $788,988 in damages, those damages would be reduced to $600,000 because Claimants had contributed to and compounded their own losses. The Panel also awarded Claimants $1 million in punitive damages, $25,000 as a sanction for delay caused by Bear, and $75,000 in attorney's fees as a sanction against Bear for failure to cooperate with discovery. It also held that Bear should be responsible for two-thirds of the forum fees. All of the compensatory award and all but $68,135.60 of the prejudgment interest was offset by the $743,436 that Claimants had already received from the restitution fund financed by Bear.

II. LEGAL STANDARD

* * *

In very limited situations, a court may vacate an award because arbitrators have manifestly disregarded the evidence. *See Halligan*, 148 F.3d at 202 (vacating an award where arbitrators "manifestly disregarded the law or the evidence or both"); *Beth Israel Med. Ctr. v. Local 814*, No. 99 Civ. 9828, 2000 WL 1364367, at *6 (S.D.N.Y. Sept.20, 2000); *Green v. Progressive Mgmt. Inc.*, No. 00 Civ. 2539, 2000 WL 1229755, at *2 (S.D.N.Y. Aug. 29, 2000) (noting that Halligan extends "manifest disregard" standard to review of the evidence); *Daily News, L.P. v. Newspaper & Mail Deliverers' Union of New York and Vicinity*, No. 99 Civ. 5165, 1999 WL 1095613, at *7 (S.D.N.Y. Dec.2, 1999) (same). "[J]udicial review of an arbitrator's factual determinations is quite limited." *Beth Israel Med. Ctr.*, 2000 WL 1364367, at *6. A court may only vacate an arbitrator's award for manifest disregard of the evidence if "there is 'strong evidence' contrary to the findings of the arbitrator and the arbitrator has not provided an explanation of his decision." A court may not review the weight the arbitration panel accorded conflicting evidence. Nor may a court question the credibility findings of the arbitrator.

The party seeking vacatur of an arbitration award bears the burden of proving manifest disregard. But, even if that party proves that the arbitrators' decision is based on a manifest error of fact or law, a court must nevertheless confirm the award if grounds for the decision can be inferred from the facts of the case.

III. DISCUSSION

A. Aiding and Abetting Award

Bear claims that the Panel's finding of aiding and abetting fraud should be vacated because the Panel: (1) manifestly disregarded well-settled law regarding clearing firm liability for acts of an introductory firm; (2) manifestly disregarded the evidence in finding the intent required to establish aiding and abetting fraud; (3) manifestly disregarded the burden of proof required for aiding and abetting fraud; and (4) failed to find proximate cause.

* * *

2.   Manifest Disregard of the Evidence

Bears also argues that the Panel's finding of fraudulent intent—an essential element of aiding and abetting fraud—was in manifest disregard of the evidence. It argues that the Panel's determination that Harrington and Bressman were "close personal friends" was "a fiction" created by the Panel and that, without this factual finding, the Panel could not have determined that Bear acted with the requisite fraudulent intent. According to Bear, the Panel had to "manufactur[e]" this finding of fact because it knew that a mere finding that Bear was on notice of Baron's fraud or that Bear knowingly or recklessly disregarded several indicia of fraud was insufficient evidence of fraud.

Bear's argument does not justify *vacatur* because Bear has not proven that the Panel manifestly disregarded "strong evidence contrary" to the contested factual finding. Neither Harrington nor Bressman testified at the hearing, so there is no direct evidence with regard to their personal relationship. The only witness with knowledge of Harrington's relationship with Bressman was Murphy, who testified that "[t]hey seemed to have a good, you know, a good relationship on some level." He also testified that Bressman had free access to Harrington's office other than through the front door so that Murphy "used to joke and wonder how he did it," and that Harrington allowed Bressman to taunt Murphy in Harrington's presence and to make remarks such as "it's funny to see Murphy frustrated or running around."

With respect to Murphy's testimony, the Panel found that "Murphy knows much more than he was willing to say in his testimony," and explained that it "took that into consideration in making its findings and conclusions." To the extent that the Panel believed that Murphy was concealing his true knowledge of Harrington's relationship with Bressman, it was entitled to do so, and this Court has no authority to question the credibility findings of the arbitrators. Because the Panel could have inferred from Murphy's testimony that Harrison and Barrington were close personal friends, and Bear has provided no evidence to the contrary, Bear has not met its burden of proving that the Panel manifestly disregarded the evidence.

Even absent this factual finding, the Panel could have inferred fraudulent intent. Fraudulent intent may be inferred from facts showing either (1) circumstances indicative of conscious misbehavior, or (2) a motive for participating in a fraudulent scheme and an opportunity to do so. Here, the Panel found evidence to support both of these tests.

First, the Panel found that Bear had actual knowledge of Baron's fraud. See Award at 24 ("[Bear was] aware of Baron's risky circumstances and fraud.") ("[Bear had] knowledge of Baron's unlawful and fraudulent conduct."). Second, the Panel found that, even if Harrington and Bressman had not been close personal friends, Bear had both the motive and the opportunity to engage in Baron's fraud. One factor motivating Bear was the simple desire to continue to collect clearing fees and other income it received from Baron as part of the Clearing Agreement. As Bear properly notes, the mere desire "to prolong the benefits" of an ordinary clearing relationship is not enough to support the scienter element of an aiding and abetting claim. But the Panel also found that Bear was motivated by its desire to recover from Baron's on "loans above and beyond the normal clearing debt"—loans the Panel described as "extraordinary". Where a defendant's "economic motives were extraordinary," a court may infer fraudulent intent.

* * *

E.   Evidentiary Rulings

Bear contests three of the Panel's evidentiary rulings: (1) the exclusion of excerpts from the SEC's deposition of John LaFond, one of the NASD regulators responsible for Baron, which was an exhibit to the Wells Submission, see Def. Mem. at 17 & n. 15, 34 n. 25; (2) the exclusion of Okin's testimony in McAndris' criminal trial, which was also an exhibit to the Wells Submission, see id. at 18; and (3) the acceptance of the OIP related to BSSC into evidence, id. Def. Repl. at 6–7.

1.   LaFond's and Okin's Testimony

Bear contends that it was "substantially prejudiced" by the exclusion of LaFond's deposition testimony because that testimony would have established that "there is nothing extraordinary about a clearing firm having contact with the NASD concerning the net capital of one of its introductory firms." Bear claims that Okin's testimony was improperly excluded because that testimony would have helped to explain how Baron tried to hide its conduct from Bear.

The Panel provided a number of explanations for its decision to exclude the testimony attached to the Wells Submission. First, the Panel explained that much of the testimony was hearsay. Second, the Panel explained that "depositions aren't favored in arbitration," particularly where those depositions were not "taken in anticipation of this proceeding." Third, the Panel noted that, if Bear needed to address some of the issues in the excluded exhibits, it could call witnesses to testify about those issues. Id. ("[I]f there are witnesses that have to be produced, in order to deal with some of these issues [in the excluded depositions and trial testimony], so be it."). In addition, much of the purportedly excluded testimony was actually received into evidence because it was summarized and referenced in the body of the Wells Submission. Given the Panel's reasoned explanation for excluding LaFond's and Okin's testimony and its acceptance of Bear's summary of the relevant portions of that testimony, Bear has not shown that the Panel violated "fundamental fairness."

2. The OIP Related to BSSC

Bear argues that the Panel erroneously received into evidence the OIP related to BSSC because it was a settlement agreement with the SEC. According to Bear, settlement agreements between private companies and federal agencies cannot be used in subsequent litigation.

Although not bound by the Federal Rules of Evidence, the Panel explicitly recognized the rules precluding the use of settlement agreements as admissions or evidence of guilt. The Panel stated that it would not consider the OIPs "binding on the panel or preclusive in any way, that the findings would not be regarded as res judicata or collateral estoppel, they would [not] be considered as an admission of facts or liability by Bear or shift the burden of proof from Claimants to Bear." It also stated that "it would not consider and would disregard the 'settlement' provisions in the SEC Consent Orders . . . and [would] consider only the factual findings and evidentiary materials set forth in the SEC Consent Orders."

Instead, the Panel admitted the OIPs pursuant to Rule 803(8)(c) of the Federal Rules of Evidence, which excepts from the hearsay rule statements setting forth, in civil actions and proceedings, factual findings resulting from an investigation made pursuant to authority granted by law. As the Panel explained, it considered the SEC findings of fact as simply one type of evidence offered for its consideration. The Panel stated that it "would consider the weight, relevance and materiality of the findings as well as the parties' arguments in that regard, any other evidence relevant to the issues set forth in the SEC findings and would not necessarily conclude that the SEC findings establish a prima facie case for Claimants." It also stated that it would not "defer to the findings of the SEC contrary to the duty of the panel to find the facts in this arbitration."

Finally, the Panel made a conscious effort to ensure that Bear had an opportunity to rebut the SEC's findings. When admitting the Wells Submission, the Panel explained that it sought to give Bear a type of "rebuttal" against the

OIPs in order to ensure "an element of fairness." Thus, the Panel did not manifestly disregard the law, exceed its authority, or violate "fundamental fairness" when it admitted the OIP related to BSSC into evidence.

IV. CONCLUSION

For the foregoing reasons, Bear's motion to vacate the Award is denied and Claimants' motion to confirm the Award is granted. Consistent with the Award, the following judgment is hereby entered against Bear:

1. *Compensatory damages in the amount of $600,000.00, which is completely offset by SIPC payments to Claimants;*

2. *Prejudgment interest equal to $211,571.60, which is offset by SIPC payments to Claimants in the amount of $143,436.00, resulting in a balance of $68,135.60 which remains due to Claimants;*

3. *Punitive damages in the amount of $1,000,000.00;*

4. *A sanction for delay in the amount of $25,000.00 (and it shall pay two thirds of the forum fees);*

5. *Legal fees in the amount of $75,000.00;*

6. *Interest at the rate of 9% per annum simple interest on the remaining amount due ($1,168,135.60) if that amount was not paid within thirty (30) days of the Award, which interest shall commence thirty (30) days from the date of the Award on any amount remaining due.*

SO ORDERED.

NOTES

Facts

1. Why did the parties treat the evidentiary rulings separately from manifest disregard of evidence? Would it be possible to link both together and create a plausible factual link between both pleadings?

2. What is the gist of the allegation of manifest disregard of evidence? What evidence should have been considered?

3. What is the evidence the Court considered probative of the issue—thus obviating the need to consider further evidence on point?

4. The Court provides an alternative basis to reject the manifest disregard of evidence claim. What is it? Is it more plausible or less plausible? Why do you think the court did not simply stop? Did mean to "pile on" or could it

have been concerned that Bear in fact had identified a significant evidentiary problem?

5.   What evidence did evidence did the tribunal exclude? How relevant was this evidence to your mind?

6.   What evidence did the tribunal admit over objection? How prejudicial do you think this evidence was? How important do you think it was in giving the arbitrators "cover"?

Law

1.   What elements must be met for a court to set aside a manifest disregard of evidence? Does it require that the panel disregarded the only record evidence on a point in question? Or does it require less, i.e., that the panel relied upon evidence that was not sufficiently probative for its conclusions.

2.   The decision states that it will not review credibility findings. Is that inconsistent with the standard it announces for finding a manifest disregard of evidence? How so? How could the two be reconciled?

3.   How free is the Court in finding alternative rationales for the tribunal's conclusions? Can create legal conclusions out of unrelated findings of facts? Can it intuit findings of fact from record evidence upon which the tribunal did not comment? How far should a court go in order to "save" an award that exhibits significant evidentiary problems?

4.   What is the standard of materiality applied in the context of the discussion of the exclusion of evidence?

Tripi v. Prudential Securities, Inc.

303 F.Supp.2d 349 (S.D.N.Y. 2003)

SCHEINDLIN, DISTRICT JUDGE.

Petitioner Rick Tripi moves pursuant to 9 U.S.C. §§ 9–10 to vacate an arbitration award ("the Award") issued on May 2, 2002. Respondent Prudential Securities Incorporated ("Prudential"), in turn, cross-moves to confirm the Award. For the reasons stated below, this action is remanded to the arbitrators for clarification of the damages award.

I.   FACTUAL AND PROCEDURAL BACKGROUND

A.   Tripi's Account

Tripi maintained an investment account ("the Account") at Prudential starting in August 1998. The Account was managed by Glenn Malloff, a broker employed by Prudential since January 1998. Malloff previously was censured and subjected to a twelve week suspension by the New York Stock Exchange ("NYSE"). As a result, Malloff was placed under heightened supervision for his first six months at Prudential.

Although Tripi's Account initially realized some gains, it dropped precipitously from its high of approximately $980,000 in January 1999 to less than $110,000 in November 1999. The Account was selected for two compliance reviews in the first eight months. On or about September 17, 1999, the Account was restricted to liquidating orders only.

B.   Tripi's Claim and Prudential's Response

On October 25, 2000, Tripi filed a Statement of Claim ("Claim") with the National Association of Securities Dealers Dispute Resolution Office ("NASD-DR"), alleging, among other things, that Prudential: (a) effected transactions without Tripi's knowledge or consent; (b) failed to follow Tripi's instructions; (c) used discretion in option trading without written authorization; (d) effected transactions in contravention of the stated goal of the Account as a retirement fund; (e) effected excessive trades solely to increase the commissions; and (f) failed to properly supervise employees, including Malloff.

Prudential responded to the Claim, alleging that Tripi was a knowing investor who sought aggressive investments and interposing several affirmative defenses, including that Tripi had ratified the transactions in the Account and failed to mitigate his damages.

C.   The Arbitration Hearing and Award

A hearing was held on April 15, 16, and 17, 2002, before Denzil J. Klippel, Arnold Wagner, and John J. Duval, Sr. (collectively, "the Panel"). On May 2, 2002, the Panel issued a decision awarding Tripi $25,000 in compensatory damages and requiring Prudential to pay all forum and filing fees. On May 12, 2002, Tripi requested that the Panel clarify the Award because no rationale for the Award was given. By letter dated May 22, 2002, the Panel denied Tripi's request for clarification.

D. The Petition

On August 2, 2002, Tripi filed a petition with this Court seeking to vacate the Award on the grounds that the Panel manifestly disregarded the law and evidence presented at the hearing. Tripi did not provide a transcript of the arbitration proceedings with that application because the NASD had not located the tape recordings. Prudential cross-moved to confirm the Award.

In March 2003, the Court denied Tripi's motion "without prejudice and with leave to re-file and/or amend the motion within ninety days of when the tapes of the arbitration proceeding are located and forwarded to him." Prudential's cross-motion to confirm the Award was "deemed withdrawn" with leave to renew and/or amend "if and when Tripi re-files his motion to vacate."

Shortly thereafter, the tapes were forwarded to Tripi's counsel. Tripi refiled his petition on June 20, 2003 and Prudential refiled its cross-motion.

II. STANDARD OF REVIEW

"It is well-established that courts must grant an arbitration panel's decision great deference." "Arbitration awards are subject to very limited review in order to avoid undermining the twin goals of arbitration, namely, settling disputes efficiently and avoiding long and expensive litigation."

The Federal Arbitration Act ("FAA") lists four specific instances where an award may be vacated, all of which involve corruption, fraud, or some other impropriety on the part of the arbitrators. See 9 U.S.C. § 10(a). In addition to the statutory grounds for vacatur, a court may vacate an arbitration award that was rendered in "manifest disregard of law." However, review for manifest disregard is "severely limited." The doctrine is reserved for those "exceedingly rare circumstances where some egregious impropriety on the part of the arbitrators is apparent, but where none of the provisions of the FAA apply."

* * *

"In very limited situations, a court may vacate an award because arbitrators have manifestly disregarded the evidence." *McDaniel v. Bear Stearns & Co., Inc.*, 196 F.Supp.2d 343, 351 (S.D.N.Y.2002) (citations omitted). However, "judicial review of an arbitrator's factual determinations is quite limited." *Beth Israel Med. Ctr. v. Local 814*, 2000 WL 1364367, at *6 (S.D.N.Y. Sept.20, 2000). "A court may only vacate an arbitrator's award for manifest disregard of the evidence if there is strong evidence contrary to the findings of the arbitrator and the arbitrator has not provided an explanation of his decision." *McDaniel*, 196 F.Supp.2d at 351 (internal quotation and citation omitted). "A court may not review the weight the arbitration panel accorded conflicting evidence." "Nor may a court question the credibility findings of the arbitrator."

The party seeking vacatur of an arbitration award bears the burden of proving manifest disregard. *See Greenberg*, 220 F.3d at 28 (citation omitted). However, even if that party proves that the arbitrators' decision is based on a manifest error of fact or law, a court nevertheless must confirm the award if "any colorable justification for the arbitrator's judgment" can be inferred from the facts of the case. *Westerbeke Corp. v. Daihatsu Motor Co. Ltd.*, 304 F.3d 200, 212 n. 8 (2d Cir.2002) (citations omitted).

III. DISCUSSION

Tripi argues that the Panel manifestly disregarded the law and evidence presented at the hearing, which require an award of greater damages upon a finding of liability. Prudential contends that there is a plausible reading of the Award that is consistent with the law and evidence. While the record is replete with evidence of Prudential's liability, there is also evidence supporting a reduction of the claimed damages. There is, however, no apparent basis in the record for the specific amount the Panel chose to award.

A.   Evidence Supporting a Reduction in Damages

There is some evidence in the record to support Prudential's defenses of ratification and failure to mitigate damages, thereby justifying an apportionment of damages. Tripi acknowledged that he received written confirmations of all trades in his account (which calculated Malloff's commissions for each trade), received monthly account statements, and sometimes accessed his account on the computer. Tripi testified, however, that he did not often look at the confirmations and monthly statements because he "cared about the bottom line"—rather than how the account was grown. Tripi also testified that he never objected, either orally or in writing, to any transaction or to Malloff's alleged failure to follow his instructions. The Panel may have found, based on this evidence, that Tripi either ratified the transactions or failed to mitigate his damages, thereby warranting a reduction in his damages award.

Tripi argues that the Panel disregarded uncontroverted evidence that Malloff failed to follow Tripi's January 1999 instruction to liquidate his stock into cash. However, Malloff denied receiving any such directive, and Tripi presented no written evidence of the instruction. Thus, the Panel could have found that Tripi never gave the instruction to Malloff, which is a credibility determination that I cannot question. Even if the Panel found that Malloff failed to follow Tripi's instruction, the Panel could have found that Tripi failed to mitigate his damages by not complaining to anyone at Prudential about Malloff's failure to follow his alleged instruction.

Tripi additionally argues that the Panel manifestly disregarded evidence of churning because Prudential employees testified that the commission velocity, account turnover, and number of trades in Tripi's account were unprecedented. There is, however, conflicting evidence in the record regarding Tripi's investment objectives. Compare 4/15/03 Transcript of Arbitration Proceeding ("4/15/03 Tr."), Ex. C to Pet., at 44, 58 (portraying himself as an inexperienced investor who could not afford to lose his retirement fund) with 4/16/03 Tr. at 376, 390 (admitting that he wanted to be "aggressive" about his investments). Thus, the Panel could have found that the trading in the account, while active, was not excessive in light of Tripi's desire to trade aggressively. As a result, there is a basis in the record for the arbitrators' decision to award Tripi less than the full amount of his losses.

B. Compensatory Damages Award

However, it is hard to imagine any justification for the arbitrators' award, which holds Prudential responsible for only three percent of Tripi's losses. The arbitrators have provided no clue as to how they arrived at a 97/3% split. In fact, when questioned about the arbitrariness of the apportionment, the Panel specifically declined to provide an explanation. Nor has Prudential pointed to any facts in the record to support such a bizarre award.

Given the strong evidence in the record of Prudential's liability, the Court cannot discern how the Panel arrived at such a disproportionate allocation of liability. Such a meager award shocks the conscience of this Court. Indeed, I would not hesitate to set aside such an incomprehensible award if it were a jury verdict. *See United States v. Chin*, 934 F.2d 393, 398 (2d Cir.1991) (acknowledging that a verdict may be set aside where it is "so offensive that it shocks the conscience"). In light of the highly deferential standard due an arbitral award, however, I will remand to the Panel with instructions that it explain its allocation of damages. After the Panel provides its explanation, either party may return to this Court to confirm, modify, or vacate the Award.

IV. CONCLUSION

For the foregoing reasons, this action is remanded for clarification of the compensatory damages award.

NOTES

Facts

1. What was the evidentiary failure in the case alleged by Tripi? Specifically, what evidence did he assert the panel disregarded?

2. What evidence does the court rely upon in order to rehabilitate, at least in part, the conclusions of the tribunal?

3. What explanation would a tribunal have to give for its split of damages? Could it fairly be inferred from what the panel did (as opposed to what it said)?

4. How do you expect the panel to react to Judge Scheindlin's directive?

Law

1. Under what FAA ground does the court treat "manifest disregard of the evidence"? Should this fairly be treated as an imperfect execution by the arbitrators of their powers under FAA, section 10(a)(4) or does it belong under FAA, section 10(a)(3)? Does it matter?

2. The court "remanded for clarification". Is this consistent with the pleadings of the parties in this case? Did either party pray for that remedy? How is the court even empowered to grant it under the FAA? Consider FAA, section 10(b), which states "[i]f an award is vacated and the time within which the agreement required the award to be made has not expired, the court may, in its discretion, direct a rehearing by the arbitrators". Is this what Judge Scheindlin did in this case?

3. Consider section 11 of the FAA. Could it be appropriately applied in this case?

> In either of the following cases the United States court in and for the district wherein the award was made may make an order modifying or correcting the award upon the application of any party to the arbitration—
>
> (a) Where there was an evident material miscalculation of figures or an evident material mistake in the description of any person, thing, or property referred to in the award.
>
> (b) Where the arbitrators have awarded upon a matter not submitted to them, unless it is a matter not affecting the merits of the decision upon the matter submitted.

(c) Where the award is imperfect in matter of form not affecting the merits of the controversy.

The order may modify and correct the award, so as to effect the intent thereof and promote justice between the parties.

Wallace v. Buttar

378 F.3d 182 (2d Cir. 2004)

POOLER, CIRCUIT JUDGE.

This case raises questions regarding the scope of federal court review of a decision issued by an arbitral panel. We resolve the case through the application of the familiar principle that the scope of such review is highly constrained. This is especially true with regard to an arbitral panel's assessment of whether the documentary and testimonial evidence presented to it is sufficient to satisfy a particular legal claim. Federal district judges are, of course, highly skilled in matters of weighing evidence. As illustrated by the result we reach here, however, district judges must put these skills aside when faced with the question of whether a decision issued by an arbitral panel should be confirmed.

FACTS

A. The Buttars' Claim.

Daljit and Paramjit Buttar, who are husband and wife, are residents of Raleigh, North Carolina. Daljit Buttar (hereafter "Dr. Buttar") is a physician specializing in neurology, and is currently in solo practice.

Dr. Buttar has assumed sole responsibility for managing his family's finances. In 1999, he happened to meet Vivek Verma, a stockbroker based in New York City, at a social event in North Carolina. At this event, and in a series of subsequent telephone calls, Dr. Buttar and Verma discussed the Buttar family's current investments and future investment goals. In July 1999, Verma persuaded Dr. Buttar to open the first of a series of investment accounts at the firm for which he worked, Montrose Capital Management ("Montrose"). The application signed by Dr. Buttar when he opened this account contains the following provision:

All controversies which may arise between us concerning any transaction, or the construction, performance or breach of this or any other agreement between us, whether entered into prior, on, or subsequent to the date hereof, shall be determined by arbitration in accordance with the Federal Arbitration Act to the fullest extent permitted by law. The arbitration shall be determined only before and in accordance with the rules then in effect of either the New York Stock Exchange, Inc., or the National Association of Securities Dealers, Inc. or any other exchange or self-regulatory organization of which [Montrose is] a member as I may elect. The award of the arbitrators, or of the majority of them, shall be final . . . .

We note that, immediately preceding the arbitration clause, the application sets forth the following "understanding" in bold lettering: "The arbitrator's award is not required to include factual findings or legal reasoning and any party's right to appeal or to seek modification of rulings by arbitrators is strictly limited."

Soon after opening this initial account, Dr. Buttar also began to discuss his investments with Robert Winston. Winston's actual responsibilities at Montrose are not entirely clear from the record, but Dr. Buttar testified that Winston "talked to me like he was the owner" of the firm. Verma himself testified that while he worked at Montrose he was under the impression that Winston ran the firm.

Verma and Winston successfully urged Dr. Buttar to make substantial investments in the securities of two firms: (1) Skynet Holdings, Inc. ("Skynet") and (2) CNF Technologies ("CNF"). Dr. Buttar was also persuaded to provide a "bridge loan" to CNF in the amount of $150,000.00. Eventually, Dr. Buttar alleges, Montrose "had invested virtually all of [his] liquid assets in CNF and Skynet." It is undisputed that Dr. Buttar suffered substantial losses as a result.

B.   The Arbitration Proceeding.

On September 11, 2000, the Buttars instituted an arbitration proceeding by filing a statement of claim with the National Association of Securities Dealers, Inc. ("NASD"), which names Montrose and Winston as respondents. The statement of claim alleges that Winston and Verma made numerous false statements to Dr. Buttar regarding the wisdom of investing in Skynet and CNF. These included characterizing Skynet as "a long-term safe investment" when it was in fact "a thinly traded bulletin board stock," falsely representing that Skynet's immediate prospects were particularly favorable because it "was in the process of a buyout by Federal Express," and assuring Dr. Buttar that the principal amount of his loan to CNF would be returned to him "plus ten percent within two months, 'guaranteed.' " The Buttars sought compensatory damages in the amount of $1,375,000.00 and an unspecified amount of punitive damages.

The Buttars filed an amended statement of claim with the NASD on March 9, 2001, which repeats the factual allegations of their original pleading, but which names Michael E. Wallace, David Jacaruso and Joseph Scotti as respondents in addition to Montrose and Winston. Liability as to Wallace, Jacaruso, and Scotti is set forth in the following allegation:

> *Respondents Wallace, Jacaruso and Scotti are liable as control persons of Respondents Montrose, Winston and Verma. See 15 U.S.C. § 78t(a); 15 U.S.C. § [77o1]; [North Carolina General Statute] § 78.A–56(a)(2)(c) . . . .*
>
> *Respondents possessed the power to control and supervise the operations of Montrose, Winston and Verma and knew or should have known that Montrose, Winston and Verma were handling Claimants' accounts in an unsuitable manner, making unauthorized trades [and] were making misrepresentations to Claimants. Respondents, as control persons, failed to properly superivse the activities of Montrose, Winston and Verma, but benefitted from the improper and illegal activities conducted by Montrose, Winston and Verma.*
>
> * * *
>
> *. . . . Respondents Montrose, Wallace, Jacaruso and Scotti are responsible for the wrongdoing of its registered representatives due to the doctrine of respondeat superior, for failing in all respects to supervise the account activity. Respondents Wallace, Jacaruso and Scotti are liable as control persons. The conduct of respondents violated the federal securities laws, state statutory and common law, and the rules and regulations of the National Association of Securities Dealers, Inc. and the securities industry.*

The Buttars' claim was assigned to a three-person arbitration panel ("the Panel"). None of the Panel's members is an attorney, but they are all seasoned business executives with substantial experience as arbitrators. On May 29, 2001 the Panel granted Winston's motion, which was joined by Wallace, Jacaruso, and Scotti, to assert a third-party claim against Verma.

The Panel conducted a three-day hearing on the Buttars' claim in November 2001. Although they were all represented by counsel at the hearing, Winston, Jacaruso, and Scotti chose not to appear in person and did not give any testimony. Wallace was also represented by counsel and testified very briefly by telephone.

A central issue on this appeal is whether the Panel could conclude that Wallace, Jacaruso, and Scotti are liable to the Buttars as control persons of Montrose. During his opening statement to the Panel, counsel for Wallace, Jacaruso, and Scotti denied that the three men could be found liable as control persons and alerted the Panel to his intention to move for dismissal on this ground at the close of evidence. This motion was in fact made, but the Panel declined to rule on it "until all of the various written pleadings and memoranda have been reviewed." The Buttars submitted a post-hearing memorandum to the Panel which sets forth the basic principles of control person liability under North Carolina and federal law. Counsel for Wallace, Jacaruso, and Scotti, however, submitted a post-hearing memorandum which is notable for its use of invective, but which is almost completely devoid of legal discussion of any type. It devotes slightly more than one-half of a page to the law of control person liability, and does not discuss North Carolina law at all. The Buttars and Wallace, Jacaruso, and Scotti also submitted reply memoranda to the Panel regarding the common law issues of laches and respondeat superior.

The evidence before the Panel regarding the status of Wallace, Jacaruso, and Scotti as control persons was neither non-existent nor overwhelming. In the first place, documents filed by Montrose with the Securities and Exchange Commission tend to support a finding of control person status. On a "Form BD"-a Uniform Application for Broker-Dealer Registration-filed by Montrose in May 1999, Wallace is identified as the firm's president. On the same form, Jacaruso and Scotti are identified as directors who each owned a 50% share of Montrose, but only Wallace is actually identified as a "control person." On an amended Form BD, however, dated November 11, 1999, Jacaruso and Scotti are listed as each owning a 25% to 50% interest in Montrose and each, along with Wallace, is listed as a "control person." Two subsequent Form BD amendments, dated December 17, 1999 and December 21, 2000, repeat this listing.

The Panel also heard the testimony of Michael Kavanagh, a stockbroker who came to work at Montrose upon a promise that he would be given a 5% ownership interest in the firm. Kavanagh testified that upon his arrival at Montrose, Winston urged him to buy Skynet and CNF securities for the accounts of the clients he had brought with him to the firm. Upon meeting with representatives of both companies, however, Kavanagh decided that he "wasn't too impressed with either one of them."

As time went on, Kavanagh became increasingly concerned that other brokers at Montrose "were being forced [by Winston] to buy . . . securit[ies] that they didn't want to buy for their customers." Kavanagh testified that he eventually brought his complaints about Winston's conduct to Jacaruso, whom he identified as "the Chairman" of Montrose. Kavanagh recalled that Jacaruso "made an agreement with me that he was going to deal with this Robert Winston issue" and that Jacaruso told him "[j]ust don't pay any attention to Robert's antics, and I'll take care of it." Kavanagh also averred that Winston's misconduct was "the topic of numerous conversations on my part in the partners' meetings," and that such meetings "were really never held without all the partners there." Nowhere in his testimony does Kavanagh state that his complaints about Winston were ever acted upon. Kavanagh eventually left the firm, testifying that he did so because "Montrose is a criminal activity. It's a pump and dump operation. It's a fraud. It's a scam . . . ."

Dr. Buttar himself testified that, prior to filing the arbitration claim, he had never heard of Wallace, Jacaruso, or Scotti. The Buttars also offered the testimony of William Collison as an expert witness in securities investing. With respect to the responsibility of Jacaruso and Scotti for the losses suffered by the Buttars, Collison testified that "they are directors of the firm. They are on the Form BD [as] the owners of the firm and . . . responsibility for what goes on in that firm ultimately rests with them." Collison further declared that Jacaruso and Scotti "as owners of the firm acquiesced, approved, sanctioned, use whatever term pleases you, the activities of Mr. Winston . . . ." Collison also testified, however, that he had no basis for concluding that Jacaruso and Scotti had actual knowledge of the trades being made in the Buttars' particular accounts.

As already noted, Jacaruso and Scotti did not testify before the Panel. Wallace, however, testified that he "was in control of everyone performing their functions" at Montrose. Wallace also acknowledged that he signed the Securities and Exchange Commission documents which name him, Jacaruso, and Scotti as control persons of Montrose and that he believed that this information "was true, accurate and complete." Kavanagh, however, characterized Wallace as being "closer in power to the janitor than the president" of Montrose, and that he believed "a lot of things that happened at the firm were done without Mike Wallace's knowledge."

C.   The Panel's Award.

The NASD served all parties with a copy of the Panel's determination of the Buttars' claim ("the Award") on March 8, 2002. On December 7, 2001 the U.S. District Court for the Southern District of New York had issued a stay of all legal proceedings against Montrose pursuant to § 362(a) of the Bankruptcy Code, 11 U.S.C. § 362(a). Accordingly, the Award states that the Panel "made no determination with respect to the claims asserted against" Montrose, but that the stay "does not apply to Respondents Winston, Wallace, Scotti and Jacaruso."

The Award contains no factual findings beyond briefly outlining the terms of the parties' claims and defenses. The determination of liability is set forth in relevant part as follows:

1.   The Panel finds Respondent Winston liable for misrepresentation; unauthorized, unsuitable and over-concentrated trading in Skynet and CNF Technologies; and fraud. The Panel finds Respondents Wallace, Scotti and Jacaruso liable for fraud and also as "Control Persons". See 15 U.S.C. 78t(a); 15 U.S.C. [7702]; [North Carolina General Statute] 78A–56(a)(2)(c).

2.   Respondents Winston, Wallace, Scotti and Jacaruso are jointly and severally liable and shall pay to Claimants compensatory damages in the amount of $1,064,543.00, plus pre-judgment interest from June 1, 2000 through January 30, 2001 in the amount of $127,629.00. Post-judgment interest shall accrue in accordance with Rule 10330(h) of the [NASD Code of Arbitration Procedure].

3.   Respondents Winston, Wallace, Scotti and Jacaruso are jointly and severally liable and shall pay to Claimants punitive damages in the amount of $604,805.00. The Panel finds Respondent Winston liable for punitive damages based upon the Panel's finding of fraud. The Panel finds the control persons, Respondents Wallace, Scotti and Jacaruso, liable for punitive damages based upon the Panel's finding of fraud. See Hunt v. Miller, 908 F.2d 1210, 1216 n. 15 (4th Cir.1990). "An employer is liable for an agent's fraud when committed within the scope of the agent's apparent authority, even when the principal did not know or authorize the commission of the fraudulent acts." Also, "a master is liable for punitive damages awarded when the servant or agent causing the injury was acting in the course and scope of the master's business." See also Black's Law Dictionary, 6th Ed.1991, 455ff. Post-judgment interest shall accrue in accordance with Rule 10330(h) of the [NASD Code of Arbitration Procedure.]

D.   The District Court's Decision.

* * *

The district court granted the motions to vacate the Award, and consequently denied the cross-motion to confirm the Award. The district court took it to be "undisputed that Winston, a broker employed by Montrose, committed a primary violation of the securities laws, that Jacaruso and Scotti were directors and shareholders of Montrose and Wallace was its president." The question then became whether the Panel could have properly found Wallace, Jacaruso, or Scotti in any way liable for Winston's acts.

The district court held that, in addition to the grounds for vacating an arbitration award set forth in the Federal Arbitration Act ("FAA"), see 9 U.S.C. § 10, "the Second Circuit[] recognize[s] two additional bases for vacating arbitration awards: manifest disregard of the law and manifest disregard of the facts." In the district court's view, the Panel could not have found Wallace,

Jacaruso, or Scotti liable for the Buttars' losses without engaging in both sorts of disregard. First, secondary liability pursuant to the doctrine of respondeat superior could not lie because the doctrine "imposes liability on the employer of those committing fraud in their employment. The entity that could have been held liable for Winston's fraud under the doctrine . . . was Montrose, Winston's employer." Second, Wallace, Jacaruso, and Scotti could not be found liable as co-participants in Winston's scheme to defraud the Buttars because "[i]n order to commit fraud, one must act with intent to defraud." The district court held that no evidence put before the Panel could serve as the basis of a finding of such intent on the part of Wallace, Jacaruso, or Scotti:

> *The totality of the evidence . . . overwhelmingly indicates that Wallace never dealt with the Buttars, lacked awareness of all wrongdoing in respondents' account, [and] had no duty nor reason to educate himself of the activity in the Buttars' accounts . . . . There was no evidence of any action taken by Jacaruso and Scotti in connection with the transactions in which Winston defrauded the Buttars.*

Clearly the arbitrators could not have found that Wallace, Jacaruso and Scotti possessed the requisite intention to defraud the Buttars without manifestly disregarding this evidence, or lack of evidence.

* * *

DISCUSSION

* * *

2.   Manifest Disregard of the Evidence.

Citing *Halligan v. Piper Jaffray, Inc.*, 148 F.3d 197, 202, 204 (2d Cir.1998), the district court held that an arbitral award may be may be vacated on the ground of "[m]anifest disregard of the facts" when the award "runs contrary to 'strong' evidence favoring the party bringing the motion to vacate." We note that a number of other district courts in our Circuit, directly relying on *Halligan* or on district court authority purporting to rely on that case, have asserted the same principle. See, e.g., *Hakala v. Deutsche Bank AG*, No. 01 Civ. 3366, 2004 WL 1057788 at *6 (S.D.N.Y. May 11, 2004); *Gwynn v. Clubine*, 302 F.Supp.2d 151, 167–68 (W.D.N.Y.2004); *Ono Pharmaceutical Co., Ltd. v. Cortech, Inc.*, No. 03 Civ. 5840, 2003 WL 22481379 at *2 (S.D.N.Y. Nov.3, 2003); *Tripi v. Prudential Securities, Inc.*, 303 F.Supp.2d 349 (S.D.N.Y.2003); *Raiola v. Union Bank of Switzerland LLC*, 230 F.Supp.2d 355, 357 (S.D.N.Y.2002); *GFI Securities LLC v. Labandeira*, No. 01 Civ. 00793, 2002 WL 460059 at *4 (S.D.N.Y. March 26,

2002); *McDaniel v. Bear Stearns & Co., Inc.*, 196 F.Supp.2d 343, 351 (S.D.N.Y.2002). Such reliance is mistaken.

In *Halligan*, we reviewed a district court's confirmation of an arbitration award which rejected an employment discrimination claim. We reversed, finding that the award had been made in the face of "overwhelming evidence" that discriminatory conduct had occurred. This evidence included the employer's admission that the claimant's "performance was not so unsatisfactory as to justify [his] discharge," and considerable circumstantial evidence that we found to be "consistent only with a finding that [the claimant] was pushed out of his job" by discriminatory animus. Id. Further, the arbitration panel issued no explanation for its rejection of the claim, and we concluded that any explanation it could have given "would have strained credulity." We held that the district court had erred in confirming the award because the evidence in the claimant's favor was so strong as to engender "the firm belief that the arbitrators here manifestly disregarded the law or the evidence or both."

Our later cases, however, have cautioned against an over-broad reading of Halligan. In *GMS Group*, we noted that Halligan confronted "the unique concerns at issue with employment discrimination claims." These concerns included "whether the composition of industry-specific panels were ill-suited to the nature of the claims, and whether employees were receiving due process in the course of arbitration." We concluded, however, that "[t]hese concerns do not translate to the claims at issue in this case." *GMS Group* dealt with a securities fraud claim, as does the instant case.

Further, in *Westerbeke* we explicitly characterized *Halligan's* suggestion that arbitral awards may be vacated on the ground of manifest disregard of evidence as *dicta*. 304 F.3d at 213, n. 9. We explained this conclusion in the following way:

> *Halligan presented the special circumstance in which the arbitration tribunal did not issue a written explanation of its factual findings. The reviewing court was therefore placed in the situation of attempting to discern what possible findings the arbitrators could have made that would justify their disposition of the case. Unable to come up with any findings that would not "strain credulity," the court concluded that the tribunal must have "manifestly disregarded the law or the evidence or both." [Halligan, 148 F.3d at 204.] Halligan does not stand for the proposition that factual findings put on the record by the arbitrator are subject to an independent judicial review, however.*

Id. (first emphasis in original; second emphasis added).

Moreover, if a federal court is convinced that an arbitral panel has reached a merely incorrect legal result-that is based upon an irrational application of a controlling legal principle-the court should not conduct an independent review of the factual record presented to the arbitral panel in order to achieve the "correct" result. In Hardy, as set forth above, an arbitral panel, which had provided no explanation of its award, found an employee, Skelly, to be secondarily liable "based upon the principles of *respondeat superior*," for primary acts of securities fraud committed by his fellow employee. The district court, as did this Court, found this to be a patently illogical holding that could not be confirmed. The district court, however, conducted its own review of the evidentiary record and concluded that "a permissible view of the evidence" supported the conclusion that Skelly could be held primarily liable for securities fraud based upon his own conduct. We held that the district court should not have undertaken such an assessment of the evidence:

> *The district court correctly found that a court must "confirm [an arbitrator's] award if [it is] able to discern any colorable justification for the arbitrator's judgment, even if that reasoning would be based on an error of fact or law."* Westerbeke, *304 F.3d at 212, n. 8. There may indeed be more than enough evidence in the record to find that Skelly should have been found primarily liable. But that is not what "the arbitrator's judgment" is in the instant case. The arbitrator's judgment is that Skelly was liable "upon the principles of respondeat superior," and no one points us to any evidence in the record that provides a colorable justification for this conclusion.*

In sum, "the Second Circuit does not recognize manifest disregard of the evidence as proper ground for vacating an arbitrator's award." *Success Sys., Inc. v. Maddy Petroleum Equip., Inc.*, 316 F.Supp.2d 93, 94 (D.Conn.2004). We recognize only the doctrine of manifest disregard of the law, which doctrine holds that an arbitral panel's legal conclusions will be confirmed in all but those instances where there is no colorable justification for a conclusion. To the extent that a federal court may look upon the evidentiary record of an arbitration proceeding at all, it may do so only for the purpose of discerning whether a colorable basis exists for the panel's award so as to assure that the award cannot be said to be the result of the panel's manifest disregard of the law. A federal court may not conduct a reassessment of the evidentiary record, as did the district court here, upon the principle that an arbitral award may be vacated when it "runs contrary to 'strong' evidence favoring the party bringing the motion to vacate" the award. Instead, whatever the weight of the evidence considered as a whole, "[i]f a ground for the arbitrator's decision can be inferred from the facts of the case, the award should be confirmed." *Fahnestock & Co., Inc. v. Waltman*, 935 F.2d 512, 516 (2d Cir.1991) (internal quotation marks and citation omitted). Only this approach to the evidentiary record is consistent with the "great deference" which must be paid to arbitral panels by federal courts. *Duferco*, 333 F.3d at 388.

B. Is the Award Supported by a Colorable Justification?

1. Control Person Liability.

The Buttars alleged before the Panel that Wallace, Jacaruso, and Scotti were liable as control persons under both federal and North Carolina law. The district court acknowledged this, but it made no finding as to whether the Buttars' claim under North Carolina law, at least as such law was presented to the Panel, provides a colorable justification for the Award. We find that it does and that the Award should therefore be confirmed. Having found that state law provides a colorable justification of liability, we express no opinion as to whether federal law does as well.

Section 20 of the federal Securities and Exchange Act of 1934 provides for control person liability as follows:

> *Every person who, directly or indirectly, controls any person liable under any provision of this chapter or of any rule or regulation thereunder shall also be liable jointly and severally with and to the same extent as such controlled person to any person to whom such controlled person is liable, unless the controlled person acted in good faith and did not directly or indirectly induce the act or acts constituting the violation or cause of action.*

15 U.S.C. § 78t(a).

North Carolina securities regulation statutes contain an analogous provision:

> *Every person who directly or indirectly controls a person liable under subsection (a), (b) or (b1) of this section, every partner, officer, or director of the person, every person occupying a similar status or performing similar functions, and every dealer or salesman who materially aids in the sale is also liable jointly and severally with and to the same extent as the person, unless able to sustain the burden of proof that the person did not know, and in the exercise of reasonable care could not have known, of the existence of the facts by reason of which the liability is alleged to exist.*

N.C.G.S.A. § 78A–56(c)(1).

In their post-arbitration brief to the Panel, the Buttars, citing our opinion in *SEC v. First Jersey Securities, Inc.*, 101 F.3d 1450, 1472 (2d Cir.1996), stated that a prima facie case of control person liability under federal law requires a showing of "a primary violation by the controlled person, control of the primary violator by the targeted defendant, and that the controlling person was in some meaningful sense a culpable participant in the fraud perpetrated by the controlled person." The Buttars argued, however, that North Carolina law is "broader" than federal law. While it may by the case under federal law that, as the district court put it, "the power to direct the management and policies of a person must be a real, de facto power and not just de jure," the Buttars argued before the Panel that this is not true under North Carolina law, stating as follows: "Under North Carolina law, controlling shareholders, officers and directors are control persons within the meaning of N.C.G.S.A. § 78A–56(c)(1), as a matter of law. *Waterman v. Alta Verde Industries, Inc.*, 643 F.Supp. 797, 809 (E.D.N.C.1986), aff'd., 833 F.2d 1006 (4th Cir.1987)." Further, while the district court stated that Wallace, Jacaruso, and Scotti could not be liable as control persons under federal law unless "they were knowing participants in Winston's breaches of the securities laws," *Wallace*, 239 F.Supp.2d at 396, the Buttars told the Panel that North Carolina law is "more favorable" to plaintiffs. Specifically, the Buttars noted that § 78A–56(c)(1) states that control person liability can be imposed unless the defendant "in the exercise of reasonable care, could not have known" of the primary violator's fraudulent acts. This, they argued, "is the language of negligence. In other words, even if Jacaruso, Scotti and Wallace did not know of the fraud, they clearly were negligent in not knowing, and are jointly and severally liable as control persons under North Carolina law."

In their post-arbitration memorandum to the Panel, as already noted, Wallace, Jacaruso and Scotti take notice of the requirements of control person liability under federal law, but they make no statement whatsoever regarding control person liability under North Carolina law. That is, they made no attempt to counter the Buttar's argument that North Carolina law is "more favorable" to plaintiffs. This was unwise on their part because, as we have stated, "under the test of manifest disregard [an arbitrator] is ordinarily assumed to be a blank slate unless educated in the law by the parties." *Goldman*, 306 F.3d at 1216 (emphasis added); *see also Duferco*, 333 F.3d at 390 ("In determining an arbitrator's awareness of the law, [courts should] impute only knowledge of governing law identified by the parties to the arbitration."); *Westerbeke*, 304 F.3d at 209 (explaining that manifest disregard of law test "look[s] to the knowledge actually possessed by the arbitrator"); *DiRussa*, 121 F.3d at 823 (rejecting the argument that the failure to award attorney's fees in case brought under federal age discrimination statute was in manifest disregard of the law, because party seeking fees told panel that he was entitled to fees, not that statute required that they be awarded); *Ahing v. Lehman Bros., Inc.*, No. 94 Civ. 9027, 2000 WL 460443 at *14 (S.D.N.Y. April 18, 2000) ("Because plaintiff has not shown that the arbitrators were aware of any clearly governing law precluding the panel from ordering plaintiff to pay half of the arbitrators' fees, their assessment of forum fees against her does not amount to manifest disregard of the law.").

If a party fails to identify governing law to an arbitrator, "we will infer knowledge and intentionality on the part of the arbitrator only if we find an error that is so obvious that it would be instantly perceived as such by the average person qualified to serve as an arbitrator." *Duferco*, 333 F.3d at 390. Thus, counsel forego their obligation to educate arbitral panels as to governing legal principles at their great peril. A motion to vacate an arbitral award because of manifest disregard of the law requires a showing that an arbitrator disregarded "a governing legal principle [that] is well-defined, explicit, and clearly applicable to the case, and [that] the arbitrator ignored it after it was brought to the arbitrator's attention in a way that assures that the arbitrator knew its controlling nature." *Goldman, 306 F.3d at 1216* (emphasis added; citation and quotation marks omitted). Having made no attempt to educate the Panel as to North Carolina's control person statute, Wallace, Jacaruso, and Scotti certainly cannot make such a showing. Nor do they make any argument on this appeal that demonstrates that the Panel misapprehended North Carolina law to an extent that would be instantly recognizable to the average person qualified to serve as an arbitrator.

"We do not sit in judgment over the wisdom of [an] arbitrator's holdings." *Westerbeke*, 304 F.3d at 216. We do, however, review an arbitral panel's decision to assure that it rests upon "a barely colorable justification for the outcome reached." *Banco de Seguros del Estado,* 344 F.3d at 260 (citation and quotation marks omitted). We conclude that North Carolina's control person statute, as it was explained to the Panel, provides such a justification for the Award. First, the Buttars directed the Panel's attention to case law which holds that "controlling shareholders, officers and directors . . . are . . . 'control persons' within the meaning of N.C.G.S. § 78A–56(c)." *Waterman*, 643 F.Supp. at 809. As we have described, Wallace, Jacaruso, and Scotti are identified on numerous Securities and Exchange Commission filings as "control persons" of Montrose. Kavanagh testified that he directly informed Jacaruso of Winston's fraudulent activities and that he raised this same issue at numerous Montrose partner meetings. Collison, the Buttar's expert, opined that Jacaruso and Scotti, "as owners of the firm acquiesced, approved, sanctioned . . . the activities of Mr.

Winston." Wallace, Jacaruso, *196 and Scotti offered no expert testimony to counter Collison's opinion. Wallace testified that he "was in control of everybody performing their functions" at Montrose.

Considered as a whole, this evidence is sufficient to provide a colorable basis for control person liability under North Carolina law as that law was explained to the Panel by the parties. We therefore reject the contention of Wallace, Jacaruso, and Scotti that the Award was based on "the Panel's own brand of frontier justice without regard to the law or facts." Instead, we believe the Award is at least colorably based upon the facts and the law as presented to the Panel.

NOTES

1. The decision suggests that there is "manifest disregard of evidence" is not an independent ground for set aside. How does the decision leave any ability for the court to review evidence?

2. Consider the actual disposition of both *McDaniel* and *Tripi*. Would either of those two cases have been decided differently under *Wallace*? If you do not think so, is there a way to reconcile *McDaniel*, *Tripi* and *Wallace*? In other words, what is an arbitrator *not* entitled to do?